Implementing Microsoft Dynamics NAV 2009

Explore the new features of Microsoft Dynamics NAV 2009, and implement the solution your business needs

David Roys

Vjekoslav Babić

BIRMINGHAM - MUMBAI

Implementing Microsoft Dynamics NAV 2009

First published: December 2008

Production Reference: 1171208

Published by Packt Publishing Ltd.
32 Lincoln Road
Olton
Birmingham, B27 6PA, UK.

ISBN 978-1-847195-82-1

www.packtpub.com

Cover Image by Vinayak Chittar (vinayak.chittar@gmail.com)

Credits

Authors

David Roys

Vjekoslav Babić

Reviewers

Chandru Shankar

Eric Wauters

Richard Malloch

Vincent Bellefroid

Senior Acquisition Editor

Douglas Paterson

Development Editor

Ved Prakash Jha

Technical Editor

Mithun Sehgal

Editorial Team Leader

Akshara Aware

Project Manager

Abhijeet Deobhakta

Project Coordinator

Neelkanth Mehta

Indexer

Hemangini Bari

Proofreaders

Chris Smith

Camille Guy

Production Coordinator

Aparna Bhagat

Cover Designer

Aparna Bhagat

Foreword

For me, the best way to tell the story of Microsoft Dynamics NAV is to describe my first encounter with it. When I joined the product team in February of 2008, I installed the product to get familiar with it. As soon as I saw the new RoleTailored user experience, I knew it was something special. It was beautiful and modern, flexible and fast. Over time, I'm comfortable admitting now, I developed a crush for this product. Sometimes, in the middle of the work day, I would open up the application and create business documents just to interact with its user interface! Today, I fully appreciate its brilliance. Here's why.

At the heart of a good business solution is end user productivity. Questions that come to mind are, 'How much time does the system save?' Or, 'How much higher is the quality of the work?' To engineer a product that ignites end user productivity, our team realized that we needed to formalize a definition and create a framework for measurement.

In cooperation with a third-party research firm, we decided that end user productivity had to take into consideration familiarity, ease-of-use, business insight, collaboration, and flexibility, in addition to transactional efficiency. The user experience in Microsoft Dynamics NAV 2009 was crafted to capture all these characteristics. It is familiar—role centers make users feel at home with the data and work they see upon entering the product; it is easy to use—activities and the action pane make it very apparent how things are done and what needs to be done; it provides insight through integrated reports and data that are showcased in the context of actions to be taken; it makes collaboration easy through notifications and by working well with Office; it is flexible—personalization permeates the experience and is very simple to make; and, finally, it is efficient—keyboard shortcuts and data positioned well with actions make performing tasks fast.

But this isn't *brilliant*. This isn't a *work of art*. This is just good engineering. What makes the user experience brilliant is that users *fall in love* with it, just like I have. This is incredibly important, because people who love the tools they work with end up loving their work more. People who love their work more end up being more successful. They make fewer mistakes, they treat each other better, and they get to work on time. Creating a Microsoft Dynamics NAV user experience that users love is a win-win-win situation. The customer wins. The customer's employee wins. And we at Microsoft win. That's why this user experience is brilliant.

That's not all there is to love about this version. Microsoft Dynamics NAV 2009 has a lot more to it under the hoods. We've made a conscious effort to modernize the core architecture. For instance, in addition to giving the user experience a new look and feel, we've also built this part of the product from scratch on .NET. It has a modern, modular architecture that will help us introduce future innovations, such as a new 'channel' like SharePoint or visualization controls based on Silverlight or WPF, quickly and without compromising quality. We've also made the architecture three-tier from a two-tier fat client. In addition to improving security, such as running the business logic from one, trusted place, this change gives partners the ability to do application-to-application integration much more easily with Web services. With a click of a button in C/SIDE, a new Web service reusing existing business logic and security is exposed for consumption by a third-party application.

On the 'Server Tier', we've taken advantage of .NET once again. C/AL business logic written in C/SIDE now compiles down to MSIL via a C# transformation. We thus leverage the innovations that the .NET runtime team has worked on for the past eight years. Similarly, we've done this with SQL Server Reporting Services, which are now our tool of choice for charts and table reports that can be viewed in context in the user experience. These architectural investments have a tremendous impact on this release and future releases. Good, modern architecture gets the best technology in your hands over time and maintains high quality.

It's true that this release has largely been about technology. That was intentional. We made a commitment to modernize the product, and we've finished those changes that impact partners and customers the most: user experience, reporting, and the tiered architecture. With such changes, a fine balance must be made between innovation on the one hand and maintaining partners' and customers' investments on the other hand. There is no perfect formula here. Sometimes there are innovations that break changes that our customers and partners have made. In these cases, you have a couple of strategies to minimize the pain—you make the innovations 'opt-in' and you create tools and provide support for completing the transformation. In Microsoft Dynamics NAV 2009, we've done both.

We allow our customers to run the Classic client and the RoleTailored client concurrently, giving them flexibility to transition to RoleTailored client over time. We've also made sure that Classic reports, the objects most commonly customized by customers and partners, run in the RoleTailored client, so the customer isn't forced to take advantage of Reporting Services capabilities. Though the runtime has changed from C/AL to MSIL via C#, the actual code itself has not: business logic changed or added by partners and customers is protected and migrates to the new version as-is. Finally, for partners, we've maintained the C/SIDE development environment, extended it with a Page Designer, and provided tools for converting Classic forms and reports to pages and Reporting Services reports, respectively.

Perhaps the thing I'm most proud about in this release is that we've substantially improved its quality. We're upping the bar considerably in a number of ways. As a result of the Technical Adoption Program (TAP) and the Beta Access Program (BAP) programs, by the time Microsoft Dynamics NAV 2009 was released, we had 9 customers already running it in production, and over 80 different partners, including ISVs and implementers, trained and familiar with the new version. We had over 1 year of server uptime and over 135 user-months on the RoleTailored user experience. In addition, we made a number of other quality investments, including improving our stress test environment, improving our code coverage and automation, and testing on 100 configurations of the operating system, database, and other system elements. You're getting the highest quality Microsoft Dynamics NAV product yet.

For me the story of Microsoft Dynamics NAV 2009 is one of tremendous success. The value proposition of end user productivity is core to our long-term vision and very compelling to our customers; the investments in modernization of the architecture set the stage for innovation and product improvements in the future; the attention to partner and customer investments has made this release the best in terms of readiness; and, the quality achievements have set the bar higher than it has ever been. This is the release that I believe takes Microsoft Dynamics NAV, our partners, and our customers into a new, modern era of ERP.

In your hands, you have a fantastic resource to get you familiar with Microsoft Dynamics NAV 2009. As you read this book and learn about the product, I hope you too fall in love with the RoleTailored user experience, Reporting Services, Web services, and the three-tier architecture!

Dan Brown
General Manager, Microsoft Dynamics NAV

About the Authors

David Roys is a Microsoft Most Valuable Professional (MVP) for the Microsoft Dynamics NAV product. He has worked in the computer industry since 1992 and currently works in New Zealand for Intergen Ltd., a leading Microsoft Gold Partner and Dynamics Presidents Club member.

Since getting his honors degree in Computing Science from Staffordshire University, England, he has worked with a variety of custom-written and packaged financial solutions in a variety of roles. His first programming job provided experience of financial systems using CICS, COBOL, and JCL on an IBM 3090 series mainframe. From being a very junior developer in a large organization, he went on to be a one-man IT department at a small food manufacturing company in a role that allowed him to learn and develop solutions for a Danish ERP package called 'Concorde XAL'.

David moved into the world of consulting and ERP reselling in 1996 where he enjoyed working with some truly brilliant people at Columbus IT Partner and was able to work on international projects in South Africa, Hungary, Poland, and Ireland.

With many years of experience in XAL and Axapta he moved to New Zealand in 2002 to work as a consultant for Ernst & Young in their IT Consulting practice delivering financial solutions in Navision Attain. He now works in his dream job as a Dynamics NAV consultant and developer for Intergen Ltd., a bunch of fun-loving, incredibly smart people. David firmly believes that ERP systems are boring and is committed to bringing some entertainment to this dull and listless world.

This book could not have happened were it not for the significant sacrifice from three special people in my life: Nikki my wife, and Katie and Annabelle, my daughters. This book is dedicated to you as a small token for the family time lost and the extra work endured.

My thanks go to the Naylor family for feeding and entertaining my family for many Sunday lunches and afternoons.

Thank you to all Intergenites that have helped with this book: to Tony Stewart and Tim Mole for your encouragement and support, to Olmec for your creative brilliance, and to those that helped with technical reviewing and provided feedback (Scruff, Matt, Jolann, Stefnie, Ian, and Michael).

Special thanks to Eric 'Waldo' Wauters, who was an absolute star technical reviewer for my chapters. Eric, your knowledge, insight and humor has helped me enormously. Some fantastic last-minute contributions from Lars Hammer are much appreciated; thank you Lars!

Thanks to Dad; he knows why.

Thanks to David Studabaker. If it weren't for your book *Programming Microsoft Dynamics NAV*, this book would not exist.

Finally, a big warm thank-you to Vjeko, my co-author and friend, who was crazy enough to take on this project when he had no time to spare. I look forward to meeting with you and sharing that glass of wine one day. You have been an inspiration to me, and have taught me many things.

Vjekoslav Babić is a Microsoft Dynamics NAV expert, consultant, and architect with ten years experience in the IT industry and six years experience delivering project success on large-scale, high-risk, and international implementations of Microsoft Dynamics solutions. He has project experience in various industries, including telecommunications, insurance, pharmaceuticals, industrial gasses, chemicals, food and beverage, manufacturing, printing, distribution, and retail.

He is a Project Management Institute certified Project Management Professional, an accomplished Microsoft Certified Trainer with a track record of successful trainings and presentations, a Microsoft Certified Business Management Solutions Professional with several Microsoft Dynamics NAV and Microsoft Dynamics CRM specializations, and holds a number of Microsoft technical certifications.

Vjekoslav has published more than forty articles on business solutions, software development, database design, and internet technologies; he is the author of the NAV Insights column and an Editorial Advisory Board member with MSDynamicsWorld.com. An active blogger, he frequently writes about Microsoft Dynamics implementation methodologies, Sure Step, and Project Management topics on his blog NavigateIntoSuccess.com.

Based in Zagreb, Croatia, he is employed as a consultant at Microsoft.

If there were only one person whom I should thank, then I would be in lots of trouble. Because there are two: my wife Selma, and my daughter Dora. Countless evenings and weekends that I spent writing these pages, my wife spent acting as a single parent, watching our daughter master her first steps and words. This was their time. And this is their book.

A big thank-you goes to Frank Fugl, a product manager in Microsoft Dynamics NAV team; Chandru Shankar, a member of Sure Step team; Vincent Bellefroid, partner at Plataan, a professional trainer, and an avid Microsoft Dynamics NAV evangelist; and Eric Wauters, a Microsoft Dynamics NAV MVP and development coordinator at iFacto, who all took time to review the early drafts and point out inaccuracies, inconsistencies, or points missed, or otherwise helped this project, and whose insight was priceless.

Finally, special thanks to Dave, my co-author and friend, who initiated the book idea, made me believe in it, and kept motivating me with his enthusiasm throughout this project.

About the Reviewers

Eric Wauters is one of the founding partners of iFacto Business Solutions (`www.ifacto.be`).

With his 7 years of technical expertise, he is an everyday inspiration to its development team. As development manager he continually acts upon iFacto's technical readiness and guarantees that he and iFacto are always on top of the latest Microsoft Dynamics NAV developments.

Apart from that, Eric is also very active in Microsoft Dynamics NAV community-life where he tries to solve technical issues and strives to share his knowledge with other Dynamics NAV enthusiasts. Surely, many of you will have read some of Eric's posts on Mibuso.com, Dynamicsusers.net, or his own blog (`www.waldo.be`), which he invariably signs with 'waldo'.

Lately he co-founded the Belgian Dynamics Community, a platform for all Belgian Dynamics NAV users, consultants, and partners, enabling knowledge sharing and networking.

His proven track record entitled him to be awarded MVP in 2007 and 2008 (Microsoft Most Valuable Professional).

Richard (Scruff) Malloch is a Business Development Manager for Intergen, a New Zealand-based Dynamics NAV implementation practice. Richard works alongside David Roys and has worked with the NAV products for over 5 years implementing Dynamics NAV into a variety of industries.

Richard is a huge fan of Dynamics NAV 2009 and wishes every success to the readers of this book who will be implementing Dynamics NAV.

Vincent Bellefroid is a Microsoft Certified Trainer (MCT), founder and co-owner of Plataan. Plataan is an independent training and consultancy bureau specialized in Microsoft Dynamics. He is an experienced implementation consultant and trainer and is specialized in Project Management. Vincent has a distinguished ERP implementation career and is the author of multiple Microsoft Official Courseware manuals related to Microsoft Dynamics and Project Management.

Table of Contents

Preface 1

Chapter 1: Introducing Microsoft Dynamics NAV 2009 7

And now for something completely different 7

Why RoleTailored? 8

New architecture—a real deal 9

Implementing Microsoft Dynamics NAV 2009 10

What is this book all about? 11

Microsoft Dynamics NAV 2009 application areas 13

A new architecture explained 15

Two-tier versus three-tier 15

Architectures of Microsoft Dynamics NAV 17

The Client Tier 18

The Microsoft Dynamics NAV Service Tier (NST) 18

The future of Microsoft Dynamics NAV 21

Summary 23

Chapter 2: The RoleTailored Client 25

What is the RoleTailored client? 26

First impressions 26

New terms for the RoleTailored client 28

The navigation window 29

The address bar 29

The command bar 31

Local commands 33

Customize and Help commands 33

The navigation pane 34

Where are all the options? 35

The status bar 36

The Role Center navigation page 37

The Departments page 48

Task pages 50
Cards 51
Lists 56
Documents 56
Journals 57
List plus 58
Matrices 59
Wizards 60
The Report Viewer 61
Print and export 63
How to use the RoleTailored client 64
Create a customer 65
Create a sales order 68
Post an invoice for a sales order 72
Enter a cash receipt 79
Concluding using the RoleTailored client 82
How to personalize the RoleTailored client 83
Make it your own 83
Customize the navigation pane 83
Adding list places to menus 85
Personalizing pages using the customize menu 86
Customize Actions 86
Customize Reports 87
Customize This Page 88
Customize This Page (task page with FastTabs) 91
Customize This Page (role center) 93
Summary 98
Chapter 3: Roles and the Customer Model 99
The Dynamics Customer Model 99
Too much information 100
A fresh beginning 100
Departments, roles, process groups, and tasks 101
What is a role in Dynamics NAV 2009? 101
The roles available in Dynamics NAV 2009 102
Role-centric thinking 105
Discovering the existing roles 105
What's in a role center? 108
Customizing a role as a super user 111
Customizing the Accounting Manager profile 111
Clearing the configured pages for a profile 113
Adding actions and reports to a profile 114
Changing the layout of the Customer Card 119
Extending existing roles as a developer 120
Find the Page ID and source table of the activities part 122

Adding the Priority Customer field 124
Extending the Sales Cue table 128
Creating a new role 132
Further Reading 133
Summary 134

Chapter 4: The Implementation Process 135
What is an implementation? 135
Implementation tasks 137
Business process reengineering 137
Configuration 139
Customization 140
Third-party solutions 140
Choose the right approach 140
The role of methodology 141
Microsoft Dynamics Sure Step 141
Phases of an implementation 142
Diagnostic phase 143
Drafting the project scope 144
Mind the gap 145
What if it's not there? 147
Detailed analysis 149
Technical requirements 150
Should we do all of it? 150
Wrapping up 151
Analysis phase 152
Prepare the path 152
Plan the resources 153
Plan approvals 154
Get the ball rolling 154
Train the key users 154
Data migration 156
Master data migration 156
Past transactions 156
General data migration analysis considerations 157
Detailed analysis 158
User roles 159
Integration and interfaces 159
Document the requirements 160
Design phase 162
Understand the standard application 162
Understand the problem 163
Use your imagination 163
Prototype, demonstrate, and iterate 163

Learn how to eat an elephant 165
Products of design 165
When to stop 165
Development phase **166**
Planning 166
Setting up the environment 167
Finally, development 168
Application functionality 168
Data migration development 169
Security issues 170
Document the changes 170
Customer testing and acceptance 171
Deployment phase **172**
Plan your steps 172
Environment configuration 172
User acceptance test 173
Load test 174
End-user training 175
Go-live 175
Operation phase **176**
No planning? 176
Documentation 177
Transition 177
Closing off 178
Final acceptance 179
Who died? 179
Did we go bananas? **180**
Betting a business on a mad horse 181
Summary **182**
Chapter 5: Configuring the System **183**
What is system configuration? **183**
A programmer's guide to accounting **184**
The hippo's bottom 184
The black art of bookkeeping 184
Finding dimensions with the five Ws (and the H) 185
The chart of accounts 190
Income statement 191
Balance sheet 192
Other reading 193
Feeding the hippopotamus 193
Is it a debit or a credit? 194
Using dimensions to analyze financial data 200

Accounting understood? 204
Groups, groups, and more groups **205**
G/L entry 209
VAT entry 210
Vendor ledger entry 210
Detailed vendor ledger entry 211
G/L entries revisited 211
Vendor posting group 211
VAT Bus. Posting Group and VAT Prod. Posting Group 212
More groups 215
Where do dimensions come from? 220
RIM **223**
The setup questionnaire 224
General Ledger setup (before RIM) 224
General Ledger setup (using RIM) 226
Data migration 232
Hurray for the Data Migration tool 233
Limitations of the Data Migration tool 240
What's missing 245
Summary **245**
Chapter 6: Modifying the System **247**
Understanding the tools **247**
Modifications for non-programmers **248**
Object Designer basics **249**
Extending the data model **251**
Creating tables 252
Adding fields 254
Table relationships 254
Table keys 256
Field groups 257
Customizing forms **257**
Creating forms 258
Form properties 259
Adding controls 260
Subforms 262
Menus and buttons 263
Customizing pages **264**
Page properties 265
Page types 265
Card 265
List 266
RoleCenter 267
CardPart 268

ListPart 269
Document 270
Worksheet 271
ListPlus 271
ConfirmationDialog 273
NavigatePage 274
Page Designer 275
Containers 276
Groups 276
Fields 277
Parts 278
Positioning controls 279
Spur some action 280
Form Transformation tool 287
Customizing reports **287**
Reporting in the Classic client 288
Creating reports 288
Components of a report 288
Report logic 295
Reporting in the RoleTailored client 295
RoleTailored report creation 298
Transforming layout 299
Transforming request option forms 300
Customizing MenuSuites **301**
A little bit of theory 302
And some practice 303
Customizing other objects **308**
Codeunits 308
Dataports 308
XMLports 309
Summary **309**
Chapter 7: Extending the Application **311**
Learning to fish **311**
What's a Web service? **312**
It's not just for the Web 313
What can we do with them? 314
Calling a NAV Web service 314
Creating a Web service 316
Calling the Web service 317
WinForms application **323**
Item look-up requirements 323
Exposing the Web service 323
New Windows application project 325
Getting some data 330

Filter Box and Find Button 333
Testing time 333
WinForms application summary 334
Sidebar gadget **334**
Design time 335
What are little gadgets made of? 335
The gadget 338
Flyouts 339
Options 340
The tricky bits 341
Just a little bit of SOAP 342
An HTML page that calls a NAV Codeunit 344
Hey, Good Lookin' 348
Calling a Web service from NAV **351**
Always take the weather with you 352
Calling out around the world 355
Service oriented or service enabled? **358**
When is a service not a service? 358
Service repository 358
Service bus 359
Don't worry, be happy 359
Any questions? **359**
Document Pages as Web services 360
Role Center as a Web service 361
Records as parameters to Codeunits 362
Codeunit functions that return complex data types 362
XMLports as parameters to Codeunits 362
More functions on a Page 363
Can I break it? 363
Presentation layers **364**
Summary **364**
Chapter 8: The Development Lifecycle **365**
Why is development different than programming? **365**
Development in Microsoft Dynamics NAV 366
The lifecycle **366**
Microsoft solutions framework 367
Understanding the requirements **368**
Designing the solution **370**
Extending existing functionality 370
Designing a completely new functionality 371
Designing tasks 373
Data model 373

User interface 378
Reports 379
Application logic 379
Planning for performance and scalability 381
Keys 381
User interface 382
Build **382**
Team approach 383
Building the data model 384
Building the user interface 384
Beware the page 384
Pages 389
Reports 389
User interface integration 390
Building the application logic 392
Security 393
Testing 393
Feature Complete 394
Object versioning 394
Should I change the Modified flag? 399
When customers play developers 400
Documentation 400
Stabilization **401**
Issue Convergence 402
Issue Log Cleared 403
Final tests 404
Release Readiness milestone 404
Finalizing development work 404
Deployment **405**
Documentation 405
Deployment Stable and Deployment Complete 405
Summary **406**
Chapter 9: Troubleshooting **407**
Identifying problems **407**
Debugging **408**
Debugging the Service Tier 409
Debugging the Classic client 415
Code Coverage 419
Performance tuning **421**
Client Monitor 423
Built-in Client Monitor functionality 424
Client Monitor helper objects 427
Analyzing performance with Excel 428

Analyzing data 431
Multi-user issues 441
Combining Code Coverage and Client Monitor 447
How about the RoleTailored client? 448
Other tools 448
Event Viewer 449
SQL Server Profiler 449
Performance Monitor 449
Dynamics management views and functions 450
Task manager 450
Planning ahead 451
Hardware Guide 451
Indexes 452
Database Resource Kit 452
Technical Presales Advisory Group (TPAG) 452
Getting help 453
Microsoft Dynamics NAV tools overview 453
SQL Server Technical Kit for Microsoft Dynamics NAV 454
Summary 454
Chapter 10: Sample Application 455
Sample code download 456
Gathering requirements 456
The scenario 456
Functional requirements 461
Process flow diagram 461
Use-case modeling 462
Defining the actors 462
Defining the use-cases 463
Use-case diagram 465
Glossary of terms 466
The domain model 469
Use-case workshop 471
Explaining the ORM diagram 471
Mobile expense claim 473
Finishing the functional requirements 480
Architectural design 481
Supplementary requirements 481
Existing architecture and framework 482
Budget 482
What's cool? 483
And the winner is... 483
Build—technical design 483
Tables 484

Expense (new table) 485
Expense Claim (new table) 486
Location (Modify Table ID=14) 486
Department (no changes to existing table) 486
Customer (no changes to existing table) 487
Expense Claim Setup (new table) 487
User Setup (modify Table ID=91) 487
Points raised by table design 488
New items to consider 489
Additional development tasks 489
Working through the use-cases 491
Do you want the good news or the bad news? 493
Build—prototype **493**
Additional tables 494
User Setup (modify Table ID=91) 494
Expense Claim Schedule (new table) 494
Customer (modify Table ID=18) 494
Time to build 494
I love the Classic client 495
Transformers, robots in disguise 498
MenuSuite and navigation pane 505
Dynamics Mobile **508**
Overview tasklet 509
Capturing Expense 510
Editing Captured Expenses 513
Synchronize 514
Prototype, demonstrate and iterate **514**
Summary **514**
So long, farewell, Auf Wiedersen, Adieu **515**
Index **517**

Preface

Microsoft Dynamics NAV 2009 is the latest release of the NAV application (formerly known as Navision) from the Microsoft Dynamics family of products that brings a three-tiered architecture, Web services enablement, and many more exciting features, to the well established Enterprise Resource Planning (ERP) solution.

Although Dynamics NAV is carefully designed for ease-of-use, attaining measurable business gains requires an understanding of business, finance, analysis and design techniques, programming skills, and the ability to manage complex projects coupled with an expert knowledge of the product itself.

This book distils hard-won experience into an easy to follow guide to implementing the full power of Dynamics NAV in your business. It won't just tell you how to do it; it will show you how to do it. It will help you to become a better consultant or developer by providing practical examples and expert advice.

From an introduction to the new RoleTailored user interface to a series of practical Web services programming tutorials, you will gain a deep understanding of what NAV 2009 has to offer compared to previous versions. With a strong emphasis on practical examples, we take you through the implementation process and provide guidance on configuring the Chart of Accounts and Dimensions for financial analysis, how to use the Rapid Implementation Toolkit (RIM) to reduce implementation effort, and an overview of the Sure Step implementation methodology. You will learn how to take a business problem through to a working solution using industry-standard techniques such as use-case modeling and object-role modeling. We will teach you how to design and develop NAV objects including the new Page object and the Client Reporting Services report layouts.

What This Book Covers

Chapter 1: The purpose of this chapter is a teaser introduction to get you excited about the product, what's in it in general, and what's in it as compared to previous versions, to give you a little taste of what's coming up in the book, and explain what the fuss about this new release is all about.

Chapter 2: The RoleTailored client is the new user interface for users of Microsoft Dynamics NAV 2009, and it is completely different to the pervious versions. We'll take you through the different components of the interface, introduce the terminology, explore the navigation components and page types, and teach you how to personalize the application to meet your own requirements using the extensive personalization features.

Chapter 3: Microsoft Dynamics NAV 2009 introduces a new paradigm to ERP. Instead of the system being focused on the forms that capture and present data and the functions the user can perform, the system is based around the individuals within an organization, their roles, and the tasks they perform. We cover how Microsoft researched the roles and explore the departments, roles, and tasks that have been identified in the Microsoft Dynamics Customer Model. We also show the reader how to assign the standard roles to users, how to create new roles, and how to allow departmental super users to configure the application for their role so that the change is applied to all users with the same profile.

Chapter 4: Microsoft Dynamics NAV is not a product with a Next-Next-Finish type of installation, and it takes a lengthy project to deploy it successfully. We focus on the six phases of the implementation process, and explain each phase with detailed dos and don'ts for a typical implementation. Based on the Dynamics Sure Step implementation methodology with advice liberally sprinkled throughout, special attention is given to new features of Microsoft Dynamics NAV 2009, and where the new capabilities must be taken into account to make most out of the implementation project.

Chapter 5: Every implementation of Microsoft Dynamics NAV 2009 will require the system to be configured to meet the needs of the business. This chapter tells the implementation consultant how to do this from a core financials perspective and provides valuable information that will allow developers to understand more about the application they are changing. We cover basic accounting for programmers, dimensions, and posting groups, and how to use the Rapid Implementation Methodology (RIM) Toolkit to speed things along.

Chapter 6: Hardly any standard system can fit the needs of a business out of the box. Either the customer must shape their processes to match the system, or the consultant must shape the system to match the processes, and usually the latter prevails. This chapter explains the process of modifying the system, how to design a viable data model, and how to design and develop a functional user interface for both RoleTailored and Classic clients, without writing any code.

Chapter 7: The three-tiered architecture of Microsoft Dynamics NAV 2009 and native Web Services Enablement open up a whole new world of possibilities for NAV implementations. We cover some of the many possibilities for extending the application, allowing the consultant and developer to understand the technologies that are available and their respective design considerations. Our practical examples introduce the NAV programmer to the world of .NET and show how you can use the information available on the internet to develop your own killer .NET add-ons.

Chapter 8: There's much more to development than programming. It starts with understanding what customer really needs, and usually extends way beyond the system being deployed to a test environment. This chapter focuses on the development phase, and what it takes to get from a concept to a live and working solution.

Chapter 9: After the system goes live, or as it grows, there are periods when new problems may arise, and often their source is far from obvious. This chapter explores the tools and techniques available for detecting problems, pinpointing the source, and helping to remove them from the system quickly and painlessly. It explains how to debug the Service Tier, how to troubleshoot performance issues, what can be done to avoid problems, and how proper planning before design can help to get it right the first time.

Chapter 10: Our sample application focuses on requirements gathering, functional specification creation, solution design, and the eventual build of a prototype. We look at how a business problem can be explored using techniques such as interviewing, use-case modeling, and object-role modeling to create a solution design that can be molded into a working prototype.

What You Need for This Book

To successfully follow the examples in this book, you need the following:

- PartnerSource access. If you are an employee of a Microsoft partner company, which specializes in implementing Microsoft Dynamics solutions, then you should have this access already enabled. If you don't have this access personally, but your company does, ask your company Microsoft partnership program administrator. If your company doesn't have this access, and you believe it should, contact your local Microsoft office.
- An installation of Microsoft Dynamics NAV 2009, which you can obtain at PartnerSource, at the following URL: `https://mbs.microsoft.com/partnersource/downloads/releases/MicrosoftDynamicsNAV2009.htm`.
- Alternatively, you can obtain a marketing virtual machine. Look for it at the following PartnerSource URL: `https://mbs.microsoft.com/partnersource/solutions/nav/`.
- An active Microsoft Dynamics NAV license with Solution Developer granule included. Also, make sure that your license is upgraded to Microsoft Dynamics NAV 2009.

Who is This Book For

- Dynamics NAV implementation consultants and developers that want to quickly understand the new features offered in the 2009 release.
- NAV consultants that want to learn more about programming and extensibility without needing to learn a programming language will also benefit from this book.
- NAV programmers that want to learn about finance configuration and solution design in order to be a better programmer and design better solutions can also use this book.

Conventions

In this book, you will find a number of styles of text that distinguish between different kinds of information. Here are some examples of these styles, and an explanation of their meaning.

Code words in text are shown as follows: "If you were to change the code to assign `myString` with text that is longer than 50 characters, you would get an exception when the code is run."

A block of code will be set as follows:

```
private void button1_Click(object sender, EventArgs e)
{
    FindRecords(textBox1.Text);
}
```

When we wish to draw your attention to a particular part of a code block, the relevant lines or items will be made bold:

```
private void button1_Click(object sender, EventArgs e)
{
    FindRecords(textBox1.Text);
}
```

Any command-line input and output is written as follows:

```
net time \\computername /set
```

New terms and **important words** are introduced in a bold-type font. Words that you see on the screen, in menus or dialog boxes for example, appear in our text like this: "From the **Role Center**, the menu contains: **Customize Actions**, **Customize Reports**, **Customize This Page**, and **Customize Navigation Pane**."

Warnings or important notes appear in a box like this.

Tips and tricks appear like this.

Reader Feedback

Feedback from our readers is always welcome. Let us know what you think about this book, what you liked or may have disliked. Reader feedback is important for us to develop titles that you really get the most out of.

To send us general feedback, simply drop an email to `feedback@packtpub.com`, making sure to mention the book title in the subject of your message.

If there is a book that you need and would like to see us publish, please send us a note in the **SUGGEST A TITLE** form on `www.packtpub.com` or email to `suggest@packtpub.com`.

If there is a topic that you have expertise in and you are interested in either writing or contributing to a book, see our author guide on `www.packtpub.com/authors`.

Customer Support

Now that you are the proud owner of a Packt book, we have a number of things to help you to get the most from your purchase.

Downloading the Example Code for the Book

Visit `http://www.packtpub.com/files/code/5821_Code.zip` to directly download the example code.

The downloadable files contain instructions on how to use them.

Errata

Although we have taken every care to ensure the accuracy of our contents, mistakes do happen. If you find a mistake in one of our books—maybe a mistake in text or code—we would be grateful if you would report this to us. By doing this you can save other readers from frustration, and help to improve subsequent versions of this book. If you find any errata, report them by visiting `http://www.packtpub.com/support`, selecting your book, clicking on the **let us know** link, and entering the details of your errata. Once your errata are verified, your submission will be accepted and the errata added to the list of existing errata. The existing errata can be viewed by selecting your title from `http://www.packtpub.com/support`.

Piracy

Piracy of copyright material on the Internet is an ongoing problem across all media. At Packt, we take the protection of our copyright and licenses very seriously. If you come across any illegal copies of our works in any form on the Internet, please provide the location address or web site name immediately so we can pursue a remedy.

Please contact us at `copyright@packtpub.com` with a link to the suspected pirated material.

We appreciate your help in protecting our authors, and our ability to bring you valuable content.

Questions

You can contact us at `questions@packtpub.com` if you are having a problem with some aspect of the book, and we will do our best to address it.

1

Introducing Microsoft Dynamics NAV 2009

Enterprise Resource Planning (ERP) systems are like wine: they get better with age. Microsoft Dynamics NAV **2009**—a member of a broader Microsoft Dynamics family of products—is an ERP system targeted at small and medium-sized businesses, which didn't just get better with its latest release, it brought a revolution. It has got a new face, and new brains, and it is off to change the ways of all participants of the ERP food chain: the consultants, the developers, and the end users alike.

In this chapter you will learn:

- Why Microsoft Dynamics NAV 2009 is so special
- Whether the **RoleTailored** client is worth all the buzz
- Why the new architecture is so important
- What it takes to implement Microsoft Dynamics NAV
- How the future of Microsoft Dynamics NAV will look

And now for something completely different

Microsoft Dynamics NAV 2009 is the most significant release of the product ever made. What's new in Microsoft Dynamics NAV 2009? Nothing. And everything.

If you're looking for additional enterprise resource planning application functionality (something that an ERP system should be all about), indeed there is nothing new. Just compare Microsoft Dynamics NAV 2009 to the previous version (Microsoft Dynamics NAV **5.0 SP1**), and you'll find the same old application areas, the same old functionality. Not even one new business process is covered. If you're shopping for these things, you're going home empty handed.

So, nothing is new.

But there's more to life than application functionality. Previous releases have included plenty of new features, new modules, and some cosmetic changes to the user interface. This release is about something else, so let me announce in my best Monty Python voice: *And Now for Something Completely Different*!

If you're an old-hand with Microsoft Dynamics NAV, when you start the new client, you'll see an application unlike any version you've seen before. It doesn't look like the Microsoft Dynamics NAV you've been used to, and has very little in common with previous user interfaces. Meet the RoleTailored user interface.

If you are new to Microsoft Dynamics NAV, you're going to fall in love with this little puppy in no time at all. It's simple and intuitive, so intuitive in fact that you'll start clicking around it productively the moment you see it. It redefines user friendliness.

However, if you are a Microsoft Dynamics NAV veteran (one of those that still remembers what **NAV** is short for), if you can keyboard your way around the application, reconcile a bank account or cancel a purchase return order blindfolded, the RoleTailored user interface is going to challenge you and it may be a while before you grow fond of it. But make sure you do grow fond of it, and do it fast: the RoleTailored interface is here to stay, it's about to define the future of all Microsoft Dynamics ERP products, and will change the way users interact with Microsoft Dynamics NAV for ever.

Why RoleTailored?

The RoleTailored user interface gets its name for a reason: at its core are user roles that define sets of specific actions and tasks that different types of users perform in the course of their daily job. Users belonging to different roles will have a different view of the system, each of them seeing only those functions they need to be able to perform their daily tasks.

The RoleTailored user interface hides the complexity of the system away from the users, and replaces it with clarity; so users can spend more time productively working with the application instead of searching for functions among dozens of unneeded ones.

If you had a chance to work with Microsoft Dynamics NAV **4.0** or **5.0**, you might remember how difficult it sometimes was to locate a specific feature in the jungle of the **Navigation Pane**. Switching back and forth the specific menus in search of a menu item, especially for users performing tasks in several functional areas of the application, was a frustrating experience.

Unless you used shortcuts, accessing any feature required three of four clicks—provided you knew exactly where it was. The system also didn't do much to help users focus on what needed to be done, and after you found the feature you needed, you typically had to spend extra time searching for documents or tasks that needed your attention. For example, if you needed to post a released invoice, you first had to click your way through to the **Invoices** feature, and then you had to search for those that were ready to be posted. This required too many clicks and far more interaction than really necessary. All in all, productivity was hindered by technology.

With the RoleTailored client, the feature jungle is gone, and the application isn't even showing you the features you don't need. Your role is defining what tasks you need to perform, so your screen isn't cluttered with functions you'll never use. Work that needs your immediate attention—such as invoices waiting to be posted, or production orders to be released—is always one click away and readily presented using visual cues. Thus, your focus is never taken away and you don't waste time on unnecessary human-machine interaction.

Consultants implementing Microsoft Dynamics NAV 2009 for their customers will need to master a completely new understanding of the customer's business model: an understanding that is focused on user roles. This understanding is necessary to successfully map the end users to existing roles, or to define new ones—a prerequisite for achieving any benefit from the RoleTailored experience and improving the user productivity. We'll help you to get that understanding in our chapter on Roles and the Customer Model.

New architecture—a real deal

Microsoft Dynamics NAV 2009 has a nice-looking user interface but true changes are beneath the surface in the new architecture, and many benefits it has brought along. Building a distributed system, deploying a hosted environment, or achieving higher scalability are among the most obvious ones.

The true beauty of the new architecture is that it breaks down the barriers that kept Microsoft Dynamics NAV a relatively closed system, one that was difficult to extend beyond the boundaries of its own user interface. Integrating ERP functionality into workflows having their start or endpoint in external systems (such as master data management procedures or e-commerce scenarios) was difficult, expensive, or both in earlier versions.

Old, two-tiered architecture didn't scale too well; you were normally limited to a couple of hundred concurrent users, and that was only if you had a top-notch multiprocessor database server with gigabytes of RAM. You couldn't extend it easily outside of the realm of the C/SIDE development environment and C/AL language, unless you got medieval on yourself venturing into realm of C/FRONT and its arcane techniques. The new architecture changes all this.

With the new architecture, these boundaries are gone, and you can go as far as your creativity allows. Exposing almost any application functionality as a Web service ready to be consumed by external applications is a matter of simple configuration settings, and connecting just about anything that can speak **SOAP** (**Simple Object Access Protocol**, the Web services communication standard) to Microsoft Dynamics NAV can be accomplished on the fly. Meet the Web services-enabled three-tier architecture.

Three-tiered architectures generally provide better scalability; in fact, they are a prerequisite for it. The Microsoft Dynamics NAV 2009 three-tier architecture improves the overall scalability of Microsoft Dynamics NAV, and its central component—the Microsoft Dynamics NAV Server—is what makes it possible. You can also deploy several Microsoft Dynamics NAV Servers in parallel, and connect them to the same database, thus achieving higher scalability levels, especially when you want to separate the workload of several departments to dedicated machines.

Microsoft Dynamics NAV Server takes over a substantial share of the chores from the client, namely the execution of business logic. This reduces network traffic because only a small amount of data travels between the server and the client. It also shortens locking times because no or very little data exchange needs to happen between the server and the client during long transactions.

The new Web services-enabled architecture means that now you can use Visual Studio to write applications that build upon Microsoft Dynamics NAV functionality, and to seamlessly integrate it into workflows that start or end completely outside Microsoft Dynamics NAV.

All of this was next to impossible in the previous versions. Microsoft Dynamics NAV of old is no more—it has grown from a simple application into a fully-fledged platform. It gives much more out of the box, and makes it possible for you to take your implementations far beyond anything possible with the previous version.

So, everything is new.

Implementing Microsoft Dynamics NAV 2009

A business is like a living organism; it contains dozens of functions, which all work towards a common goal: success. Business departments, while all being a part of a much bigger system, have their own needs, targets, and processes, and sometimes can thrive totally oblivious of the existence or function of other departments.

Marketing can launch campaigns totally unaffected by the headaches manufacturing might be going through, warehousing can ship and receive pallets regardless of what accounting might have on their mind, and all of them can be successful in their own right. But the success of a business is not just the sum of successes of individual departments—for a business to succeed, all departments must work in harmony.

Enterprise Resource Planning, or ERP, is a paradigm that integrates data and processes from all departments into a single software platform, which not only serves the needs of each individual department, but also the needs of the business as a whole.

Every business is unique: they all do accounting, purchases and sales, but each of them does it in its own unique way. The software they use to run business should play along, and allow them to operate successfully, while giving them freedom to do it their way.

What is this book all about?

Microsoft Dynamics NAV 2009 is a feature-rich and highly customizable ERP solution: it comes bundled with a lot of standard functionality, which can be used as is, or customized to exactly match specific processes of a company. To put it to work successfully, it takes much more than merely installing it. The process which transforms it from a generic solution to a highly specialized one able to cope with mission-critical requirements and carry the bulk of the day-to-day business operations is called implementation.

Implementation is a journey, which starts with understanding the application. You need to know the user interface, how to operate it, how to customize it to fit the requirements of a business, and how to personalize it to best match the users' preferences and unique needs. The RoleTailored interface of Microsoft Dynamics NAV 2009 offers a wealth of personalization capabilities: users can add or remove screen elements and functions and make the interface feel comfortable to them. This allows users to focus on their tasks and activities instead of wasting time on unnecessary interaction with the system.

Microsoft has developed a customer model with a set of pre-defined user roles, based on the roles typically found in today's businesses. During implementation, you'll meet your end users and learn their daily routine. This knowledge will help you map your customer's model to the Microsoft Dynamics NAV's default one, and develop the role centers custom-tailored to specific needs of your users to boost their productivity and increase satisfaction.

To successfully implement Microsoft Dynamics NAV 2009, you need to know its standard functionality, and the kinds of business processes it can support. During the implementation, you'll analyze the business processes of your customer and understand how they relate to Microsoft Dynamics NAV 2009 application areas.

Microsoft Dynamics NAV 2009 is not a my-way-or-the-highway kind of application: its rich configuration capabilities make it possible to establish many business rules using application setup alone. Application setup is a central part of every implementation, and you'll spend a lot of time discussing various settings with your customer: general ledger, posting rules, dimensions (just to name a few).

When it is not possible to achieve what you need using setup, you'll reach for built-in customization and development tools that allow you to modify existing functionality or to develop a new one. Depending on the complexity of your customer's requirements, you might be able to modify the application without any programming knowledge, and even if you are not a programmer you can go a long way in developing a data model, user interface, or reports.

Microsoft Dynamics NAV 2009 is more than just an ERP system or a business management solution—it is a true platform that can be used to build upon. Developing inside it, using built-in development tools is not what makes it a platform; it's the architecture that does it. The Web services enablement allows publishing application functionality as a Web services, and makes it possible to develop distributed applications over Microsoft Dynamics NAV, or include and seamlessly integrate its functionality in third-party or custom-developed applications without hassle.

While implementing Microsoft Dynamics NAV you should bear in mind that you are not merely introducing an application into a business environment; you are dealing with business-critical processes. The solution you are implementing will be used on daily basis, probably throughout the company; it will run or control high-stake processes, such as invoicing, tax reporting, and inventory management, and it will have potential to enhance the way your customer does their business, or to bring it to a complete halt. That's why it is important to understand what the implementation process looks like, and how to smoothly drive it from initiation to a successful closure.

Microsoft Dynamics NAV 2009 application areas

Like any other ERP application, Microsoft Dynamics NAV 2009 comes with many application areas that can be used independently of each other. In ERP terminology these are called modules, and they allow great flexibility in dealing with an enormous variety of business requirements. Customers in different business branches, or verticals, will use different modules: a manufacturing company might use all of the ERP modules, while a government agency or a public-sector company might only need financials, purchases, and human resources functionality. Even though these modules are separate in ERP systems, they are all integrated into a single application, and all use the same integrated database.

Strictly speaking, Microsoft Dynamics NAV does not have modules in the typical ERP meaning of the word: the functionality is so tightly integrated that there is no clear boundary between *functional areas*. And this is exactly what we call them in Microsoft Dynamics NAV.

Microsoft Dynamics NAV 2009 comes with the following functional areas:

- **Financial Management**: As a cornerstone of every business management system, this functional area includes functionality necessary for managing finances of a company. Financial management consists of general ledger, cash management, accounts payable, accounts receivable, fixed assets, and inventory costing. Comprehensive financial analytics and history of financial transactions is also included.
- **Sales & Marketing**: Usually this functional area comes as a series of modules in other ERP systems, but they all have one thing in common—they all cover the customer-facing activities of a company. Microsoft Dynamics NAV packs all this functionality into a single functional area, which includes sales order processing, marketing, pricing, and Customer Relationship Management.
- **Purchase Management**: As an important component of what other ERP systems usually bundle as Supply Chain Management, this functional area provides functionality for handling the input of goods into the company. It includes planning and purchase order processing.
- **Warehouse Management**: This too belongs to Supply Chain Management; this functional area takes care of warehouse processes and handling of goods once they enter the company. In Microsoft Dynamics NAV, this functional area consists of order management, planning, goods handling, and inventory management.

- **Manufacturing**: Usually this functional area is at the very core of every Supply Chain Management system; the manufacturing module delivers all the functionality necessary for tracking and managing conversion of raw materials into finished products. In Microsoft Dynamics NAV, this functional area comprises product design, capacity planning, production planning, production order management, and manufacturing costing.
- **Jobs**: This functional area is what other ERP systems usually call project management; it is used to track projects undertaken by the company, and it consists of job planning and costing. This should not be confused with project management tools, because it is primarily used to track projects from a financial perspective.
- **Resource Planning**: If you sell services, this functional area contains the necessary functionality for planning and managing the resource availability and usage. It includes resource planning, pricing, and resource capacity management.
- **Service Management**: Typically, the Service Management module is part of Customer Relationship Management, but in Microsoft Dynamics NAV it is a separate functional area comprising contract management, service planning and dispatching, and service order processing.
- **Human Resources**: This manages the workforce through the functionality of employee record management and time and attendance. While most other ERP systems include comprehensive functionality including payroll and benefits, Microsoft Dynamics NAV stays at the most basic functionality allowing partners to build upon it.

Many features of one application area can also be found in another, such as inventory management or costing functionality, which is interspersed through the Financial Management, Sales & Marketing, Purchase, Warehouse, and Manufacturing functional areas. This improves user experience for users of the Classic client, because it is one of the mechanisms that reduce the time spent on searching for functions.

Most of the functional areas in Microsoft Dynamics NAV 2009 also include analytics functionality, which allows detailed analysis of information stored in the system. Another important common functionality is transaction history, which allows fast and easy finding of literally any transaction and the effects it had on the system.

Contemporary ERP systems rarely exist in isolation. The imperatives of agile business demand that anything that can be automated gets automated, and anything that can be integrated gets integrated. Microsoft Dynamics NAV 2009 readily integrates with lots of other products, raising productivity to a completely new level.

Microsoft Dynamics NAV can utilize Microsoft BizTalk Server for business-to-business communication and automation of Supply Chain Management, through the built-in Commerce Gateway functionality. In much the same way, Microsoft Office SharePoint Server (MOSS) can be used to enable access to the system through a web browser interface. Microsoft Dynamics NAV 2009 also bundles a feature-rich integration with Microsoft Outlook. All of this functionality saves a lot of time and spares the system from human error, which otherwise can't be completely avoided.

A new architecture explained

The architecture of any system is among its most important components. It affects many aspects of it: how the system will perform, how it will be able to scale, how secure it will be, how difficult it will be to integrate it with other systems. These depend a great deal, if not exclusively, on architecture.

With Microsoft Dynamics NAV, architecture was a constant for a long time and it withstood dozens of releases almost completely intact. There was certain lore to it among developers and consultants—functionality could change, features got included or dropped, but you could depend on the architecture, it remained the same release after release. Then the advent of Microsoft Dynamics NAV 2009 turned the architecture upside down.

Two-tier versus three-tier

Business applications usually have three discernible layers: presentation, business logic, and data. How exactly these layers are structured is defined through architecture. While the term may seem somewhat outdated these days, Microsoft Dynamics NAV has long been built around a Client/Server architecture.

A Client/Server architecture presumes that there are two layers, or tiers, in the system—a client and a server. The client is used for presenting the user interface to the user, while server is used to store the data. The most important part, however, is the business logic, and either of the tiers can do the processing, effectively resulting in two possible two-tier architectures.

The first one, popularly called the *thin client* architecture, uses the client as a mere data presentation and entry device, while all business logic is processed centrally at the server. The server sends the data to the client, which presents the data to the user. When the user changes data, the client submits it back to the server, and any necessary processing is done away from the client. With thin client architectures, clients are very simple and cheap, while the servers are big, powerful, and usually very expensive.

The second one, called the *fat client*, goes the other way around, putting the burden of processing the business logic on the client. The server is used just to handle the data storage and management operations, while the client does everything else. This approach leverages the fact that most of the client computers are powerful, and that all this power remains largely underutilized. With so many resources readily at the disposal of a system, the fat client approach results in relieving the server from the work that can be done at the client, saving the costs of building an expensive server system.

Although neither of these approaches is inherently good or bad, and both come with their share of pros and cons, two-tier architectures in general leave a lot to be desired. Just to start with, they can't scale. Two of the three mentioned components are particularly resource-hungry: business logic and data processing.

If you put the burden of business logic on the server, then the server has to do both logic and data processing. These two tasks can easily and quickly eat up all system resources if done simultaneously for bigger number of concurrent connections. Even though the server is perfectly capable of accepting more connections, or in other words *scaling up*, its nailed-down system resources are preventing it from doing so.

On the other hand, if the burden of business logic is on the client, and the client only needs to process a single connection at a time, the client resources are utilized in a rather effective way, but the concurrency is affected terribly. Hardly any transaction consists of just a single write operation, and there are many reads and writes going on all the time. This results in many locks being placed all over the database, and with a network being a far slower a resource than a server bus, while one client processes a transaction through the network, most other clients need to queue up and wait for their turn. Even the fastest of network environments will hit their limits with a fairly low number of users working concurrently in the system.

Three-tier architectures introduce a middle tier, which takes over the business logic processing, thus completely isolating all the components of the system to separate tiers. This brings significant improvements over two-tier approaches, by combining the benefits of both fat-client and thin-client approaches, while effectively overcoming their limitations.

The middle tier takes business logic processing away from the database tier, leaving the database to handle a single task of data processing. At the same time, with business logic being processed at the server, clients only need to feed the data to the middle tier once per transaction. Instead of having dozens of clients attacking the database server randomly and locking its resources at will, the middle tier can efficiently marshal the requests, resulting in more synchronized communication, which doesn't adversely affect concurrency as much as random access does. This results in considerably increased scalability.

Architectures of Microsoft Dynamics NAV

Microsoft Dynamics NAV has long been a fat client two-tier Client/Server architecture system. It consisted of a client, which processed both the user interface and business logic, and a server, which only processed the data. Obviously, with this approach, achieving high scalability levels was difficult.

Microsoft Dynamics NAV 2009 comes with both two-tier and three-tier architectures. For backward compatibility, the two-tier architecture is retained through the Classic client, which is basically the same C/SIDE client that most of us have been used to working with in previous versions. For new features, such as the RoleTailored client or Web services enablement, there is the new three-tier architecture:

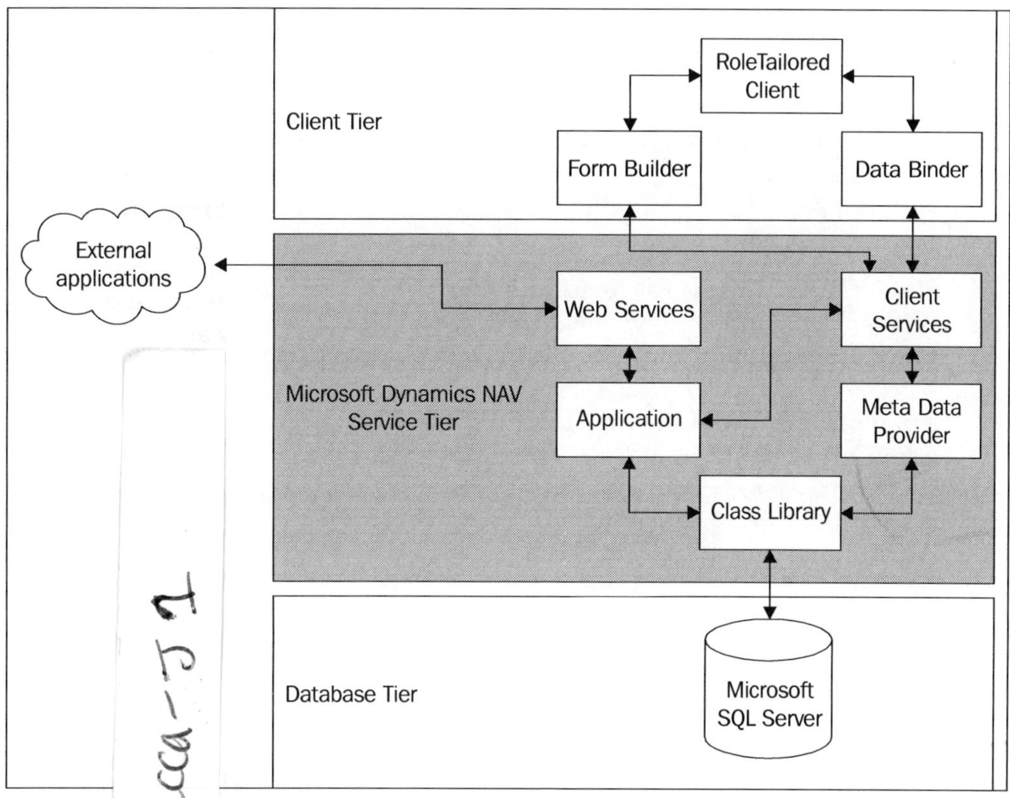

Let's get to know the important components of Microsoft Dynamics NAV's three-tier architecture: the RoleTailored client and the Service Tier. Note that the database tier is the same one used in two-tier architecture, and is used only to store the data, so we are not going to investigate it in detail.

The Client Tier

Microsoft Dynamics NAV 2009 has introduced a new Client Tier component that is completely different from the fat Classic client. The main design goal of the new Client Tier was not to develop the shiny new RoleTailored client application, but to allow for a future inclusion of any number of different client applications which could run on different hardware or software platforms and still provide the same functionality and the same RoleTailored user experience.

The following components of the Client Tier make this possible:

- **Data Binder**: Data is just stored in the database, but it doesn't live there. It is continually transferred between the client and the server, courtesy of the Data Binder component. It is also in charge of all notifications sent back and forth between the user interface and business logic layers.
- **Form Builder**: The trickiest of components, the Form Builder builds logical display-independent forms, based on Pages metadata stored in the database. These forms contain all functionality regardless of the display target, including data binding, input validation, and any business logic. Any display target builds its own specific version of the form, based on this logical form.
- **RoleTailored Client**: The logical runtime which is bound to a concrete display target technology. The architecture of previous two components allows for more than only one possible display target. Currently, only WinForms display target is released, which is called the RoleTailored client, but more could be built in the future. This open design will allow Microsoft Dynamics NAV to expose a single set of pages across a wide variety of display target technologies, with very few or no modifications of the page definitions.

The RoleTailored user interface is one of the most important additions to Microsoft Dynamics NAV 2009, and you will get a chance to learn about the role-based experience and RoleTailored user interface of Microsoft Dynamics NAV 2009 in great detail in the next chapter.

The Microsoft Dynamics NAV Service Tier (NST)

The middle tier of any three-tier architecture is usually the one that is responsible for most of the legwork the system has to do. Microsoft Dynamics NAV 2009 is no different, and the Service Tier, which comprises several components, carries the bulk of the processing of the whole system.

The Microsoft Dynamics NAV Service Tier is not a single component, and the work is distributed among the following components:

- **The Microsoft Dynamics NAV Service**: A workhorse of Microsoft Dynamics NAV 2009 Service Tier, this is the connection point between the client and the system. It works in the context of a Windows service built on Windows Communication Foundation (WCF) and .NET. It also handles authentication and thread management, and functions as a broker which receives and validates requests from the client, and then routes them to the proper service component for execution. After the execution completes, the response is returned back to the client.
- **The Application Component**: Although this component is really a new gadget in the Microsoft Dynamics NAV arsenal, it is just a shiny wrapping around the well-known application logic. The application logic is still written in C/AL, but is compiled into a .NET assembly at design time. At run time it executes on top of Microsoft Dynamics NAV Class Library.
- **Microsoft Dynamics NAV Class Library (NCL)**: As the most interesting part of the Service Tier, this is actually the Microsoft Dynamics NAV runtime wrapped as a .NET class library. It is a non-public library, which means that developers will not be able to inherit from it or extend it directly, in much the same way as the Classic client itself has always been out of the reach of developers. This component is hence used only to port the functionality of the Microsoft Dynamics NAV environment into the world of managed code and .NET interoperability, which makes it possible to run it in the context of Web services.
- **The Metadata Provider**: This handles all sorts of metadata that circulates between the client and the server, and there is a decent share of it. It is primarily used to feed the form metadata, the personalization metadata, and table metadata to the Form Builder and Data Binder components of the RoleTailored user interface. It also handles the filtering of the metadata based on licensing and permission restrictions, and language settings.
- **Business Web services**: This component provides interfaces necessary for connecting external or third-party applications to Microsoft Dynamics NAV 2009. It supports operations such as reading, creating, modifying, and deleting of data in Microsoft Dynamics NAV, while invoking any necessary business logic and executing any code pertinent to such operations. Examples of these would be execution of any field validation triggers, or initialization of proper number series when inserting new master data records. It resides in the same .NET assembly as Microsoft Dynamics NAV Service.

Web services confusion: When talking about Web services in context of Microsoft technology, it is natural that people immediately assume that Internet Information Services (IIS) is involved. However, this assumption is wrong.

Microsoft Dynamics NAV Service Tier doesn't use IIS. Instead, it is built on Windows Communication Foundation (WCF), a set of .NET technologies (formerly code-named *Indigo*). Compared to IIS, WCF has much less overhead, both in the number of execution layers and in setup and administration, thus resulting in faster and more streamlined communication.

Microsoft Dynamics NAV Service and Business Web services components are both built upon WCF and reside in the same .NET assembly, which publishes two separate Windows services: one used for native communication between the RoleTailored client and the Service Tier, and one for Web services enablement.

Obviously, Microsoft Dynamics NAV 2009 goes much further than just providing a new fancy user interface—it finally introduces the product into the ubiquitous world of Service Oriented Architecture. While extending the application with genuine non-C/SIDE functionality in previous versions of Microsoft Dynamics NAV was almost literally restricted to programming the arcane C/FRONT interface, which never truly saw much action, the new architecture provides the entire infrastructure needed to have external applications access and integrate with the Microsoft Dynamics NAV functionality.

The biggest excitement with these components is that they are not here only to carry the weight of the RoleTailored user interface, but they pave the road for many other user interfaces to take advantage of Microsoft Dynamics NAV infrastructure. The RoleTailored client is just the first one that does so, and many more, such as the SharePoint interface, which is planned to follow the release of Microsoft Dynamics NAV 2009 shortly, can be expected to follow.

The simplest of examples of what you can effortlessly achieve with Microsoft Dynamics NAV 2009, but which called for a tremendous amount of work previously, is a web interface that will fully and consistently execute the Microsoft Dynamics NAV business logic. Writing a web application, such as a web shop or a self-service portal for customers or vendors, which consumes Web services published through Microsoft Dynamics NAV and seamlessly integrates with its business logic, is as simple as writing any Web services-aware application, and doesn't require any black-belt programming knowledge or skills.

Therefore, the new architecture provides as much opportunity to third-party solution providers as it does to customers.

The future of Microsoft Dynamics NAV

Ever since Microsoft took the helm of the Danish company called Navision A/S in 2002, one of the great benefits for Microsoft Dynamics NAV customers has been the clear and up-to-date roadmap of the product. Customers have never been kept in the dark regarding what future versions will bring, or where the product would be in years ahead, reassuring them of the security of their investment into Microsoft Dynamics NAV technology.

Microsoft's ongoing strategy for Microsoft Dynamics NAV is to continually deliver a competitive product, which brings more value to mid-size businesses than its rivals. This is going to be done by improving application functionality and enhancing user experience.

With Microsoft Dynamics NAV 2009 paving the way for role-based and role-centric customer models, future versions might build upon this foundation, and deliver broader user roles functionality. Also, new application features have consistently been introduced over past versions, so any future releases can be expected to come packed with new features and application functionality. Another trend has been evident since version **5.0**, which is inclusion of broader global functionality, and with Microsoft's official introduction of modules such as Kitting or Cost Accounting, it can reasonably be expected that more such functionality will be introduced in future versions.

From development perspective, Microsoft Dynamics NAV 2009 has made a big step forward. With Visual Studio debugging of C# code it is now possible to integrate non-C/AL developers into development and testing teams. While not that exciting for .NET veterans, introduction of features such as color-coding in the C/AL editor really reassure the partners that the improved development experience is in focus for future versions of Microsoft Dynamics NAV.

Microsoft Dynamics NAV SQL Server option has been getting better in performance with every new release, while Microsoft Dynamics Classic database server has reached its limit a long time ago. This, along with the fact that three-tier architecture doesn't even support the Classic database server, makes it obvious that Classic database will gradually be phased out.

A major driver for the development of future versions of Microsoft Dynamics NAV, as well as of all products within the Microsoft Dynamics line, is customer-driven innovation—a simple concept of delivering what customers really need. Microsoft has invested significant effort into engaging in dialogue with customers and partners about the future of Microsoft Dynamics products and their roadmaps.

As a result of this research, three major areas of Microsoft Dynamics NAV 2009 can be expected to go through many improvements over the several next product versions:

- **Business Vision + Software**: An area that has always gone through the most improvements in every new version, with application feature list getting ever more comprehensive. This trend can be expected to continue, probably with some shift towards more vertical and industry-ready solutions. Future versions may bring even more productivity enhancements, such as those already achieved with the RoleTailored client, together with better integration with Microsoft Office and the Server System stack of products. Improvements in SQL Server integration have always been among the top priorities. Teaching old dogs new tricks has never been a simple job, and converting a two-tier solution—initially not architected to leverage the benefits of a true relational database management system such as SQL Server—to a fully scalable multi-tier system and not causing any regression issues in the process, is a fantastic feat. Now that Microsoft Dynamics NAV has finally got its middle tier, and that SQL Server 2008 is out, true improvements are yet to be seen.
- **People + Processes**: Microsoft's focus on overall user experience is evident—and not only in Microsoft Dynamics line of products—therefore significant enhancements can be expected here as well. The use roles might get richer and deeper, and might support more processes and more scenarios. Tight integration with Microsoft Office, together with Web services enablement, will provide the possibility to use Microsoft Office applications as the actual frontend, in much the same way as Microsoft Dynamics CRM already uses Outlook. Also, introduction of contextual business intelligence, and integration with mobility platform, both of which have already been enabled to an extent, are the two areas that could go through considerable improvements.

- **Company + Ecosystem**: Microsoft Dynamics NAV has a track record of providing great integration capabilities, and Web services in Microsoft Dynamics NAV 2009 are just the latest addition to the arsenal. With Web services in version 2009, Microsoft Dynamics NAV has just made the first steps on a Software + Services path. Integration with Microsoft Office is one of those features that get better in each version. Two of the best examples are Word and Excel export functionality through XML stylesheets, and fully customizable integration with Outlook, both introduced in version **5.0**. With the Microsoft Office family growing in members and functionality, many enhancements can be expected in this area. Last, but not least, companies are doing increasingly more business with their customers and suppliers electronically. Future versions of Microsoft Dynamics NAV are going to bring a lot of enhancements in the area of collaboration and data exchange with business partners, something that has already been supported to an extent with the Commerce Gateway feature, but which can be expected to include more out of the box scenarios.

Summary

In this chapter, we journeyed through the world of Microsoft Dynamics NAV 2009, and all the bells and whistles it brings along. We discovered what makes it so special and so different from anything Dynamics so far. Then we covered the topic of implementation of an ERP system—what an implementation process might include, and what is important to know about implementing Microsoft Dynamics NAV. We went through the new architecture, and learned what Microsoft Dynamics NAV comprises, and what lies behind the RoleTailored client and Microsoft Dynamics NAV Service Tier (NST). At the end, we've taken a sneak-peek at the future of Microsoft Dynamics NAV and what we can expect to see over the next version or two. All in all, in this chapter we've introduced Microsoft Dynamics NAV 2009; let's now get our feet wet in it, and move on to the next chapter to meet the RoleTailored client up close and personal.

2
The RoleTailored Client

In a three-tiered application, such as Dynamics NAV 2009, we have a database layer, a business logic layer, and a presentation layer. The presentation layer is often referred to as the client and, for the end users, it's the most important part; for the majority of NAV end users, the client *is* the application.

We therefore need to understand the client, how it works, and the design principles it is built upon, so that we can provide killer sales demos, in-depth training, and effective support of the application and design customizations that are in keeping with the standard user experience.

NAV 2009 has two clients that will be used by the majority of users: the **Classic** client and the **RoleTailored** client. If you're an administrator or a programmer, the Classic client will provide the tools you need to perform your day to day tasks, and if you've used previous versions of Dynamics NAV, the Classic client will be instantly familiar.

For end users, the RoleTailored client provides a new and colorful user experience. It is built around people and offers a user experience that is tailored to the role they play in the organization. It readily exposes the information that is important to the users and facilitates easy access to the tasks they need to perform.

In this chapter, we're going to explore the RoleTailored client and will cover:

- Some new terminology and an overview of the new application components
- How to perform some common business activities using the RoleTailored client
- How an end user can personalize the RoleTailored client

What is the RoleTailored client?

The RoleTailored client is all about people, the roles they play in an organization, and the tasks they perform. The Classic client, and the client available in NAV versions prior to the 2009 release, is focused around data entities (such as customers, vendors, items) and the functions that can be performed on those entities, and as such can often be overwhelming (too many menu options, too many fields on data entry forms).

The RoleTailored client has an attractive visual appearance and provides the impression to each user that the application has been written just for them. We'll be looking at the concept of *Roles and the Customer Model* in the following chapter, but for now it's time to explore what the RoleTailored client has to offer.

First impressions

The start screen for the RoleTailored client is called the **Role Center** and contains a wealth of information. The user doesn't need to click a single thing and is immediately shown information pertinent to their job.

The most visually prominent feature of the **Role Center** is the **Activities** part containing stacks of documents, called **Cues**, that each represent an inbox of items that require action to be taken by the user.

The previous image shows the **Role Center** for the Sales Order Processor profile (just one of the twenty-one profiles available in NAV 2009). Let's compare the starting page for the Classic client to see just how simple and friendly the RoleTailored client is.

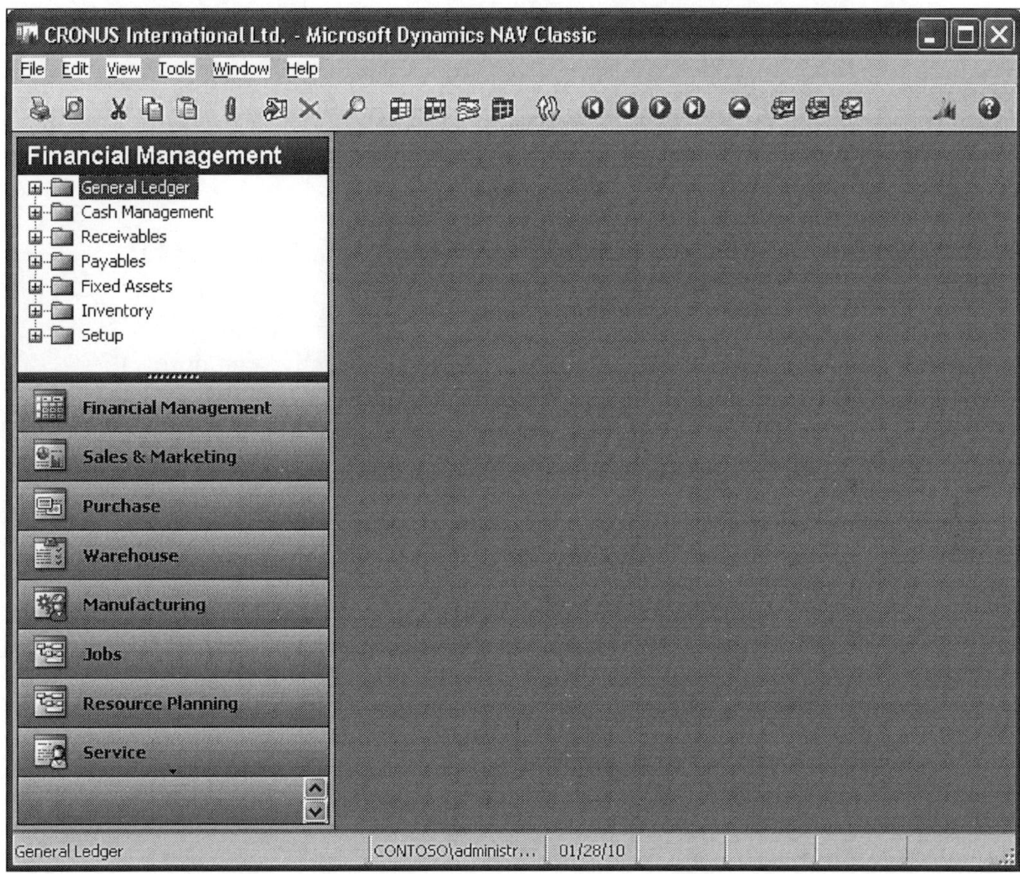

As the Classic client is the only client that provides development and administration tools, it will still be used frequently, and the NAV 2009 architecture allows the RoleTailored client and Classic client to co-exist over the same database. Some third-party add-ons may make it necessary for certain tasks to be performed in the Classic client, particularly if there is a need to take control of hardware (such as cash-registers, weighing scales, or scanners) from within the application.

Speak to me NAV

As you can see, the RoleTailored client is welcoming and attractive. If it could talk, it would sound like HAL from the 1968 science fiction film *2001: A Space Odyssey*. I imagine it saying: "Hi Dave, how are you? Shall we sell something today?"

The Classic client, on the other hand, would have a voice like John Cleese's Basil Fawlty (short, abrupt, and more than a little bit rude), and would say: "Yes. What do you want? I haven't got all day you know!"

There's nothing wrong with the Classic client; indeed some NAV veterans may prefer it to the RoleTailored client. New applications take some time getting used to, but the users are going to love the RoleTailored client; so the sooner you get to love it, the easier it will be.

New terms for the RoleTailored client

When we work with a product like NAV, we need to talk about it and write about it; we'll need to train our end users on how to use the system and communicate clearly with developers and other consultants. The first step in effective communication is for all parties to use the same language and terms. We don't want to cover every control in detail here, it's better to figure things out by playing with the client; you're only going to get good at this by trying it first-hand. Instead, we'll focus on what's new and what's important to help you use the right terms and approach design in the right way.

RoleTailored client terminology links

It is likely that you'll want to provide an overview of the user interface to your end users as part of their introductory training. Rather than providing all details here, we've provided links on our book web site (`www.teachmenav.com`) to download the *User Experience Guidelines for Microsoft Dynamics NAV 2009* and links to some useful topics in the online help.

The RoleTailored client has two main types of window: the **navigation window** and **task pages**. The navigation window for the RoleTailored client is similar in behavior to Microsoft Outlook 2007. The application has a navigation pane on the left hand side for accessing the different areas of the system (in Outlook, the areas accessed by the navigation pane include mail folders, calendars, and tasks; in NAV, we access list places, the role center, and the departments page).

The navigation window, which can be thought of as the main application, can display three types of pages: the **Role Center**, **List Places**, and the **Departments**

Page. From the navigation window, the task page is launched and opens in a window of its own to allow the user to carry out a specific task, such as create a sales order, edit customer details, or post a journal. There are seven types of task pages with different layouts: **Card, Document, Journal, List, List Plus, Matrix,** and **Wizard**.

In addition to the main window types of navigation window and task page, there are the usual dialogs, message boxes, and print preview windows that compose the RoleTailored client user experience.

The navigation window

At the top of the navigation window we see some new controls that will be familiar to users of Vista or Internet Explorer but are new to NAV. The **travel buttons** provide a back button, a forward button, and a travel history drop-down button.

As you navigate to different places in NAV 2009, your last ten places will be saved in your travel history (although the history is erased once you exit the application). If you click the travel history button, a drop-down list of the places you have been to is displayed and you can select a place from this list to navigate directly to that place.

The address bar

The **address bar** allows you to see where you are and where you have come from. It works in a similar way to the address bar used by Explorer in Windows Vista.

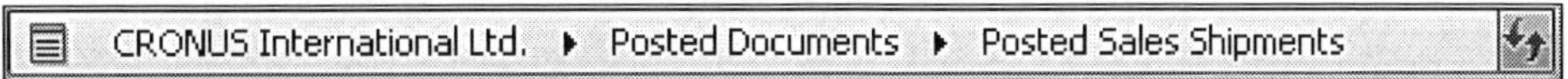

The address bar starts with the company name (in our case **CRONUS International Ltd.**) and is followed by the menu groups and menu option you have selected from the navigation pane. You can click the triangles that separate the different elements of the address and a drop-down list will appear allowing you to select a different menu group.

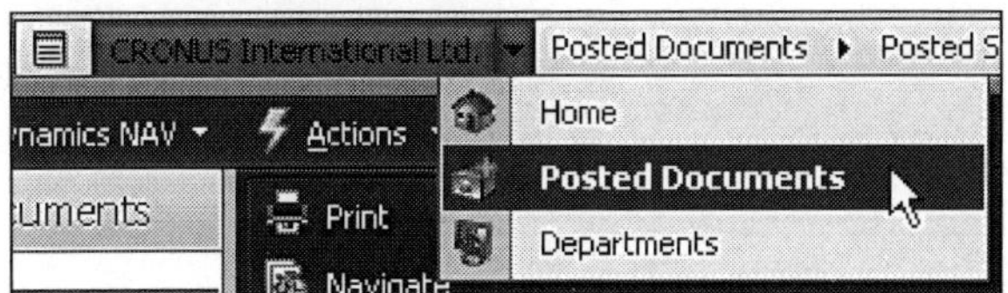

If you click to the right of the address, or right-click the address bar and chose **Edit**, your current address will be transformed into edit mode and will change in appearance from the following:

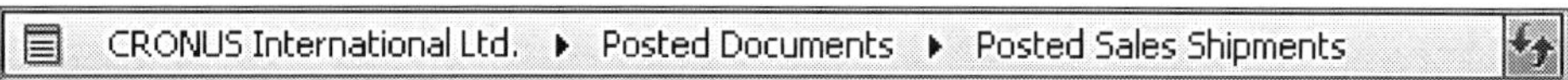

...into this:

Once the address bar is in edit mode, you can type the address directly or edit the text to give you the address you want. Notice that the refresh button at the right of the address bar has changed to a **Go to** button (which has the same effect as pressing the *Enter* key).

Copy and paste with the address bar

In addition to the **Edit** option, a right-click on the address bar will also show **Copy** and **Paste** menu options. This is a real help for anyone needing to write technical documentation for Dynamics NAV as instead of writing:

Open the **CRONUS International Ltd.** company and from the Main Menu select the **Financial Management**, **General Ledger** menu group, and choose the **Chart of Accounts** menu option.

You can now write:

Go to **CRONUS International Ltd./Departments/Financial Management /General Ledger/Chart of Accounts**.

Not only is it easier to follow but you can copy-and-paste the address directly from the address bar into your document.

You should encourage your users to copy the address and paste it into any emails when they are logging a support issue, and when you send instructions to them, you should do the same.

The **refresh button** to the right of the address bar will re-read data from the database and update the screen controls accordingly. As an alternative to clicking the button, you can also press *F5* to refresh the screen.

As a developer it's useful to know that this will also re-read the latest objects from the database, meaning that it is no longer necessary to close and re-open the database in order to see programming changes.

The command bar

Underneath the address bar we have a row of command buttons called the command bar that includes system-wide commands (such as **Help**, **Customize**, and **Exit**), and context-sensitive commands that appear in the **Actions**, **Related Information**, and **Reports** buttons relative to the page being displayed.

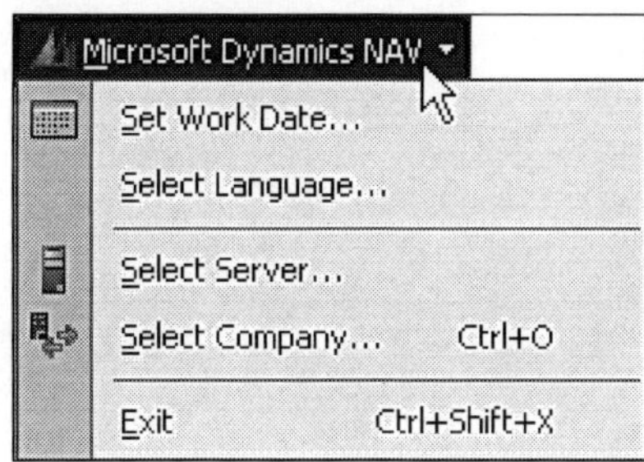

The Microsoft Dynamics NAV command button provides options to **Set Work Date**, **Select Language**, **Select Server**, **Select Company**, and **Exit**.

The work date

The **Set Work Date** option allows you to work with the system as though you were working on a day different to today's date (when you first enter the system, the work date is set to today's date).

A typical use would be when you need to post the journals required to close the accounts for a previous period. Since the default date on a number of pages in NAV is the work date, you can set your work date to a previous date temporarily, and as far as the system is concerned, you are working on that date.

The current work date is displayed on the status bar, and the **Set Work Date** dialog can also be activated by clicking the date shown in the status bar at the bottom of the navigation window.

You may notice that there is no open database option in the menu (this is available in previous versions and the Classic client). Instead, we have a **Select Server** option that refers to the URL of a **Dynamics NAV Server**, which is our middle tier in the three-tiered architecture. The URL is specified as **servername/DynamicsNAV**, where **servername** is the name of the computer on which the service is installed and **DynamicsNAV** is the name of the **server instance**.

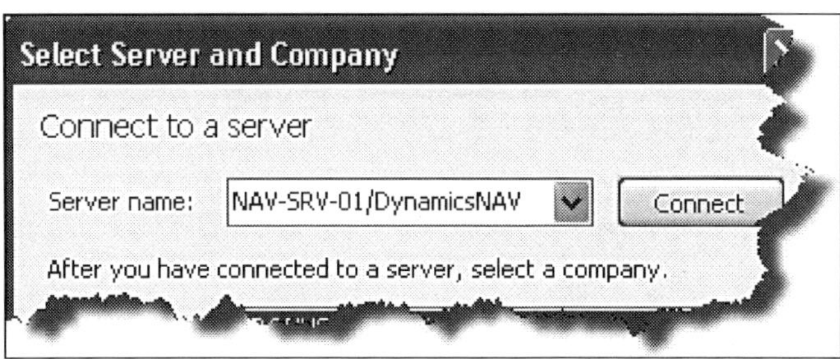

Once you have connected to the server, you can select the company to work in.

Renaming the NAV Server instance

The NAV Server instance name is specified in a configuration file in the install directory on the server. On a default install the file is located in `C:\Program Files\Microsoft Dynamics NAV\60\Service` and is called `CustomSettings.config`.

You can change the **ServerInstance** key to a new value by editing the XML file. You should take a backup copy of the `CustomSettings.config` XML file before editing it just in case you delete or edit the wrong key.

After a change to the server instance, you'll need to restart the **Microsoft Dynamics NAV Server** service. When your RoleTailored client restarts, it will look for the last server instance it connected to and, after a long pause, will display the following message.

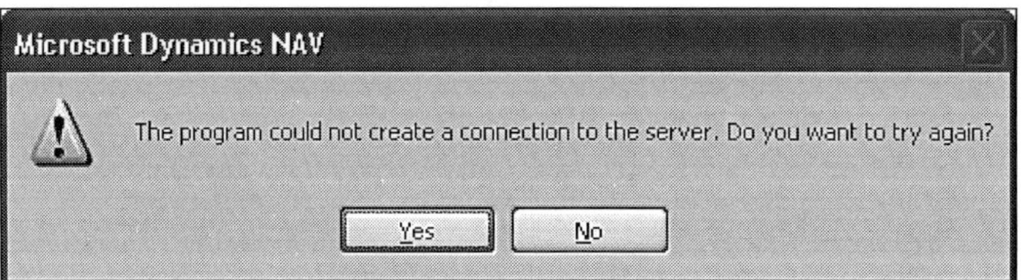

Select **No** and you will be able to specify the correct URL in the **Connect to a server** window.

Local commands

The **Actions** command button will reveal different things depending on which page is currently displayed and to what extent you have personalized the system.

We'll cover this in more detail in our section on how to use the RoleTailored client. Typical actions include: **View**, **Edit**, **New**, **Delete**, **Notes**, **Links**, **Print**, **Open in New Window**, **Refresh**, **Clear Filter**, **Send To**, and **Print Page**.

The **Related Information** command button comes and goes depending on which list place or task page you happen to be on.

As you would expect, the menu provides links to the related information for the current page. In older versions these options lived on the **Menu Buttons** at the bottom of the form.

Similar to the **Actions** menu, the **Reports** command button will show different options depending on the page you are currently viewing.

Each option on the drop-down menu represents a single NAV report.

Customize and Help commands

The **Customize** command button is the key to personalizing the application, which is arguably one of the greatest features of NAV 2009. We'll be covering the customization options in more detail in the *How to personalize the RoleTailored client* section later on in this chapter. To give you an overview, here are some of the menu options available.

- From the **Role Center**, the menu contains: **Customize Actions**, **Customize Reports**, **Customize This Page**, and **Customize Navigation Pane**.

- From a **List Place**, you'll see additional items for: **Action Pane, Filter Pane, Chart Pane, FactBox Pane, Choose Columns, Choose FactBoxes**, and **Customize Actions Pane**.
- When using a **Task Page**, you'll see an additional option: **Limit Totals To**.

The **Help** command button includes the **Microsoft Dynamics NAV Help** option that displays the vastly improved online help and the **About Microsoft Dynamics NAV** option that displays information about the application.

The **About Box** for the application includes the all-important Version number (all-important if you ever need to log a support call with Microsoft).

The navigation pane

The navigation pane exists in older versions of Dynamics NAV (and the Classic client) but in the RoleTailored client takes on a much sleeker, smarter look.

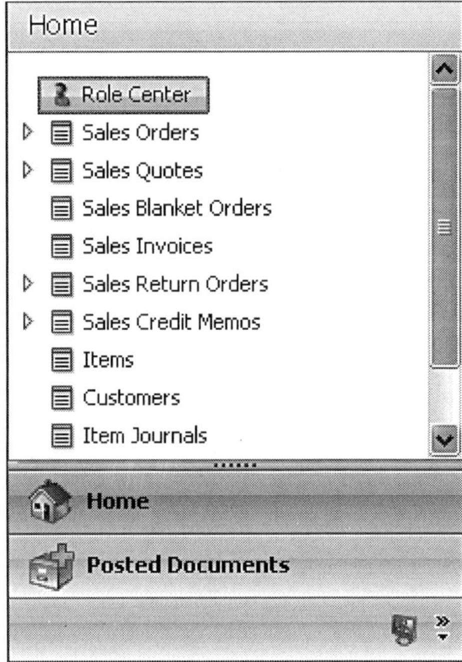

The pane has three **Activity Buttons** in the image, although the **Departments** activity button is shown in miniature at the bottom (because our activity pane is sized so that the full activity button will not fit).

The **Home** activity button is used to display the role center and the list places that are linked to a user's role. The customization options allow users to add new list places to the home part of the navigation pane.

The home navigation pane is kept deliberately simple, and you should avoid the temptation of adding too many options when modifying the system. One good guideline is to ensure that the home pane does not need to scroll in order to display all the options. It is better to add new activity panes than to keep adding to the home pane.

Rather than having menus that are related to functional areas of the system (such as Financial Management, Sales & Marketing, and Purchase in the Classic client navigation pane), the activity buttons are focused on the activities that are being covered such as billing customers or reviewing posted documents.

Where are all the options?

If you've been looking at the new sleek, trimmed down user interface that is offered by the RoleTailored client and wondering where all of the other stuff from the old Dynamics NAV application has gone, then you can wonder no more—it's in the **Departments** page, which can be accessed by clicking the **Departments** activity button.

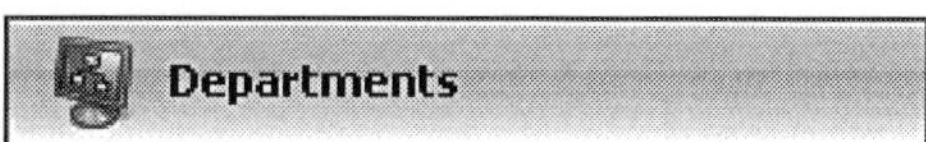

They could have called the Departments page the 'Everything Else Page', but I guess that's not as catchy.

The users can see those options that they have permissions to see (and there are a lot of options), and can copy any useful links to other sections of the navigation pane. We'll look at the Departments page in more detail later on in this chapter.

Tucked away at the bottom of the navigation pane there is one little drop-down button with a single option of **Customize Navigation Pane**.

If you right-click on any of the existing navigation pane activity buttons, the same menu option appears.

The status bar

The status bar runs along the bottom of the navigation window for the RoleTailored client and contains fields that show company name, work date, and user name.

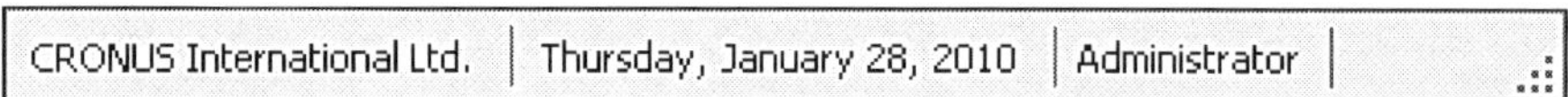

Both the company name and work date areas are buttons that, when clicked, will activate the dialogs used to select these values. The buttons activate the same options that can be triggered from the Microsoft Dynamics NAV command button discussed earlier.

We've dealt with the outside edges of the navigation window by looking at the travel buttons and address bar, command bar, navigation pane, and status bar. This surrounding area is known as the **navigation frame**. Inside the navigation frame we can have one of three types of pages displayed: a Role Center, a List Place, or a Departments Page.

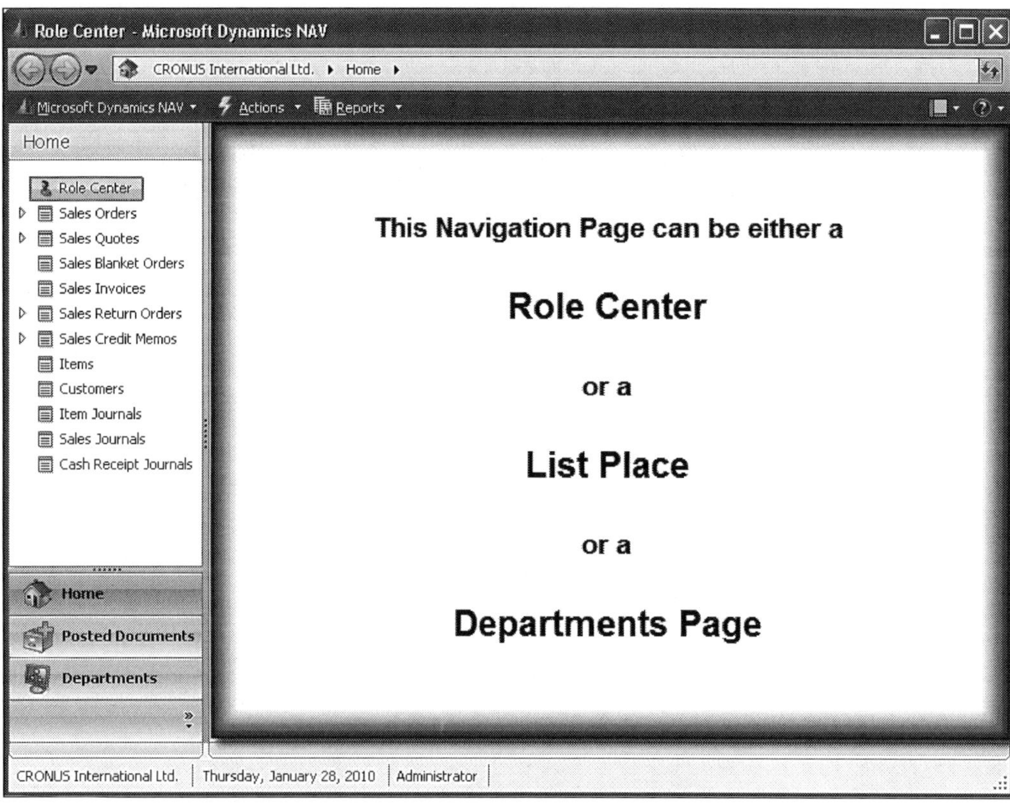

The Role Center navigation page

The **Role Center** page provides quick access to the list places and task pages that are needed by people in a given role, and as such allows users to feel that the application has been created just for them. We'll discuss user roles, profiles, and role centers in more detail in the following chapter, but first we need to understand what a role center is and what parts are used to display the information and navigate to the task pages.

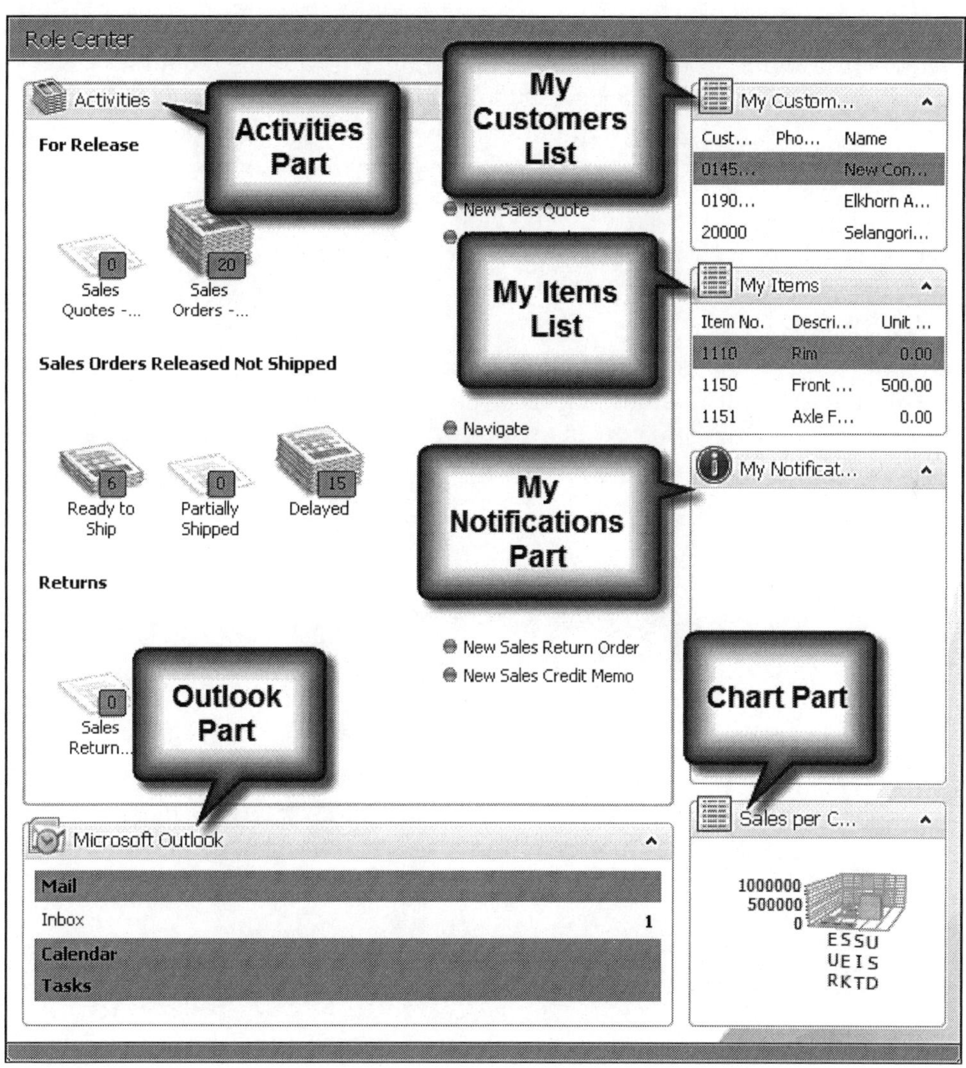

There are twenty-one role centers available in NAV 2009, although with access to development tools, new Role Center pages can be created by those with programming skills.

End users have the ability to personalize the role center according to their requirements by hiding, moving, and configuring the parts contained on the page, but it is up to the analysts and developers to create role centers that match the activities performed by the users of the system.

The role center has two columns that contain parts such as Activities, Outlook Part, List Part, Notifications, or Chart. Each part contains two additional buttons at the top of the part that show a list of relevant actions and provide the ability to collapse or expand the part. End users may add multiple chart parts to either column in the role center, with a maximum of seven parts allowed in any one column.

The RoleTailored client does a pretty good job of trying to size the columns to give you the best possible view of the parts you have selected.

Activities part

The **Activities** part is the meat of the Role Center while the other parts are merely vegetables and gravy. It contains graphical **Cues** depicting stacks of documents that grow or shrink depending on how many documents there are on which the user must take action.

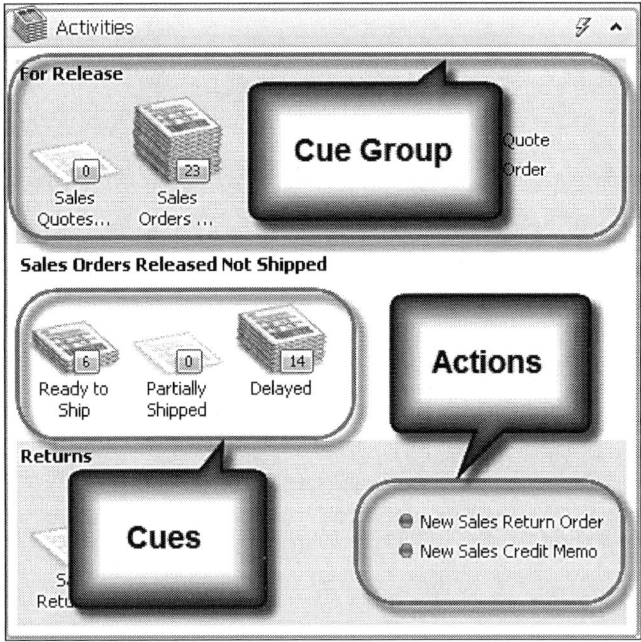

When you click a stack of documents, the relevant list place is opened in the navigation window. The user may remove cues from the part by selecting the **Customize** option from the **Actions** menu for the part (shown as a lightning bolt at the top-right corner of the part).

The cues are organized into groups and within each group there are actions such as **New Sales Return Order** or **New Sales Credit Memo**. We'll explore customizing the activities parts in greater detail later on in this chapter.

Actions for the activities part are **Remove** and **Customize**.

Outlook part

The **Outlook** part in the Role Center page allows users to see the number of unread emails in their inbox (with the ability to select which folders to display including RSS feeds), calendar appointments, and tasks. The user can click on the items to open the folder in Outlook.

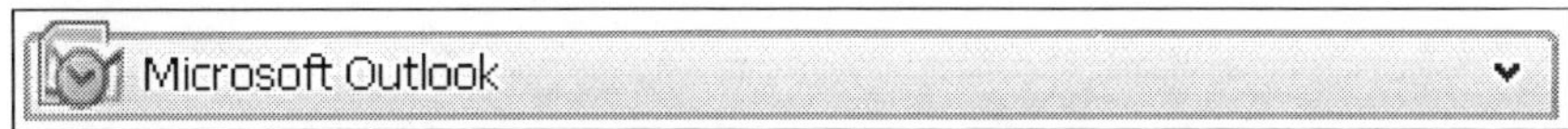

Actions for the Outlook part are **Remove** and **Customize**.

List parts

The list parts available in the **Sales Order Processor** role center are: **My Customers** and **My Items**.

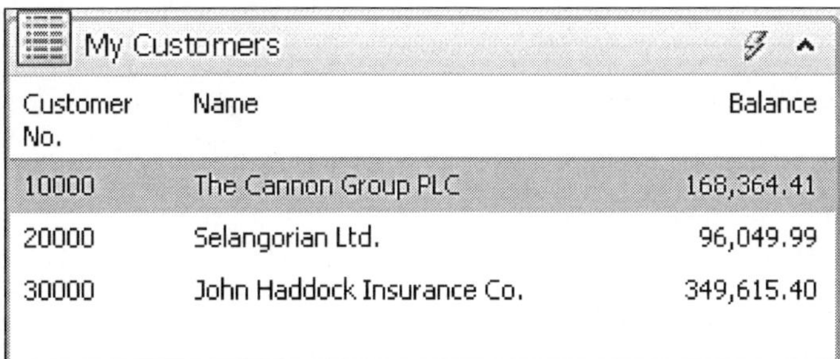

The list parts for **My Customers**, **My Items**, and **My Vendors** are based upon tables that include two fields: a user ID, and a link to the other table (such as a customer number). This simple technique provides an easy way for users to add their favorite items to their own role center.

Actions for the list part are: **Manage List**, **Open**, **Sort**, **Choose Columns**, **Remove**, and **Customize**.

Chart Part

The neat thing about the chart part is that you can add any number of them to your role center as long as you don't exceed seven parts in any given column. You can also select which chart a chart part will display, and they can be any color you want, as long as it's green.

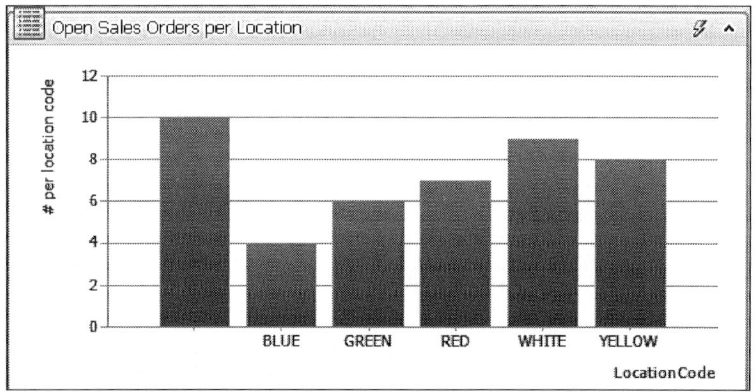

This is an incredible feature allowing Key Performance Indicator (KPI) type reporting straight out of the box. Although not all of the charts offer any obvious value, the salespeople are gonna love this!

You can hover over the bars in the chart with your mouse pointer to display a tooltip containing more details, such as the dimensions the bar corresponds to and the amount being represented.

It's not easy being green

There are forty pre-defined charts, and new charts can be created by importing an XML chart definition into a blob field of a new **Chart** table. If this all sounds a bit too complicated, you can take a look on our book's downloads page at `www.teachmenav.com` to get hold of a tool to help you create your own charts.

Actions for the chart part are: **Remove** and **Customize**.

Notifications part

Notifications provide a way to pass notes around, a kind of mini internal email system. The notes are linked to documents or records such as Sales Orders and Customers, and the user can double-click the note to display the record to which the note relates. In addition to notes being surfaced on the role center, the note will be visible on the Page for the record it is linked to, that is, a Sales Order Document or Customer Card. It is also shown in the list place if the Notes FactBox is shown.

Actions for the notifications part are: **Remove Notification**, **Delete**, **View**, and **Remove**.

Remove Notification and **Delete** look suspiciously alike but they are different in function. The **Remove Notification** option will stop displaying the note in your role center's notification part while leaving the note attached to the record for all to see. The Delete option will remove the note from your notification part and delete the record from the database so that the note is no more, has ceased to be, has expired and gone to meet its maker—it is an ex-note!

The List Place navigation page

The **List Place** forms a large part of the new NAV 2009 user experience and, with the exception of the role center, every menu option in the **Home** activity pane will launch a list place. Clicking on cues in the role center will display a list place; clicking on items in the navigation pane (such as Sales Orders, Customers, Items, even Journals) will display a list place. The list place allows you to see the list of records, and you can filter the results, see related information in the various parts that accompany the list, and double-click a record in the list to open a card task page.

This new approach of launching a list from a menu option is opposite to the old approach (or the Classic client approach), whereby a menu option launched a card form showing a single record. Microsoft's Dynamics usability studies found that in the old client, after launching a card form via a menu option, the first thing the user typically did was press the *F5* key to launch the list showing all records so that they could search for the record they wanted. This new approach makes perfect sense but may take some getting used to for experienced users.

List places are read only; if you want to edit records, you need to use a task page. You can launch the list place in a new window by right-clicking the menu option and selecting the **Open In New Window** option; this works in a similar manner to Microsoft Outlook (where clicking on a folder in the navigation pane will display a list of the items the folder contains in the main window, unless you select the **Open in New Window** option by right-clicking the menu for the Outlook folder).

The list place contains much more than a list of records such as **Filter Pane**, **Action Pane**, **FactBox Pane**, **List**, and **Chart Pane**. Let's start at the top with the action pane.

Action pane

Any of the options from the Actions command menu, Related Information menu, or Reports menu can be promoted to the action pane. Being promoted is not as good as it sounds: the options simply get more work for no extra money.

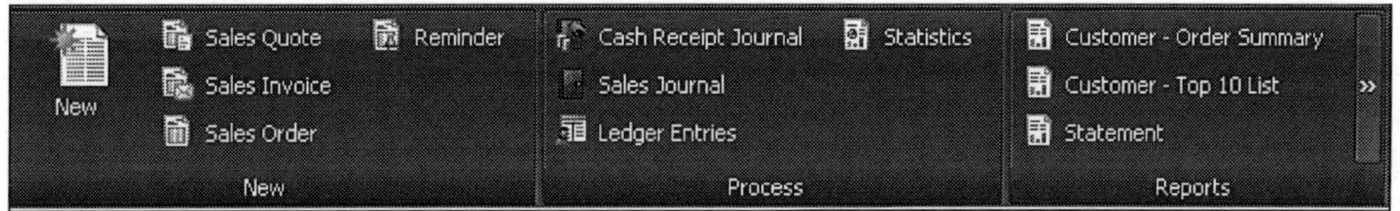

The intention of the action pane is to make the most commonly used features more accessible to the users, and to enable them to tailor the pane to their exact requirements.

In addition to promoting commands from the **Actions** menu to the action pane, the options can be promoted within the action pane by giving them a large appearance. In the previous image (taken from a Customer list place) the **New** action is clearly more dominant than the actions to create a new **Sales Quote, Sales Invoic**e, **Sales Order**, or **Reminder**.

If you promote more options than can fit in the available space (as in the reports group on the previous image), a button appears to the right allowing you to select from the additional options.

If you are short of screen space, the action pane can be hidden completely by using the customize menu. Beneath the action pane and above the list is the filter pane.

Filter pane

The filter pane can be hidden by using the Customize button, but in its minimized state it shows the useful quick-filtering controls that allow you to filter on any column included in the list. Simply select the field from the drop-down button (in the image, it is showing the **No.** field) and type your filter in the box that has the ghosted text ***Type to filter***.

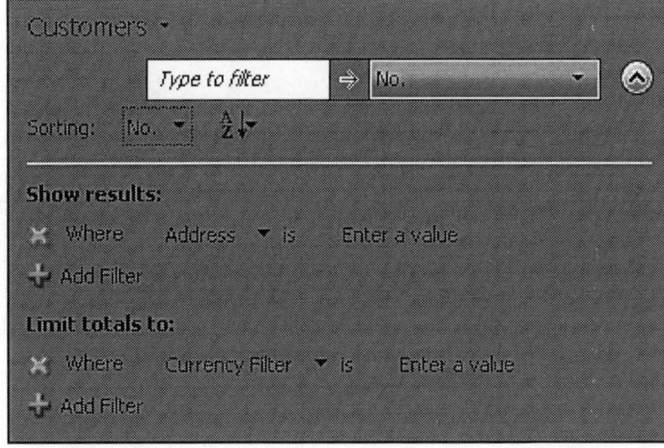

The filter pane appears above your List and is used to filter the records that are displayed, change the sort order, and apply limits to any totals displayed in the list. In older versions, the apply limits to any totals option was called **flow-filters**.

The sorting of records is done through two buttons: the first allows you to select from the pre-defined indexes on the table and the second allows you to decide if the records are in ascending or descending order.

If you want to apply filters to multiple fields simultaneously, you can click the **Expand** button to reveal the **Show results:** area. Once the expanded area is displayed, it is simply a matter of using the **Add Filter** button, selecting a field, and then clicking the **Enter a value** button to enter a filter.

Filter limits

The filtering options in the RoleTailored client are not as powerful as ones in the Classic client. For example, when you have an option field, you can only filter on what it is, and not what it isn't. This means that you cannot show all customers that are not blocked (that is their **Blocked** field is neither **Ship**, **Invoice**, nor **All**). I expect we may be seeing a change to this in a service pack some time soon. In the meantime you could change the caption for the first option in the option string property on the table definition from a single space to some words such as *Not Blocked*.

If you want to limit the totals on the list to a given filter for pre-defined filters, you can select the **Advanced filter** option from the record drop-down menu (in the previous figure, the **Customers** drop down).

And now on to the main purpose of the list place: the list.

List

The list is the star attraction of the list place, but it doesn't really do much. It shows the records that match the filters you have entered on the filter pane. You can select multiple records but you cannot select all records in one go.

If you right-click you will get a menu as shown below that allows you to view or edit the record on a task page. You can also select the columns to show in the list and select the height of the headings. This is useful for those columns that have long titles such as the **Sell-to Customer No.** column pictured below.

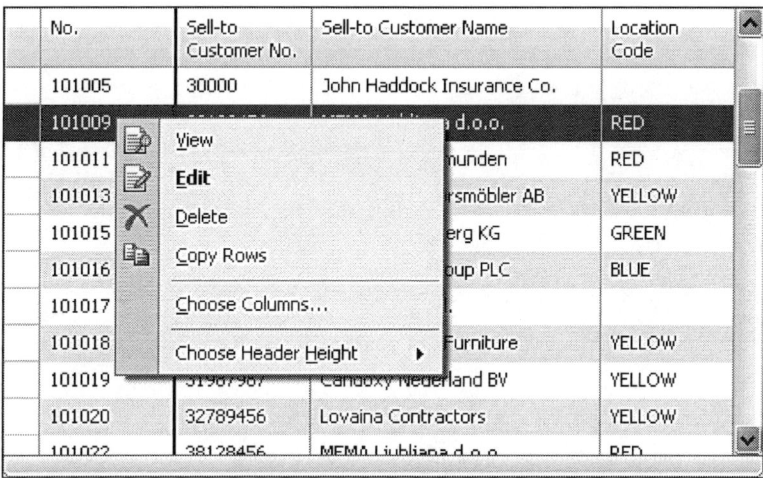

Lists are non-editable, so the **Copy Rows** option is only useful for transferring to Excel and not for inserting into another list (as it was in the Classic client).

It is not possible to drag columns around to change their order of appearance, and there is no option to hide a column if you right-click on the column header. You can, however, do these things with the customize options and we'll cover these in our section on customization later on in this chapter. There is a nice Excel-like feature that allows you to double-click the divider between two column titles in order to resize the column to fit the largest data field.

Chart pane

Not shown by default but possibly the nicest looking part in the list place is the chart pane.

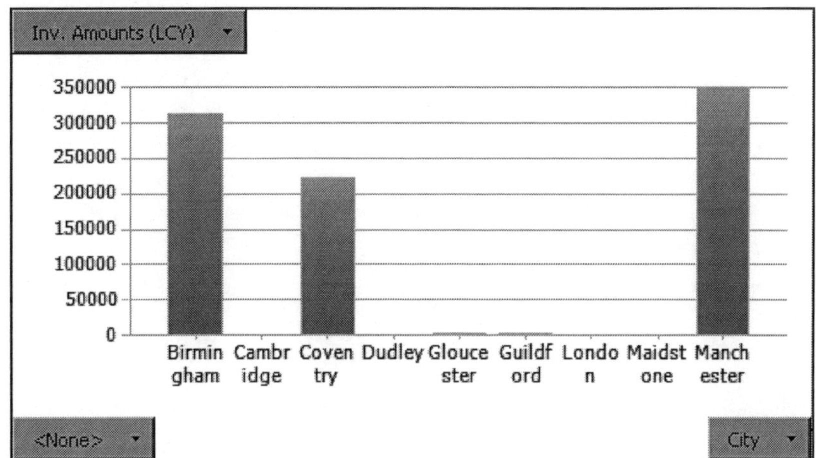

The chart pane allows you to show two-dimensional and three-dimensional charts for the data that is contained in the list. Any filters you apply in the filter pane will also filter the data displayed in chart.

You can select a measure (in our example, this is **Inv. Amounts (LCY)**) and up to two dimensions. Here we have selected a single dimension of **City**, and you can see the chart displays the data quite nicely (note that I filtered the data so that **Country/Region Code** is GB).

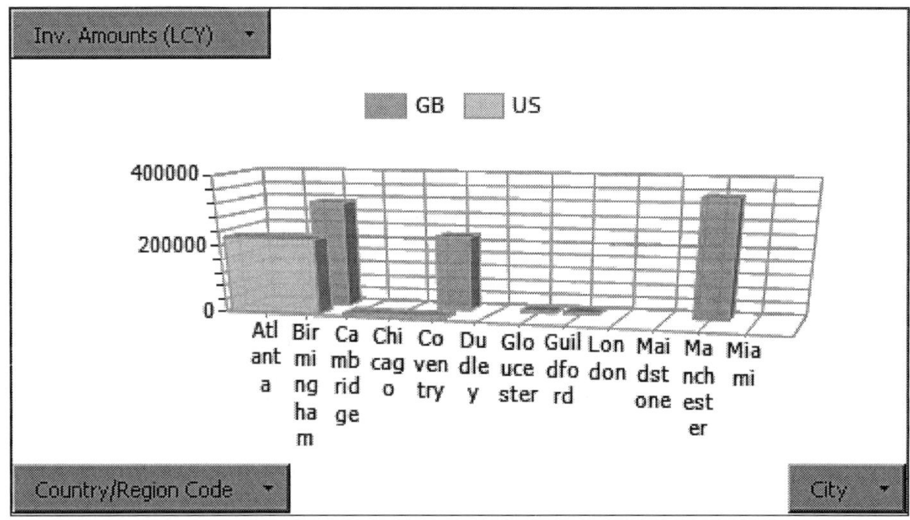

If I add a second dimension (**Country/Region Code** in my example), then the graph is rendered as three-dimensional chart. In the previous image, I changed my filter so that **Country/Region Code** is **GB | US** (meaning either GB or US), as this makes the chart a little less cluttered.

This chart control is full of features. You can add multiple measures if you are not using a secondary dimension, which would allow you to compare things like amount and discount side by side. A right-click menu allows you to save the chart as a bitmap (`.bmp`) or portable network graphics (`.png`) file, or copy the picture to the clipboard. If you are using a three-dimensional chart (two dimensions and a single measure), you can use the left mouse button to click on the chart and drag the chart to change the viewing perspective.

When the chart gets really busy, you can hover the mouse pointer over a bar to see which dimension values it relates to and the actual amount the bar corresponds to.

The chart pane does not remain on a list place after you close the client. We expect this to change in a later service pack release, but make sure your users are aware of this feature before they spend hours setting up their favorite charts only to lose them when they exit the application.

On the right of the list place, we have the FactBox pane; let's see what it does.

FactBox pane

Customer Sales History - Sell-to Customer	
Customer No.:	10000
Quotes:	0
Blanket Orders:	0
Orders:	4
Invoices:	0
Return Orders:	0
Credit Memos:	0
Pstd. Shipments:	6
Pstd. Invoices:	3
Pstd. Return Receipts:	1
Pstd. Credit Memos:	1

The **FactBox Pane** can contain any number of FactBoxes depending on how many are available for selection on the list place. Each available FactBox can appear only once within the pane. You will always be able to select Notes (which shows notifications for the record) and Links (which shows links to external documents or files).

The action button allows you to select the fields to show in the FactBox or to remove the FactBox from the pane.

Each value shown against a field is a link to either a Card page (such as **Customer No.**, which links to the Customer Card) or a list place in a new window (such as **Pstd. Invoices**, which links to the **View - Posted Sales Invoices** list page).

You can expand and collapse the FactBox using the expand/collapse button at the top right, and the Customize menu offers an option to choose the FactBoxes to display.

The FactBox was our last part of the list place, so now it's time to look at everything else or, as Microsoft calls it, the Departments page.

The Departments page

The **Departments** page has a navigation pane that looks reminiscent of the one in the Classic client; the following image shows them side by side. You can see that everything on the Classic client has been moved down a level: Financial Management is no longer a menu in its own right but is instead a sub-menu of the Departments menu.

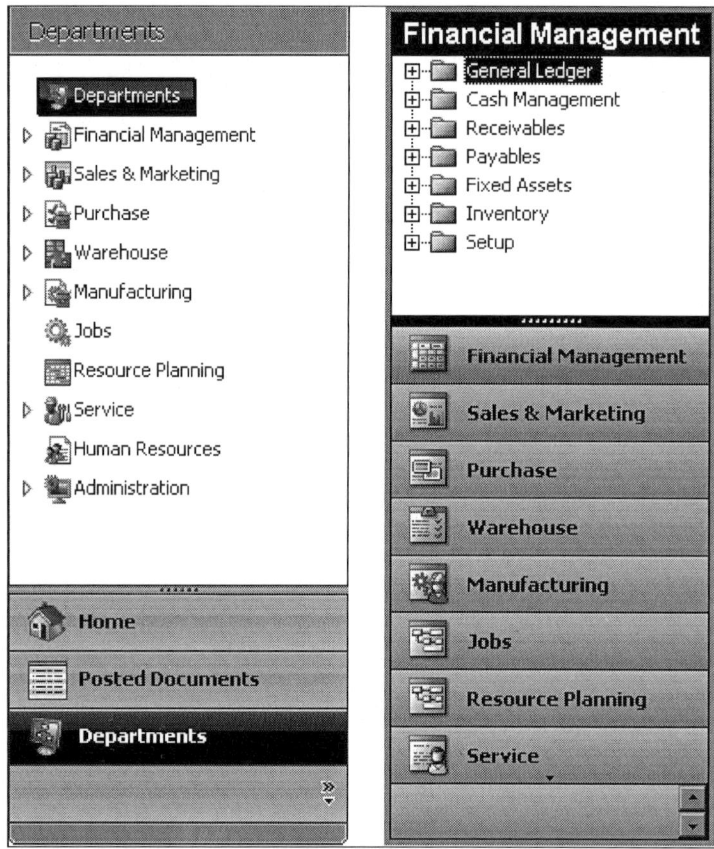

You'll also notice the extra option at the top of the **Departments** page menu called **Departments**. This is similar to the **Home** button in the **Role Center**, and when it is selected the main window displays the following image:

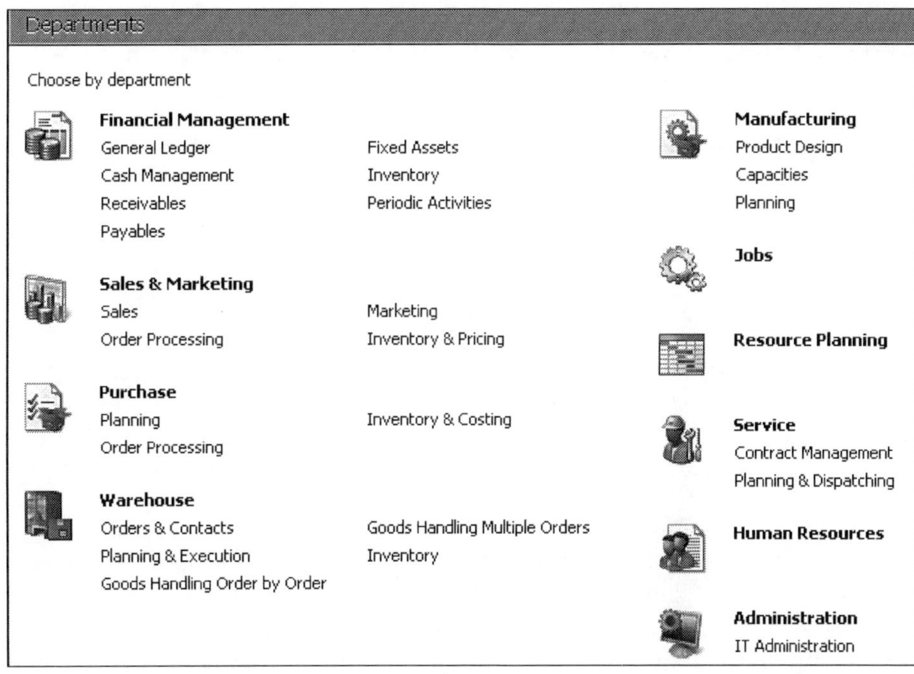

As you select menu options from the navigation pane or click on options within the main window, the main window menu display changes, helping you to narrow your selection until you see the option you want. For example, clicking the **Financial Management** menu will show the following page.

Financial Management

Choose by department

General Ledger

Cash Management

Receivables

Payables

Fixed Assets

Inventory

Periodic Activities

General Ledger	Consolidation
VAT	Receivables
Currency	Payables
Fiscal Year	

...or choose by category

Lists
Tasks
Reports and Analysis
Documents
History
Administration

The first level of submenus is treated as departments: **General Ledger**, **Cash Management**, **Receivables**, etc. You can also select the option to view the menu items by category such as **Lists**, **Tasks**, or **Reports and Analysis**.

If you click enough options, you will navigate to the point where the link you click will open a list place in the main window or a new task page or report in a window of its own. For example, if you expand the **General Ledger** menu and click **Chart of Accounts**, you will see the Chart of Accounts list place displayed in the main window. If instead you expanded the **General Ledger** menu and clicked **General Journals**, this will open the **Edit - General Journal** task page.

For menu items that represent a list place, you can select **Add to Navigation Pane** from the right-click menu. This is just another way of customizing the navigation pane and adding a new option. We'll cover the other way of doing this later on in our section on how to personalize the RoleTailored client.

For menu items that are not lists, you can right-click and select **Add to Reports on RoleCenter** or **Add to Actions on RoleCenter** depending on whether the option is a report or a task page. Again, there are other ways of doing this and we will cover that in a later section. If you select one of these options to add the menu to the actions or reports menu on the RoleCenter, the option gets added to the bottom of the menu but you can customize the menu to move it somewhere else if you prefer.

That concludes our review of the navigation window. Now it's time to look at the part of the application where the real work happens: the task page.

Task pages

Task pages is the broad category used to describe a page that is used to edit data or carry out a specific task. When you double-click a record from a list place or select certain actions, a task page will open in a new window. Task pages fall into seven subcategories with different layouts: Cards, Documents, Journals, Lists, List Plus, Matrices, and Wizards. Many of the components on a task page are the same as those found in the Navigation Layer; we'll still list the components for completeness but tell you to look for the definition that was provided earlier.

Let's start with the most common page type: the card.

Cards

The following image shows the customer card. You'll notice that the title for the window now includes the word **Edit** to inform you that you are able to edit the data as opposed to **View** which means it is for view only.

At the top of the card task page, you'll notice the command bar and action pane that we covered in the previous section on the navigation window, so we'll skip those and move on to the fast tabs that make up the main part of the card task page.

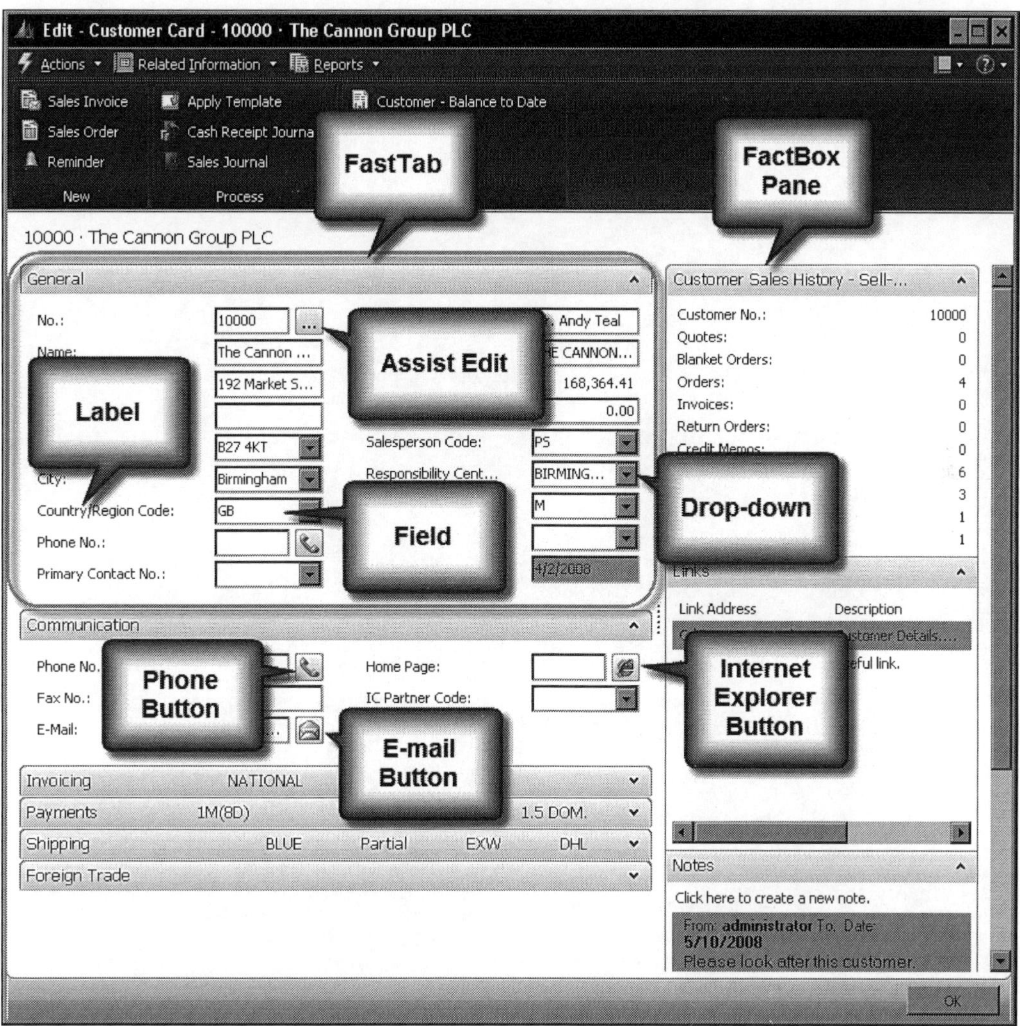

FastTab

The card has a number of FastTabs that stack on top of each other, unlike the tab control in the Classic client where the pages sit behind one another. The following is an image of one of the FastTabs from the customer card in its expanded state.

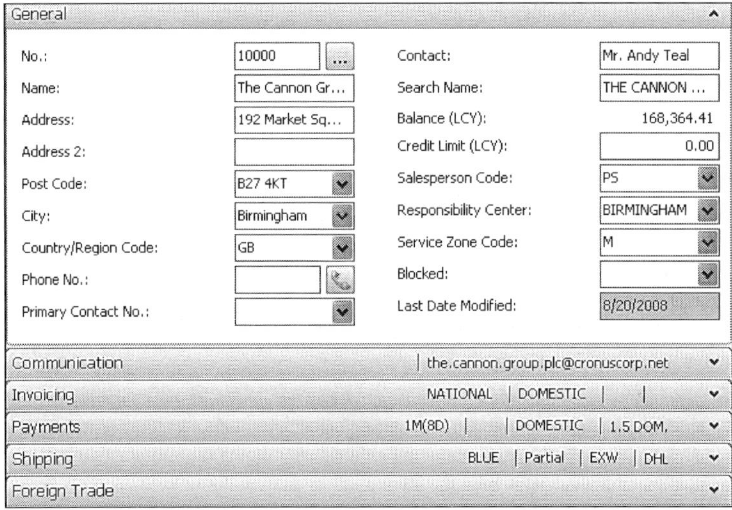

By stacking the tabs vertically, the card has a number of nice features. If you are not familiar with older versions or the Classic client, next is a picture of how the tabs for the customer card look there.

Notice that things look a lot less cluttered in the RoleTailored client compared to the Classic client, even though the same fields are being displayed. The white background, slightly larger field size, and removal of the **leader dots** makes for an altogether tidier appearance.

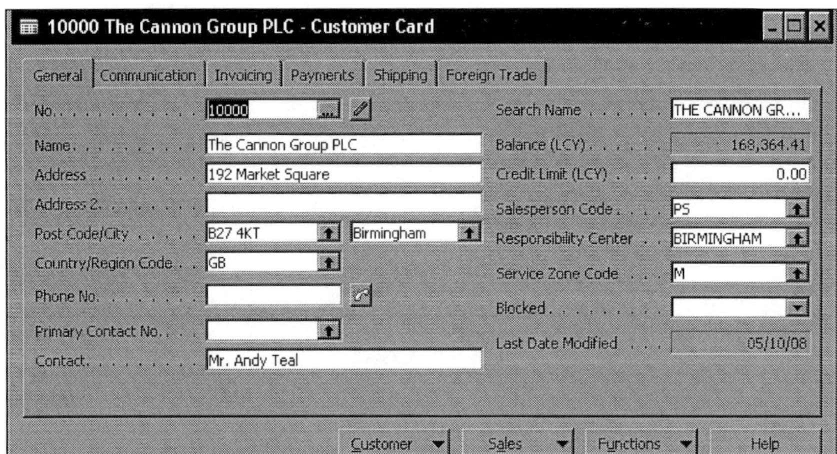

By stacking the FastTabs vertically and providing the ability to collapse and expand the tabs, you can have multiple tabs open simultaneously. This means that (providing your screen is large enough) you can see the fields on the **General** FastTab and the **Communication** FastTab at the same time without needing to click on the tab to reveal the information.

When the FastTab is collapsed, you can still see the most important information on the FastTab. For example, in the following image, even though the **Payments** FastTab is collapsed, we can still see the customer's payment terms, reminder terms, and finance charge terms.

Don't worry if these fields are not important to you; the RoleTailored client allows you to select which fields get **promoted** to the FastTab title, which fields are **additional** and should be initially hidden, and which fields are simply **standard**. We'll cover more on how to configure the FastTab fields later on in our section on customizing a page with FastTabs.

On each FastTab there are a number of controls: **Labels**, **Fields**, and **Buttons**. Labels and fields are pretty intuitive, so there's no need to go into details.

Mandatory fields now have a visual indicator telling you that the field must be filled in. To see this in action, try to create a new account in the chart of accounts and you will see a red star against the code field.

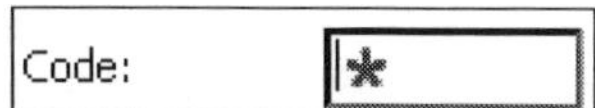

If you neglect to fill in the mandatory field, and attempt to move to another field, an error message is displayed at the top of the page and another visual cue is added.

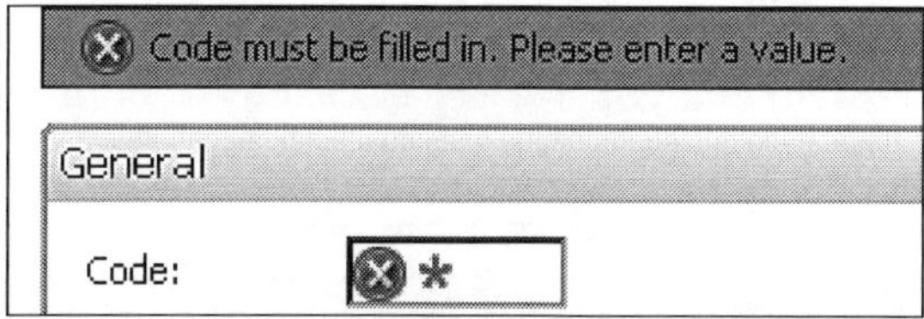

Errors

Error messages are now displayed in an error bar at the top of the page. Multiple fields can contain errors simultaneously, and the error bar will change to show which error is displayed (1/2, 2/2, etc.)

It is possible to press the *F5* key and revert all fields with errors back to their previous state, and therefore be able to save the record and continue.

Fields can be calculated from other records (the **Balance (LCY)** field, for example, is calculated from the sum of the **Amount (LCY)** field from the Detailed Cust. Ledg. Entry table). If this is the case, the field will be shown as text with no field border and when you hover your mouse pointer over the field, an underscore will indicate that you can click the field similar to a hyperlink on a web page. Clicking the link will display a drill-down list page showing the details of the records that were used to calculate the value in the field. This behavior replaces the drill-down button in the Classic client.

Drop-down buttons

If a field is related to another table or may only contain a pre-determined set of values, a drop-down button is drawn to the right of the field. In older versions of NAV and the Classic client, a different button was used to indicate if the field was related to another table (look-up) or if only a limited set of options were allowed (drop-down); in the RoleTailored client, the same button is used for both purposes.

Depending on where the data for the field comes from, you will see one of three things: a simple list of options, a drop-down control, or a selection list task page.

For a related table, you will see that multiple fields are displayed in the drop-down box and a column heading is included. These new lists are created by the RoleTailored client based upon the **DropDown** field group on the table definition. We'll cover field groups in more detail in Chapter 6.

The new drop-down list also provides a resizing gadget at the bottom-right of the box, and two buttons at the bottom-left—**New** and **Advanced**. When you select the **New** button, a **Select Card** task page is displayed that allows you to fill in the details for a new record and then click OK to select it. If you click the **Advanced** button, you will see a full **Select List** task page. If a DropDown field group has not been defined or there is some special logic behind the lookup (as in the case of the Post Code field on the Customer Card), then you will see a select list by default when trying to select from the field.

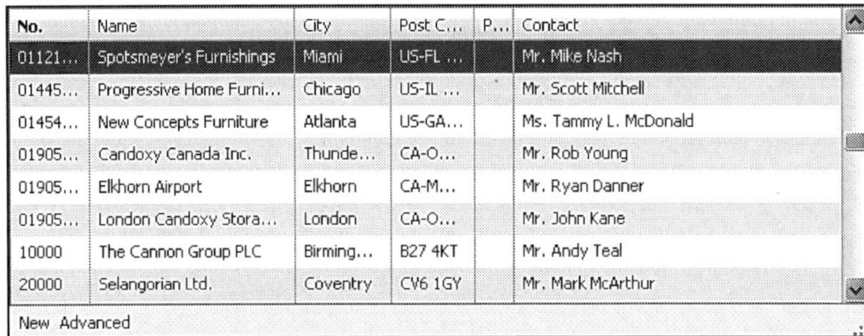

No.	Name	City	Post C...	P...	Contact
01121...	Spotsmeyer's Furnishings	Miami	US-FL ...		Mr. Mike Nash
01445...	Progressive Home Furni...	Chicago	US-IL ...		Mr. Scott Mitchell
01454...	New Concepts Furniture	Atlanta	US-GA...		Ms. Tammy L. McDonald
01905...	Candoxy Canada Inc.	Thunde...	CA-O...		Mr. Rob Young
01905...	Elkhorn Airport	Elkhorn	CA-M...		Mr. Ryan Danner
01905...	London Candoxy Stora...	London	CA-O...		Mr. John Kane
10000	The Cannon Group PLC	Birming...	B27 4KT		Mr. Andy Teal
20000	Selangorian Ltd.	Coventry	CV6 1GY		Mr. Mark McArthur

New Advanced

The new drop-down list can be sorted according to any of the columns shown and the **Find As You Type** feature can also be used. In the previous image, the **No.** field is shown in bold indicating that this is the current sort order of the list. By clicking on the title of the list or using the cursor-down arrow on the keyboard, you can activate the heading so that you can use the cursor-left and cursor-right keys to select different fields for sorting. You may notice that the Find As You Type works as a filter and not a find meaning that only those matching records are shown.

Assist Edit

The assist edit button exists to help you enter a value into a field.

You will see this against every code field that is linked to a number series, as this will allow you to select the number series to use for a new record.

Phone, email, and browser buttons

The phone button, email button, and browser buttons will dial phone numbers (for users with a TAPI phone system), launch a new email, and open the URL in a web browser respectively.

The same functionality existed in older versions and the Classic client, but for developers it is now a lot easier to add these buttons to a page.

The new buttons are drawn by the RoleTailored client when a new **ExtendedDatatype** property is set on the field definition to be either **Phone No.**, **E-Mail**, or **URL**.

There are two other types available in the ExtendedDatatype options: Ratio and Masked. A Ratio type field is displayed as a read-only progress indicator with a percentage value. A Masked field does not show input when you type into a field (such as a password field).

FactBox pane

We've already covered the FactBox pane when looking at the list place in the navigation layer. The FactBox pane allows you to display FactBoxes that can contain summarized data for the entity such as Customer Sales History, Dimensions, Links, and Notes. The difference here is that the Notes and Links FactBoxes can be used to add notes and links instead of just viewing them.

Lists

There are no new elements to discuss for a list task page, as it is simply a list place from the navigation layer but displayed in its own window.

Documents

A document task page is used to display any document-type entities that comprise a header and multiple lines such as Sales Order, Sales Invoice, Purchase Order, Purchase Invoice, and so on.

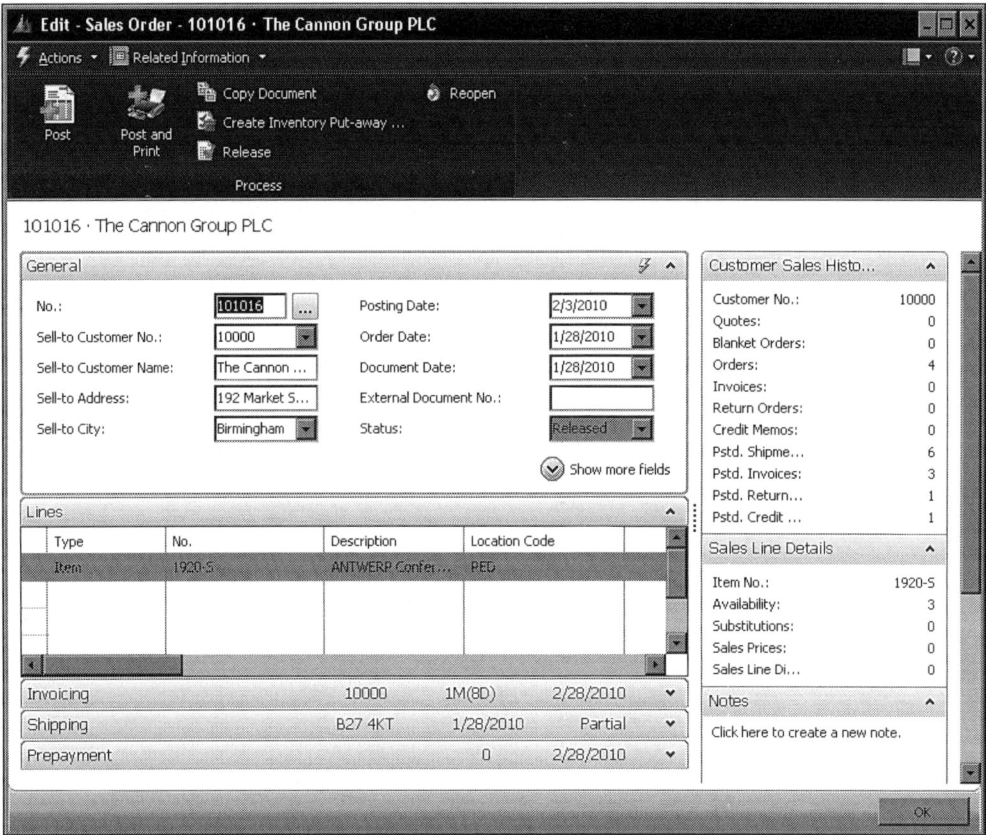

At first glance it looks just like a card task page with FastTabs and FactBoxes. However, one of the FastTabs is a list that contains the lines of the document and you can edit the values and add new lines.

Journals

A journal task page is an editable list and is used for entering batches of transactions that will be posted simultaneously. Examples of journals are G/L Journals for entering financial transactions, Sales Journals, Cash Receipts Journals, etc.

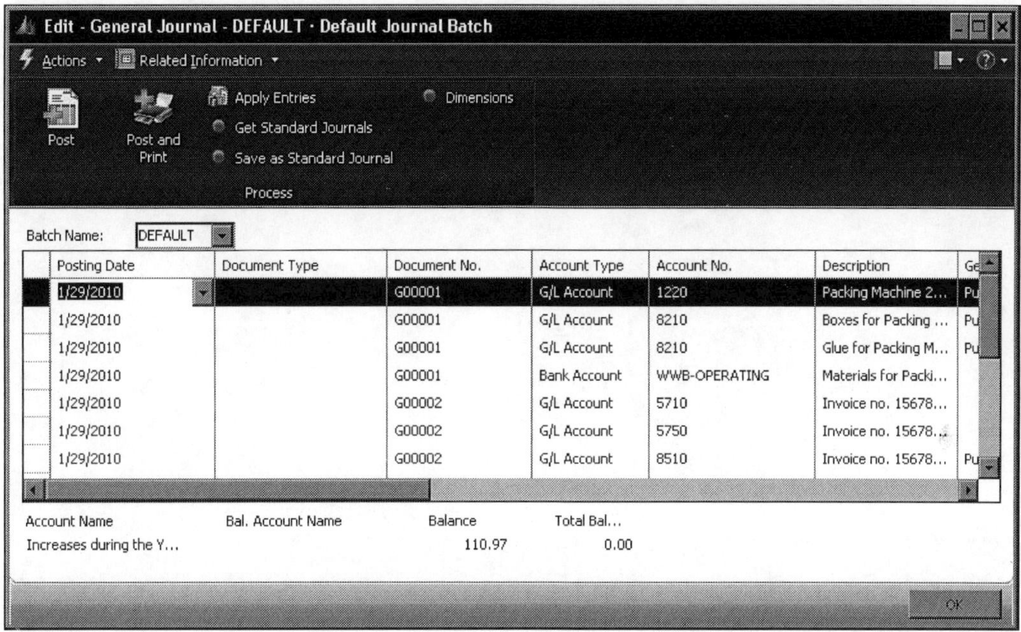

This type of task page doesn't look like the task pages we have already covered but it uses all of the same components. There are no FastTabs or FactBoxes as the main area of the window is filled with the journal lines and some additional fields.

List plus

A list plus task page is similar to a document in that the page shows several FastTabs, one of which is a grid FastTab that shows multiple related records. Unlike the document page which always has the lines FastTab as the second FastTab on the page, the list plus can have a grid on any fast tab, and it is also possible to have multiple grids on a single list plus page.

It is difficult to find a typical use of a list plus page. Statistics is one of the quoted examples but many of the list plus pages simply look like lists. A list plus will not contain chart parts but can display FactBoxes. A good indication of when you should use a list plus type page is when you need more than one grid or you want to display fields and grids that are not in a document relationship.

Matrices

A matrix task page is one where values need to be entered for a given combination of two items. A good example is a G/L Budget where a row of the matrix typically represents the G/L Account and the columns of the matrix may represent the accounting period. Each cell for a given row and column (or G/L Account and Period) represents the budgeted value.

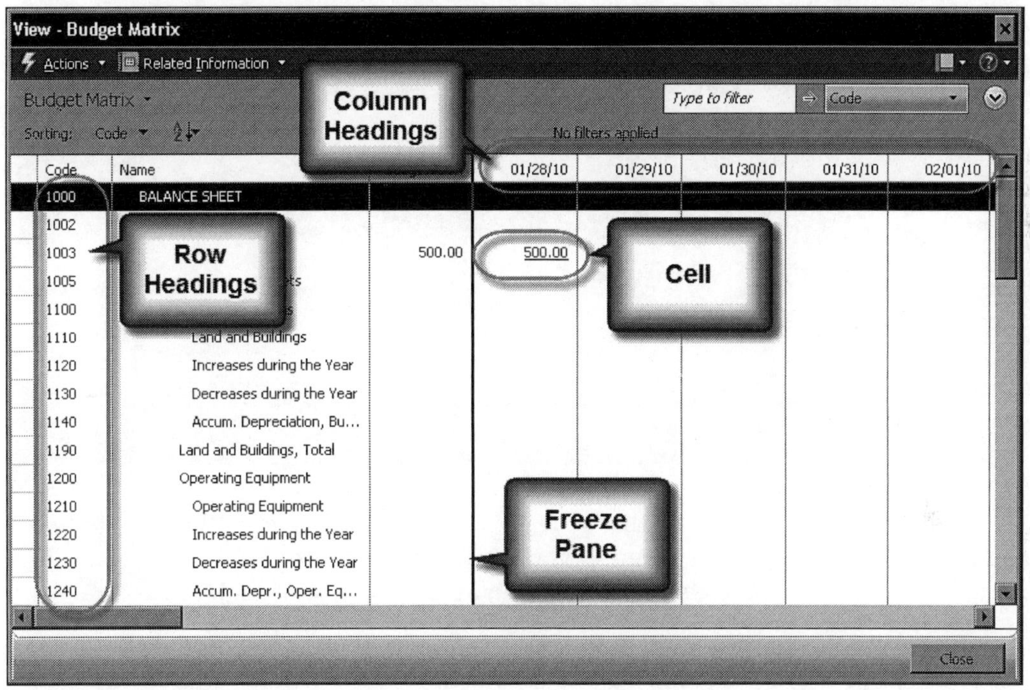

In the previous image, I have used the freeze panes feature to lock Code, Name, and Budgeted Amount columns so that they are always visible on the screen. The freeze panes feature exists on lists and any type of data grid and not just matrix pages. The matrix control in previous versions and the classic client had a fixed set of columns and a scrolling set of columns, which can be recreated in the RoleTailored client through using this feature. Scrolling right with the scroll gadget will move through the Accounting Periods but leave the other columns in place. We'll show you how to add a freeze pane in our Configuration section later on.

In order to change the number in the cell of a matrix, you must click on the field that contains the value you want to adjust and this will display another list task page as follows:

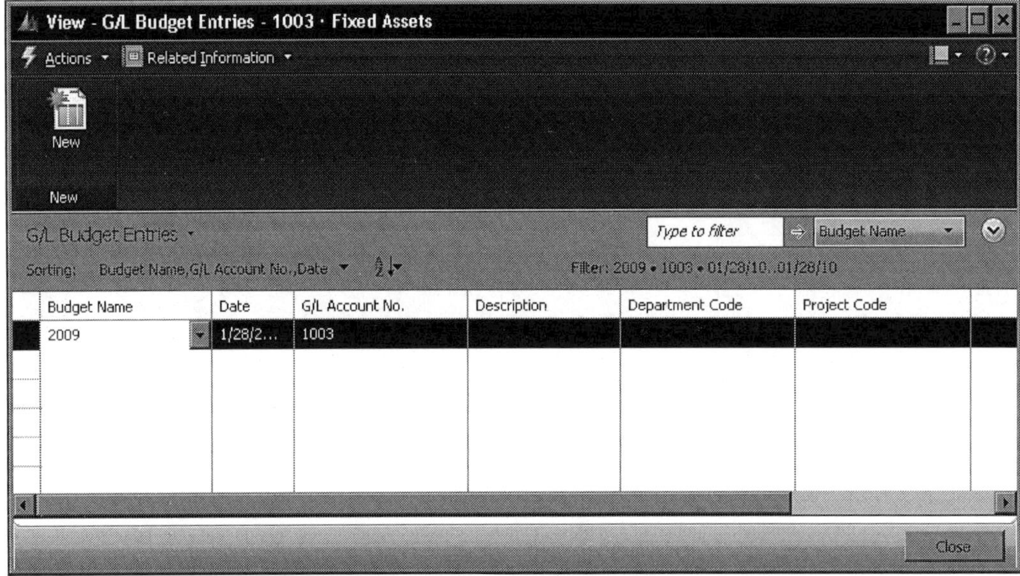

To add a new adjusting entry in the list task page that appears, click the **New** button and complete the adjusting amount. If you're used to the matrix controls in earlier versions of NAV, this new version may take a little getting used to. Matrices are typically used for ad hoc reporting type functions such as Analysis by Dimensions.

For experienced users of NAV, you may be thinking that this new matrix control is a lot harder to use than the previous one—the main disadvantage being that you cannot edit data directly in the matrix grid. Thankfully, if you have a lot of data to punch in to a budget, you can prepare the data in an Excel spreadsheet and import it directly, and the matrix task page will then only be used for fine-tuning and minor adjustments.

Wizards

A wizard task page is a task page that guides you through a particular task by offering advice, fields to complete, and navigation buttons to move forwards and backwards through the steps of the task. A good example of a wizard task page is the page displayed when you select the option to create a new interaction from a Contact record.

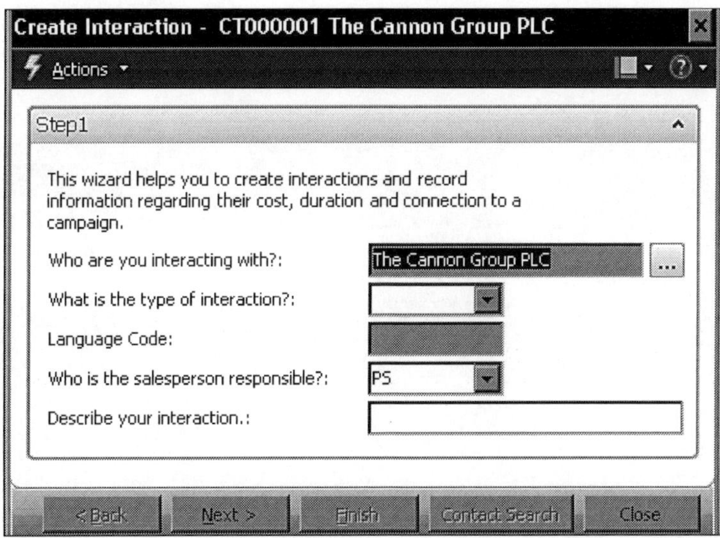

Each step of the wizard behaves like a FastTab although unsurprisingly, you cannot configure the fields that will be displayed.

The Report Viewer

When you select an option to run a report, you will see a Print Report task page.

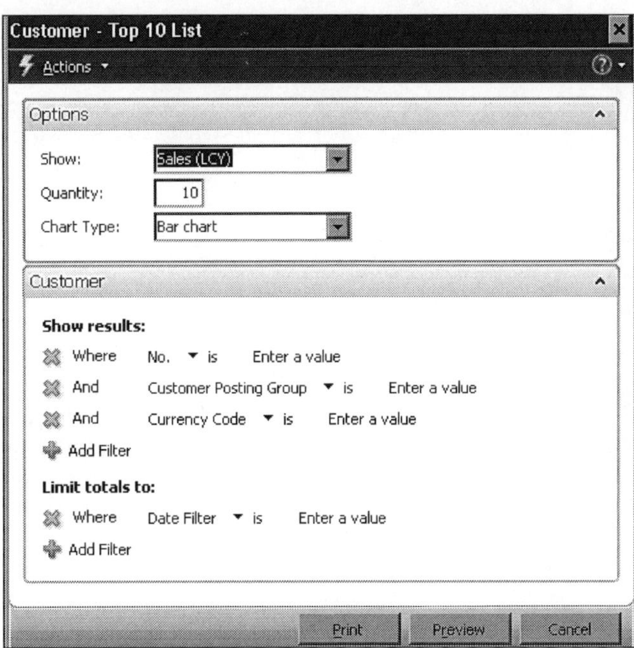

The page contains an **Options** FastTab and filtering FastTabs to allow you to select the data used on the report. When you click the **Preview** button, the report will render in a **Print Preview** page.

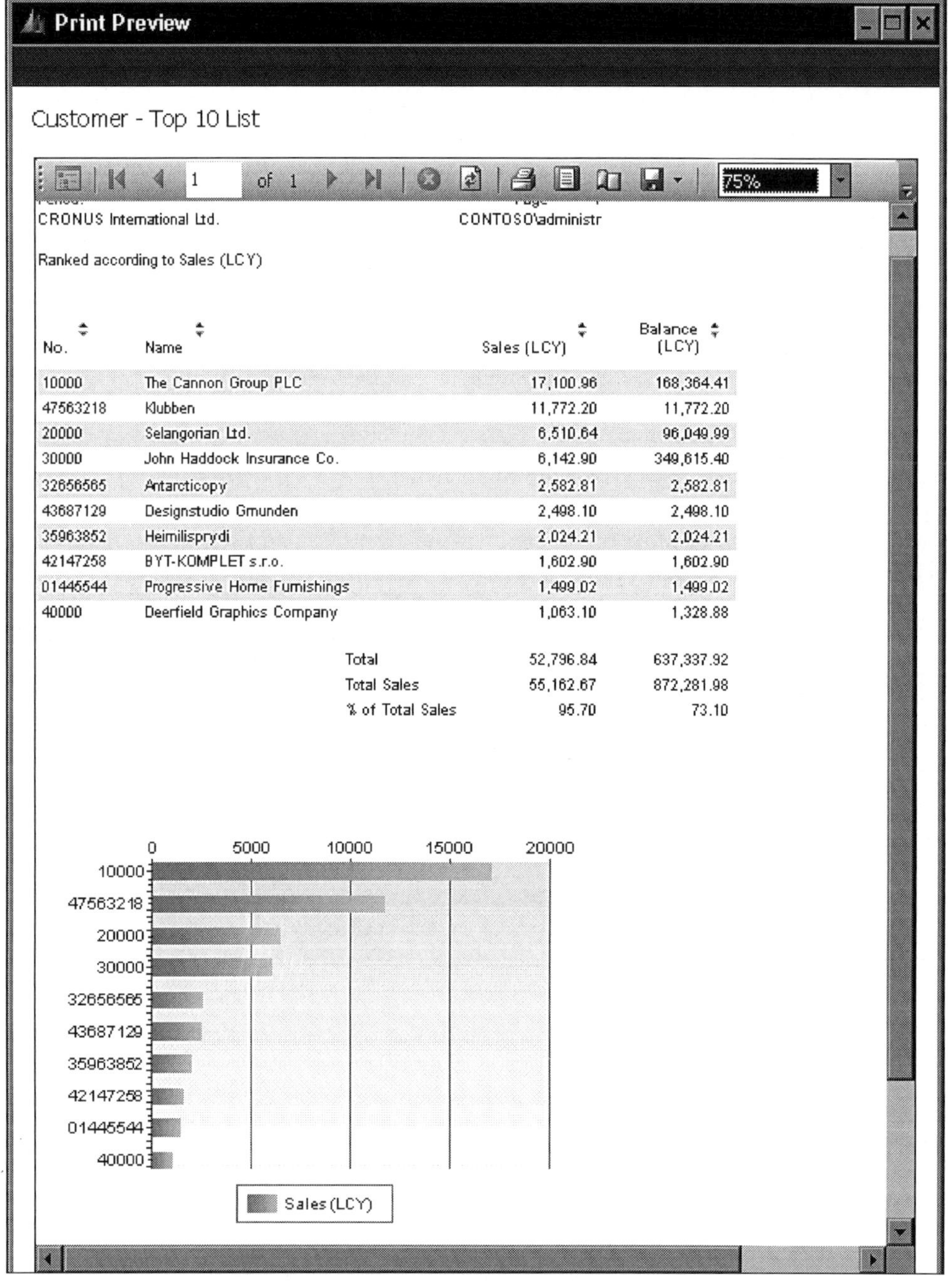

The report is being rendered in a **ReportViewer** control that was introduced in the .NET Framework 2.0, and uses a new reporting services client report definition (`.rdlc`) file to determine the layout. We'll cover more on how the new reports work from a developer's perspective in Chapter 6 but for now, let's see what additional features the Report Viewer provides to our end users.

Reporting Services reports can be developed to include a table of contents by marking sections in the report as being included in the document map. The table of contents shows as a Document Map that can be used to navigate the report or hidden completely using the following button.

The toolbar for the Report Viewer allows you to navigate the pages as you would expect with the following controls:

These two controls allow you to **Stop Rendering** and **Refresh** a report. The Stop Rendering is for those times when you started running a report that is going to take five minutes to render and you didn't enter the filter correctly.

The Refresh button is for those reports that are so good that you want to render them again—sadly, if you want to read the data from the database in order to pick up the very latest figures, you will need to run the report again; the refresh does not re-read.

Print and export

Reporting Services reports are great in that the presentation of the data (the rendering) can support different output formats. The **Save As** button (shown here as a floppy disk with a drop-down) allows reports to be saved as Excel or PDF files.

The other controls pictured in the previous screenshot allow you to: **Print** the report, view the report in **Print Layout** mode, and adjust the **Page Setup**. You should note that the Print Layout mode disables the **Find** and **Sort By** interactive features of the Report Viewer.

Over on the right of the toolbar, a new control group allows you to search for text within the body of the report.

This has got to be my favorite group of controls in the Report Viewer. You can type text into the Find box and hit the **Find** button to jump to the place in the report where the text appears. The **Next** button will take you to the next instance.

If your report definition has included the **UserSort** property, then the report will include Sort By buttons that allow you to change the sort order of the data on the report.

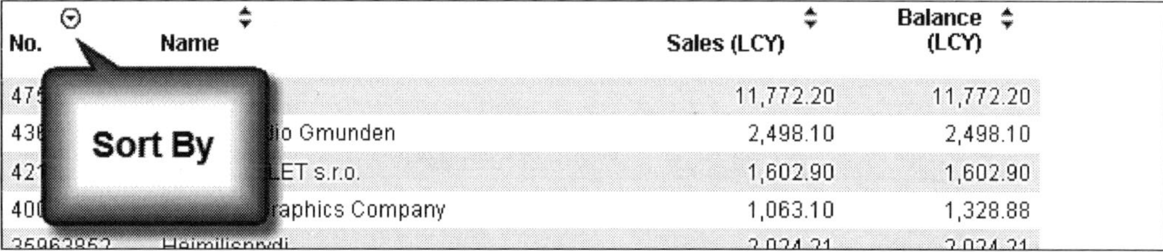

We've finished looking at the various places, pages, panes, and controls that the RoleTailored client has to offer. Now it's time to see the RoleTailored client in action.

How to use the RoleTailored client

You should now be familiar with most of the features of the RoleTailored client from an end-user perspective. We'll look at the personalization features later on in this chapter, but now it's time to walk through some exercises to understand how the application works. You will find that the online help that accompanies NAV 2009 has been dramatically improved over previous incarnations with the addition of process-oriented help topics. Open the help from the Help menu or by pressing *F1* and take a look within the General Ledger section. You'll see topics such as:

- Creating Purchase Invoices
- Filling In and Sending IC Sales and Purchase Documents
- Calculate Invoice Discount
- Invoicing Purchases with Multiple Currencies

This is a big improvement and you can spend time learning how to use the product by using the online help and the product itself—something that was never possible in older versions.

The purpose of this section is not to teach you how to use Dynamics NAV as an application; it's huge! There are training courses, manuals, online help, e-learning courses, and online forums and communities available to help you learn NAV, and the scope of the product is far more than we could possibly hope to cover in this book.

What we will do is give you some easy exercises that will help you understand how to do things in the new RoleTailored client, using most of the elements we have previously discussed.

There are several ways of skinning a cat (allegedly) and we're not saying that these are the best or only ways of carrying out these particular business processes. The processes are here to illustrate the features of the RoleTailored client and are deliberately simple.

Create a customer

In this process we are going to create a new customer record. This will show you how to use a card task page to enter details for a new record. There are many fields on the customer card but we are going to focus on just those that are needed to allow us to work with the customer and post some transactions.

1. Go to **CRONUS International Ltd.** | **Home** | **Customers**.
2. The customer list place is displayed.

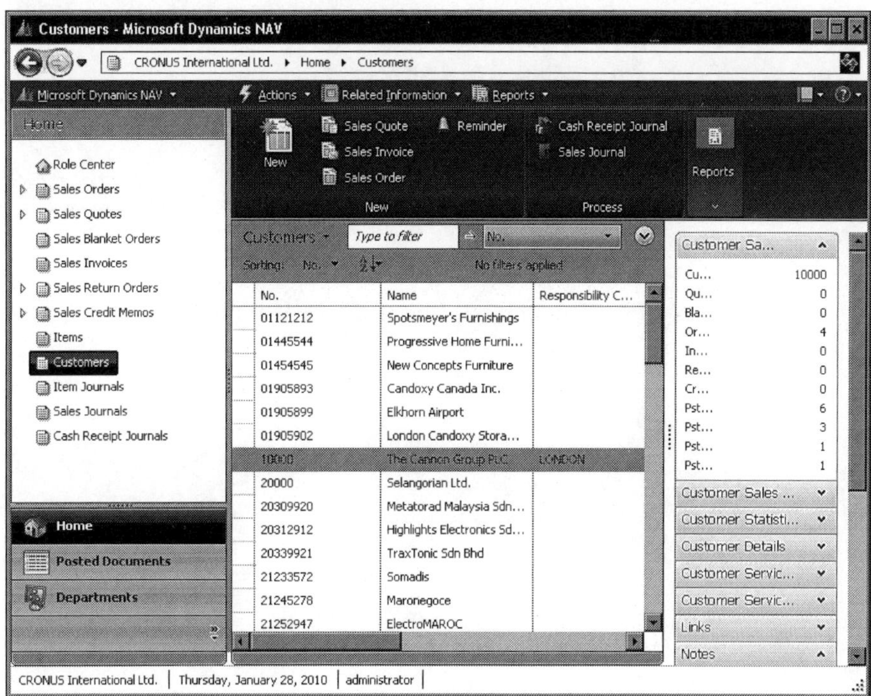

3. Click the **New** button on the action pane to create a new record or press the *Ctrl+N* key combination.
4. The **New - Customer Card** task page is displayed and your cursor is in the **No.:** field waiting for you to enter a number for the new customer.

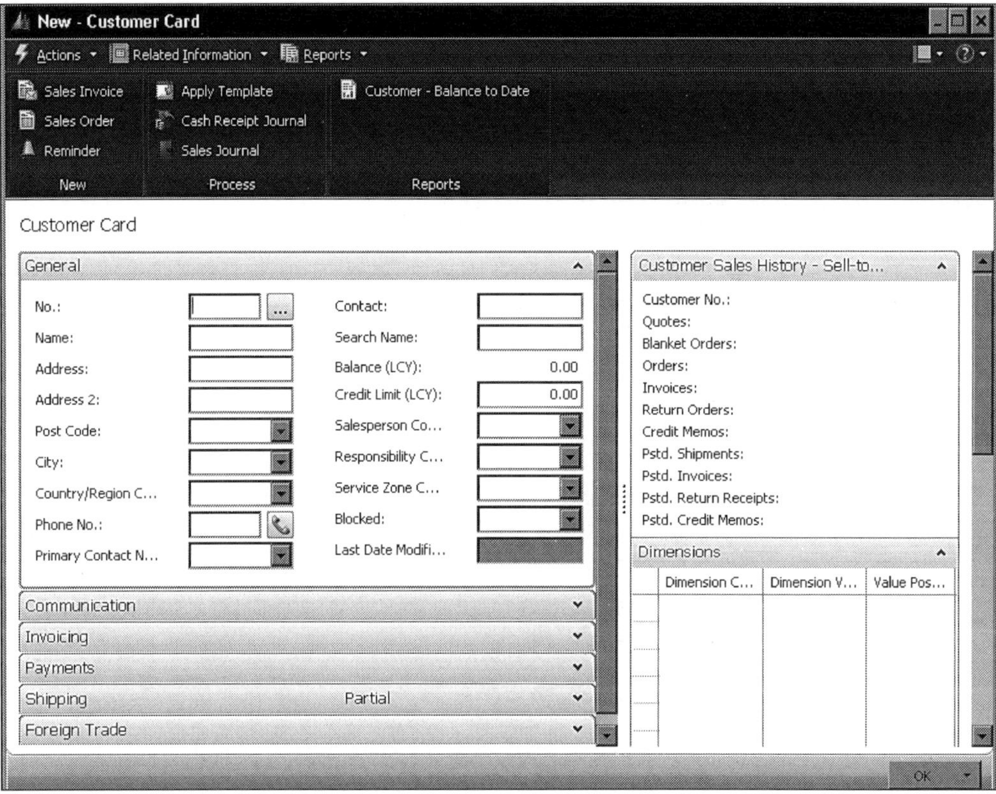

Press the *Enter* key to move from the **No.:** field.

5. The system allocates the next customer number from the number series and moves the cursor to the **Name** field.

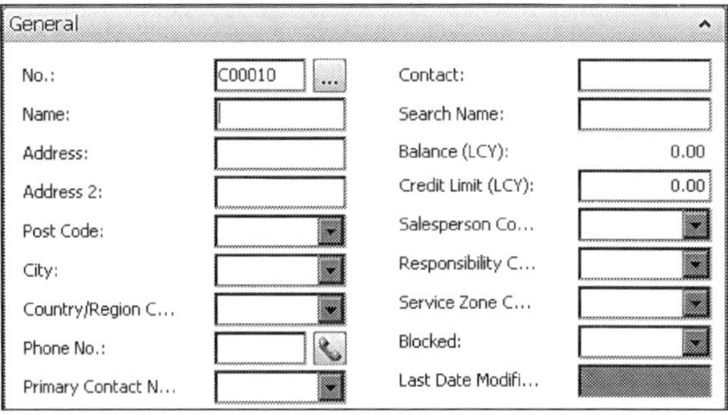

6. Enter the following details on the **General** FastTab:

Field	Value
Name	**Nicholas Claus Inc.**
Address	**Cliff House**
Address 2	**Near the North Pole**
Country/Region Code	**US**

7. Click the **Invoicing** FastTab and ensure it is expanded.
8. The **Invoicing** FastTab is displayed.

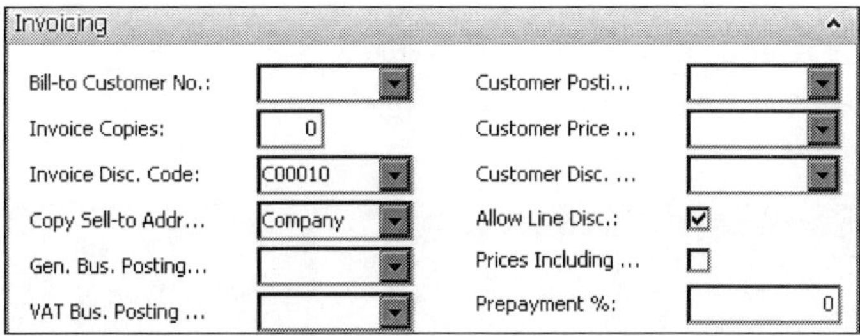

9. Enter the following details on the **Invoicing** FastTab:

Field	Value
Gen. Bus. Posting Group	**NATIONAL**
VAT Bus. Posting Group	**NATIONAL**
Customer Posting Group	**DOMESTIC**

10. Click the Payments FastTab and ensure it is expanded.

VAT Bus. Posting Group

When you are completing your data, you'll notice that this value gets set automatically when you enter the **Gen. Bus. Posting Group**. Don't worry if you don't understand the purpose of these fields as we'll be covering their purpose in Chapter 5—*Configuring the System*.

11. The system displays the **Payments** FastTab.

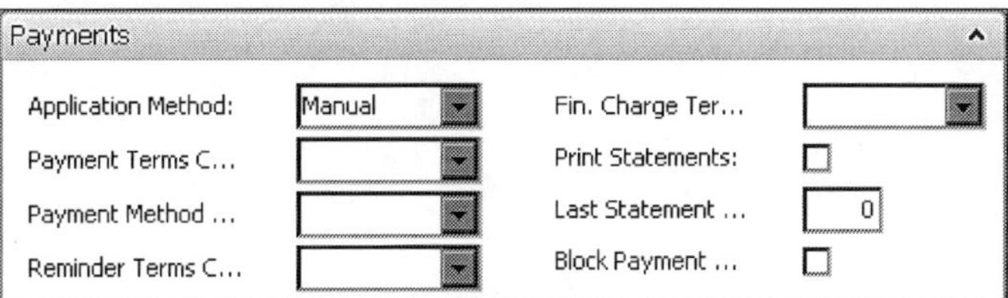

12. Set the **Payments Terms Code** to **CM** and click the **OK** button on the **Customer Card** to save the record and return to the Customer List Place.
13. The *Create a customer* process is now complete.

Create a sales order

Now we are going to create a sales order for our new customer. We're going to have a single inventory item on our sales order just to keep it simple. This example covers using a document task page and also shows how to use a drop-down to filter and select a customer.

1. From your **Role Center**, click the **New Sales Order** action button or select the **New Sales Order** option from the **Actions** menu.
2. The **New - Sales Order** document page is displayed, and your cursor is in the **No.** field waiting for you to enter a number for the new sales order.

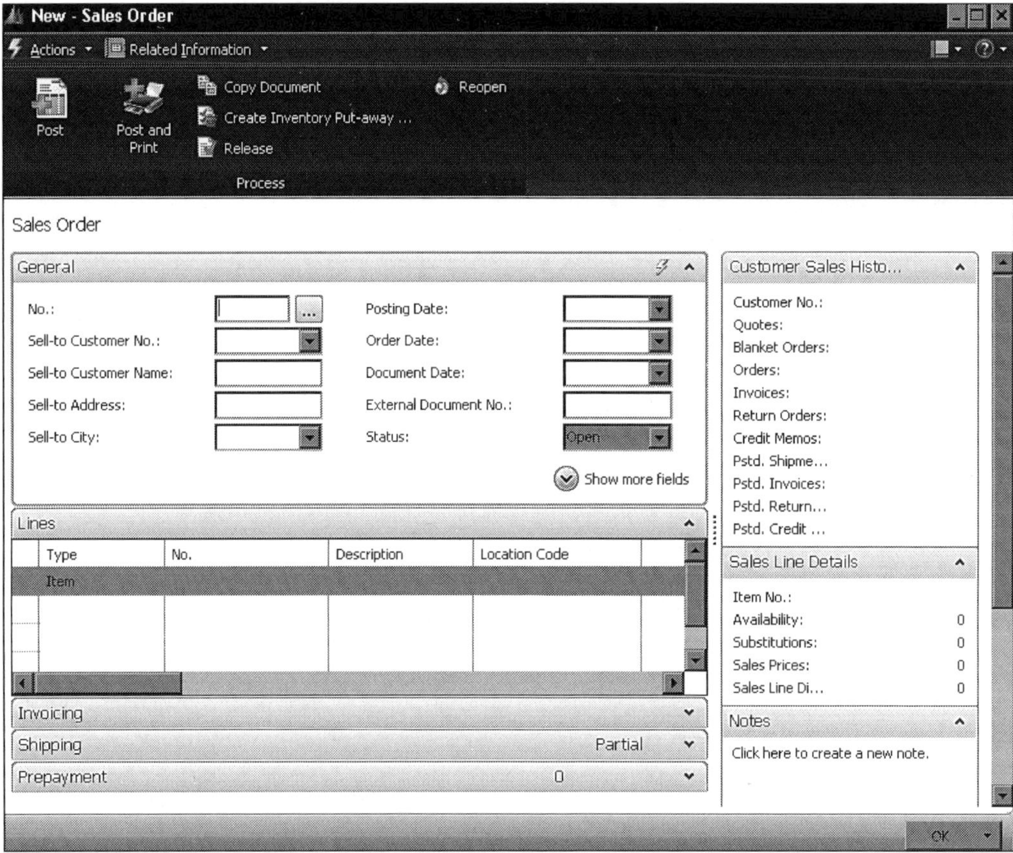

Press *Enter* to move away from the No. field.

3. The system allocates the next sales order number from the number series and moves the cursor to the **Sell-to Customer No.** field.

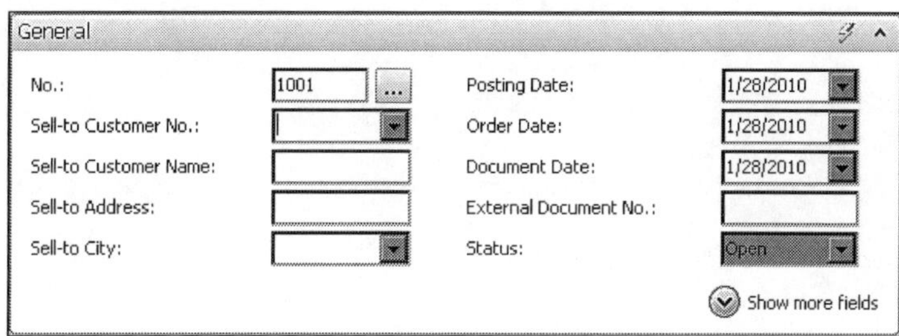

4. Click the drop-down button against the **Sell-to Customer No.** field.
5. The **Sell-to Customer No.** drop-down list is displayed.

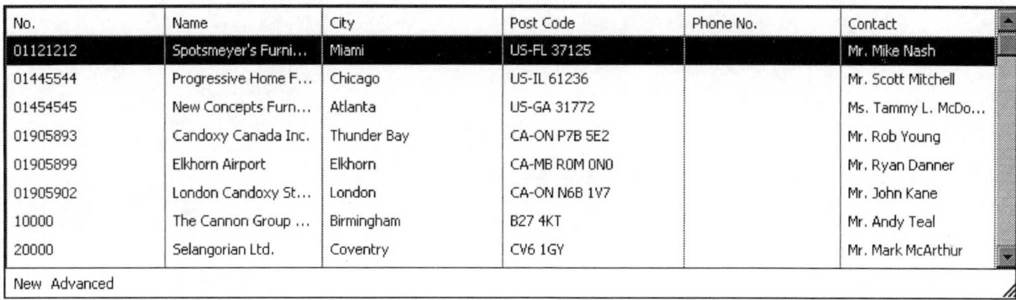

No.	Name	City	Post Code	Phone No.	Contact
01121212	Spotsmeyer's Furni...	Miami	US-FL 37125		Mr. Mike Nash
01445544	Progressive Home F...	Chicago	US-IL 61236		Mr. Scott Mitchell
01454545	New Concepts Furn...	Atlanta	US-GA 31772		Ms. Tammy L. McDo...
01905893	Candoxy Canada Inc.	Thunder Bay	CA-ON P7B 5E2		Mr. Rob Young
01905899	Elkhorn Airport	Elkhorn	CA-MB R0M 0N0		Mr. Ryan Danner
01905902	London Candoxy St...	London	CA-ON N6B 1V7		Mr. John Kane
10000	The Cannon Group ...	Birmingham	B27 4KT		Mr. Andy Teal
20000	Selangorian Ltd.	Coventry	CV6 1GY		Mr. Mark McArthur

New Advanced

Press the cursor-down arrow on your keyboard so that the first record is highlighted, and then use the cursor-right key to activate the **Name** column. You should see that the **Name** column heading text is now shown in bold.

Start to type **Nicholas** and you will see that as the characters appear in the **Sell-to Customer No.** field the records in the drop-down list are filtered to show those that start with the value you are typing. Another way of searching for records is to use the Select List.

6. Click the **Advanced** button at the bottom left of the drop-down list.

7. The **Select – Customer List** page is displayed.

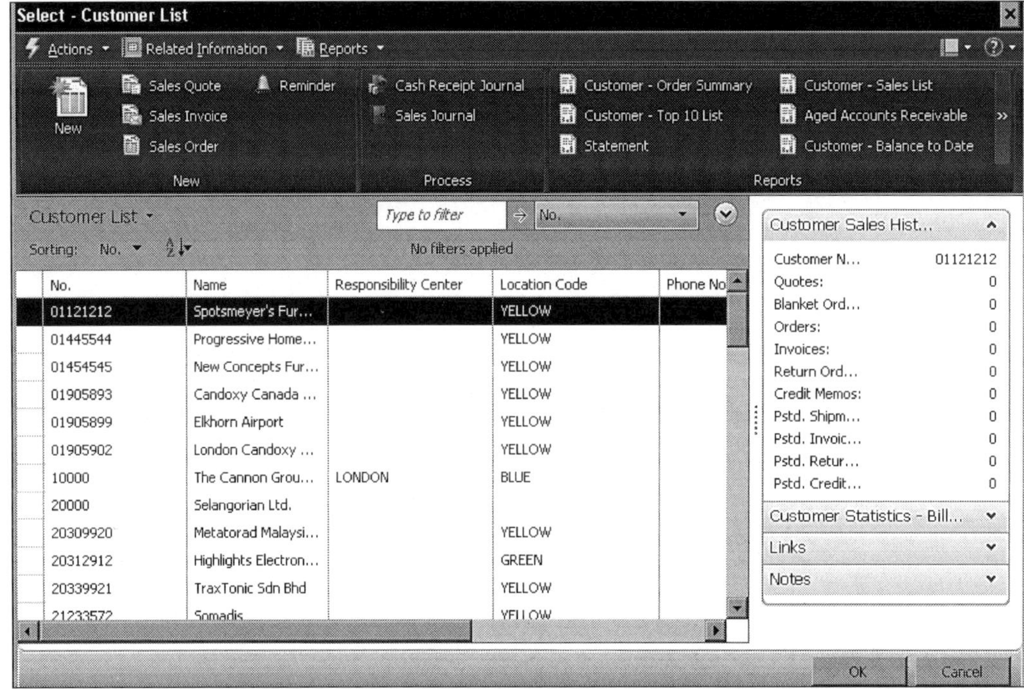

We would like to search for our customer by name; click the **Quick Filter** drop-down button in the filter pane (currently showing the **No.** field) and select the **Name** field.

8. The **Quick Filter** field is changed to **Name**.

9. Click in the ***Type to filter*** field, type **Nich**, and press the *Enter* key.
10. The **Customer List** is filtered to show those customers with names starting with the characters **Nich**.

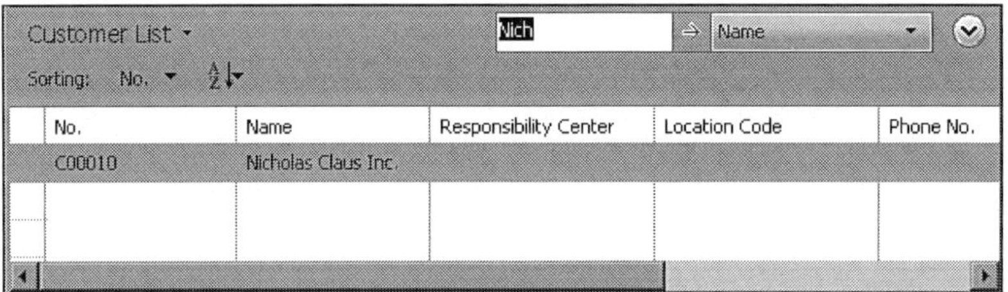

11. Click the **OK** button to select the record for customer **C00010**. Your customer may have been allocated a different number but you should recognize the customer as the one you created earlier.
12. The customer number is entered into the **Sell-to Customer No.** field.

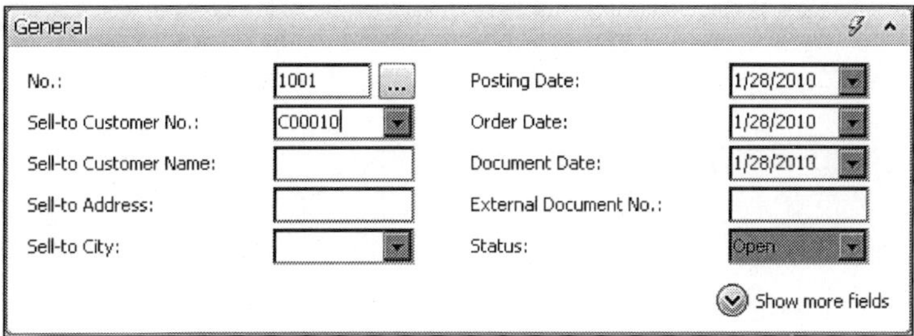

Press the *Enter* key to move away from the **Sell-to Customer No.** field.

13. The customer-related details such as **Sell-to Customer Name, Sell-to Address,** and **Payment Terms** are copied from the customer card to the sales order.

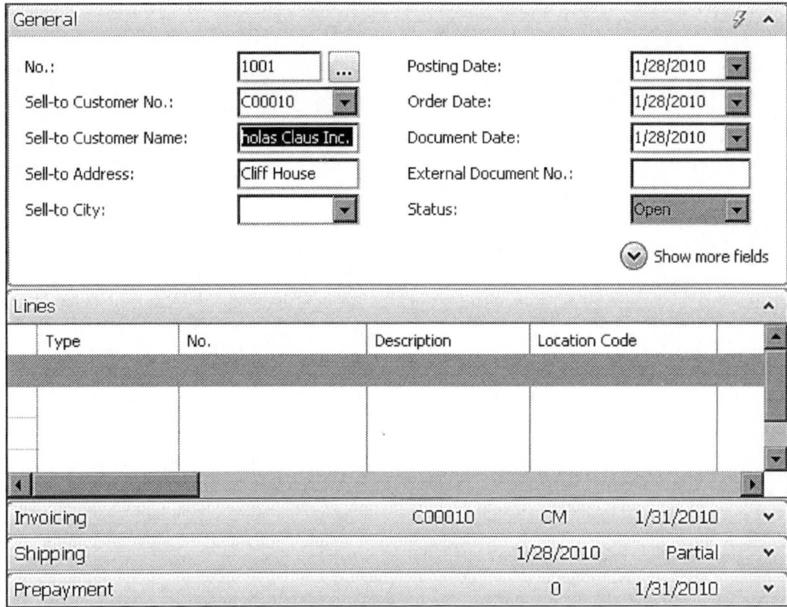

Use the mouse to click on the **Type** field for the first line on the sales order, or use the *Tab* key to move to that field (you will have to press the key several times to get there).

Type **I** for item and press the *Enter* key.

14. The **Type** field is set to **Item**, and the cursor is in the **No.** field waiting for you to enter an item number.

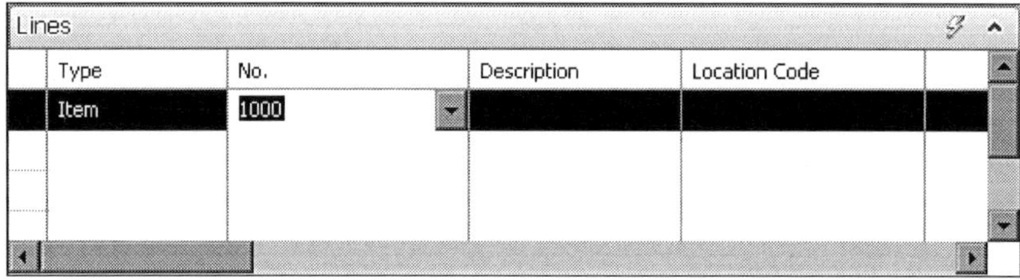

15. Enter **1000** and press *Enter*.
16. The system copies the **Description** and other item-related data from the Item Card to the Sales Order Line.

17. Use the *Tab* key to move to the Quantity field. Type **1** and press *Enter*.
18. Click **OK** to save the sales order.
19. The *Create a sales order* process is now complete.

Post an invoice for a sales order

It is likely that somewhere between creating your sales order and posting an invoice you will have other processes to perform such as picking and shipping goods. For our exercise, we're keeping it simple so that we can show you a list task page and a report.

> **Posting an invoice—no stamp required**
>
> Just in case you're not familiar with financial or ERP systems, the term posting used in this context means committing the document to the various ledgers within the system—such as the Customer Ledger and the General Ledger—and not putting an invoice in an envelope, sticking a stamp on it, and putting it in a post box.

1. From your **Role Center**, select the **Customers** list place.
2. The **Customers** list place is displayed.

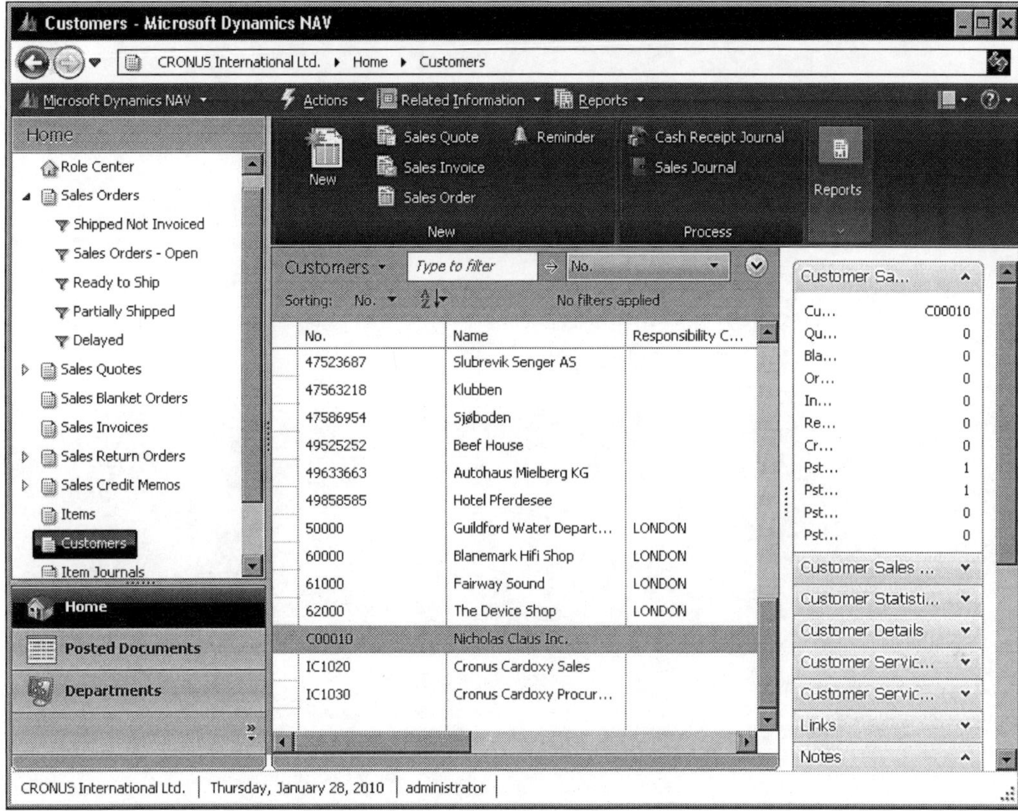

3. Click the Quick Filter drop-down button in the filter pane (currently showing the **No.** field) and select the **Name** field.
4. The Quick Filter field is changed to **Name**.

5. Click in the ***Type to filter*** field and type **Nich** and press the *Enter* key.

6. The **Customer List** is filtered to show those customers with names that start with the characters **Nich**.

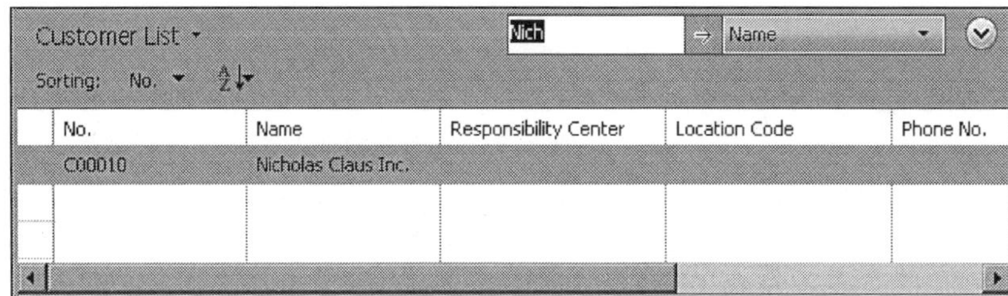

7. Click the **Related Information** menu button and from the **Sales** submenu, select the **Orders** menu option.
8. The **View - Sales Orders** list task page is displayed.

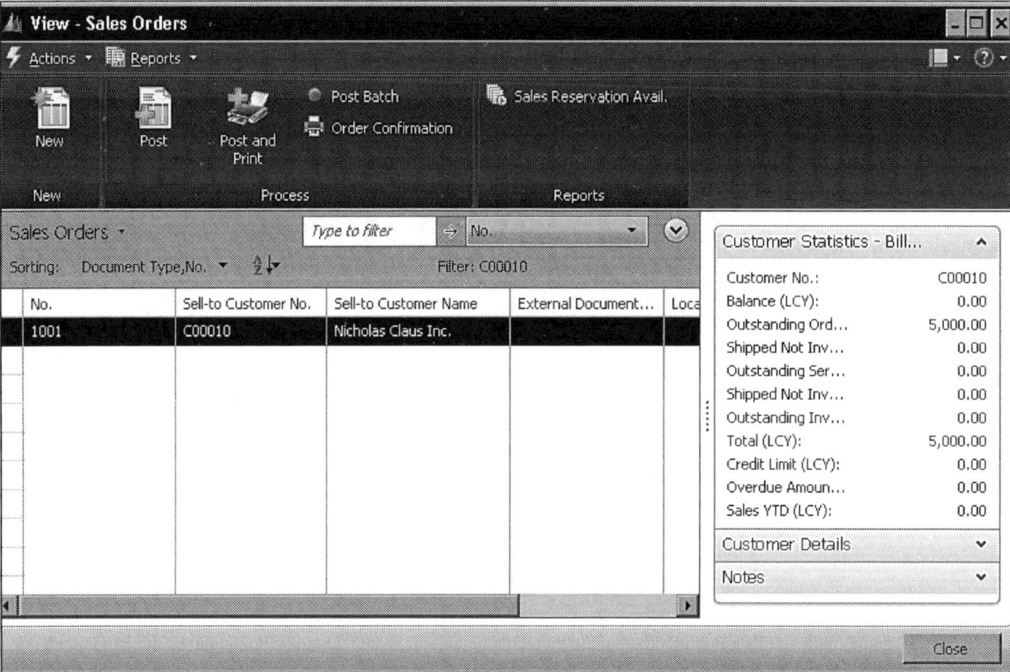

Since there is only one order for this customer, it is already selected. Click the **Post** button in the Process group of the Action Pane or select Posting, Post from the Actions menu or press the F9 key.

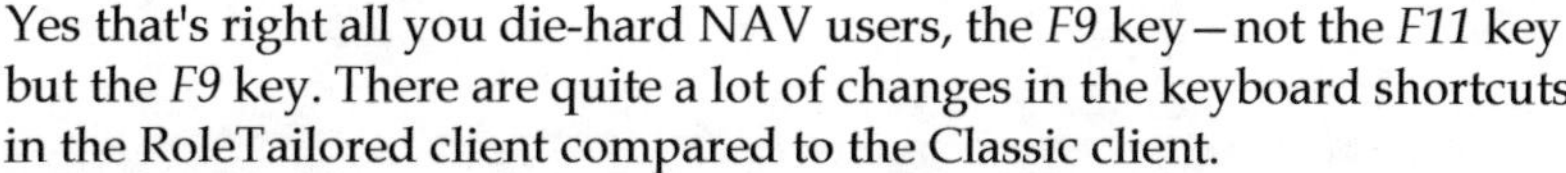

F9 to post? No way!

Yes that's right all you die-hard NAV users, the *F9* key—not the *F11* key but the *F9* key. There are quite a lot of changes in the keyboard shortcuts in the RoleTailored client compared to the Classic client.

For new users, this will be fine as the new key assignments are more in keeping with Windows standard key-presses. For NAV veterans, you're going to need to learn some new shortcuts, but thankfully the online help has a topic called Microsoft Dynamics NAV Keyboard Shortcuts—Comparison Table that gives the Classic client and RoleTailored client shortcuts side by side.

9. The system displays a dialog box asking you to select the type of posting you want to perform.

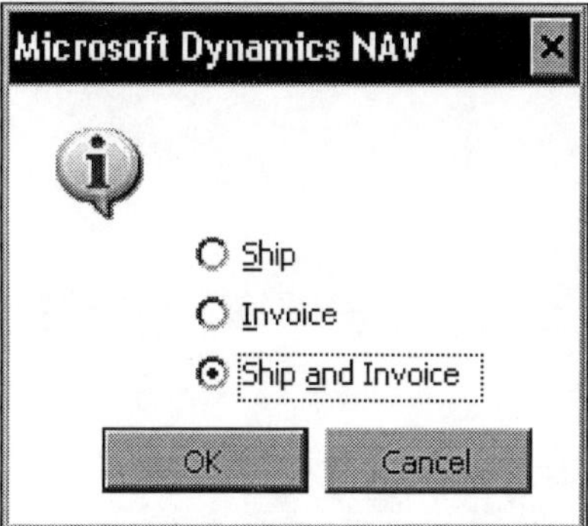

The **Ship and Invoice** option is fine, so leave that as selected and click the **OK** button.

10. The system returns you to the navigation layer.

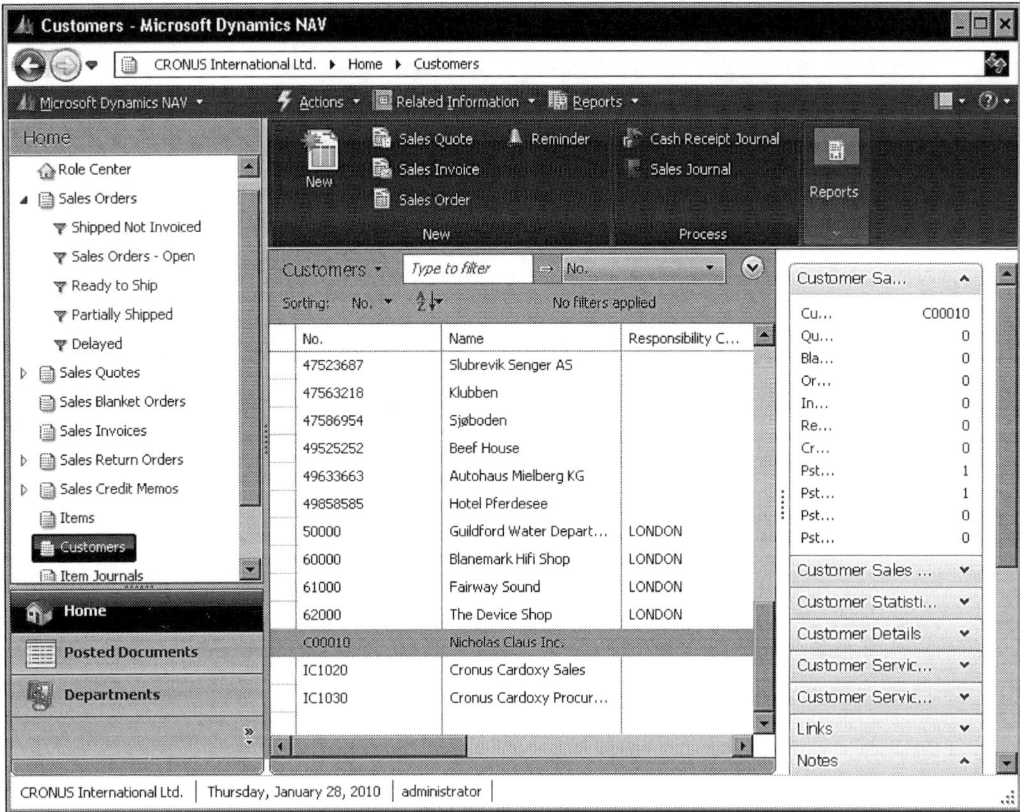

11. Select the **Posted Documents** menu button from the navigation pane and click the **Posted Sales Invoices** list place, or type **CRONUS International Ltd./Posted Documents/Posted Sales Invoices** in the address bar.

12. The **Posted Sales Invoices** list place is displayed.

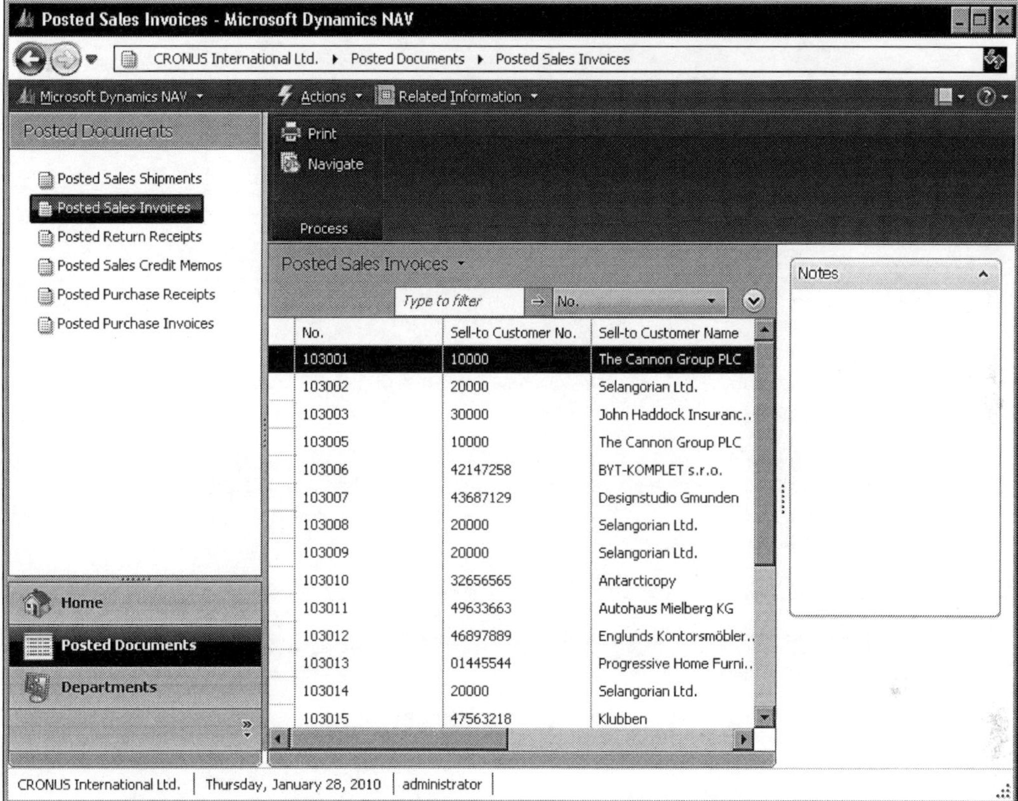

Press the *Ctrl+End* key combination to move to the last record (which is the invoice we just posted) and from the action pane, click the **Print** button.

13. The **Sales – Invoice** print dialog is displayed.

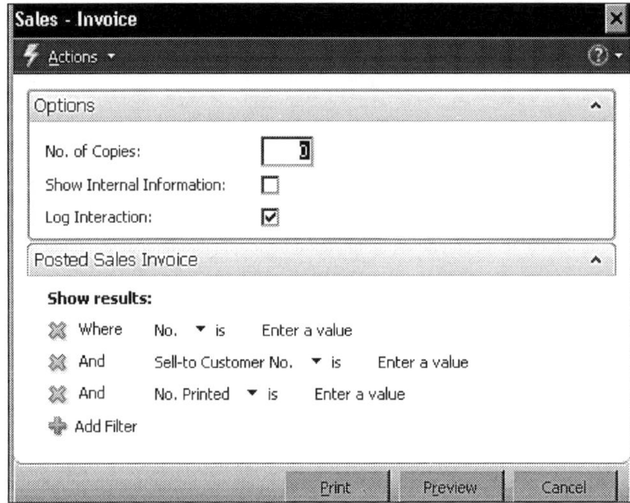

14. Click the **Preview** button.
15. The **Sales - Invoice Print Preview** page is displayed.

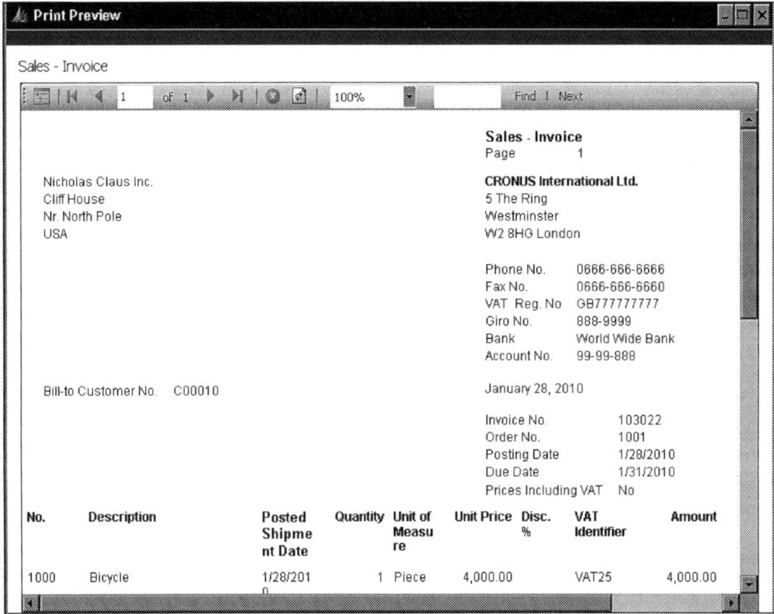

Close the preview window by pressing *Esc*.

16. The *Post an Invoice for a sales order* process is now complete.

Enter a cash receipt

In this process we'll use a journal task page to post a cash receipt for the invoice we previously posted, and use a list plus task page to apply the payment to the outstanding invoice.

1. Go to **CRONUS International Ltd.** | **Departments** | **Financial Management** | **Cash Management**.
2. The **Cash Management** departments place is displayed.

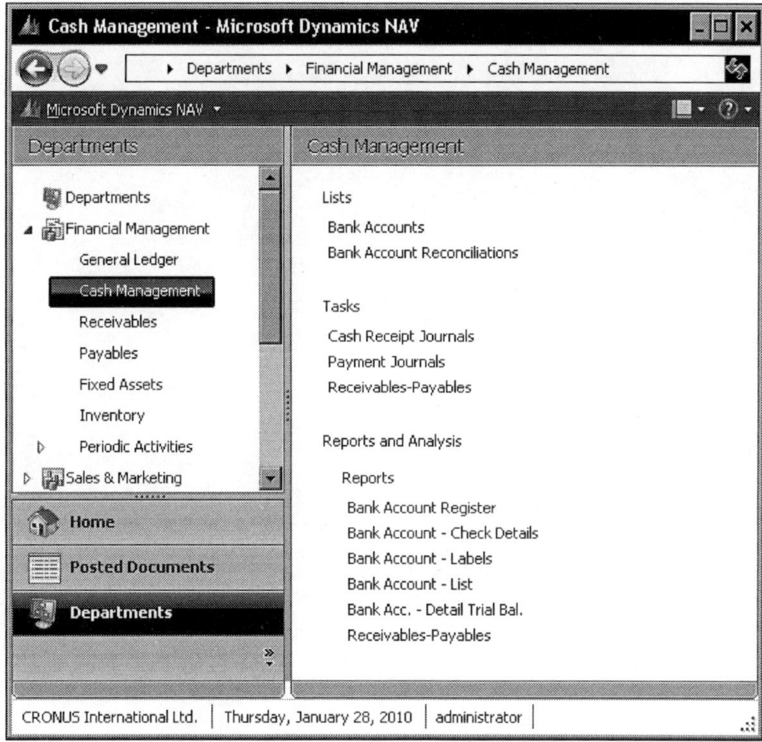

3. Click the **Cash Receipt Journals** option.

4. The **Edit - Cash Receipt Journal** page is displayed.

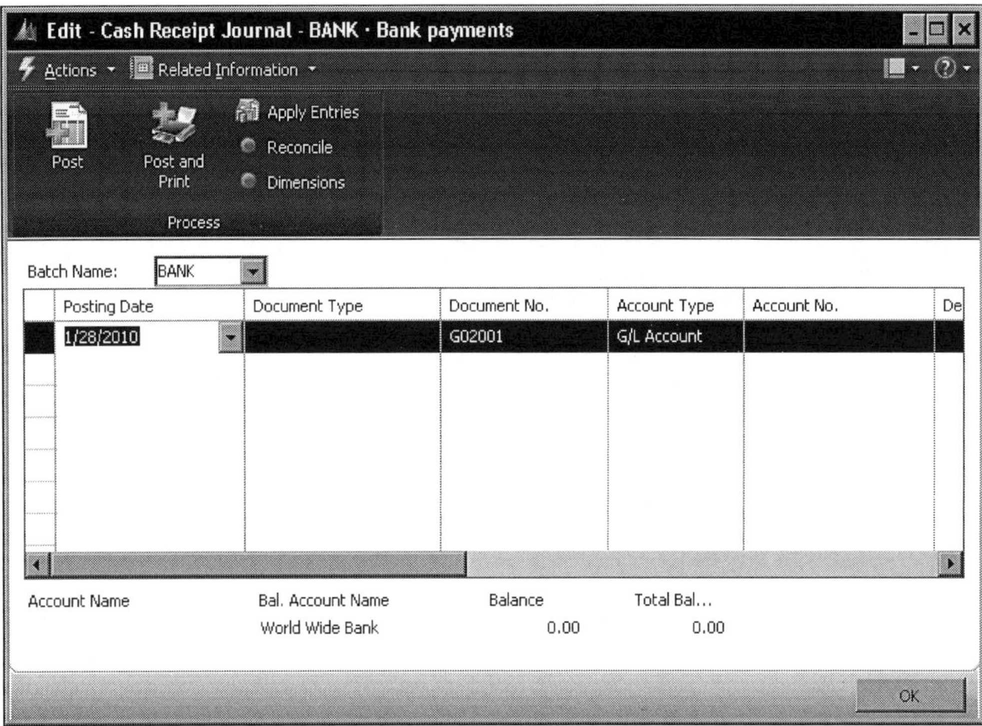

Enter the details as follows:

Field	Value
Posting Date	**1/28/2010**
Document Type	**Payment**
Document No.	Leave as suggested value. For me this was **G02001**.
Account Type	**Customer**
Account No.	**C00010** (use the number for the Nicholas Claus Inc. account we created earlier—your number may be different).
Amount	Leave this blank as it will get set when we mark the invoices we want to pay later on.
Bal. Account Type	**Bank Account**
Bal. Account No.	**WWB-OPERATING**

5. Click the **Apply Entries** option in the action pane.

6. The **Apply Customer Entries** task page is displayed.

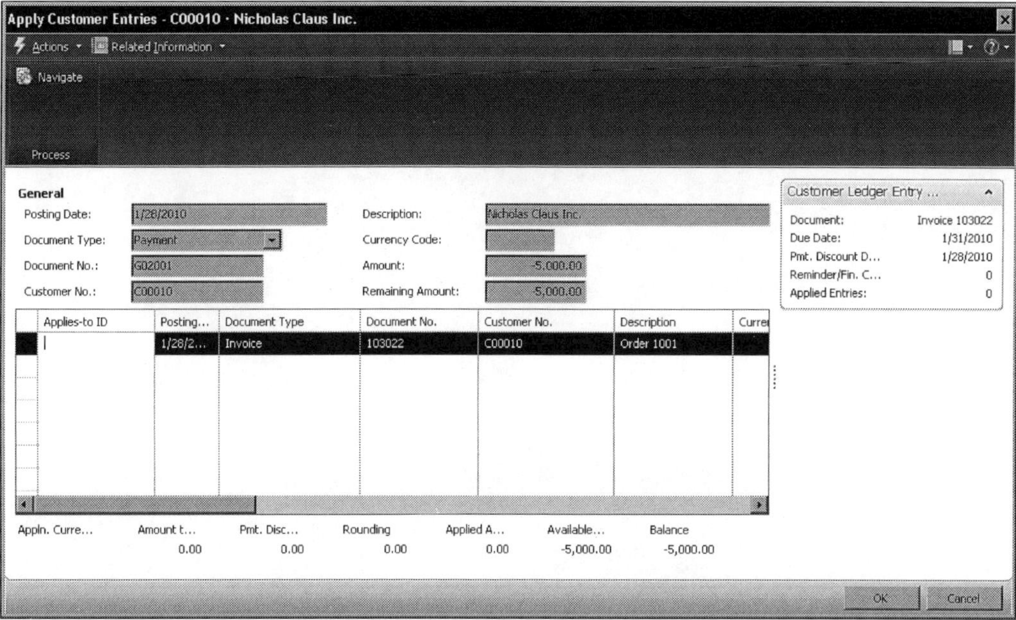

7. Press *Ctrl+Shift+J* to set the **Applies to ID** on the current line. Click **OK** to accept the application.
8. The **Edit - Cash Receipt Journal** page is displayed.

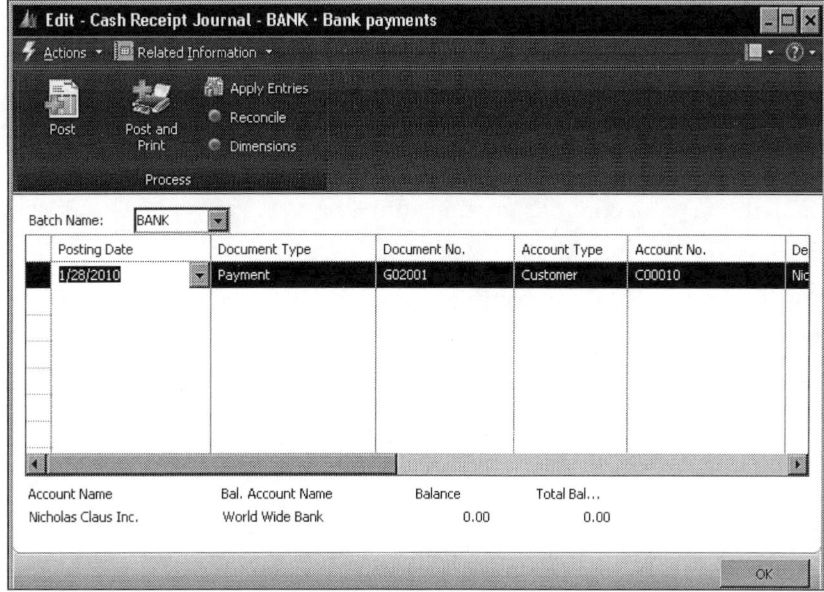

9. Click the Post button on the action pane or press the *F9* key.
10. The system prompts you to confirm whether you want to post the journal lines.

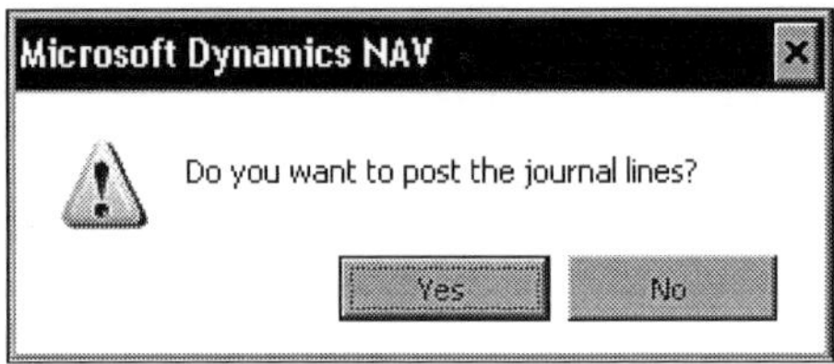

11. Click **Yes** to post the journal lines.
12. The system displays a message confirming that the journal lines were posted successfully.

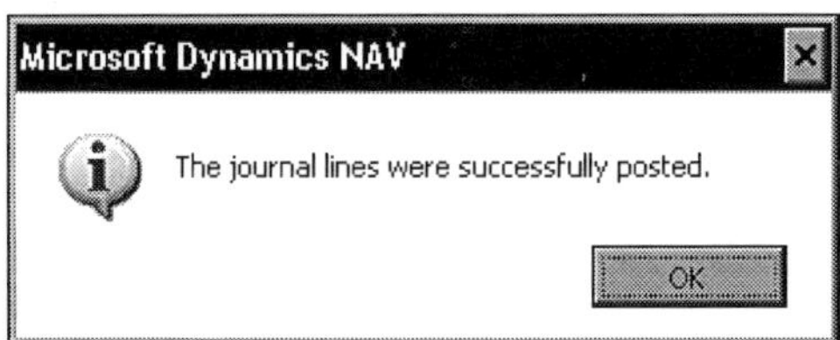

13. Click the **OK** button.
14. The *Enter a cash receipt* process is now complete.

Concluding using the RoleTailored client

Now we've looked at a series of business processes and have seen how they are performed using the RoleTailored client. Apart from the few changes in key-presses we saw (such as *F9* for posting instead of *F11* and *Ctrl+N* to create new records instead of *F3*), if you've used older versions of Dynamics NAV you should have found the exercises similar to what you are used to.

Now it's time for you to try things out for yourself. Use the online help to guide you through some other common business processes such as creating a purchase order, entering a purchase invoice, and making a vendor payment.

How to personalize the RoleTailored client

Older versions of Dynamics NAV allowed some personalization of the user interface but only to a limited extent. It was possible to personalize the navigation pane by hiding menus and menu options, creating shortcuts, and generally moving things around. It was also possible to customize list controls on forms by selecting the columns that should be shown and changing the height of the heading row. Unfortunately, by the standards of other ERP products I have worked with (particularly Dynamics AX), this was a pretty poor show. It's sad but true that NAV would get teased and bullied by AX because of its limited personalization capabilities; but not anymore. NAV has grown up and has a personalization capability to be proud of.

Now let's take a look at how to personalize the RoleTailored client or in the words of Simon Cowell, 'Make it your own!'

Make it your own

There are two levels of personalization for the RoleTailored client: those changes that can be made by an ordinary user that will only affect their own interface and changes that can be made by a department super-user that will change the interface for all users within that role.

We're going to cover the second form of customization in our chapter on the Dynamics Customer Model later on. For now, we'll focus on what the average user will be able to do to tailor the application to suit their role.

Customize the navigation pane

If you want to customize the navigation pane—when it comes to options to select—you are spoilt for choice. You can do any of the following to achieve the same effect:

- Right-click on any of the navigation pane buttons in the navigation pane and select the **Customize Navigation Pane** option.
- Click the customize menu and select the **Customize Navigation Pane** option.
- Click the **Configure Buttons** button in the navigation pane and select the **Customize Navigation Pane** options.

Once you have selected your preferred method of customizing the navigation pane, you are presented with a **Customize Navigation Pane** page.

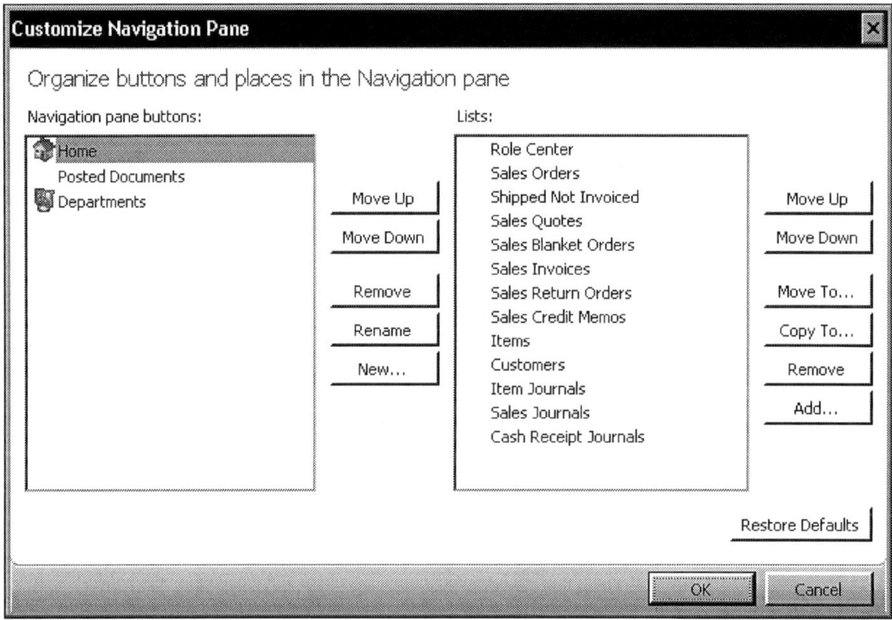

As you select the navigation pane buttons on the left-hand side, the **Lists** pane on the right-hand side updates to reflect the options available.

The navigation pane buttons comprise two fixed buttons **Home** and **Departments** that cannot be moved, removed, or renamed and any number of additional navigation pane buttons. The above role has a single additional navigation pane button called **Posted Documents**, but you can use the **New...** button to create more.

The **Departments** navigation pane is the odd one out because it is not possible to personalize the departments place in any way. This makes sense because the departments place is where *everything else* is when you have refined your navigation pane to only include the options you need. If you were able to remove options from the departments place, you could be left with no option other than clicking the **Restore Defaults** button to get the options back.

The departments place is really just the menu suite from the Classic client that has been transformed to work with the RoleTailored client. If you want new options to be available in the departments place, you need to use the Classic client and the **MenuSuite** designer to add them. MenuSuite objects for the RoleTailored client have a 10 in front of the ID that is used for the Classic client and have additional properties that are specific to the RoleTailored client, such as **Department Category**

The **Move Up** and **Move Down** need no explanation although the **Home** activity button will always be at the top and the **Departments** will always be at the bottom, so, unless you add some more activity buttons, not a lot is going to happen when you click these.

The **Remove** button will remove the navigation pane buttons without a prompt, so use it wisely. If you make a mess, you can either hit the **Cancel** button to exit without saving your changes or use the **Restore Defaults** button; nothing is saved until you click **OK**.

The **New...** button allows you to create activity buttons of your own, and you can select from an extensive range of standard icons. The **Rename** option allows you to change the name or change the icon for one of the existing activity buttons, but you cannot rename or change the icon for **Home** or **Departments**.

Adding list places to menus

After clicking on the **Home** button, you will see the **Lists** panel updated to show all of the list places that are available from your **Home** menu group. The **Role Center** is at the top of the list places in the **Home** group and unsurprisingly, this list cannot be moved, removed, or edited.

The other items can be configured although it is not possible to rename an item. You'll also notice that when some of the items are displayed in the navigation pane, they are not a single item but instead comprise a group with filtered options underneath. These filtered groups are added through the Classic client development tools and are only present for the default options in the role. Users cannot add their own list places with filters.

To add a new option, click the **Add...** button.

The dialog box that you see contains all of the options from the MenuSuite in the Classic client or the departments page in the RoleTailored client. Expand the menu groups until you see an option you want to select. You can only select options at the lowest level of the tree and only those options that have been set up in the MenuSuite as a Department Category of **Lists**. We'll cover this in more detail when we look at how to create your own Role in Chapter 3—*Roles and the Customer Model*.

Personalizing pages using the customize menu

The customize menu button looks like the following:

When we discussed the customize menu back at the start of this chapter, we discovered that different options are available depending on which place you have active when you select the menu. In reality there are only three customization pages to know about: Customize Actions, Customize Reports, and Customize This Page. All of the other options will open a specific part of one of these pages.

Customize Actions

From the customize menu, select the **Customize Actions** option and you will see a page that looks very similar to the following. The actions that are available will depend on the task page or place you had active at the time you selected the option.

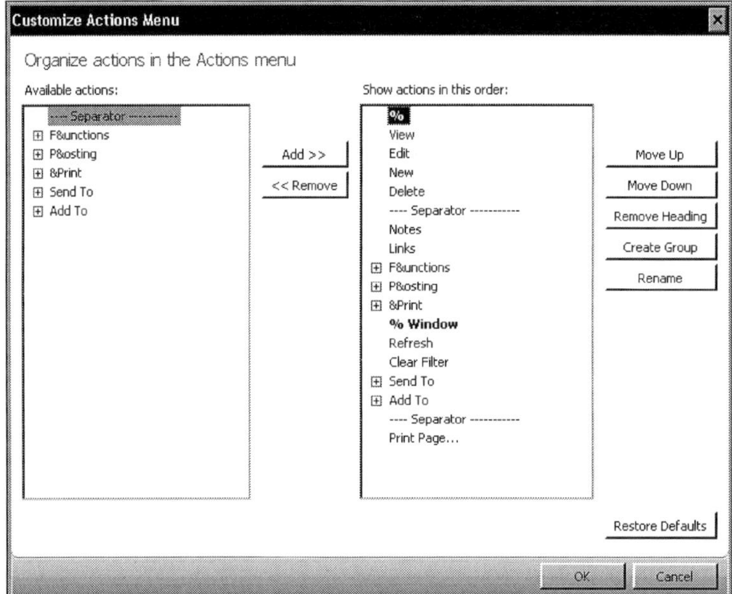

You can configure the available actions using the **Add** and **Remove** buttons between the two panes.

The ampersand (&) in the text of the action represents the hotkey for the menu option, and this is the key you will be able to use to select the option using the keyboard. You can change the & position to use a different hotkey but this is not recommended; the system will allocate a hotkey automatically if one is not defined, and by allocating your own keys, you are only likely to confuse other users if you are showing them your system.

Customize Reports

Now hold on a second, this looks familiar:

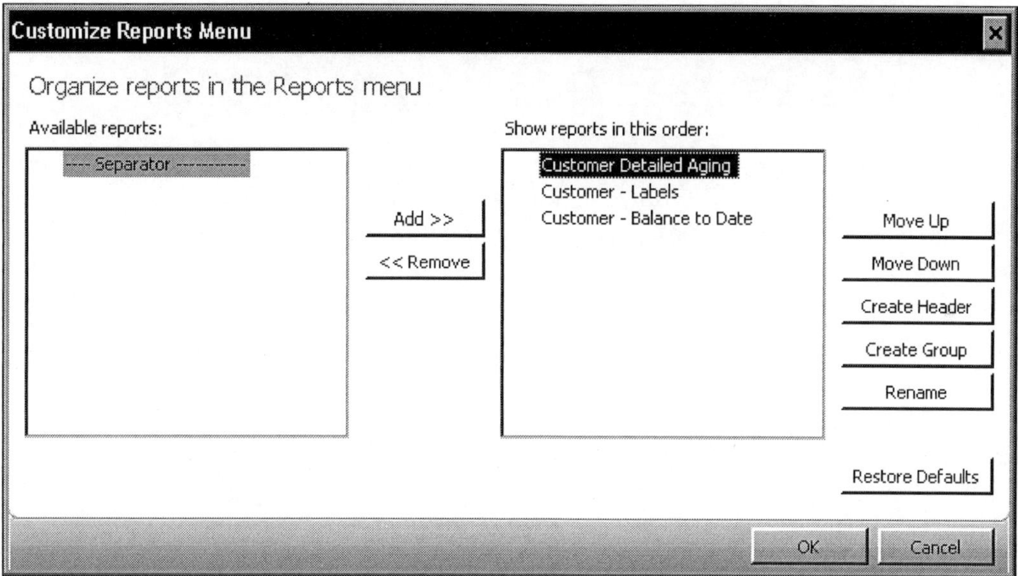

The **Customize Reports Menu** page looks and works exactly like the **Customize Actions Menu** page, except that you are working with the available reports and not the available actions. If you want to add a completely new report to your page, you will need to talk nicely to a developer as this needs to be done in the object designer using the Classic client.

Customize This Page

For any page other than the Role Center (which has a different customization page) and the departments page (which does not allow customization), you will see a variation on this page when you select the **Customize This Page** option from the customize menu.

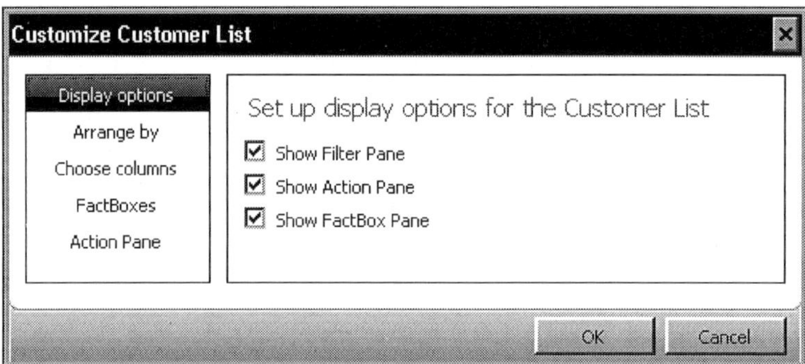

The **Display options** group allows you to select which panes are to be displayed on the page. Removing the tick from the **Show Filter Pane** on this form has the same effect as selecting the **Filter Pane** option from the **Panes** group of the customize menu button.

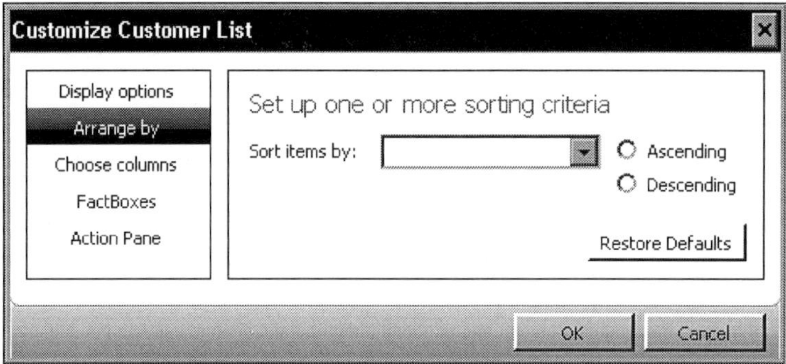

The **Arrange by** group allows you to change the sort order for the items on the list place. You can only select from the pre-defined keys on the table. It's a shame that you cannot select the sort order of your choice, but at least you know the lists will display quickly (unlike some other ERP solutions that allow end users to select non-indexed sort orders that can degrade performance when drawing the screen).

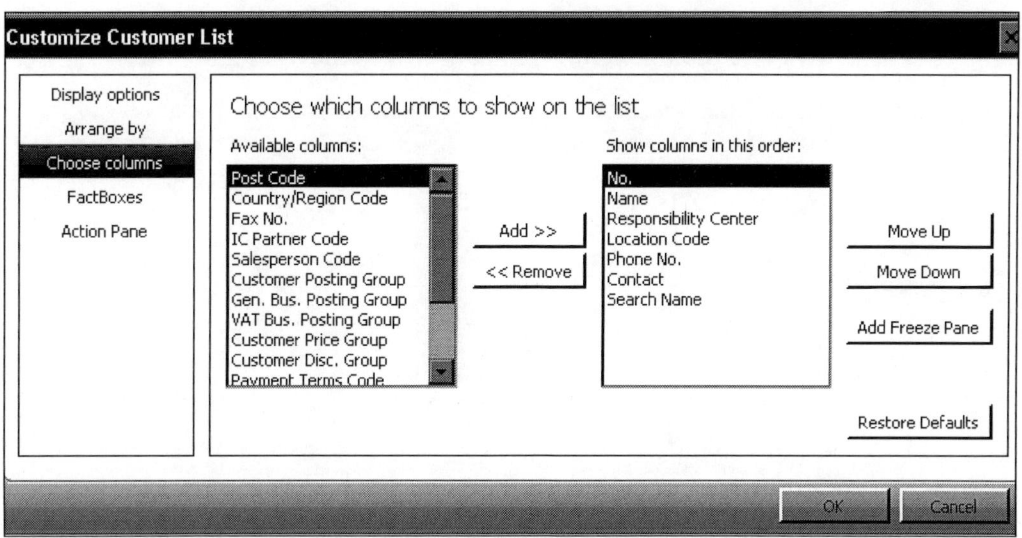

The **Choose columns** group looks similar to the options used for configuring action menus and reports with an additional **Add Freeze Pane** button.

The freeze pane allows you to lock columns on a list so that they will always be displayed as you scroll right.

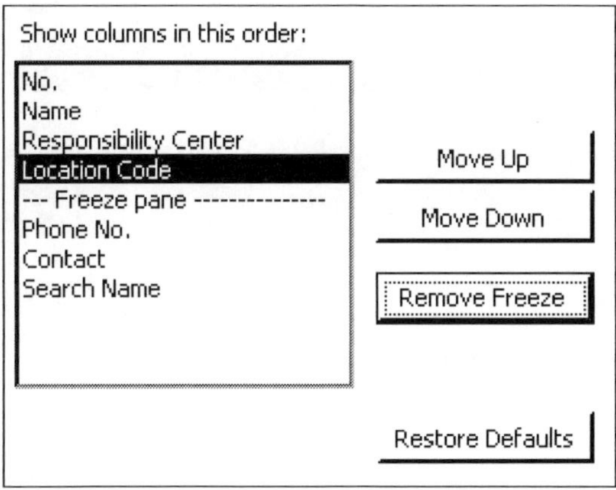

When you click the button, the freeze pane is inserted after the currently selected column and the **Add Freeze Pane** button changes to a **Remove Freeze** button.

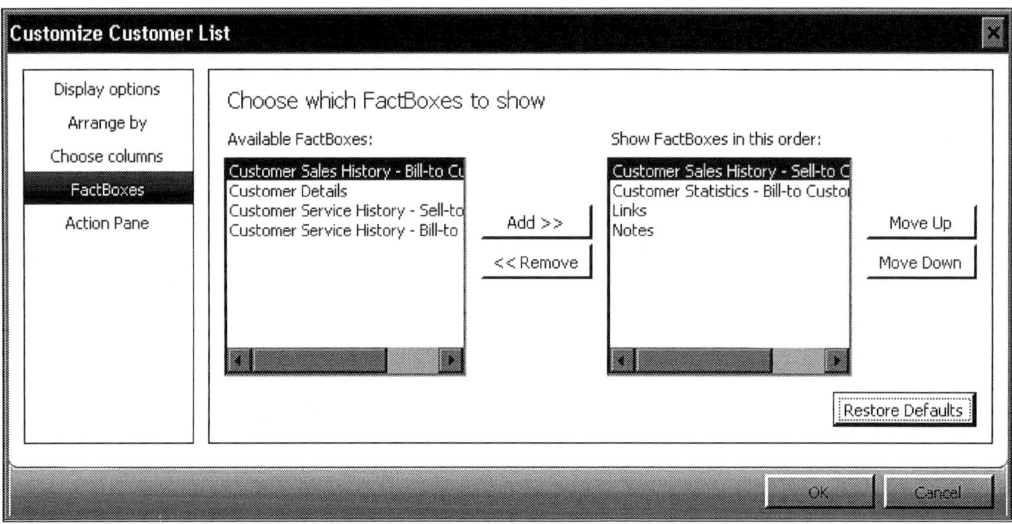

The **FactBoxes** group allows you to select from the available FactBoxes on the page. Again, to add new FactBoxes to the Available list, you'll need to use the development tools in the Classic client.

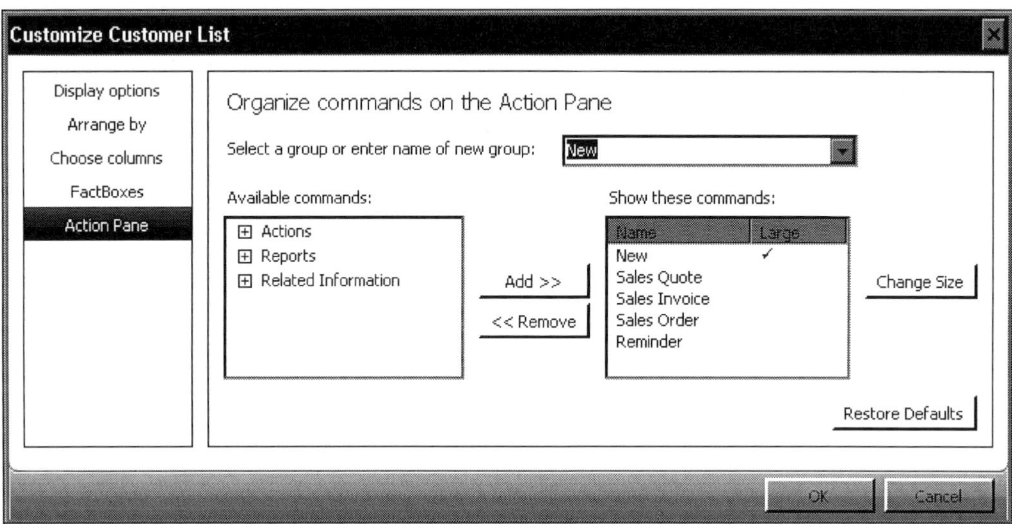

You can create new groups by typing a new group name in the text box with the label **Select a group or enter name of new group:**, although this does not allow you to change the order of the groups. The groups are ordered alphabetically. To create a new group, you need to type some new text and then click on another part of the page.

Take care when adding groups

If you want to remove a group, you are in trouble, because the only way to remove a newly created group is to click the **Restore Defaults** button (which will remove all newly created groups), so be careful when adding groups and ensure your spelling is accurate or be prepared to redo your customizations. Thankfully, the **Restore Defaults** button only applies to the currently selected page group, so you won't lose your FactBoxes changes if you are on the action pane group when you click it.

The other new feature on this group is the **Change Size** button that allows you to make an icon large or remain regular sized.

Customize This Page (task page with FastTabs)

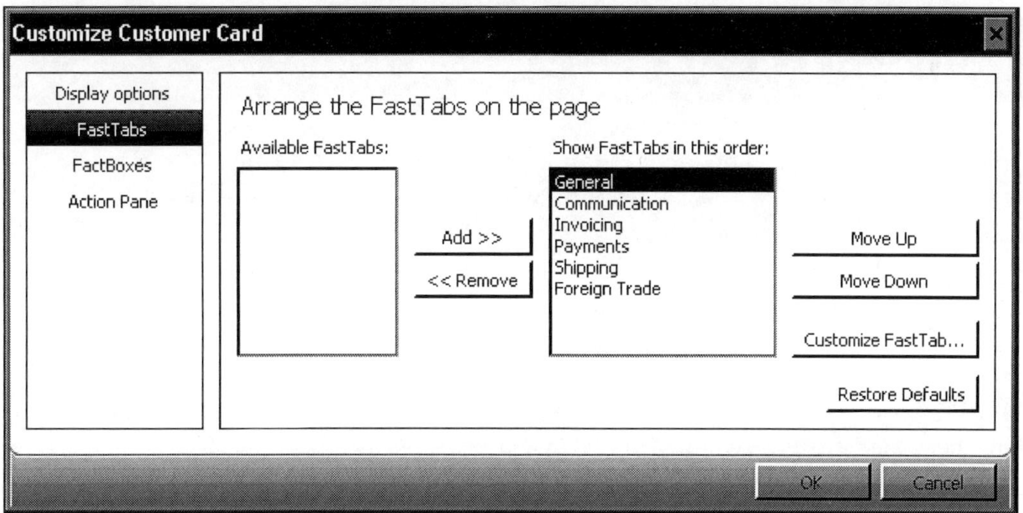

When you look at the **Customize This Page** option from a task page with FastTabs, such as the **Customer Card**, you'll see that the list-related options such as **Arrange by** and **Choose columns** are gone and in their place is a **FastTabs** option.

This group allows you to select those FastTabs that are to be displayed on the page using the usual **Add** and **Remove** buttons. There is, however, an extra button labeled **Customize FastTab...** that allows you to promote and demote fields within the FastTab.

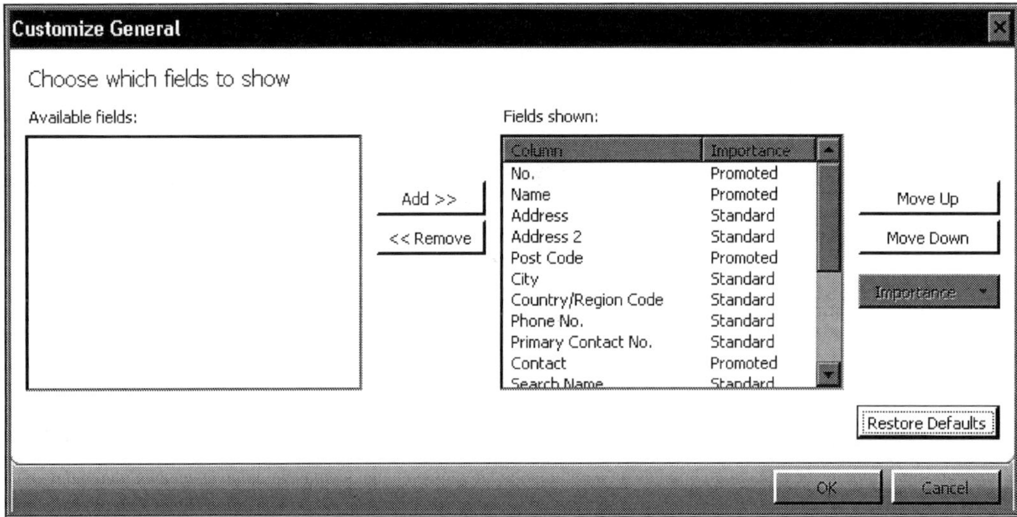

The **Importance** field can be set to **Standard, Promoted**, or **Additional**. A Promoted field will appear on the FastTab heading when the FastTab is minimized. An Additional field will be hidden from the form but can be displayed by clicking the **Show more fields** button on the FastTab.

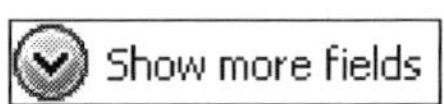

The **Show more fields** button only appears on a FastTab when some of the fields have been set to an **Additional** importance level.

Customize This Page (role center)

The **Customize the Role Center** page is shown in the following image:

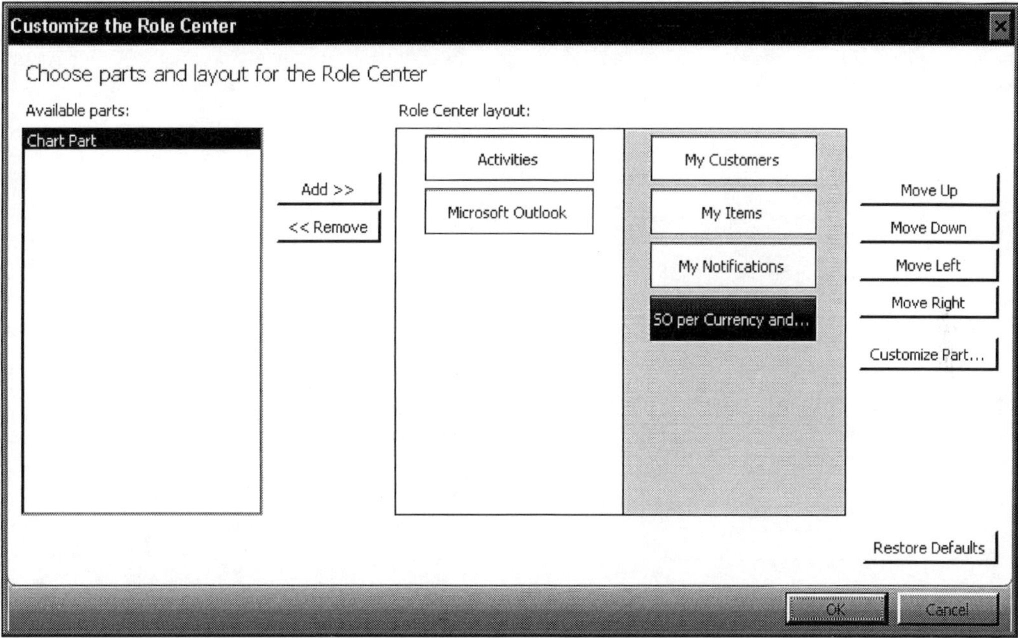

The **Customize This Page** option when called form the role center has a completely different look to the page used for list places and task pages.

The **Available parts** are determined by the development team when they create the role center page. You may add any number of chart parts but cannot exceed seven parts in any one column.

Each part type has different configuration options, with the exception of the **My Notifications** part, which cannot be customized. Let's look at each in turn.

Activities

The **Customize Activities** page looks like the following:

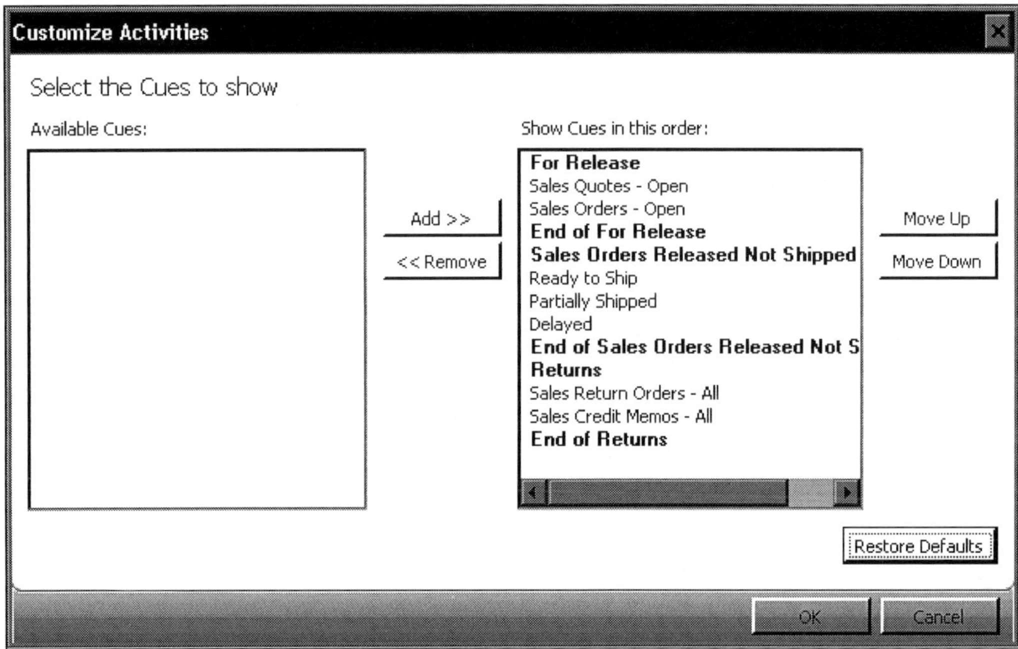

Customizing the activities part is simply an opportunity to move the cues around or remove them altogether. In reality, you don't have a lot of control here; you can remove cues but not group headings and you can change the order of cues within a group but not move cues from one group to another.

Microsoft Outlook

The **Outlook Part** looks like the following:

The options on the **Customize Outlook Part** page are pretty obvious, and the user is provided with as much control as they could possibly wish for. Personally, I would never want my Outlook items to be surfaced in my role center, and for me this part is the first to go, but that's why *personalization* is so great.

My Customers and other list parts

Customizing a list part provides similar options to those available when configuring a list place.

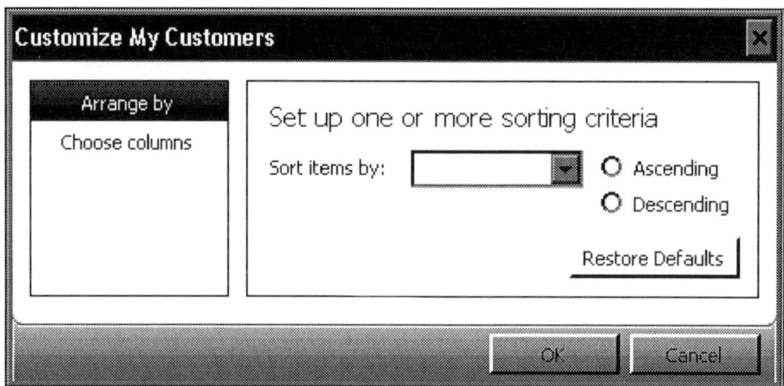

You can select the sort order of the items in the list.

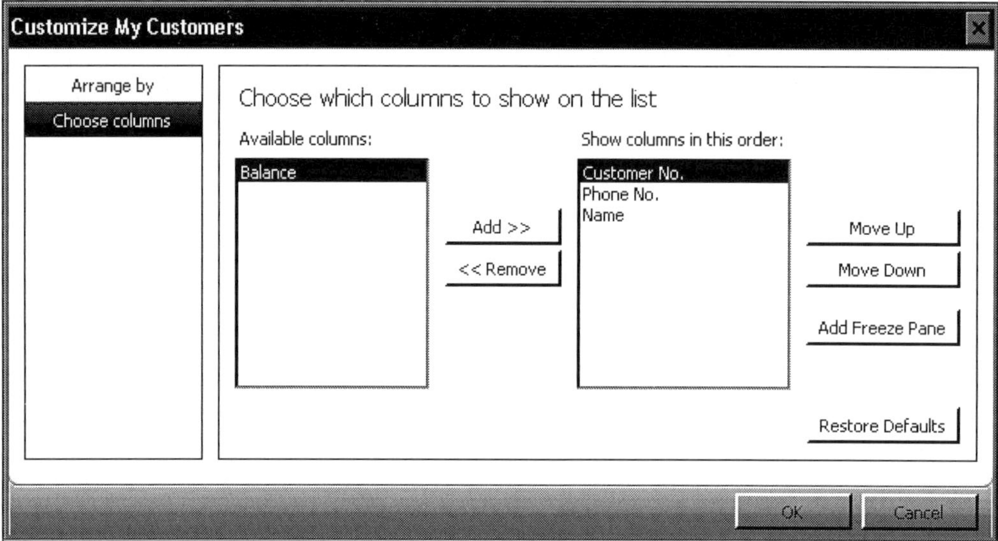

And you can select the columns that are displayed and optionally set a Freeze Pane.

My Notifications

There are no customization options for the My Notifications part.

Chart part

Configuring a chart part allows you to select the chart you wish to display. There are thirty-five charts to choose from and new charts can be created by the development team. After selecting the chart, there are no other configuration options available, meaning it's WYGIWYG.

WYGIWYG

This is my play on the WYSIWYG (what you see is what you get) acronym. WYGIWYG stands for what you get is what you're given.

Summary

The RoleTailored client is pretty special and there's a lot to it. We've looked at most of it (excluding a lot of the obvious stuff) and introduced some new terms that will help us discuss and understand NAV 2009 going forward. We've looked at some of the changes in the new client compared to the Classic or old client, and have seen that the new client provides a superior user experience, although it may take a while for NAV veterans to get used to it. Finally, we've explored the extensive personalization capabilities of the RoleTailored client, and have seen that the majority of users are going to be very happy indeed.

In the next chapter, we'll look more at the RoleTailored paradigm and learn about Roles and the Dynamics Customer Model from which they are derived. We'll see how the techniques we have learned in personalizing the application can be applied to all users for a given profile.

3

Roles and the Customer Model

Have you ever had one of those ideas that was so brilliant that you couldn't contain yourself? Then, when you explain the idea to someone, they say, 'But of course! How else would you do it?'

The Dynamics Customer Model is a bit like that. It's totally brilliant and yet blindingly obvious. The Dynamics Customer Model is a new approach to ERP and together with the RoleTailored client offers a completely new user experience. In this chapter we're going to look at what the model is, how it came about, and what you should do with it.

You'll learn about:

- The Dynamics Customer Model
- The roles available in Dynamics NAV 2009
- How to customize an existing role
- How to create a new role

The Dynamics Customer Model

There is quite a wealth of excellent material on the Dynamics Customer Model available on the Microsoft web site, and we'll provide references for further reading at the end of this chapter. We'll give you an executive summary in a few pages and then move on to what the Dynamics Customer Model means to you and how it is implemented in Dynamics NAV 2009. Let's start by looking at some of the problems with the old approach to ERP.

Too much information

A big problem for the old Dynamics NAV user interface was that there was way too much information: thousands of menu options that launched hundreds of reports and forms containing hundreds of fields and menu options. This overwhelming interface led to stress for new users, and on occasions, fear during implementations, and it often made for difficult training sessions. It seemed that the key to success for users was to develop the skill of mentally removing superfluous information from the screen in order to focus on what was important. For example, users eventually learned which half of the fifty fields they needed to complete in order to create a new customer record, but the 'one-size fits all' approach meant that although you had a system that had everything everyone needed, it was not a good fit for anyone. A new approach was needed to allow users to become more productive; it was time to go back to basics.

A fresh beginning

The Microsoft Dynamics team worked hard to get an understanding of businesses and the people that worked in them by conducting research, usability studies, interviews, and site visits. Years of research has culminated in the documentation of a 'standard' company called the 'Microsoft Dynamics Customer Model'. As you would expect, there is a large degree of commonality between businesses, and the information contained in the model makes an excellent platform on which to base any implementation of Microsoft Dynamics. It provides a common reference point for the product development team, the implementation consultants, and for the end users.

Prior to Dynamics NAV 2009, in order to implement NAV as an ERP solution, it was down to the implementation consultant to interview people and analyze the business in order to understand the departments, roles, people, and the daily routines and business processes that constituted the business. The consultant also needed to understand the business processes that could be performed in NAV. Since older version of NAV were not task-oriented, it was often necessary for the implementation consultant to use their own experience or work through the application in order to determine which business processes were covered. This approach was time-consuming and relied upon having experienced consultants with a depth of business knowledge and experience.

With the Dynamics Customer Model, the consultant can draw upon the work the Microsoft Dynamics Research and Development team has done. The consultant can focus on the gaps and differences between the Dynamics Customer Model and the business, knowing that the bulk of the processes have already been covered.

Departments, roles, process groups, and tasks

The model is represented in two views: **People and Departments** and **Departments and Work**, and you can download illustrations from the Microsoft web site reference provided at the end of this chapter.

The People and Departments view shows eighteen typical departmental organization charts for different types and sizes of business. It shows how fifty-eight roles are organized into five departments: Operations, Sales & Marketing, Human Resources, Finance, and IT & Partners.

This is a great diagram and we recommend that you print a nice large version of it and put it on the wall when doing the initial training and analysis sessions for your implementation. Ask the users to identify which role they play in the business and to identify any roles or departments that are not covered in the model. This will immediately provide a level of comfort for the users that the software has been designed to fit their needs, and is a superb way to quickly determine if the product is a good fit for the business.

The Departments and Work view shows thirty-two process groups (such as Pay, Collect, Treasury Management) that contain over one hundred and fifty processes (such as Pay for product or service, Collect for product or service, Deposit Bank funds, and so on). Similar to the other illustration, you can quickly put this in front of your prospective users and ask them to identify the business processes that are not covered by the standard model. The gaps identified in this process are a golden opportunity to question the need for the missing processes. Any processes that are not covered are quickly identified and can be analyzed further in order to determine what modifications, if any, will be required to allow the system to cater for those processes.

What is a role in Dynamics NAV 2009?

Now we know what a role is at a conceptual level: it represents the role a person may play within an organization. It makes perfect sense to define an ERP system in terms of roles, departments, processes, and tasks, but how do we realize this conceptual entity of a role as a real user experience in NAV?

The answer is really quite simple: we build a Role Center page and link this to a person. We also need to ensure that the security permissions are granted so that the user can perform the tasks for their role and not see data that is not pertinent to them. When the person logs in to the RoleTailored client, the Role Center page that is linked to the user's Windows user name is displayed providing the immediate visual cues, actions, and list places that are necessary for the user to carry out their tasks and business processes.

In the programming and configuration world, a role is called a profile. This is to avoid confusion with the existing security roles, which are still used to grant access to table data and other functionality. The user is linked to the Role Center page via a property on a profile. Each user may belong to zero or one profile. Each profile must have a single Role Center page associated with it. If a user is not linked to a profile, they will see the Role Center for the default profile when they log in to NAV.

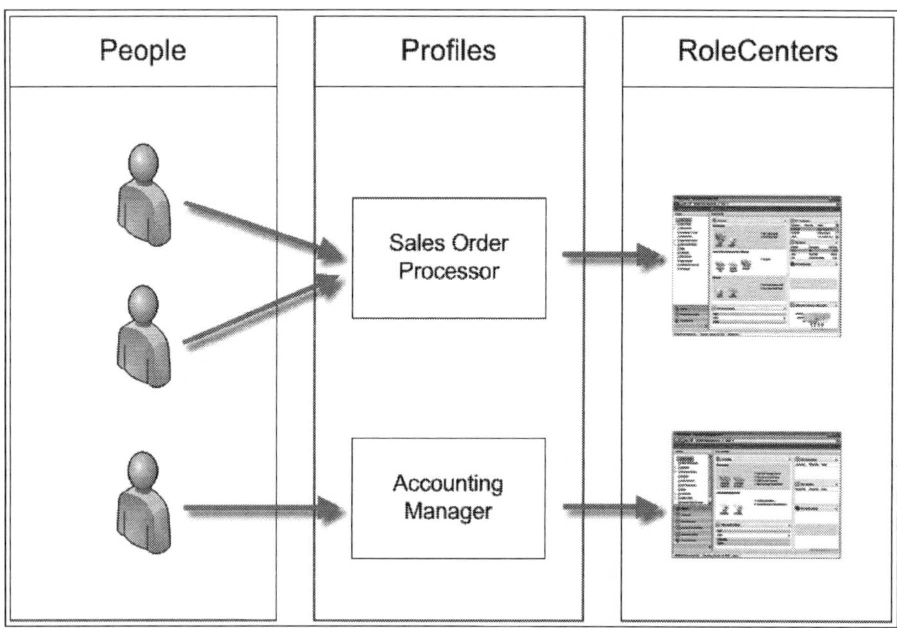

The roles available in Dynamics NAV 2009

Not all of the roles in the Microsoft Dynamics NAV Customer Model are implemented in NAV 2009. The product ships with twenty-one pre-configured profiles. We'll look at each of the roles grouped by department. You'll notice that each of the roles has a person's name attached to help you identify with that role—the whitepaper and illustrations even include photographs of the people that play the role within the model. I notice there's no Dave or Vjeko role, so I guess we'll have to build one of these later on. For now, let's look at what you get as standard. First we'll go through the meaning and context of these roles in business terms and then we'll look at how to explore the Role Center pages to see what they contain.

Role	Description
President—Charlie	Charlie keeps the business viable by determining product and company direction. He is involved with all departments and depends on accurate information from his staff. His Role Center is page 9019: **CEO and President Role Center**.
Small Business Owner—Stan	Stan manages the business from start to finish. He is responsible for everything and has to understand every aspect of the business. His Role Center is page 9020: **Small Business Owner RC**.
Finance, Accounting Manager—Phyllis	Phyllis manages the accounting department, processes general ledger (GL) transactions, reviews and approves accounts receivable (AR), accounts payable (AP), payroll, and bank transactions, and reviews aging reports. She also ensures that her team accurately completes financial procedures on time. Her Role Center page is 9001: **Account Manager Role Center**.
Finance, Accounts Payable Coordinator—April	April verifies paperwork matches and applies criteria from Ken (Controller) or Phyllis (Accounting Manager) to determine which invoices to pay, and then processes supplier payments. She may also reconcile bank statements. Because April sees data from so much of the company, people come to her with all types of questions. Her Role Center page is 9002: **Acc. Payables Coordinator RC**.
Finance, Accounts Receivable Administrator—Arnie	Arnie verifies shipment paperwork and creates invoices. He processes and applies cash receipts to appropriate invoices. He may follow up on past due accounts to obtain payment. His Role Center page is 9003: **Acc. Receivables Adm. RC**.
Finance, Bookkeeper—Annie	Annie handles the day-to-day financials of a small business. She is involved with creating invoices, paying bills, and balancing the bank statements. Annie hands off, to the external accountant, the more complex tasks of payroll, depreciation, and creating financial statements. Her Role Center page is 9004: **Bookkeeper Role Center**.
Operations, Logistics, Warehouse Worker—John	John puts received items away and picks items that need shipping. John waits for Sammy (Shipping and Receiving) or Ellen (Warehouse Manager) to tell him what to do. John's Role Center page is 9009: **Whse. Worker WMS Role Center**.
Operations, Logistics, Shipping and Receiving—Sammy	Sammy manages shipping, and also receives goods and verifies them against purchase orders. He also supervises the other warehouse employees. Sammy has two Role Centers depending on whether you are using Warehouse Management Systems (WMS) or just the standard inventory locations. The Role Centers are 9000: **Whse. WMS Role Center** and 9008: **Whse. Basic Role Center**.

Role	Description
Operations, Logistics, Purchasing Agent—Alicia	Alicia orders materials and supplies. She follows up on purchase order (PO) confirmations and partial receipts. She also researches suppliers to get the best quality products at the lowest price. Alicia reports to Inga (Purchasing Manager). Alicia's Role Center page is 9007: **Purchasing Agent Role Center**.
Operations, Production, Production Planner—Eduardo	Eduardo manages scheduling and planning of production. He often needs to reshuffle existing orders to make room for more urgent orders. He considers exceptions to be the rule. His Role Center page is 9010: **Production Planner Role Center**.
Operations, Production, Shop Supervisor—Lars	Lars ensures that the machine operators are productive, trained, and motivated. He can perform any job in the shop, but rarely has to do so. Once again there are two Role Center pages covering Manufacturing Foundation and Manufacturing Comprehensive. The Role Centers are 9011: **Shop Supervisor Mfg Foundation**, and 9012: **Shop Supervisor Role Center**.
Operations, Production, Machine Operator—Shannon	Shannon is trained to work her machine. She works hard to meet her production quotas so that she can get her bonus. Shannon does not use a computer at all, which would make for a pretty simple Role Center. The Role Center page provided is for Manufacturing Comprehensive and the page is 9013: **Machine Operator Role Center**.
Operations, Professional Services, Resource Manager—Reina	Reina manages and schedules Project Team Members. She ensures they are hired, trained, and available to Prakash (Project Manager) and June (Product Division Manager) for projects. Her Role Center page is 9014: **Job Resource Manager RC**.
Operations, Professional Services, Project Manager—Prakash	Prakash is responsible for project delivery. He works with Reina (Resource Manager) to provide adequate resources and staff. He has approval authority for all project-related charges from Tricia (Project Team Member), as well as any other materials charges. Parkash's Role Center page is 9015: **Job Project Manager RC**.
Operations, Customer Service, Dispatcher—Daniel	Daniel organizes the fleet of service technicians. He decides which customers they will call on and in what order. His Role Center page is 9016: **Service Dispatcher Role Center**.
Operations, Customer Service, Outbound Technician—Terrence	Terrence works in the field performing maintenance and installations as directed by Daniel (Dispatcher - Customer Service). Terrence's Role Center page is 9017: **Service Technician Role Center**.

Role	Description
IT & Partners, IT Manager—Tim	Tim is the IT decision maker and owns the IT budget in a company with 4–15 servers. As the senior IT admin, Tim manages Chris (IT Engineer) and completes some tasks to help balance his workload. Tim's Role Center page is 9018: **Administrator Role Center**.
Sales & Marketing, Sales Manager—Kevin	Kevin manages sales reps for his area and tracks what they are doing. He helps them to close sales and may do limited selling himself. His Role Center page is 9005: **Sales Manager Role Center**.
Sales & Marketing, Sales Order Processor—Susan	Susan enters orders and performs sales support tasks. She takes orders from sales reps and repeat orders directly from customers. She works closely with the sales reps as she may talk to the customer more often than they do. Susan's Role Center page is 9006: **Order Processor Role Center**.

Role-centric thinking

As consultants, we need to become familiar with the Dynamics Customer Model. We need to start using the terminology that Microsoft has used, and start thinking in terms of roles and processes and not forms and functions. When analyzing businesses, we should be looking for gaps in the Dynamics Customer Model and in the NAV 2009 implementation of the customer model. In order to fill those gaps, we need to be extending the model before we extend the application. This means thinking about the role that the requirement relates to and the process that is missing features. After we look at how departmental super users can personalize the roles, we'll see how we can add new features to existing roles and create new roles from scratch.

Discovering the existing roles

You can see the profiles available in the standard product by going to **CRONUS International Ltd.** | **Departments** | **Administration** | **Application Setup** | **RoleTailored Client** | **Profiles**.

If you want to have a play around with the roles in the standard product, you'll need a way of starting the application using a profile different to the one that is assigned to your user. Thankfully, the boffins at Microsoft have provided a startup option for the RoleTailored client that allows you to do just that.

RoleTailored client startup options

To find the various startup options for the RoleTailored client, open a command prompt and go to the folder that contains the `Microsoft.Dynamics.Nav.Client.exe` executable and type the name of the executable, followed by `/?`. For example, on a typical installation this will be:

```
"C:\Program Files\Microsoft Dynamics NAV\60\
RoleTailored Client\Microsoft.Dynamics.Nav.
Client.exe" /?
```

When you start the application with a `-profile:` option, you can specify which profile you want to use, regardless of your user ID. If the profile name contains a space, you must enclose the profile name in double quotes.

Here's a useful tip to get you started. Use Windows Explorer to open the folder containing your RoleTailored client executable.

Then, using your right mouse button, click on the `Microsoft.Dynamics.Nav.Client.exe` file and drag it to your desktop. When you release the button you will see a menu giving the options to **Copy Here, Move Here, Create Shortcuts Here**, or **Cancel**.

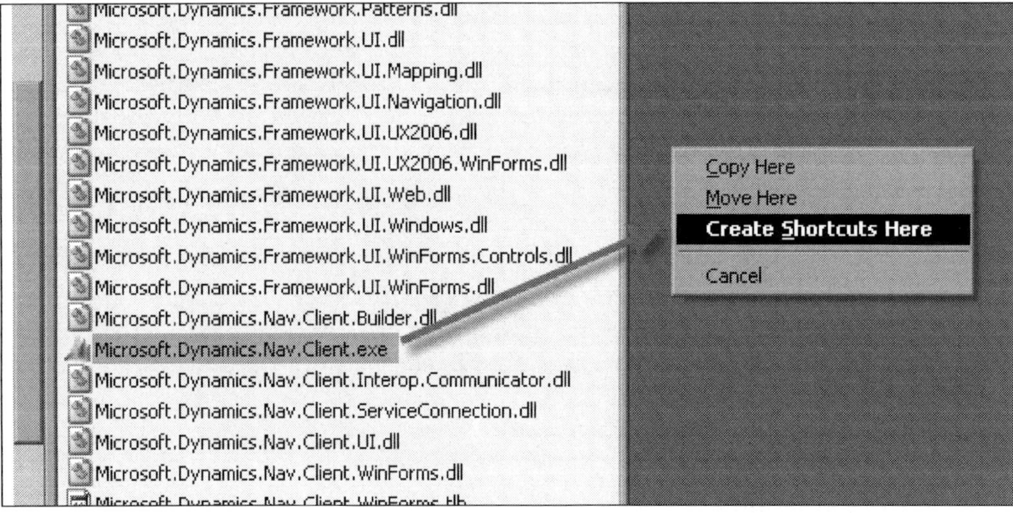

Select the option to create a shortcut. Next, click the newly created shortcut and press *F2* to rename it. Rename the shortcut to **Accounting Manager Profile**. (The name you provide is up to you, but try to use something that identifies the profile you intend to start the application with.)

Now, right-click the shortcut and select **Properties**.

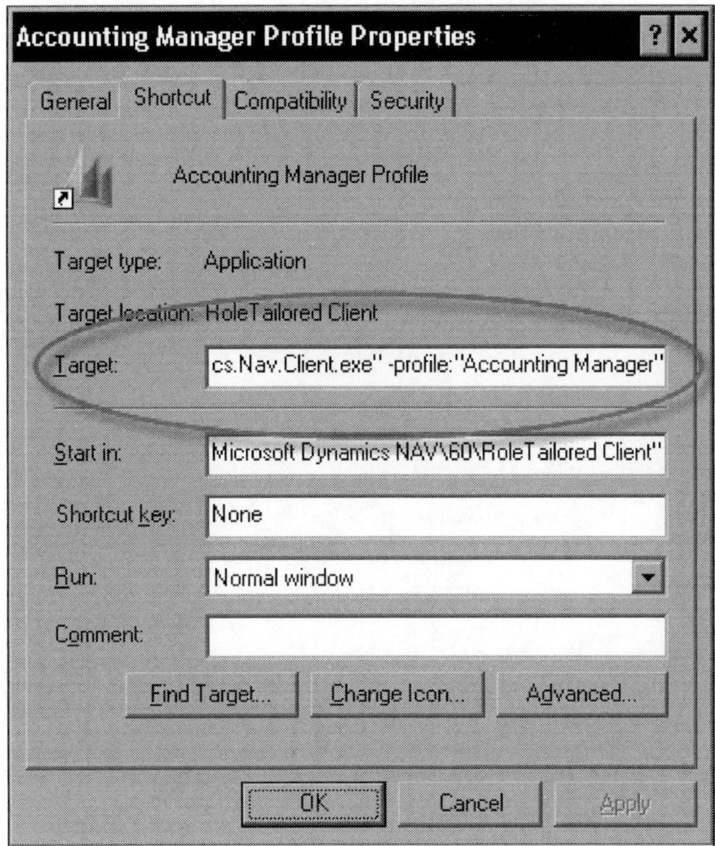

Add the text `-profile:"Accounting Manager"` to the end of the **Target** field.

Once this is done, click **OK** to save the changes you made to the shortcut. When you double-click this shortcut, the RoleTailored client will be started using your current Windows credentials but with the **Accounting Manager Profile.**

Repeat this exercise for each of the available profiles:

Profile ID
ACCOUNTING MANAGER
AP COORDINATOR
AR ADMINISTRATOR
BOOKKEEPER
DISPATCHER
IT MANAGER
MACHINE OPERATOR
ORDER PROCESSOR
OUTBOUND TECHNICIAN
PRESIDENT
PRESIDENT - SMALL BUSINESS
PRODUCTION PLANNER
PROJECT MANAGER
PURCHASING AGENT
RESOURCE MANAGER
SALES MANAGER
SHIPPING AND RECEIVING
SHIPPING AND RECEIVING - WMS
SHOP SUPERVISOR
SHOP SUPERVISOR - FOUNDATION
WAREHOUSE WORKER - WMS

What's in a role center?

Another trick for finding the contents of a Role Center page is to use the export as XML feature from within Dynamics NAV 2009. Since we know the pages for the various role centers are within the range of object IDs 9000 to 9020, we can select these objects from within the Object Designer and export them as XML. You can export all pages in this way but the resulting XML file is quite large and doesn't open properly in Excel.

Obviously, you can just design the various pages in the Object Designer, but this does mean you don't get the ability to easily look across all Role Center pages at once.

To illustrate this, here's an example. Let's say we want to see which profiles have the report ID 111: Customer - Top 10 List.

1. You'll need to be running on a developer's license in order to do this. First, you need to open the Classic client and run the **Object Designer**.
2. Click the button to show objects of type Page, and select objects from range ID **9000** to **9020**. Now select the **File** menu and choose **Export...**.

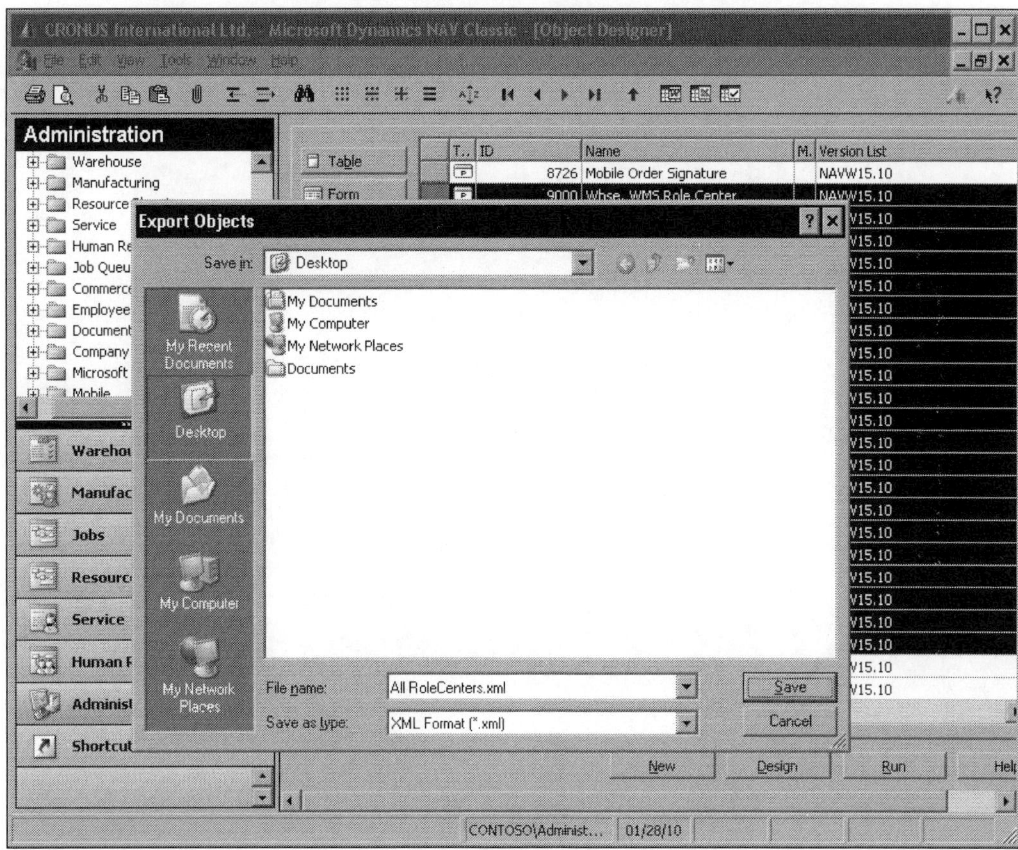

3. Change the **Save as type** field to **XML Format (*.xml)** and enter a suitable file name. Click **Save** to save the file.

4. Now you can open the XML file in the XML tool of your choice. For me, the features in Excel 2007 are just right. Launch Excel and choose to open the XML file.

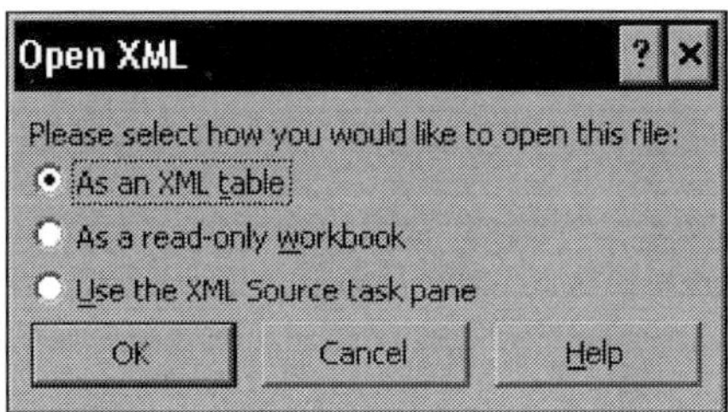

When prompted, select the option to open the file **As an XML table**.

5. You now have an auto-filtered Excel table with all of the nodes from the XML document containing all of the Role Center pages. Click the filter button for the **RunObject** column, and select to show only those lines where the value is **Report 111**.

6. You will now see a list of four role centers that have the report we're interested in—**Sales Manager**, **Order Processor**, **CEO and President**, and **Small Business Owner**.

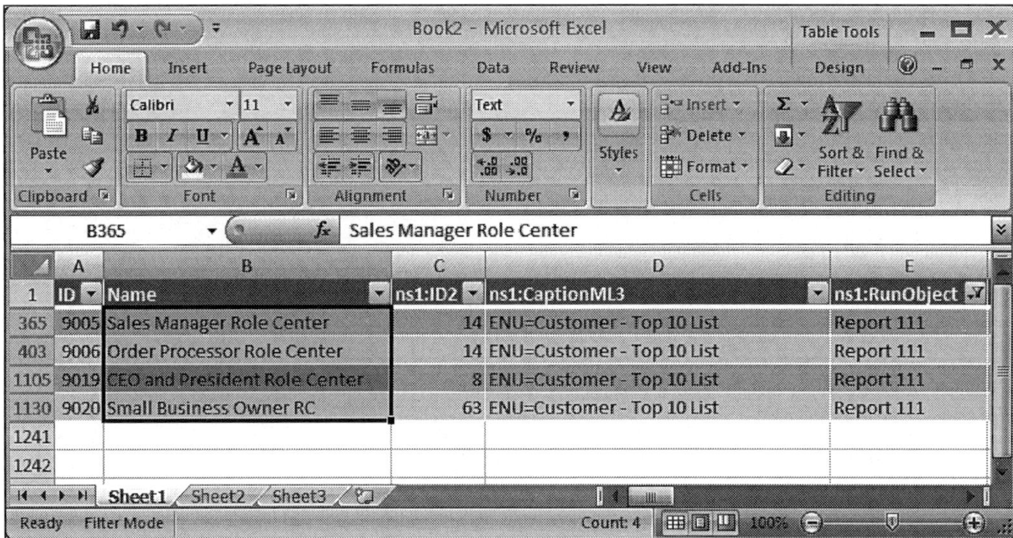

I can recommend using Excel to explore the XML export of the Role Center pages as a great way to get to know the role centers in the system; take some time to explore the various reports and actions made available to the profiles.

Customizing a role as a super user

It is likely that as well as allowing individual users to personalize their own RoleTailored client (something we covered in Chapter 2) you will want to have your departmental super users provide configuration, such as adding list places, configuring FastTabs, and so on for all members of a role.

Customizing a role is done in the same way as a user personalizing their individual experience, except that the RoleTailored client is started in configuration mode.

To be able to configure a role center, you must be a member of the SUPER security role, and must also be the owner of the profile you wish to configure. To check to see the owner of the profile, go to **CRONUS International Ltd.** | **Departments** | **Administration** | **Application Setup** | **RoleTailored Client** | **Profiles** and ensure your user name is in the Owner ID field; if it isn't, you'll need to edit the profile to ensure it is.

Customizing the Accounting Manager profile

In a previous example, we looked at how to create a shortcut that would start the RoleTailored client using the Accounting Manager profile. In this example, you need to copy that shortcut and rename it as **Customize Accounting Manager Profile**.

Once again, we need to open the properties dialog box for the shortcut; but this time, add the **-configure** option to the **Target** field. The order of the options is not important, so you can add the text at the end. Your field should look like the following:

```
"C:\Program Files\Microsoft Dynamics NAV\60\RoleTailored Client\
Microsoft.Dynamics.Nav.Client.exe" -profile:"Accounting Manager"
-configure
```

If you remember from Chapter 2, the configuration you can perform in a role center is limited to:

- Moving, removing, and promoting actions or reports in the Actions pane
- Adding chart parts to the role center or changing the chart used in existing chart parts
- Moving, removing, or configuring parts in the role center
- Adding activity buttons to the navigation pane that can contain any other options available from the departments place
- Changing the columns displayed in a list place
- Changing the appearance and priority of FastTabs and the fields they contain

By providing the ability to customize the application for other users, Microsoft has opened up a whole new area for Dynamics NAV and has reduced the reliance on programmers in order to deploy simple customizations. Try to ensure that your departmental super users capture some documentation around the changes they are making. This will certainly help should the changes need to be reapplied for any reason. The configuration changes apply to any page in the system, not just the role center, and they are stored in the database. (No longer will the mysteries of the ZUP file plague users.)

Whatzup?

In previous version of Dynamics NAV, user customizations could be made and stored but only for an individual user. The settings were stored in a file commonly referred to as a *ZUP file,* as it had a file extension of `.zup`.

ZUP files were not human readable, meaning it was not possible for consultants to find out what was in the files if users were experiencing problems. ZUP files lost their settings for objects when those objects were recompiled. Opening two sessions of NAV would put up a cryptic message for the users asking if they wished to replace their ZUP file. All in all, not ideal!

Now our customizations are stored in the User Metadata table, and the customizations themselves are stored inside a blob field that contains an XML document describing the changes made.

You will also find some other personal settings, such as your preference for column sizes, are stored in a `PersonalizationStore.xml` file that can be found in your `%AppData%\Microsoft\Microsoft Dynamics NAV\` directory—but don't go trying to read this file unless you like reading cryptic XML.

Profile customization changes get stored in the Profile Metadata table, and the RoleTailored client is smart enough to take the standard page metadata (the definition of the page itself) and merge this with the Profile Metadata and then the User Metadata to provide a finished page for the user.

Let's take a look at a couple of examples to illustrate how this works. We're going to add a new report to the Accounting Manager profile role center, add a new action item, and finally make some changes to the FastTabs on the Customer card.

Clearing the configured pages for a profile

Before we start, let's make sure there are no customizations for the profile already.

1. Go to **CRONUS International Ltd.** | **Departments** | **Administration** | **Application Setup** | **RoleTailored Client** | **Profiles**.
2. The RoleTailored client **Profiles** list place is displayed.

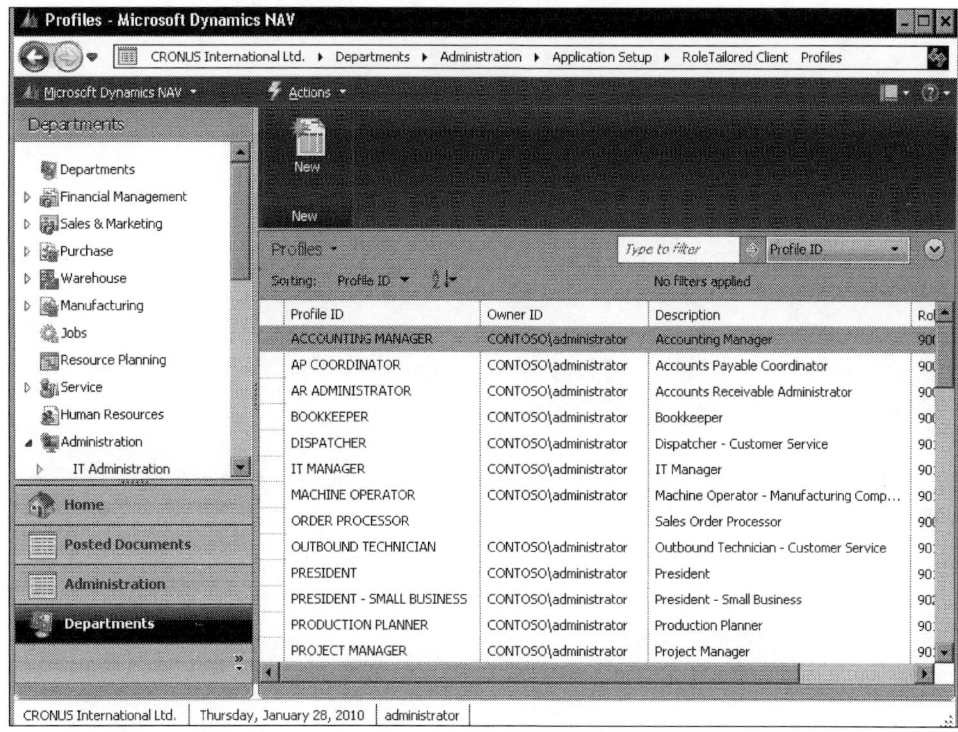

3. Double-click the **ACCOUNTING MANAGER** profile to open the **Profile Card** page.
4. The **ACCOUNTING MANAGER** profile card is displayed.

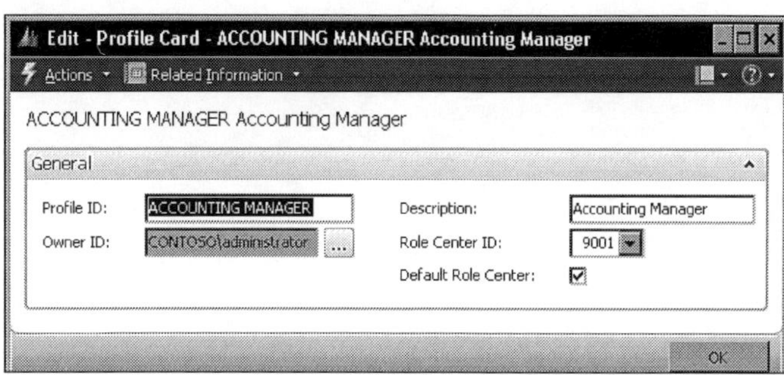

5. Click the **Actions** menu, and from the **Functions** submenu, select the **Clear Configured Pages** menu option.
6. The system displays a confirmation box to ensure that you wish to continue.

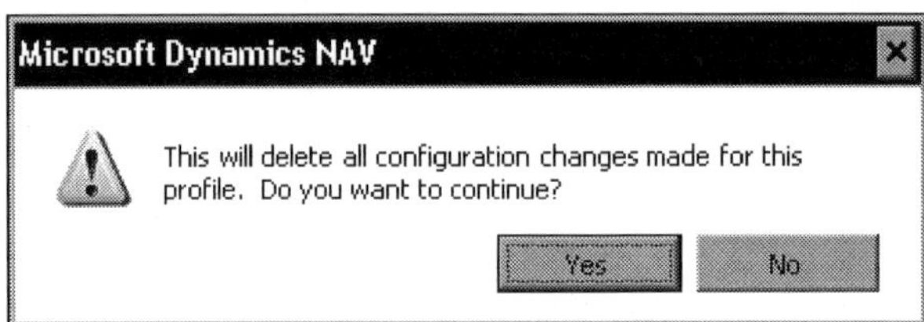

7. Click **Yes** to delete the configuration changes.
8. The *Clearing the configured pages for a profile* process is now complete.

When you start the application in configuration mode, the system does not apply the User Personalization that you may have. Instead, you are looking at the system as though you are a new user that belongs to that profile. Now let's make the first of our changes.

Adding actions and reports to a profile

In this scenario, we want to add the BizTalk Inbound Sales document worksheet to the Actions available to the Accounting Manager profile. We also want to add the **Sales Reservation Avail.** report so that all users of this profile will be able to easily run the report from their role center.

1. Start the RoleTailored client in configuration mode for the Accounting Manager profile by executing a shortcut with the target:

   ```
   "C:\Program Files\Microsoft Dynamics NAV\60\RoleTailored
   Client\Microsoft.Dynamics.Nav.Client.exe" -profile:"Accounting
   Manager" -configure
   ```

2. The RoleTailored client launches the Accounting Manager profile role center in configuration mode.

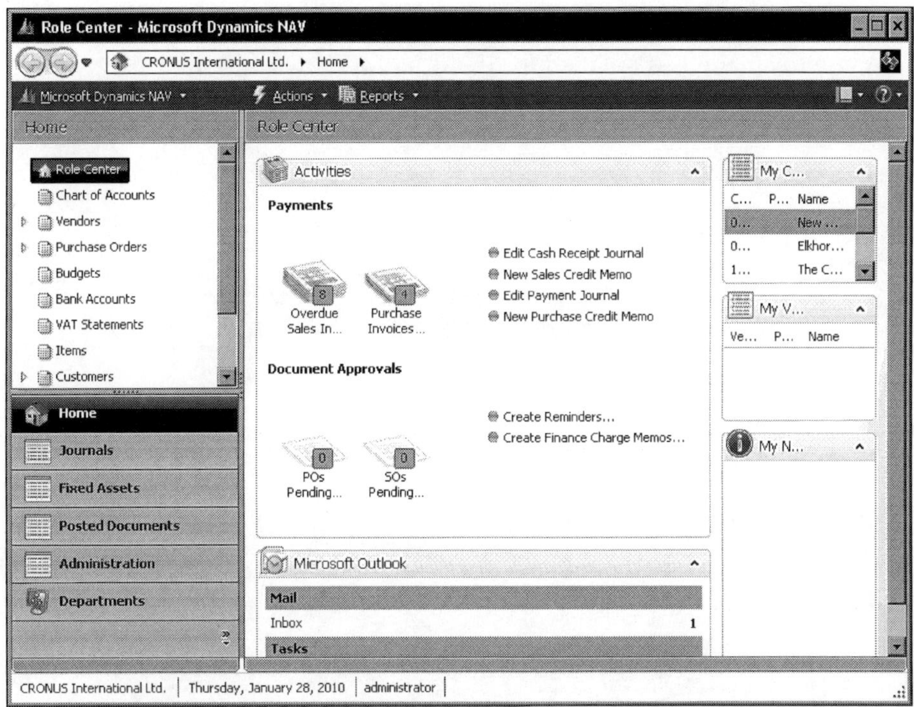

Go to **CRONUS International Ltd. | Departments | Sales & Marketing | Order Processing**.

3. The **Order Processing** Departments place is displayed.

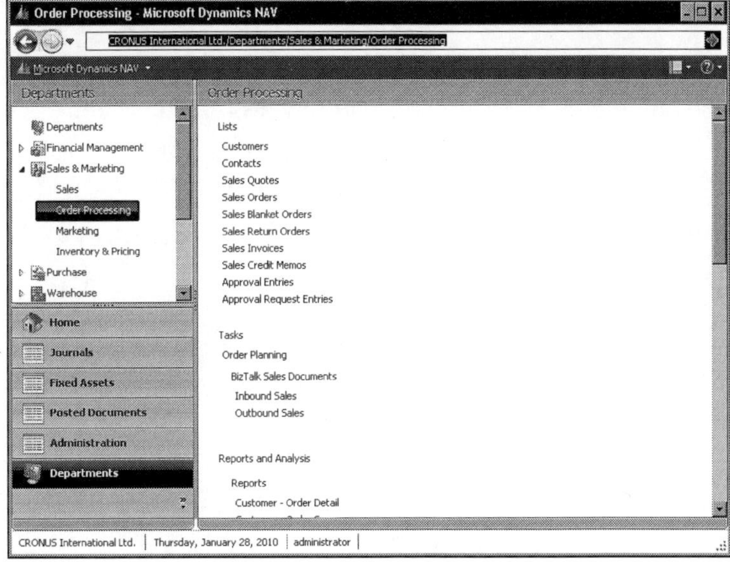

4. Right-click on the **Inbound Sales** option.
5. A context menu is displayed for the **Inbound Sales** option.

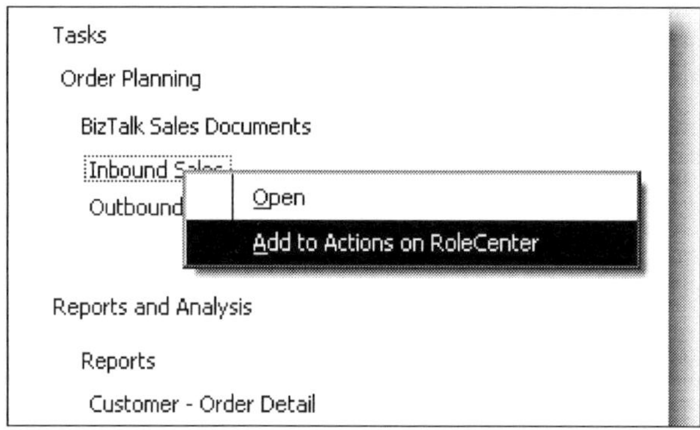

6. Select the **Add to Actions on RoleCenter** option.
7. The system displays a confirmation dialog box asking if you want to restart the application in order to pick up the latest changes.

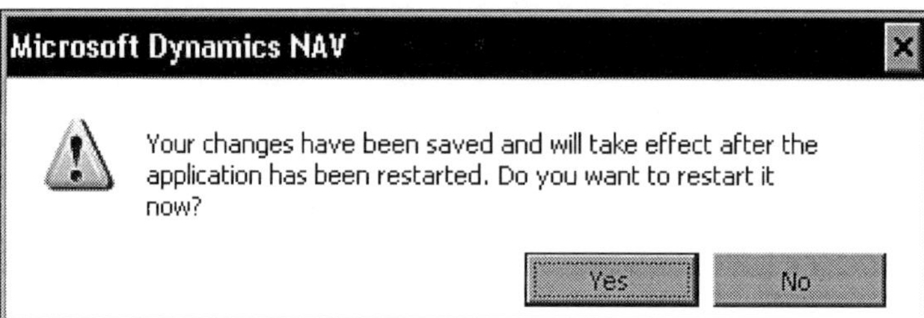

8. Click **Yes** to restart the RoleTailored client.
9. The RoleTailored client is refreshed and the Role Center home page is displayed.
10. Click the **Actions** menu button.
11. The system displays the **Actions** menu with a new option at the bottom of the menu for **Inbound Sales**.

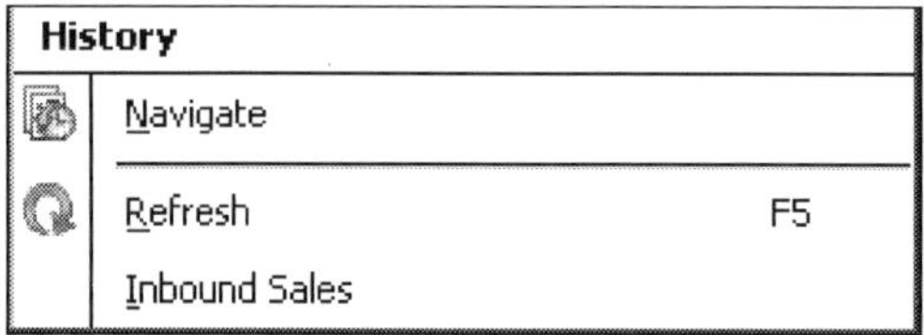

Select the option from the menu.

12. The **Inbound Sales Doc. Worksheet** is displayed.

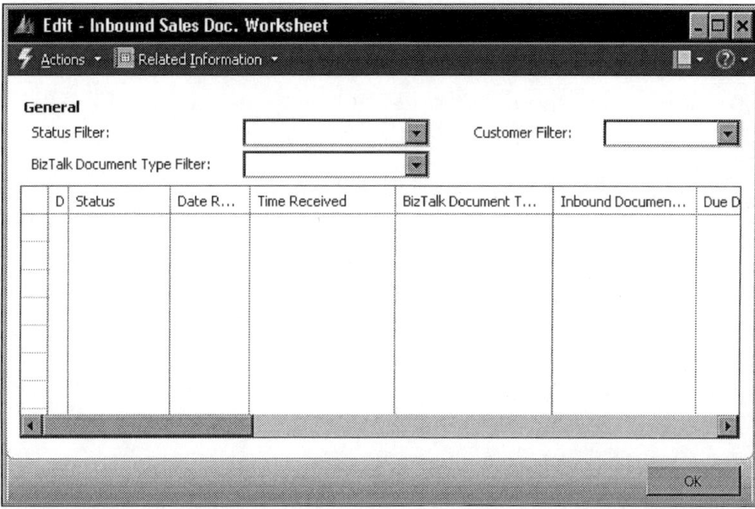

13. Close the worksheet, and on the role center, click the customize menu button and select the **Customize Actions** option.
14. The **Customize Actions Menu** page is displayed.

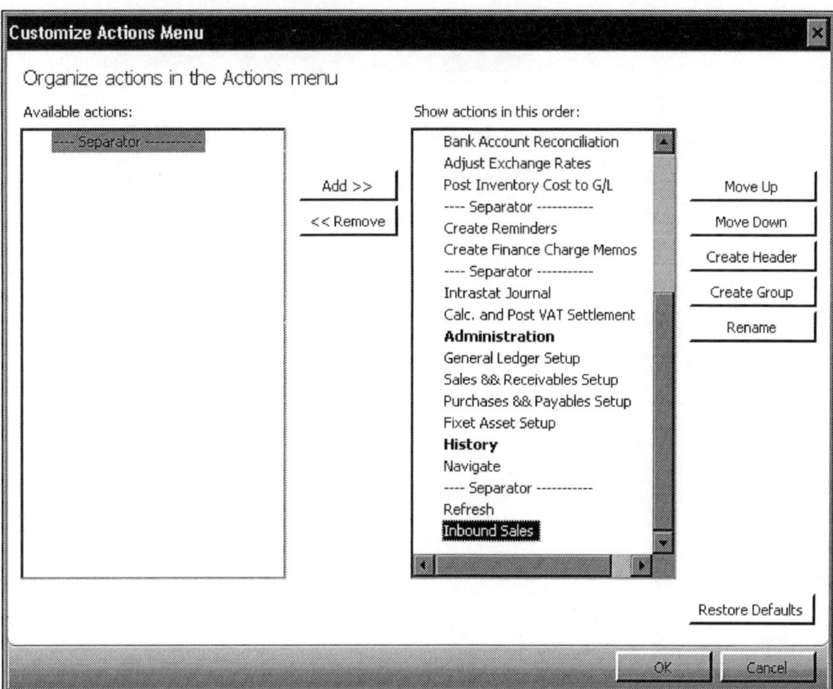

15. In the **Show actions in this order** list on the right-hand side, scroll down until you see the **Inbound Sales** option you have just added. Use the **Move Up** button to position the new action just beneath the **Payment Journal** task. Click **OK** to save the changes.
16. You are returned to the Role Center home page. Go to **CRONUS International Ltd. | Departments | Sales & Marketing | Order Processing**.
17. The **Order Processing** Departments place is displayed. Scroll down to find the **Reports** section and right-click the **Sales Reservation Avail.** report.
18. A context menu is displayed for the **Sales Reservation Avail.** report.

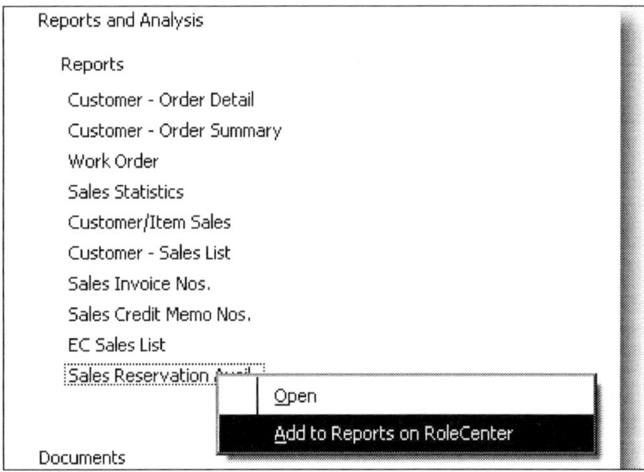

19. Select the **Add to Reports on RoleCenter** option.
20. The system displays a confirmation dialog box asking if you want to restart the application in order to pick up the latest changes.

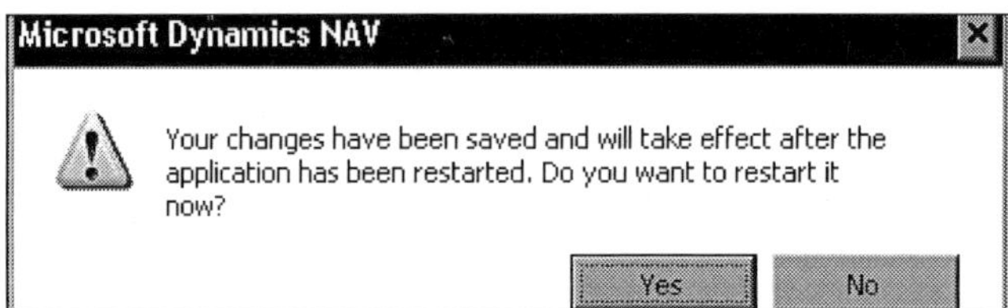

21. Click **Yes** to restart the RoleTailored client.
22. The report has now been added to the Reports menu. The exercise is now complete. Don't forget you are still in configuration mode, so you will need to exit the application before you make any changes you don't want to apply to all the users of this profile.

Changing the layout of the Customer Card

You should now know how to start the application in configuration mode for a particular profile. Once in configuration mode, the application behaves exactly as it would normally, except that any changes you make will be propagated to all users of that profile.

Now it's your turn. See if you can use the information in this section and the *Personalizing pages using the customize menu* section in Chapter 2 to complete this exercise.

1. Start the application in configuration mode for the **ACCOUNTING MANAGER** profile.
2. Modify the **Customer Card** to remove the **Foreign Trade** FastTab.
3. Change the importance to **Additional** for the following fields on the **General** FastTab: **Primary Contact No., Contact, Search Name, Responsibility Center,** and **Service Zone Code**.
4. Exit configuration mode and verify your changes by starting the application for the **ACCOUNTING MANAGER** profile and launching the **Customer Card**.

If everything went well, your Customer Card page will look something like the following:

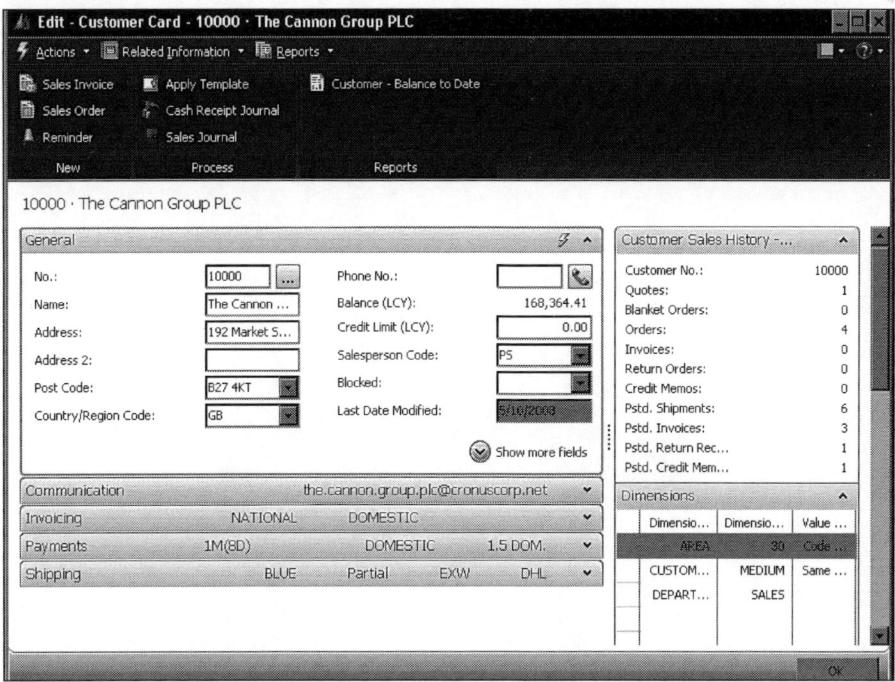

Notice the missing **Foreign Trade** FastTab and the **Show more fields** button at the bottom of the **General** FastTab.

What's in the blob?

If you want to know what NAV is storing when you make your customizations, you can export the contents of the blob from the Profile Metadata table.

If you don't feel up to writing a program that will export the blob contents, you can download a sample program from the PACKT web site (`www.packtpub.com`) or from our book web site (`www.teachmenav.com`).

Extending existing roles as a developer

The ability to configure the application for all users of a given profile is a really nice feature, and it certainly removes the need for a lot of customization work that could previously only be done by a developer (or a brave end user with sufficient access rights). There are, however, some things that still need a developer to help with, for example:

- Adding new parts to the role center
- Adding cues to the role center activities part
- Adding actions to the role center activities part

Let's take a look at making some changes to the **Activities** part for the **Sales Order Processor** profile.

In this example, we are working in an organization that does not use **Sales Quotes** but they do have priority customers. They have asked for sales orders for priority customers to stand out from all other orders. They also requested that the Sales Quote related cues and actions be removed from the order processor's activities part.

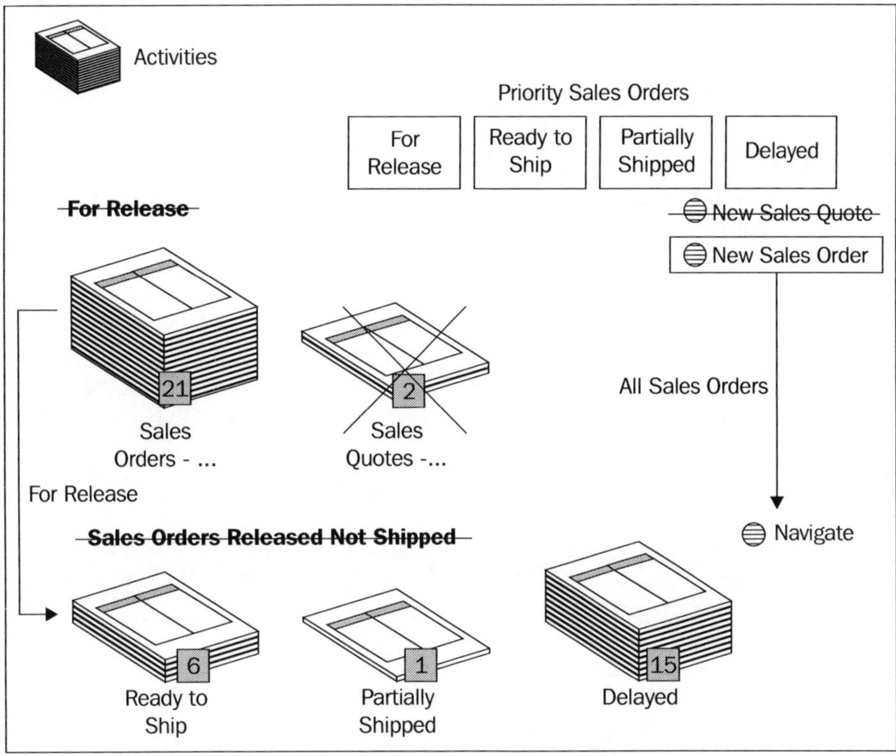

As with any development, it's a good idea to get an idea of the change on paper before you start hacking code. The previous image shows the results of the discussion with the client showing what has been agreed.

- The **For Release** cue group is to be replaced with a **Priority Sales Orders** group.
- The **Sales Orders Released Not Shipped** group will be renamed as **All Sales Orders** and will have the **Sales Orders - Open** cue moved to it. The **New Sales Order** action will also be moved to the **All Sales Orders** cue group.
- The **Sales Quotes - open** cue and the **New Sales Quote** action will be deleted.
- The **Priority Sales Orders** cue group will contain the same four cues as the **All Sales Orders** cue group. There will be no actions for this cue group.

Now we are ready to do some programming; so it's time to fire up the Classic client with a developer's license.

Before we start, make sure you have a backup of the database or at the very least an export of the programming objects—if you break something, it's nice to know you can get it back.

Find the Page ID and source table of the activities part

We know from looking at the **Order Processor** profile that the role center ID for the profile is **9006**. Although we're not going to be editing the Role Center page 9006 in this example, we can open up the page to see what the page ID of the activities part is. We're not going to worry too much about what all the various properties of the page mean, as we'll be covering development of pages in NAV 2009 in Chapter 6—*Modifying the system*.

1. Start the Classic client and press *Shift+F12* to launch the Object Designer; find page **9006** and click the **Design** button.
2. The **Page Designer** for page **9006** is displayed.

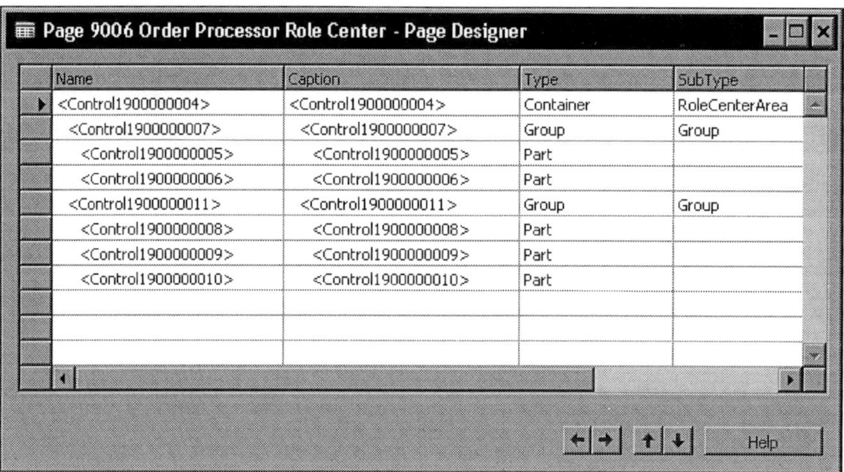

3. Click on the line for the first control with a **Type** value of **Part**, which in the previous image is **<Control1900000005>**. Press *Shift+F4* to bring up the properties for the part.

4. The **Properties** for **<Control1900000005>** are displayed.

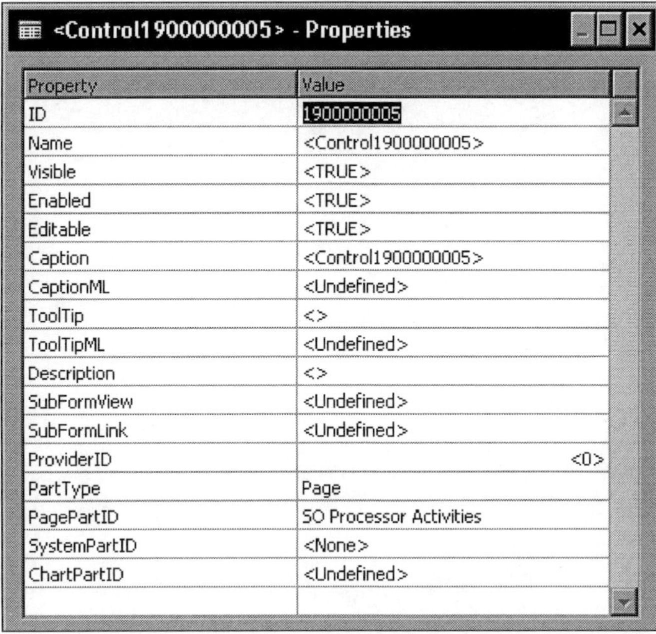

5. Look at the **PagePartID** property and make a note of the value or copy it to the clipboard. Press *Esc* to exit to the Object Designer and find the page with a name **SO Processor Activities**. Click the **Design** button to edit the page.
6. The **Page Designer** for page **9060** is displayed.

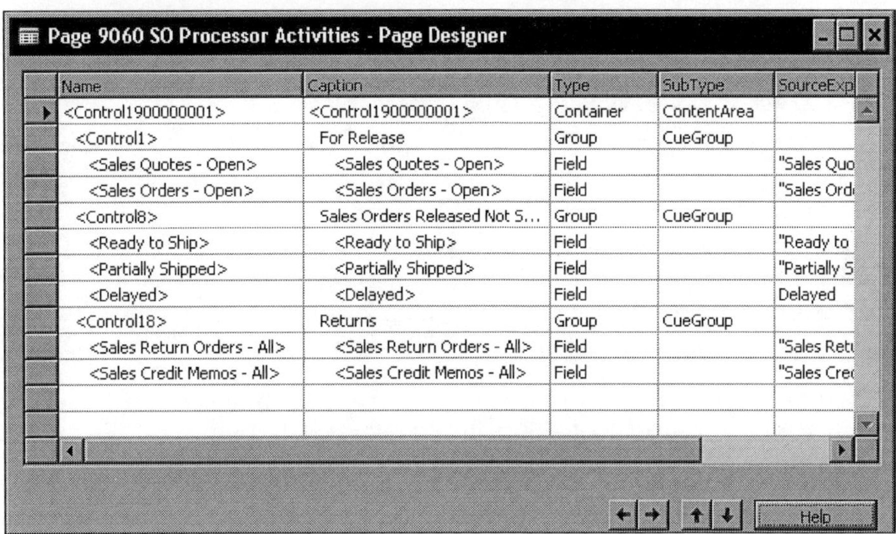

7. Click on the first blank line at the end of the list of controls and press *Shift+F4* to display the properties for the page.
8. The **Properties** sheet for the 9060 SO Processor Activities page is displayed.

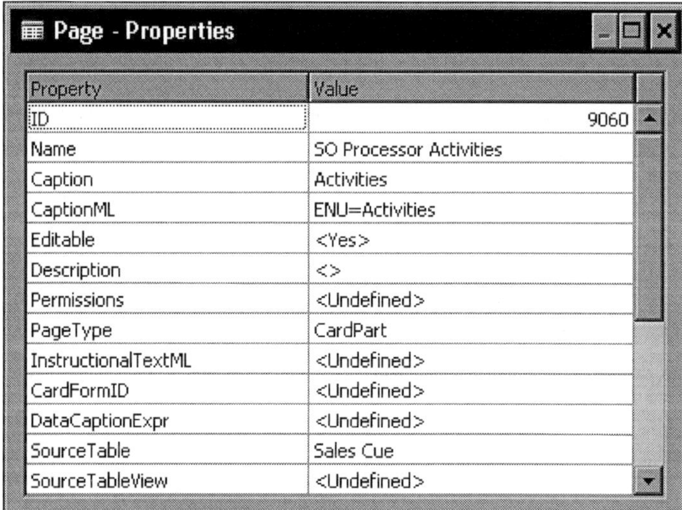

9. Find the **SourceTable** property and make a note of the value **Sales Cue**. Press *Esc* to exit the page and choose **No** if prompted to save any changes.
10. The *Find the page ID and source table of the activities part* process is now complete.

Before we can add our new cues for Priority Sales Orders, we need to be able to determine what a priority sales order is.

Adding the Priority Customer field

A priority sales order is an order that exists for a priority customer. To realize this in the application, we are going to add a new Boolean type field to the **Sales Header** table called **Priority Customer.** We will also add this to our Sales Order page so that we can set it in order to test our changes. In reality, we would be adding the Priority Customer field to our customer table and ensuring that it gets copied across to the sales header when the **Sell-to Customer No.** field is validated. In this example, we are simply showing how to create new cues and will not be going into that level of detail.

1. Start the Classic client and press *Shift+F12* to launch the **Object Designer**; find **Table 36 Sales Header** and click the **Design** button.
2. The **Table Designer** for table 36 is displayed. Each line represents a field on the table.

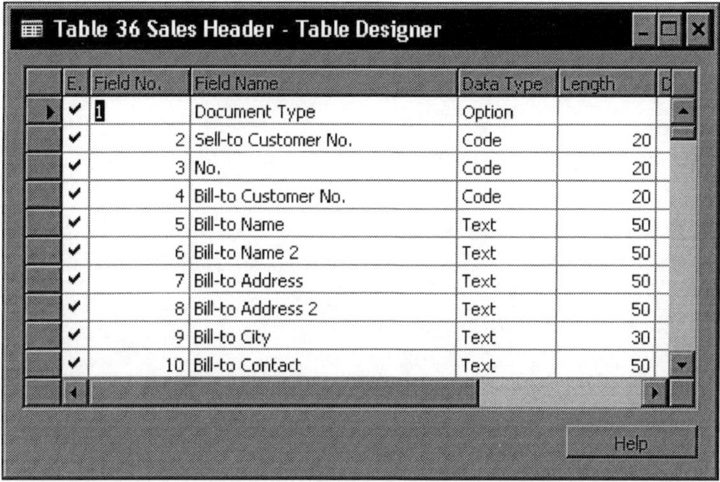

3. Press *F3* to insert a new line and set the details as follows:

   Field No.: 50000

   Field Name: Priority Customer

   Data Type: Boolean

   Press *Esc* and select **Yes** when prompted to save your changes.

4. From the **Object Designer**, find the **Sales Order** page (page ID=42, which is co-incidentally the answer to the meaning of life, the universe, and everything).

   Click the **Design** button.

5. The **Page Designer** for **Page 42** is displayed.

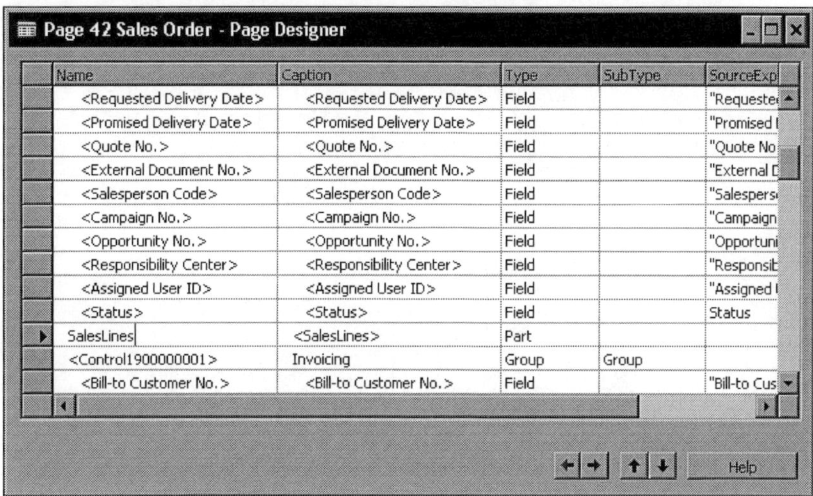

Scroll down and click on the line with the **SalesLines** Part as shown in the screenshot.

Click the Field menu button or select the **Field** menu option from the **View** menu.

6. The **Field Menu** is displayed.

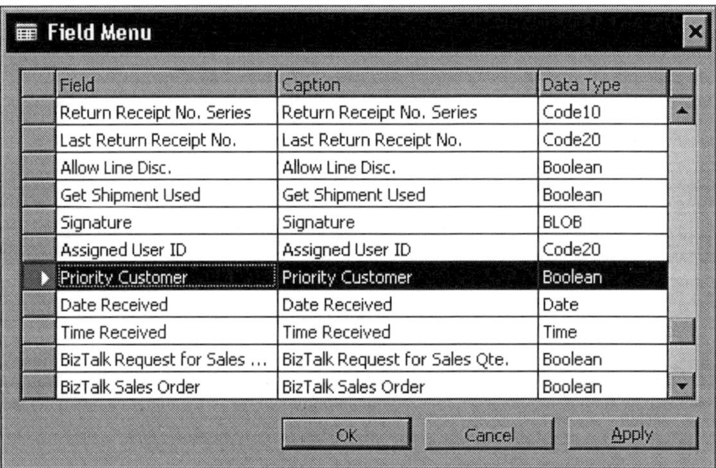

Scroll down to find the **Priority Customer** field and click to select the entire row, then, click the **OK** button to insert the field.

7. The system prompts to ensure that you want to add the selected field.

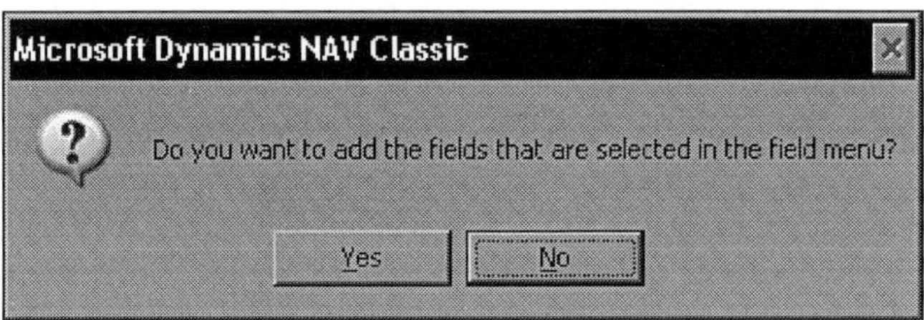

Click the **Yes** button.

8. The **Page Designer** for **Page 42** is displayed with the newly inserted **Priority Customer** field.

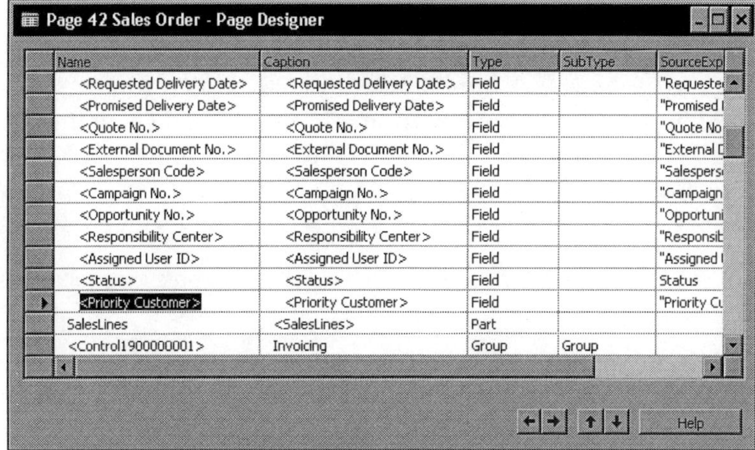

Press *Esc* to exit the **Page Designer,** and choose **Yes** when prompted to save the changes.

9. The exercise is now complete.

There is no need to restart your Microsoft Dynamics NAV Server service in order to pick up the table changes.

To verify that the modification has worked correctly, use the RoleTailored client and look at the **Sales Order** card. You should see the newly added **Priority Customer** field on the **General** FastTab, as shown in the following screenshot:

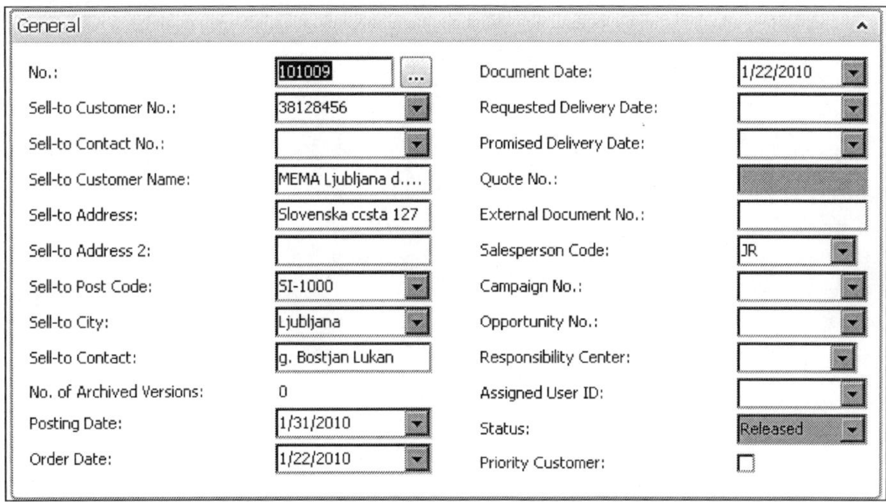

Now's a good time to check the **Priority Customer** field for a few of your sales orders, as we are going to need some Priority Customer orders before we can test our new role center.

Extending the Sales Cue table

The Sales Cue table provides the information that is used to display the cues in the activities part on the role center. In this exercise, we're going to create some new flow fields on the sales cue table that will show us the counts of orders for priority customers.

1. Start the Classic client and press *Shift+F12* to launch the **Object Designer**; find **Table 9053 Sales Cue** and click the **Design** button.
2. The **Table Designer** for table 9053 is displayed. Each line represents a field on the table.

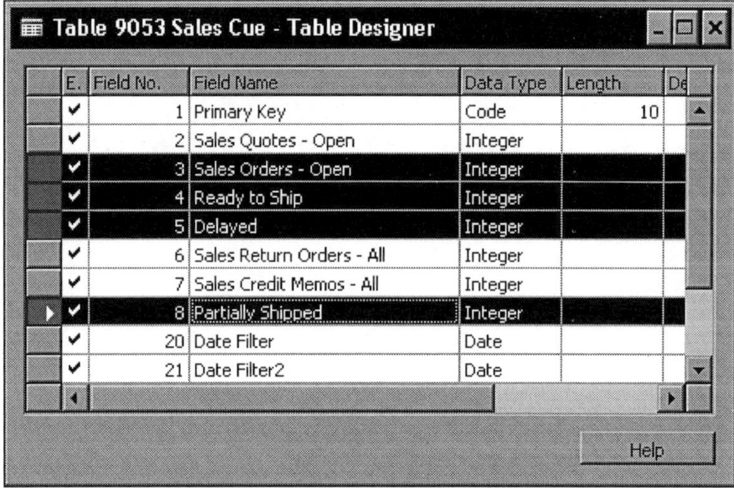

Highlight fields 3 to 5 and 8 and copy them to the clipboard with *Ctrl+C*.

Then scroll to the last newly inserted blank line and paste the copied fields. Overtype the **Field No.** values so that the field numbers are within the 50000+ developer range. Also add the word Priority to the start of the field name.

3. The **Sales Cue Table** is displayed with four new fields added.

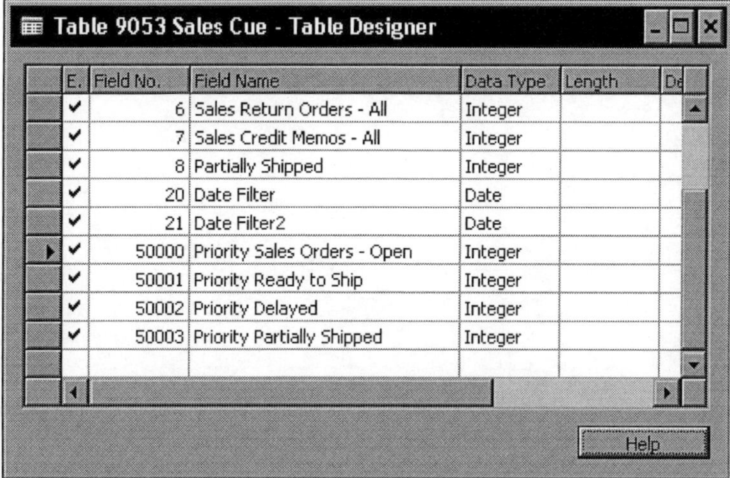

Click the 50000 field, **Priority Sales Orders – Open,** and press *Shift+F4* to bring up the properties for the field.

4. The **Properties** for the **Priority Sales Orders - Open** field is displayed.

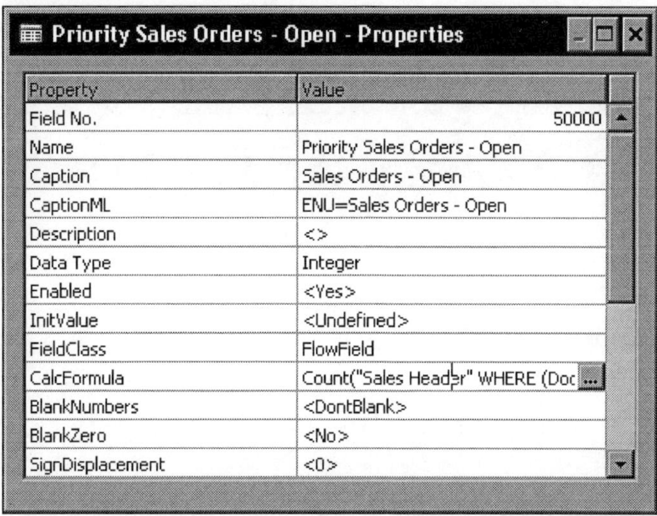

Copy the contents of the **Name** field and paste it into the **Caption** field.

The field is a Count FlowField showing the count of sales orders that match certain criteria. Scroll down to the **CalcFormula** field and click the Assist Edit button (the three dots to the right of the field).

5. The **Calculation Formula** form is displayed.

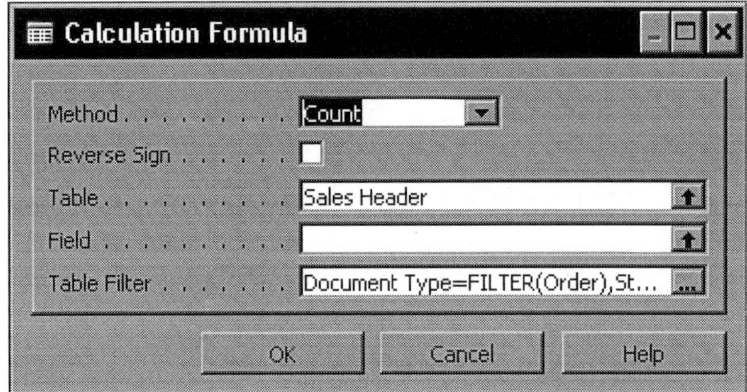

Click the Assist Edit button to the right of the **Table Filter** field.

6. The **Table Filter** form is displayed.

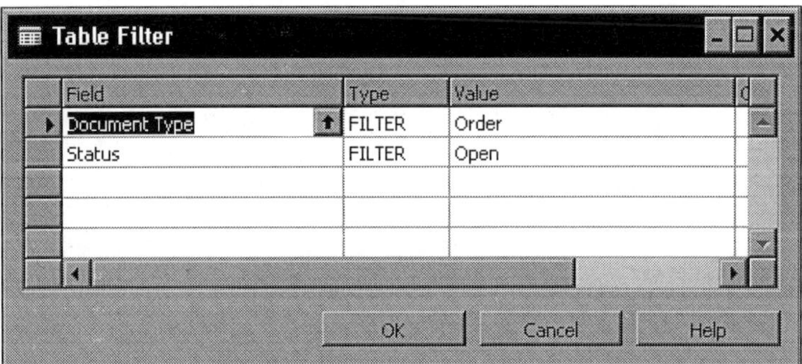

Insert a new line with the following values:

Field: Priority Customer

Type: FILTER

Value: Yes

Click the **OK** button, and then click **OK** again to exit back to the properties form. Press *Esc* to return to the Table Designer.

7. Repeat steps 3 to 6 for each of the new fields in order to add the Priority Customer filter to the Calculation Formula property, and set the **Caption** property for each field.

8. Press *Esc* to close the **Table Designer** and select **Yes** to save your changes.

We now have the count fields we need to display our priority customer cues. You should have seen enough development to be able to make these changes yourself.

1. Use the **Object Designer** (*Shift+F12*) to open page **9060** in the page designer.
2. Change the captions of the cue groups to **Priority Sales Orders** and **All Sales Orders**.
3. Delete the cues from the first cue group.
4. Use the **Field** menu to add the **Priority Customer** fields to the first cue group and the **Sales Orders - Open** field to the second cue group. Make sure the **DrillDownFormID** property for each cue is set to **Sales Order List**. Without this, your cues will not work.
5. Click on the first cue group control, and from the **View** menu, select the **Actions** option. Delete the **New Sales Quote** action and cut the **New Sales Order** action.
6. Click on the second cue group control, and from the **View** menu, select the **Actions** option. Press *F3* to insert a new action before the **Navigate** option, and paste the previously cut action. Remember to set the **DrillDownFormID** property.
7. Exit the **Page Designer** and select **Yes** to save the changes.

If everything went well, your final page should look like the following:

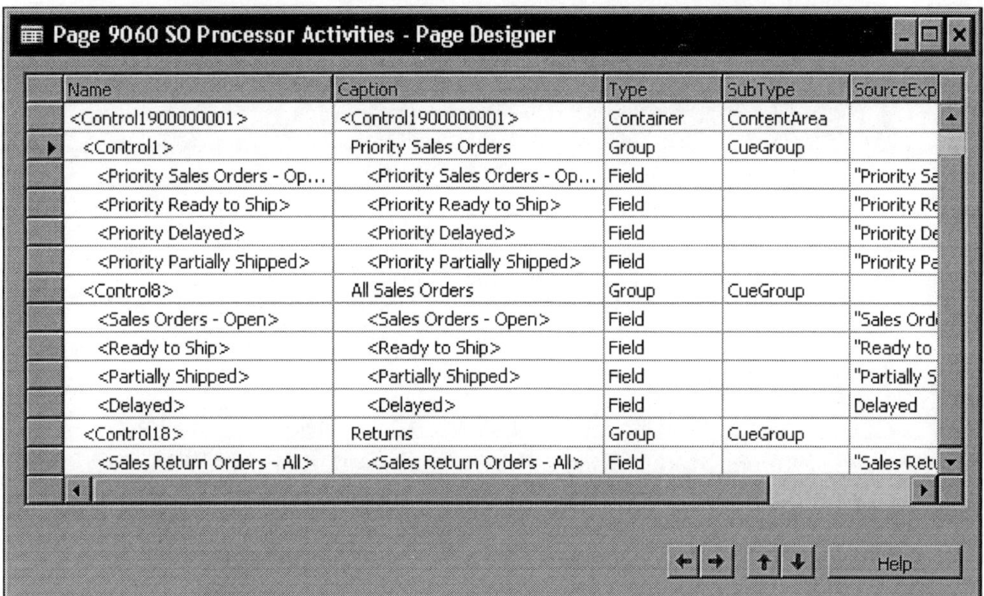

You may need to restart your Microsoft Dynamics NAV Server service in order to pick up the table changes. If things went really well, when you start the RoleTailored client, your **Role Center** will look like the following image.

Notice that in addition to the new cues that have been added to the **Activities** pane, as an extra bonus, the filtered views of the **Sales Orders List** have been added beneath the **Sales Orders** option in the navigation pane.

Creating a new role

When it comes to creating a new role in NAV 2009, your first step is to look at the Dynamics Customer Model to see if the role has been identified in the model but simply not implemented in NAV 2009. This will help you to find the correct terminology for the role. It is likely that later releases of NAV will include more roles, and it would be nice for your new role to be phased out and replaced with a standard role when it becomes available.

The next step is to find an existing role that is close to the one you want to create and copy it. There is really nothing to be gained by building your role from scratch, so why not cheat? Open the existing **Role Center** page you want to copy and then choose **File**, **Save As**, and save the page as a new ID in the 50000+ range and give the role a new name. Do the same for the **Activities Part** page, and then edit your new pages to make the role work as you want. Some people may find it easier to start from scratch rather than copying an existing role—try it both ways before deciding which is best for you.

Building the role center and activities part is fairly simple, especially when you are mainly copying the existing pages. The majority of effort required in designing a new role will be spent determining precisely what information is most important for users of the new role and which actions and reports the role will require. The best way to develop the skills needed to be able to consult in this area is to study the existing profiles that ship with the product, and see how the product team has implemented profiles to meet the requirements described in the Microsoft Dynamics Customer Model.

Further Reading

The following URL provides more details on RoleTailored productivity in the Microsoft Dynamics product range:

`http://www.microsoft.com/dynamics/product/familiartoyourpeople.mspx`

The following resources can be downloaded from the site:

- Microsoft Dynamics RoleTailored Business Productivity whitepaper
- Microsoft Dynamics Customer Model: People & Departments, illustration 1
- Microsoft Dynamics Customer Model: Departments & Work, illustration 2

We recommend you take some time to download and read the whitepaper and study the illustrations.

Summary

The RoleTailored client is wonderful. Not only does it solve the 'too much information' problem for users, it looks nice and is really easy to configure. The Dynamics Customer Model is there to guide you in your analysis of customer roles, and the pre-configured profiles are there for you to copy and learn from.

We've seen how to customize the existing profiles, how to make modifications to a profile, and have offered some advice on how to create profiles of your own for your implementations. Now it's up to you. Take some time to download the further reading and examine the standard profiles. See if you can create your own role center by copying an existing page and activities part page—look at some of the roles in the customer model that have not been implemented in Dynamics NAV 2009, and see if you can work out how to implement a profile to meet one of those roles.

4
The Implementation Process

"Cheshire Puss," she began... "Would you tell me, please, which way I ought to go from here?"
"That depends a good deal on where you want to get to," said the Cat.
"I don't much care where – " said Alice.
"Then it doesn't matter which way you go," said the Cat.
" – so long as I get SOMEWHERE," Alice added as an explanation.
"Oh, you're sure to do that," said the Cat, "if you only walk long enough."

Lewis Carroll, Alice's Adventures in Wonderland

Microsoft Dynamics NAV 2009 is not just a software product. It is a business management system, and is a very generic one at that. Coming from a **Finish** button in the installation procedure to a fully functional solution tailored specifically for your customer's business takes a lengthy implementation project before success is achieved.

In this chapter you will learn:

- What an implementation is
- Why methodology is important
- What the six phases of Microsoft Dynamics Sure Step methodology are

What is an implementation?

Imagine building a house. A house is made of a lot of stuff: bricks, mortar, paint, tiles, doors, windows, pipes, cables, you name it. You usually start by laying the foundation. Then you continue with the walls and eventually finish with the roof. But masonry is hardly your only concern. Your walls need to have windows to let air and light in; you need doors to get from room to room, also to get in and out. You need water in your bathroom and your kitchen, and electricity all over. You get the picture. To build a house, it takes much more than just piling all the material, then calling it a day.

A business management system is no different, and to bring one to life it takes far more than a next-next-finish installation procedure. You need to consider many variables, and the software itself is just one of them. But why is it so?

One word alone answers this question: **diversity**.

If all the beers tasted like Heineken, and all the singers sang like Sting, this world would be a boring place to be. Diversity makes it otherwise.

In business world, diversity abounds, with companies making money in many different ways: some manufacture goods, some buy and resell goods, some provide services, some arrange for others to provide services.

Even companies in the same vertical conduct their business diversely, handling finances, manufacturing, purchases, sales or human resources in very specific ways. To businesses, diversity provides competitive edge, and encourages positive change and innovation. All in all, no two companies are the same.

Business management software needs to be able to cope with this diversity. It must provide a stack of horizontal functionality that can be put to work regardless of how complex, or simple, the business processes it supports are. At the same time it has to be flexible enough to adapt to any specific vertical requirements, initially not covered by it at all. In effect, business management software needs to be as diverse as the market it covers.

Vertical and Horizontal Solutions

Companies doing the same kind of business by producing similar goods or providing similar services, with specific set of needs or conforming to a specific common set of requirements, are said to belong to the same vertical industry, or simply *vertical*. Some typical examples of verticals are healthcare, banking, insurance, telecommunications, and publishing.

A software application not pertaining to any specific vertical industry is called a *horizontal solution*. Typical examples of horizontal solutions are word processing or spreadsheet applications. In the language of business management software, the term *horizontal functionality*, or *core functionality*, refers to those application modules (such as financial management or human resources) that are not intended to cover requirements of any specific vertical industry, and are therefore applicable to any industry.

Microsoft Dynamics NAV 2009, like any other ERP software, comes with dozens of application modules, consisting of hundreds of separate functions. All this is called *standard functionality*. It doesn't necessarily mean it is standardized by an international standards authority, but rather that this is how the software vendor has decided to standardize these functions and how the system behaves out of the box.

The idea behind ERP standardization is to provide a kind of best-practice functionality to users of such software. Typical examples of best practice functionality are journals in financial management, or production orders in manufacturing. Sometimes these practices are best simply because they are mandated by government; sometimes they are best because the industry has been applying them for a long time and determined that they are best indeed.

To its customers, standardized software also gives a reassurance that their investment won't go in vain, because if the software worked for thousands of other companies, it should work for them as well.

Standard functionality is generic—it is designed to match the needs of most of businesses as closely as possible. However, on a scale ranging from 'Not at all' to 'Exact match', most companies would classify ERP functionality as 'Close, but not exactly there'.

The process of getting from generic functionality to an exact match is called *implementation*.

Implementation tasks

Two parties are usually involved in a business management software implementation process. The central one—the company implementing the software to use it later on—is usually called *the customer*. The other party, helping the customer implement the software, is usually called *the consultant*.

There are four ways in which standardized software can be put to work when the functionality is close, but not exactly matching the way the customer goes about its business:

- Business process reengineering
- Configuration
- Customization
- Third-party solutions

Let's take a closer look at each of these.

Business process reengineering

Over time, this one has grown into a buzzword, and has even evolved into an acronym, so nowadays it simply goes under BPR. When a customer has been doing a process in a way not compliant with the standards represented by the ERP solution they are implementing, BPR is a viable approach. So, the customer changes the way they do certain business processes.

A look back...

Business Process Reengineering (**BPR**) kicked off in late 1980s in United States as a scholarly theory, soon to boom to a $50 billion industry by 1995, with consultancies all over the country selling their services to Fortune 500 companies. The theory basically rode the continuous improvement wave, but insisted that the change should be revolutionary, rather than evolutionary. Like any revolution, this one ate its own children too when companies misunderstood the core and started laying off thousands of employees under the banner of BPR. By 1996 the concept was nearly stigmatized, with the initial proponents regularly criticizing the abomination of the practice.

Nevertheless, the aftermath is positive, as it has been learned that business methods and processes need to be reflected upon and optimized. Although it doesn't mean the same thing as it did originally, the term stuck, and today business process reengineering is a common management approach, albeit a far less radical one.

Although not initially related to each other, BPR and ERP implementations usually go hand in hand. Implementation of ERP software opens many opportunities for improvement, so companies sometimes decide to change the way they do business and adapt to the way standard software recommends.

Changing, or reengineering, a business process is not a simple task. Processes have their roots in people, and any attempt at changing people often equals tickling the dragon's tail. Without strong support from top management, you shouldn't really attempt this.

A perpetual question of ERP implementation consultants is should they, or should they not, engage in business process reengineering activities at all. To this question, there is no correct answer. If you are experienced in the industry, and you understand the customer's business problem, and are sure beyond reasonable doubt that you can help them, then the answer is *Heck, why not*?

The point of being a consultant is to consult, or advise your customers in their best interest and to their benefit. If you see that they can benefit most from changing their own processes, and you can support the implementation of this change by standard best-practice functionality of the ERP system you are implementing, then you should go for it. At the very least, you should let the customer know that you believe a business process change will bring them the most benefit.

Implementation of business management software after all involves much more than just the software itself. Software, people, and processes are seamlessly interwoven in every business, and voluntarily or not, you are going to affect all of these anyway. If this is the case, it is better to proactively manage the change, rather than cluelessly stand by with your customer and passively watch as the change occurs.

As much as there is opportunity in BPR, there is threat. A true danger lurking behind BPR is that the best-practice functionality as covered in the software doesn't really fit the customer's needs. If the customer initiates changing their ways, and this is the case, disaster is imminent. Another reason against BPR is the fact that a non-standard business process might have been driving your customer's success and providing competitive edge—if this is the case, your customer will be justifiably reluctant to change it.

Configuration

People like to choose their own pizza toppings, credit card designs, desktop wallpapers, and things tailored to their specific fancies in general. Technology is exceptionally good at complying.

Instead of sporting a my-way-or-the-highway attitude, most of business management software offers a wide range of features allowing for fine tuning its behavior to better match the user needs. This is achieved through various parameters and configuration settings, which specify how the system should behave. This is called configuration, and for ERP systems it sometimes takes days or even weeks to complete.

Configuration may be as simple as choosing a costing method for an item or specifying whether to automatically post a shipment on invoice, or as complicated as configuring a supply planning system for goods flow of thousands of items through dozens of inventory locations or designing complete approval workflows for sales or purchase documents.

The concept of configuration in itself is simple, and there is no arcane knowledge or fancy theory behind it: if you can achieve what you need through configuration, you should go for it no questions asked. Not only the risks a customization brings along are avoided, but in any upgrade scenario the value of a configured solution, as opposed to a customized one, is priceless.

Customization

When neither of the previous situations applies, it's development time. If a requirement can't be met by configuration, and customer is not willing to give in, there is no alternative but to cut open the system and make it do what it wasn't designed to do in the first place. Customizations are as easy to go for as they are risky, and there is but a thin line between a surgeon's knife and a butcher's axe.

Customizations can mean small changes such as modifying the layout of sales invoice, or adding an extra field to the item table, but can often get downright complex with requirements such as engineer-to-order manufacturing or retail point-of-sale functionality.

The biggest caveat with customizations is that the developer doing the change, or the architect designing it, must have a thorough understanding of the system and what impact the change will have not only on the functionality but also on scalability, supportability, and especially upgradeability to future versions. Before going down this path, the consultant and the customer should exhaust all other options, including possible third-party solution add-ons.

Third-party solutions

Sometimes the scale of customizations is so huge that your implementation project really turns into a custom development one. This can easily happen if the customer has very specific needs that are not met with what Microsoft Dynamics NAV can offer out of the box. If this is the case, you may decide to look for a third-party solution tailored to cater for these specific needs. For Microsoft Dynamics NAV there are just about 1,700 registered third-party solutions, and it is very likely that you can find one that matches customer needs perfectly.

So instead of custom-developing a one-off solution, which is typically a lengthy high-cost and high-risk project, a better approach might be to implement Microsoft Dynamics NAV together with an existing third-party solution. Implementing such a solution usually consists of configuration, but it may include some business process reengineering, and some limited custom development.

Choose the right approach

With such a wide range of possibilities with implementation, it is crucially important that there is common understanding between the customer and the consultant. The consultant must understand what the customer really needs, but also know how to map these needs to Microsoft Dynamics NAV, to create a working solution for the customer.

Ultimately, the duty of the consultant is to present his or her view of the solution back to the customer, and come to an agreement that such a solution is what the customer really needs. Only when an agreement is reached, can the consultant start working on delivering this solution.

Now that we've seen *why* it takes an implementation process to get from a generic solution to the one that really works for the customer, let's see *how* to get there, and learn the steps of a Microsoft Dynamics NAV 2009 implementation process.

The role of methodology

Whether you are building a house or an airplane, growing crops or writing a book, you have the benefit of many years of collective experience summed up into a methodology. Methodology helps us understand the goals, and the methods to reach the goals. A good methodology brings to the surface the risks and pitfalls involved, which will keep us from making the same mistakes that someone else has made in the past.

Failures can be costly. Had the first guy who ran marathon length, poor Pheidippides, known how the marathon was supposed to be run, he may not have died of a heart attack!

Fifteen years ago, the majority of software projects were either cancelled, or exceeded heavily the allocated time and budget. Today, the situation is much better, and increasingly more projects are successful. The reason behind this positive change is the development and adoption of formal methodologies.

Microsoft Dynamics Sure Step

The best methodology that exists for implementing Microsoft Dynamics NAV is Sure Step—Microsoft's methodology developed specifically for implementing the ERP and CRM products in the Microsoft Dynamics family.

This methodology is far more than just a set of methods and a knowledge base about implementation projects, and it consists of:

- **Best practices** that let the consultant know how an implementation task or a set of tasks should be performed to achieve the best possible result, or to avoid mistakes that have already been made by someone in the past.
- **Tools** that make it easier to perform tasks by automating or streamlining time-consuming and error-prone tasks, such as organization and business process mapping.

- **Templates** that boost productivity by providing a documentation framework. Preparing documentation using these templates ensures that every important aspect of the documentation has been touched, and that nothing important has been missed.

Phases of an implementation

An implementation of Microsoft Dynamics NAV 2009 is conducted in phases, which are carried out one after another in sequence, usually with output of one phase serving as input for the next.

Per Sure Step, there are six phases of a typical implementation:

- Diagnostic
- Analysis
- Design
- Development
- Deployment
- Operation

If this approach reminds you of the waterfall model of software development, you are right: implementation of Microsoft Dynamics NAV indeed adheres to a lot of the principles of the waterfall model.

The waterfall model is a systems development lifecycle model that requires that the software product is developed in a sequence of phases, and that one cannot move to the next phase before the previous one has been fully completed. Phases of the waterfall model include requirements analysis, design, coding, integration, testing, installation, and operation.

A lot of software development experts are quick to criticize the waterfall model, demonstrating how inferior it is to other models and concepts, such as the iterative model, the spiral model, agile development, or extreme programming. In the case of software development, they are right most of the time. A new software product developed from scratch stands a much better chance of success if more iterative and evolutionary models are applied.

But there is an important distinction to be made: implementation of Microsoft Dynamics NAV *is not* a software, or software development project.

The crucial difference between development of a new software product and development of customizations for a complex existing system such as Microsoft Dynamics NAV 2009 is that for the former we are writing code from the ground up, so we can shape the new piece of software as we like, without much ado about factors outside the domain of our work. With such products, requirements are rarely completely articulated at the beginning, and some concepts need several iterations of requirement specification, design, coding, and testing before they are ready to be released. Applying a waterfall model to these kinds of projects usually doesn't work out.

However, when we are customizing a complex product, such as Microsoft Dynamics NAV 2009, we aren't building anything from scratch, and there is this huge working system with hundreds of functions and hundreds of thousands of lines of code already in place. When we are developing over such a huge code base, we must be extra careful that whatever we do doesn't bring the whole system down.

Before a single line of code has been written, we must completely understand the customer's needs, and the customer must agree to the defined scope of work, or else we better prepare for the inevitable scope creep issues.

And while most implementations of Microsoft Dynamics NAV will probably include some development and programming, an implementation can easily go without any of it at all. Even during highly customized implementations, development, or programming, represents only a portion of the tasks that need to be completed, and belongs to only one of the phases necessary to achieve success.

Diagnostic phase

To my customers, I usually like to put it this way: If you don't see a problem, you don't need a solution.

When a company decides to implement a business management solution, such as Microsoft Dynamics NAV, it usually means that there is a business problem, and that the company is aware of it.

Examples of business problems that may call for an implementation of Microsoft Dynamics NAV include:

- The company has a jungle of unrelated applications, which are prone to human error and cause inefficiency.
- Business processes, such as manufacturing or sales, require automation.
- Current processes are not optimized and incur too many operational costs to the bottom line.

- Existing business management software does not provide the necessary level of automation, isn't flexible enough, or is not reflecting the current state of business processes.
- The company has poor or no insight into, or control of, execution of its operations.

Any of these can be a valid business problem which triggers the need for a new business management solution. Such a need is a starting point for every implementation. Of course, these are just for illustration purposes, and there may be a whole lot of other triggers.

Identify the goals

Many companies jump into an implementation of a business management solution, without articulated goals. Not having a clear goal, and still going for an implementation of an ERP solution, is a bad decision. When there are no clear goals, you are likely to waste a lot of time and effort in an endless cat-and-mouse game of managing new requirements, unnecessary development, failed acceptances, and possibly a lot of obstruction from users chronically frustrated by not seeing the point. If you find yourself in a situation like this, the best you can do for your customer, and yourself, is to advise that the whole project be postponed until a final set of requirements is developed.

Strictly speaking about implementation, diagnostic phase really fits within the sales cycle, rather than implementation itself. The goal of the diagnostic phase is to answer an important question: is Microsoft Dynamics NAV the right solution for the customer? The search for this answer will take the customer on a journey aimed at providing compelling reasons to implement Microsoft Dynamics NAV.

To the consultant, diagnostic phase gives an understanding of the customer's situation which triggered the need for acquiring and implementing the software. It sets the expectations, defines project goals, and focuses the whole implementation process on solving the problems that led to the project in the first place. Without this understanding, the implementation may easily wander away from its intended objectives.

Drafting the project scope

Among the most important goals of the diagnostic phase is defining the high-level project scope. Project scope is the sum of all requirements that must be met during an implementation. Especially from the customer perspective, it is usually regarded as the sum of features that the deployed application must contain.

As diagnostic phase is more about sales than about implementation, defining the project scope helps prepare a proposal for the customer. Therefore, during proposal preparation, it is useful to regard the project scope also as the sum of work that has to be done to complete the implementation project—it makes it much easier to estimate duration and costs.

To define project scope, we must engage in an activity called requirements analysis. In typical software projects, analysis of requirements is usually a tedious task, because requirements usually need to be defined from scratch. With Microsoft Dynamics NAV, thankfully it is not the case.

As a generic business management application, Microsoft Dynamics NAV already contains a lot of functionality that is likely to satisfy the majority of customers. Obviously, not all functions will satisfy all the customers, but most of the customers will be pretty happy with the functionality as-is. This makes it considerably easier to analyze and define the requirements, because we presume that most of the requirements are already met, at least to a certain degree.

Microsoft Dynamics Sure Step methodology contains several *decision accelerators*, packaged offerings with well-defined steps and templates, which help conduct the diagnostic phase in a managed, predictable way. The decision accelerators address the customer pain from various perspectives, and gradually build a clear picture of how exactly Microsoft Dynamics NAV will solve the customer's problem, while providing the consultant with all the information necessary to initiate a successful implementation project.

Mind the gap

Diagnostic phase starts with an identification of requirements and business processes that the customer wants to cover in their solution. At this point we are interested in collecting as much information as possible in order to prepare the high-level analysis of business processes, called *Fit/Gap Analysis*. As its name suggests, this analysis focuses on detecting gaps between what the customer needs, and what the application provides. Anything that the customer needs, and that exists in the application in the form that will satisfy the customer, is a *fit*. Anything that the application provides, but customer needs supported in a different way, and anything that the customer needs, but the application doesn't provide at all, is a *gap*.

The Requirements and Process Review activity of Sure Step diagnostic phase helps collect necessary information about requirements and business processes. The results of this activity will prove an indispensable input for a successful *fit/gap* analysis.

To conduct a *fit/gap* analysis, you start at a very high level with identification of business processes. Your goal is to identify which processes the customer needs included in their Microsoft Dynamics NAV solution, and draft your high-level approach to closing the identified gaps.

When analyzing business processes, you generally need to answer two questions: *what*, and *how*. *What* is the process itself—the identification that the customer uses and needs a process. *How* is the process conducted—the steps that the customer takes when performing it, the tasks and subtasks the process consists of, as well as all input that goes into it, and output that comes out of it.

How about the Why?

When you have got the answers to what the process is and how it is performed, if you notice the gap between the customer needs and Microsoft Dynamics NAV, and you believe that the process is ineffective, don't miss the opportunity to ask a simple question: why? The customer may be doing a certain process in a certain way, because they didn't have means to automate it, or because their old software was inflexible and had them do it exactly that way. Automating an ineffective process won't give any benefit to the customer. Also, having an existing process in place, and supported by the old inflexible software exactly as the software expects, can be a good sign that the customer has already adapted their processes sometime in the past, and shaped them to match the software. If it was the case in the past, it is very likely to be the case in the present too, so this may be a good opportunity to close the gap with a business process reengineering approach, rather than by customization.

As you might guess, the *what* is far less of an issue than the *how*. But in diagnostic phase, you don't need to get too much of the *how* part of it. You need to get just enough. How do you know what is just enough, but not too much?

When you identify that the customer needs a process, you generally want to inquire a little bit about this process to gain an understanding of how the process is performed. With this information, you typically know how complex the process is, and whether it is a *gap* or a *fit*.

The following matrix can help you decide how to approach the overall analysis of a business process:

	Simple	**Complex**
Fit	No further analysis	Detailed analysis in analysis phase
Gap	Detailed analysis in analysis phase	Detailed analysis in diagnostic phase

For example, during *fit/gap* analysis, you may find out that your customer sends quotes during the sales process. This process is covered by default in Microsoft Dynamics NAV, so it looks like a *fit*. However, before you mark it as fit, ask a few questions to find out what this process looks like, and what the steps to complete it are. If after several questions you find out that the quoting process includes automatic merging of all quotes for the same customer into a single document, you see that this process is really a *gap*. Being a simple *gap*, it doesn't need any further analysis in the diagnostic phase, and you may move on.

Fit Gap Solution Blueprint decision accelerator streamlines the process of analyzing high-level requirements and mapping them to standard functionality of Microsoft Dynamics NAV. It gives you the *degree of fit*, an important metric which explains how far away from standard application you will have to go before you meet all the requirements.

What if it's not there?

The biggest issue with *fit/gap* analysis is not the processes that are there, but the ones that don't exist by default in Microsoft Dynamics NAV. You usually don't have these processes in your templates, but this doesn't make them any less eligible to be included in the analysis.

In these cases, you need a lot of help from your customer. Some customers start the project with a **Request For Proposal** (**RFP**) document, which explains all of their needs, and solicits a high-level *fit/gap* response from consultants, based on which final decision is made about the solution and the vendor. If the project has started this way, you already have the list of non-standard processes, and you are half done.

But what if there is no such document? In this case, you are basically on your own, and you must conduct a comprehensive analysis of the customer's business, which has traditionally been a difficult and a risky job. When the customer doesn't have a clear set of requirements, and you don't conduct the *fit/gap* analysis properly, new requirements are going to pop up all the time, which may jeopardize the project outcome.

A good approach in this situation is to start with the organizational structure. Draw a map of company's organization, and make sure all the departments are listed. Then find out what each of these departments does, and who are the key people performing these tasks.

With Microsoft Dynamics NAV 2009, the job of detecting non-standard processes is made easier using Microsoft Dynamics Business Modeler, a tool available free of charge to all Microsoft Dynamics partners. This tool helps you diagram the organizational structure, process groups, processes and tasks, key people owning these processes, and relationships between them. These diagrams are an effective communication tool between you and your customer, and really help achieve deep understanding of real customer needs.

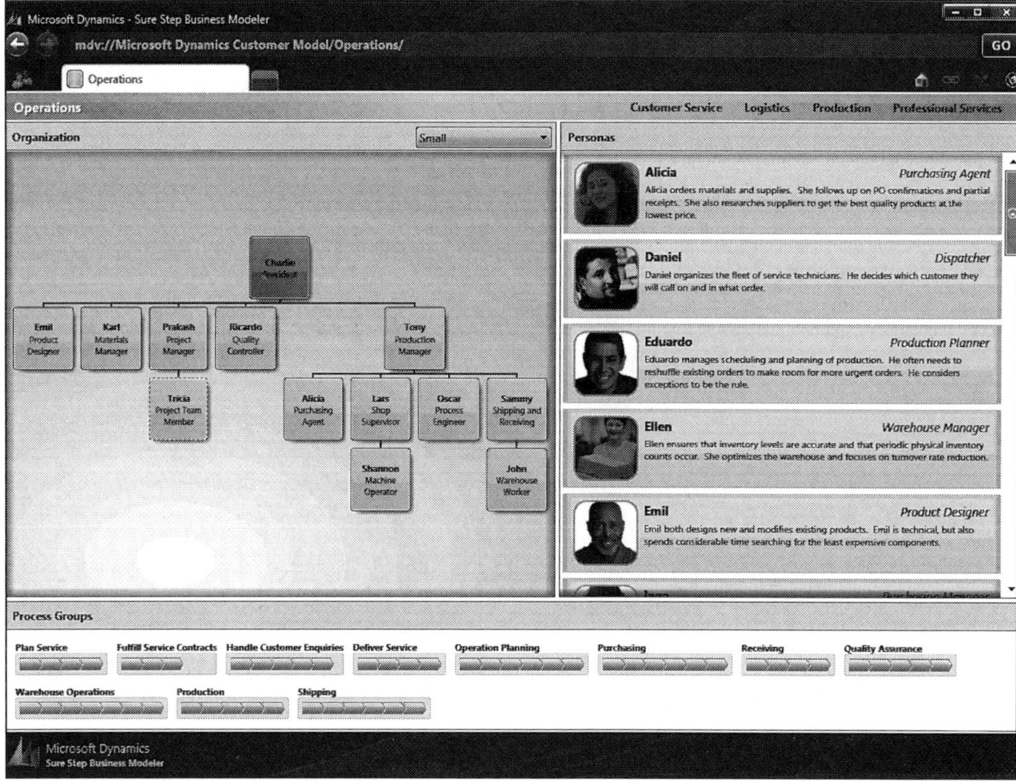

The benefit of using this tool is twofold: it helps you better understand the customer's business, and it streamlines your implementation by mapping directly to the Microsoft Dynamics NAV 2009 customer role model of the RoleTailored user interface. By modeling your customer's business using this tool, you make it much easier to design and customize the RoleTailored user interface to exactly match the customer needs.

It's about people, too

Microsoft Dynamics NAV 2009 is not only about processes, but also about people. Business Modeler is an exceptionally good tool because it addresses a completely different dimension of all business processes in existence: the fact that they are tightly integrated with the people. As much as you can't separate people from processes in real life, you shouldn't separate them in a business management system.

Analyzing just the processes themselves addresses only half of the issue. By focusing on people as much as on the processes, you have a much better chance of success. Microsoft Dynamics NAV 2009 is efficiently bridging the gap that has traditionally existed between people and processes in an ERP system, by tightly integrating business processes with role-specific tasks, and through the RoleTailored user interface.

When you have identified all the business processes, and determined which of them are *fit*, and which of them are *gap*, you can move on to the next step.

Detailed analysis

During diagnostic phase, you sometimes need to analyze certain processes in more detail. These are typically those processes that you have identified to be *gaps*, and which are complex in nature.

Although there will be dedicated time to perform the detailed analysis of all business processes later in the analysis phase, do not skip this step in diagnostics. The point of detailed analysis during diagnostic phase is to help you define the high-level project scope, which in the end helps you estimate the total project cost. Without analyzing the complex processes that are obvious *gaps*, we can't really know how much time and effort will it take to deliver a solution, and any estimate we make in the proposal will be just a wild guess at best.

In essence, detailed analysis in diagnostic phase doesn't differ from that in analysis phase, so let's just move on.

Proof of Concept decision accelerator takes selected business processes and demonstrates in a lab environment (but with the customer's live data) how these processes can be solved in Microsoft Dynamics NAV. While preparing this demonstration, you get a chance to analyze these processes in more detail.

Technical requirements

After processes have been analyzed, in more or less detail, we are now acquainted with the customer's functional needs. That's good, but not good enough. Usually, there are also some technical needs that must be met for the project to succeed. We must make sure we don't forget about them.

Technical needs are about hardware, software and network infrastructure, and data and process integration with external systems. Synchronizing customer information with a CRM system or a call center, or submitting purchase orders to vendors electronically, are obvious examples.

Now is a good time to analyze the existing network and server infrastructure, and to determine whether it is going to provide adequate performance. Performance in general is a topic to be discussed at this point, because we need to know what kind of expectations the customer has from Microsoft Dynamics NAV, so we can prepare accordingly. Waiting five seconds for a purchase invoice posting routine to complete might be acceptable for one customer, but it might be simply too much for another. If we don't know the performance requirements, whatever we end up with might simply not be good enough.

Architecture Assessment decision accelerator takes all technical requirements into account and defines infrastructure and hardware recommendations for an optimized deployment of Microsoft Dynamics NAV.

Should we do all of it?

After all functional and technical requirements are gathered, we need to define the scope. It is important, because not everything we have been discussing with our customer so far needs to go into the implementation. Sometimes it makes perfect sense to implement Microsoft Dynamics NAV in several phases, to start with financials, sales, purchases, and inventory in one project iteration for instance, then add warehouse management and manufacturing in another. So, from all gathered requirements, we need to decide what is in scope, and what's out of it. This is far from simple.

When deciding what should go out of scope, we need to classify the requirements by importance. In order to do so, we can ask two fundamental questions.

The first question is straightforward: *is this critical*? Another way to ask this question can be: *can you live without it*? For a pharmaceutical company, it is critical to keep track of lot numbers of all materials and products they are handling. For a toy retailer, this might not be of any concern. Another example would be regulatory compliance; it is always critical to be compliant to local legislation. If the answer to this question is *yes*, then we don't even need to ask the second one.

The second question is a tough one: *does this add value*? This can also translate into: *what do you accomplish by this*? If there is a process or a task that the customer does, and it doesn't really contribute to the bottom line, not even indirectly, then not only should it not be automated by the system, it should be scrapped altogether.

If it is not business critical, and it doesn't add any value, then it is only a nice-to-have feature. Nice-to-haves look better when out of scope.

Out of scope doesn't necessarily mean it won't ever be implemented: it is simply not considered for the first rollout. As implementations often go through several additional, but smaller cycles, we may take all the out-of-scope requirements into consideration for a later rollout. **Scoping Assessment** decision accelerator helps a great deal with defining proper scope, and breaking down the implementation into several successive rollouts as necessary.

Wrapping up

After the processes have been analyzed, and the scope defined, we are ready to close the diagnostic phase. It is important that our diagnostic phase has produced as much documentation about the customer requirements as possible. This documentation is at a high level—it handles processes from a big-picture point of view, rather than from a zoomed-in close-up one. Also, we probably have some *fit/gap* worksheets, explaining where the biggest pain points are, and what we should focus on mostly during later phases.

Another helpful document that diagnostic phase usually produces is the **Work Breakdown Structure**, which contains the high-level plan broken down into more focused phases and tasks. This is not a final document; it is currently at a very high level, with only as much detail as we need to give a rough estimate of the expected implementation timeline and costs.

All of this documentation helps us prepare the implementation proposal, and present it to the customer. When we have done so, our diagnostic phase has been completed, and as soon as the customer accepts the proposal, we are ready to draft the contract, and move on to the next phase.

Presenting the diagnostic results to the customer is made easier through **Business Case** decision accelerator, which presents the findings of the diagnostic phase in executive language, and estimates the investment scale, return on investment, and total cost of ownership of the new Microsoft Dynamics NAV solution.

Analysis phase

If you have got to this point in the project, it probably means your customer has accepted your proposal, so congratulations! With the analysis phase initiated, your implementation project has begun.

During the diagnostics phase, we learned a lot about our customer—what they do, and how they do it. We have become familiar with our key users, and the tasks they perform, but we only have the big picture.

Imagine gazing around from the top of the Empire State Building in New York. We see the city of New York: a seemingly infinite stretch of buildings reaching far beyond the horizon. That's the view we get from the diagnostics phase, but can we say we know New York City yet? No way.

To get to know the city, we need to get down to street level and take a look around. We must stroll down Broadway Avenue, from Times Square to SoHo, see the mingling crowds and the lines of yellow cabs. We need to take a hike through Central Park, have a hot dog with everything from a street vendor, feel the frenzy of the Wall Street, take a ferry to Liberty Island. Now we're starting to get a feel for the city.

That's the analysis phase. After taking a bird's eye view of our customer's business, we now need to meet our customer close-up. We need to analyze their business processes in detail, in order to gain a deep understanding of their needs and pains. This will help us prepare for the hard work ahead.

Prepare the path

In order to plan the analysis phase, we must first review the documentation from the diagnostics phase.

The diagnostic documents, especially the *fit/gap* analysis report, serve as a starting point for the detailed analysis conducted in this phase. While we were selective in the diagnostics phase and analyzed only a few processes in detail, in analysis phase we need to conduct a detailed analysis of all the processes that the customer needs covered in the system. This includes *gap* and *fit* processes alike.

Mind the Fit

One common mistake in performing analysis is to ignore the processes that were identified as *fits* and concentrate solely on the *gaps*.

It is inevitable that the customer has a different idea of how to conduct a business process compared to what the system actually allows. We can only discover these differences by analyzing the *fits*. Ignore them at your peril.

Analyzing the processes that fit doesn't mean we need to modify the system to match the customer's expectations. Very often, the customer will change their processes to match the system; however, if we don't explore the processes that fit, the mismatch is going to be found quite late in the project—on occasions, depending on how good the customer is at testing, after go live. This is definitely a situation we want to avoid.

Plan the resources

Analysis is an important task with a fairly high risk of project failure if done poorly, and we therefore need to allocate our most experienced application consultants. A successful implementation is built upon the foundation of understanding. The consultant must understand the customer's business at the analysis stage and the customer must understand what the product is capable of and what modifications are required. It may appear that savings can be made by skimping on the analysis phase. Tight project deadlines may also put pressure on us to simply stop talking and get building. Do not give in to these pressures; take time to prepare your foundations carefully to give your project the best chance of success.

Our resources are only half the story

The resources we assign to the process are only half the story; the other half is the customer's own people. As much as analysis calls for the best consultants to conduct it, it calls for the best of the customer's people, also called *key users*, to participate and share valuable insight.

Unfortunately, key users are often the ones that carry the bulk of the business, and analysis is a lengthy process. Dedicating these people to a project can put the normal flow of business at risk. What customers sometimes fail to realize is that by not relieving these users from their daily duties, and having them actively participate in analysis, the business as a whole is at a much higher risk. Project success depends upon properly conducted analysis, which includes having the right business people involved. Make sure your customer is aware of this.

Plan approvals

The next thing we need to plan is the approval process. Consultants and key users may define the best requirements specification in the world, but before it is released into design and development, it must be approved by the customer. We need to plan and agree how the approval process will work, who will be involved, who will need to revise the documentation before it is approved, and whose signatures are necessary before moving on—and yes, approvals must be in writing.

Get the ball rolling

With the responsibilities assigned and formal approval procedures in place, we're ready to move on. Our next step has a very fitting name: *Kick-off meeting*. This is the moment that the consultant and the customer teams sit together for the first time to discuss the project.

The goal of this meeting is to formally introduce the team members, explain their roles and responsibilities, explain the methodology and project management approach. It provides a good chance for all the participants to state their expectations and discuss the project goals. It is also a good place to start activities in many project management disciplines related to the implementation, with scope management and risk management being the most important.

The kick-off meeting is an important milestone that signifies, after long preparation, that the implementation project has officially begun.

Train the key users

At some point we must teach the users how to work with Microsoft Dynamics NAV 2009. Contrary to what might seem common sense, the sooner we do this, the higher the chance of success. The principle driver of early key user training is to establish a common language. Among the best things you can do for yourself and your customer is to acknowledge that there is a huge gap between how your customer sees their business, and how you see it. There is an even larger gap between how you see the implementation process, and how your customer does.

Early key-user training comes with more than a handful of benefits for the consultant and the customer alike. Put yourself in your customer's shoes for a moment. You know your business inside-out and have been using your old software for as long as you can remember. Now there's this new thing called Microsoft Dynamics NAV 2009 to learn and although the consultant uses some familiar terms, it doesn't look, feel, or smell like your old system. If that isn't bad enough, the consultant is using strange new terms like role center and action pane; it's good that you're getting some training.

Now get back to your shoes, there's work to be done.

You as a consultant speak your lingo; the customer speaks their lingo. You first need is to bridge this gap, and fuse these two into one common language that you *both* understand. There is no better way to do this than to conduct key user training early on.

Training is delivered in two environments. The first one, the *training environment*, can be deployed at your site, or at the customer site, and it is going to be used for structured training led by an application consultant in a series of classroom sessions.

The second environment is more vital to the overall project success, and it is called the *sandbox environment*. This is a semi-live environment, deployed within customer's infrastructure right after or during the classroom training. The idea is to give users a continuous access to the application with sample data, so they can literally play around with it at their convenience.

Early training exposes key users to Microsoft Dynamics NAV 2009, and helps them understand the new solution. Key users are key for a reason; they are best at understanding their business, or their old software, most likely both. They can quickly map their existing knowledge to the new information they will be receiving throughout the project, and they will be the quickest to grasp the principles of Microsoft Dynamics NAV 2009, and to become true masters with it.

Once they get familiar and comfortable with Microsoft Dynamics NAV 2009, key users are going to be able to help you conceptualize the solution or design a process. When there is a problem to be solved, they will be able to point you to the right solution, because of this unique skill set you help them build.

A more compelling reason why you should really engage in key-user training activities early in the analysis phase is that key users can quickly notice any gaps that might somehow have slipped your scrutiny during the diagnostics phase, or that would otherwise be missed during analysis. Key users will learn how to use the application, and will try to match their existing knowledge with the new one. They will also try to detect the touching points between the processes they are involved in, and the way they are handled in Microsoft Dynamics NAV 2009. While doing so, they will easily notice if there is a *gap*, where you have seen a *fit*. This is going to save you a lot of rework later during deployment, or even operation, when undetected gaps tend to surface and create mayhem.

Last, but not least, your key users will ultimately deliver the end-user training to your customer's employees. If you train them early, they will get a chance to become the kind of experts, application gurus, who will relieve you from burden of what-does-this-button-do type questions once the solution goes live, and enters the support phase.

Data migration

A critical part of every implementation is the data migration process. The customer has been doing their business for some time, creating data, as much they will create data in Microsoft Dynamics NAV 2009. When implementing Microsoft Dynamics NAV, some of the data already existing in the customer's existing system will need to be migrated from the old system to the new one.

There are two kinds of data that are generally considered for data migration:

- Master data
- Past transactions

Master data migration

Master data describes the business. The term master data refers to information such as customers, vendors, items, charts of accounts, and such.

When implementing Microsoft Dynamics NAV 2009, master data is usually migrated from the old system to the new one; typing it by hand is rarely a viable approach. When you have the list of processes, collected during the diagnostic phase, you can easily define which master data will be transferred.

Typically, you will need to migrate the chart of accounts, fixed assets, customers, vendors, and items information. Depending on your customer's business, you may also need to include warehouse locations, bills of materials, employee records, and such.

The goal of master data migration analysis is to list the master data that will be migrated once the system goes into production. Do not focus on the mapping of master data between the old system and Microsoft Dynamics NAV 2009; that's something you will do later during design phase.

Past transactions

Transactions include all information posted into accounting books, or ledgers. Examples of transactions are posted invoices, shipments, receipts, credit memos, but also postings to general ledger and various supplementary ledgers that may exist in the system.

Sum of all transactions represents the accounting backbone of a system, and has value and importance from several standpoints. It is invaluable for tax reporting purposes, and even has to adhere to accounting standards prescribed by international accounting bodies and local authorities, but is also important for management reporting purposes such as decision making.

Migrating transactions is quite a different story from migrating master data. While errors in master data migration may affect certain operations, they seldom have long-lasting effects on the course of business. However, errors in migrating transactions can sometimes be very hard to detect, and cause long-term problems of the kind you usually don't want the tax authorities to discover for you.

Instead of migrating individual transactions to Microsoft Dynamics NAV, you may want to migrate the opening balances only, as opposed to transaction data, which keeps individual transactions recorded as they were in the old system. Opening balances are just summary figures. Instead of posting ten invoices and three payments for a customer, you simply post a single line that posts the total balance for this customer. These are easier to do, less prone to errors, but don't provide any detail.

In the end, it's your customer's call to decide which way to go.

General data migration analysis considerations

Obviously, migrating data from previous systems to Microsoft Dynamics NAV is not an easy task, and you must take care to perform it accurately, because your customer's business depends on it, as does your project success.

With data migration analysis, try to answer the following questions:

- Which categories of master data will be migrated? You might need to migrate the customers, vendors, and items, but it may be the case that the customer will want to start with a brand new chart of accounts to sort out their accounting issues.
- Do you need to migrate the historical data and how much of it, or will it be enough just to post the opening balances? Influence the customer to decide on this early, because a change in data migration strategy can affect the project timeline. The best practice is to simply post the opening balances if possible. Migrating heaps of historical transactions may take a lot of time and cost too much, and still result in limited value for the end user.
- Where will the data be taken from? The customer's existing system may not be integrated at all, and data can easily reside in several disconnected repositories, such as Microsoft SQL Server, Oracle, Access, but also in less structured formats such as Excel or Word documents.
- How will the data be migrated? You may pull the data directly from the old system using a data integration technology such as Microsoft SQL Server Integration Services, or you may use Microsoft Dynamics NAV XMLport objects to import data from files prepared to an agreed standard. For the majority of tasks, we recommend using the data migration tools within the Rapid Implementation Methodology (RIM) toolkit, which we will cover more in the following chapter.

With these questions answered, you will have enough information to design and develop good data migration routines later in the project.

Detailed analysis

Detailed analysis is really just a shorthand name for detailed *fit/gap* analysis. If you have completed the high-level *fit/gap* analysis during diagnostic phase, you will have a fairly good feeling of what a detailed analysis should be all about.

Your task is to go through all identified business processes and review them once again, this time more deeply than you did it before. You need to do this even for those processes you identified as *fit*, because after analysis phase is completed, you will need to have all of the customer requirements collected, not only the *gaps*. *Fits* will make your job easier, but won't make it unnecessary.

For very simple processes that you have deemed to be *fit* during diagnostics, you don't need to spend extra effort. If there are any possible *gaps* with these processes, key users have likely already spotted them during key-user training or their own at-will investigation of the system. Your primary concern should stay with those processes that you immediately identified as *gaps*, as well as any complex processes that you classified as *fit*.

Complex processes bring the biggest risks, no matter whether they are *gap*, or *fit*. Actually, for complex processes it is rarely possible to say up front whether they are *gap*, or *fit*, and frankly, complex processes are hardly ever a *fit*. Therefore, you should document them first, and try to collect as much detail about them as possible.

The best way of documenting a business process is to prepare diagrams in Visio, or another application capable of producing flow charts or similar diagrams.

When business processes are documented like this, your goal is to identify as many *gaps* as possible, and then work together with key users to define how these gaps will be closed. At this point, this is about detailed gap resolutions, not the high-level ones. This means that with every identified *gap* you should explain your approach to resolving it, which can be a reengineered existing process, a new process, custom development, or a third-party solution. Have in mind that configuration isn't a gap resolution activity—anything that can be fully resolved using configuration should be considered a *fit*; however, you should make sure you document the configuration settings required to meet the requirement, otherwise you risk introducing problems by making incorrect configuration settings later on.

User roles

Processes are not the only things that require detailed analysis. Remember that any business management system consists of software, hardware, people, and processes, and all of these are eligible for detailed analysis.

In previous chapters you've seen that Microsoft Dynamics NAV 2009 puts a strong emphasis on users and their role in the system as a whole. While analyzing business processes, you have an indispensable chance to get to know the customer organization from the inside, meet the users and talk to them about the processes they are involved with and what their role in the system is.

Once again, you can make use of Microsoft Dynamics Business Modeler to document all of the key users, their relationships to other users, and their involvement in processes. This will help you map your customer's model to Microsoft Dynamics NAV standard Role Model.

Integration and interfaces

We have addressed data migration, a one-off process that pulls the data from old systems and stores it in Microsoft Dynamics NAV 2009. Sometimes this just won't be enough, and you will need to exchange data between your Microsoft Dynamics NAV solution and other applications on regular basis. This is called integration and interfaces.

A typical example of an application you would want to integrate with Microsoft Dynamics NAV is another product from Dynamics family—Microsoft Dynamics CRM. These two systems serve two completely different purposes, but have several touching points, such as master data and sales transactions. If you want to have the same customer information in both of the systems, you will need to establish a data integration mechanism that will synchronize this information on demand or by schedule.

It is during the analysis phase that you need to find out about all data integration requirements, the systems with which the integration will be necessary, whether it will be a unidirectional or bidirectional integration, how the information will be synchronized, which of the systems will be the master system, and what kind of schedule would be necessary to achieve smooth information flow and unobstructed processes.

Microsoft Dynamics NAV 2009 comes with a lot of out-of-the-box integration functions. You may achieve direct integration with Microsoft Office Outlook and exchange information about any entity that is supported in Outlook. There is also integration with Microsoft BizTalk Server, which provides an easy **Business to Business** (**B2B**) communication with customers and vendors, allowing for direct exchange of sales documents. When analyzing integration needs of customers, you should take this functionality into account, and try to see whether you can use any of it instead of developing your own.

Document the requirements

After you have completed the detailed analysis of processes, user roles, and data integration and interfacing requirements, it is time to systemize all of these in a structured document called the *Functional Requirements Document*. This is a central document upon which many later project deliverables will be based: design specifications, development, deployment, user documentation, acceptance tests, and probably many others.

The functional requirements document is much more than its name suggests, and it comprises the following information:

- **Business Process Analysis** should contain description of all the processes that went through the detailed analysis.
- **Fit/Gap Analysis results** explain the gaps between existing processes, or any new processes that should be introduced, and Microsoft Dynamics NAV 2009, together with resolutions.
- **Data Migration and Data Integration Requirements** explain how the data should be migrated when the project goes live, and what kind of continuous data flow between Microsoft Dynamics NAV and external systems will be established.
- **Configuration Requirements** explain your configuration plan for addressing the *fit* processes. These should be documented as well, because design, development, and deployment of *gap* processes shouldn't interfere with the settings explained here.
- **Security Requirements** are very important because you need to protect the sensitive data in the system. It is much easier to plan for a secure implementation of Microsoft Dynamics NAV in advance, than it is to add security later during deployment. You should do your best to define a sustainable security model that will cover not only immediate security requirements, but also any future ones. By logically linking security roles with user roles, this task is a lot easier.

- **Test Requirements** provide information about testing and acceptance requirements that the project will need to go through before it is accepted by the customer.
- **Training Requirements** are often overlooked, but are extremely important. Without properly trained end users, whole projects may be put at risk. Therefore, explain what kind of training will be required for which roles, and how it will need to be delivered to achieve maximum benefit and efficiency.

Of course, after you finish the work on this document, you need to have it reviewed and approved by the customer. From the moment this document is approved, the bureaucratic part of the project is essentially over, and all hands involved in the project are about to get dirty with real work.

The functional requirements document serves a twofold purpose. The obvious one is to explain the scope of the project, and try to freeze, as much as possible, the project goals and requirements. When the customer accepts this document, the ideal scenario would be that it is not changed, and that all following phases completely adhere to it. However, as this world is far from ideal, this document will serve only as a baseline, and will be governed by scope management discipline and change processes.

The second purpose, a very important, but less obvious one, is to review and adjust the proposal for implementation if necessary. So far, the proposal has been through two different stages. The first stage was the pre-diagnostic stage when it was a rough high-level estimate of time and cost. This was updated after the diagnostic phase, when more information was collected and a clearer picture of requirements was obtained. After the analysis phase is completed, you have your final list of requirements and solutions, so you should be able to estimate with much higher precision how long the project will take, and how much it will cost, and then give your customer an updated proposal.

The latest version of Sure Step has a different logic about the Functional Requirements Document: instead of it being a cornerstone document of the analysis phase, it merely documents the high-level business requirements and serves as input to detailed *fit/gap* analysis, while other requirements mentioned here belong to a document called the Non-Functional Requirements Document. Either approach is valid, as long as your requirements have been properly documented.

Design phase

Each phase of the implementation lifecycle is totally dependent on its predecessor. The design phase is critical to the success of the project—very often it is where your implementation comes to life. A good design can create a system that your users will love, that is easy to maintain, and is not too hard to develop. A poor design can kill your project.

No matter how good you are at designing solutions, you are totally reliant upon the upstream activities. If you have identified the wrong requirements, your design is sunk before it sets sail. I cannot emphasize this point enough: Make Sure You Are Solving the Right Problem.

The design of solutions to software problems is an interesting area: it's where the science meets art. It relies upon creative thinking and problem solving skills as much as it does analytical processes. Being able to solve problems and find creative solutions is something that is hard, if not impossible to teach. There is a certain element of magic in solution design; sometimes you just fill your head with information and see what comes out. Some of my best designs come to me in the shower. The human brain is an incredible thing and I cannot begin to understand how this process works; however, there are some tricks that that will help you become a good designer. To become a great designer is going to be down to you and your natural abilities.

Understand the standard application

The greatest resource for improving your design skills is Microsoft Dynamics NAV 2009, out of the box, in all of its unmodified glory. You need to go on training courses, study the application, read everything you can find on the product, and use the application. The more you understand about the standard product, the easier you will find it to fill those gaps. Your goal in design is to make something that the users cannot tell from the standard product. In order to do that you need to know the product inside out.

When you are looking at the standard product, think about the problems the product development team members were trying to solve and learn from how they did it. Look for the patterns they use. Search the product for the different page types and where they are used; you will benefit from mimicking this use of page types.

Understand the problem

Your first step in solving problems is to fully understand the problem being solved. Don't rely on a written statement of requirements as being the sole source of information, talk to people and ask questions, look at existing systems and processes. When you have a good understanding of the problem, only then you can design the solution. If we don't know what the gap is intended to achieve, how can we possibly hope to come up with a successful solution design?

Use your imagination

Imagination is the most powerful problem solving tool you have available to you. Once you have your knowledge of the problem, imagine using the system to solve it. Imagine sitting down at your computer and using the application to carry out the tasks required to meet the requirements. Understand your target audience (users) and try to think of how they work and what they would like to see.

Very often, you can carry out design workshops with your users by drawing screen mock-ups on a whiteboard and talking about how we use the screen to carry out the task. On some occasions, you really just need to think about the problem in a quiet environment and let the creative juices start flowing.

Prototype, demonstrate, and iterate

Everyone strives to get it right the first time, but this goal does not apply to the world of solution design. Good designs come about through a series of checks and alterations. As soon as you have an idea for a solution design, get it down on paper and talk it through with the users. Learn how to draw sketches that look like the kinds of pages used in the application: Cards, Documents, Journals, Lists, List Plus, Matrices, and Wizards. This type of design is called 'paper prototyping' and it is really fast. Don't be tempted to draw your screens in Visio or build them in NAV; we are only trying to convey meaning at this stage and once you have reached a level of understanding, you will know when to move on from the paper sketches to a real prototype. Try to remember that *form follows function*; once we have the functionality of the solution agreed, we can worry about the presentation.

Writing long descriptions of processes doesn't work. Users will agree to functional specifications rather than say they don't understand them. This is based upon the assumption that we, the consultants, know what we are doing and that once the users get to see the working solution, they will be able to suggest changes.

Users understand screens. When you put a piece of paper in front of them with a drawing of a screen and talk about how you fill it in, the menu options you select, the next screens that are presented, your users will start to understand the solution design. It is only now that they can start to contribute to the design process. Don't be too precious with your design. It can be hard to have users telling you how the system should behave, but you need to listen to them and steer them away from bad design; however, you will need to make compromises. If the users do not feel that they have been listened to, and do not buy in to the solution design, you are heading for trouble.

In an ideal world, your analysis will have captured all of the requirements, your design will be perfect, your documentation of the functional requirements and solutions design will be read by the users and understood, but let's face it; this world is far from ideal. Don't torture your users with pages and pages of design specifications. Talk the users through the design and observe their reactions. Don't be driven by getting a signature on a piece of paper indicating that the solution design meets the users' requirements; this can serve only one purpose and that is to give you a stick with which to beat the users when they eventually tell you they want something different to your original design. Instead, let the users own the solution and shape it to their requirements as they imagine using the screens that you have drawn.

As you discuss the prototype, you need to refine your data model. Each field that needs to be completed must be identified, by name, type, and purpose. Beware fields that have no known purpose—they are either truly without purpose, in which case you must remove them from the design now, or they are an unexploded bomb waiting to go off when you least expect it. Every field has a purpose; find it and record it.

More often than not, information is pulled from customer's old system into Microsoft Dynamics NAV 2009 during a one-off process called *data migration*. You need to think about it now. Describe the data mapping between the information in the old system and Microsoft Dynamics NAV 2009. There will be many fields, such as customer number, name, address, or telephone, that will map directly between the two systems. There will probably be other fields that won't map directly, and will require some additional work.

For example, if you encounter a field named **Discount** % in the source customer master table, you shouldn't add a new field to the **Customer** table in Microsoft Dynamics NAV. You need to think of clever methods of mapping this information to the standard sales discounting system of Microsoft Dynamics NAV instead.

Once your paper prototype has reached a certain stage, you can build a real prototype. In order to do this, you need to have your data model relatively complete. Building tables and pages is fast in NAV, so make use of that speed. Get something built quickly, and get it in front of your users; you'll benefit in the long run.

Learn how to eat an elephant

How do you eat an elephant? One bite at a time. Don't try to do too much at once. You may be tempted to get all of your gaps designed before presenting them to the users, but this is a mistake. There are no efficiencies to be gained by doing all the design and then putting the users through a mammoth acceptance exercise. Instead, take a few related gaps, design them, and iterate until you have an accepted solution design, then move on to the next set of features. Your users will thank you for breaking your solution into manageable chunks. If you try to cram all of your walk-throughs into a single session, you may find the feedback starts to die off. If this happens, it either means your designs have suddenly started being right the first time or your users are tired and are no longer able to give the problem their full attention. Pushing on because project timelines are tight is a false economy; short-changing your design activities will cost you dearly later on.

Products of design

Design is not only about customizations and development, much as the implementation of Microsoft Dynamics NAV 2009 is not only about development. There is much more to it.

During design phase, what we are designing is a whole solution, not just part of it. The solution includes custom development, but it also includes standard functionality, and we need to pay some attention to it too. Our design specifications should address the configuration of standard application features for two reasons. First, sometimes the customizations we do in the development phase will work only with certain application settings. And second, we need to specify somewhere how we plan to parameterize the final solution. Design specification is the right place to do so.

We also need to take care about interfacing and data migration functionality. It's never too early to think about these, because often there is a complex interdependency between integration and application functionality.

Data migration is important in its own right, and it should really be addressed here. Unfortunately, it is postponed for deployment far too often.

When to stop

The design phase and development phase can overlap, so don't feel you need to have the design fully complete before the development can begin. Towards the end of the design phase, you will have completed the implementation of you data model. You may also have built a number of pages required for the solution. The remaining work should be the tricky development tasks that require typing a lot of code. This is where the development phase really kicks in.

Development phase

We've talked the talk, now it's time to walk the walk. With all requirements agreed upon, and design prototypes accepted, you might be feeling tempted to open the C/SIDE designer and start coding away. Well, don't! The sooner you start coding, the later you'll finish.

Before you write your first line of code, you need to review the design specifications. Usually, there will be many features to be developed, and many existing functions to be modified, and with an integrated system such as Microsoft Dynamics NAV there may be many not-so-obvious dependencies. So, let's make some plans first.

Planning

Let's start with a list of features to be developed. Before we start actual development, we should prioritize the features. Obviously, some features need to be developed before the others, but how do we decide?

The easiest way around is to ask two questions about every feature:

- What kinds of dependencies exist between this feature and the other ones? In complex projects, you will encounter a lot of complex dependency patterns. You will see different features mandating changes to the same objects and same data entities, and seemingly unrelated features, such as reports, depending heavily on several distinct modifications. Detecting such dependencies before you begin coding will save you many days of chasing your own tail. Groups of dependent features should go into development together.
- How critical is the feature? Not all features are equally significant for the customer. Printing out the name of the salesperson's manager on sales invoices may be important to the customer, but it is not critical. Giving priority to items with earlier expiration date in requisition planning may cut or incur significant costs after the system goes live.

With prioritization, we need to address another important issue: the resources. For small projects there will usually be only one developer, but for complex projects you may require five or six developers working on several different features in parallel. If you skip the prioritization, there will be increasingly more confusion and panic as your project goes on.

Prioritization makes it easy to plan for contingency. Deadlines are usually tight, and sometimes not all the features are necessary for the solution to pass pre-deployment acceptance. Some minor features may even be postponed for after the go-live date. Without clear priorities, the level of panic in the development team will be inversely proportional to the number of days left, and panic is hardly a good productivity and quality driver.

After the plan is completed, you need to present it to the customer. It is crucial that you explain the development process to the customer. When you enter the development phase, customers often want to see the results as soon as possible. They sometimes even organize some early reviews with project sponsors to increase their buy-in and support, and these can easily disrupt your development plans. Try not to fall into a trap set by a customer project manager eager to show off this new custom-developed delivery route optimization functionality to their bosses.

Things like these have a huge potential to seriously disrupt the development plans, because they shift priorities at random, and features that should have enough development time end up having little or none. As a result, instead of drawing expected *ooh's* and *aah's* from project sponsors, such show-off meetings easily end up decreasing confidence in project success and trust between the customer and the consultant.

Present your project plan to the customer and try to get their agreement. If the customer would like to have several reviews with project sponsors, then include these in the development plan too.

Setting up the environment

It's still not time for the C/SIDE object designer. After you complete planning, and everything is ready for the development to begin, you need to set up the development environment.

There are at least two separate environments to start with, and these should be configured before actual development activities commence. The first one is the development environment itself, where you will be writing code, modifying and extending the application. The other one is the testing environment, used to test the features. These two environments should ideally be physically separated.

Development tools that you will deploy in the development environment depend on your functional requirements and design specification, but at the very least you will need Microsoft Dynamics NAV 2009 Classic client for C/SIDE development, RoleTailored client for testing, and Microsoft Visual Studio for debugging. Depending on requirements, you might also use Visual Studio for data integration development using Integration Services, Analysis Services development for Business Analytics functionality rework, and possibly some Reporting Services reports design.

It is a good practice to separate the development environments, and have one for application customizations, one for reporting, and one for data integration. It makes it possible to work comfortably, without interfering with other developers and their work, and allows for safe rollbacks of separate features.

The testing environment doesn't need any of the development tools. If you're testing everything in a single testing environment, then it should resemble the future production environment as much as possible.

Finally, development

Only this far into the implementation project are you safe to actually start programming. Functional requirements, design specification and technical design specification are all completed, and you pretty much know what you need to do.

Development consists of two separate development activities. In the first one, you address the application functionality, all the modifications, customizations, and new features, as well as the data integration functionality. The second activity comprises development of data migration functionality.

Application functionality

We start application features development from as low as we can. With Microsoft Dynamics NAV 2009 it's the data model, consisting of tables and their relationships. After the data model has been completed, we can continue to the user interface, which is really a presentation layer over underlying data. After these two are completed, we conclude the feature development by programming the business logic. It may be that a lot of work on the data model and presentation layer has been started during the design phase, in which case you may be simply tidying up and ensuring that all development standards are being met and that changes are properly documented.

At this point the necessity of planning the development activities ahead becomes crystal clear. If we have analyzed and planned development activities, then we are developing dependent features together. This means that there will be no interference between us and other developers working on other feature sets.

If we didn't bother to plan development activities, many developers working at the same time on different features affecting the same standard objects may easily trample over other developer's work.

After development of a feature has been completed, the developer is the first to test it. A developer should make sure that everything that was specified in the design specification is really included, and that no obvious errors or bugs exist. At this point we don't need to make sure that the business process is supported fully and that it goes smoothly; this is the application consultant's job. We only need to ensure everything is there, and it doesn't collapse when blown upon. If you are developing a report, run it with several different filters if possible, and if it throws an error, go back and correct it. Remember that the point of testing is not to prove something works, but to try to make it go wrong. If you found no errors, is that because you are a great developer or a lousy tester?

Only when all specified requirements are there, and there are no more errors coming out at you, can you move the feature into the test environment for an application consultant to test its functionality. The application consultant once again needs to make sure everything is there, but the focus is on the business process integrity and functionality, as defined in the test plan. Of course, the consultant should still keep a close eye on any bugs or errors, and return the work immediately to the developer, if any of these pop up.

There may be several cycles of testing and rework necessary before a feature can be declared completely developed.

Data migration development

As soon as changes to the data model are completed by the feature development team, data migration development can commence. It can be conducted in parallel with feature development, by another developer, or a team of developers, or it can be developed by the same developers at any appropriate time during the development phase.

The appropriate time depends mainly on the complexity and quality of the available source data and the testing plan. If there are many different data sources with lots of garbage information, the sooner you start working on data migration, the more chances of success you have. If specific functionality can't be tested without the customer's data already loaded into the test environment, then data migration development should be completed before feature development. If customer's data is not a prerequisite for testing, then you may postpone the data migration development until after the features have been developed.

The best approach is to have a dedicated developer who will work on data migration functionality only, and to start working on it as soon as possible after data model has been finalized.

Data migration can easily take as much time as feature development because the customer's original data may reside in various data sources. When data sources are structured, it might not be a big problem to pull it out using SQL Server Integration Services, but sometimes data may be residing in unstructured Excel spreadsheets, SharePoint libraries, or even Word documents.

An important part of data migration is data quality. Even with structured data sources, garbage data is accumulated over time. Dummy items and for-test-purposes-only customers are all too common, but not such a big problem. The problems start with bad data integrity. Text columns containing date values or numbers are a typical example of seemingly innocent issues that can turn into real showstoppers. If your customer used an ERP system before deciding to move to Microsoft Dynamics NAV, you might not need to worry about these, but expect to encounter proportionally as many of these problems as there are separate applications from which the data needs to be pulled.

Data migration needs to be thoroughly tested many times, and you can expect many more rework cycles than with application functionality. The reason is that data is volatile, and your data migration procedures need to be able to cope with unexpected situations. Although not very likely, it may be the case that you have a text field used for storing document dates, and that every single date entered into this field is correct up to the point you start development. Don't rely on this, and make sure your data migration procedure expects to get an incorrect value in this field. Bear in mind that after you have completed and tested a data migration procedure, and before you perform the final production data migration, there will be new information in the system, and your procedure needs to cope with it as well. Either prepare to get garbage and handle it, or prepare to have a panicky go-live.

Security issues

When all the development has been completed, don't forget to test and validate the security requirements. You must first take care that your data is secure, and that data sensitivity is consistently observed throughout the standard Microsoft Dynamics NAV application and all your customizations. You must also ensure that functions and processes are secure and that only authorized users can perform sensitive tasks. If unauthorized, being able to see a customer's credit limit may be bad. Being able to release a sales order for shipment may be disastrous.

Document the changes

After all the development has been completed, one more chore remains to be done—documentation. There are two kinds of documentation:

- **End-User Documentation** is a set of documents describing the customized application functionality, and is used by end users during training, and later as a reference. Most end-user documentation comes from the Functional Requirements Document, and if there weren't many change requests, most of it can be copy-pasted.

- **Technical Documentation** is a set of documents describing the development work, and can be used by systems and database administrators, and developers and application consultants supporting the solution. Sometimes technical design specification will suffice, with appropriate updates reflecting the changes implemented since it was approved, but sometimes different sets of documents will need to be written.

Customer testing and acceptance

Development has been completed, and tested by the consultant team. Now it's time for the customer to see the fruits of your labor. Customer testing doesn't differ too much from the testing your own application consultants did. It's the same thing, only done from a different perspective.

Of course, you don't need to wait for customer testing to occur only after all the development work has been completed. Just as you are able to release designs to the development team as they are complete, you can also release completely developed chunks of functionality for customer testing.

This testing work will be done by a completely new group of people, selected from each department as representatives well-versed in processes and daily routines. It will be necessary to conduct another series of user training, this time focusing on the customized application and processes as required by the Functional Requirement Document. Users conducting this test will be concerned to validate that the processes as covered in the customized Microsoft Dynamics NAV solution conform to their needs. This is why this testing is also called process testing.

It is important to note that customer process testing is not the final customer acceptance testing, and that often users will complain that a process is not satisfactory. As long as the process complies with the functional and design specification approved by the customer, you don't need to worry. It is normal behavior for end users to sometimes obstruct the change, because with the system, they will need to change their habits.

After process testing has been completed, you need to collect the feedback and act accordingly. More often than not a few rework iterations will be required to get the functionality straight, but if everything so far has been done as suggested, there shouldn't be many issues preventing the customer from signing off on the development work.

Once all the customer tests have been conducted according to the plan, and the application consultants agree that all the application functionality, data integration, and data migration features have been developed, it is time to sign off on the development phase and prepare for deployment.

Deployment phase

Now we are getting serious. All has been said, all has been done, now it only takes a little push before the thing goes live.

Plan your steps

One last time in our project, we begin with planning the activities. Deployment is a joint effort of customer and consultant; it's a phase where all the people involved in the project join forces, so it takes twice as much planning as it took in previous phases.

There are many tasks that need to be synchronized during the deployment process. Major activities during deployment are final systems and environment configuration, user acceptance testing, load testing, end-user training, and final data migration. If any of these fails, go-live may be at risk.

The first activity that is going to occur during deployment is the configuration of the production environment. Hardware sizing and software requirements have already been specified during design phase, and adjusted as necessary based on feature and process testing results, so there shouldn't be any surprises regarding what kind of server hardware we need for our solution to function as expected. Where surprises usually come is when the technical consultant gets on site with installation CD's, only to find out that servers are about to arrive in five days. Prevent these situations by preparing a configuration plan, which will clearly identify tasks to be performed, as well as prerequisites.

The burden of planning activities will, however, stay with planning for the most important process of the deployment phase: the **User Acceptance Testing** (**UAT**). These tests can take a significant while, and will require intensive engagement of both the customer's key users and your application consultants, so schedule these activities carefully. You won't want to test every single action or button, but whole process groups and the system functionality as a whole. Make sure that all test case scenarios have been prepared, that all test scripts exist together with input and expected output specifications.

Environment configuration

The first step in deployment is the simplest one. We need to configure hardware and software, and if properly planned for, it shouldn't bear many risks. Our technical specification we carried over from the design phase specifies exactly how the software needs to be installed. Whether it will be a single server deployment, or there will be separate servers for Microsoft SQL Server and for Microsoft Dynamics NAV

2009 Service Tier, installation should be simple. If you need to deploy Microsoft Dynamics NAV 2009 RoleTailored (or Classic) client to many machines, consider using an unattended installation approach.

After the Microsoft Dynamics NAV 2009 infrastructure has been installed and configured, we need to configure the application itself. This shouldn't be difficult either, because we have all of our configuration settings documented during analysis and design phases, but it may take a while to complete it. Everything that is not migrated from the old environment, and that is not integrated with external systems, must be configured manually. This consists of simple tasks such as module setups, but usually includes configuring all sorts of supplementary setups, such as posting groups, units of measures, payment methods, dimensions, approval workflows, security roles, and so on.

In order to avoid the human error factor, you can maintain a setup database throughout development and testing. Initially, you configure it according to functional and design specification, then as development progresses you update both the documentation and the application setup according to the latest changes in requirements. Finally, during deployment you simply restore this database into the live environment, preserving all configurations, and significantly reducing both the time needed to complete this activity, and risk of going live with an incorrectly configured application.

Another reason why you would want to approach the system configuration this way is that during deployment it is best practice to work in two separate environments: production environment and test environment. The production environment is going to wait for final data migration and go-live, but the test environment will be heavily used during the final testing activities of the deployment phase. If you have your Microsoft Dynamics NAV 2009 database with the application set up, you can use it to apply the same environment configuration to the testing environment as will be used in production.

After both production and test environments have been installed and configured, it is time to migrate the data into the test environment for the last, but the most important of all rounds of testing: the **User Acceptance Test** (**UAT**).

User acceptance test

Let's sit in a car. It's a brand new Aston Martin V8 Vantage, a hand-crafted beauty-and-the-beast you customized and personalized to your fancies. Start the ignition, and the engine roars. Test passed. Switch the lights on, and here they go. Another test passed. Turn the steering wheel left and right, and the wheels are turning accordingly. From what we have done so far, this car would seem to be working. But that's not quite it.

So far we have been testing various aspects of the application. During development we have had several rounds of feature tests, and then after development work has been completed we have conducted process testing with end users. The goal of these tests has been to show whether specific features work as required, and whether specific processes can be used to achieve their specific goals.

In this final round of testing, we are taking our system for a test drive. The User Acceptance Test, comprising several system tests, will put the system as a whole under scrutiny by key users and selected end users whose goal is to determine whether the system as a whole can be accepted or not. During UAT, users will follow a series of test cases prepared during design and development phases, which test the system functionality thoroughly, not from the perspective of a single process such as sales order processing, but from the perspective of many processes working together. An example test case might include sales order processing, requisition planning, purchase order processing, production order processing, and manufacturing costing, with a focus on the information flow between separate processes.

The UAT is our last chance to find out if something somewhere is wrong and needs rework. Although after several rounds of internal and customer testing this final series of tests can seem redundant, we need to devote as much time as necessary to accurately conduct these tests as defined in test plans, and carefully document the test results.

The idea behind UAT is to test the real-life situations and their coverage by the system. These tests need to be designed in such a way as to mimic as closely as possible the actual work end users perform during the course of a day. In theory, if these tests are really designed like this, everything that would otherwise surface in production should also surface during testing.

Detecting an issue during UAT and not letting it slip into production can indeed save many pennies. Any issue that was detected must be carefully analyzed, and traced back to its root. After the source has been established, we need to go through another, small-scale cycle of design-development-test, and then repeat not only the test that exposed the error, but also all other functionally and logically related tests.

Load test

Microsoft Dynamics NAV 2009 is not the most scalable solution in the world. In optimized deployments, it typically reaches about 250 concurrent users, but depending on customizations and user activity, as few as 100 concurrent users can push it over the edge. The least suitable moment to find out that your hardware wasn't properly sized, or that performance of your customizations is far from optimal, is after the system has already gone live. Therefore, include load testing as a standard activity in all of your deployments.

Load tests put the system under high stress, simulating much more transactional and concurrency pressure on it than expected, with the goal to find out whether the system as designed fits within constraints imposed by hardware infrastructure. These tests are not obligatory. If you are deploying an as-is Microsoft Dynamics NAV 2009 for a ten-employee umbrella manufacturing company, there aren't that many things load tests would explain to you that you didn't know before. Complicated business processes, heavy customizations of standard functionality, third-party add-ons, combined with high number of concurrent users, mandate carefully planned load tests.

For load tests, you should try to make your test environment resemble the production environment as closely as possible. Ideally, it should consist of the same or comparable servers and desktop machines, because otherwise test results won't be too meaningful. As with UAT, the idea behind load tests is to detect critical problems and address them accordingly before the system goes live.

End-user training

Sometime during deployment phase we need to train our end users on how to use our customized Microsoft Dynamics NAV 2009 application. As simple in content as it might seem, end-user training can be a true monster. If our customer is a large corporation, with several hundreds of users requiring training, and with optimal classroom setup of not more than a dozen trainees, end-user training can take forever.

In such scenarios, key users or end users who participated during process and system tests typically deliver this training to their peers. For smaller organizations, consultants can deliver this training themselves.

Before we start training, we need to make sure that our documentation is complete and up-to-date. We will be conducting our training based on it, so it would be a good idea to distribute all the necessary manuals to end users attending this training.

Go-live

There. The system is ready to be deployed. There are just a handful of chores remaining, and off we go to uncork that champagne.

If all of the discussed phases have gone as planned, go-live itself won't be even a nuisance. What we need to do is to perform the final data migration into the soon-to-be-live environment, validate this data, and then shut down the old machines. Well, not literally. Old software won't go out the moment Microsoft Dynamics NAV 2009 enters the daily operation; it will still stay there to conduct a few checks every now and then, or to access historical data deliberately left out of new system.

The final go-live activity is customer sign-off on the deployment phase, a milestone confirming that everything that has been planned to be delivered was delivered according to plans and specifications, and to customer satisfaction.

Champagne time!

Operation phase

OK, the project is live, we've celebrated it, maybe even got drunk over it, do we go home now? Er, not quite. Depending on the panic factor influencing your activities in the final days of deployment, and the number of open issues from testing, there will be a few open tasks left that you need to close before calling it a day.

No planning?

Exactly. For the first time in the project we don't actually need to plan anything. Our Microsoft Dynamics NAV 2009 solution is alive and kicking—the customer is using it and is managing their business through it. What's remaining are a handful of unstructured tasks not really affecting the schedule, the project scope, or the project plan. We may execute them at a leisurely pace over the next few weeks.

Most likely we've carried a few tasks over from previous phases. These usually include tweaking layouts of some non-critical reports or fine-tuning role centers. These tasks weren't enough to stop the go-live, but are absolutely necessary for the final project sign-off.

No matter how much effort was invested into the testing cycles during development and deployment, issues still make their way into production. An item will end up having an incorrect costing method, a field will be missing, a security role will prevent a user from accessing the data they need. These issues will be popping up all over the place for the next few weeks but don't let it get you down—it's perfectly normal.

It happens because you couldn't prepare test plans for every application feature, button and action, nor could you prepare or execute test cases for every possible real-life scenario. If your testing plan included the most important, business-critical scenarios, and you got them through rigorous user acceptance tests, whatever emerges during the operation phase won't cause any serious headaches.

Documentation

Another task that usually gets carried all the way over to operation phase is documentation. Documentation is important, but is not critical. If the deadline was tight, and time was scarce, this one sank deep on the list of priorities. It is likely that if you made it through go-live without producing documentation, there ain't gonna be none. But let's assume that we intend to diligently document the work we have done.

End-user documents sometimes don't get finished in time because of the pressures surrounding go-live. If you didn't finish them before go-live, do so now. Ignoring them won't do you any good; it will just cause trouble when users start asking for help with the simplest of features that could have easily been explained in a 'how-to' document.

Design specifications and functional requirement documents scream for an update at this point. Although the best practice is to update the design document as soon as a change request is accepted, late in development or throughout deployment phase, you sometimes simply didn't have time for too much paperwork, and you simply concentrated on delivery. If that's the case, now is the right time to make up for it.

Finally, there will be a series of documents that are best written after the system has gone live, such as backup procedures, operation manuals, and system maintenance guidelines.

Transition

The ultimate goal of the operation phase is to gradually transfer the deployed solution from the consultant to the customer. After go-live, the consultant is still working closely with the end users, with the majority of activities focused around end-user support. Support is at its peak in the first days after go-live, with dozens of questions and issues raised daily. We need to address and resolve all of them.

Immediately after go-live we may feel overwhelmed by the volume of support requests, but as the time goes by, and as users get more proficient with the new system, the number of requests will gradually decrease. When the rate of new issues falls below our capability to handle them, it's time to start wrapping up the project.

Transitioning the project from the consultant to the customer means relieving the consultant from the responsibility for end-user support, and moving it to the customer's IT department or key users. It's not necessary to wait until each and every support request has been resolved, before the project is officially closed. As soon as there are no major issues left, and the customer is ready to take over the support, we can initiate the transition. This may require an additional round of training, probably focused on administration and maintenance, and raises the possibility of a knowledge transfer workshop.

A good practice is to establish a knowledge base and to document all the problems that may repeat, together with their resolutions. If there is a bug with specifying the Item Category Code for an item, and six people report it, it doesn't need to go into the knowledge base, because once you fix it, it won't repeat again. But if six people turn to you asking about how to create a new item with a non-default number series, this calls for a knowledge base article that explains step by step how to do it. SharePoint can do this job quite nicely.

Closing off

Operation phases can get tricky. When the system goes live, and end users start using it on daily basis, many of them will want to voice their strong opinion and request changes or new features, which were never originally planned. There is nothing wrong with these, and change requests are normal, even expected, during all phases following analysis. However, operation is where these issues can easily get out of control.

Sometimes the customer simply doesn't feel ready to declare independence, and it seems as though they would rather have the consultant perpetually by their side. Change requests come in extremely handy with this agenda, because they provide a perfect excuse for not closing the project.

If this happens, we must not fall into this trap. It's OK to accept a few change requests even if they are irrelevant and we honestly think the customer can do without them. But as soon as we notice a slightest hint that these might escalate, we need to start pushing for final acceptance. If the original scope has been completed, and all mission-critical functionality is in place, but the customer still didn't go flat on new ideas, we probably need to agree on some kind of permanent support, but outside the boundaries of the project.

Final acceptance

The last step of our long project journey is to obtain customer's final acceptance and project sign-off. At this point the customer is working comfortably in Microsoft Dynamics NAV 2009, the old system has been decommissioned and is not used in parallel any more, and no new issues are appearing. This means that the project can be declared officially completed, with a final customer's sign-off on the entire project.

Sign-off needs to be obtained in writing. Although the customer's project manager can be one of the people who participate in the final sign-off, it is important to note that for sign-off to be relevant, it needs to go as high up the executive ladder as possible. Ideally, it should be signed by the project sponsor, or a senior executive.

Who died?

The room for improvement is the largest room in the world. No matter how successful our project was, if we didn't learn something from it, we have wasted an opportunity. After the final sign-off has been obtained, the project is officially closed, but we may want to do one more thing: project review.

It's funny that project review meetings usually go under the morbid name of *Post Mortem*. I never really understood why someone would call a project review meeting a post mortem, unless the project bit the dust. Hopefully, our project is very much alive, so we can rather call this meeting a *Post Go-Live Review*, or simply a *Project Review*.

The point of a project review meeting is to gather the *lessons learned*. This project wasn't the last project we would do, and probably wasn't the customer's last one either. Gathering lessons learned can help both the consultant and the customer rethink the whole project, see what went well and what might have gone a bit better. This kind of activity and candid information sharing is beneficial for all project participants, and can result in the future projects being conducted more effectively. This is not an opportunity to apportion blame or to give each other a good slap on the back. Find out what you can learn from the project in a short and to-the-point meeting and then go out for dinner or a few drinks.

Did we go bananas?

And now for a tough one: do we really do projects this way? With so much paperwork, analysis, planning, designing, revisions, approvals, and acceptances, it must cost a fortune! And it does.

The only problem is, without all that paperwork, analysis, planning, designing, revisions, approvals, and acceptances, it still costs a fortune. And a far bigger one at that.

Remember our house from the start of the chapter? Let's try building it without a methodology.

What kind of house do you need? *A house*. Do you need one floor, two floors? *Well, just start building it, then we'll see where we get*. Would you like an entrance from the street, or from the court side? *Just put one somewhere, we'll move it later if we need to.* Plastic window frames or wooden window frames? *Doesn't really matter.*

Uh-oh!

With this approach, it's going to be a long journey before this house is built, and I don't want to be there when the bill arrives, and it will probably go down with the first breeze.

The same is true with software projects, especially with large scale projects such as implementations of ERP systems, including Microsoft Dynamics NAV 2009. There are many components, many considerations, and many different needs that one single system must address, and to make it stable and reliable, we need to take some preemptive steps.

When customers decide to implement a business management system, they usually start with a predetermined budget, and often they already have a desired go-live date in mind. Often they have an idea of what kind of business problem they want to solve. They want to control time, cost, and scope. Unfortunately, this is the project equivalent of wanting to have your cake and eat it.

This situation is often described as a triangle, with three sides representing three project constraints: time, cost, and scope (the features). The customer can grab and control any two sides, but the third one slips out of their control. It is not possible to control all three, much as it is not possible to build a 100-storey skyscraper in three months on a 450,000 US$ budget. If we have this budget, and it needs to be built in three months, it's not going to be a 100-storey skyscraper. Or if it needs to be a 100-storey skyscraper, and it needs to be finished in three months, it will cost a sheer fortune. That's how it works.

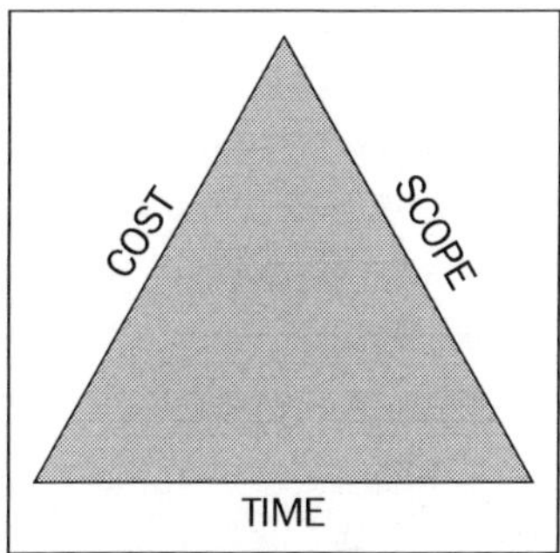

This is obvious, at least with skyscrapers, but software projects often start with unrealistic expectations. Budgets are OK, as are time constraints. What doesn't fit this triangle is features. Customers want features, they want many of them. This is called *scope creep*, and it's consistently taking projects down.

Consultants often swallow this bait. Customers ask for a proposal, consultants go ahead and propose, analyze the requirements provisionally, then jump into programming. As soon as a feature has been completed, customers think of five other nice-to-haves that would go perfectly with that one, and bury the consultant under piles of new requests. After a while, when it is developed, an end user comes and says it isn't even close to what they need. Then rework cycle is initiated, and all of this is repeated as often as unnecessary.

Things like this do happen.

In the end, it becomes obvious that the budget won't be enough, and a tough choice is presented. Either the project switches from a fixed-priced one to a time-and-material based one, or it is cancelled. Both choices are equally bad. If it goes the time-and-material way, it's going to cost a fortune. If it's called off, whatever has been spent to this point may as well have been burnt. This is nothing a lawsuit wouldn't sort out, but that wasn't a project goal, or was it?

Betting a business on a mad horse

Methodologies exist precisely to mitigate these problems. Yes, it's true that a continuous engagement of a dedicated project manager will increase the costs of project delivery. It's also true that extra paperwork adds a lot of overhead, which prolongs the deadline. But that's one side of the truth. The other one is that with a systematic and disciplined approach to an implementation, the project becomes predictable and manageable.

The problem with projects led without a formal methodology is that they only appear cheaper at first, but they rarely finish on time, within budget, and hardly ever deliver against the expectations. With an implementation of Microsoft Dynamics NAV, predictability is important. As for any ERP system, the majority of implementations of Microsoft Dynamics NAV are mission critical. They are there to support the business, and carry the bulk of it.

The question of implementing Microsoft Dynamics NAV therefore ceases to be a question of technology success. It becomes a question of business success. The outcome of a large-scale implementation can boost a business, or bring it down altogether. With business success at stake, predictability is a must, and in spite of higher perceived costs, methodologies help keep the costs down by reducing risk. Proceeding with an implementation without formal procedures in place is like betting your whole business on a mad horse. It can win the race, but it can as well start running in the opposite direction. You can never tell.

Summary

Microsoft Dynamics NAV 2009 is not just an application that can be installed and used out of the box. It is business management software, and for businesses to get true value out of it, it must be shaped to the specific needs of its users. To get from standard functionality to a custom-tailored one, it takes a lengthy process, which consists of several important phases aimed at understanding the customer's problem, defining a proper solution, and delivering it, while observing principles and constraints embedded in Microsoft Dynamics NAV. Implementation projects are not development projects, and although development is usually one part of the process, focusing just on development is a sure path to failure. On the other hand, Microsoft Dynamics Sure Step methodology provides a path to success.

5
Configuring the System

Dynamics NAV 2009 is a powerful system and, as my Uncle Ben once told me, with great power comes great responsibility. In order to make the system work correctly, it is our responsibility to configure it according to the requirements of the users. This configuration process can be time-consuming and requires a lot of deep product and business knowledge. Thankfully, if you just want to have a play around, the product ships with a demonstration company that is fully configured and ready to use, but eventually you will need to configure a new system from scratch. When that time comes, this chapter will help you through the process.

In this chapter you'll learn:

- Enough accounting and finance knowledge to make you dangerous
- About the **Rapid Implementation Methodology** (**RIM**) Toolkit
- How to configure the parts of the system not covered by the RIM Toolkit

What is system configuration?

System configuration can be divided into three broad categories:

- Defining your chart of accounts, dimensions, and various posting groups
- Setting the parameters that control the system's behavior
- Loading the 'master' data such as customers, vendors, and inventory items

Don't panic if 'dimensions' and 'posting groups' are terms of mystery—all will become clear. Microsoft has provided a **Rapid Implementation Methodology** (**RIM**) tool that helps you through the configuration process. Before we look at the tool, we're going to go through some of the system, accounting, and business basics that will help make the configuration process make sense.

A programmer's guide to accounting

It's rare that you'll do anything in Dynamics NAV that doesn't require some knowledge of accounting and finance. If, like me, you're from a technical background, some of the accounting terms and practices you've encountered may seem strange and illogical. This section will guide you through the financial jungle and give you the confidence you need to configure like a pro. If you're a programmer, you may mistakenly think a chapter on accounting and configuration doesn't apply to you. A good programmer tests their work by using the application; to use the application, you will need to be able to configure it and understand it. You'll need to get some understanding of finance, just enough to be dangerous. Let's start by looking at the chart of accounts—I'll try to make it as painless as possible.

The hippo's bottom

If Dynamics NAV were a hippopotamus then the chart of accounts would be its bottom; no matter what you feed into it, the chart of accounts is where it ends up. It should be no surprise to learn that whichever parts of NAV you intend to use, you will have to plan your chart of accounts and dimensions to be able to use them. Once the chart of accounts has been decided, you can configure the rest of the system. Later we'll see how configuration is principally done to decide how the financial information should be collected.

If you are replacing an existing system with Dynamics NAV, designing the chart of accounts and dimensions can be relatively simple as the important business information has already been determined. Don't be surprised, however, if the accountants in the business see the new financial system as a golden opportunity to do a bit of tweaking.

If you have no accounting experience, you are going to need to learn some basics. If you are a qualified accountant or an experienced NAV consultant you can skip ahead but I warn you, by skipping forward you may miss more exciting analogies on hippopotami.

The black art of bookkeeping

Businesses are relatively simple beasts—we buy stuff, we sell stuff, and if our business is successful we'll make some money along the way. As our business grows, so does our need for information; good information helps us to answer the important questions we face every day. Can we afford to buy another machine or hire a new employee? Should we expand our product line? How can we make more money or reduce our costs? Without information we cannot answer these questions. Without good information our business will not realize its potential, and, if we're unlucky, it may go bust.

Bookkeeping will not only help us understand how well the business is doing but it will also help us to plan for the future. By recording information about expenses and income, we can track a company's actual performance against its planned performance. By looking at past performance we can learn to make better plans for the future. Dynamics NAV is the perfect tool to help us record financial information, and the place to do this is the chart of accounts.

Some lingo explained

The term General Ledger is often used interchangeably with chart of accounts. Individual records within the chart of accounts are called G/L Accounts (or General Ledger Accounts). The ledger entries that are summed to provide the G/L Balances are called G/L Entries.

The General Ledger departments place in Dynamics NAV comprises the chart of accounts, budgets, intercompany postings, journals, and a host of reports and analytical tools.

We'll start by focusing on the chart of accounts and dimensions—NAV's dynamic duo.

Finding dimensions with the five Ws (and the H)

It is rare that we will be asked to design a chart of accounts for an implementation of Microsoft Dynamics NAV. Businesses that are implementing an ERP solution are often mature enough to have an existing chart of accounts and a pretty good idea of the financial information they want to capture and report on. It's easy to get an understanding of what a G/L account is and what a dimension is from a technical point of view, but understanding why they are needed is a different story.

If you know anything about accounting, you'll know that financial transactions are posted to G/L accounts. They have a value; they are either a debit or a credit (don't try too hard to figure out which way round things should be), and they have a date. You can think of the amount as a thing you can measure and the G/L account and date as classifications of the data that will help you perform analysis. The classification adds different dimensions to the data, so this is probably why we call them 'Dimensions'. Are there any more dimensions apart from *G/L Account* and *Date* that we can use to make our reporting even better? This all depends on what you are doing and what you are interested in. Let's consider an example.

Example

Susan buys some toner cartridges for a laser printer in the accounts department on July 17, 2008.

This is a financial transaction. It cost us money, so it's an expense, but how can we classify it?

I keep six honest serving-men

(They taught me all I knew);

Their names are What and Why and When

And How and Where and Who.

- Rudyard Kipling, Just So Stories 1902

There are six important questions that will serve you well in business, and these are often referred to as the five Ws and the H. The questions are who, what, when, where, why, and how. I use these questions all the time when performing analysis. They're not always relevant but I always know that if I have considered these questions, I have not missed anything. If you take our six questions and apply them to our transaction, you will uncover the potential measures and dimensions.

Let's take each one of our six words in turn, and try to formulate a question about the transaction using that word. Once we have worked out our question, we can try to answer it with what we know. We can also determine if the answer to that question is likely to be of importance to our business. If it is, it's a dimension.

Who?

Who bought the toner?

Susan bought the toner. That was easy, wasn't it? The problem is we don't really care about the answer in this case. Susan is responsible for buying office stationery and consumables, and I don't need to analyze who is buying the things my business needs. Are there any other *who* questions we can ask?

Who was the toner bought for?

Now it's getting interesting. The toner was bought for the Accounts Department. 'Department' would be a good thing to be able to analyze my expenses by. Are there any more *who* questions?

Who did we buy the toner from?

We bought the toner from a vendor. I may well want to group my vendors in some way in order to perform analysis. Possibly a 'Vendor Group' would be another dimension for my transaction.

'Who' dimensions

Department, Vendor Group

What?

What did Susan buy?

She bought toner. At the lowest level I could record the specific item that was bought as a dimension, but I think we are more likely to want to group this item. Toner is a type of consumable, and would probably be grouped under stationery and consumables. If I have the ability to analyze my expenses by categories like 'stationery and consumables', then I will be able to track how much I am spending on this type of expense and possibly control the expense. Let's call this dimension 'Expense Type'. Are there any other *what* questions?

What did it cost?

We are definitely interested in the amount things cost. Let's call this 'Amount'.

What was Susan wearing when she bought the toner?

OK, that one's a little creepy—stay focused on questions that reveal business information!

'What' dimensions

Expense Type, Amount

When?

When did Susan buy the toner?

Another easy one! This is the date the transaction took place, or possibly a posting date for the transaction. In financial terms, we are only really interested in the financial period.

'When' dimension

Posting Date

Where?

Where did Susan buy the toner?

It is unlikely we would be interested in the geographical region in which Susan buys her toner, but at least by asking the question we can tick this off the list and be confident we have explored all avenues. Maybe this would be more important for a sales transaction. If we are importing goods from overseas as opposed to buying stationery, this may be an extremely interesting question.

'Where' dimension

Region

Why?

Why did Susan buy the toner?

Probably because we ran out over three weeks ago, and have been managing until now by taking the old toner cartridge out of the printer, shaking it, and putting it back to get a few more faint, stripy prints. Are there any *why* questions we could use for analysis? Maybe there was some 'Purpose' to the expense that we would want to record. It could have been needed for a 'Sales Campaign', or maybe it was to be used for a 'Project'.

'Why' dimensions

Purpose, Project, Campaign

How?

How did Susan buy the toner?

Did Susan buy this through an account with the vendor, or did she buy it with her own money and claim it on expenses? Maybe she used an internet account or a purchasing card. These transactions could have significantly different handling costs which could provide some useful information. Let's call this 'Transaction Type'.

'How' dimension

Transaction Type

Well that wasn't too hard, was it? Now we have asked our questions, go through the answers and see how many 'things' you might want to know about our transaction.

- Department
- Vendor Group
- Expense Type
- Amount
- Posting Date
- Region
- Purpose
- Project
- Campaign
- Transaction Type

One of these things is not like the other ones. Can you guess which one I am talking about?

Give yourself a lollipop if you said 'Amount'. The amount of the transaction is something we can measure or add up. Funnily enough this is called a 'Measure'. The other things all provide some aspect or category to the transaction. We call these things 'Dimensions'.

You can now repeat the exercise for different types of transactions. It could be that your expenses are internal charges for using fixed assets. This may mean that the 'Asset Group' is interesting for analysis. Try to think of the typical transactions for the customer's business, list them, and work through the six questions to find the important information. Once you have been through all of the different types of expenses, repeat the exercise for the different types of revenue.

When you're identifying dimensions with the business people, don't just identify the dimension names, but try to collect a set of sample data. For example, if Department is clearly important, try to capture a few departments as you are going through the exercise. On many occasions I have seen workshops where everyone has agreed on the important dimensions only to find that in a follow-up session no one can remember why they wanted the dimension or what values it was meant to contain. Capturing sample data will help you later on when you need to configure the dimensions and the possible values those dimensions can contain.

That exercise should have helped you to understand dimensions, but what about the chart of accounts? Believe it or not, we've just covered that as well.

The chart of accounts

Your chart of accounts is split into two parts: the income statement and the balance sheet, but if you've ever looked at an income statement in the chart of accounts you will have noticed that it looks more like a list of expense types and revenue types from our list of dimensions. The dimension that we identified as 'Expense Type' is typically the G/L Account Number, and in NAV terms this is not a dimension. The principal, however, is the same: it's a piece of information we know about a transaction that will allow us to group similar transactions together for analysis.

If you were designing a chart of accounts from scratch, a good place to start would be to consider all of the expense types and revenue types that you would want to record amounts against and how these should be grouped. Let's not get too carried away here—we're looking to strike a balance between having good classification of data for analysis and still allowing people to do their jobs. Don't force the users to study sheets of dimension and account codes just to be able to submit their expenses. We're not going to improve the business reporting by making people's jobs harder; instead we'll make day-to-day transactions more difficult and bureaucratic. Good judgment and pragmatism will help us greatly in this task. If you're an implementation consultant, relax: you're not going to be able to tell the business people what accounts and dimensions are right for them, but you need to be able to give them advice on how to discover the right ones and what factors should be considered.

Fortunately if you're not an accountant, and you simply want to learn about the application, you can look at the chart of accounts that exists within the demonstration company; this will give you a good idea of what to expect (although the demonstration company needs to be able to show many different types of businesses, so there are more accounts in here than you would typically see in a single type of business).

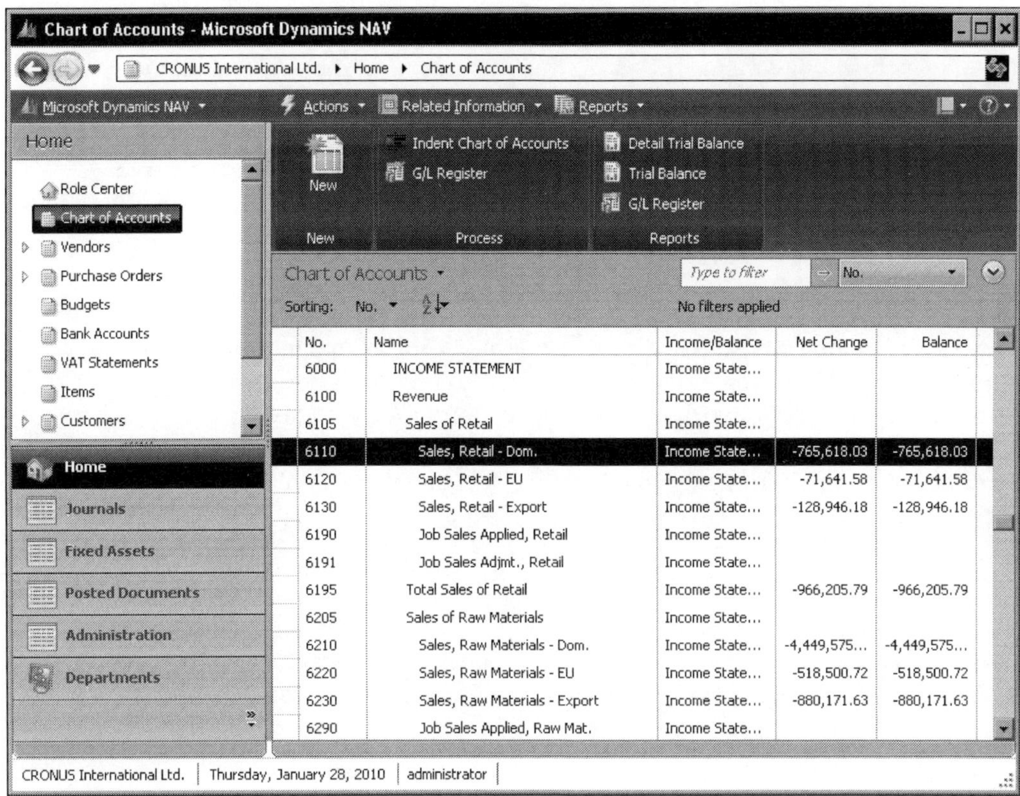

If you haven't done so already, now's a good time to open up the RoleTailored client using the Accounting Manager profile and open the Chart of Accounts list place.

We've discussed revenue and expense accounts, which can be found in the income statement starting at account number 6000 along with gains and losses (not covered yet). In addition to these income statement accounts, there are another four types of account that you'll find in the balance sheet: assets, liabilities, shareholder's equity, and dividends. Let's go through each of these account types and new terms in order to gain some understanding.

Income statement

The income statement (or profit and loss) represents the money going in and out of the business. If you add up all the transactions for a given time period, you can measure the company's performance. You could think of this as being like your bank account. Your salary goes in, your expenses go out, and you hope that the monthly closing balance has an upward trend. Within the income statement, there are four account types you are likely to come across.

Income/revenue

Revenue is the money that comes in to the business. You may call it income. Typically it's the result of selling something but it could be a grant from the government or income on investments. Don't confuse income with being given money in the form of a payment; receiving cash doesn't affect your performance for the period, it merely changes the state of accounts in the balance sheet (but more about that later).

Expenses

I think most people have a really good understanding of expenses. An expense account is probably the easiest type of account to relate to, and no matter which part of the business you work in, you'll be responsible for some of the transactions in the expense accounts: salaries, training, and entertainment. Hopefully, if you're a consultant or programmer, you also make some contribution to the revenue accounts.

Gains

A gain is any money coming in to the business that is not the result of normal trading activities. It could be that you sell a long-term asset such as a car, and the income from the sale less the cost (accumulated depreciation for an asset) is the gain. Sometimes this appears as "other income".

Losses

A loss is the opposite of a gain, and is any other expense for the period that is not related to normal trading. Let's face it if you do sell your car, it is more likely you will be posting a loss to your income statement and not a gain.

Balance sheet

The balance sheet represents the value of the business: what it is worth. At any point in time, the balance sheet lets you see what you owe and what is owed to you. The following are the four account types in the balance sheet:

Assets

An asset is something you own, such as cash or something that could be turned into cash. Some of your assets will be real things that you can get your hands on (often called tangible assets). There are other assets that you cannot get your hands on, such as the amount of money owed to you by your customers (and believe me for some customers getting your hands on this can be quite a task).

Liabilities

My wife thinks I am a liability. In accounting terms this represents something you owe. It could be a bank loan, the money you owe to your vendors; maybe it's the tax you have collected that must be paid to the government.

Shareholder's equity

Equity accounts tell you the value of your business. This could be the amount of money your shareholders have invested in the business. Another equity account is the retained earnings account. This is the difference between your income and expenses. If you make more money than you spend, then your retained earnings will increase. Dynamics NAV has an end-of-year routine that will take your result from the income statement and transfer it to your retained earnings equity account; at the same time the income statement is cleared to zero and you are ready to start a new year.

Dividend

This is a distribution of a company's profits to the shareholders. After you have calculated your retained earnings, it is likely a dividend will be taken from any earnings.

Other reading

I have read a few 'Accounting explained to stupid people', 'Accounts for non-financial geeks' type books but I can't really recommend the ones I've read. I will however recommend that if you are feeling particularly masochistic, and want more of this accounting mumbo jumbo, you go check out AccountingCoach.com at `http://www.accountingcoach.com/`. This has some great articles; it's free but the most valuable resource is the definition of accounting terms in the accounting dictionary at `http://www.accountingcoach.com/accounting-terms/accounting-dictionary/index.html`.

Feeding the hippopotamus

If you are skimming through this book, and come across this section without having read the previous text, you may wonder what a heading on hippopotami has to do with accounts. Shame on you for skimming, now go back and read from the beginning! The thing is, all that stuff about account types, assets, liabilities, and so on. was getting a bit heavy, and I really couldn't bring myself to write the subject heading 'posting transactions to the general ledger' which is what this section is really about. We have gone through what our chart of accounts is and how to define it, now we must look at how we get the transactions in there—how to feed the hippopotamus.

There are a number of ways of getting our financial transactions into the system. The most obvious and immediate way is to simply post a general journal. You can think of a general journal as a place to prepare your transactions. Your transactions are the adjustments you want to make to your balances in the chart of accounts. Once you have prepared your journal, you can post it. The act of 'Posting' the journal is simply when the system checks the lines to ensure the business and accounting rules are followed and creates the actual transactions. I'm not an accountant and, as such, I tend to think of posting a journal as a way of fiddling with the account balances. I'm sure there are some very serious and sensible reasons why accountants do this.

You cannot edit General Ledger entries (well you can if you are a developer, but you really shouldn't). If you want your balance of 3,000 to be a balance of 2,000, then you will post a transaction of -1,000. You never write directly to the General Ledger entry table, or edit the amounts of general ledger entries.

I wanted to give a real-world example of a journal that could be posted with dimensions to the chart of accounts that did not involve any of the other parts of the system. Each example I came up with had another part of the system involved. Take a look at the list and you'll see what I mean:

- Departmental wages to expense account—opposite posting involves the bank module
- Expenses to expense account—opposite entry probably involves a creditor account so we can make a payment
- Sales income—involves the sales module and transactions to a debtor account
- Post utility bills such as electricity—opposite entry will again involve a creditor account
- Depreciation expense of fixed assets—involves fixed assets module

The only real-world examples I could think of were bringing on opening balances for a new company and making adjustments to incorrect entries (fiddling). Let's use the example of posting the departmental wage costs, as this is great use of dimensions and not worry about the bank module. (We'll just post the balancing entry to a G/L account for Cash instead of one that represents our bank account.)

Is it a debit or a credit?

First of all we need to consider which way round our entries will be (will they be debits or credits?) I'm a programmer and my world is founded upon logic and reason, and I believe that a credit is positive and a debit is negative. Accountants, on the other hand, live in a world that is based upon voodoo and confusion; for some strange reason in accounting a transaction can be either positive or negative depending on where you put it.

When we talk about debits and credits we are not talking about negative and positive. (If you are a programmer reading this, fasten your seatbelt because it's going to get a little bumpy.) It's better to think of there being two columns in our ledger. The one on the left is for debits and the one on the right is for credits. Some of our accounts normally have a debit balance (on the left) and get increased by debit transactions. Other types of accounts normally have a credit balance (on the right) and get increased by credit transactions. For our chart of accounts to balance, the sum of the debits must equal the sum of the credits.

The best thing to do is just to learn the difference and leave it at that. Assets and expenses are expected to always have a debit balance. Income and liability and equity accounts are expected to always have a credit balance. Remember *left and right* not *negative and positive*.

Account Type	Debit	Credit
Dividends	Increase	Decrease
Expenses	Increase	Decrease
Asset	Increase	Decrease
Losses	Increase	Decrease
Gains	Decrease	Increase
Income/Revenue	Decrease	Increase
Liabilities	Decrease	Increase
Shareholder's Equity	Decrease	Increase

There are a couple of tricks that have helped me in the past to remember these differences. A friend and colleague once told me 'you debit your debtors'. I always pieced this little gem together with my knowledge that an asset is a good thing and the money your debtors owe to you is a good thing, therefore you debit asset accounts. Not very elegant, I'll admit, but I got by on this for a good number of years.

Another way to learn the debit and credit accounts is to make use of an acronym from the first letters of the accounts (DEAL and GIRLS.)

DEAL and GIRLS

Dividend, Expense, Asset, and Losses (abbreviated as 'D-E-A-L') accounts increase in value when debited and decrease when credited, whereas Gains, Income/Revenues, Liability, and Stockholder's (Owner's) equity (abbreviated as 'G-I-R-L-S') accounts decrease in value when debited and increase when credited.

Computers don't really have the concept for numbers that can be either on the left or on the right, so in accounting packages they use negative numbers to represent credits and positive numbers to represent debits. That's right (for all you programmers out there—I hope you fastened your seatbelts when I told you to), it's backwards! Don't try and reason this. Don't try and use logic, just learn it. Repeat this mantra:

Debit Positive, Debit Positive
Credit Negative, Credit Negative
Debit Positive, Debit Positive
Credit Negative, Credit Negative

If you are an accountant reading this, you're probably giggling to yourself, but believe me the computer people are getting close to melt-down.

OK, enough voodoo. Let's get back to our example. We want to post some departmental wage expenses. We are increasing our staff wages expenses, and we know that expense accounts are debit accounts, so we'll be posting a debit entry, which will be a positive number. Our opposite entry is going to go to a cash account, which is an asset. Assets normally have a debit balance but paying our staff is going to decrease our balance, so we will be posting a credit entry, which will have a negative balance.

1. Start the RoleTailored client using the Accounting Manager profile and go to **CRONUS International Ltd. | Journals | General Journals**.
2. The **General Journals** list place is displayed.

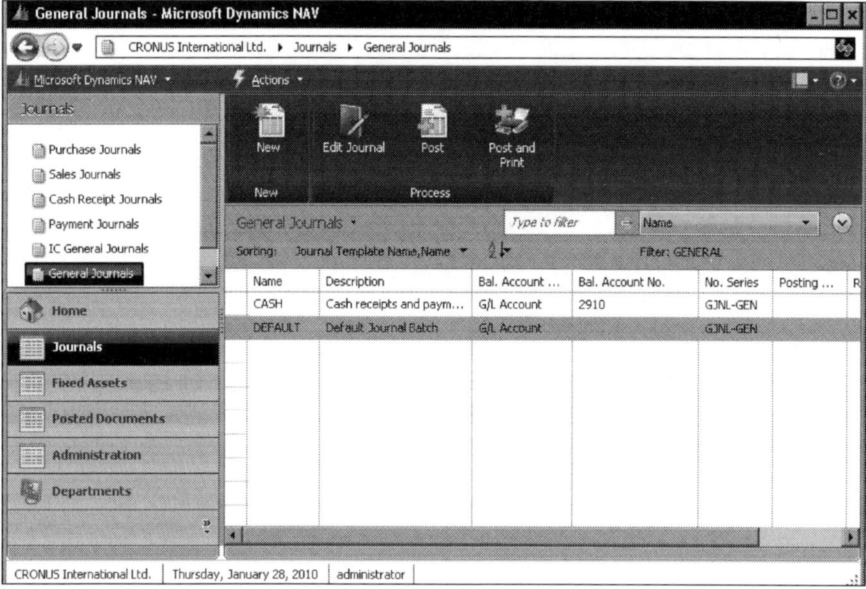

Double-click the **DEFAULT** general journal batch.

3. The **Edit - General Journal** page is displayed.

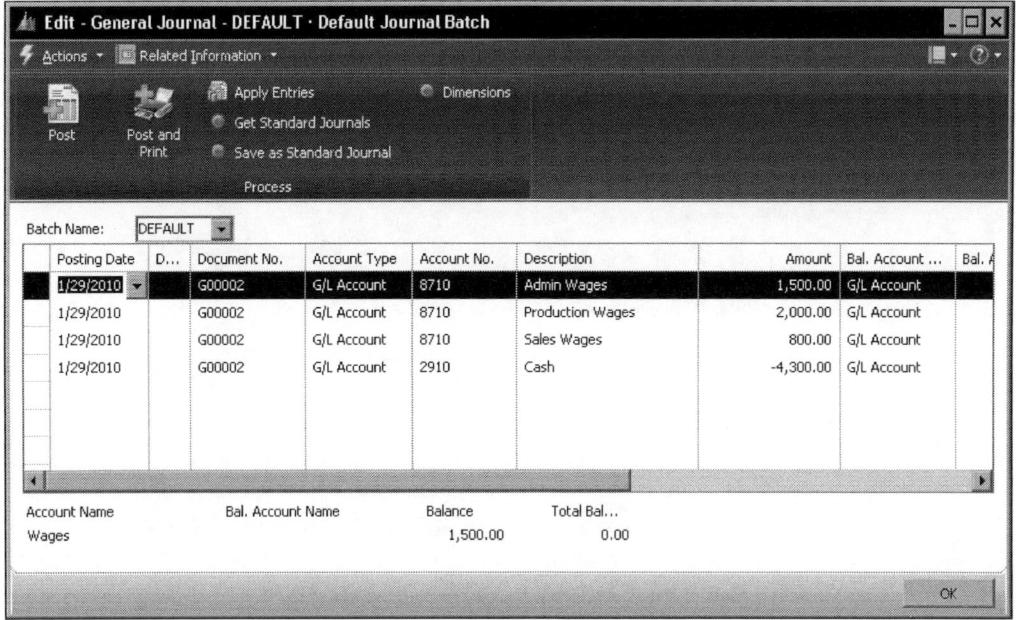

If the journal is not empty, press *Ctrl+Home* to go to the first record, then with the *Shift* key held down press *Ctrl+End*. This will select all records in the journal. Press *Ctrl+D* to delete the records.

On the first line, enter **8710** in the **Account No.** field. Enter **Admin Wages** in the **Description** field as we are going to be posting this amount to the admin department. Press *Enter* to move to the next field.

Press the *Tab* key, or *Enter* key, until the cursor is in the *Amount* field, and then type **1500** and press *Enter*.

We will now enter our admin dimension value against this line. Click the **Dimensions** button in the **Actions** pane.

4. The **Edit - Journal Line Dimensions** page is displayed.

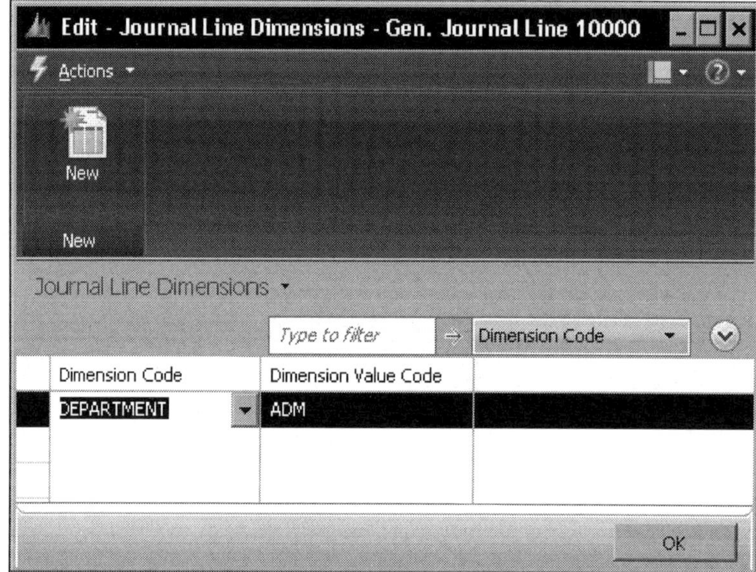

In the first field (the **Dimension Code** field) enter **DEPARTMENT**, and press *Enter*.

Use the drop-down button by the side of the **Dimension Value Code** field and select the line that has a code of **ADM** and description of **Administration**. Click the **OK** button to continue entering the journal lines.

Use the down-arrow cursor key to move to the next blank line. A few things have happened now. The **Posting Date** has been automatically filled in, and the **Document No.** has also been automatically completed for you.

Complete the rest of the expense lines in the journal with the following details:

Account No.	Description	Amount	DEPARTMENT
8710	Production Wages	2000	PROD
8710	Sales Wages	800	SALES
2910	Cash	-4300	

Notice that the last line is the balancing line and has no dimensions attached.

All being well your **Balance** and **Total Balance** fields now show **0**.

Click the **Post** button in the **Actions** pane.

5. The system displays a prompt asking you if you really want to post the journal.

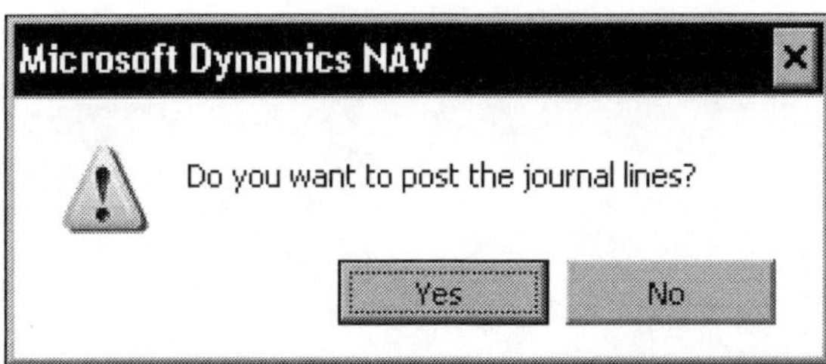

6. The journal lines were successfully posted and the exercise is complete. Close the **Edit - General Journal** page and return to the role center.

Now whenever I do something like this, the first thing I want to know is what happened. NAV provides a rather neat feature called Registers that keeps track of all the transactions that were posted together in one go. To launch the G/L Registers list place, go to **CRONUS International Ltd. | Posted Documents | G/L Registers.**

Press *Ctrl+End* to get to the last record. If you have done everything correctly, the **G/L Registers** should be displayed and the last one will have today's date as the creation date.

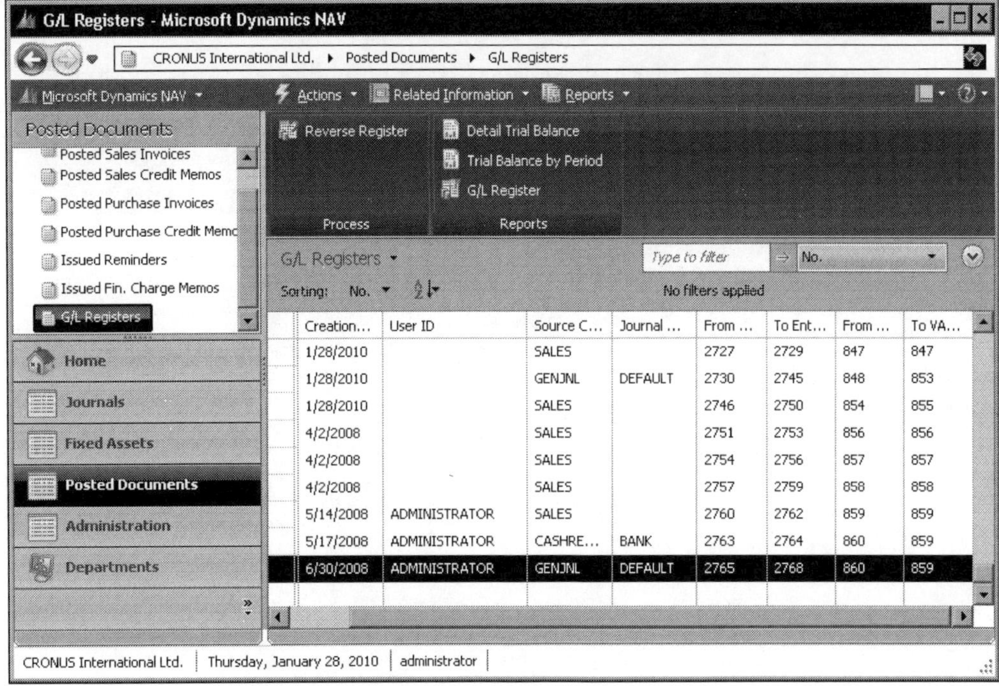

Creation...	User ID	Source C...	Journal ...	From ...	To Ent...	From ...	To VA...
1/28/2010		SALES		2727	2729	847	847
1/28/2010		GENJNL	DEFAULT	2730	2745	848	853
1/28/2010		SALES		2746	2750	854	855
4/2/2008		SALES		2751	2753	856	856
4/2/2008		SALES		2754	2756	857	857
4/2/2008		SALES		2757	2759	858	858
5/14/2008	ADMINISTRATOR	SALES		2760	2762	859	859
5/17/2008	ADMINISTRATOR	CASHRE...	BANK	2763	2764	860	859
6/30/2008	ADMINISTRATOR	GENJNL	DEFAULT	2765	2768	860	859

Click on the **Related Information** button, and from the Register menu select the **General Ledger** option. The **View - General Ledger Entries** page is displayed.

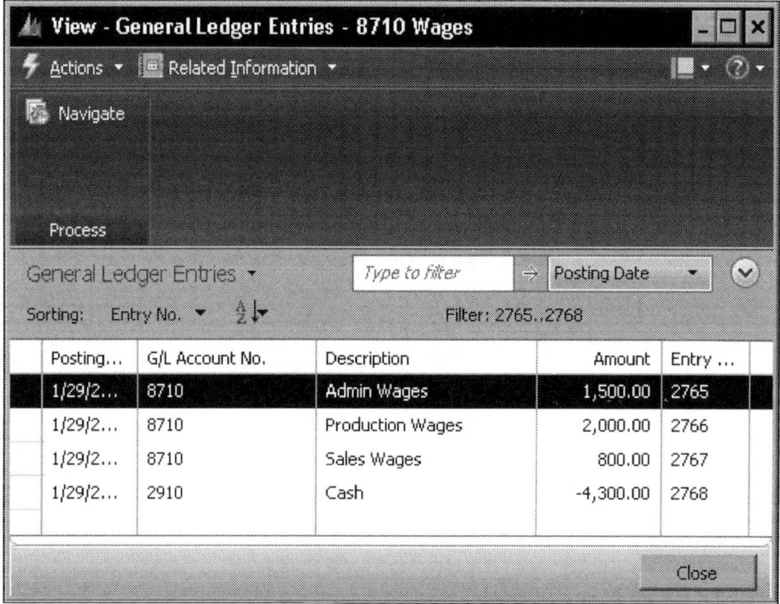

It looks a bit like the data we typed into our journal, doesn't it? Make a note of the posting date as we'll use that later on to filter our results. Tucked away behind the scenes is our dimension information. You can view that by selecting **Related Information | Entry | Dimensions**, or by pressing *Ctrl+Shift+D*.

Using dimensions to analyze financial data

If you worked through our example, you will have now posted transactions for various departments to our Wages G/L account (and a single balancing entry to the Cash account).

We've seen the direct results of our posting by looking at the registers, but let's now use the **Chart of Accounts** page itself to analyze our balances.

Go to **CRONUS International Ltd.** | **Home** | **Chart of Accounts**.

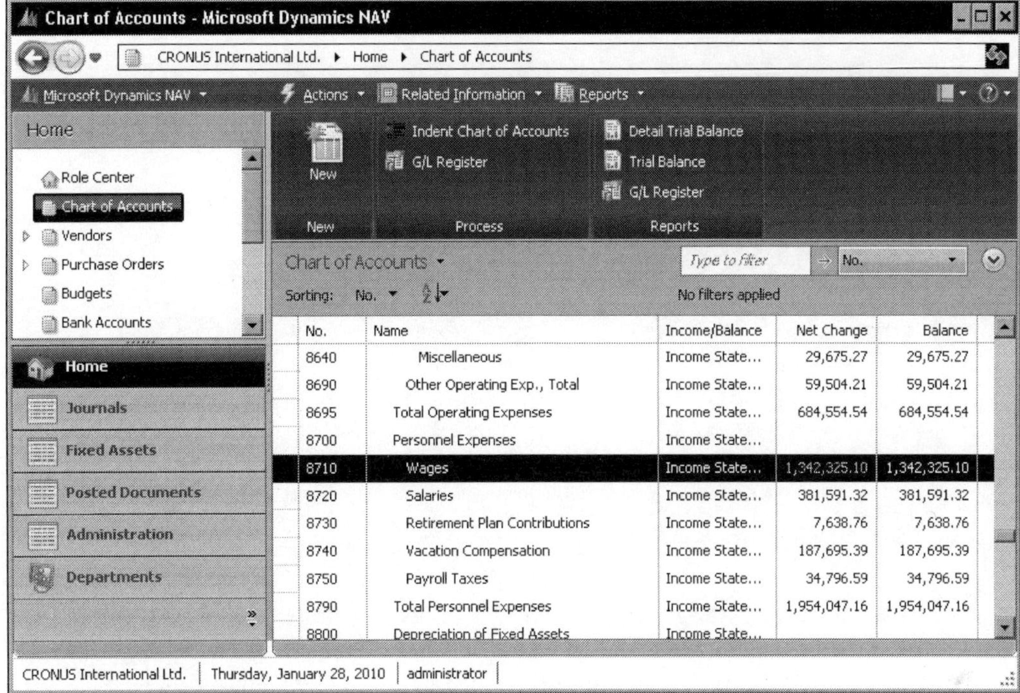

Scroll forward until the current record is shown as the **8710 Wages** account.

You may notice that the **Balance** and **Net Change** fields contain amounts considerably larger than the journal we posted. This is because the demonstration company already has transactions posted to it. To change the figures to only show the period we are interested in, click on the **Chart of Accounts** button in the filter pane and select the **Limit totals** option.

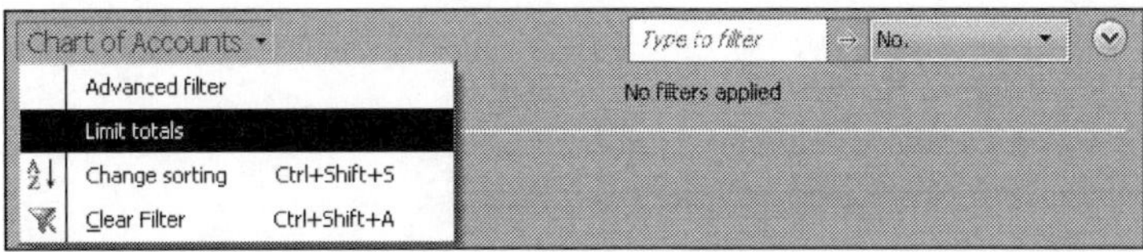

The **Limit totals** option replaces **FlowFilters** from older versions and the Classic client. The new name certainly makes it easier to understand, and the results are the same. Applying a **Limit totals** filter will filter the underlying records that are being totaled in order to show different values in certain fields on the current page. In this case we are going to filter on the **Posting Date** in order to change the value of the **Net Change** field.

Select the **Limit totals to:** filter to show the Date Filter with a value that you noted previously. You did write it down didn't you? In our demonstration company the date was **01/29/2010**.

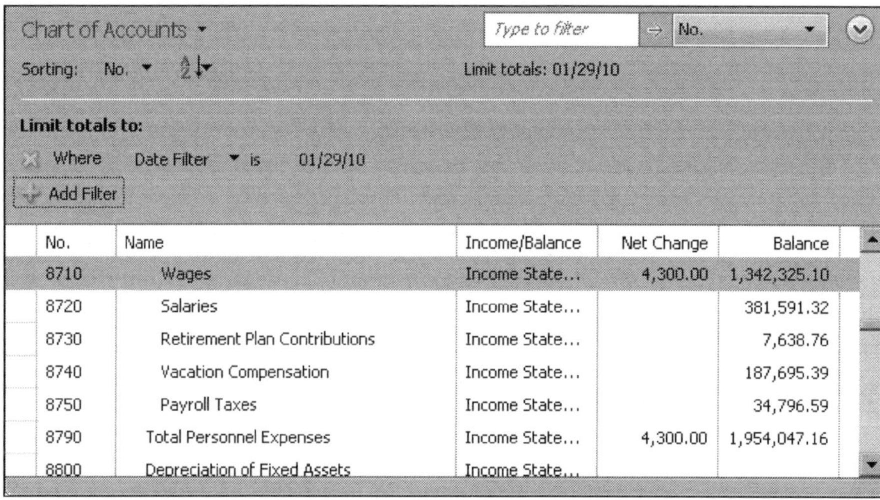

As you can see the **Net Change** now shows our expected value of **4,300**. The **Balance** field still contains a large number but that's OK. The Balance field shows the balance 'as at' the date we have entered and so it is including all of the transactions up to and including the date range we entered into the filter (in this case we entered a single date and not a 'from and to' date range.)

Click the **Add Filter** button once again, and this time add a filter for **Global Dimension 1** and use a value of **PROD**.

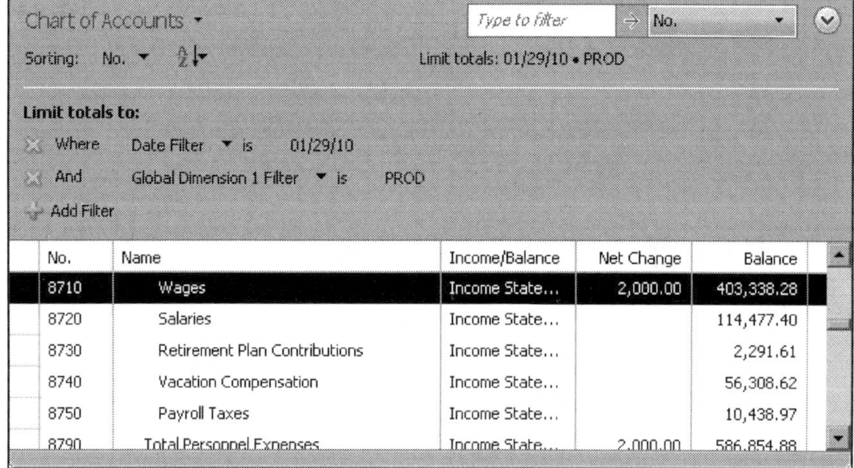

You'll see that the **Net Change** field has changed once again, but this time it is displaying the amount that we posted to the **PROD** department and not all departments.

Repeat this experiment for the different departments of 'ADM' and 'SALES' to see the values in the **Net Change** field change.

To finish off this section, let's take a look at another way of analyzing our chart of accounts data using a page called **G/L Balance by Dimension**.

From the **Chart of Accounts** list place (**CRONUS International Ltd. | Home | Chart of Accounts**), click the **Related Information** button, then select **Balance, G/L Balance by Dimension**. A new page is launched with some fields to fill in to control what data we want to display in our matrix.

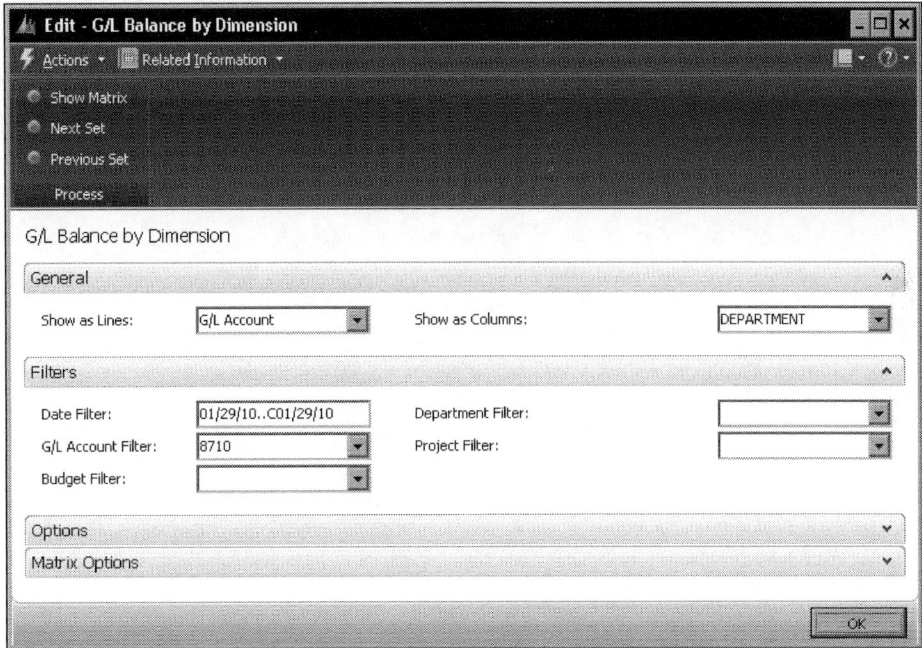

Complete the information as shown in the image on the **General** and **Filters** FastTabs so that we are showing lines as **G/L Account**, columns as **DEPARTMENT**, and we are filtering the G/L Account as **8710**. With the values filled in, click the **Show Matrix** button in the **Actions** pane.

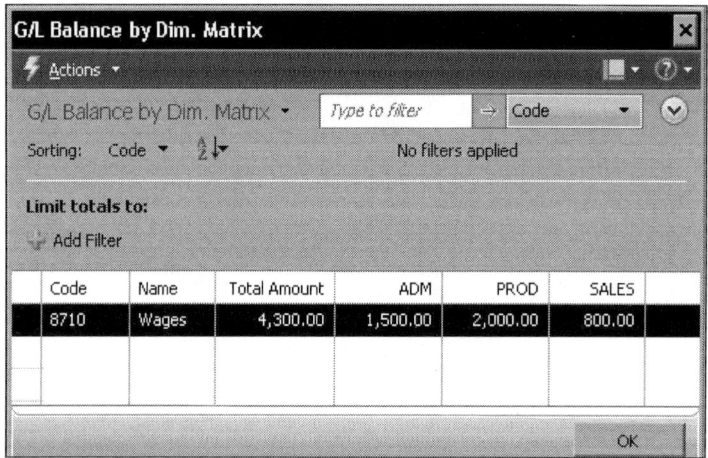

You can now see an analysis of the Wages expenses broken down by department. Notice that although we have many dimensions available to us, only two of them (**Department** and **Project**) are available on the **Filters** FastTab on the previous page. This is because in the demonstration database Department and Project are defined as Global Dimensions 1 and 2, which provides additional functionality in some areas (such as this one). When choosing your dimensions you should carefully consider which are likely to be most useful for Global Dimensions 1 and 2.

Accounting understood?

OK, so we're not going to be passing any exams with what we've learned so far but just to recap, let's take a look at what we've covered. So far you have learned:

- What the general ledger is, what dimensions are, and why accounting is governed by voodoo and not logic
- Some useful tricks for helping you to unearth the dimensions that are important to a business without unleashing a bureaucratic monster
- Why dimensions are so cool, and a few simple ways to use them to analyze financial transactions
- That no matter how many exciting hippopotami analogies there are, accounting is still pretty dull

Now it's time to take a look at how the system decides which accounts to post transactions to in the General Ledger.

Groups, groups, and more groups

In the previous section we looked at how important it is to identify your chart of accounts and dimensions when configuring your installation of Dynamics NAV. In terms of financial analysis and reporting, there is probably nothing more important. I also mentioned that a lot of the work required in setting up the 'other' parts of the system is done in order to decide how the financial information related to those other parts is collected. Well now it's time for us to grab the hippo by the ears and look at how those 'other' parts of the system are to be configured.

To begin, let's consider our purchase of toner example we used to discover dimensions in the previous section:

Susan buys some toner cartridges for a laser printer in the accounts department on July 17, 2008.

We are going to create a purchase invoice for this transaction, post it, and then look at what happened. Afterwards, I'll show you how to configure the system so that you can decide where things go when invoices are posted.

1. Start the RoleTailored client using the BookKeeper profile and go to **CRONUS International Ltd. | Home | Purchase Invoices.** Click the **New** button to create a new purchase invoice.
2. The **New - Purchase Invoice** page is displayed.

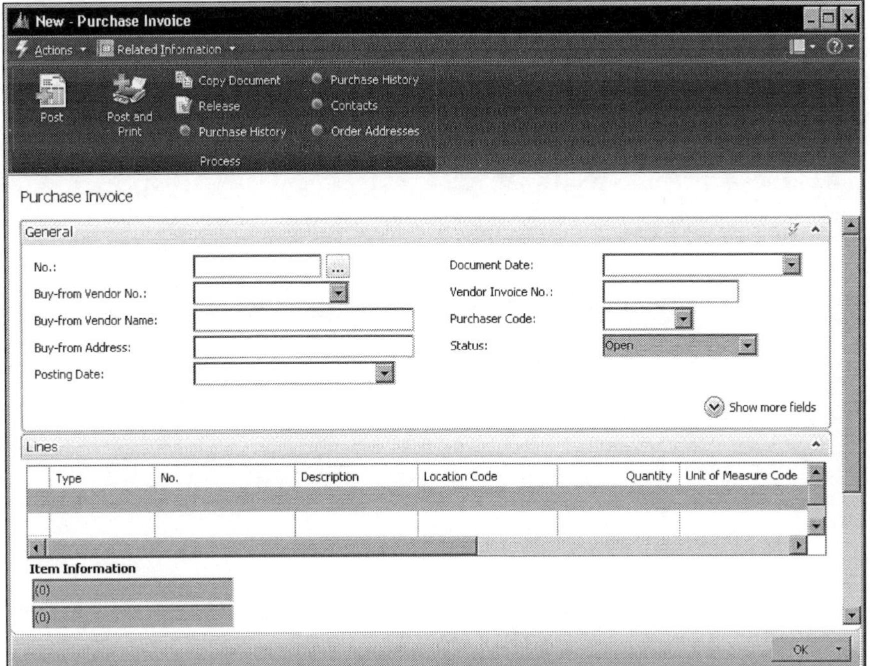

Your cursor will be in the **No.** field as the system is waiting for you to enter a new purchase invoice number. We want to take the next number from the number series, so just press *Enter*. The system will complete the purchase invoice number for you (this is just an internal number, so don't worry about it too much) and move to the next field.

Type **30000** into the **Buy-from Vendor No.** field and press *Enter*.

3. The vendor details are copied to the **General** Tab.

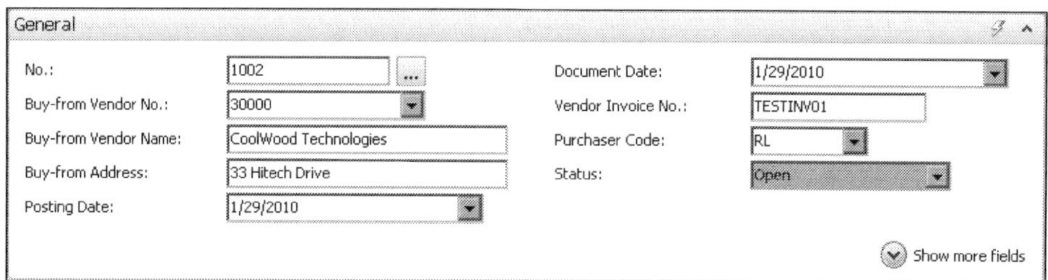

The system looked up the vendor number and copied across the name, address, and other details from the vendor card. This is good because you don't need to think about those fields on the header part of the document. The only field you'll need to fill in is the **Vendor Invoice No.** over there on the right. Just put anything in there for the time being. (For a real invoice, this is where you would enter the invoice number from the invoice document sent to you by the vendor.) Now we can enter our purchase line (the thing we bought).

Click in the **Type** field in the grid at the bottom of the form and select **G/L Account** from the available options.

4. The **Lines** FastTab is ready for you to enter details of the expense.

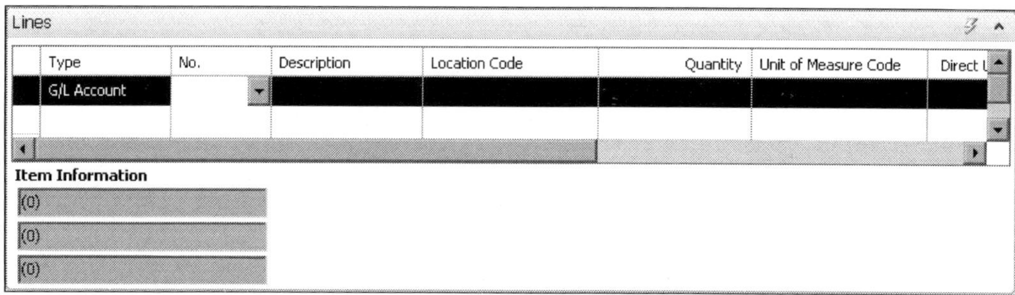

We are going to enter our toner cartridge as a G/L expense because the toner cartridge is not an inventory item, it's a consumable. Complete the line details as follows:

No.	Description	Quantity	Direct Unit Cost Excl. VAT
8210	Toner Cartridge	1	100

You'll notice that when you entered **8210** into the **No.** field, the **Description** was automatically set to **Office Supplies**. That's just the description of the particular expense account.

We've now entered enough information to be able to post the invoice. Posting is just another way of saying we want to lock the document so that it cannot be changed and transfer the financial values to the General Ledger and write entries to the other ledgers (such as the ledger that tracks the amounts we owe to our vendors).

Click the **Post** button in the **Actions** pane.

5. The system prompts to ensure you really want to post the invoice.

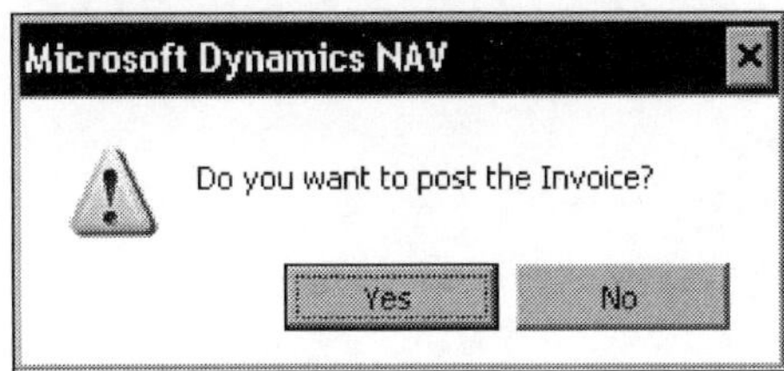

6. The exercise is now complete.

From our previous discussions on expenses and the G/L we could safely expect that the transaction we created would create a debit (positive) transaction for 100 dollars against our Office Supplies expense account. We know that according to our double-entry book-keeping rules, there must be an opposite entry somewhere—but where?

First of all let's take a look at what actually got posted to see if our guessing is right.

Go to **CRONUS International Ltd. | Posted Documents | Posted Purchase Invoices.** The Posted Purchase Invoices list place is displayed, although the list is probably not showing the invoice you posted, you can press *Ctrl+End* to get to the last record in the list.

If you double-click the record, you'll see the **Posted Purchase Invoice** document page. Notice that the posted invoice looks just like the invoice we just keyed except that we cannot edit any of the fields. Now we want to see what the results of posting the invoice are. Return to the list place and click on the **Navigate** button.

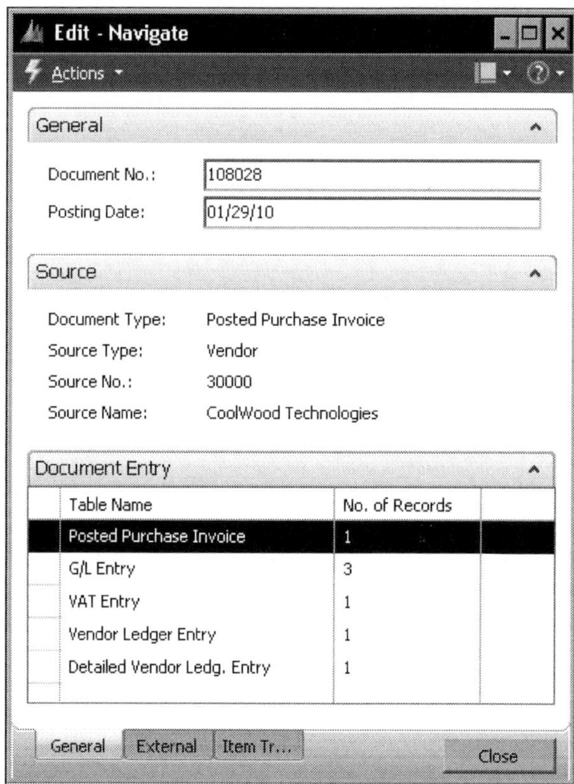

The **Navigate** page shows all of the different ledger entries that were created in relation to the **Document No.** and **Posting Date** you selected. In this case we can see one **Posted Purchase Invoice** (this is where we started), three **G/L** entries, one **VAT** Entry, one **Vendor Ledger Entry**, and one **Detailed Vendor Ledg. Entry**. Phew—what a lot of entries! Where did they all come from?

We know all about the **Posted Purchase Invoice** because we created it ourselves by keying in a purchase invoice and then posting it, but what about the other entries? Let's look at each of the types in turn.

G/L entry

The Navigate page allows us to drill down to show the underlying transactions that have been counted, so to see the G/L entries, click on the number **3** in the **No. of Records** field to the side of the **G/L Entry** table name. Alternatively, you could have selected the **G/L Entry** line and selected **Show** from the action pane or **Actions** menu.

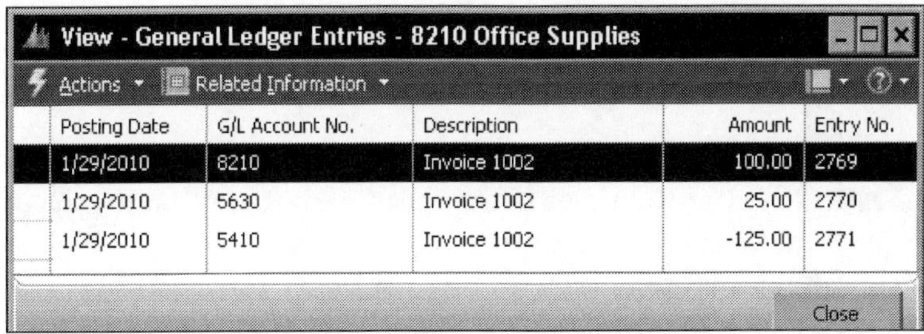

We have three lines in the **General Ledger Entries** page. The first line is recognizable as the line we entered on the purchase invoice. The **G/L Account** is **8210 (Office Supplies)**, and the **Amount** is **100** dollars. This is the one entry that we could have guessed would be there. The next entry down is for VAT—to see the account name for the G/L Account you can click on the line and look at the title bar of the window. In the picture shown, the title of the window shows **8210 Office Supplies**. When you click on the second line, the title changes to show **5630 Purchase VAT 25%**.

To find out more details about this G/L Account, go to **CRONUS International Ltd. | Home | Chart of Accounts** and do a quick filter on **No.** to show the **5630** account.

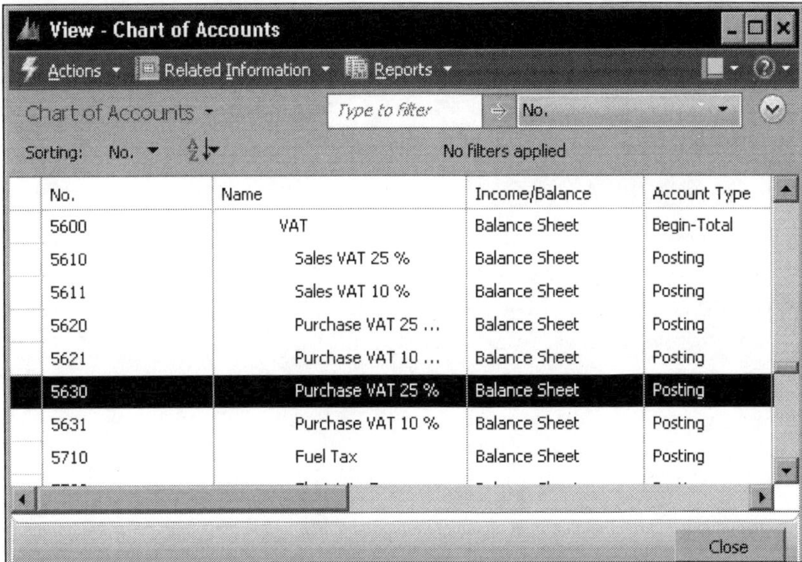

We can see this is a **Balance Sheet** account, and if we scroll further down we can see it is included in the **Total Liabilities** section of our chart of accounts. A liability is something we owe, and its normal posting is a credit (which is a negative number), but we are going to pay the tax to the vendor when we pay for the invoice they send us, which means we can offset the tax against the tax that we collect for the tax man when customers pay our invoices. For this reason the entry is a debit (positive), which will decrease the balance in a liability account. In other words, we are reducing the amount of tax we owe to the tax man by paying the tax part of the invoice to the vendor (who is then responsible for paying it to the tax man.)

Click on the final line with the **-125.00** dollar amount and you will see account **5410 Vendors, Domestic**. If you find this account again, you'll see that the account is a **Balance Sheet** account, and it is within the **Accounts Payable** section of the **Total Liabilities**. Normally we call this the vendor control account. It is the account that tells us how much we owe to our vendors, and we must be able to reconcile this balance to the open transactions in our vendor ledger.

It is the G/L Entries that we are really interested in, and in particular we want to discover where the accounts for the Tax and Accounts Payable came from, so we'll come back to the G/L entries after first considering the other types of ledger entries attached to this transaction.

VAT entry

Depending on what tax rules you have in your country, you are going to need to submit a tax return at some point in time. You could probably figure out the details you need for your tax return from the G/L entries, and I have worked with ERP systems that use this technique. Thankfully, Dynamics NAV has the **VAT Entries** table which makes the process of calculating and posting your tax settlement a lot easier.

Vendor ledger entry

The vendor ledger entry is principally used to tell you how much you owe to the vendor. If you think of your account statement with the vendor, this is a charge that you have to pay. When you add together the remaining amount of all your vendor ledger entries, you have your vendor account balance.

Detailed vendor ledger entry

If the vendor ledger entry tells me how much I owe the vendor, then what on earth is the detailed vendor ledger entry there for? There are some things that can change the amount of money you owe on a vendor invoice. If the invoice is in a foreign currency, then the fluctuating exchange rates can mean the actual amount owing will also change. It would be a bit scary if the amount could simply fluctuate and you had no idea why. This is where the detailed vendor ledger entries come in. Every time the amount on the vendor ledger entry changes, a detailed vendor ledger entry is written to provide an audit. These entries can be created for early settlement discounts (money off for paying early), fluctuations in exchange rates for foreign currency invoices, rounding amounts for settlements, and foreign currency rounding.

G/L entries revisited

OK, so now we have looked at the entries that got created during the posting, let's go back to those pesky G/L entries and find out why the system created the entries it did.

We have already worked out our first entry—it's what you keyed in on the invoice line, so let's not even consider that. The next easiest one to figure out is the vendor control account 5410 Vendors, Domestic. The fact that the vendor control account 5410 is set amongst a handful of other vendor control accounts should convince you that it must be possible to link the account to be used as the vendor control account to the vendor record in some way. This linking of G/L accounts and sub-ledger accounts in Dynamics NAV is done through groups, and for the vendor control account, we use the vendor posting group.

Vendor posting group

When we posted our sample invoice, we posted it to the vendor account 30000, which is CoolWood Technologies in the demo company. If you open this vendor card (you can go to **CRONUS International Ltd.** | **Home** | **Vendors** and then fast filter on account number 30000, then double-click the record to open it) you will see that the **Invoicing** FastTab shows a number of different groups. Let's not worry about the first three groups for the moment—we'll get to those later.

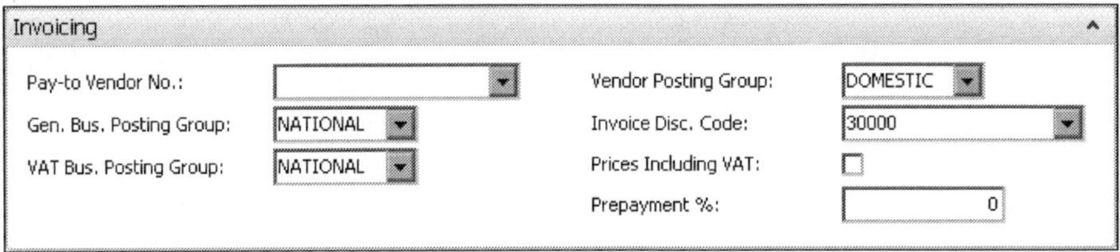

You can see the **Vendor Posting Group** is set to **DOMESTIC**. If you click on the drop-down button to the right of the field, you will see a list of vendor posting groups. Click the **Advanced** button to display the **Vendor Posting Groups** page.

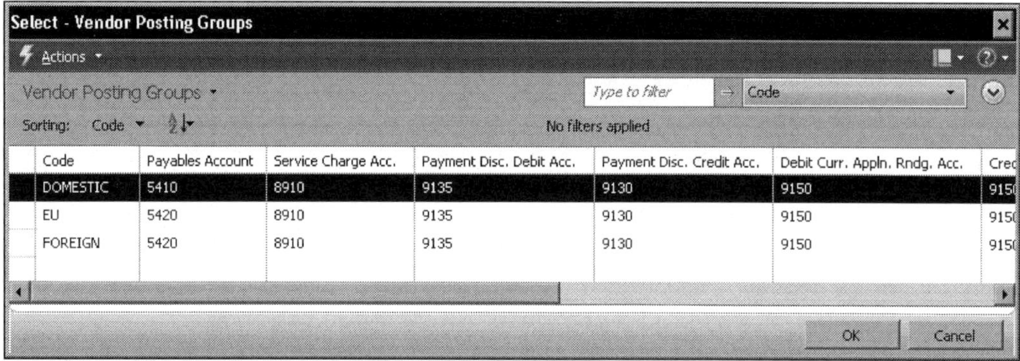

Once you have picked yourself up off the floor from the shock of seeing so many accounts, take a look at the second column on the screen. The **Payables Account** contains our trusty **5410** account, so this is the answer to why the system decided to post the transaction there. I'm going to go through all of these account settings later on (there are eleven in total) and tell you what they are used for, but that's a topic for another day, and I recommend you prepare yourself with a good stiff drink (or two) before trying to go through them all.

VAT Bus. Posting Group and VAT Prod. Posting Group

Now we're getting to the nitty gritty—the point where most users consider batting their head against the nearest hard vertical surface. In order to figure out where to put the VAT entry, the system is going to use not one but two posting groups. These two groups form a kind of matrix, but you won't find any PVC-clad pistol-toting ladies or Kung Fu action in this matrix. Oh no! This matrix is there to confuse and confound you (actually a bit like the end of *The Matrix Revolutions*).

What is the matrix?

Apart from being one of my all-time favorite movies (see `http://whatisthematrix.warnerbros.com/`), a matrix is commonly used in NAV to show information that relates to two different categories, similar to the way Excel displays a pivot table.

In our example, the VAT is dependent on two things: what you are buying, and who you are buying it from. The same applies for sales as well: what you are selling, and who you are selling it to.

These *what* and *who* attributes are handled by the two groups: **VAT Prod. Posting Group** tells us what category of product we are buying and the **VAT Bus. Posting Group** tells us who we are buying from.

If you look at the **Invoicing** FastTab on the vendor card, you will see that the **VAT Bus. Posting Group** is set to **NATIONAL**. The **VAT Prod. Posting Group** is nowhere to be seen. That's because it relates to the *what* and not the *who*. So what did we buy? We bought some toner. How does the system know what we bought? We coded it to a G/L Expense account for Office supplies (8210). Let's take a look at the G/L account to see if there is any mention of VAT.

Go to **CRONUS International Ltd. | Home | Chart of Accounts**, find the account with Code **8210** and double-click to open the **G/L Account Card**.

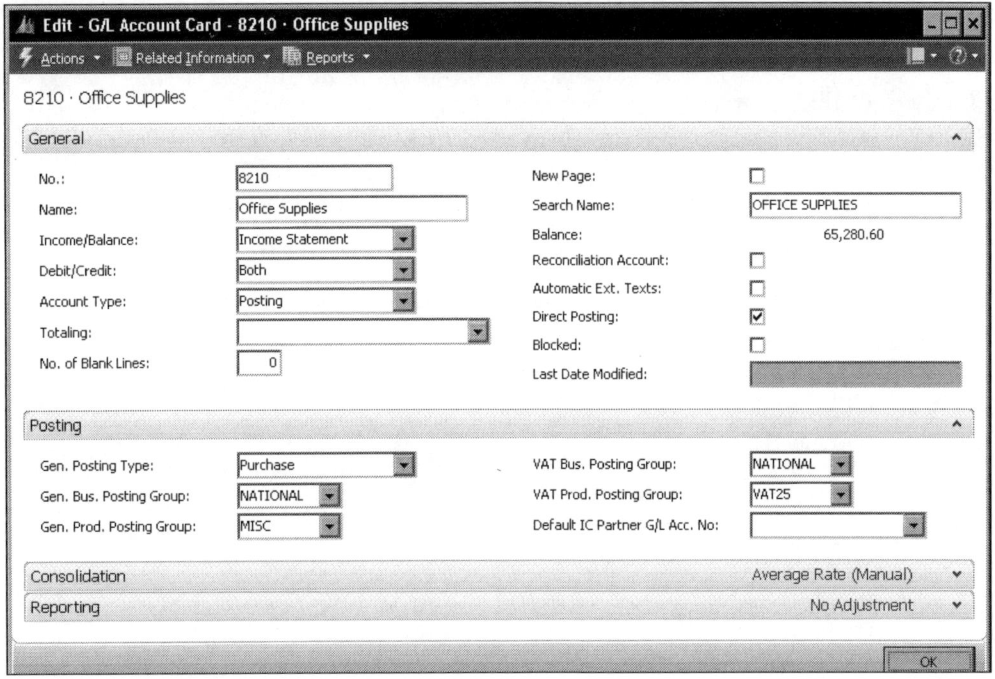

If you take a look on the **Posting** FastTab, you will see the **VAT Prod. Posting Group** is set to **VAT25**. Now it's time to enter the matrix. Click on the **Related Information** button and select **VAT Posting Setup**.

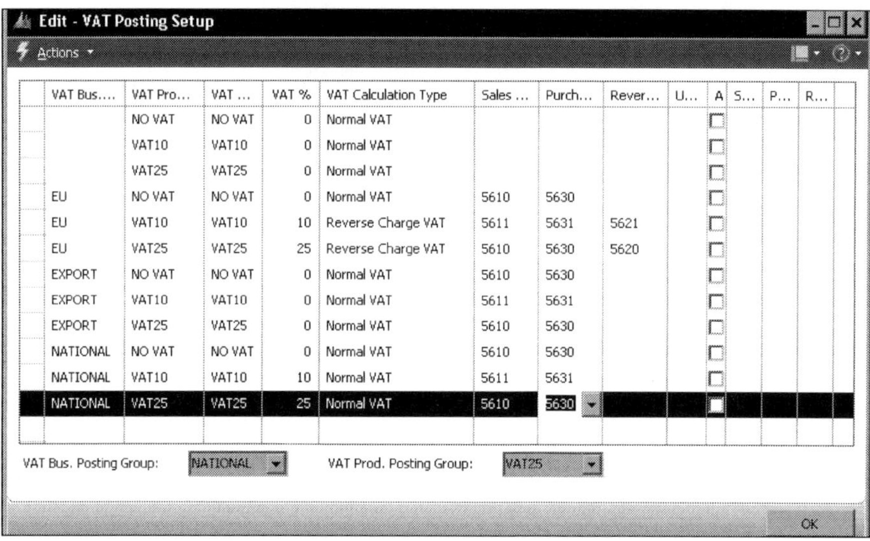

What a scary screen. I decided to show some of the columns that are normally hidden to add to the fear factor. First of all, look for the account we are interested in and try to ignore the rest. We are looking at the **Purchase VAT Account** because this is where the VAT amount for purchases is going to be posted.

Not only does this setup screen tell us to use G/L account **5630** for the **NATIONAL**, **VAT25** combination, but it also tells us to use **25** as the **VAT %** rate to calculate the tax.

Wow, we've figured out where all of our G/L entries came from. Let's recap:

G/L Account	Account Name	Debit Amount	Credit Amount	Reason for Account Selection
8210	Office Supplies	100.00		We keyed it in to the invoice.
5630	Purchase VAT 25%	25.00		The combination of the **VAT Bus. Posting Group** from the vendor card, the **VAT Prod. Posting Group** from the G/L Expense Account, and the fact that this is a **Purchase** transaction.
5410	Vendors, Domestic		125.00	The **Payables Account** field for the **Vendor Posting Group** that is specified on the vendor card.

It's time to take a deep breath because there are other groups to discover.

More groups

Let's create another invoice. We want one that is the same as our previous example, so we're going to use the copy document feature.

1. Start the RoleTailored client using the BookKeeper profile and go to **CRONUS International Ltd.** | **Home** | **Purchase Invoices**. Click the **New** button to create a new purchase invoice.
2. The **New - Purchase Invoice** page is displayed.

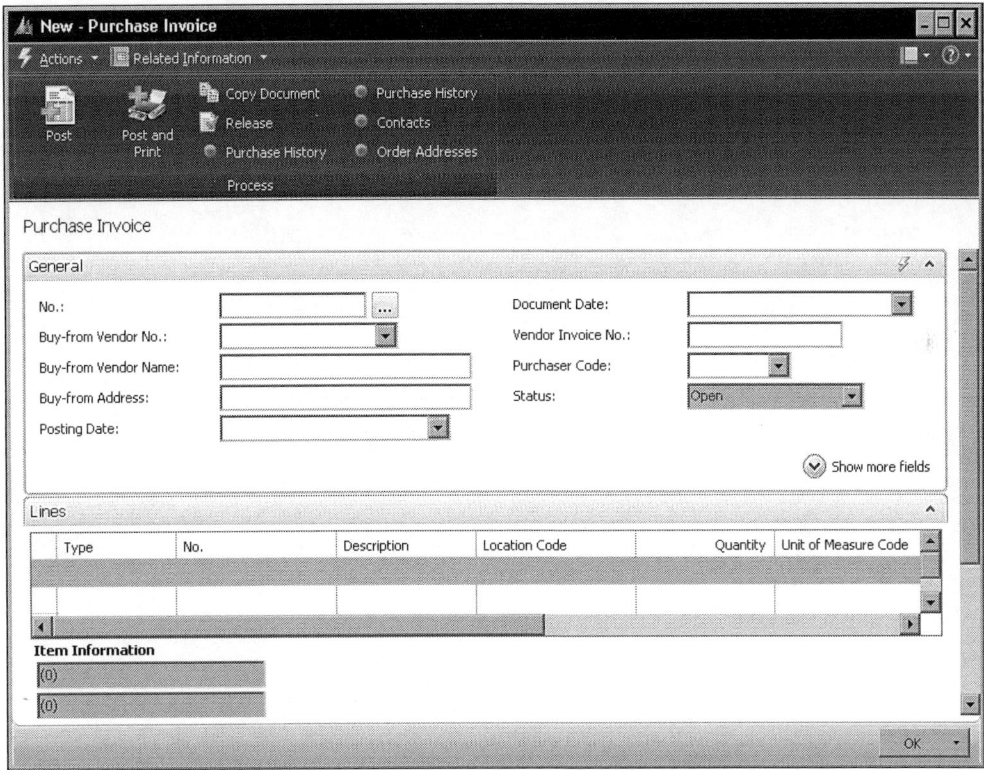

Your cursor will be in the **No.** field as the system is waiting for you to enter a new purchase invoice number. As in the last exercise, we want to take the next number from the number series so just press *Enter*.

Click the **Copy Document** button in the **Actions** pane.

3. The **Copy Purchase Document** page is displayed.

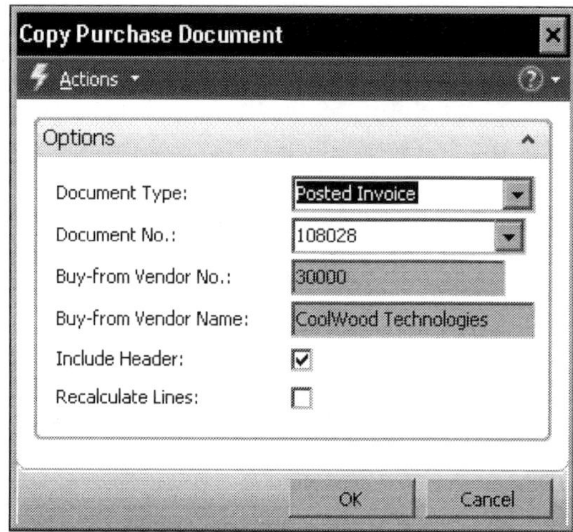

Change the **Document Type** to **Posted Invoice**, and use the drop-down button to select the posted purchase invoice from our previous example. Tick the **Include Header** box, and press the **OK** button.

4. The invoice details are copied to our new invoice.

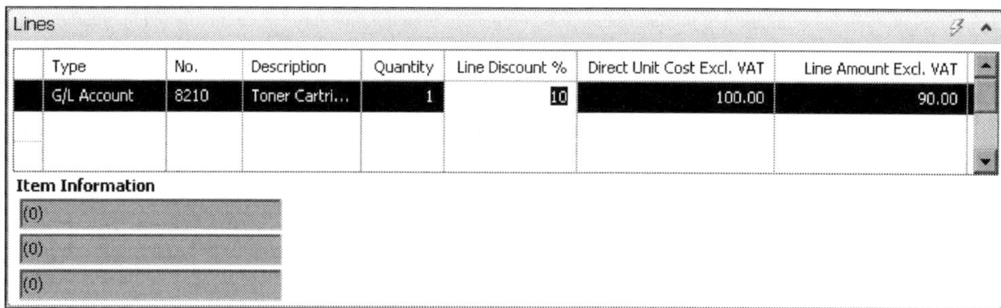

Because we are nice guys, our vendor has offered a 10% discount on this order, so on the purchase line, key **10** into the **Line Discount** % field.

If you try to post this invoice now, you'll get an error message telling you that the vendor invoice number has already been used for this vendor. It's good to know the system is looking out for us. Change the **Vendor Invoice No.** field to a different value, and press *F9* to post the invoice (or click the **Post** button).

Select **Yes** when asked if you want to post the invoice.

5. The exercise is now complete.

You should know the drill now; we want to find the G/L entries that were created by posting this invoice. This time we'll use the Registers feature of Dynamics NAV. Go to **CRONUS International Ltd. | Posted Documents | G/L Registers.**

Find the last record by pressing *Ctrl+End* and click the **Related Information** menu and select the **Register | General Ledger** menu option. The G/L entries that relate to our new invoice are displayed:

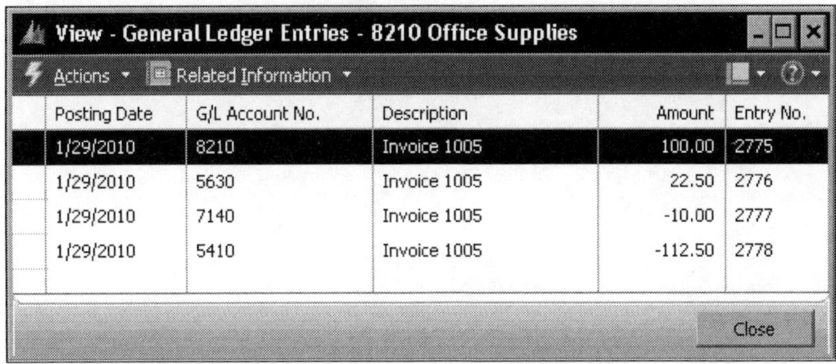

Posting Date	G/L Account No.	Description	Amount	Entry No.
1/29/2010	8210	Invoice 1005	100.00	2775
1/29/2010	5630	Invoice 1005	22.50	2776
1/29/2010	7140	Invoice 1005	-10.00	2777
1/29/2010	5410	Invoice 1005	-112.50	2778

Although the amounts are different for the transactions, most of these lines are the same as in our previous example, but now we have an additional line. The third line down has a posting of **-10** dollars to account **7140**. Click on the line and you'll see the title of the window change to show that this is the **Disc. Received, Retail Account**.

We knew that the system would need to do something with the **10%** discount we entered against the line but how did it decide to put the discount to account 7140?

We can make a good guess that the account selection has something to do with the vendor and the G/L account we selected on the invoice line. Let's start by looking at the **Invoicing** FastTab on the vendor card.

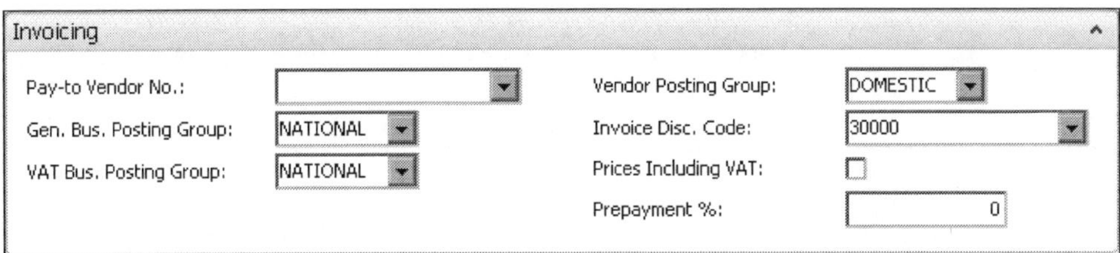

The first posting group shows a **Gen. Bus. Posting Group** of **NATIONAL**. This is the general business posting group for the vendor. It works in a similar way to the **VAT Bus. Posting Group** we looked at earlier in our investigation of the VAT account. Click the drop-down button to the right of the field, and click the **Advanced** button.

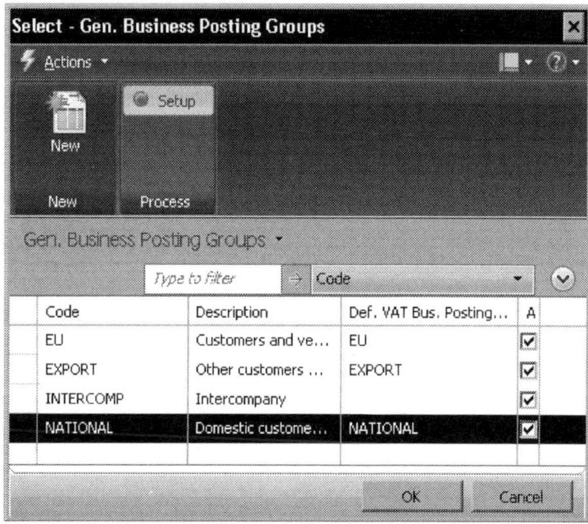

Notice the **Setup** button lurking at the top of the screen. Click this button to reveal probably the scariest setup screen in the entire system.

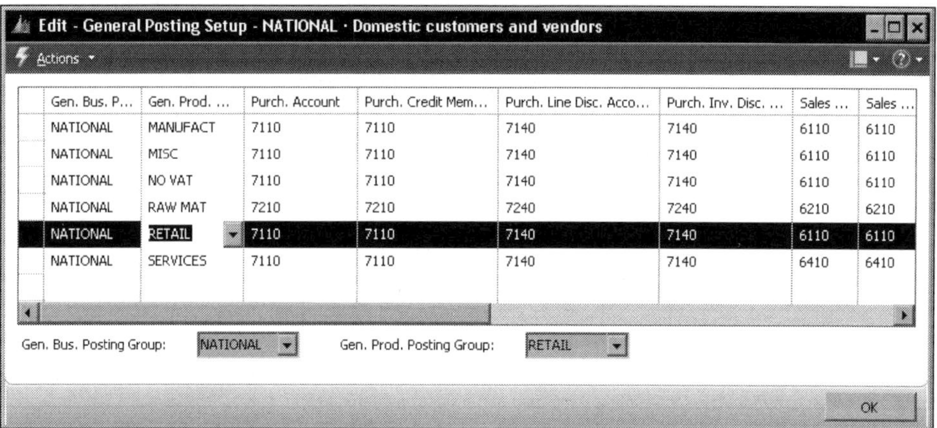

It's another one of those screens that shows one line for each combination of the two fields **Gen. Bus. Posting Group** and **Gen. Prod. Posting Group**. We can probably guess that the **Gen. Prod. Posting Group** we are interested in is the **RETAIL** group (as our discount got posted to a retail discount account), but we don't need to guess do we? Find the **8210** G/L account, and take a look on the **Posting** FastTab.

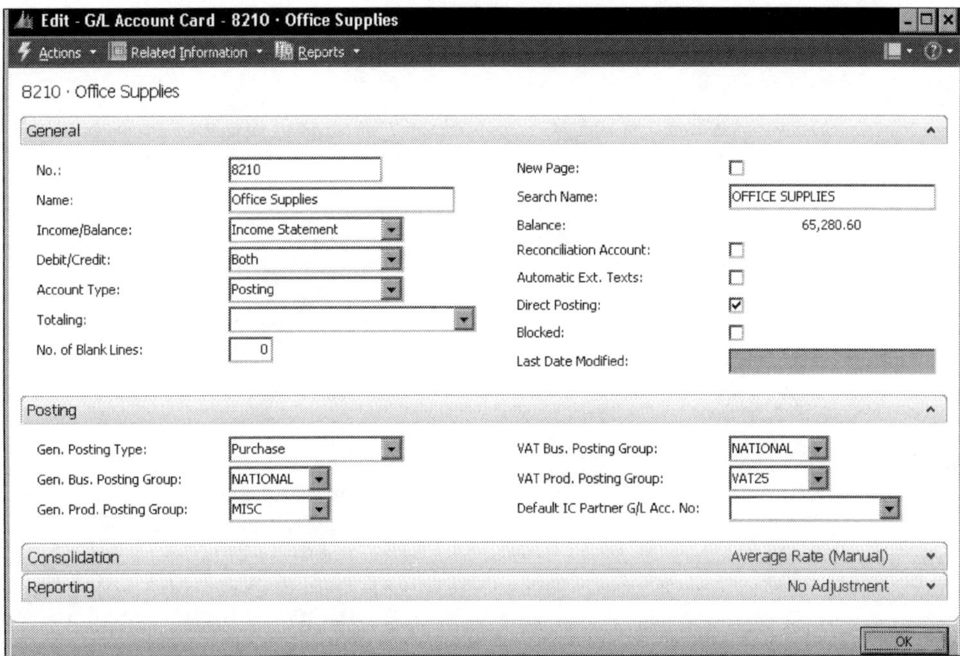

You can see that the **Gen. Prod. Posting Group** is **MISC**. Oops—it's not **RETAIL** as I predicted—this is why you don't guess: if you don't know, find out.

So now that we know our combination of general business and general product posting groups, we can go back to our posting setup form. Look for the line with **NATIONAL** and **MISC** and scroll over to the right. One of the many accounts shown on this setup screen is called **Purch. Line. Disc. Account**.

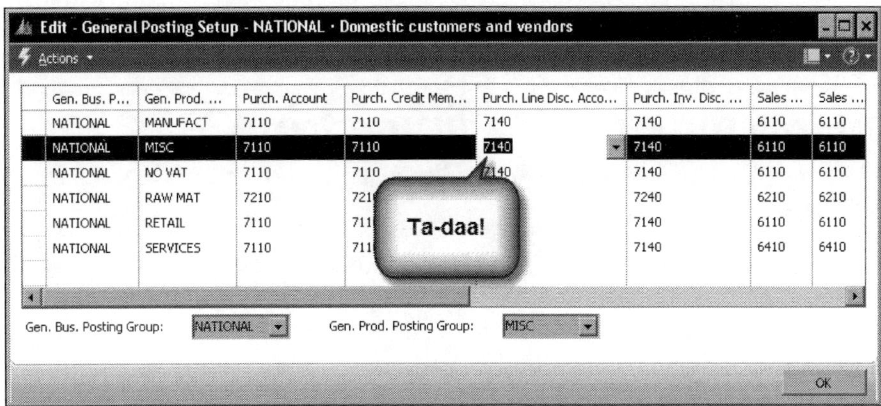

Hey look, it's **7140**, that's our account! I feel like a magician pulling the correct card from the deck.

Let's put all our entries together with the reasons for account selection:

G/L Account	Account Name	Debit Amount	Credit Amount	Reason for Account Selection
8210	Office Supplies	100.00		We keyed it in to the invoice.
5630	Purchase VAT 25%	22.50		The combination of the **GST Bus. Posting Group** from the vendor card, the **GST Prod. Posting Group** from the G/L expense account, and the fact that this is a purchase transaction.
7140	Disc. Received, Retail		10.00	The combination of the **Gen. Bus. Posting Group** from the vendor card, the **Gen. Prod. Posting Group** from the G/L expense account, and the fact that this is the amount of line discount on a purchase.
5410	Vendors, Domestic		112.50	The **Payables Account** field for the **Vendor Posting Group** that is specified on the vendor card.

As you can see, the posting groups used in Dynamics NAV give you incredible flexibility for capturing your financial information in the General Ledger. Hopefully, you can see that the planning of your chart of accounts and your posting groups go hand in hand. You should understand the posting groups and what they can do for you, and the additional analysis capabilities you will get from using dimensions before you draft your chart of accounts.

Where do dimensions come from?

Well, a Mummy Dimension and a Daddy Dimension, who love each other very much, get certain urges...

We've seen where the system gets the G/L account code from, but so far the only dimensions we have seen are those that are keyed in on a journal line. There is a better way to get the dimensions on to the posted ledger entries, and now that we understand some of the fundamentals, we can delve a little deeper.

There are actually five main types of dimensions, and in our previous section we covered two of them: journal line dimensions and ledger entry dimensions. The other main types are default dimensions, document dimensions, and posted document dimensions. The following diagram shows the basic flow between the different dimension types.

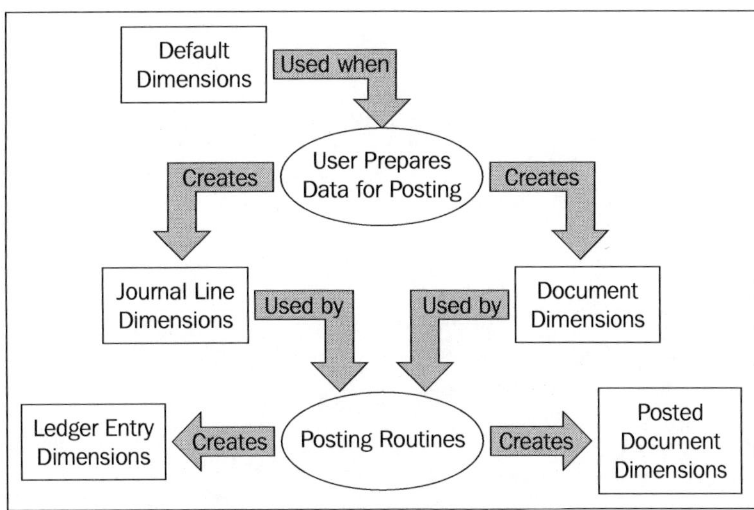

Understanding this flow of information is going to get us through a lot of scenarios and, as far as system configuration is concerned, it is the **Default Dimensions** we need to concentrate on. There is always the option for the user to key in the dimensions they want to use when preparing the data (as we did in our previous example), but for now we'll look at how the default dimensions can be used to automatically populate the dimensions.

We can set default dimensions against master card type records such as customer, vendor, or item. Here is a complete list of the tables that can have default dimensions specified against them.

Table ID	Table Name
13	Salesperson/Purchaser
15	G/L Account
18	Customer
23	Vendor
27	Item
152	Resource Group
156	Resource

Table ID	Table Name
167	Job
270	Bank Account
413	IC Partner
5071	Campaign
5105	Customer Template
5200	Employee
5600	Fixed Asset
5628	Insurance
5714	Responsibility Center
5800	Item Charge
5903	Service Order Type
5904	Service Item Group
5940	Service Item
5965	Service Contract Header
5968	Service Contract Template
99000754	Work Center

When a user of the system is preparing data for posting (creating a journal or keying in a document such as a sales order or purchase order), the system will use the default dimension to copy the default dimension values to the un-posted document, document line, or journal line. This can save a lot of time when entering data, and can also ensure that where you require a particular dimension to always be used for a given transaction concerning a master record, this can be configured.

There are occasions when the data being entered can relate to more than one of the master records. For example, consider a sales order that has a customer and a salesperson, and a sales line that has an item. Now there is no good reason I can think of to have the same dimension specified on all three of these master records, but what if that were the case? How would the system resolve this conflict?

Fortunately there is an option called **Default Dimension Priorities** that can resolve this. For each of the various source codes in the system, you can specify the priority for default dimensions for all of the tables with which you believe you may have conflicts.

If you take a look at **Financial Management | Setup, Dimensions | Default Dimension Priorities** in the Classic client, and select the **SALES** source code, you will see the following.

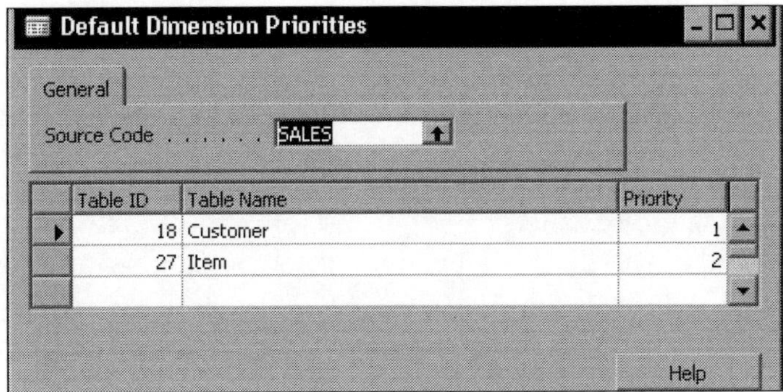

The screen shows that when preparing data that uses the **SALES** source code, the default dimensions that are attached to the **Customer** table will take priority over those on the **Item** table.

RIM

Dynamics NAV is a big product and there's a lot to configure; we've looked at how to determine some of the financial setup but there's an awful lot more to do. Thankfully, the nice people at Microsoft have made life easier for us by creating a **Rapid Implementation Methodology (RIM)** toolkit that takes away some (but not all) of the pain of configuring the system.

Every implementation requires the same basic steps to get the system ready for use. The RIM Toolkit provides an easy way to get things going quickly, and also allows the customer to do a lot of the configuration work for themselves. You can find the Dynamics NAV RIM Users Guide 2.0 in the `Documention\Application Guides` directory of the product DVD. The toolkit comprises the following:

- A Microsoft Project (mpp) project plan for a RIM implementation of Dynamics NAV
- A set of industry-specific XML files that contain:
    - Standard configuration data such as: Currencies, Posting Groups, Setup Tables, Countries, and so on
    - A series of setup questionnaire questions that will help you configure the setup data
    - A set of data templates to help you quickly create master data records with default values pre-filled

- NAV forms and programs to help you prepare, and import XML files for setup data (questionnaire answers)
- NAV data migration forms and programs to help you prepare and import master data (such as G/L accounts, customer accounts, vendor accounts, and so on)

Now hold on a second, if the RIM Toolkit contains the posting groups and posting group setup tables, why on earth did we spend so much time discussing finance and posting groups? Why can't we just use the RIM Toolkit? Well, the RIM Toolkit will create the posting groups and posting group setup records for you, but your chart of accounts and the accounts that go in to those posting group records must be completed by you. Capisce? The RIM Toolkit will make your life easier but you still have work to do.

You can, of course, decide to ignore this tool and carry on configuring the system the 'old way', by going through each of the setup screens with the user and asking them how they want the values to be set, writing dataports to read in data, and creating a document with details of what has been agreed, but why would you? We'll take a look at what the RIM Toolkit does for you, and by the time we have finished, I'm sure you'll be convinced that this is definitely the way to go.

The setup questionnaire

To understand why the setup questionnaire is good, you need to understand how you would configure the system without it.

There are twenty-eight setup tables in NAV (set a filter on the table name in the Object Designer to look for names with setup to see what I mean) although it is unlikely you would ever need to configure every one as this would require you to use Financials, Sales, Purchasing, Inventory, Job Costing, Relationship Management, Human Resources, Manufacturing, Fixed Assets, Warehousing, Service Management, Employee Portal, Business Notifications, Mobile Sales, and Commerce Gateway, all within the same implementation.

Let's take just one of these areas and see how you would configure the system if you were not using RIM.

General Ledger setup (before RIM)

In the before-RIM configuration process, you needed:

- An installation of NAV
- A consultant with enough knowledge to lead the process
- At least one decision maker from the company being configured

In reality, rather than one decision maker you'll have a room full of users (or at least a handful) in order to complete this configuration workshop.

The consultant will start by explaining the process and will then launch the **General Ledger Setup** page by selecting **CRONUS International Ltd.** | **Departments** | **Administration** | **Application Setup** | **Financial Management** | **Finance** | **Tasks** | **General Ledger Setup**.

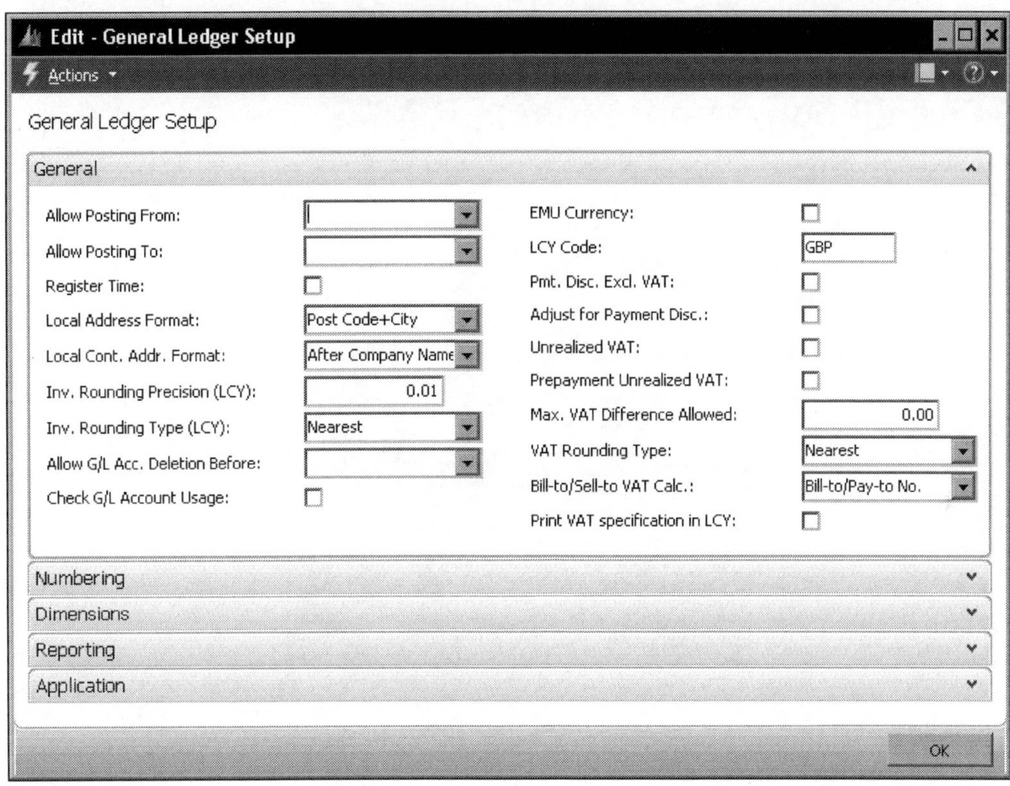

The consultant will then patiently go through each of the fields on each of the tabs on the setup form and explain what the field is used for, and get the users to decide on a suitable value.

If the consultant isn't entirely sure of the meaning of the field, she or he can try to use the online help to describe the field in more detail. On occasions the online help is not sufficient to determine the purpose and so the consultant is forced to do a bit of preparation.

Any fields that cannot be decided upon will be noted down, so the consultant can follow up or answer more questions at a later date. This process needs to be repeated for each of the setup tables that cover the application areas that are in scope for the new installation.

This method of configuration requires the attention of a lot of people; it is time-consuming and is therefore expensive. The process does not produce documentation automatically and so, if documentation of the agreed configuration is required, there is even more work to do following the session.

General Ledger setup (using RIM)

The RIM configuration of the General Ledger (and all other setup tables) can be done by the users themselves using Excel. No NAV installation is needed, no NAV consultant required, the users decide among themselves on the settings and send the results back via email. The configuration will typically follow the following process:

1. Start the Classic client and select **File** | **Company** | **New**.
2. The **New Company** window is displayed.

   Type the new company name and click **OK**.

3. The System creates the tables for the new company, initializes some data, and then displays the **Company Setup** prompt.

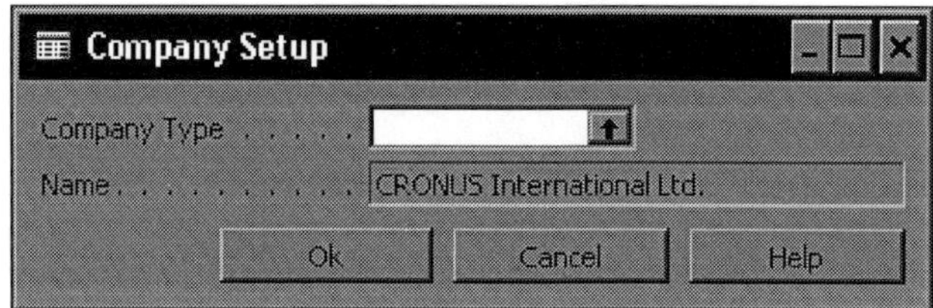

   Click the **Company Type** look-up button.

4. The **Company Type Selection** form is displayed.

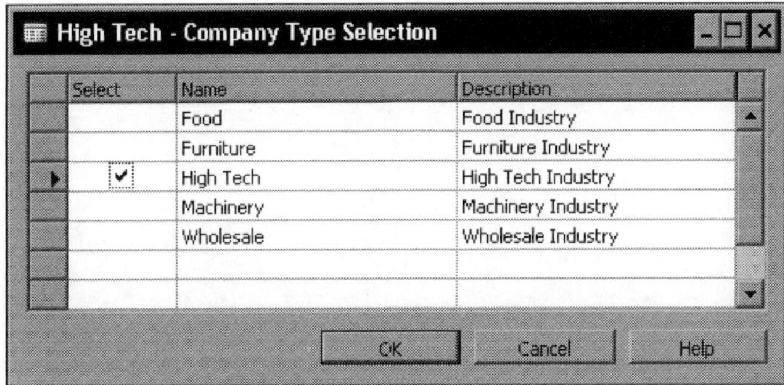

Place a check mark against the company type that has the configuration that most closely resembles the company you are configuring and click **OK**.

5. The **Company Setup** window is displayed with the **High Tech** company type selected.

Click **OK** to continue with the configuration.

6. The system imports the data from the XML file related to the **Company Type** selected, validates it, and inserts it into the NAV tables.

If all goes well, the success message is displayed.

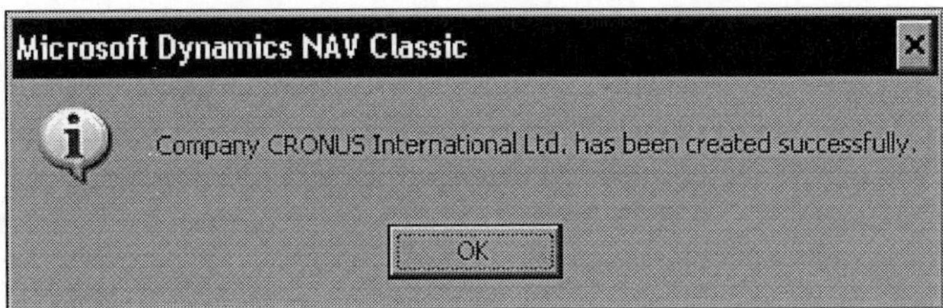

Click **OK**.

7. The exercise is complete.

The company creation process is only possible in the Classic client; as we're in the Classic client we'll use it to generate the Excel spreadsheet to give to the customer.

1. Select **Administration | Application Setup | Company Setup | Setup Questionnaire**.
2. The **Setup Questionnaire** form is displayed.

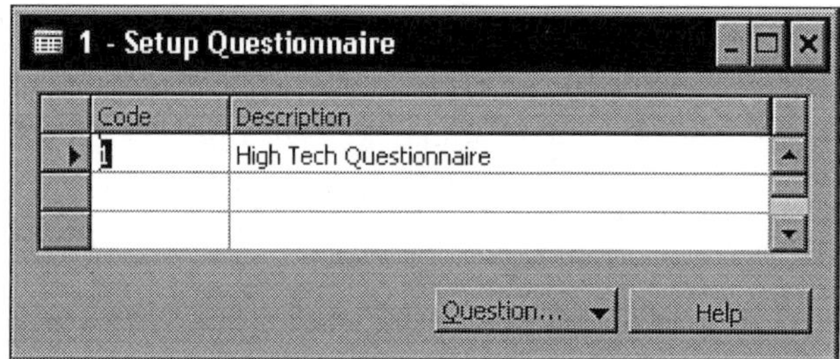

Click the **Questionnaire** menu button and select the **Export to Excel** option.

3. The **Save as Excel Workbook** file requester is displayed.

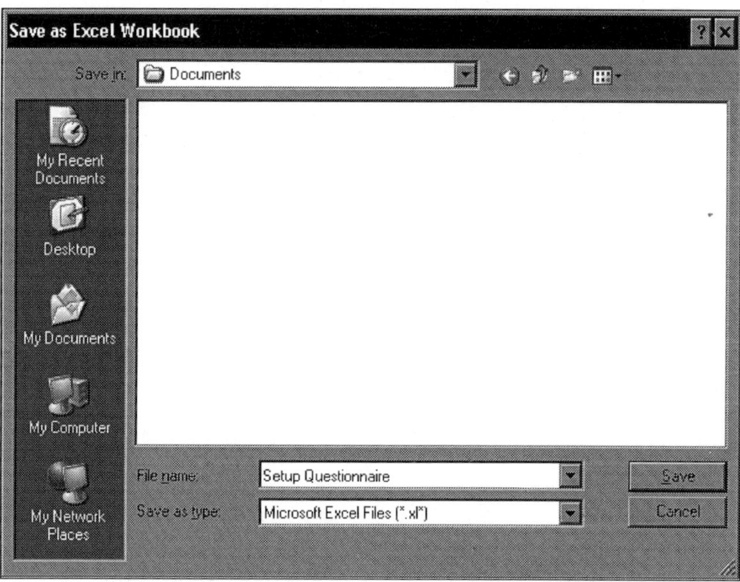

Type a **File name** and click **Save**.

4. If all went well the success message is displayed.

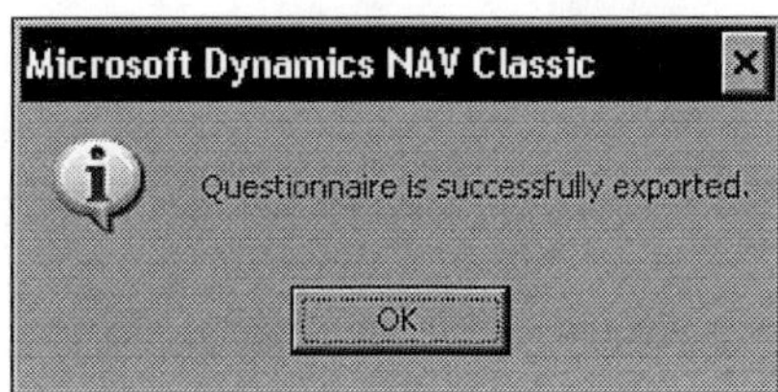

Click **OK**.

5. The exercise is complete.

The system has generated an Excel spreadsheet containing one worksheet for each of the ten setup tables included in the setup areas that were imported from the RIM industry-specific XML file. Let's open the Excel spreadsheet and take a look at the **General Ledger Setup** worksheet.

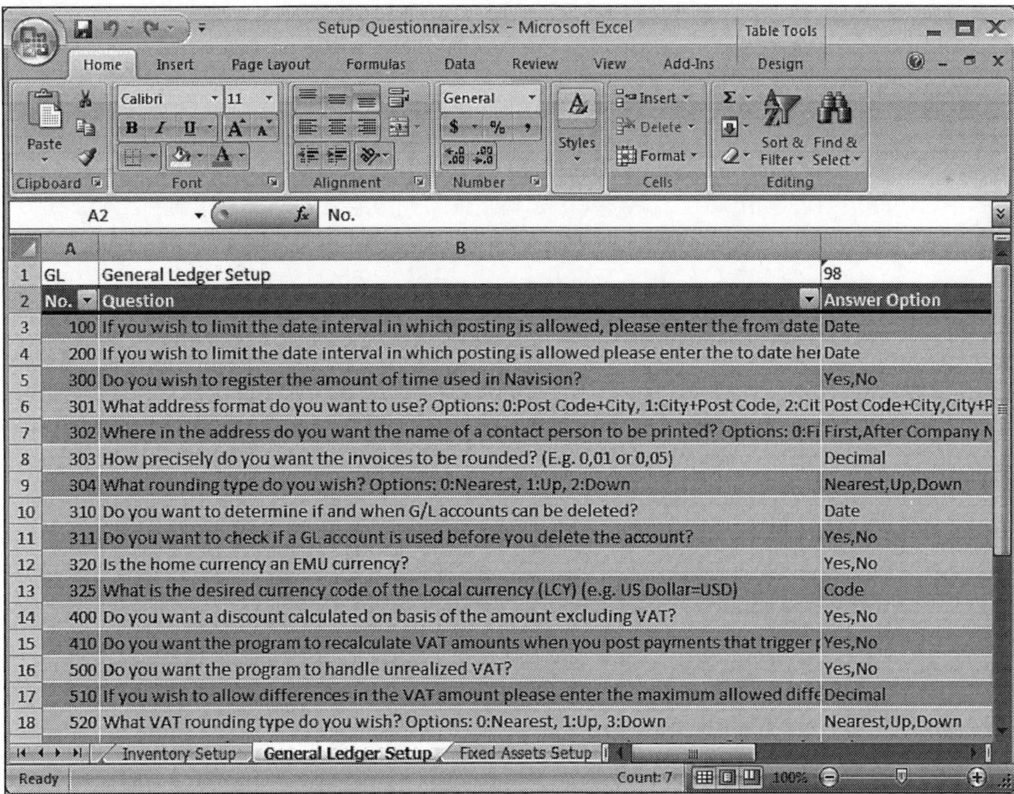

	A	B	
1	GL	General Ledger Setup	98
2	No.	Question	Answer Option
3	100	If you wish to limit the date interval in which posting is allowed, please enter the from date	Date
4	200	If you wish to limit the date interval in which posting is allowed please enter the to date hei	Date
5	300	Do you wish to register the amount of time used in Navision?	Yes,No
6	301	What address format do you want to use? Options: 0:Post Code+City, 1:City+Post Code, 2:Cit	Post Code+City,City+F
7	302	Where in the address do you want the name of a contact person to be printed? Options: 0:Fi	First,After Company N
8	303	How precisely do you want the invoices to be rounded? (E.g. 0,01 or 0,05)	Decimal
9	304	What rounding type do you wish? Options: 0:Nearest, 1:Up, 2:Down	Nearest,Up,Down
10	310	Do you want to determine if and when G/L accounts can be deleted?	Date
11	311	Do you want to check if a GL account is used before you delete the account?	Yes,No
12	320	Is the home currency an EMU currency?	Yes,No
13	325	What is the desired currency code of the Local currency (LCY) (e.g. US Dollar=USD)	Code
14	400	Do you want a discount calculated on basis of the amount excluding VAT?	Yes,No
15	410	Do you want the program to recalculate VAT amounts when you post payments that trigger (	Yes,No
16	500	Do you want the program to handle unrealized VAT?	Yes,No
17	510	If you wish to allow differences in the VAT amount please enter the maximum allowed diffe	Decimal
18	520	What VAT rounding type do you wish? Options: 0:Nearest, 1:Up, 3:Down	Nearest,Up,Down

It's probably not going to replace a consultant entirely, but there is a lot of information in this spreadsheet. Here's a sample of the data from question 301.

Question	**What address format do you want to use? Options: 0:Post Code+City, 1:City+Post Code, 2:City+State+Post Code, 3:Blank Line+Post Code+City**
Answer Option	**Post Code+City,City+Post Code,City+County+Post Code,Blank Line+Post Code+City**
Comment	**Select the format in which addresses must appear on printouts. If an address includes a country/region code, the format defined for that country/region code will overrule the format that is defined here.**

The sheet also includes fields for the user to complete the **Answer** and the **Question Origin** (which is an option for the users to record who decided on the answer).

Now the users can work through the questions and decide on the settings in the system. If they are not sure, they can send an email to the consultant for clarification, or save up the answers they are not sure of for the next site visit. All in all this is a much quicker way to complete the configuration of the setup tables.

But what about the setup tables that aren't included in the Setup Questionnaire or new fields that you may add to your setup tables? A number of the missing tables are for parts of the system that the users are not going to be able to configure on their own, such as Commerce Gateway or Employee Portal. Some of them could be added to the questionnaire, and you can do this yourself and then save the questions for later use. The techniques explained next can also be used to refresh the existing tables with newly added fields.

Let's take the Jobs Setup table as an example. There are only two fields on this table, so it's understandable that it's not included as standard.

1. Select **Administration** | **Application Setup** | **Company Setup** | **Setup Questionnaire**.
2. The **Setup Questionnaire** form is displayed.

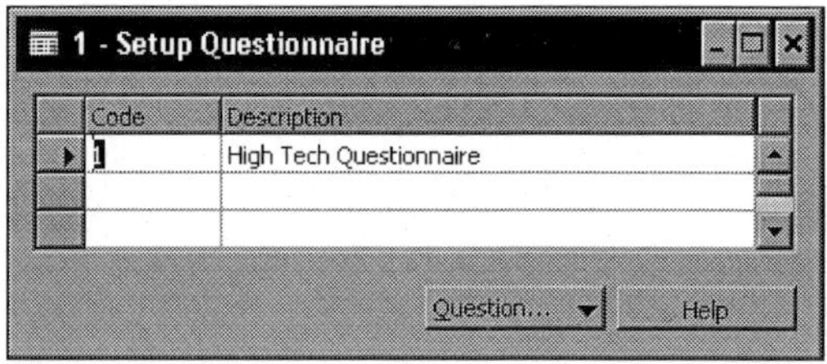

Click the **Questionnaire** menu button and select the **Show Questions** option.

3. The **Question Area** form is displayed.

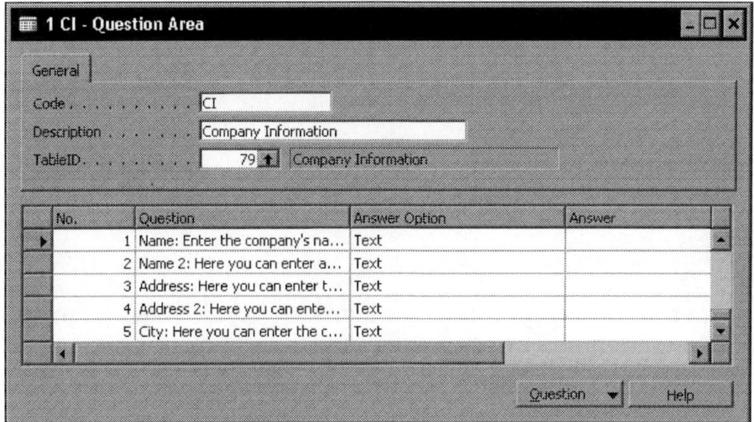

Click in the header part of the form and press *F3* to create a new record. Enter the following details:

Code: **JOB**

Description: **Jobs Setup**

TableID: **315**

Now the header is created but there are no questions. Click the **Question** menu button and select the **Update Questions** option.

4. The **Question Area** form is displayed with one line inserted for each field on the setup table.

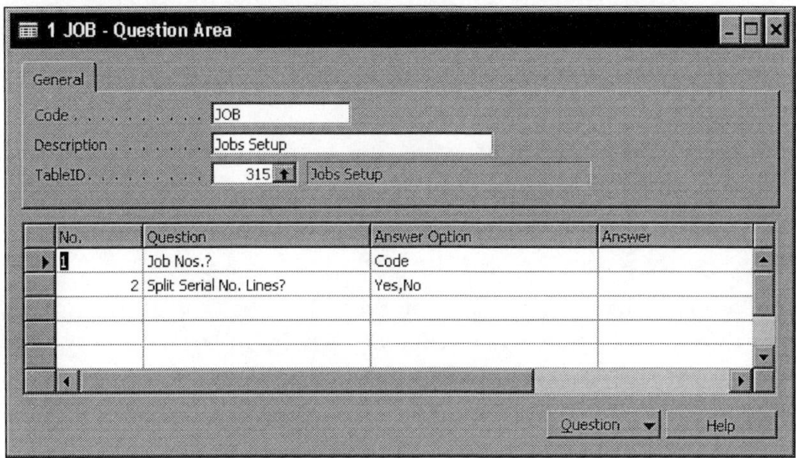

The questions are fairly basic, just the field name with a question mark at the end.

You can enter your preferred question, default answer, and some comments to help with the setup. If you're unsure of what the field does, run the real setup form (Jobs, Setup, Jobs Setup) and use the field help by pressing *F1* on each of the fields.

Once you have completed the questions, press *Esc* to return to the **Setup Questionnaire** form.

5. The exercise is now complete.

If you want to save your new questions for using on a later project, you can select the **Questionnaire** menu button and choose the **Export to XML** option. This will create an XML file that you can import for new projects using the **Import from XML** option.

If you are prepared to get your hands dirty with some XML, you can even incorporate your new questions into the industry-specific setup XML files so that new companies can be created with the questions of your own design ready to be configured.

Data migration

In order to understand why the data migration components in the RIM Toolkit are so good, you need to understand how data migration can be handled without RIM. The process prior to RIM was quite simple, you identified the tables that needed to be populated and then got a programmer to write Dataports for each of the tables to be populated. Typically, the Dataport was written to import data as a CSV (comma separated values) file that could be prepared in Excel. It doesn't sound like a huge problem but in reality, this process was painful for a number of reasons:

- Dataports are an all-or-nothing kind of creature. If the system encounters a problem after importing a million records, it will display an error message and abort, rolling back the changes. This is time-consuming and very annoying.
- Dataports are difficult to debug, and the standard error messages often fail to tell you exactly where the problem lies.
- CSV files get complicated when you have data that contains quotes or commas. An alternative is to change to TAB delimited, but this can make preparing the data more difficult.
- Dataports don't use column headings as standard, so the files that are prepared in Excel need to be manipulated before they can be imported.

Another problem with Dataports is they are seemingly innocent little creatures. Everyone knows they are simple in construction and anyone can build them, so we never really allocate much time to their development, however; they nearly always take longer than expected, and take a lot of tweaking to get them right. Usually it is the data that needs to be massaged to fit the Dataport, but all in all this is a lengthy process.

Hurray for the Data Migration tool

The Data Migration tool in the RIM Toolkit addresses all of the shortcomings of the previous approach and adds a whole heap of other advantages. Probably, the greatest feature is that it's really easy to drive, which means even the most technically illiterate consultants are going to be able to use this tool, and after a little practice, your customers may even be doing it for themselves.

Let's take a look at a simple example. We're going to create an Excel spreadsheet that will allow us to key in our chart of accounts and then import it into our new company.

Before we start, we're going to need to know a couple of things about the table we want to import. We need to know the table name (ideally we want the table ID), and we also want form ID for the form we want to use to manage the data.

To find these details, start by running the form that is used to display the data you want to import. For us this is **Financial Management | General Ledger | Chart of Accounts**.

With the form displayed, press *Ctrl+F2* to launch the designer.

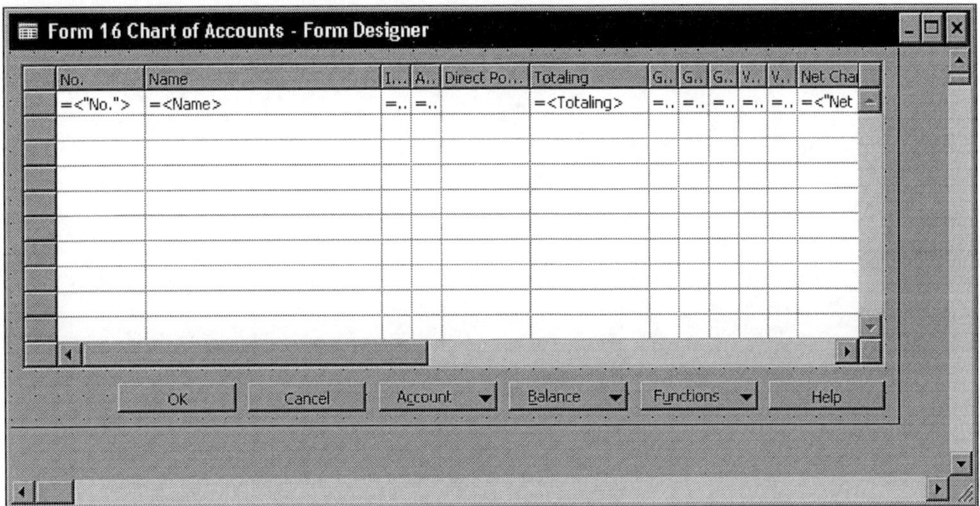

Notice that the title of the window tells us the Form ID, so you can make a note of that, but how do we find the table ID? Make sure you don't have any form controls selected (when you first open the designer, no controls are selected, so as long as you don't click on anything you'll be fine), then press *Shift+F4* to launch the properties for the form.

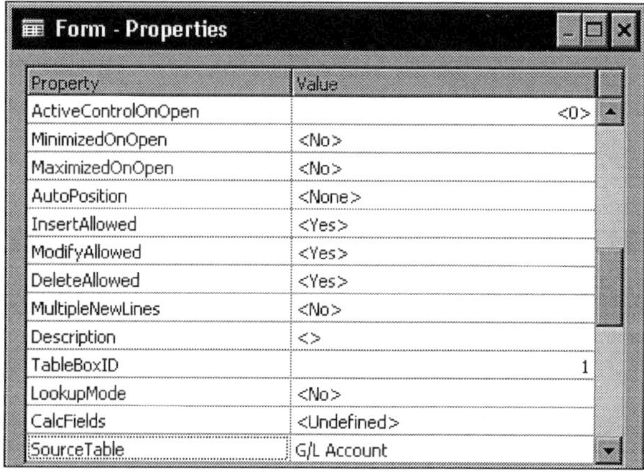

Move across to the **Property** column and press the *S* key twice. The first time the form will jump to the **Sizeable** field (the first property in the list that starts with S); the second time the form will jump to the **SourceTable** property. Move across to the **Value** field and copy the text **G/L Account** to the clipboard using *Ctrl+C*.

Nearly there; press *Esc* until you are out of the designer; you shouldn't be prompted to save changes (if you didn't change anything) but if you are prompted, say **No**. Now press *Shift+F12* to launch the **Object Designer**.

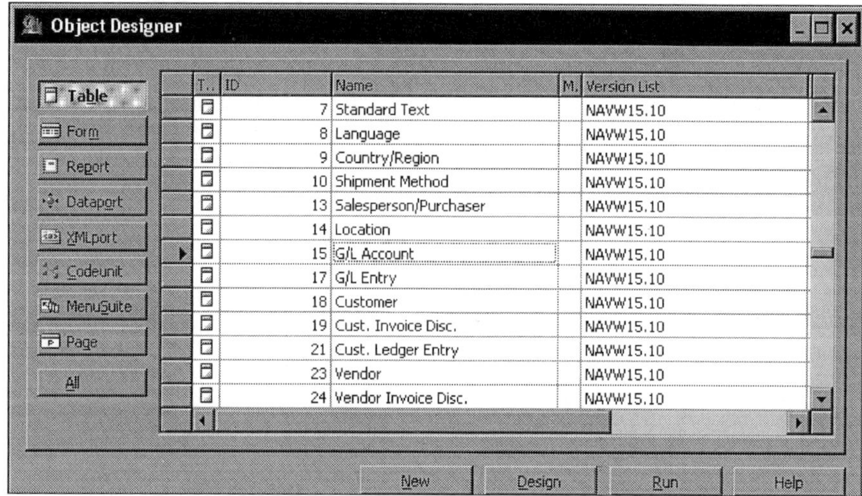

You can click the **Table** button to show the tables, and use *Ctrl+F* find feature on the **Name** field along with the table name you copied to the clipboard to find the **G/L Account** table.

Now we know the **Table ID** is **15** and the **Form ID** is **16**; it's time to do some migrating.

1. From the Classic client, select **Administration** | **Application Setup** | **Company Setup** | **Data Migration**.
2. The **Migration Overview** form is displayed.

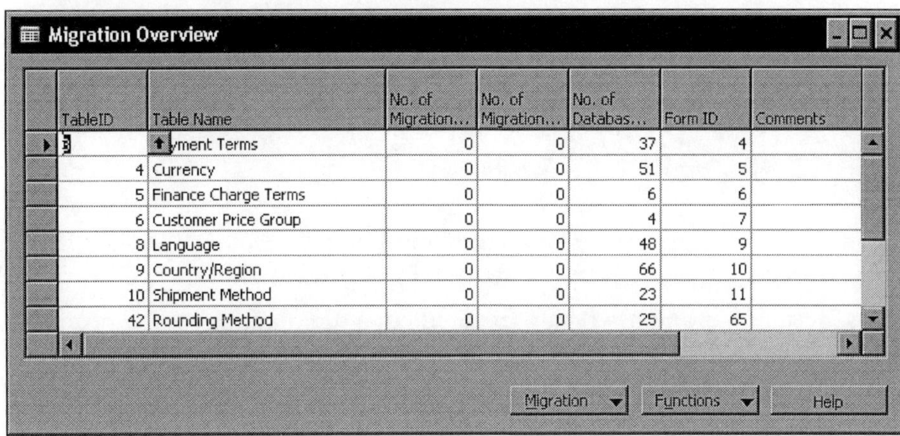

TableID	Table Name	No. of Migration...	No. of Migration...	No. of Databas...	Form ID	Comments
3	yment Terms	0	0	37	4	
4	Currency	0	0	51	5	
5	Finance Charge Terms	0	0	6	6	
6	Customer Price Group	0	0	4	7	
8	Language	0	0	48	9	
9	Country/Region	0	0	66	10	
10	Shipment Method	0	0	23	11	
42	Rounding Method	0	0	25	65	

In each line the form represents a table to be migrated. For each table, it shows the number of pending records (read from the file but not yet applied), the number of migration errors, and the number of records currently in the database for this table.

Press *F3* to create a new record and complete the details as follows:

TableID: **15**

Form ID: **16**

Click on the **Migration** menu button and choose the **Migration Fields** option.

3. The **Migration Fields** form is displayed.

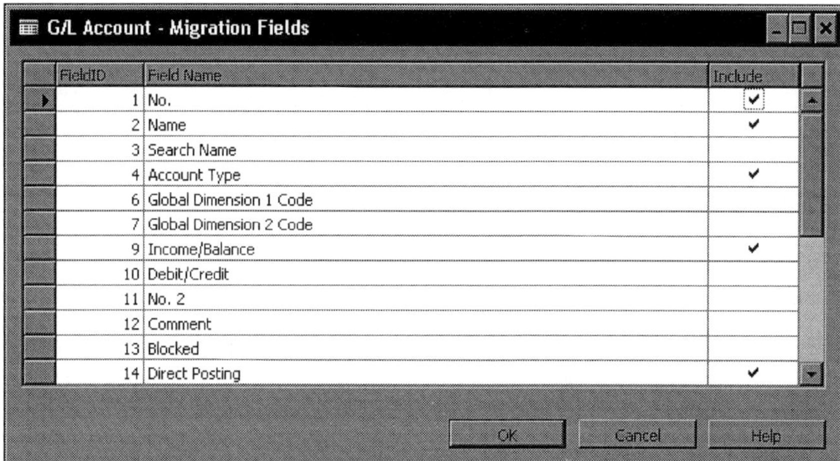

Check the fields you want be included in the interface file. In this example, we are selecting: **No., Name, Account Type, Income/Balance, Direct Posting**.

The system has already ticked the fields that are included in the primary key for this table. The primary key is what identifies one record as being different from another, and you should not remove these fields from the **Migration Fields** setup. If you do, you will find that the records cannot be imported as all fields in the primary key must contain a value.

In addition to the **Include** field, there is a **Validate** field that is not shown by default. For new tables this is set to **Yes**, but you can change the value to **No** to prevent the system from validating a field. This is good if you like importing invalid data, or have a need to import data with references to tables that do not yet exist.

Click the **OK** button when all the required fields are checked.

4. The **Migration Overview** form is displayed once again.

   Click to the left of the record to ensure the entire line is selected.

5. The **G/L Account** record is selected for export.

Migration Overview

TableID	Table Name	No. of Migration...	No. of Migration...	No. of Databas...	Form ID	Comments
9	Country/Region	0	0	66	10	
10	Shipment Method	0	0	23	11	
15	G/L Account	0	0	294	16	
42	Rounding Method	0	0	25	65	
79	Company Information	0	0	1	1	
92	Customer Posting Group	0	0	4	110	
93	Vendor Posting Group	0	0	4	111	
94	Inventory Posting Group	0	0	12	112	

Migration | Functions | Help

If the record isn't selected as shown in the screenshot, the next step is going to export all the tables, so make sure you have the line selected.

Click the **Functions** menu button and select the **Export to Excel** option.

6. The **Save as Excel Workbook** dialog is displayed.

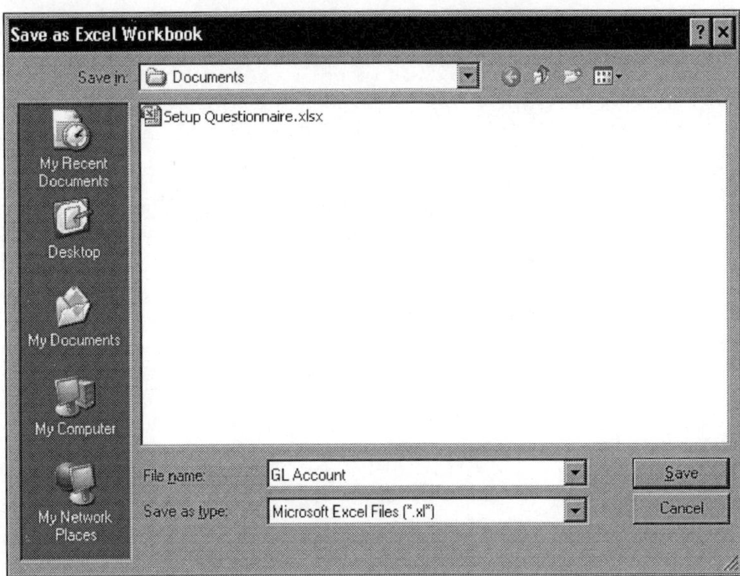

Type **GL Account** into the **File name**, make a note of the directory you are saving to and click **Save**.

7. The success message is displayed.

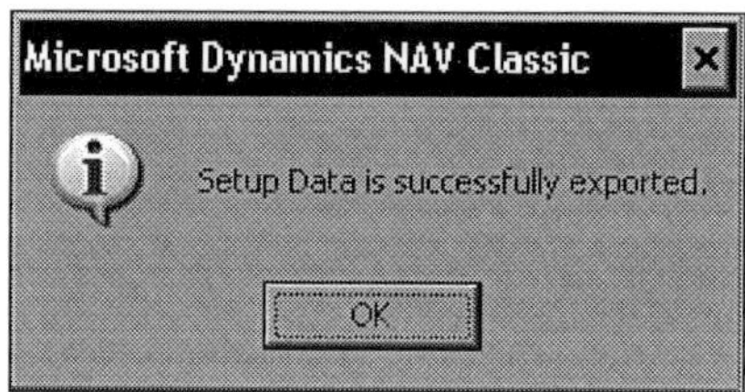

Click the **OK** button.

8. The exercise is complete.

Now it's time to take a look at the file we created. Hopefully, you made a note of where you saved the file so you can open it and take a look.

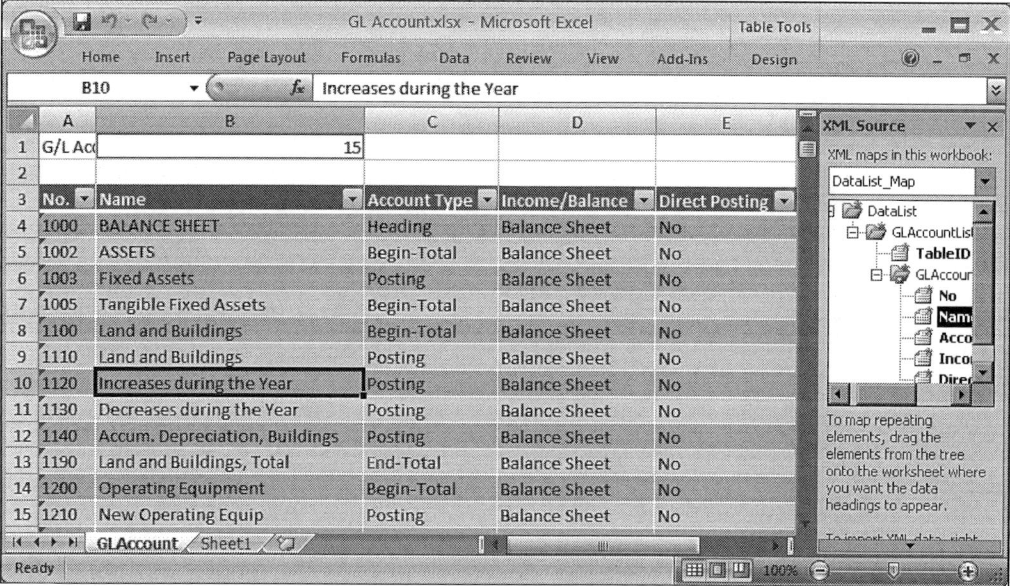

For each table you selected for export (in this case just the **G/L Account** table), there is a worksheet in our Excel workbook. This is no ordinary spreadsheet. The table is actually an XML table, and it is attached to an XML schema definition. This means that you can insert new rows in the table and NAV knows what field in the database each cell represents. It also means that you can't just knock-up any old Excel spreadsheet. The file must have the XML mappings that correspond to the data-migration setup. If you try copying the data to a new spreadsheet and importing this (a spreadsheet that has no XML schema), you will see an error message telling you the file is not valid for import.

To test the import, let's modify the account name for **G/L Account 1110** to be **Land**. Then we'll insert a new account code **1115** with an account name of **Buildings**. Finally, we'll deliberately set the **Account Type** for account **1120** to an invalid value of **Hippo**.

When you're done editing, your spreadsheet should look something like the following:

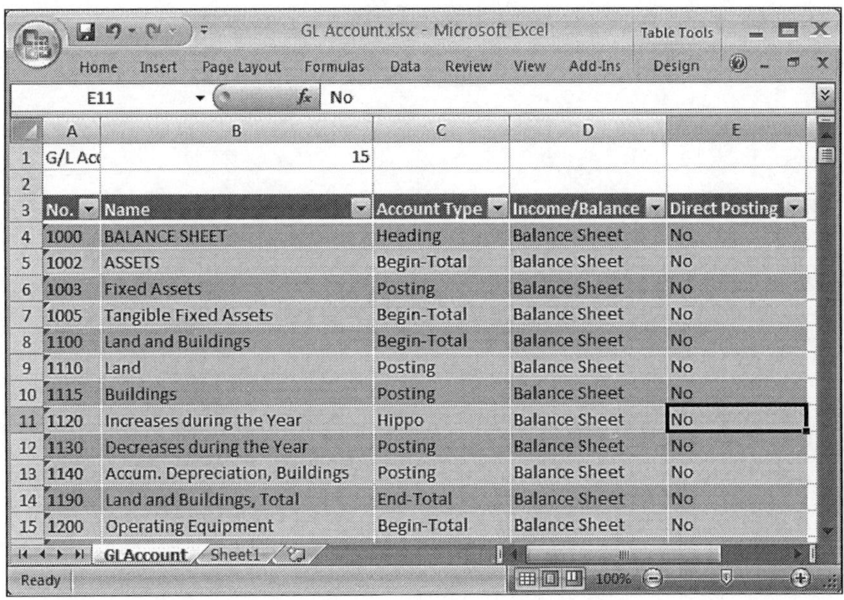

Save your changed spreadsheet, and we'll see what happens when we try to import it. Run the **Migration Overview** form once again, and with the **G/L Account** line selected, choose the **Functions | Import from Excel** option.

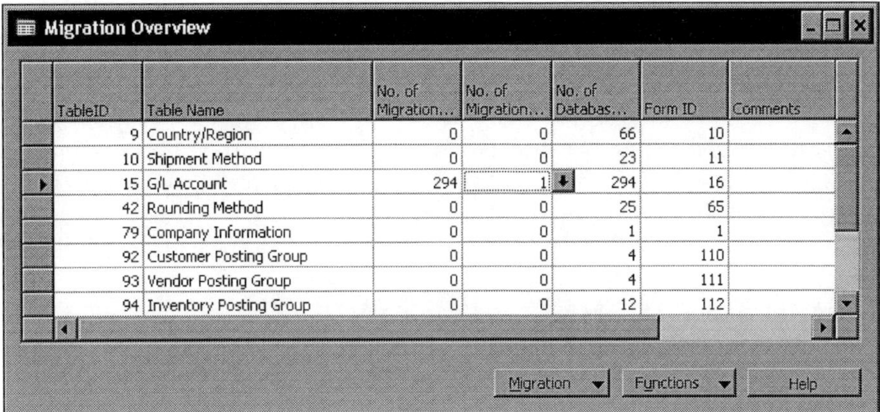

Notice that there are **294** valid records imported and 1 record in error. This is a total of 295 accounts and we started with 294 in our database—but that's **OK** because we inserted one.

Use the drill-down on the **No. of Migration Errors** field to show the error record.

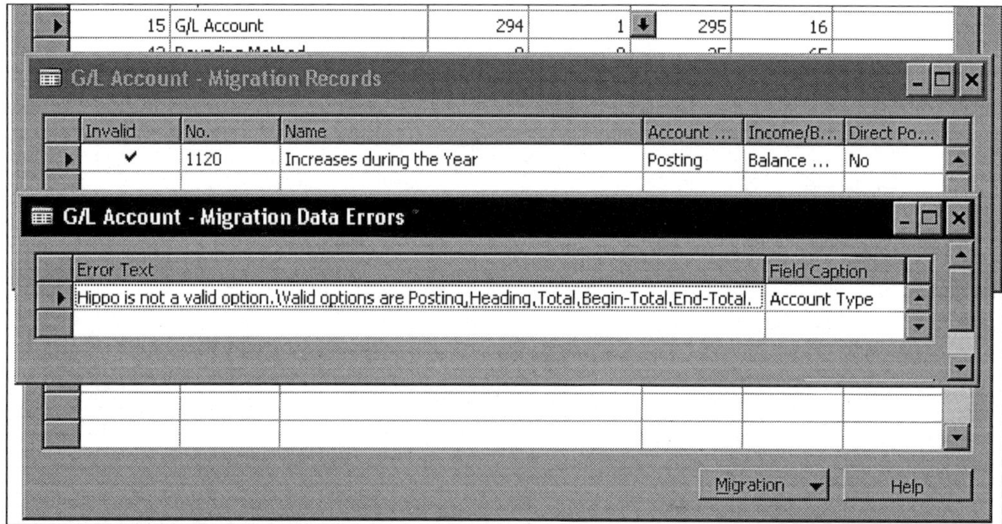

The problem record is displayed, and if you press *F9*, you will be shown the actual error message. Apparently, Hippo is not a valid option.

To apply the changes, select the **Apply Migration Data** option from the **Migration** menu button. Once you do this, you'll notice that all 295 records get imported. This is because the system corrected the erroneous account to have a valid posting type—don't get too excited there was no fuzzy logic involved here, the system simply selected the first (that is, default) option field value. You can use the **Migration Records** form to correct any data that is causing an error prior to import (watch out for those error messages—if you don't manually delete them before re-applying the data, you'll still see them in the list, which can be more than a little confusing). You should be wary of this feature that erroneous option types get 'corrected' automatically. Just because the system has selected a valid option does not mean it's the correct value, and finding the erroneous records after you have applied them may mean re-importing the data.

Limitations of the Data Migration tool

The Data Migration tool seems fantastic, but in reality it is lacking in a few areas. Even with its shortcomings, it's still a great tool, but let's take a look at some of the problems.

Dimensions

Do you remember the dimensions from earlier on? When we looked at the various dimensions, we discovered that only Global Dimensions 1 and 2 can be used in certain areas of the system; the Data Migration tool is another good example of this. When you were configuring the fields to be imported for our G/L Account table, you may have noticed that only Global Dimensions 1 and 2 were available for selection. Typically this will not be sufficient and there are two ways around this problem. Depending on your skills, you may either take the way of the consultant, or the programmer's path.

Unlimited dimensions—the way of the consultant

Some of the tables in the system have Shortcut Dimension Codes 1 and 2, which means you can simply populate those in the data migration import (although this doesn't give you the opportunity to say that the dimension code is mandatory for that record). For the other dimensions, and those cases where you want to set **Value Posting** rules, you need to be a little more creative. Fortunately you can import your dimensions using the Data Migration tool. It takes a little mind-stretching to understand the concept but, it is possible to do this without writing any programming code.

As an example, we're going to add **AREA** and **CUSTOMERGROUP** (in my setup these are dimensions three and four) to a couple of customers we are going to import as well as the **DEPARTMENT** dimension (dimension one).

First of all, we need to know which table the dimensions three and four will be stored in as they are not available as fields on the **Customer** table.

Launch the customer card in the Classic client and find customer number **10000, The Cannon Group PLC**. Click the **Customer** menu button and select the **Dimensions** option, or use the *Ctrl+Shift+D* key combination.

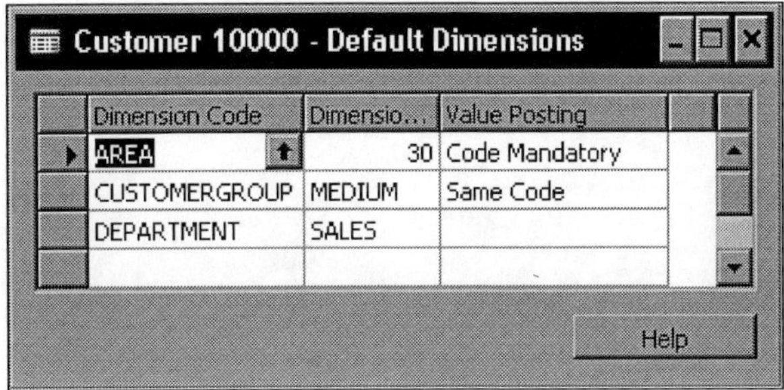

You'll notice that we already have **AREA** and **CUSTOMERGROUP** dimension values against this customer. With your cursor on the **AREA** dimension, select **Zoom** from the **Tools** menu or use the *Ctrl+F8* key combination.

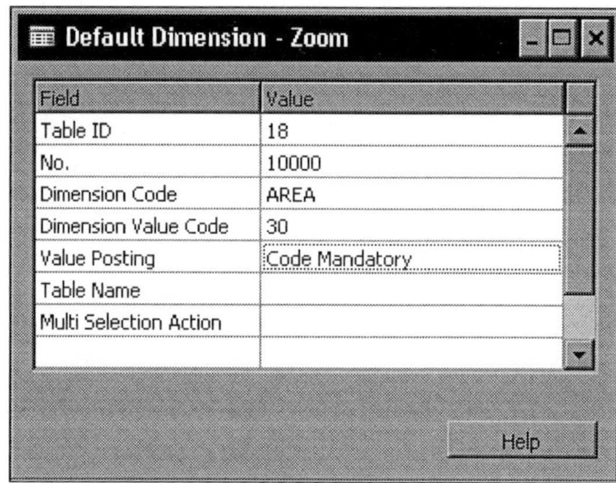

The table is **Default Dimension**, and in order to specify default dimension settings for a customer, the **Table ID** must be **18**. The customer number will go in the **No.** field, the dimension code in the **Dimension Code**.

So in order to import our customer with a **DEPARTMENT**, **AREA**, and **CUSTOMERGROUP** dimension, we will need one record in the **Customer** table and two in the **Default Dimension** table (note we do not need to specify **DEPARTMENT** as we can use the **Global Dimension 1 Code** field on the **Customer** table.) Our data will look something like this:

Customer		
No.	**Name**	**Global Dimension 1 Code**
1001	**Test Customer**	**SALES**

Default Dimension				
Table ID	**No.**	**Dimension Code**	**Dimension Value Code**	**Value Posting**
18	**1001**	**CUSTOMERGROUP**	**MEDIUM**	**Same Code**
18	**1001**	**AREA**	**30**	**Code Mandatory**
18	**1001**	**DEPARTMENT**	**SALES**	**Same Code**

Different tables will be used to attach dimensions depending on which table they are being attached to. For example, if you are importing a series of **Gen. Journal Line** records as opening balances, your dimensions will be in table **356**, **Journal Line Dimension**; the method for discovering the table to be populated and the fields that must be completed (described above) can be used for any of the tables in the system.

Unlimited dimensions – The programmer's path

When all you have is a hammer, every problem looks like a nail. So, if you are a programmer, we don't blame you for adopting a *Heck, why not* approach. If you don't want the consultant and the customer key users (or whoever will be populating the import files) to spend too much time warping their brains and filling the dimensions import worksheets the consultant way, go and program a solution that would solve the problem in a no-brainer way.

There are definitely several ways in which we could do this, and if you are technically inclined, you can use the guidelines we are proposing to write your own solution. If you really want this solution but don't want to program it, you should take a look on the downloads section of `www.teachmenav.com` to see if we created one for you; at the very least, you will find a detailed explanation of how this can be done.

In our solution, we propose something that would make it terrifically easy for anyone to set up as many dimensions as their heart desires. Wouldn't it be simply great if your users could enter the import information like this (notice the dimension columns):

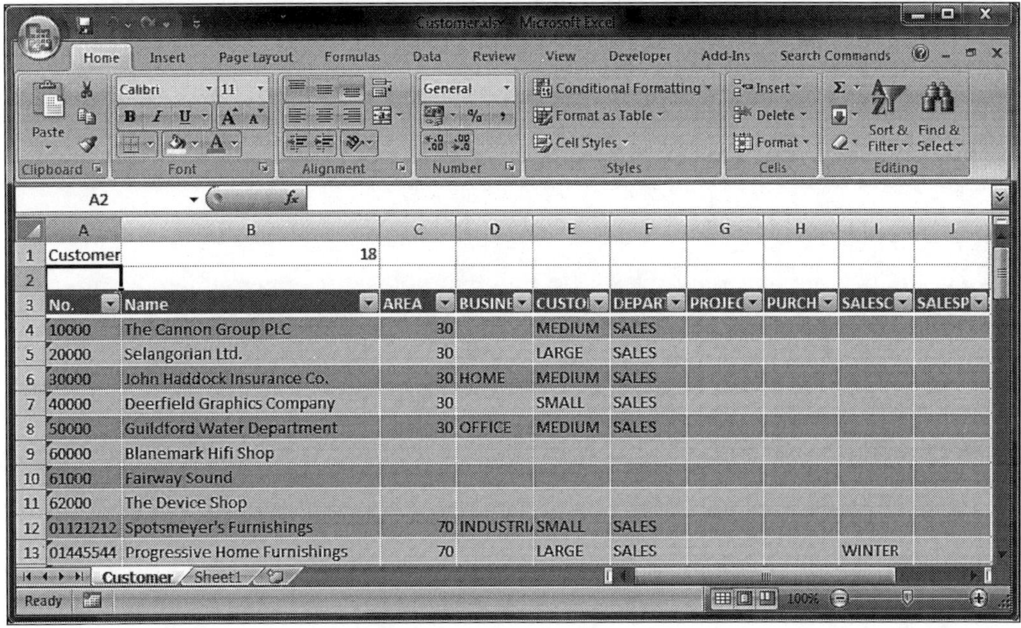

With this, you have solved a problem the programmer way, and probably earned yourself a beer from your consultants!

Known issues

There are a number of problems with the Data Migration tool that are known to Microsoft and will be corrected in later releases. You should check these areas carefully and look for hotfixes, or make some corrections to the programming, before using this tool for an implementation. You may find the following issues:

- Overflow on type conversion when text fields larger than 100 characters are imported (you can fix this by changing **FORM ID=8626** so that the **MatrixCellData** global variable is **250** characters in length and not **100**).
- Error on importing fields when the table contains a field name that starts with a number (simple: don't use field names that start with a number).
- Applying data causes date fields to be blanked (they read in **OK** but don't get applied properly).

Slow performance

The Data Migration tool is very clever; you can set it up so that it can import any field into any table. Unfortunately this flexibility comes at a price. In order to be able to achieve this, the tool treats each field as a record in a table with a table ID, field ID, and value. This dramatically increases the number of records that need to be handled when a migration is run. For the most part it's not a problem, but if you want to import millions of records, you may be better off writing a dataport, or possibly even creating a table to store the non-validated values for the record and populating this quickly with SQL statements. You can then write C/AL code to validate the fields into the correct table. For importing a few hundred customers, or inventory items, it's perfect.

Data templates

There is a data templates part of the RIM tool that I have not covered here because, well to be frank, it doesn't work terribly well. In theory, you can set up a data template for your table and use it to auto-populate fields on the item being imported. The default values field on the data template will overwrite any values you specify in your data migration file. (In my opinion a default should only apply if the value is left blank.) You can try this out and see if you like the overwrite with defaults option.

What's missing

Between the setup questionnaire and the Data Migration tool, it is possible to get nearly all of your system configured, by the end users, using little more than Excel. Well that's the theory behind it. In reality, the users are still going to need to a lot of help getting through this process.

Experience has shown that the end users are perfectly capable of using the Data Migration tool to prepare their own data, import it, and correct any errors. This in itself eliminates a lot of time spent in data conversion and configuration, and training the users to use these tools should be part of every project's implementation. The RIM tool is definitely worth using, and by using spreadsheets for preparation, the configuration is largely self-documenting; however, it isn't going to make consultants redundant from the configuration process.

If there are parts of the system that require configuration that are not covered (such as add-ons that you always deploy), you should definitely extend the standard company XML files and setup questionnaires so that the work in preparing for their configuration need only be done once.

Summary

It's been a long road, getting from there to here. We've learned about G/L accounts and dimensions, and how to configure the system to collect the financial data we are interested in. We've looked at the RIM Toolkit and seen that, although it is not as good as it could be, it is going to save us a lot of time and is therefore worth investing time in. Dynamics NAV is a big system and we have only dealt with the core issues facing a configuration consultant.

6
Modifying the System

"The best investment is in the tools of one's own trade." Benjamin Franklin

Hardly any standard business management application can fit the needs of a business out of the box. Either the customer must shape their processes to match the system, or the consultant must shape the system to match the processes. Usually, the latter prevails. This chapter will explain the process of modifying the system without programming and describe the tools we have at our disposal to do it.

In this chapter you will learn:

- How a non-programmer can develop killer applications
- How to customize data model, user interface, and reporting components
- What kind of changes can be made without breaking the whole thing
- And a few tricks from old dogs that got new bones ahead of everybody else

Understanding the tools

Have you ever held a chainsaw in your hands? Go try it, hear it roar. Quite a beast, eh? Now, what can you do with it? Was felling timber the first image that popped up?

We had something else in mind. Have you ever seen any of those ice sculptures? Did you know that sculptors often use chainsaws to carve them out? Carving them slowly over days with fine tools is often not an option—the ice can start melting in a matter of minutes. To be able to finish in time before physics takes over, power tools must be used, and specially equipped chainsaws have been selected as a tool of choice of many ice carvers.

Modifying a big system, one like Microsoft Dynamics NAV 2009, requires a lot of skill, knowledge, and experience. While skill and experience can't be learned from a book, knowledge for the better part of it can. There are two kinds of knowledge: the knowledge of the tools, and the knowledge of the product.

If you only know the tools, and don't know the object you will work on with these tools, you can easily mess up. If you only know the product, but don't know the tools, you are missing many opportunities. When you know the tools, and what they can do, and how the product will behave when it has been touched, you are on the right path.

If you are an application consultant, and you know the product and how it works, but haven't ever dared to open it up in **Object Designer** and shape it to your liking, this chapter is for you. You already have the knowledge of the product, what it is and how it works; you only need the knowledge of the tools to become a true artist.

A chainsaw artist, if you wish. The tools you are about to master are quite powerful: they can craft beautifully architectured state-of-the-art solutions, or they can leave a complete mess.

Let's become artists.

Modifications for non-programmers

In Microsoft Dynamics NAV 2009, it is possible to create a fully functioning modification without really writing a single line of code. As a matter of fact, it happens quite often. Often, customers will demand changes that are simple in nature: adding a field to a report, or rearranging the screen elements. You don't need to be a programmer to be able to accomplish that mission.

Microsoft Dynamics NAV comes with a comprehensive set of tools aimed at modifying the solution and every aspect of it, from the data model, via business logic, all the way to the user interface. Many steps along this way can be done without any programming knowledge.

Let's take a look at what can be done without writing code:

- **Extending the data model**: Application data is stored in tables, which are specifically designed to store exactly that information which is required by the application, no more, no less. When your customer presents you with new requirements, these will often spawn many changes to the underlying data model, to accommodate all those types of information that weren't originally supposed to be stored, because nobody knew they existed. You can do all of these data model modifications using special data design tools, without writing any code. True, some business logic is usually associated with data, so called *business rules*, but these should be written much later, after the model has been completed.

- **Modifying the user interface**: To put a functional user interface together requires a good understanding of the underlying data model, and of various user interface controls that can be put on screen, what they can do, and what they can't. You can compose hundreds of fully functional data-enabled pages or forms, and establish complex navigation rules between them, without ever coming anywhere close to the C/AL code editor.
- **Reporting**: Again, to compose reports mainly requires good knowledge of the underlying data, and the knowledge of tools. While some complex reports may require extensive coding, the vast majority of reports will be prepared by simply laying out fields in the report designer.
- **Data import and export**: When data needs to go in and out of the system, you can reach for built-in development tools that can create data migration objects in a matter of minutes.

One of those times when knowing how to shape the system matters, while coding doesn't at all, is prototyping. Imagine how quickly you could get the requirements straight with a customer if you were able to quickly compose a usable user interface prototype!

Object Designer basics

All of the development in Microsoft Dynamics NAV is done through the **Object Designer** feature of the Classic client.

To invoke the **Object Designer** from anywhere within the application, simply press *Shift+F12*, or go to main menu, click **Tools**, then **Object Designer**. It looks like the following screenshot:

To the left there is a series of buttons, which you can use to switch between the lists of objects of various types:

Type	Description
Table	Tables are used to store information in the system.
Form	Forms are used to provide access to information by displaying it on screen and allowing data entry and modification. Forms can only be used by Classic client.
Report	Reports are primarily used to display information in printable form, but can also be used to execute batch jobs.
Dataport	Dataports are used to export and import information to and from the system in fixed width or variable length text format.
XMLport	Dataports on steroids, XMLports are RoleTailored and can get information into or out of the system in XML and text format. XMLports can also be used to automate communication with external application in a way transparent to the users, such as with Business Notifications functionality.
Codeunit	Codeunits contain blocks of application code: the part of the system popularly called **business logic**.
MenuSuite	MenuSuites define what the navigation pane in Classic client and the **Departments** page in the RoleTailored client look like.
Page	Pages are the forms of the RoleTailored client: they are used to present the information to users and provide means for data entry using RoleTailored or any other service-tier clients (such as SharePoint client).

On the right, there is a table displaying all the objects of the selected type. The following columns are on show:

Column	Description
Type	This is actually displayed as an icon, which can represent any of the eight object types described in the previous table.
ID	An integer number representing the unique identifier of an object. Every object in the system is uniquely distinguished from every other by its type and ID.
Name	A textual identifier of the object, which has to be unique for each object type. You typically refer to objects by their names when you are declaring C/AL variables.
Caption	A localized version of the name, aware of the multi-language capabilities of Microsoft Dynamics NAV.

Column	Description
Modified	Tells if the object was modified. Upon saving, every object will automatically get a checkmark in this field.
Version List	A textual list of version tags, explaining which product releases, add-ons, or customizations have changed the object.
Date	Date of the last save operation in **Object Designer**.
Time	Time of the last save operation in **Object Designer**.
BLOB Size	Size of BLOB representation of the object in the database. The definition, and for all compiled objects an executable version of it, are saved in the database. This makes for a very portable solution, where the database is, so are the application objects.
Compiled	Flag that tells if the object was compiled, either during the last save operation, or manually by calling the **Compile** command. Only compiled objects can be executed.

On the bottom right, you have a few basic command buttons: **New** to create a new object of the selected type, **Design** to open an existing one, **Run** to execute the selected object, and **Help** to answer any questions that we might come across in the process of modifying the system.

Extending the data model

At the heart of every application functionality in Microsoft Dynamics NAV lies the data. Customer or vendor master records, open documents, posted documents, application setup or ledger entries, all these, and many more, exist as data stored in tables.

Every table represents a category of information, such as customers, or items. A row in a table represents a specific instance of such information, such as the customer *Spotsmeyer's Furnishings*, or the item *TOKYO Guest Chair, blue*. A row consists of a set of *fields*, which are attributes that describe every piece of data. Bits of information, such as customer number, or item unit cost, or invoice due date, are stored as fields.

Tables aren't isolated, and usually refer to each other using *relationships*. For example, the table **Sales Header** relates to the table **Customer** through fields **Sell-to Customer No.** and **Bill-to Customer No.**. Another table, **Sales Line**, relates back to table **Sales Header** through **Document Type** and **Document No.** fields. These relationships represent real-life properties: sales lines belong to a sales header, making a sales document, such as an invoice. An invoice is then issued to a customer.

Tables and their relationships make the *data model*, and the role of the data model is to encapsulate the real-life properties of entities, as well as their natural relationships.

Creating tables

To create a new table, click **New** in **Object Designer**, while the **Table** button is selected. This will bring up the **Table Designer**.

> Creating new objects is almost uniform throughout the application. While the **New** button is specific to **Object Designer**, there are other ways you can use to create something new, like pressing *F3*, or calling **New** from the **Edit** menu.

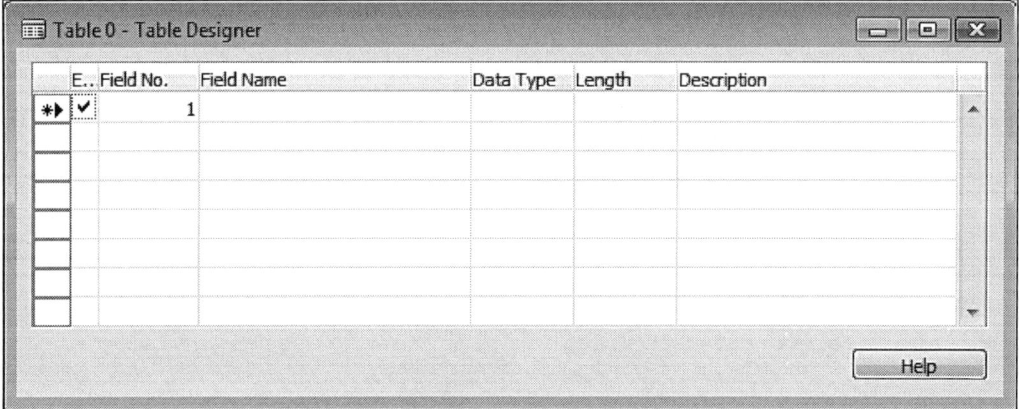

Whenever you create a new object, you'll soon want to save it. To save an object, click *Ctrl+S* or choose **Save** or **Save As...** from the **File** menu. This will bring up the **Save As** dialog window:

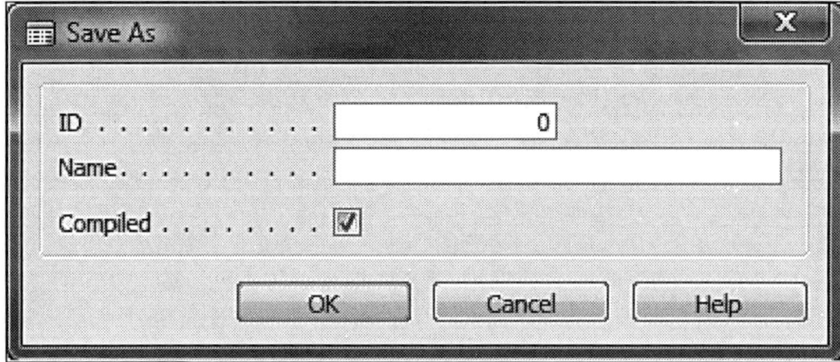

Enter the **ID** and the **Name**—both are mandatory—and click **OK**. **ID** is the object number in **Object Designer**, and **Name** is its name—make sure that both values are unique.

Depending on your license, you might be allowed to assign object ID's only in the range 50000 to 99999. Other ranges are reserved.

The **Compiled** checkbox tells the application whether you want to compile the object during saving. During design time, especially when coding, you might not be able to compile the object because of compile-time errors that will go away by themselves when you finish what you have started. In these cases, the save operation will fail if the **Compiled** checkbox is switched on.

To avoid these problems, switch the **Compile** checkbox off until you have finished designing, when you can turn it back on for the final save.

Every object in Microsoft Dynamics NAV contains properties. Every property represents a specific behavior the object can exhibit, and by setting properties we can make objects behave exactly the way we need them to.

The properties of any object in the application can be accessed by pressing *Shift+F4*, choosing **Properties** from the **View** menu, or by clicking the properties icon in the toolbar. Before displaying table properties, you must first place the cursor on the first empty row, or call the **Select Object** function from the **Edit** menu.

Many properties are common among application objects, and this is the list of those you will have to set for every object you define:

Property	Description
ID	The unique identifier of the object. This number has to be unique for any object type in the application. Think of this property as of the equivalent of the file name property for files on your disk.
Name	Unique name of the object. This is how the object is referred to in C/AL code and various C/SIDE properties.
Caption	Defines the caption that the system will display in the application title bar when the object is run. To take maximum advantage of the multi-language feature of Microsoft Dynamics NAV, you should not define this property manually, but define the **CaptionML** instead and the system will take care of the **Caption** automatically.
CaptionML	There are many properties ending in **ML**. This stands for *multi-language*, and an **ML** property always represents the multi-language version of an ML-less one. Therefore, **CaptionML** represents a multi-language version of **Caption**.

When editing properties, you'll notice that some of them have < and > around the value, such as **<Normal>**, **<Yes>**, or **<Undefined>**. These indicate the default states of these properties. When you set a property value explicitly, it loses the < and > signs to indicate that the property value has been explicitly assigned. To return back to the default state, select the property value and press *Del*.

Adding fields

Tables consist of fields, and you need at least one of these. To add fields to a table, while in **Table Designer**, position the cursor on the first empty line, and type in the name.

For each field you need to define these properties:

Property	Description
Field No.	The field's unique identifier within the table, by which the field is known to the system. Every field must have a **Field No.** assigned.
Name	The field's unique name within the table, by which the field is known to developers. The **Name** is how the field is referred to by C/AL code or C/SIDE properties.
Data Type	Determines the type of data stored in this field. When data is entered, the system automatically validates it against the data type, preventing any incompatible data entry (such as typing **Twenty** into an **Integer** field).
DataLength	Specifies the length of text that can be entered in this field. The application will automatically prevent the entry of any information longer than the specified length, both for manual and programmatic entry. This property is available for **Text** and **Code** data types.

Get familiar with the field data types and the various properties you can set on them by calling **C/SIDE Reference Guide** from **Help** menu.

Table relationships

Tables can relate to each other to represent natural, logical, or real-life relationships. You can express relationships in a technical way, using entity-relationship terms: invoice *is of* customer; item *is of* inventory posting group; sales line *is of* sales header. Or you can do it naturally, using human terms: invoice *is issued to* customer; item *uses* inventory posting group, sales line *belongs to* sales header.

A table is always related to another table through a field. In these examples, invoice is related to customer through the **Sell-to Customer No.** and **Bill-to Customer No.** fields; item is related to inventory posting group through the **Inventory Posting Group** field; sales line is related to sales header through the **Document Type** and **Document No.** fields.

In Microsoft Dynamics NAV, relationships are established through the **TableRelation** field property. To define a relationship, select the **TableRelation** property and click the Assist button to open the **Table Relation** editor. This is what it looks like for the **Sell-to Customer No.** field of table **36 Sales Header**:

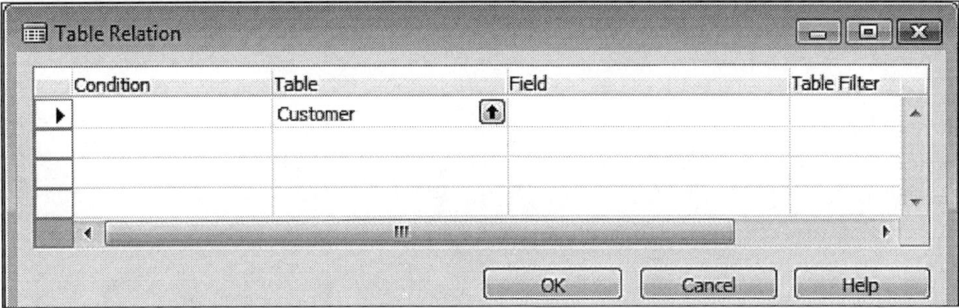

This is a simple relationship between the **Sell-to Customer No.** field and the primary key field of the **Customer** table. Relationships can be more complex: you can define conditional relationships, or explicitly declare fields you want to relate to, and you can even specify table filters to be applied during lookups.

We don't define relationships just for the heck of it—they have three important purposes:

- **They enable lookup functionality**: When **TableRelation** is set for a field, whenever you are editing a value for that field, the system will let you pick up one of the possible values by bringing up the lookup form. You can define which form is used as a lookup form for a table by setting its **LookupFormID** property.
- **They establish data integrity**: If you define a **TableRelation**, then you won't be able to just type any value in that field, because the relationship terms would be broken. You can only enter a value that exists in the related field in the related-to table. The system always takes care that only valid values are written in fields belonging to a relation. You may, however, switch off this mechanism by setting the **ValidateTableRelation** property to **No**.
- **They maintain data integrity**: If you change a value of a key field in a table, the change will be propagated to all the related tables. For example, if you change the **No.** for a customer, it will be automatically changed in all tables that are related to the **Customer** table.

Table keys

As the time goes by, handling increasing amounts of data would be difficult if there were no keys. Keys tell the system where to look for specific information. Tables, fields, and relations typically represent real-life entities, their properties and relationships; keys, on the other hand, stand for a very abstract concept.

There are two kinds of keys: primary and secondary.

Primary keys are used to uniquely identify data rows stored in tables. A record can be uniquely identified by a single field, or a set of fields. (This is called a *compound key*.) Examples of simple keys are **No.** in the **Customer** table, or **Code** in the **Unit of Measure** table; an example of compound key is **Document Type, Document No.** for the **Sales Header** table.

Secondary keys are used as indexes. An index in a table has the same purpose as an index in a book. Take this book as an example: if you want to see where the word *table* is used, you'd go to the *Index* section and see all the pages where word *table* is mentioned. A handy feature!

Let's now see how keys are defined. Design **Table 18 Customer**, and call **Keys** from the **View** menu. The key editor opens:

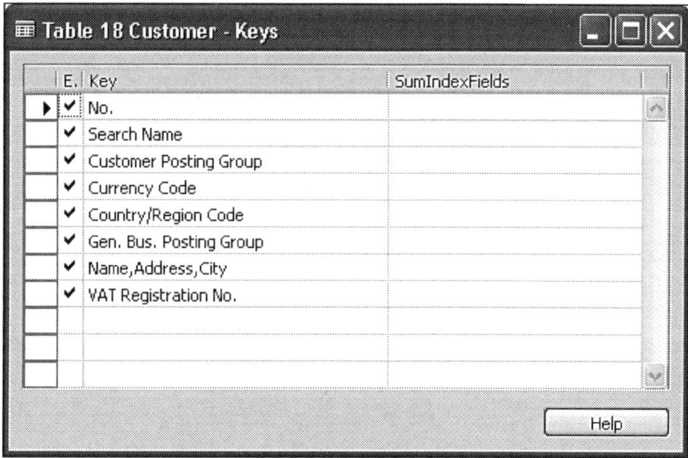

The first line always contains the primary key. Other lines are secondary keys, which are typically used as indexes that help the database find information faster. To add keys, simply add a new line and type in the fields separated by a comma.

We'll discuss keys in much more detail in the chapter called *The Development Lifecycle*.

Field groups

Microsoft Dynamics NAV 2009 introduces a new concept: field groups. They have only one purpose: to enable lookup functionality in the RoleTailored client. In the Classic client, to enable lookup functionality, you must configure the **LookupFormID** property on the table. Every time users want to look up fields from other tables, they must show the whole lookup form, which takes the user's focus away and may even be cluttered with far more information than the user needs to effectively look up a value.

In the RoleTailored client, you don't need to invoke an extra page to look up values from another table: there is drop-down functionality, which shows only those values from another table that are necessary for an effective lookup, while keeping the user's focus on the original table. Something like the following:

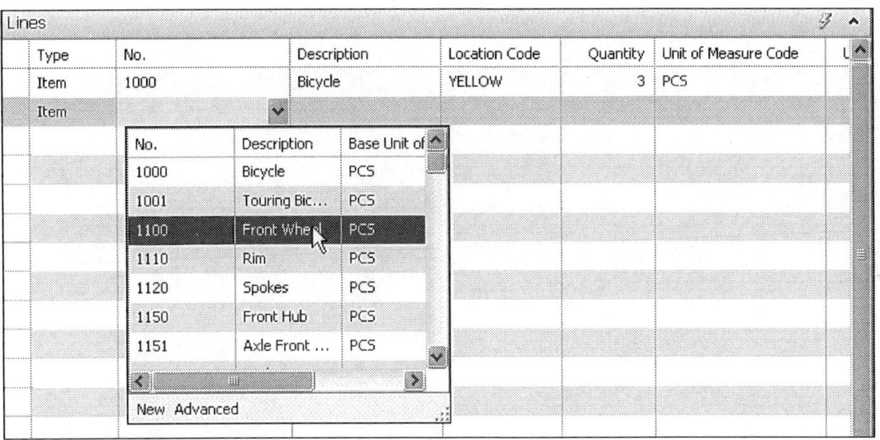

To define which fields will be shown in the RoleTailored client drop-down menus, call the **Field Groups** function from the **View** menu in **Table Designer**. There is only one field group that has a meaning, and it has to be called `DropDown`. The fields list, separated by commas, defines which fields will be shown to users in drop-down menus. Any other field groups have absolutely no meaning in this release of Microsoft Dynamics NAV, and while you might add as many field groups as you like, they won't have any effect on the system at all.

Customizing forms

No matter what our data model looks like deep down, and what we have done to it, our users are mostly unaware of any of it. Users never interact with the application directly through tables—for that they use the user interface elements of a client application.

Microsoft Dynamics NAV 2009 comes with two clients: the new one called RoleTailored, which you have already had chance to meet and play with, and the old one called Classic.

When defining the user interface, you must address both of them. Unfortunately, defining user interfaces is a double work: you must define them separately. Forms, the building blocks of the Classic client can't be used in the RoleTailored one, while pages, the building blocks of the RoleTailored interface can't be used in the Classic one.

Creating forms

Lucky for you, creating forms is mostly a trouble-free task: the **New Form** wizard, a fairly straightforward gadget, which requires very little technical skills, is there to help you kick start. To create a form, click the **Forms** button in **Object Designer**, then click the **New** button, or simply press *F3*. The wizard is there:

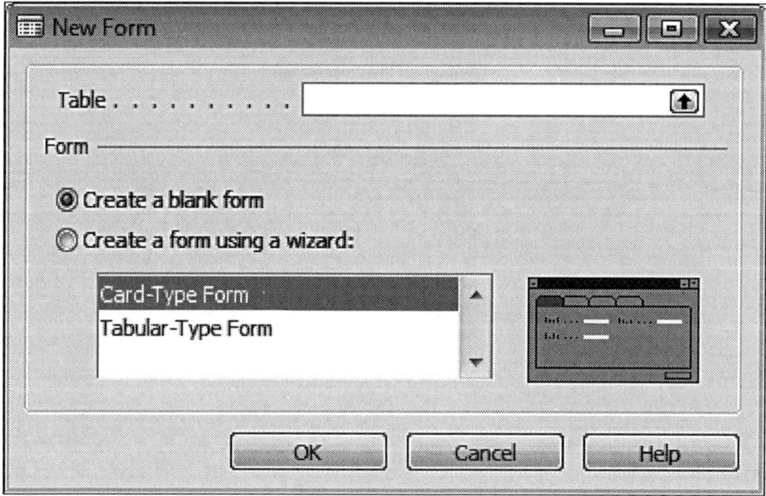

The majority of forms are data bound, which means they display information from a table. A form can only be bound to a single table, and you can choose which one by filling out the **Table** field in the **New Form** dialog. You can choose to continue with a blank form, or to use one of the two wizards: the **Card-Type Form** Wizard or the **List-Type Form** Wizard.

The **New Form** wizard helps you create forms of the two most common types: cards and lists. The wizard will help you choose which fields to display on the form, and choose their arrangement and layout.

After the wizard completes its job, your newly designed form is displayed in the **Form Designer**, where most of the design work for forms is done. A typical result of a **Card-Type Form** wizard is as follows:

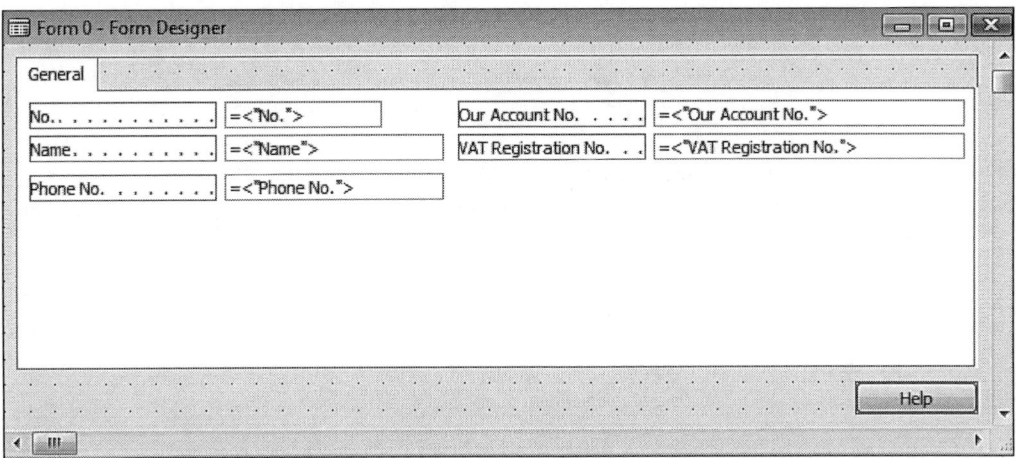

Form properties

It's a good time to inspect and get to know the most useful form properties. Most of them have been set by the wizard, but sometimes you'll just get to set them manually:

Property	Description
Width and **Height**	Define how wide and tall the form will be when displayed in non-maximized state.
Editable	Specifies whether controls in the form can be edited. When set to **No**, none of the controls in the form can be edited.
InsertAllowed, **ModifyAllowed**, and **DeleteAllowed**	By default, all data-bound forms allow all types of operations. If you want to prevent users from inserting, modifying, or deleting records in this form, set these properties to their desired state. Set these properties only when absolutely necessary, such as for setup forms that must allow modifications but not insertions or deletions.
LookupMode	A form in lookup mode displays **OK** and **Cancel** buttons, and closes when users press either of these; while in non-lookup mode these buttons are automatically hidden. Lookup mode is normally controlled by the application, and a form automatically enters the lookup mode whenever users open the form by looking up a field from another table by pressing *F6* or clicking the lookup button. By setting this property to **Yes** you can put a form explicitly into the lookup mode.

Property	Description
SourceTable	Specifies the underlying table upon which field controls in the form will be based.
SourceTableView	Specifies the default sorting and filter state of the form. Here you can explicitly declare a filter that can't be overridden by users, for example if you only want to see active customers, or documents of a certain type.

There are many more properties, but they aren't so frequently used and you'll learn them gradually as you continue to work with the application.

Adding controls

A jolly bunch of controls was added to the form when you completed the wizard, but you can add many more as you go. To add more controls to the form, you have two choices: adding fields or adding controls.

When you add a field, it is automatically converted to either a **Text Box** or a **Check Box**, depending on the field's data type, and it is automatically bound to the field. On the other hand, controls may, or may not be bound, and there is a broader choice of controls to choose from.

To add fields, select **Field Menu** from the **View** menu. The **Field Menu** is opened, and you can select the fields you want added to the form. When you are ready to add those fields, simply move your mouse pointer above the desired position in the form, and when the mouse pointer changes to a rectangle with a small cross at the upper left, double-click on the form. This will add the fields and their captions, and set their properties, all in one go. This is how it works:

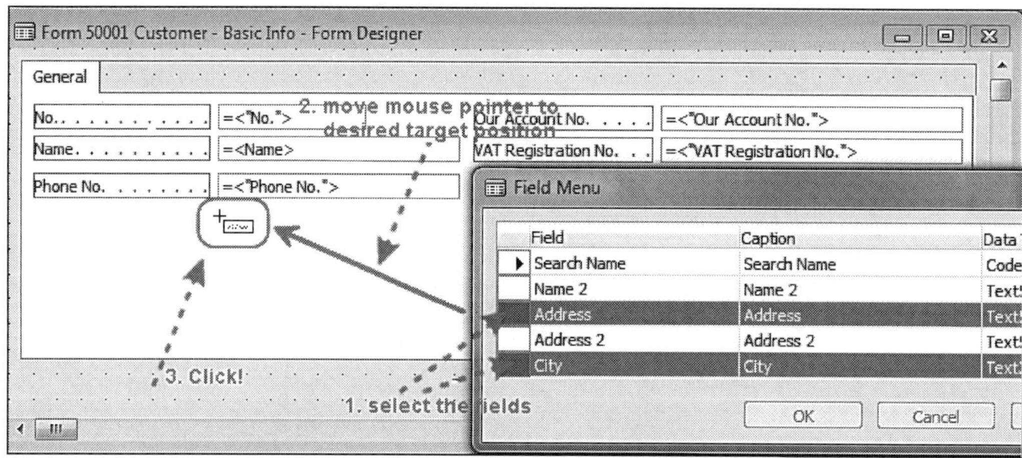

If you want to do this manually, or you want to add other controls such as buttons, progress bars, or subforms, display the **Toolbox** window by choosing **Toolbox** from the **View** menu. A small floating window will open with different icons representing different types of controls you can add.

Adding controls is as simple as adding fields; you simply select the desired control, position your mouse pointer above the desired target position, and click. These are the types of controls you can add:

Control	Description
	Label—displays a static, multi-language enabled text defined by its **Caption** and **CaptionML** properties.
	Text box—this must be bound to a source using the **SourceExpr** property. It can be bound to any of the following sources: a field in a table, a variable, a constant value, a **Text Constant**, or a valid C/AL expression. If the source is a variable or an editable field in a table, the control is editable; in any other case it is read-only.
	Check box—a small square box, which can be in two states: checked or unchecked. Similar to a text box, it must be bound to a source using the **SourceExpr** property, with one condition: the source must be of or evaluate to Boolean data type.
	Option button—a small round button, which can be in two states: checked or unchecked. It must be bound to a source using the **SourceExpr** property. The source of the Option button must be of or evaluate to Boolean or Option data type. You will typically have more than one Option button linked to the same source, and set their **OptionValue** properties to different values, representing different options users can select from.
	Command button—a plain button, which displays a static, multi-language enabled text defined by its **Caption** and **CaptionML** properties.
	Menu button—a button that displays a static, multi-language enabled text defined by its **Caption** and **CaptionML** properties and opens a menu when clicked.
	Frame—a control which is used as a container of other controls: and any controls placed inside a frame are moved together with the frame. A frame can display a caption in its top-left corner
	Image—displays a static image, defined by its **Bitmap** property. This property can be set to a numeric value (a variety of documented and undocumented numeric values can display any of the built-in application icons), or to a file path. If you specify a path, it must point to a BMP file, and the image is embedded into the form at compile time.

Control	Description
	Picture box—displays a bitmap from a table field of type BLOB. The field is specified using the **SourceExpr** property.
	Shape—displays a static shape of type defined using the **ShapeStyle** property.
	Indicator—displays a progress bar, with the **SourceExpr** property bound to any kind of C/AL expression evaluating to a numeric value in the 0 to 10,000 range (10,000 represents 100%).
	Tab control—a container control with several tabs, or pages, defined using **PageNames** and **PageNamesML** properties.
	Subform—used to display a form, typically a list, within another form, typically a card form.
	Table box—contains other controls typically of type **text box**, arranged in a tabular list. Every list form contains a **table box** control.
	Matrix box—a complex control, similar to a **table box** in the way that it displays a set of columns. However, the columns are determined at run time from a list of values from another table. Making use of this control requires a fair amount of programming.

Let's take a look at some commonly used non-basic controls.

Subforms

Imagine a form within a form. What is it good for? Well, hardly anything if you imagined a card form within another card form. But if you imagined a list form within a card form, uses are plenty: sales invoices or production orders with their lines, bills of materials with their components, sales statistics with breakdown per territory; you name it. This is achieved using the **Subform** control. Run form **42 Sales Order** to get a gist of what a card form with a **Subform** looks like.

To configure a subform control to display another form, you need to set some properties:

Property	Description
SubFormID	Specifies the ID of the form that will be displayed as subform.
SubFormLink	Specifies how the subform is linked to the main form. Subforms are used to represent parent-child or master-detail relationships between data in two tables, with a header displaying master information, and lines displaying details. This property is used to specify the master-detail relationship.

Menus and buttons

Other types of controls that you will usually want to include on your forms are menus and buttons. They are used to invoke other features, such as posting procedures, reports, or other forms.

Two controls are particularly useful for this: **Button** and **MenuButton**. A button can execute a single action, something like the **Make Order** button on the **Sales Quote** form. A menu button isn't linked to an action directly, but when clicked, it displays a menu of actions that we can then execute by clicking on them. For a feel of a typical menu button, take a look at **Functions**, also on the **Sales Quote** form.

Now that we've mastered the rocket science behind, let's see which properties we need to set to define actions:

Property	Description
PushAction	Type of action that can happen when users push the button. `<0>` indicates that no action will be taken; `OK`, `Cancel`, `LookupOK`, `LookupCancel`, `Yes`, `No`, `Close`, and `Stop` will all close the form with proper status returned to the caller; `FormHelp` will launch the online help for the form; `RunObject` will execute an object; `RunSystem` will execute an external application; and `LookupTable` will launch the default lookup form for the underlying source table.
RunObject	Specifies the type and ID of the object that will be executed when the button is pushed. **PushAction** must be `RunObject`.
RunFormView	Specifies any sort order or filters applied to the executed form. **PushAction** must be `RunObject` and **RunObject** must specify a form.
RunFormLink	Specifies the link established between the caller form and the executed form. When two forms are linked using this property, the called form can update its contents when record selection is changed in the caller from. You can think of this as showing a subform in an external window.
RunFormLinkType	Specifies whether the link specified in **RunFormLink** is an active one, or a one-time link. An active link, specified by the `OnUpdate` value, will cause the called form to update its content based on the link every time the record is changed in the caller form. A one-time link, specified by `OnOpen`, will simply display the called form, with the link in place, but will not update the called form when the record in the caller form changes.

For menu buttons, you must first define menu items. To do so, right-click the menu button and choose **Menu Items**, or choose the same command from the **View** menu. For each menu item you must at least define its **Caption**, and you can use other properties to define specific actions that will execute when a menu item is selected from the menu.

Menu items share the majority of their properties with command buttons, and all of the properties discussed in the table above apply to menu items of menu buttons as much as they do to command buttons.

Customizing pages

Pages are the RoleTailored client's equivalent of forms, and are the building blocks of the RoleTailored user interface. They are used primarily to display information from the database and to allow data entry, but we can use them simply to put anything we wish on screen for the user to interact with.

To create a page, in **Object Designer** select **Pages**, then click the **New** button. The **New Page** form will assist you through the creation process:

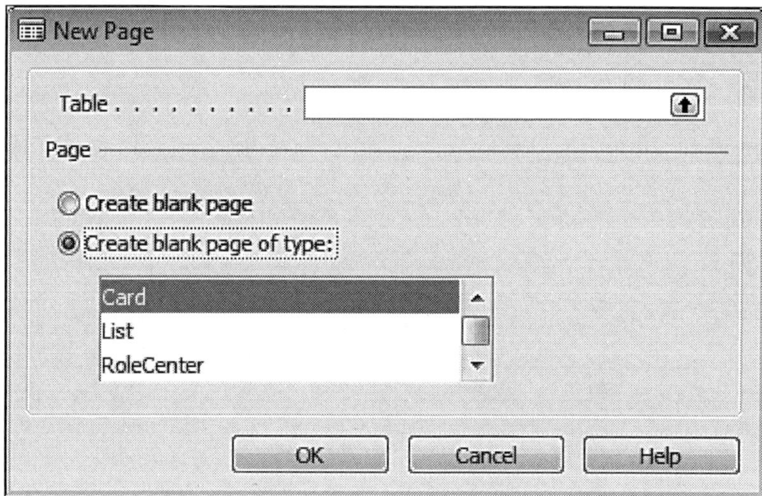

Page properties

Unlike the **New Form** dialog, here you can only choose the source table and the type of page; but as soon as you make your choice, a blank **Page Designer** is shown, with only two properties filled out: **SourceTable** and **PageType**. Most page properties are called exactly the same and exhibit the same behavior as form properties, but there are four additional ones:

Property	Description
PageType	Specifies the type of the page. Types affect the behavior of pages, and we will discuss page types in more detail later on.
InstructionalTextML	Declares the multi-language text label that will be displayed on the page before any other user interface element. It only has effect on ConfirmationDialog type forms.
CardFormID	Defines the card form that is used to display, edit, or create records of the type that is displayed in a list. For example, in **Customer List**, this property defines that **Customer Card** is invoked every time a user calls the **Edit**, **View**, or **New** action. This property affects only list type forms.
LinksAllowed	Specifies whether links functionality will be available for this page or not.

Page types

The most important of these properties is **PageType**, because it defines the behavior of the form when displayed in the RoleTailored client. There are exactly ten types of pages: **Card**, **List**, **RoleCenter**, **CardPart**, **ListPart**, **Document**, **Worksheet**, **ListPlus**, **ConfirmationDialog** and **NavigatePage**.

Let's take a closer look at their purpose, functionality, and anatomy.

Card

Similar to the card form, this type of page displays information about one record of a single table, such as one customer, one vendor, or one item. Typical examples of a card page are **21 Customer Card**, or **30 Item Card**.

The following is what a typical page looks like:

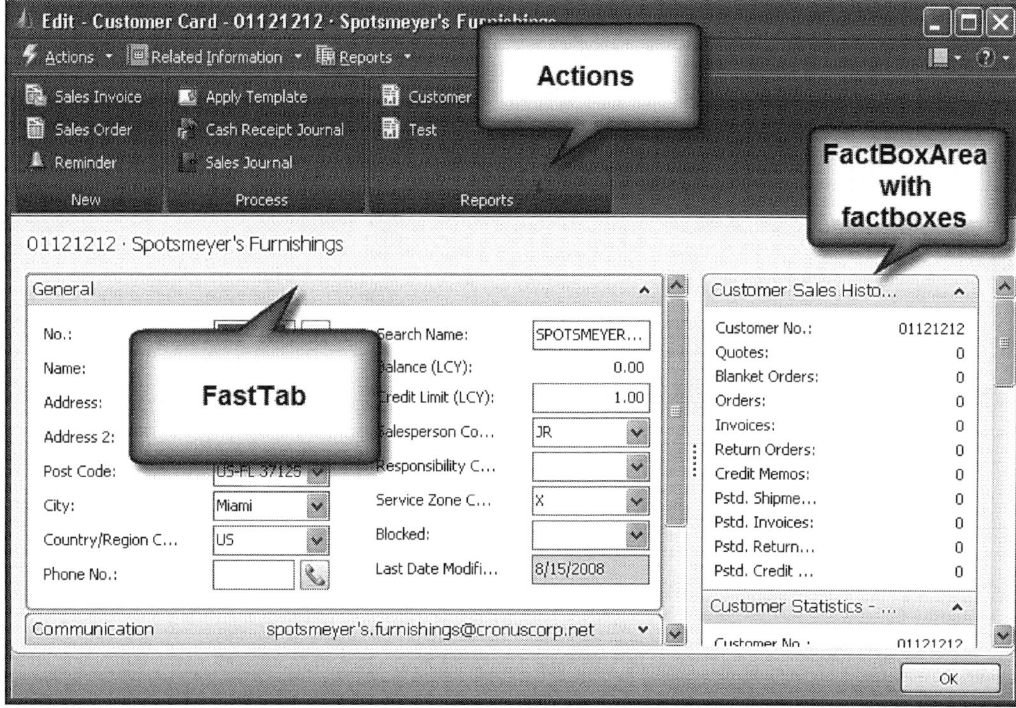

At the top of the page there are actions. Actions can be grouped into menus, or into toolbars. We'll learn all about them later.

The majority of the screen is used for information display and entry. The left part of the screen is occupied with a ContentArea, which consists of groups of fields called FastTabs. Values of fields in FastTabs are typically taken from a single record of a table.

The right part of the screen is occupied by the FactBoxArea, which contains several FactBoxes.

List

Similar to the list form, List pages display multiple records from the same table at once, such as a list of customers, list of vendors, or list of items. Typical examples are **22 Customer List**, or **27 Vendor List**.

This is what a List page looks like:

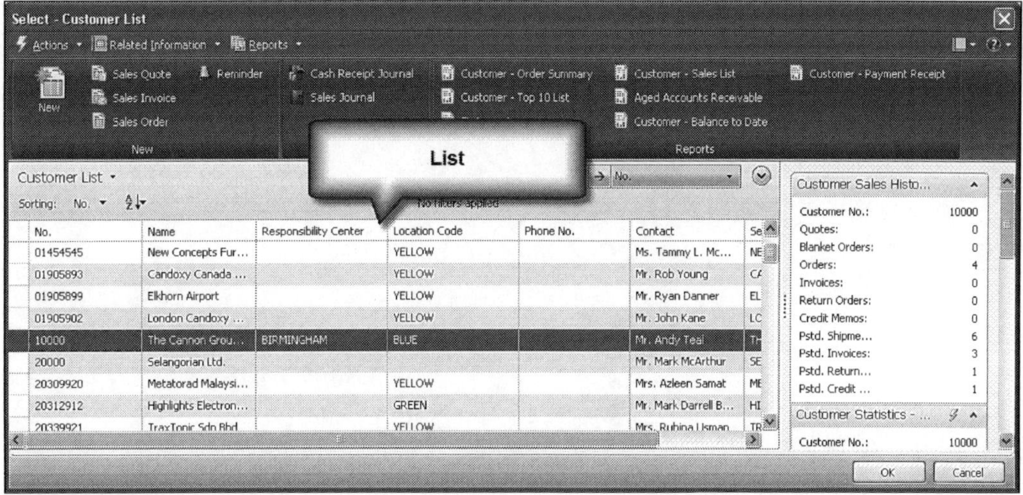

It has exactly the same elements as a card page, except its ContentArea is consumed by a single repeater group, which lists all information in a table.

RoleCenter

Pages of this type are used as home screens for different roles. They consist of different parts, and are used to provide quick access to the functionality most used by a user role, as well as the most relevant information, all at a glance. Examples of RoleCenter pages are **9005 Sales Manager Role Center** and **9010 Production Planner Role Center**.

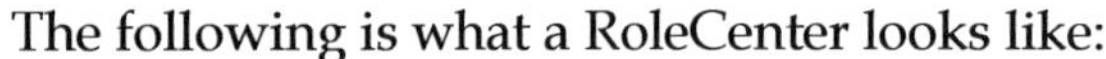

The following is what a RoleCenter looks like:

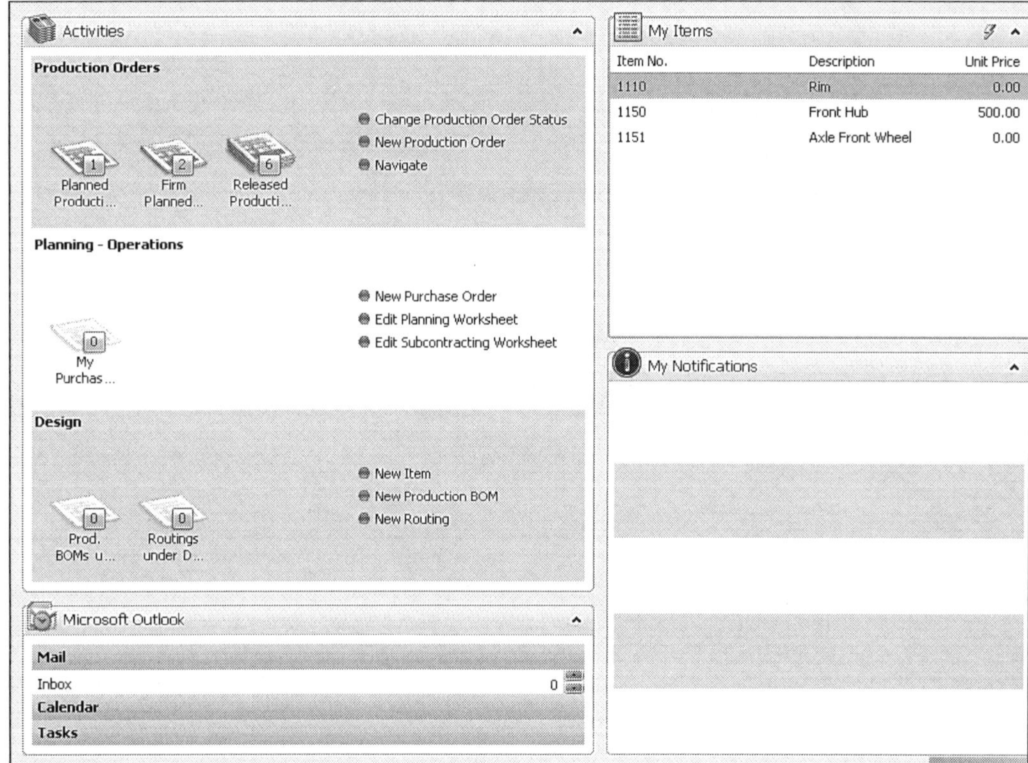

It consists of groups displayed as vertical columns. In each group it is possible to have several page parts, such as **Activities**, **My Items**, and many more.

CardPart

CardPart pages are card pages that aren't used standalone, but come as parts on other pages, such as Card, List, or RoleCenter pages. Various FactBoxes, such as **9082 Customer Statistics** or **9092 Approval Factbox**, are typical examples of CardPart pages. Most elements of a RoleCenter, as well as most FactBoxes are actually CardPart (or ListPart) pages. Here is an example of a CardPart:

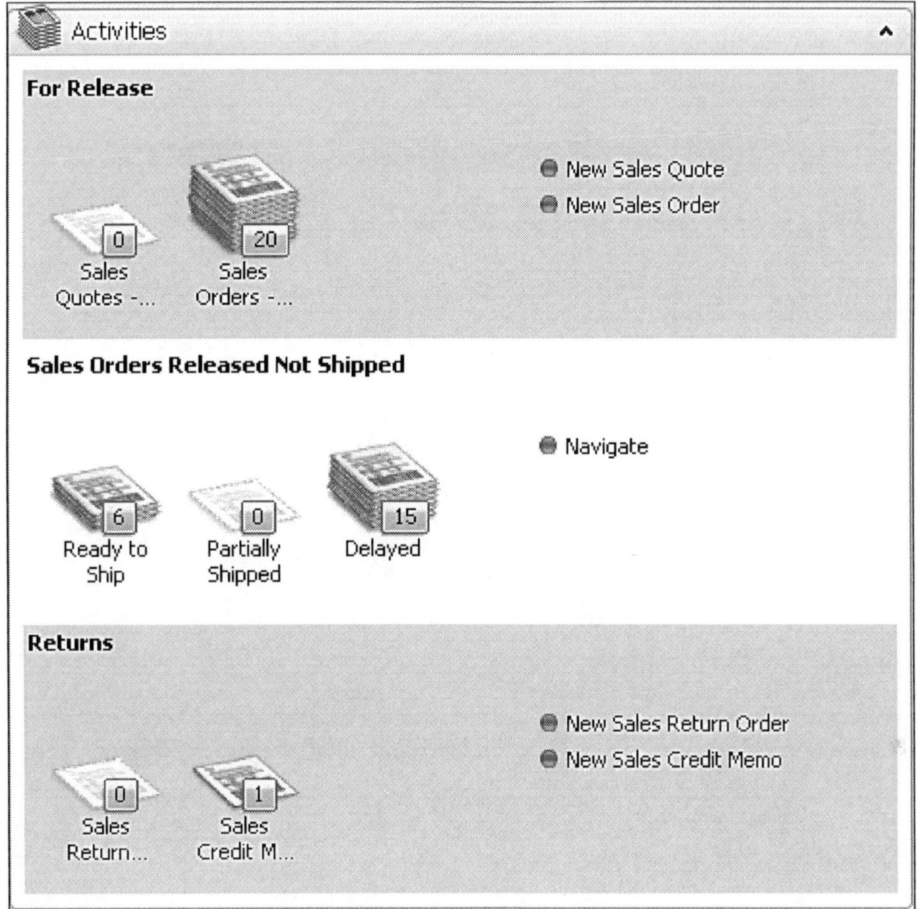

CardPart pages typically consist of several groups, which are rendered in various ways, depending on the type of elements displayed. The CardPart shown consists of three CueGroups.

ListPart

ListPart pages are list pages intended for inclusion as parts of other types of pages. Pages such as **47 Sales Invoice Subform** or **9150 My Customers** are examples of ListPart pages. Most of the list part pages are simply sub-pages of other pages, but often ListParts find their way into RoleCenter pages or FactBox areas as well.

Here goes a ListPart:

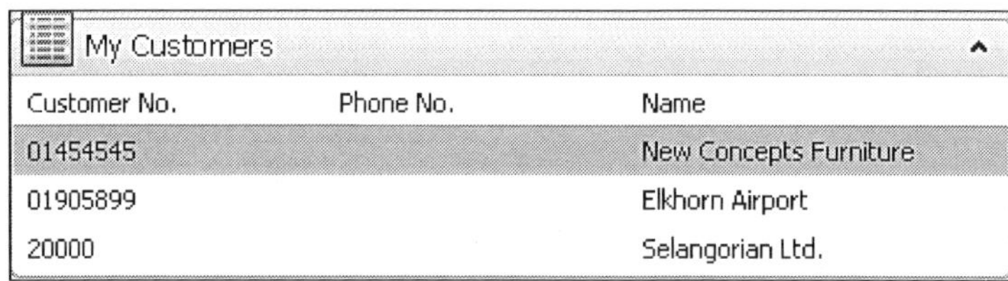

As obvious as it is, all list parts consist of columns of fields.

Document

Document pages are combinations of card and list types, and contain several groups of header information and typically one ListPart page with lines information. Information contained in header and lines of a Document page represents an indivisible entity (for example an invoice consists of both header and lines). Take a look at page **43 Sales Invoice** or **99000831 Released Production Order** to get a feel for document pages.

The following is a document page:

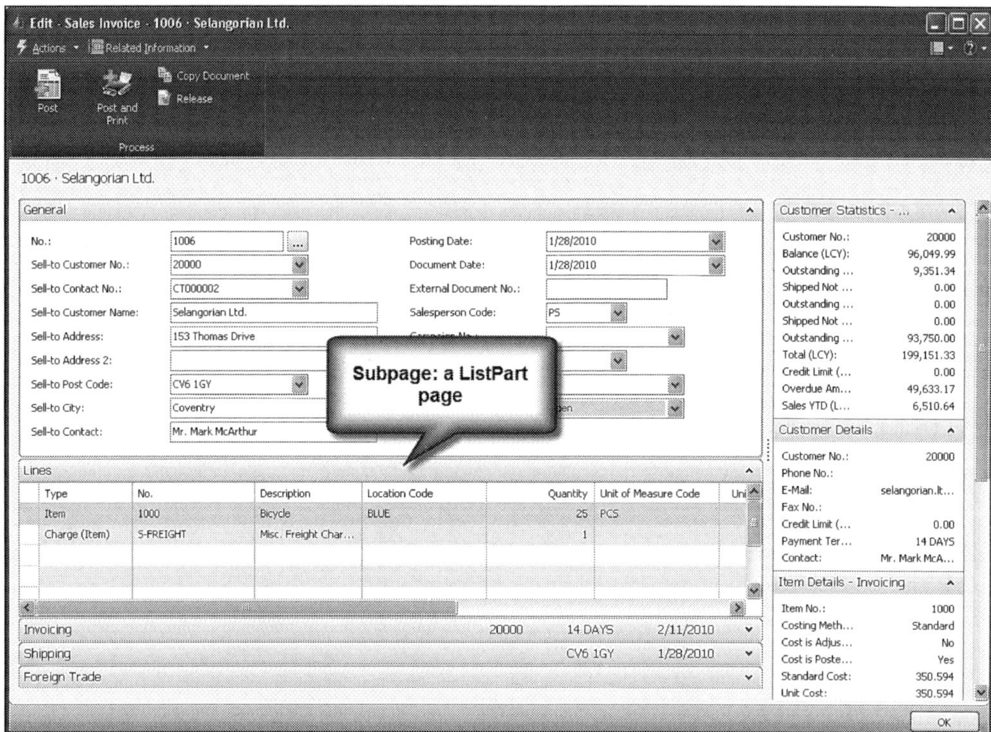

If at first it doesn't look much different from a typical card page, take a closer look. One of its FastTabs is actually a ListPart page.

Worksheet

Worksheet forms are used for various journals, such as **39 General Journal** or **40 Item Journal**, and they typically comprise a filter, lines, and a summary footer.

This is what a good Worksheet page looks like:

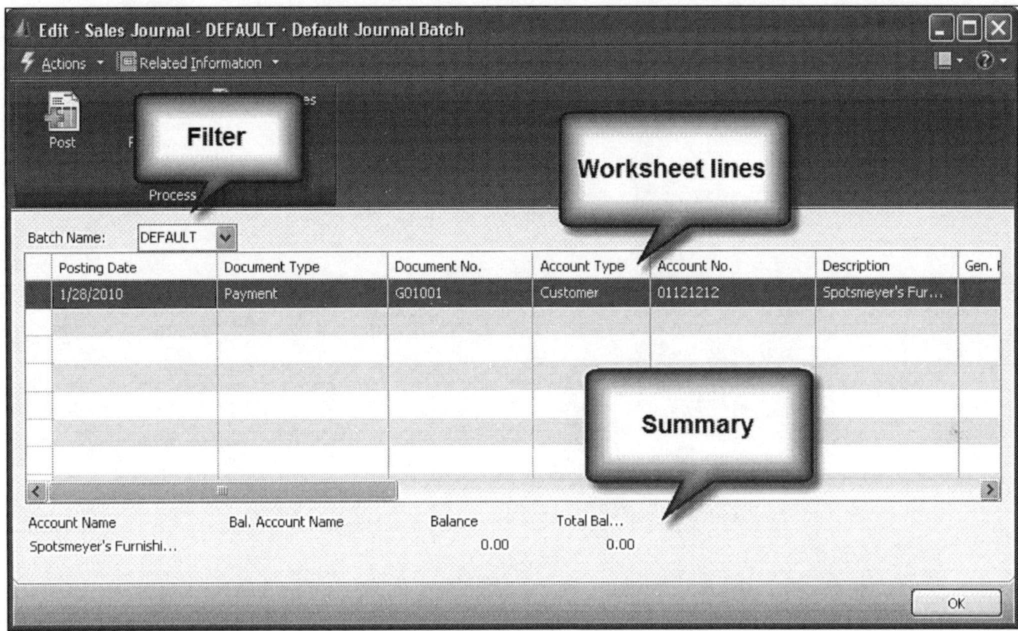

The elements of a Worksheet page are a single filter field used to choose batches (groups of lines of a worksheet that will be processed as a single transaction), lines, and a footer, which typically gives summary information about the worksheet lines.

ListPlus

This is a hybrid of list and card types, but different from document type. It contains header information and lines information; however, the lines don't belong to the header, they are only related to it. Good examples of ListPlus pages are **397 Sales Invoice Statistics** or **5091 Segment**.

The following is a ListPlus:

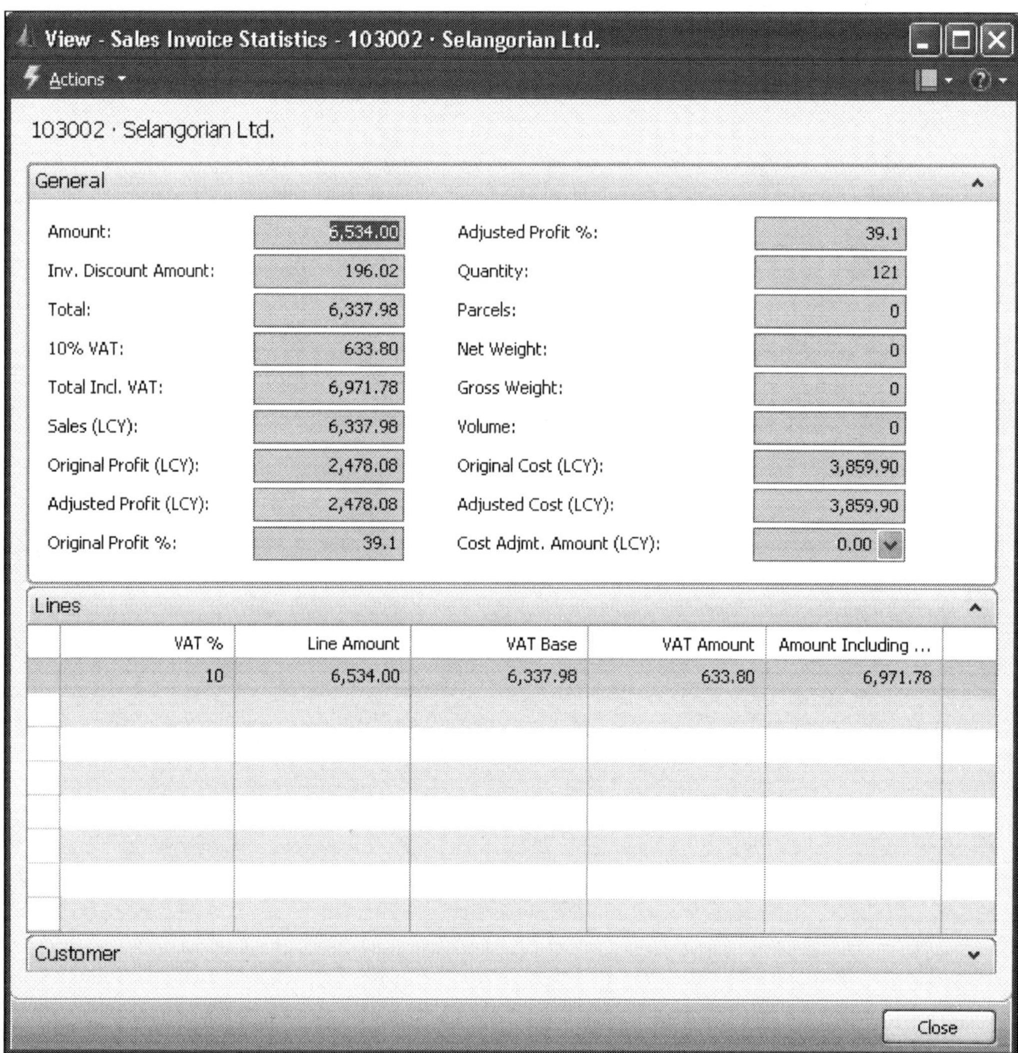

If it reminds you of a Document, it is so because it is similar. It contains exactly the same types of elements, and is rendered similarly, and the difference is purely technical. A document represents a single entity while a ListPlus contains information collected from various entities.

ConfirmationDialog

Pages of this type are used for important interruptions of user actions, when the application needs an extra confirmation from the user before the action can be completed. These pages usually contain information that will aid the user in deciding the course of action. Typical examples of ConfirmationDialog pages are pages **342 Check Availability** or **343 Check Credit Limit**.

This is a typical ConfirmationDialog:

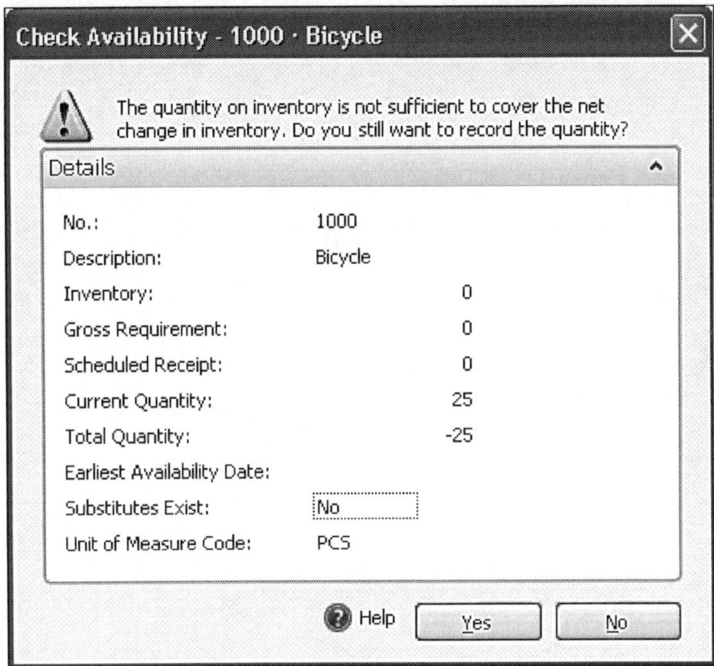

Notice the text above the FastTab: it comes from the **InformationalTextML** property, which can be defined on any type of page, but only has effect on pages of type ConfirmationDialog.

NavigatePage

For pages of this type, groups aren't displayed as FastTabs, but as normal tabs (although on the bottom of the page). The most obvious example is of course page **344 Navigate**, but as tabs can be made visible or invisible interchangeably, this type of page is very useful for wizards, such as **5077 Create Interaction** or **5126 Create Opportunity**.

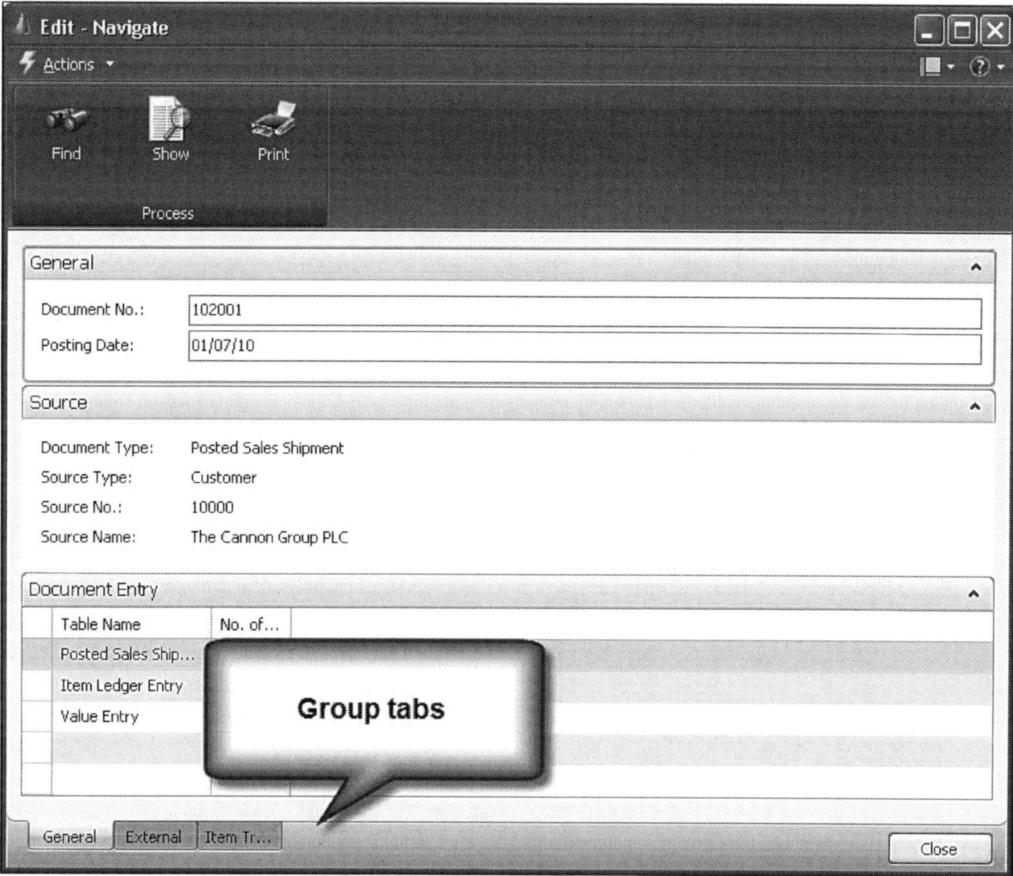

While tabs didn't find their way into card or document pages, they got their upside-down spot in NavigatePage pages. They work exactly the same way that page control works in form objects.

Page Designer

To get a feeling of how a simple page is designed, in **Object Designer** locate the page **5714 Responsibility Center Card** and click the Design button:

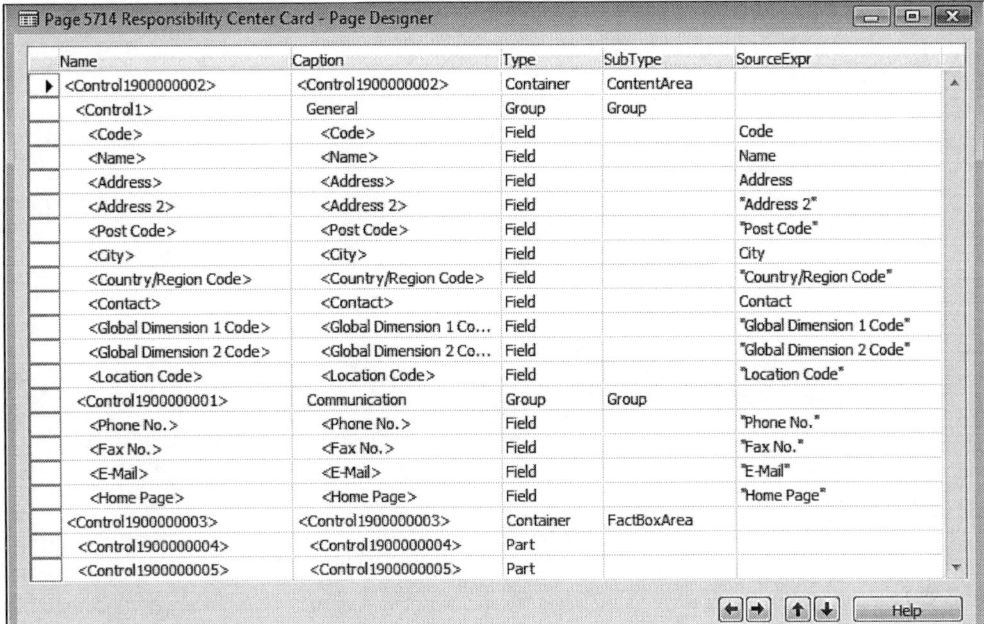

Page 5714 Responsibility Center Card - Page Designer

Name	Caption	Type	SubType	SourceExpr
<Control1900000002>	<Control1900000002>	Container	ContentArea	
<Control1>	General	Group	Group	
<Code>	<Code>	Field		Code
<Name>	<Name>	Field		Name
<Address>	<Address>	Field		Address
<Address 2>	<Address 2>	Field		"Address 2"
<Post Code>	<Post Code>	Field		"Post Code"
<City>	<City>	Field		City
<Country/Region Code>	<Country/Region Code>	Field		"Country/Region Code"
<Contact>	<Contact>	Field		Contact
<Global Dimension 1 Code>	<Global Dimension 1 Co...	Field		"Global Dimension 1 Code"
<Global Dimension 2 Code>	<Global Dimension 2 Co...	Field		"Global Dimension 2 Code"
<Location Code>	<Location Code>	Field		"Location Code"
<Control1900000001>	Communication	Group	Group	
<Phone No.>	<Phone No.>	Field		"Phone No."
<Fax No.>	<Fax No.>	Field		"Fax No."
<E-Mail>	<E-Mail>	Field		"E-Mail"
<Home Page>	<Home Page>	Field		"Home Page"
<Control1900000003>	<Control1900000003>	Container	FactBoxArea	
<Control1900000004>	<Control1900000004>	Part		
<Control1900000005>	<Control1900000005>	Part		

Help

Unlike **Form Designer**, which we saw earlier, here we can declare user interface elements (controls), but can't specify exactly how or where they will be positioned on screen.

To create a new control, select the first empty line and simply start typing something into the **Name** or **Caption** column. These two properties have exactly the same meaning as anywhere else in the system. Important properties you must set for page controls are **Type**, **SubType**, and **SourceExpr**.

Property	Description
Type	Defines the general behavior of the control. Each control belongs to one of the four types: Container, Group, Field, or Part.
SubType	For each type, there are several subtypes, which further modify the control and its behavior.
SourceExpr	For controls of type Field, this property defines the source from which the control's value is taken.

Let's take a closer look at types and their respective subtypes.

Containers

At the base of every page there is a container, and every page must have a container defined as its topmost element. The container is used to define the general behavior of the page.

There are three subtypes of containers:

- **ContentArea**: most common container subtype, used for most page types. If a page is not a FactBox or a RoleCenter page, then its topmost container must be of type ContentArea.
- **FactBoxArea**: containers of this type contain page parts of FactBox type, and place them in the FactBox pane of the page.
- **RoleCenterArea**: used by pages of type RoleCenter, these containers group page parts into vertical columns.

Don't define two containers of the same type per page. A page must contain exactly one ContentArea or RoleCenter area, and up to one FactBoxArea. Any other containers beyond these will be ignored and won't be rendered.

Groups

Groups are used to group other controls together in several different ways. Group subtype determines how exactly the group is rendered in the RoleTailored client.

There are four group subtypes:

- **Group**: groups fields into FastTabs, for easier navigation and to reduce clutter on screen. This subtype is typically used on card type pages.
- **Repeater**: groups fields into tabular lists, typically on list or ListPart pages.
- **CueGroup**: displays fields as visual cues, instead of as normal field controls.
- **FixedLayout**: displays field values as non-editable labels, without their field captions. Typically used with worksheet type pages.

Group subtype affects several other aspects of the RoleTailored client renderer. For example, it determines the type of icon that RoleCenter will display in the upper-left corner of a page part. If a part page contains a CueGroup, the icon will display a pile of papers, while for other group subtypes it will display a single document.

For other page types groups also have specific behavior. For example, in pages of type NavigatePage, groups are rendered as tabs, instead of as FastTabs. For PageCards, groups are displayed as labels printed in bold, while ListCard pages will ignore any groups other than Repeaters.

Cue groups specialty

Cue groups don't just look great on screen. They also integrate neatly into the **Home** menu when used on Role Center pages. When a field displayed in a cue group uses as its drill-down page a page that has been placed as an action into the **Home** menu, then a filter is added to that **Home** menu action, which will inherit display value and drill-down functionality from the cue group field. Thus, cue groups effectively remain accessible at all times through **Home** menu actions. Take a look at these; they all come from cue groups in the **Order Processor** role center:

Fields

The most common element of all pages is field, and most of the pages contain plenty of these. Fields are used to display actual values from the database, and to allow entry of new values. Fields can display values taken from table fields, C/AL variables, functions, or text constants.

How exactly the field will be displayed is determined by:

- **Data type of the value associated with the field**: Every data type will render a particular user interface control. Code, text, and numeric fields are rendered as text boxes, options are rendered as combo boxes, boolean values display checkboxes, and date values come with the date picker control.
- **TableRelation property**: If a field is related to another table as a lookup field, it will display a drop-down menu similar to a combo box, which allows looking up values from another table. If a field is a SIFT field, it will be displayed as a hyperlink, which will allow drilling down to actual values used for calculation of the value displayed in the SIFT field.
- **Group subtype**: Fields in Group subtypes will be rendered with their captions to the left of the field control; fields in CueGroup are rendered as visual cues (stacks of documents); fields in Repeaters will be rendered as columns of tables; and fields belonging to FixedLayout groups will be displayed as read-only labels without caption.
- **ExtendedDatatype property**: If defined on a field, this property determines additional functionality of the field. Values of **Phone No.**, **URL**, and **E-Mail** will display an icon button, which will launch a phone caller application, a web browser, or an e-mail client respectively, while **Ratio** fields will be displayed as progress bars.

Parts

The RoleTailored client allows you to embed pages and other objects, such as charts, as parts of other pages. This can be achieved through controls of type Part. It is only possible to embed pages of type CardPart and ListPart.

Parts don't have subtypes, but their behavior is controlled by an important property: **PartType**. It can have one of the following values: **Page**, **System**, or **Chart**.

Page parts

The default value of the **PartType** property is **Page**, and it's for reason: the most common type of parts is other pages. It is possible to embed CardPart or ListPart pages only, but you have a lot of flexibility with them to define whatever functionality you want to
see embedded.

When you specify **Page** as **PartType**, you must also define the **PagePartID** property, which must contain the ID of the page object you want to embed.

System parts

Other than user-defined parts, there are system provided parts, which give access to useful functionality and information.

For system parts it is necessary to specify, **SystemPartID** property, which is really a drop-down list of the following parts:

- **Outlook**: displays the Outlook integration part, which provides information about pending items, such as e-mail messages, calendar entries, or tasks.
- **Notes**: displays the notes linked to the currently selected entity.
- **MyNotes**: displays notifications other users sent to the user using Notes functionality.
- **RecordLinks**: displays the links related to the currently selected entity.

Chart parts

A particularly eye-candy feature of Microsoft Dynamics NAV 2009 is charts, a special type of parts, which can be included on any RoleCenter page without any declaration, or on other types of pages by declaring them through a **Part** property of type Chart.

There is a smorgasbord of system-provided charts, which cover most application areas from accounting to manufacturing. If you are unhappy with these, you can create and import your own. Chart definitions are stored in the system table **2000000078 Chart**, where they can be imported or exported as XML definitions using the **Charts** form or page. You can find **Charts** in the **Departments** page (or navigation pane if you are using the Classic client) under **Administration | Application Setup | RoleTailored Client**.

Positioning controls

There is little you can do about specifying exactly where a control will be rendered in the page. Properties well known from forms and reports, such as XPos and YPos, simply don't exist for pages. With this, the RoleTailored client is somewhat stubborn, so the best you can do is get to know how it works, then play along with these rules.

Generally, the objects are rendered in that order in which they are declared. Depending on page type, groups are arranged horizontally or vertically, according to their order in Page Designer. If you have a card page, and you want something to display to the right, the only option you have is to place it into a FactBoxArea.

If you are unhappy with the order of controls, you can change it by moving them up or down, using the up or down buttons (↑ and ↓). Be careful when rearranging groups, because moving a group up or down will move the group control only. Fields or parts belonging to that group will stay in the same place, and you will have to move each control individually. Furthermore, moving groups up or down will typically disrupt their indentation, so you will probably need to fix it using the indent buttons (← and →).

Fields in FastTabs are always arranged in two columns, in somewhat annoying fashion: the number of fields is divided by two, with equal number of fields displayed in each column. It's impossible to have a FastTab with only one column (unless it sports a single field), or with five controls in the left column and two controls in the right one.

Spur some action

Other than controls for displaying and entering information, pages also contain actions. Actions are used to call other objects, such as pages or reports, or to execute application logic, such as posting procedures.

Most of the pages contain actions, which are displayed in the menu bar and the actions pane. This is how actions are organized for page **21 Customer Card**:

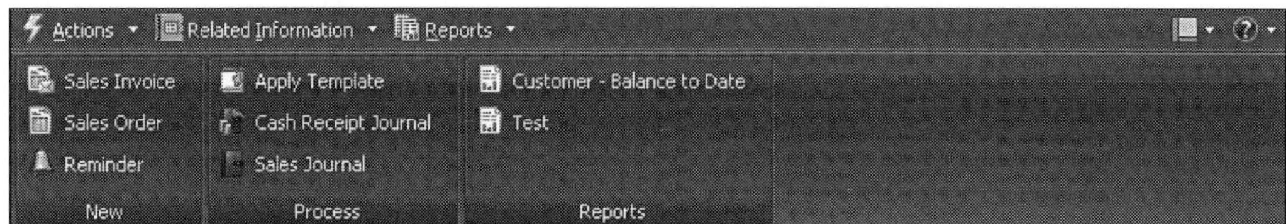

Actions are grouped into three menus (**Actions**, **Related Information**, and **Reports**), and three action categories (**New**, **Process**, and **Reports**). Menus look and function much like the menu buttons in the Classic client, while action categories are a new concept for Microsoft Dynamics NAV users. Functionally, they resemble ribbon groups in Microsoft Office 2007 applications.

To define actions for a page, in **Page Designer** scroll down to the first empty line, then select **Actions** from the **View** menu.

[It is possible to define actions on non-empty lines; however, these actions only have effect in specific cases, for example on CueGroup controls. In most other cases, the RoleTailored client will simply ignore them.]

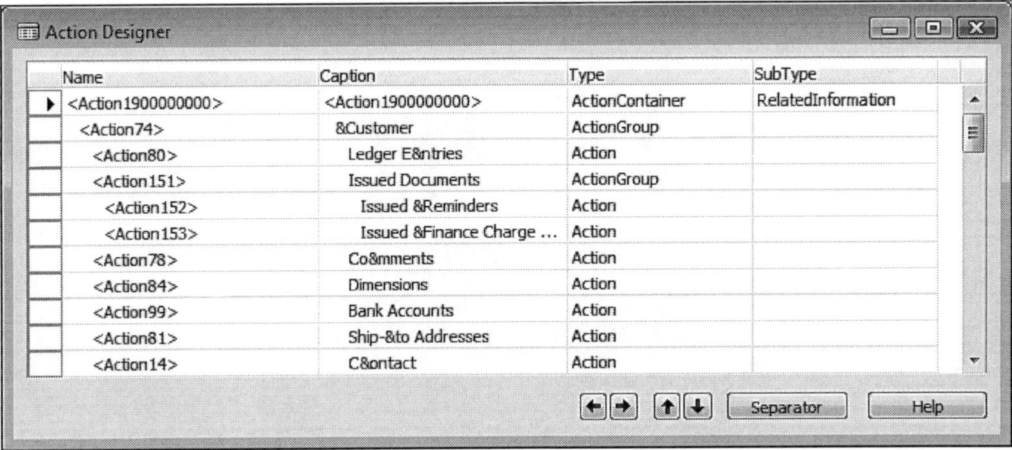

Designing actions is as simple as designing page controls, because the **Action Designer** employs the same logic as Page Designer. Indenting and moving of actions works exactly the same way as with page controls, and basic properties used to define actions are called exactly the same way as with page controls.

> Luckily, it is possible to use the magic of copy-and-paste to copy actions to the clipboard, then paste them into another object's **Action Designer**. This is something that was never possible for menu items of menu button controls in forms.

There are four types of actions that can be defined using the **Type** property: **ActionContainer**, **ActionGroup**, **Action**, and **Separator**.

ActionContainer

Yes, you've got it right: ActionContainers contain actions. Every action must belong to a container, and there are several types of containers you can use. Each container type is defined by the **SubType** property, which can have one of the following values:

- **NewDocumentItems**: Actions in this container are placed into the **New Document** submenu of the **Actions** menu.
- **ActionItems**: Actions in this container are placed into the **Actions** menu below the **Links** action.

This is how **NewDocumentAction** and **ActionItems** actions are placed into the **Actions** menu:

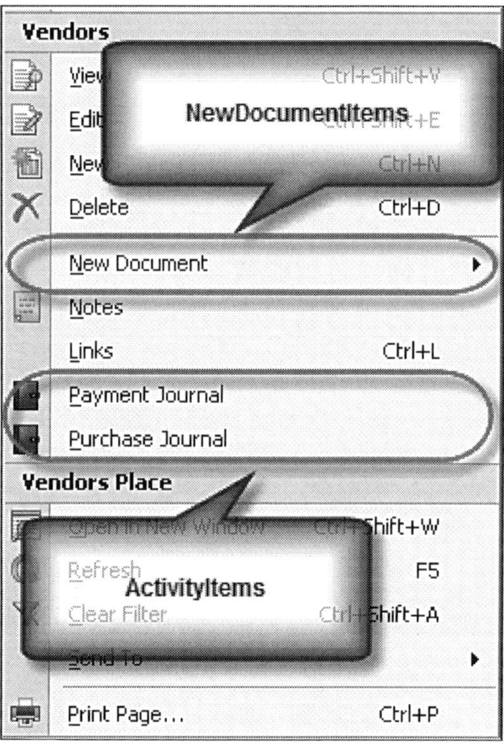

- **RelatedInformation**: Actions in this container are placed into the **Related Information** menu.

- **Reports**: Actions in this container are placed into the **Reports** menu.

- **HomeItems**: Actions in this container are placed into the **Home** menu of the **Role Center**. Understandably, this container is only relevant for RoleCenter pages, and other pages ignore any actions placed in this container.
- **ActivityButtons**: Actions in this container are placed in the navigation pane just between the **Home** button and the **Departments** button.

This is how HomeItems and ActivityButtons are placed:

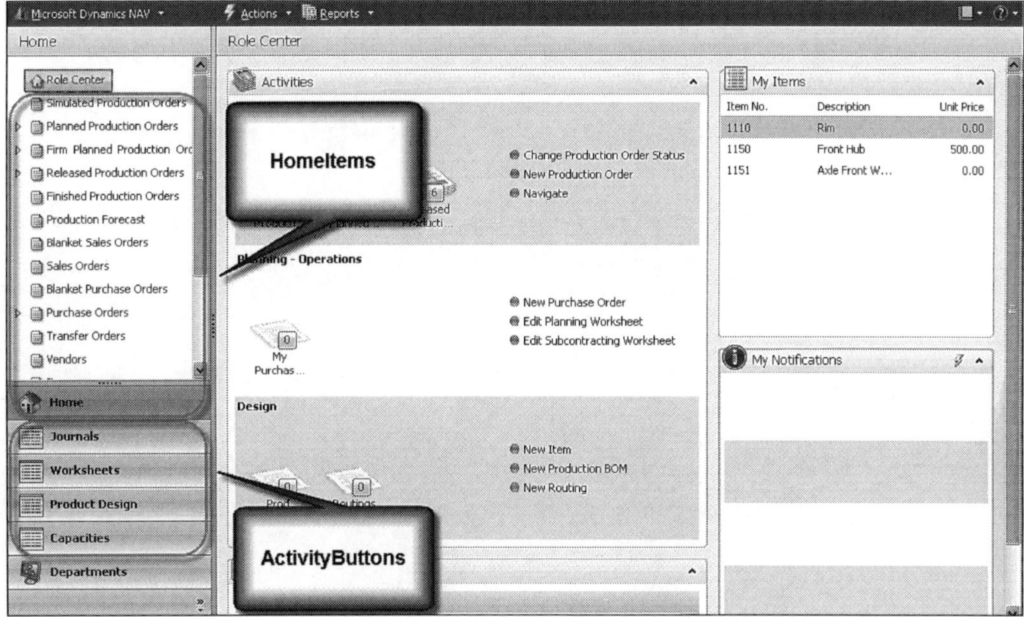

ActionGroup

You can use **ActionGroups** to group actions into meaningful sets. How exactly a group will behave depends on the **ActionContainer** subtype.

For **NewDocuments**, **ActionItems**, **RelatedInformation**, and **Reports** container subtypes, each group will be displayed as a submenu:

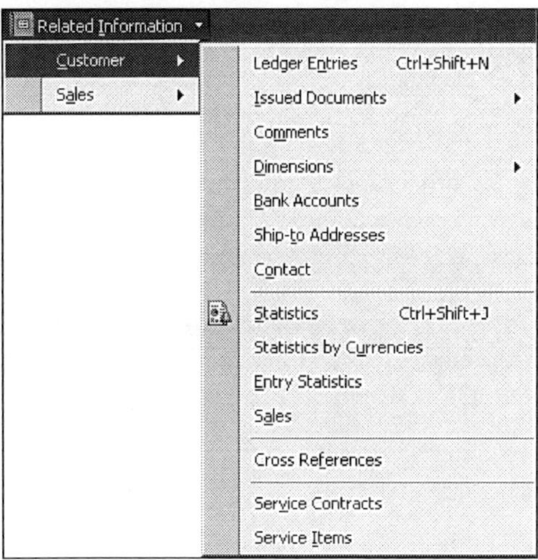

In this example, **Customer**, **Sales**, **Issued Documents**, and **Dimensions** are actions of type **ActionGroup**.

For the **HomeItems** container, groups are ignored, and all actions are rendered in one flat list.

Groups in an **ActivityButtons** container are displayed as buttons in the navigation pane:

In the screenshot shown, **Posted Documents** and **Administration** are declared as actions of type **ActionGroup**.

Action

All of these define just the skeleton—actions of type **Action** constitute the fleshy part of the page navigation. For the sake of clarity, we will simply call them *actions* (to avoid clumsy, but accurate term *actions of type* Action).

Actions are used to call pages or reports, or to execute any C/AL logic that might be defined behind them. Most navigation needs can be fulfilled without any code, though, by setting properties:

Property	Description
RunFormMode	Specifies in which state the page invoked by this action will be open. This can be **View**, **Edit**, or **Create**. **View** will display the page as read-only; **Edit** will make it editable; and **Create** will display an editable page with all fields emptied and ready to insert the new record.
Image	Specifies the icon that will be displayed with the caption. There are hundreds of icons, each of which is referred to using a textual identifier.
Promoted	Specifies whether an action is promoted to one of the action categories, for better visibility and accessibility on the screen.
PromotedCategory	Specifies into which action category in the action pane this action will be promoted. Possible choices are **New**, **Process**, and **Reports**.
PromotedIsBig	If set to **Yes**, this will make the promoted action button big.
Ellipsis	Specifies whether the action caption is displayed with an ellipsis (...) appended, indicating that clicking this action will require further input before the action is completed.
ShortCutKey	Defines the keyboard shortcut that can be pressed to invoke the action directly, without clicking on it with the mouse.
RunObject	Defines which object will be called when the action is invoked. You can run pages, reports, codeunits, and XMLports.
RunFormView	Specifies any keys, sort order, or filters that will be applied to the page specified in **RunObject** when it is run (applies only to page objects).
RunFormLink	Specifies the link between the calling page and called page (applies only to page objects). It works as a dynamic filter, because it enables filtering another page based on values of the active record in current page.

There are two major concepts that rely on setting these properties: promotion, and object running.

Action promotion

Actions are typically displayed in menus; however, you can promote the most used actions to make them more accessible and readily visible to your users. Promoted actions are displayed both in menus and in the action pane, in one of the three possible categories.

These are the promoted actions for **Transfer Order**:

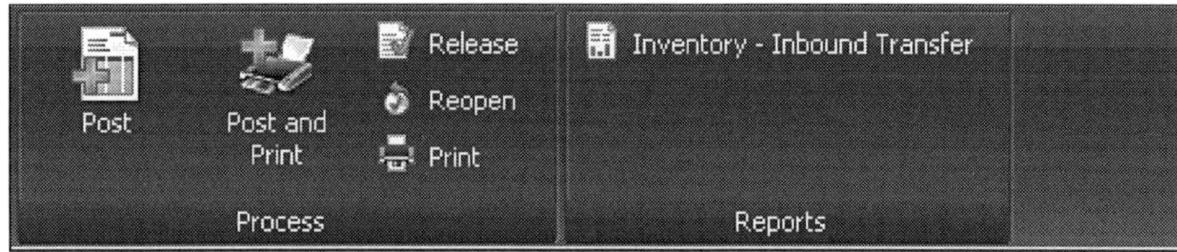

To promote an action, you need to set its **Promoted** property to **Yes**, and choose the category into which it is promoted the (default is **New**). If you need to make promoted items very prominent, you can set their **PromotedIsBig** property to **Yes**, to make them really big in the action pane.

Promotion category doesn't have anything to do with the ActionContainer type, and you can promote actions from the **NewDocumentItems** container into categories other than **New**, or actions from a non-**NewDocumentItems** container into the **New** category.

Object running

Actions are used to execute things, and there are only two ways to make them do so: to make them run objects, or to make them call C/AL code by utilizing their `OnAction` triggers. The former is easy, because it requires no knowledge of C/AL and is intended for simple navigation, such as opening specific entities from a list of entities, or running a report. The latter can be as simple as writing a single line of code, or as complex as hundreds of lines of very complicated business logic.

Never put extensive business logic directly into the `OnAction` trigger. Instead, embed the business logic into a separate function, preferably of a codeunit (a concept know as abstraction), and then call this function. This will make your code reusable, and safe from inadvertent deletions.

To specify which object will be run when the action is clicked, you need to define its **RunObject** property. You can do it by manually typing the object's **Type** and **ID**, or **Type** and **Name** (this is one of those situations where the **Name** property matters outside of C/AL variable declarations). For example, to call **Customer Card**, you simply type **Page 21**, or **Page Customer Card**.

Another possibility is to select the **RunObject** property, then press *F6* or click the Assist button, then choose from the list of all possible objects. After a while you'll catch yourself simply typing the object ID's from memory like a real pro.

If you are calling pages, you may want to specify sort order or any filters that will be applied to these objects. You can achieve this by using the **RunFormView** property. You can either type in the view syntax manually, or you can press *F6* to invoke the **Table View** editor, which will make your chore considerably easier:

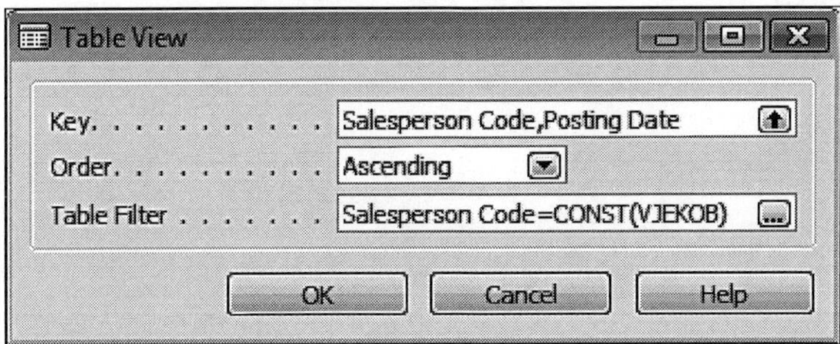

Form Transformation tool

Now you have seen how much work it is to define proper and good looking forms, and how much effort it is to create decent pages; effectively this is twice as much effort to create what's fundamentally the same thing: a user interface. Having forms and pages as separate objects is a major pain for developers. Or at least it would be if there weren't the Form Transformation tool.

As its name suggests, it is used to convert forms to pages. As you have seen, there are many differences between forms and pages, but there are many similarities as well. These similarities are the basis for the Form Transformation tool: it makes use of them to make it possible to convert almost every form to a page of mostly the same functional value.

We'll provide a detailed walk-through of this tool in the *Sample Application* chapter.

Customizing reports

In Microsoft Dynamics NAV, reports are used for printing information from the database, and to execute *batch jobs* (process information in batches). Our focus will stay with the printing part of this definition. Modifying batch jobs requires a lot of programming knowledge, so our story about them ends here.

Even though reports are traditionally seen as objects used to print data, reports in Microsoft Dynamics NAV 2009 provide a more versatile functionality: they can print information, process it, or do both simultaneously; or they can present data on screen, or export it to Excel or PDF.

To better understand how to create and modify reports in Microsoft Dynamics NAV 2009, we need to do some theory (with a bit of practice as we go).

Reporting in the Classic client

Reporting in previous versions of Microsoft Dynamics NAV, as well as in 2009's Classic client uses technology based on C/SIDE objects called Reports.

Creating reports

Creating simple reports is a fairly simple task—all you need to do is click **New** in the **Object Designer** within the **Reports** view, then the **New Report** wizard takes over.

You need to specify the table over which the report will be based, and then decide whether you are in the mood to draw the layout yourself, or you want to have the wizard do the legwork on your behalf. There are three types of layouts the wizard can create:

- **Form type report**: For each record in the table, fields will be arranged vertically one below another, and often arranged in two or three columns. For each field, the caption is printed to the left, and the value to the right. Records are arranged vertically with some white space in between.
- **Tabular type report**: The report prints a table, where each row represents a record in the underlying table, and each column represents a field. There is also a header row, which displays column captions. This is the most versatile type of report, because it can be used for documents.
- **Label type report**: The report is divided into tiles arranged horizontally, then vertically, and each record occupies a single tile. Only values are printed, and captions are omitted: good for printing mailing labels or item barcode stickers.

When you specify which table you want to use as your base and make your pick about the report type, clicking the **OK** button will launch the wizard for the report of the chosen type. Each of the types has its own wizard with a different set of questions asked and steps to follow.

Components of a report

A report consists of data set definition, report layout, and options page. Now, being proprietary all the way home, all of the folowing three use specific terminology:

- Data Items: the data set
- Sections: the layout
- Request form: the options

Data Items

Reports need to be connected to some data, which resides in tables. Data items are tables we decided to use in our reports. Data items are also the first thing we see after the **New Report** wizard has completed its chore. A typical data item looks like the following:

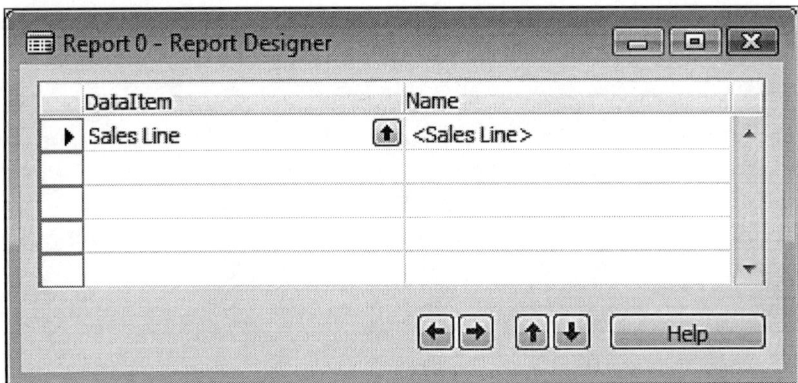

You can add as many data items as you need. To add a data item, position the cursor on the first empty line, and start typing the table name (or number) in the **DataItem** field. Alternatively, you may position the cursor on an existing data item line, then press *F3* (or choose **New** from the **Edit** menu). This will insert a new line just before the line you selected.

When the report is run, data items are executed in sequence, meaning that all the records from the first data item will be processed (and inserted into the report) before the report moves on to the next data item. In most cases, this is not how you want it to be.

Data items come with a concept of indenting. By the clicking left and right arrows you can indent a data item to the left or right. This can help establishing a parent-child (or master-detail) relationship between data items, meaning that for each parent (or master) record all its child (or detail) records will be processed before the report moves on to the next master record.

Indenting alone has not yet established the parent-child relationship. It has achieved only one thing: it will make the report execute all child records for each of the parent records. To complete the relationship setup, we need to set some data item properties:

Property	Description
DataItemIndent	Indenting level of a data item. 0 means it's the root level, 1 is first child, and so on.
DataItemTable	Specifies from which table the data item will pull data.
DataItemTableView	Defines the key and sort order used by the data item, but can also contain filters by which we want to filter the data before they are pulled from the table.
DataItemLinkReference	For data items with indent level higher than 0, this property specifies which data item is the parent data item.
DataItemLink	For child data items, here you specify the fields and conditions that are used to establish a parent-child relationship.

The most important property is DataItemLink, and we can type in the link setup manually, or we can invoke the DataItem Link editor by pressing *F6* or clicking the Assist button. It will open the DataItem Link editor, which is used to establish the mapping between the fields in the child table (Field column) to the equivalent fields in the parent table (Reference Field column).

Other than indenting, data items can accomplish a few other things as well, so you will frequently use these properties as well:

Property	Description
GroupTotalFields	If you want to group your data by a field, you can specify such a field here. Grouping is when you want to print sales headers grouped by customer, or document date. If you want to group by more fields, you can list them separated by a comma, in which case groups will be nested in the order you specified them.
TotalFields	The report can keep totals for numeric fields, so you don't have to write code, which you would otherwise have to do to achieve this. Because the report won't keep any totals automatically, here in this property, you need to specify fields you need totaled.
NewPagePerRecord	Specifies that whenever a new record is hit for this data item, the report will simply insert a page break. This is very useful when printing many documents at once; we want each of the invoices to start at a new page.

Sections

Data items simply define where the data comes from and what kind of relationships exist between different tables; sections define how this data is going to be laid out on the report. Section Designer is where you do this, and you can invoke it by clicking Sections in the View menu.

You'll immediately see that it's no state-of-the-art editor, but it accomplishes its purpose. The folowing is what a typical Section Designer will look like:

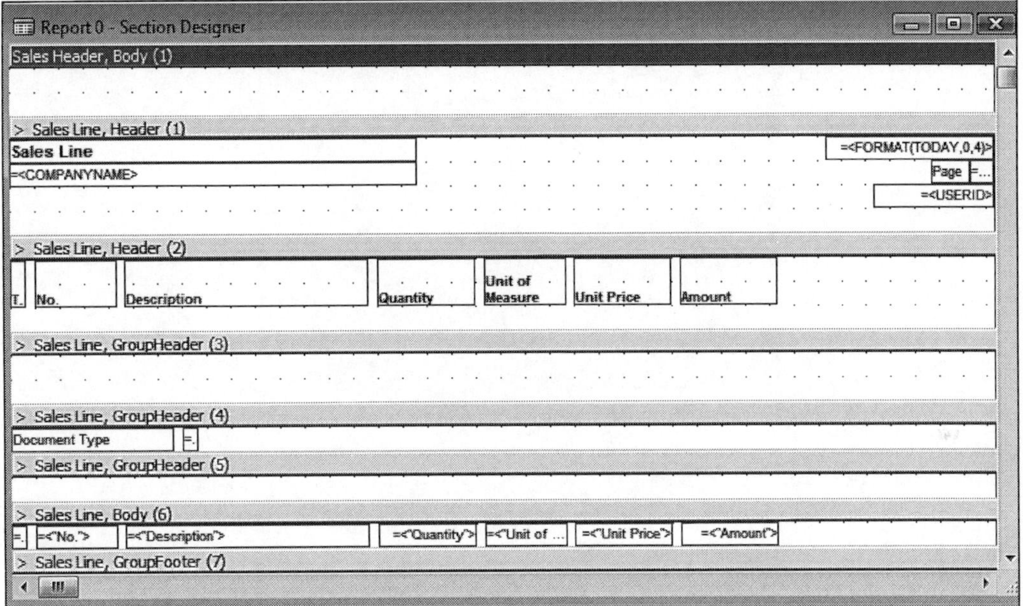

When you create your report using the wizard, it will create several sections for you, depending on the report type and choices you made. For every data item that you add manually, one section is inserted. A section is a part of a report with specific behavior. This behavior is embedded in the section type, and to see which section types there are, simply press *F3*, or select **New** from the **Edit** menu:

This is what they do:

Section Type	Description
Header	This section is printed once per data item, before any of the actual data lines, which is why it is called Header. For parent data items it means once per report, but for child data items it is printed once for each parent record. Think of the report printing this information every time it starts processing a data item—for parent data items this is only once; for child data items it is once for each parent record. This is where you typically put column captions.
GroupHeader	If you defined grouping for the data item, this section will be printed once per group. For example, if you decided to print sales headers, and group them by customer, then this header will be printed once for each customer.
TransHeader	If processing a data item has not been finished before the end of the page is reached, then it continues on the next page, at which point the TransHeader is printed there. Therefore, it prints once for each next page of an unfinished data item. This is where you typically put page totals carried over from the previous page.

Section Type	Description
Body	This section prints once for each record. If you print sales lines, for each one of them the report will print a body section. This is where you typically put data fields.
TransFooter	Similar to TransHeader, if processing of a data item has not been finished (not all body sections have been printed for it) before the end of the page is reached, then the TransFooter section will print. It prints once per page for an unfinished data item. Most often, you'll put page total fields here.
GroupFooter	If your data has been grouped, a group footer will be printed once per group, after the group has been completed. For example, if you print sales headers grouped by customer, after all records for each customer have been printed (all body sections), then a group footer is printed. Here you typically put group totals.
Footer	This section prints once per data item, after all the data lines (all body sections) have been printed. It is printed once per report for parent data items, and once per each parent record for child data items. Here you'll mostly put grand totals, and any necessary footer information, such as payment terms, instructions, and so on.

In **Section Designer**, each section is represented by a gray horizontal bar which goes all the way across the screen, and carries a label, such as **Sales Header, Body (1)**. This label is actually an identifier: **Sales Header** is the name of the data item, **Body** is the section type, and the number in parentheses is the ordinal number of the section for that data item. If there are several sections for the same data item, they will all be numbered consecutively starting at 1.

Sections contain field controls and labels. The difference is that field controls display a value from a table field (or another source, such as a variable, a constant, or a C/AL expression), while labels simply print static text.

To add table fields to a section, select **Field Menu** from the **View** menu. It will bring up the list of fields in the data item table for the currently selected section. In the **Field Menu**, select the desired fields, position your mouse pointer over the section into which you want to add them, and click the left mouse button.

When fields are added, both field controls and labels are added to the same section. Typically, you will want labels in a header section and field controls in a body section, and there is no way but to move them around manually.

Request form

When a report is started, and before it is printed, users usually have a chance to define some filters and options. This is called the request form, and this is what it may look like:

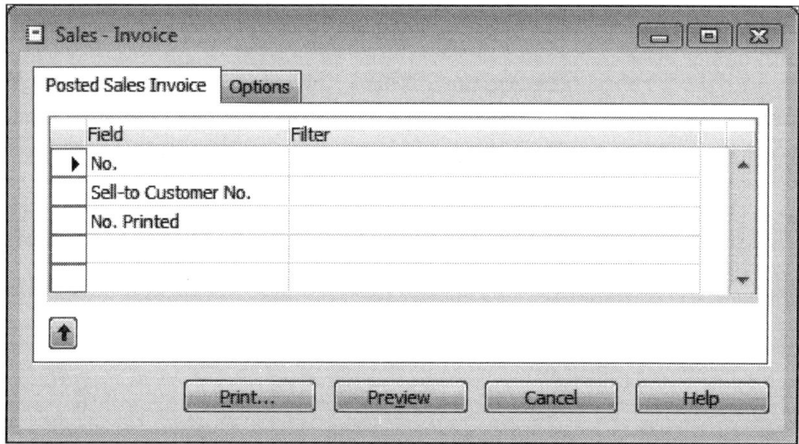

The request form consists of several tabs. If we didn't change the default properties, one tab will be shown for each data item, and we can use these to specify any filters we want applied. By setting the **ReqFilterFields** property of a data item, we may choose which fields will be included by default.

To hide a data item from the request form, clear its **ReqFilterFields** property, and set the **DataItemTableView** property to some value (typically, you set it to use ascending sort order by the primary key).

In most cases, however, enabling filtering for data items simply won't do, and functional requirements will call for much more. If you need to enable printing multiple copies, or to hide or display certain sections or even data items based on the user's choice, you'll need to do some more design and programming. This is where one more **Request Form** tab comes in handy: the **Options** tab.

To enable the **Options** tab, choose **Request Form** from the **View** menu, and it will open the **Request Options Form Designer**. It looks, feels, and functions exactly like the **Form Designer** for standard C/SIDE forms. The only difference is that you can only define one request options form per report, and that the definition for this form is embedded into the definition of the report itself.

A fully fledged request options form might look like the following (it belongs to report **5600 Fixed Asset - Analysis**):

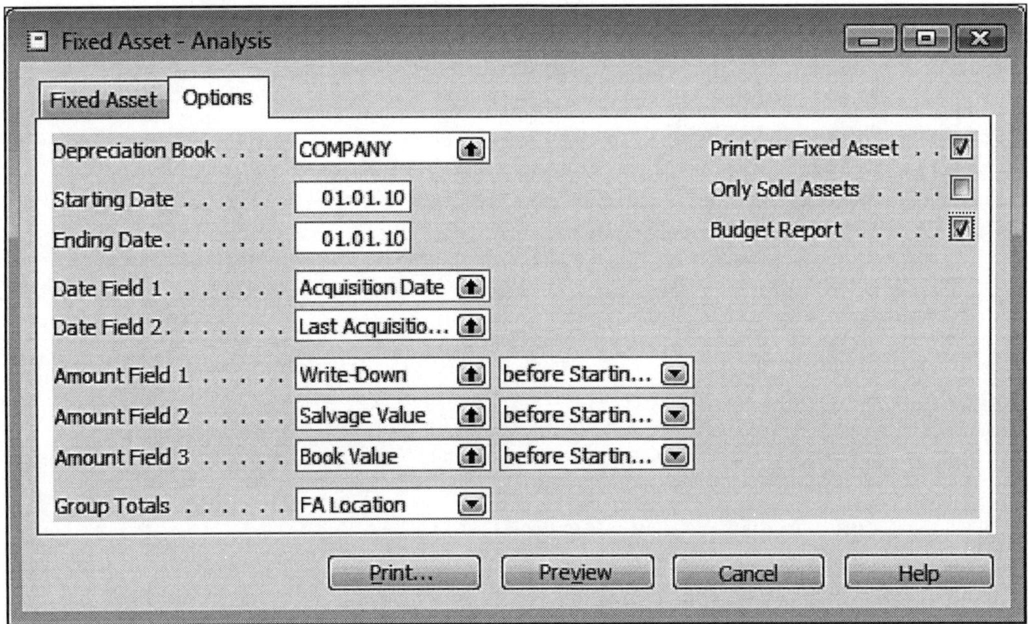

Report logic

Now for the hard part: all of these report elements can have application logic behind. And they usually do. Only the simplest of printouts can be achieved without any coding, and some reports, such as the one in the example above typically require a fair amount of coding. Just take a quick peek at the code behind dozens of triggers in this report, and you'll get the gist.

Reporting in the RoleTailored client

Things look quite differently in the RoleTailored client. As it utilizes the service tier, and no logic is ever executed on the client, the native C/SIDE reporting architecture is incapable of providing a robust and scalable reporting platform for the RoleTailored client. Instead of porting the native reporting functionality to the service tier, Microsoft has decided to make use of its standard reporting platform: Microsoft SQL Server Reporting Services.

The truth about Reporting Services

Microsoft Dynamics NAV 2009 does not utilize SQL Server Reporting Services. It makes use of the ReportViewer .NET control in local processing mode, which means it uses a client-side .NET class to render reports and doesn't require any Reporting Services components on the client or server end.

In fact, the only thing the ReportViewer control and Reporting Services have in common is that both use RDL (Report Definition Language), but the ReportViewer control uses the client version, called RDLC. The difference between RDL and RDLC is that RDLC files don't contain information about how to query the data source, while RDL files do.

Effectively, when using RDLC, the ReportViewer control is aware only of the layout; it is the host application's duty to retrieves, processes, and feeds the data to the ReportViewer control in the form of an ADO.NET DataTable object. This is why Microsoft Dynamics NAV can't publish any reports to a Report Server and why all the RDLC reports can only be used from within the RoleTailored client.

Always look on the bright side of life, however; RDLC and RDL are completely interchangeable, and can be easily converted from one to another. When future versions of Microsoft Dynamics NAV bring tighter integration with Reporting Services, reports in RDLC will be as good as those in RDL, and all the hard work that you invest into preparing good-looking RoleTailored reports now won't go in vain then.

Now that you know a little bit of reporting technology of Microsoft Dynamics NAV 2009 (still not enough to qualify as a geek, though), let's see how reporting truly works in the RoleTailored client:

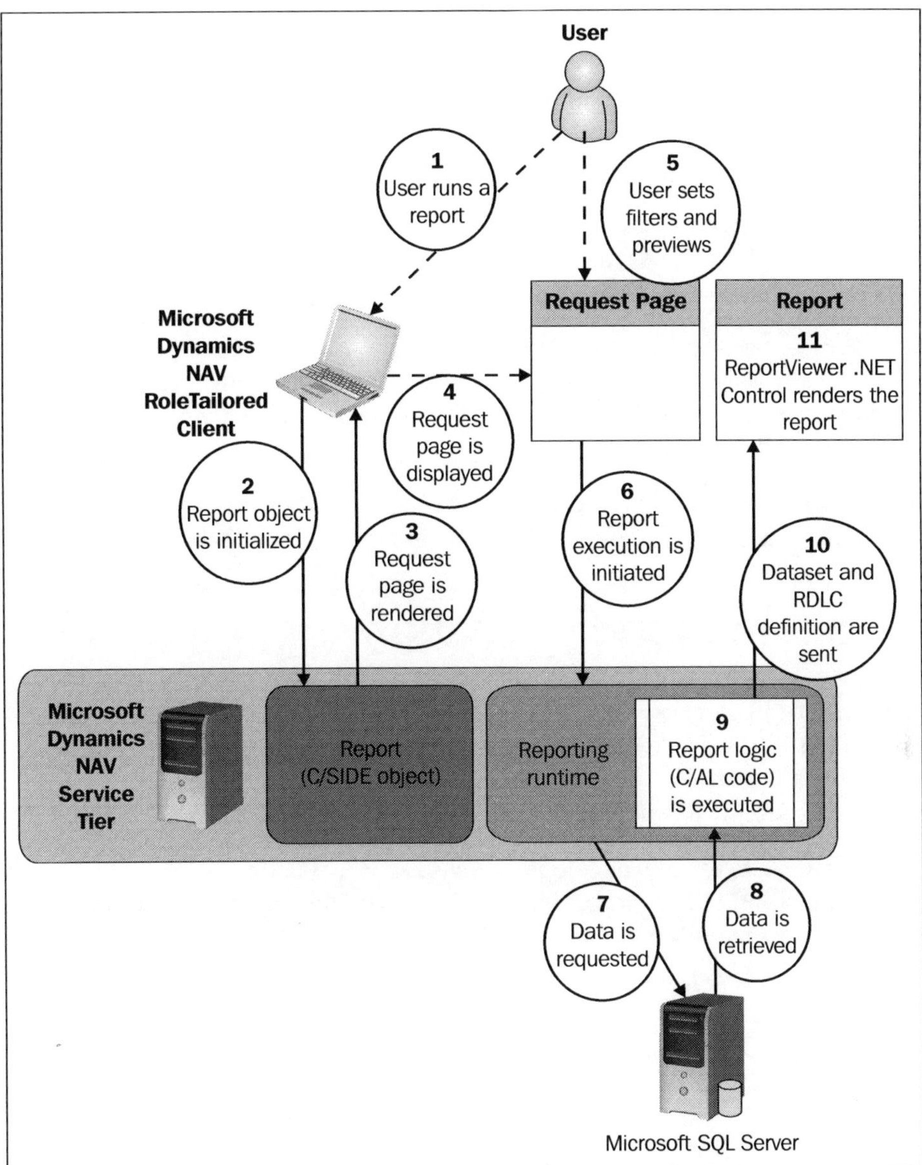

Obviously, the RoleTailored client is only in charge of presentation, and all the logic is executed on the server. Also, there have been important changes in how the report itself is executed, especially in how the data source is queried, and triggers are fired. All in all, these changes in architecture have inevitably reflected on how reports are designed.

In the RoleTailored client, reports consist of the following components:

- Data Items
- RDLC layout definition
- Request page

Although the two clients use different reporting components, all of them are stored in the same C/SIDE report object. Each of these clients will use that part of the report definition that it needs.

Data items are the same for both clients, and everything we said about them in the context of the Classic client applies here as well. The only two differences are the RDLC layout definition, which is used in place of sections, and request page, which is the RoleTailored equivalent of request form.

Thankfully, we don't need to do any of these manually; there are tools that help us translate just about everything we did from Classic to RoleTailored flavor.

RoleTailored report creation

There are two ways to create a report for the RoleTailored client: to transform a Classic report, or to create one from scratch. Transforming is the easy way around, but it presumes that you have a Classic version of the report already. On the other hand, creating a new RoleTailored report without an existing Classic version of the same can be an equally annoying experience as creating the Classic version first.

Since it's advisable to always have both versions anyway, your general approach to report creation should be to create the Classic version first, then test it thoroughly. When you are happy with the results, you can role-tailor it by using the built-in transformation tools.

The RoleTailored representation of each report is stored inside the report object, and you can access it by opening a report in **Object Designer**, then choosing **Layout** from the **View** menu. Report layout will open in your default RDLC editor.

Let's take a look at a typical standard report, from the RDLC point of view. In **Object Designer**, locate report **6 Trial Balance**, and click the **Design** button. When the report is opened, click the **View** menu, then **Layout**, and here it comes:

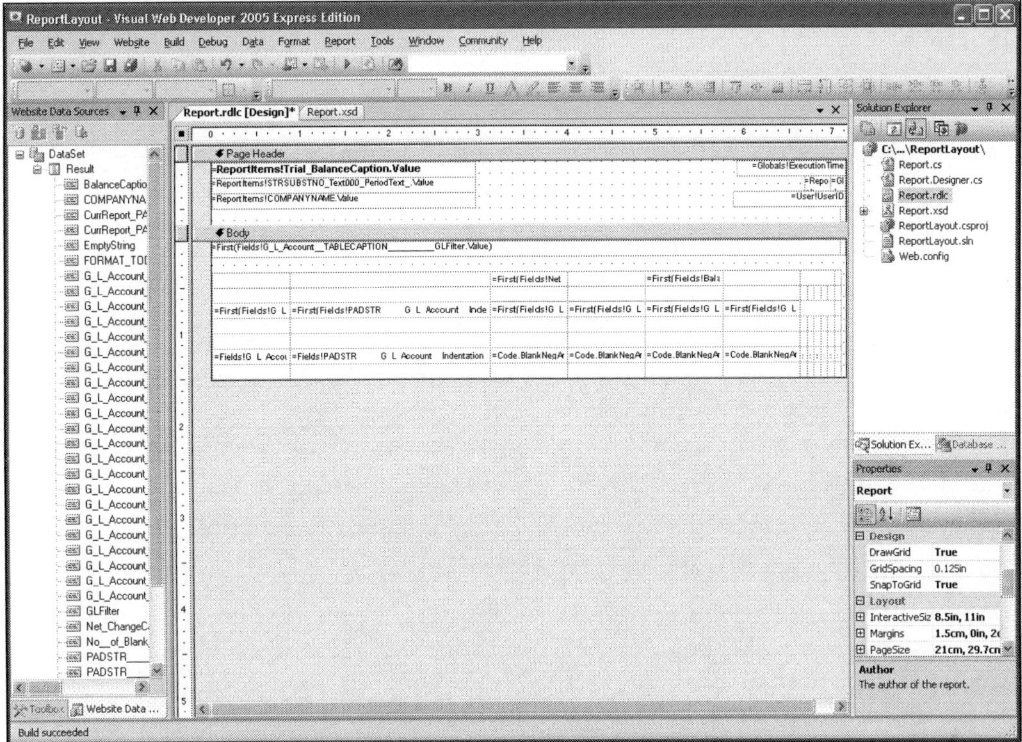

At this point feel free to go like: *Whoa, this thing's in color*! User experience of any of the RDLC editing tools is far superior to that of the **Section Designer**, and the colorful user interface is just the first hint of this.

Transforming layout

OK, we cheated a bit. We took a finished report and bragged how nice everything was. That was easy. Does it look that easy if we have to do it with brand-new reports, those that we built from scratch? See for yourself.

Create a report of any type you like using the **New Report** wizard, and look at its layout, using **View, Layout**: you'll see it's empty. That's because it was never transformed. Transforming a report for the first time is no more complicated than viewing its layout; you only need to run different commands.

Go back to **Report Designer** in the Classic client, open the **Tools** menu, then click **Create Layout Suggestion**. Again, your default RDLC editor will open; this time Microsoft Dynamics NAV will convert the report layout definition from Classic client's sections into an RDLC one.

When you close the RDLC editor and return back to **Report Designer**, it will ask you:

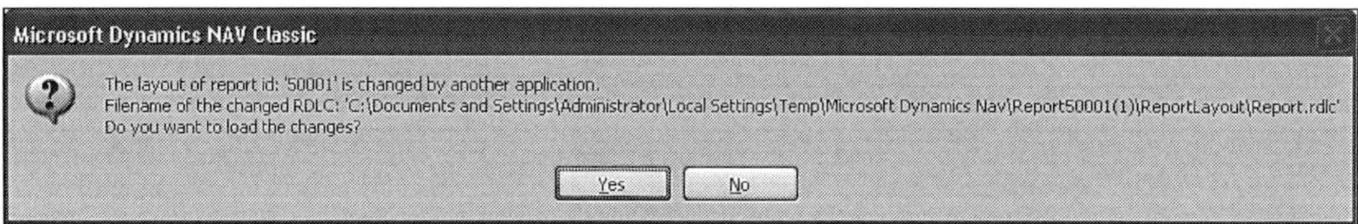

As you can see from the text message, the RDLC layout you worked on was stored in a temporary location on your disk, so any changes you made in the RDLC editor actually affected only this temporary file. Unlike sections, the RDLC layout is not saved into the report automatically, which is a good thing—in case you messed up, this confirmation dialog gives you a chance to simply rollback. If you click **Yes**, the RDLC file will be imported into report; **No** will keep the things as they are.

Transforming request option forms

You guessed it right! For those reports that have their layout converted to RDLC, request option forms can't be run in the RoleTailored environment. That's simply because they are normal forms, and forms are no good for the RoleTailored experience. The RoleTailored client will look for the request option page definition instead.

Request option page is the same thing as request option form, only RoleTailored. You can see the request option page definition if you click the **View** menu, then pick **Request Page**. It looks and feels exactly like the **Page Designer** you are already familiar with.

As with all Classic forms, you have two options with request option forms: you can transform them into request option pages using the Form Transformation tool, or you can design them from scratch. Take our advice: the few controls you need to declare aren't worth the bureaucracy of the Form Transformation tool; just go and type them directly there in **Request Option Page Designer**.

Everything you learned about designing pages can be applied equally successful to designing request option pages. The only difference is that a request option page doesn't have the **PageType** property.

You don't have to bother transforming your Classic reports to RoleTailored ones if they contain complex layout or request option forms. the RoleTailored client is capable of running non-transformed Classic reports as well.

If you omit transforming any of the Classic reports into their RoleTailored counterparts, and you access such reports from the RoleTailored client, the RoleTailored client will launch the Classic client runtime in the background and display the report as if it was accessed from the Classic client (without displaying the whole client to the user).

Of course, for this functionality to work, you must have the Classic client installed on user's machines.

Customizing MenuSuites

Now that you know how to create forms, pages, and reports—the building blocks of the Classic and RoleTailored clients—it is the time for you to integrate those elements into menu navigation for easy access by the users. You do this using MenuSuite objects.

MenuSuites work differently between the clients: in the Classic client they are displayed in the navigation pane, while the RoleTailored client displays them in the **Departments** page. Take a look and compare them:

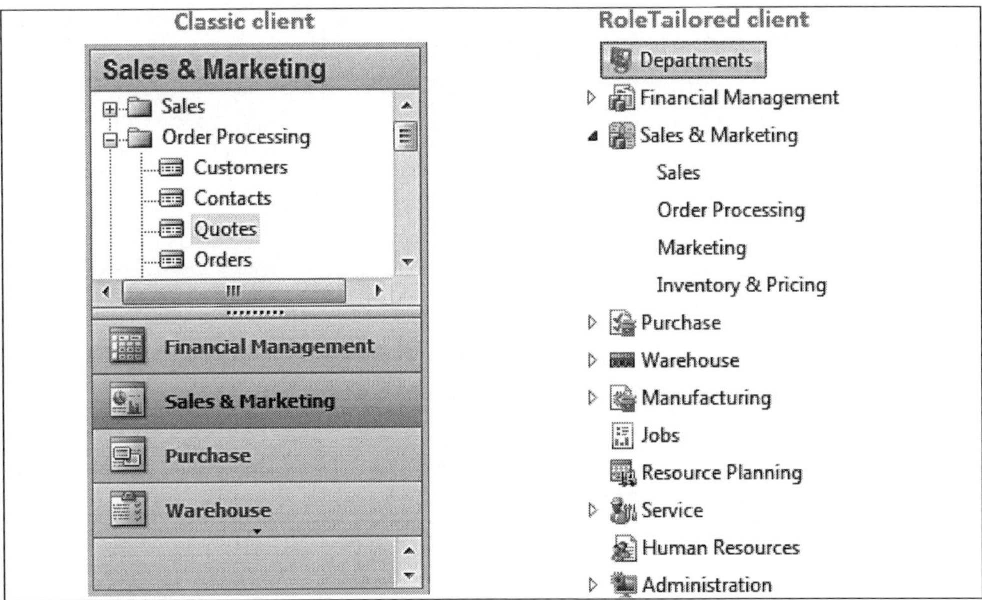

Apart from the looks, there is a huge conceptual difference between these two. In the RoleTailored client, navigation is primarily achieved through role centers where the vast majority of tasks start and users should have very few reasons to leave their role centers for the Departments page. On the other hand, in the Classic client all navigation starts in the navigation pane.

A little bit of theory

The navigation pane organizes navigation elements into *menus* (in the previous screenshot these are **Financial Management**, **Sales & Marketing**, **Purchase**, and **Warehouse**), *groups* (**Sales** and **Order Processing** in the screenshot), and *items* (**Customers, Contacts**, **Quotes**, and **Orders** in the screenshot). Menus and groups are used merely for logical organization, while items are responsible for displaying various user interface components, such as forms and reports.

The definitions of these menus, groups, and items are stored in MenuSuite objects. If you go to **MenuSuite** in **Object Designer**, you'll see that there aren't too many of them: depending on your localization, you'll probably see between three and five of them. That's because MenuSuites don't work like other objects in Microsoft Dynamics NAV—one MenuSuite doesn't represent one navigation pane (or Department page), but instead it represents one *level*. To understand how levels work, let's see how many levels there are and what they represent:

MenuSuite ID	Name	Meaning
10	MBS	Developed globally by Microsoft
20	Region	Developed by Microsoft for common regional functionality
30	Country	Developed by local Microsoft office as part of localization
51 through 60	Add-on 1 thru Add-on 10	Third-party add-ons
80	Partner	Partner customizations
90	Company	Customer's own customizations

Even though levels are fixed, and you can't change them, names are not set in stone—you may change them to whatever you like, if you see it fit.

There is another set of levels, which start with 1010 and end with 1090, and have *Dept* – in front of their name: these are used by the RoleTailored client to construct the Departments page. Numbering scheme, names, and meanings are exactly the same as here, only the ID is shifted up by 1000. This means that in Microsoft Dynamics NAV you can have at most 15 levels, or up to 15 MenuSuite objects per client (up to 15 for Classic, and up to 15 for the RoleTailored one).

When the application starts (precisely, when a company is opened), it uses the levels of MenuSuites to construct the navigation pane: it starts with the lowest level (10 MBS) and adds all menus, groups, and items it contains, then moves up to the next level to do the same, all the way up to the level with the highest number (typically 90 Company). Each of the levels contains only differences from the previous one: additions, changes, and deletions. For example, if level 10 MBS defines the menu Warehouse, and you delete the same menu on level 80 Partner, it won't be included in the navigation pane. Also, if you include it again on level 90 Company, it'll be back.

And some practice

There are three ways in which to edit a MenuSuite object:

- By creating a new MenuSuite object in **Object Designer**. As soon as you create a new one, it automatically opens in the **Navigation Pane Designer**.
- By designing the object in **Object Designer**: you select which level you want to edit, click the Design button, and it will launch the **Navigation Pane Designer** for that specific level.
- By invoking **Navigation Pane Designer** from the **Tools** menu: it will always launch the **Navigation Pane Designer** for page 90 Company.

The Navigation Pane Designer is completely integrated into the navigation pane itself, which means that it merely switches the navigation pane itself from navigation mode into design mode. Even though there are visual clues that suggest the mode you are currently in, it might not be immediately obvious. The difference is subtle: in design mode, the name of the MenuSuite being designed is displayed to the left of the selected menu name, and the titles of any menus inherited from a previous level are preceded by the guillemet (») character.

To create a new MenuSuite, you simply click **New** while in Object Designer's MenuSuite view. Whenever you are creating a new MenuSuite object, the system asks you two questions: which kind of client you intend this MenuSuite for, and which level you are creating. Only those levels that haven't already been consumed by an existing MenuSuite object can be created.

Careful with those Object IDs

Once you choose the intended client and level, you can't change your mind any more. Or better said: you shouldn't. What you actually can do is change the Object ID. Don't do this, because this can introduce a serious mess. An unfortunate fact about MenuSuites is that level and client information are hardcoded into the Object ID, and while changing the Object ID from 80 to 90 won't have any consequence whatsoever, changing it from 80 to 1080 might make a total mess, to the extent of crashing the RoleTailored client on every start.

The reason for this is that MenuSuites in Object ID range 10 to 90 can define items of type form, while MenuSuites in range 1010 to 1090 can't. However, simply changing the Object ID for a MenuSuite won't convert form references to page references. This means that with changing an Object ID from the Classic client's range into the RoleTailored one, you literally sneak items of type form into the Departments page, something that the RoleTailored client isn't resilient enough to endure. Therefore, those Object IDs aren't to be touched!

Designing MenuSuites is easy; all you'll ever need to do is available at the right click. Depending on where you place your cursor, one of two different menus will drop down. If you right-click a menu, you get the options for editing the menus. If you right-click a group or an item, you guessed it right—the options displayed allow you to edit groups and items. Simple and intuitive!

Let's see what's on the menu about menus. Design a MenuSuite and right-click the **Sales & Marketing** menu. You'll get the following options:

Command	Explanation
Create Menu...	Opens the **Create Menu** dialog, which allows you to create a new menu. The dialog will ask you about the **Caption**, **CaptionML**, and the **Bitmap**. The first two are already familiar, while **Bitmap** is a numeric value, which specifies the icon displayed to the left of the menu caption. Possible values are 0 to 15, and all of them look equally pale in the Classic, and equally vivid in the RoleTailored client.
Delete	No worries, it'll make sure you are sure before it deletes the selected menu. But anyway, don't use this option, there is a better one: **Disable**.
Rename	Allows you to edit the **Caption** property. You'll not want to call this one too often, because it only cares about the currently selected language, and doesn't care much about **CaptionML** settings for other languages you might have installed.
Move Up	Moves the menu one step up.
Move Down	Moves the menu one step down.
Hide in Designer	Hides the selected menu from the MenuSuite designer every time you are designing that MenuSuite. It only applies at design time (the menu stays displayed while in navigation mode), and only for the MenuSuite you were editing when you hid it. While you might catch yourself wondering why this feature was necessary, it comes in really handy when you are designing certain menus, such as add-on menus or partner menus: you might decide to remove all those menus not pertaining to the MenuSuite you are editing, making it much easier for you to do the proper design.
Show in Designer	Displays the list of all the menus hidden in Designer for the MenuSuite being edited, and lets you choose which ones you'd like shown again.
Disable	Disables the selected menu so that it isn't displayed in the navigation pane. It has the same effect on the end users as **Delete**, but is much less radical because it preserves the whole menu structure and items. If you need to delete a menu, think about using this one instead.
Enable	Opposite of **Disable**. This one is displayed only if you right-click a disabled menu.

Command	Explanation
Assign Users...	Opens the **Assign Users** form, which displays the list of all existing users in the system, and lets you specify which users have access to the selected menu. By default all users have access to all menus, which is represented by a checkmark to the left of each user's name. When you uncheck this checkmark the user can't access this menu any more, for the simple reason it isn't displayed for them in their navigation pane anymore. Using this feature doesn't relieve you of the obligation to define strong security using roles: even though you might have hidden a menu from all existing users, every new user will by default have access to all menus. So, don't think of this feature as a security feature, which it is not; think of this as of a per-user menu disabling/enabling facility.
Cut	Places the selected menu into the clipboard, ready to delete it from the MenuSuite as soon as you paste it. The problem is, you can paste it only into the same MenuSuite you are designing; as soon as you close the designer, any menu you put in the clipboard is gone. Not too useful.
Copy	Places the selected menu into the clipboard. You can later paste it into the same MenuSuite, which will create a copy of the same menu.
Paste	Available only if you have a menu in the clipboard. It will paste the menu from the clipboard and place it at the very bottom of the navigation pane.
Properties	Opens the **Menu Properties** dialog, which allows you to modify the same properties you could specify when creating the menu: **Caption**, **CaptionML**, and **Bitmap**.

That's about menus. Let's see about groups and items. While designing a MenuSuite, right-click on a group or an item, and you'll get the chance to pick one of these:

Command	Explanation
Create Item	Opens the **Create Item** dialog, which will create a new item. While doing so, you may specify **Object Type**, **Object ID**, **Caption**, and **CaptionML**. For RoleTailored client MenuSuites there is also the **Department Category** property. **Object Type** and **Object ID** let you specify which object will be invoked when users click the item in the navigation pane (or Departments page), and for the Classic client you can choose tables, forms, reports, dataports, and codeunits, while for the RoleTailored client you can choose pages, reports, XMLports, and codeunits. **Caption** and **CaptionML** define how the name of the item will be displayed to users in their mother tongue, and are automatically populated when you specify **Object Type** and **Object ID**. **Department Category** defines in which category of the Departments page this item will be displayed, and it can be one of the following: Lists, Tasks, Reports and Analysis, Documents, History, and Administration.

Command	Explanation
Insert Items	Opens the **Insert Items** dialog, which lets you choose a number of existing items from other menus and insert them into the current one all at once. A very handy feature.
Create Group	Does exactly that. No dialogs, no fuss, just creates a new group with an intuitive caption **New Group**. You can immediately specify the caption, which doesn't have to be unique—you may have as many **New Group** groups as you desire. As soon as you create a group, edit its properties by right-clicking the group and choosing **Properties**—this will let you specify the **CaptionML**, because by creating a group you only defined the **Caption** property.
Delete	Deletes the selected group or item, but doesn't bother to ask you if you are sure. So better be sure before clicking this one on groups, because it takes away all the subgroups and items belonging to the late group.
Rename	Allows you to specify the **Caption** property for the selected group or item. Doesn't care about **CaptionML**.
Move Up	Moves the selected group or item one step up.
Move Down	I wonder what this one does...
Cut	Places the group (including subgroups and items) or an item into the clipboard, ready to delete the original group or item as soon as it is pasted elsewhere. Now this one is useful as you'll probably want to cut-and-paste some groups around different menus in the same MenuSuite from time to time.
Copy	Places the group (including subgroups and items) or an item into the clipboard.
Paste	Pastes the cut/copied group or item from the clipboard into the menu. This option is available only if there is a group or item in the clipboard.
Properties	Shows the **Group Properties** or **Item Properties** dialog. The **Group Properties** dialog will let you specify **Caption** and **CaptionML**, while the **Item Properties** dialog will let you specify exactly the same properties as the **Create Item** dialog.

Obviously, creating and editing MenuSuites is not rocket science. They are very simple objects; they contain no code and no documentation trigger; and they come with very few properties, most of which you can't even access the way you can with other types of objects. The only other things you can do with MenuSuites besides those few listed above are export and import them as text or FOB file (don't try XML, it won't do anything useful), and compile them.

> Compiling a MenuSuite object will go through all items defined in that MenuSuite and check whether the objects referred to by the items still exist. If they don't, you'll get to know that. When working on implementation projects, make sure you compile your MenuSuites before every deployment.

One thing worth noting is that you don't have to create two versions of MenuSuite objects for the Classic and RoleTailored clients manually. If your MenuSuite objects are huge, then you can benefit from the Form Transformation Tool—it can also transform your Classic client MenuSuites into RoleTailored client ones saving you many uneventful hours of right-clicking your way through Navigation Pane Designer.

Customizing other objects

Customizing Microsoft Dynamics NAV is not just about forms, pages, reports, and MenuSuites. There are codeunits, dataports, and XMLports. Let's just see what they are all about, before we call it a day.

Codeunits

We wanted to make this chapter code-free, and show you what kind of stuff you can do with Microsoft Dynamics NAV without ever coming anywhere near C/AL. And from what you've seen so far, there's an impressive lot of development you can do without any coding at all.

Codeunits are all about code. That's why they are called that after all. They are objects used to encapsulate blocks of code with similar purpose or that accomplish a specific thing. Codeunits are the cornerstone of the business logic of Microsoft Dynamics NAV, and you should make extra sure that people modifying them have good knowledge of the functionality of the application area they are modifying and the business logic behind the code contained in them. Don't ever settle for less.

Dataports

Dataports are on their extinction path. They have been used by previous versions of Microsoft Dynamics NAV to export and import data in textual formats, and in their heyday they were even able to handle XML.

Nowadays, they are limited to the Classic client (the RoleTailored client can't run them), they can cope with text data only, their number has been decimated, and there are but a sorry few left in the standard application. Their functionality has been completely taken over by their younger brethren, the XMLports, and if you need to develop any text import or export functionality, go for XMLports, they are the new standard.

XMLports

XMLports are objects that have been used to import and export XML data into and out of the application, but in Microsoft Dynamics NAV 2009 they have been upgraded to support the variable and fixed text formats as well. Since the RoleTailored client doesn't understand dataports, XMLports are effectively the new standard for handling data import and export, and whatever import/export requirements you might have, they are best met with XMLports.

XMLports also have a powerful feature that delivers a conclusive advantage over dataports, and that's the ability to stream data directly from and into various sources and destinations. While dataports were limited to reading and writing to text files, XMLports can read and write directly or indirectly to files, memory, BLOB fields, and automation objects.

Although designing XMLports might require no programming at all, making any real use of them does. As they primarily do streaming, you'll have to program at least some C/AL code to specify streaming sources and destinations.

Summary

In this chapter we have learned how to modify the Microsoft Dynamics NAV 2009 application, something that is an integral part of literally every implementation project. We have seen the palette of tools, wizards, and designers we can use to facilitate the creation of new objects.

The C/SIDE integrated development environment makes it possible to develop new functionality quickly, and we have seen that it can even happen without writing a single line of code.

We have gone through data modeling concepts, and explained how data modeling maps real-life objects and their relationships, and how to make best use of that knowledge when designing new tables and their relations.

We have then seen how to map the data model on both Classic and RoleTailored user interface objects, and how to prepare usable and easily navigable user interfaces. We have also seen how to develop reports, and make them run equally well in both clients.

In the next chapter we are taking a step ahead: we are going to see how we can extend the application even further, by using Web services.

7
Extending the Application

The three-tiered architecture in Dynamics NAV 2009 enables wonderful things to happen. Yes, you can get better scalability by separating the business logic from the presentation layer, but there are a couple of other things you get as a result of the Dynamics NAV Service Tier: Web services enablement and Multiple Presentation Layers. The RoleTailored client is an example of a presentation layer with which you are already familiar; later on we'll see other examples of user interfaces such as the SharePoint client and Dynamics Mobile. The user interfaces are lovely, without a doubt, but it's the Web services that have got people buzzing. Web services enablement opens up a whole new world for NAV implementations and in this chapter, we're going to look at some of the things we can now do.

In this chapter you'll learn:

- What a Web service is (a geek-free definition)
- What you can do with Web services (geeks only I'm afraid)
- What clients are available as Presentation layers (a short mention)

Learning to fish

> *Give a man a fish and you feed him for a day; teach him to use the Internet, and he won't bother you for weeks!*

This is going to be a real challenge for me, and I guess I am not the only one that wants to play with the new technology that Web services enablement brings, but is a little unsure where to start. A good number of people that are experienced NAV consultants and C/AL developers are going to need to learn some new technologies if they want to start experimenting with the new extensibility options in Dynamics NAV 2009, or even simply understand what options are available for their new solution designs or sales presentations. This chapter is going to be all about practical examples—real sample applications that you can create for yourself. Some of these examples start off with one set of requirements that evolve as we progress through the design process. I deliberately kept the examples this way to help you to understand that the path to your final working solution is not always the shortest. Sometimes you get an idea for an application and as you proceed with the design, you think of things that would be better or easier to use. Sometimes your initial design simply won't work when you start to try it out. It's important to realize that designs are not precious and it's OK to change your mind. There are a couple of important issues to consider: always ensure you are solving the business problem, and don't get carried away gold-plating your design. Keep it simple, and once it is working and meets the initial requirements, you can then go back and add the bells and whistles (but you'd better check with whoever is paying the bills first).

I'm not a .NET programmer, and I have never created a web site or Web service in my life. I'm not making excuses for the programming you are about to see (much), but instead pointing out that if I can do this (and I really hope I can), I'm sure you can too! This chapter is not a place for me to tell you the best way to do these things, but instead is a place for me to show you that with a very limited knowledge of .NET, a web browser to do some research, and enough time, you can create pretty much anything you can imagine.

First of all, let's get some theory out of the way so that we have a basic understanding of what we're dealing with.

What's a Web service?

Web services have been around for a few years now but they are new to NAV (well, sort of— but more on that later). A good way to distinguish between technical and non-technical NAV consultants is to ask them if NAV supports Web services and watch to see if their eyes glaze over. There's no wonder some NAV consultants struggle to understand Web services as a concept; if you're not a developer and you have never worked with Web services, learning the basics might be more than a little bit scary. Here's a typical definition you might find on the Web; don't be put off by the geek-speak.

A scary geeky definition of a Web service

A 'Web service' (also Web Service) is defined by the W3C as 'a software system designed to support interoperable machine-to-machine interaction over a network'. Web services are frequently just Web APIs that can be accessed over a network, such as the Internet, and executed on a remote system hosting the requested services.

There are a lot of acronyms and jargon phrases to learn if you want to talk the talk, but let's take a look at what a Web service is in simple terms.

To start with, let's consider a comparison between web sites, something we are all familiar with, and Web services.

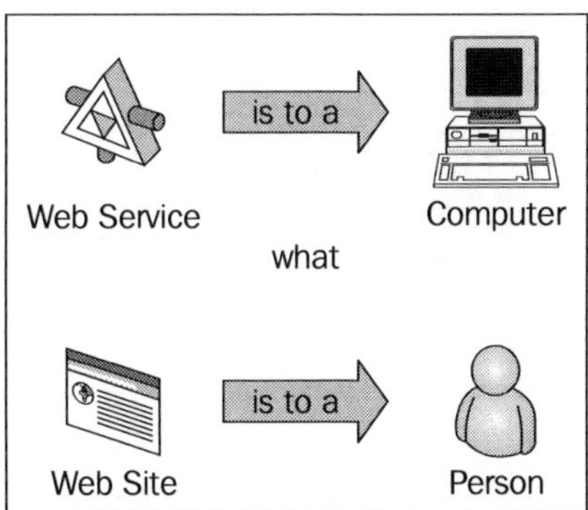

I like to think that a Web *service* is to a computer what a web *site* is to a person. If you want to know what's on TV tonight, you can type the URL for a TV Listings site into a web browser and bring up a page with details. It's not going to take you long to find the required information, but what if you wanted to write a computer program to send an e-mail when your favorite TV show was about to start, how would you go about that? This is a more complex problem, we know the data is there on the web site, freely available to all humans, but we can't just tell our computer to go off and read the web site (well we can—but deciphering it may require a fair amount of clever programming). Wouldn't it be great if there was a computer-friendly version of the data on the web site that allowed computers to ask for information and get answers back? Wouldn't it be great if you could write your program to make the call to this service without the need to install any special software components on your computer? Yes, it is great, and that's why Web services came into being and have now become so popular.

It's not just for the Web

It's not immediately obvious why we would want to expose our precious company data that we keep locked up in our ERP system on the Web, but just because they're called *Web* services doesn't mean they're just for the World Wide Web. Let's consider the *intranet* compared to the *internet*. It didn't take long for companies to realize that the popularity of internet sites and the ease of use that everyone was experiencing through the world wide web could provide great benefits within the boundaries of a company's safe internal network—a kind of mini-internal-internet or *intranet*. For Dynamics NAV, the analogy between Web Sites and Web services works even better when we consider an intranet. What if different departments could pull data directly from the ERP system and use it in their own specialist applications? This is where the real value of Web services enablement in Dynamics NAV 2009 comes into its own. It is now possible to take any functionality from within the ERP solution and expose it to other applications as Web services; it's not just possible, it's dead easy!

What can we do with them?

OK, so it's easy to expose NAV functionality, so what? Well if you can call any Codeunit or Page from within NAV with pretty much any software package that you can extend, there are limitless possibilities to create fantastic productivity applications for the business. Here are just a few examples:

- Let staff submit their expenses from Excel, or from their mobile phone, without needing to re-key them into the finance system.
- Allow users to create new customer accounts from within Word or from an intranet web page.
- Provide a Vista Sidebar gadget that shows the number of documents requiring approval and allows the user to approve the document without needing to open the ERP.
- Provide a simple single-task Windows application that will let staff see where stock is.

These examples are just a few that spring immediately to mind, but if you have the know-how, you can do pretty much anything. So how easy is it to expose NAV functionality as a Web service? Let's find out.

Calling a NAV Web service

There is a great series of articles on MSDN by Manuel Oliveira that explain how to expose NAV functionality as a Web service. If you have never read these, you may want to skim through them after reading this example to see just how easy we have it with the new version of NAV.

Talking with NAV—the hard way!

Visit `http://msdn.microsoft.com/en-us/library/ms952182.aspx` and `http://msdn.microsoft.com/en-us/library/ms952079.aspx` for a couple of examples that explain the multiple hoops we needed to jump through in order to access NAV functionality using Web services. That's before NAV 2009 came along!

Since these early examples of NAV extensibility, the Windows Communication Framework has made things easier, and Kris Rafnsson has provided a blog posting and sample application that allows you to call NAV functionality as a Web service without using message queues. This example is pretty amazing, but there is still a fair amount of work required to get this up and running and build new solutions. Although this is a big improvement on the Message Queue approach, it is nothing compared to the simplicity and elegance of the NAV 2009 Web services enablement. You can read through Kris's post at `http://blogs.msdn.com/nav/archive/2008/04/15/using-web-services-to-access-microsoft-dynamics-nav-5-0.aspx`.

In Manuel's first example (although not actually a Web service), he creates a simple NAV function that will accept a text string and return the text string back but converted to upper case. This example spans 15 printed pages and uses a lot of geeky stuff. As a bare minimum, we are going to need a Codeunit to expose and a .NET program to call the thing, so let's forget about these and just compare the components that are needed to take care of the plumbing:

- Microsoft Message Queue
- Navision Communication Component
- XMLDOM automation control
- Navision Application Server
- A lot of complicated C/AL code using InStreams and OutStreams and XML manipulation

Manuel's examples were written in 2004 and, although they're very well written, the whole thing is just too hard! After reading the articles, you'll understand why there hasn't been a glut of NAV components on the market using Web services exposed by NAV. Our example by contrast requires the following (again ignoring the Codeunit we are exposing and the .NET program needed to call it):

- Dynamics NAV 2009 Business Web services
- A new record in a table with a check in a box

Creating a Web service

Let's start by creating our very simple Codeunit. In this example, I have created Codeunit **50001** called **NAV Codeunit**, which has a single function called **ConvertStrToUpperCase** that takes a 50 character text field and returns a 50 character text field that has been converted to upper case.

```
Codeunit 50001 NAV Codeunit - C/AL Editor

Documentation()

OnRun()
IF GUIALLOWED THEN
  MESSAGE('Input: %1\'+
          'Output: %2',
          'hello world!',
          ConvertStrToUpperCase('hello world!'));

ConvertStrToUpperCase(p_Str : Text[50]) : Text[50]
EXIT (UPPERCASE(p_Str));
```

It wasn't absolutely necessary for this example, but I put some code in the **OnRun()** trigger of the Codeunit that will demonstrate the Codeunit working when run. Here is the output from running the Codeunit in NAV:

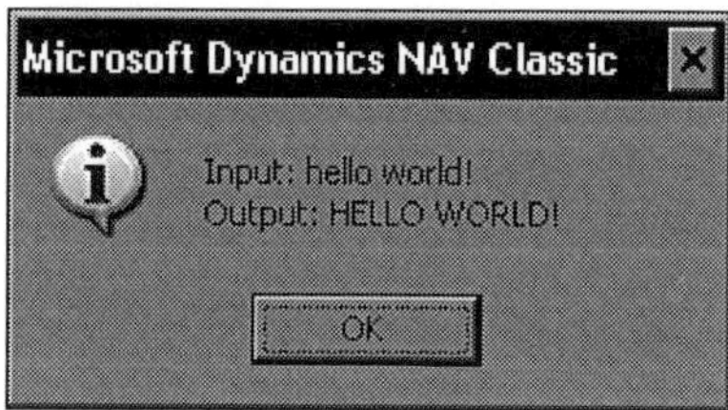

Now we can expose this Codeunit as a Web service. In the Classic client, select **Administration | IT Administration | General Setup | Web Services**.

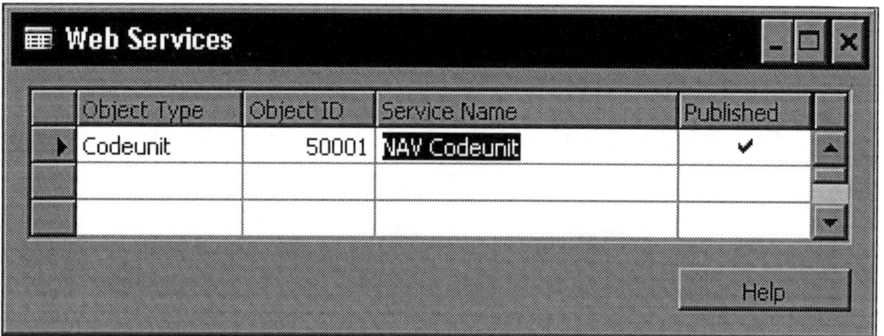
Web Services

Object Type	Object ID	Service Name	Published
Codeunit	50001	NAV Codeunit	✔

Help

This is just a regular NAV form, so fill in the details on a new record with **Object Type** as **Codeunit**, **Object ID** as **50001**, and **Service Name** as **NAV Codeunit**. To publish the Web service, tick the **Published** field. I just happened to give the Web service the same name as the Codeunit, but this is not necessary, you can call it whatever you like.

We have now exposed NAV functionality as a Web service—how easy was that?

Calling the Web service

The .NET program to call the Web service is going to be a little harder. I'm going to create a simple C# console application using Microsoft Visual Studio 2008 Professional Edition. (This is installed on the Marketing Beta release of the product which all partners can download from PartnerSource.)

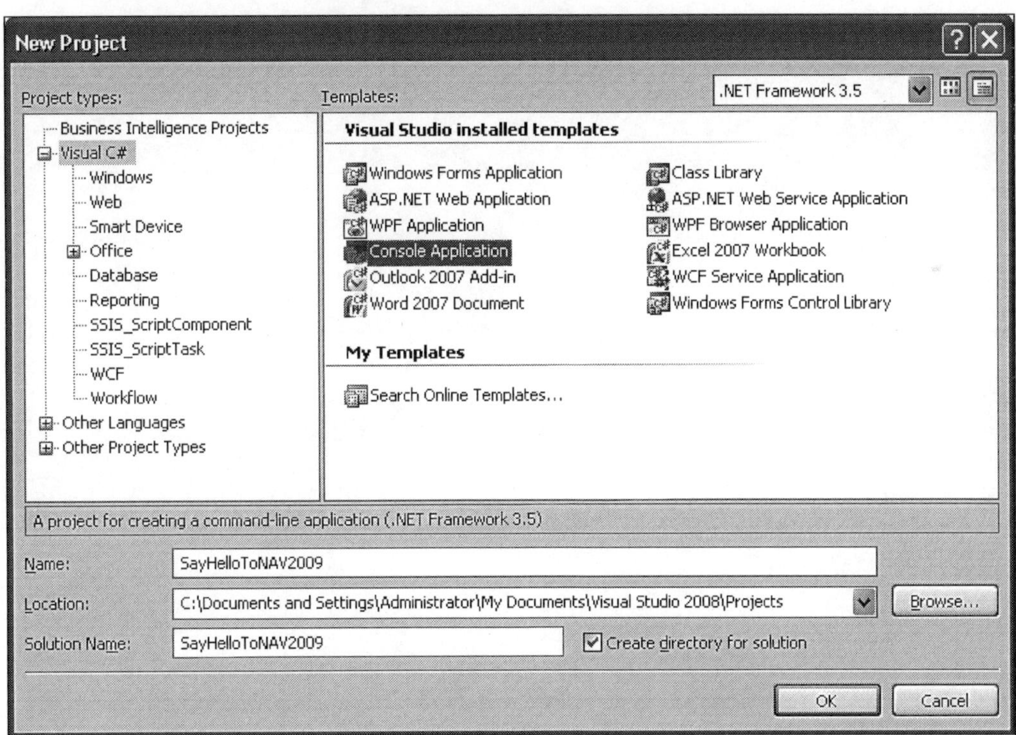

Create a new Console Application, I called mine **SayHelloToNAV2009**.

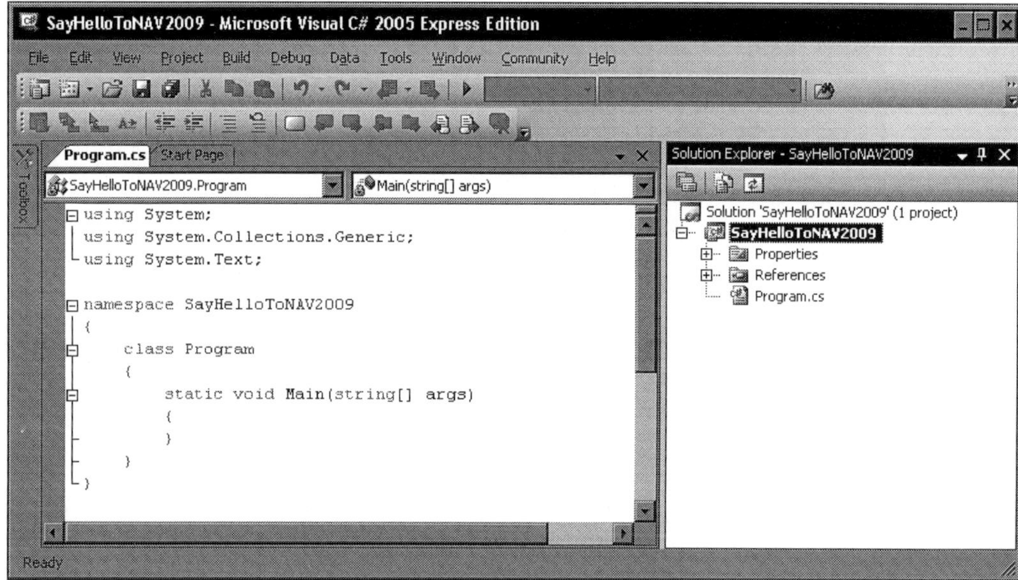

The project gets created with a `Program.cs` file with enough code generated for you to allow the project to compile and run. There's no way I can teach you to program in C# in this chapter, there are whole books dedicated to the subject; instead what I'll do is give you the details you need to be able to recreate our examples for yourself. If you like what you see, maybe you'll go on to do some more .NET programming and your next book will be one on C#. The great thing about .NET languages and Visual Studio is there's a huge amount of knowledge freely available on the Web.

The first thing we need to do is add our Web service to the project. To do this, right-click on the **References** node in the **Solution Explorer** window and select **Add Service Reference**.

Visual Studio 2005 is different

These instructions are for adding a web reference using Visual Studio 2008. In 2005, things work a little differently. Instead of selecting **References** | **Add Service Reference** | **Advanced** | **Add Web Reference**, you simply selected **Add Reference** | **Add Web Reference**.

In the dialog that is displayed, click the **Advanced** button, and then click the **Add Web Reference** button.

In the **Add Web Reference** dialog form, enter `http://nav-srv-01:7047/DynamicsNAV/ws/CRONUS_International_Ltd/Services` as the URL for the Web service. This will display the group of Web services that are exposed by NAV.

Where do I find that URL?

The format of the URL is quite straightforward. Let's break it up into chunks.

URL Part	Meaning
`http://`	Tells the browser which protocol to use (Hypertext Transfer Protocol)
`nav-srv-01`	Is the name of the computer on which the Web services run
`:7047`	Identifies the port on which the service is listening for service calls – this can be specified in the `CustomSettings.config` file by changing the value of the **WebServicePort** key value.
`DynamicsNAV`	Is the name of the Dynamics NAV Server service and can be changed by setting the **ServerInstance** key value in the `CustomSessiongs.config` file.
`ws`	Needed to identify this as a Web service call.
`CRONUS_Int...`	This is the company name with spaces and full stops and minus signs removed and replaced with an underscore. I find this a little unpredictable, but thankfully there is a **SystemService** Web service that has a `Companies()` operation that will return a list of company names in the correct format.
`Services`	Tells the system to return a list of services available. We could use page followed by the name of the page Web service or Codeunit followed by the Codeunit service name.

You may need to alter the given URL to use the machine name that is running the Microsoft Dynamics NAV Business Web services, but for the Marketing Beta VPC image, this one will work just fine.

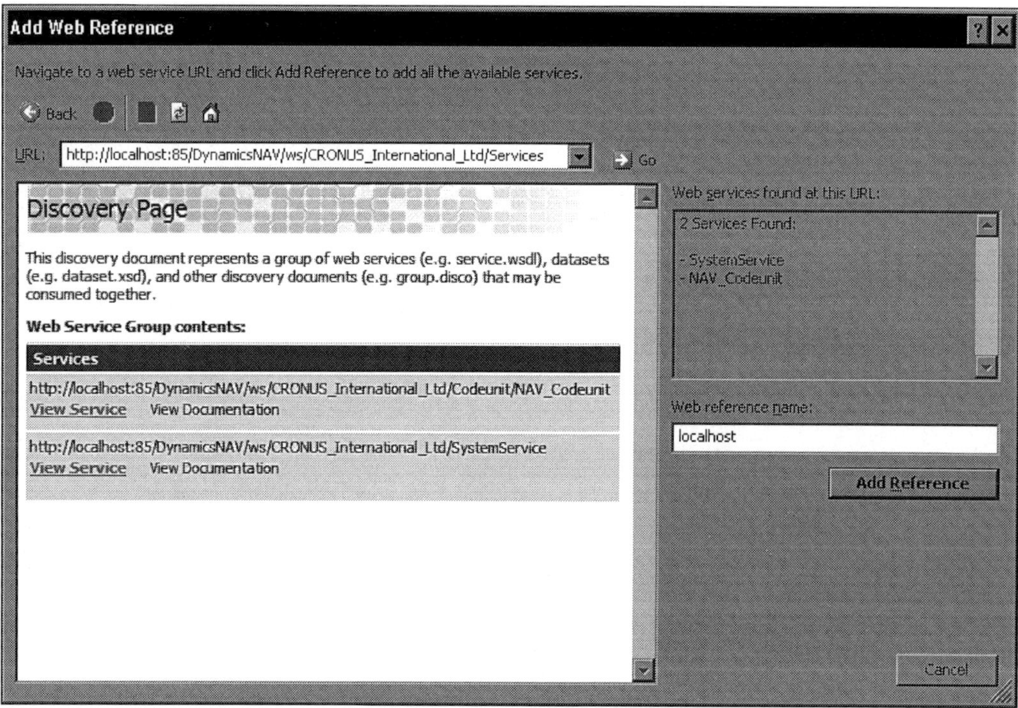

The form shows two available services: **SystemService** and the Codeunit we added called **NAV_Codeunit**. Click on the **View Service** link for the **NAV_Codeunit** service.

The form changes to show the **Methods** available for the **NAV_Codeunit** Web service.

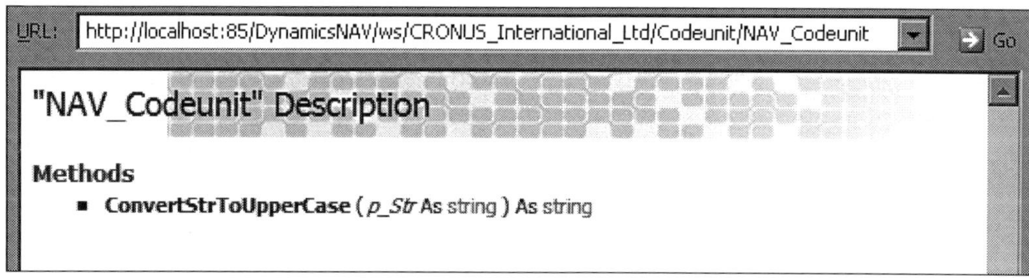

The web reference name on the right of the window (not shown in the screenshot) is set to `nav-srv-01` (or whatever the computer name happens to be for you), which is a little bit confusing as to me this represents a computer, but we are using it as the name of our web reference to our NAV Codeunit. You cannot actually use this suggested name, so let's overtype it with **NAV_Codeunit_Reference**. Click the **Add Reference** button to add the web reference to our project.

Now we have our web reference, we can write our code. Here is what my code looks like in Visual Studio:

```
using System;
using System.Collections.Generic;
using System.Linq;
using System.Text;

namespace SayHelloToNAV2009
{
    using NAV_Codeunit_Reference;     // NAV_Codeunit_Reference
                                      // is the name
                                      // of our web reference
                                      // the using command means
                                      // we don't
                                      // need to type it.
    class Program
    {
        static void Main(string[] args)
        {
            // Create a new instance of our Codeunit Web Service
            NAV_Codeunit navCU = new NAV_Codeunit();

            // Set the Web Service to use default credentials.
            // NAV Web Services need the Windows credentials
            // of a valid NAV user otherwise they won't work.
            navCU.UseDefaultCredentials = true;

            // Declare a string variable to feed into the Codeunit
            // and initialize it.
            string myString = "hello nav2009!";

            // Output the string to the console.
            Console.WriteLine("Input : {0}", myString);

            // Output the results of my Codeunit function
            Console.WriteLine("Output : {0}",
                        navCU.ConvertStrToUpperCase(myString));
```

```
                // Keep the console window open until enter key pressed.
                Console.Write("\nPress ENTER to Continue...");
                Console.ReadLine();
            }
        }
    }
```

I'm being a bit lazy here as I am not trying to trap any exceptions that may be thrown by calling the Web services. For example, I defined my `ConvertStrToUpperCase` function to accept a 50-character text variable as input, but in the method description for the web reference, it was simply shown as a string. If you were to change the code to assign `myString` with text that is longer than 50 characters, you would get an exception when the code is run. It's good practice to put your call to the Web service within a `Try`/`Catch` statement so that you can handle the exception in a nice way. Once you have got this working, why not change the preceding code to use a `myString` value that is larger than 50 characters and see what happens?

New tricks for old dogs

The .NET programming environment is fantastic compared to the C/SIDE, but if you're not used to Visual Studio.NET, you may find yourself pressing *F5* to bring up a list of methods and fields. This key-press will actually attempt to compile and run your solution. The Visual Studio equivalent of the C/SIDE *F5* key is called intellisense, and will pop up automatically as you type full stops after objects, or you can use the *Ctrl+K, L* key combination.

Let's run our example (press *F5*) and see what happens:

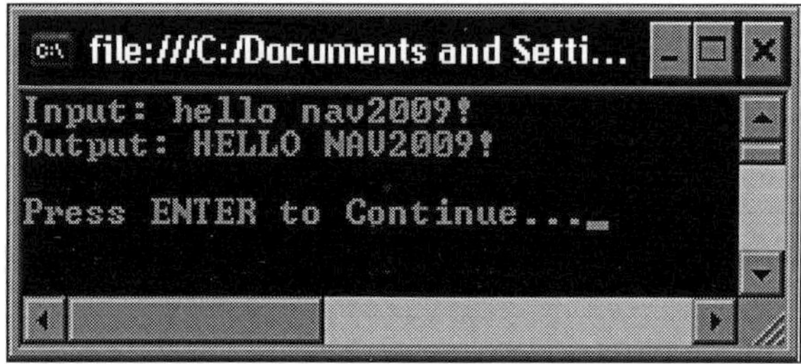

We did it! We did it! We did it! Yeah! (I think my kids have brainwashed me with too many hours of Dora the Explorer.)

That was really quite easy. Now let's take a deep breath and do some real-world examples.

WinForms application

Our first example was more a proof of concept than anything else—a simple demonstration of how easy it is to expose NAV functionality as a Web service and create a .NET application that will consume it. Now we want to make something that could be of some use. I thought of this example when watching warehouse workers try and use NAV for the first time. All they wanted to do was find out where some stock was, and they had a tiny17-inch monitor that was showing NAV **5.0**'s large menu structure where they had to navigate through several layers in order to be able to search through the item card and find the bin contents.

Now we have NAV 2009, and the RoleTailored experience means the few simple functions that a warehouse worker needs can be exposed on the role center, but I figured maybe there would be some simple activities that don't really warrant having a full NAV license tied up. This 'Stock Look-up' application is intended to provide that functionality. As always, before we start writing code, we need to define what the functional requirements for our application are.

Item look-up requirements

Our application will have a single input field that allows a user to type a piece of text that can represent an item number, part of an item number, or part of an item description, and hit a search button (a bit like using a web search page). The system will apply some wildcard filters around the words so that the users don't have to be bothered with learning about wildcards, and display a list of potential matches including the Item No., Item Description, Unit of Measure Code, and Quantity available. Possible extensions to this application would be to allow the Quantity to be interrogated further to show which bin locations the stock was in, using Warehouse Management functionality. For now, we'll keep it simple to see if we can use a page type Web service and create a WinForms application.

Exposing the Web service

We know that our requirements will mean using a Page type Web service since we are going to need to set filters and bring back multiple records. It makes sense to use the Item Card page (Page ID=30) since this has all the fields we need: **No.**, **Description**, **Base Unit of Measure**, and **Inventory**. If you've read through the sample Web service call at the beginning of this chapter, it should be no surprise to learn that exposing our Item Card Page as a Web service is as easy as 1, 2, 3.

1. Open **Administration | IT Administration | General Setup | Web Services** in the Classic client.

2. Create a new record for **Object Type** = **Page, Object ID** = **30, Service Name** = **Item Card**.
3. Tick the **Published** field.

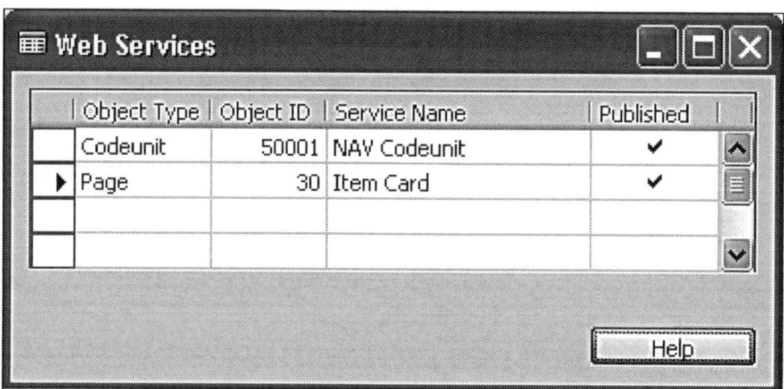

Now we have our page exposed as a Web service, let's see if it shows up by entering `http://nav-srv-01:7047/DynamicsNAV/ws/CRONUS_International_Ltd/Services` in our web browser.

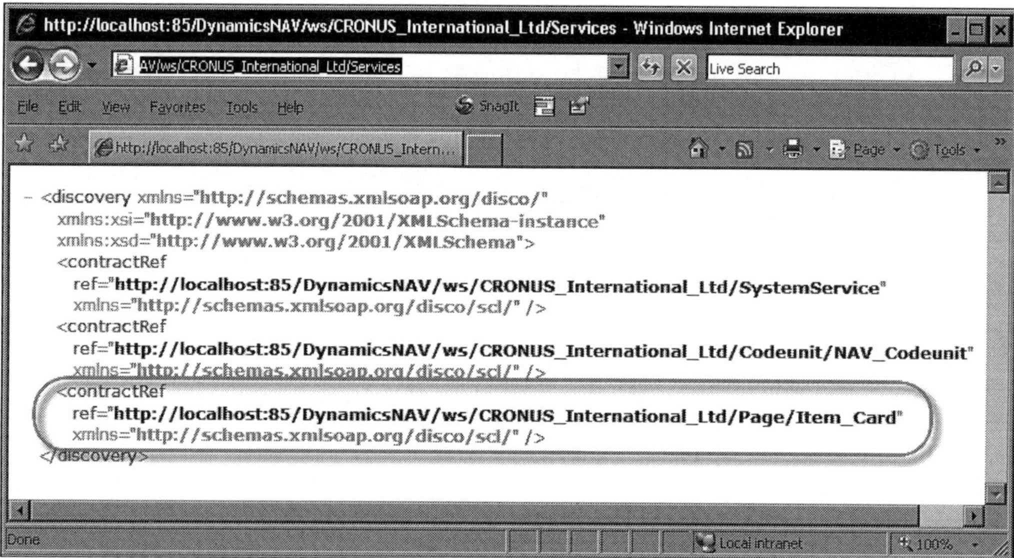

Bingo! Now let's take a look at the WSDL for that service and see what methods and properties we have available. Whoa—lots of code—over 500 lines, way too much to include here. Instead of digging in to the WSDL, we'll create our WinForms application.

New Windows application project

Start up Visual Studio.NET and select the option to create a new project using the **Windows Forms Application** template.

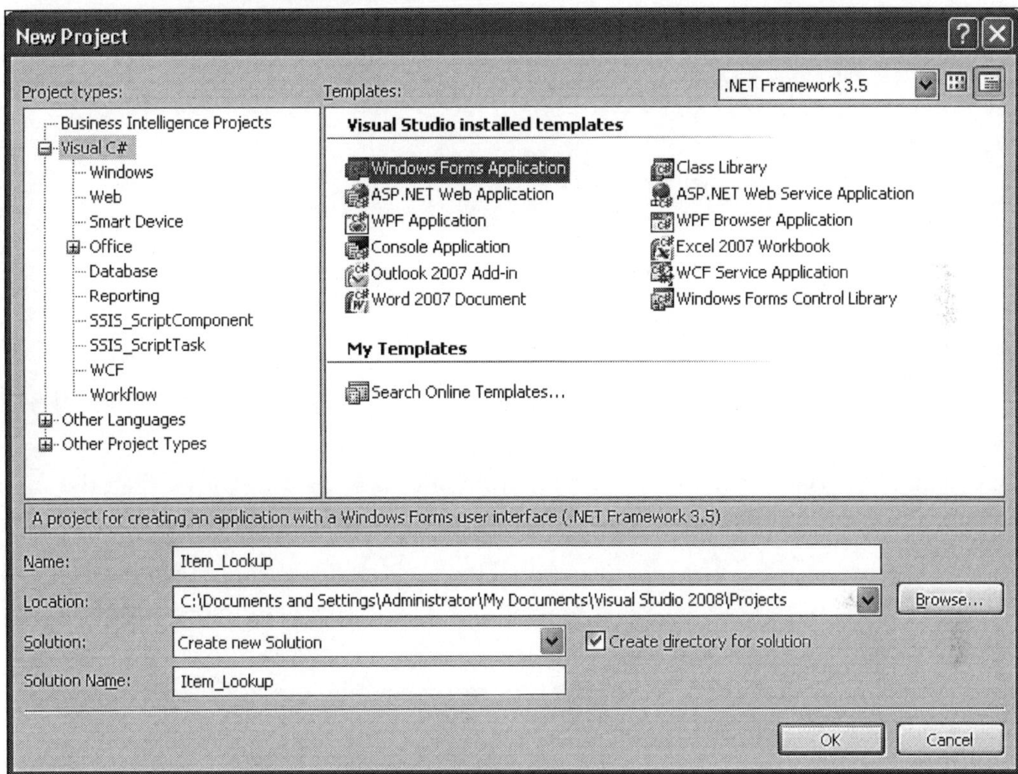

Give the project a name, I called mine **Item_Lookup**.

Visual Studio makes a new project for us with a **Form1.cs** class that is our Windows Form. You could run this form now by pressing *F5* but since it has no controls on it, you won't be able to do anything other than resize it, move it around, and close it.

The first thing to do is add our web reference. You can follow the same steps as we did for our **Hello NAV 2009** example, but use the URL for the new page Web service instead. If you get it right, you should see the following service description:

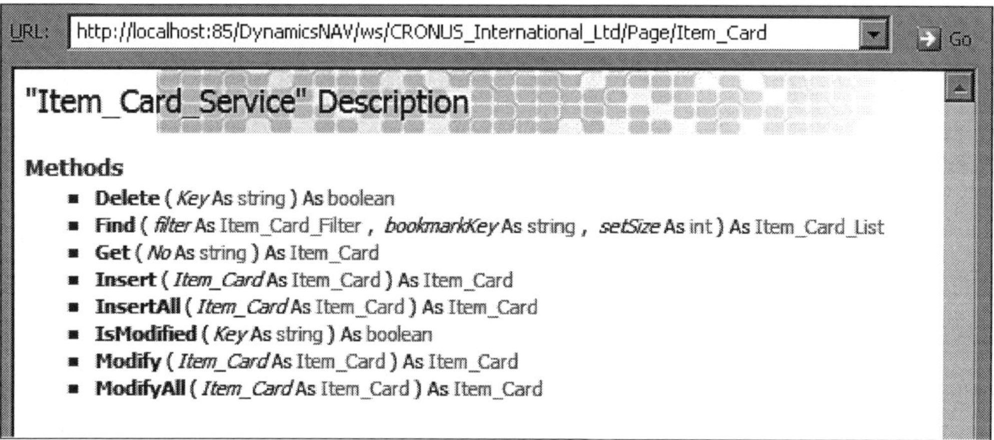

Once again, I'm going to change my service reference to something other than the machine name (I used **Item_Card_Ref**), and click the button to add it to my project.

Now we can add some controls to our form. I took a look down the list of controls and found one called **DataGridView** that sounded about right. I dragged one of these on to my form.

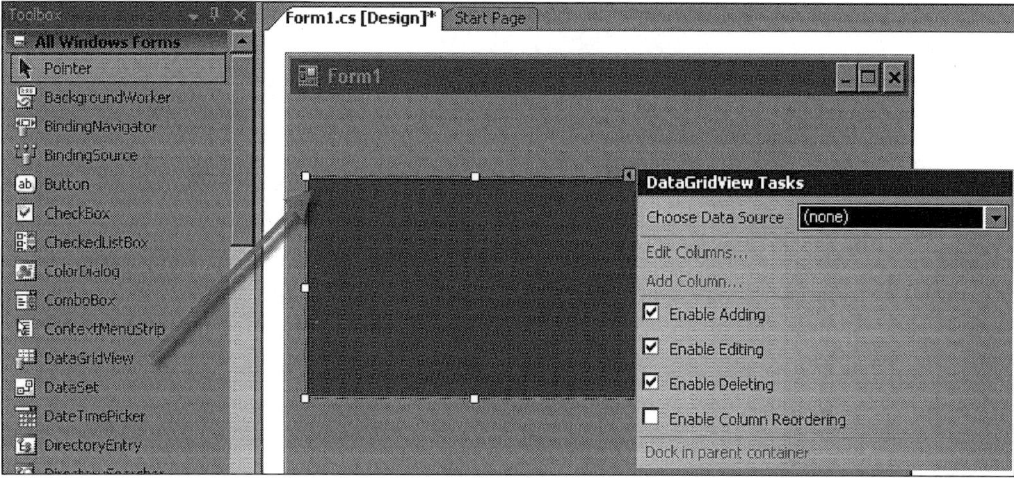

When we drag this control on to a form we get a nice little pop-up window asking where our data will come from.

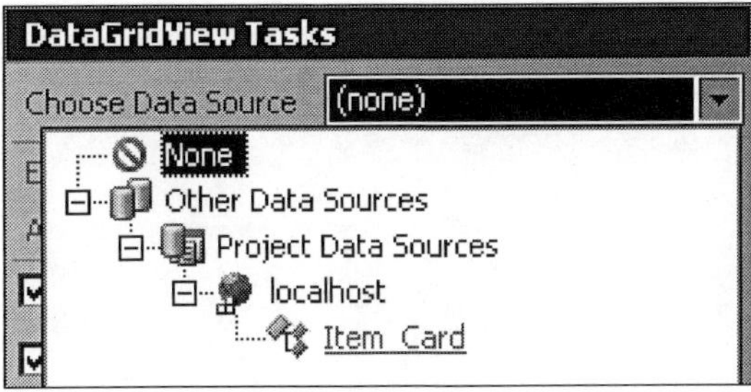

You can expand the tree nodes until you find the **Item_Card_Ref** Web service reference, and there in the list is our **Item_Card** data source. Select it and a new BindingSource control is added to the form.

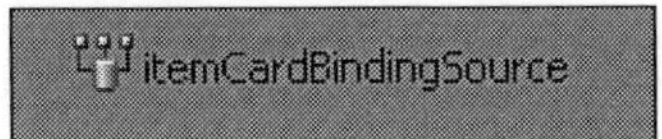

With the **DataGridView Tasks** window still open, you can remove the tick from the **Enable Adding**, **Enable Editing**, and **Enable Deleting** check boxes; we really don't want our warehouse staff accidentally deleting our inventory items.

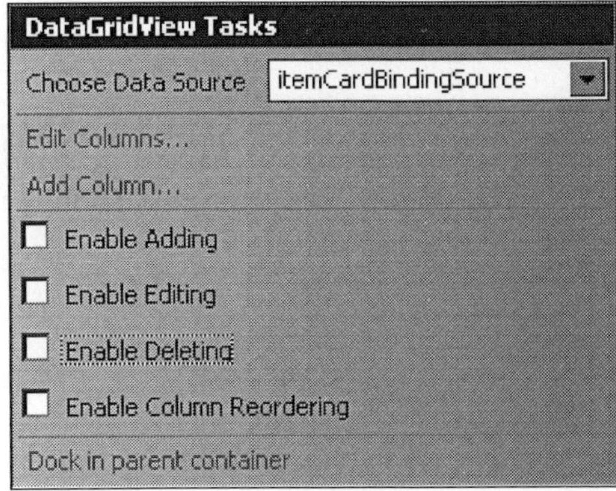

Now we can drag our DataGridView control so that it fills the bottom part of the screen, and in the properties pane, change the **Anchor** property to **Top, Bottom, Left, Right**. This is a bit like setting Horizontal Glue and Vertical Glue properties in C/SIDE to both so that the control will resize when the form is resized.

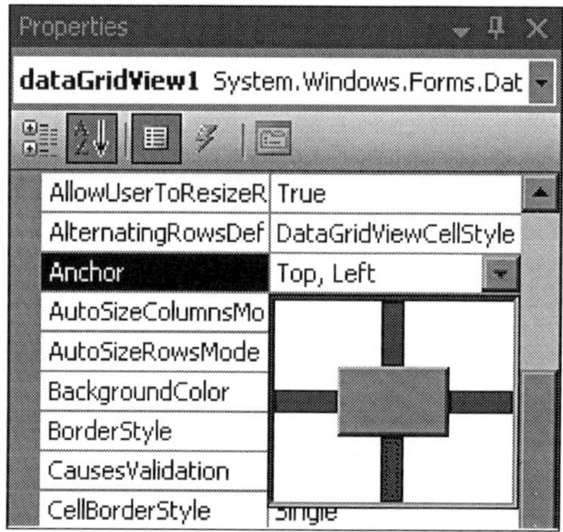

Now we need to change the columns on the DataGridView so it only shows the four fields we are interested in. Click the tasks button, and from the **DataGridView Tasks** form, select the **Edit Columns** option.

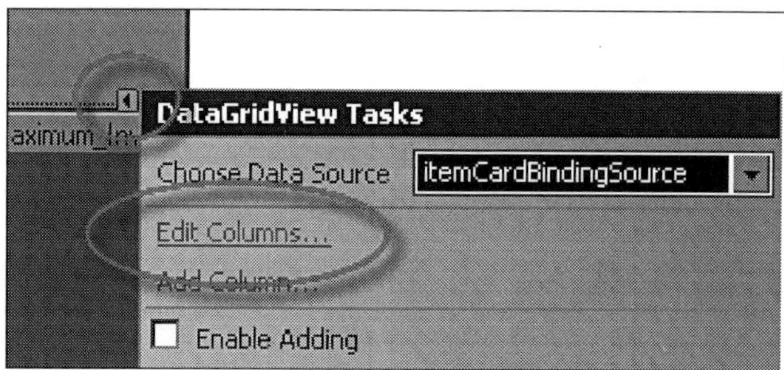

With well over a hundred fields to remove and no multi-select option, the best thing you can do is press *Alt+R* to remove the current field and keep the keys held down until all fields are removed. Once all fields are gone, click the **Add** button to bring up the **Add Column** dialog.

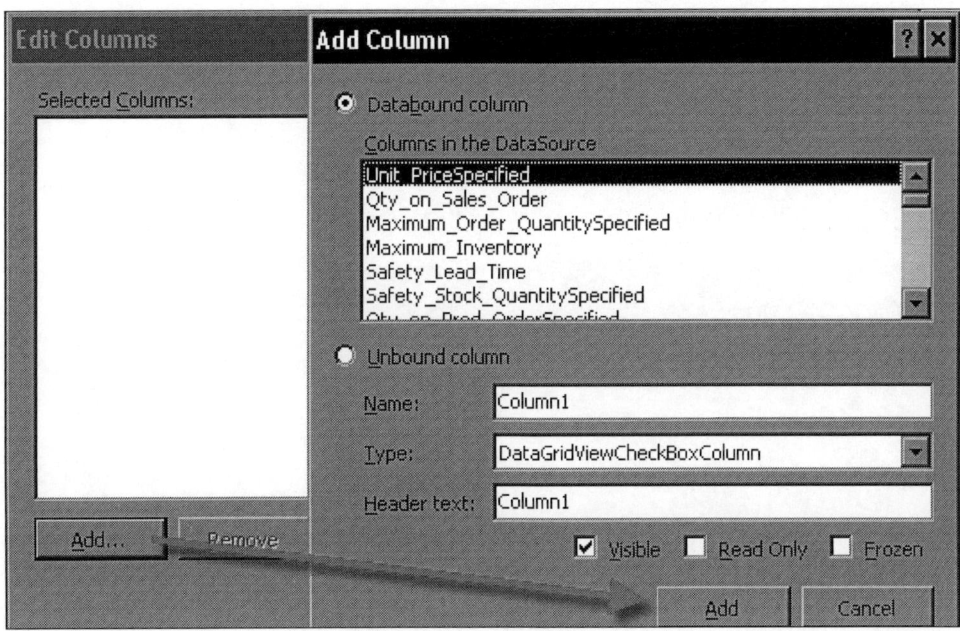

The list works in the same way as the lists in the C/SIDE environment in that if you want to find a specific item, you can jump to the first item by pressing the starting letter; if it's not the column you want, you need to keep pressing the start letter until the required column appears.

Add the **No**, **Description**, **Base_Unit_Of_Measure**, and **Inventory** columns, and close the form.

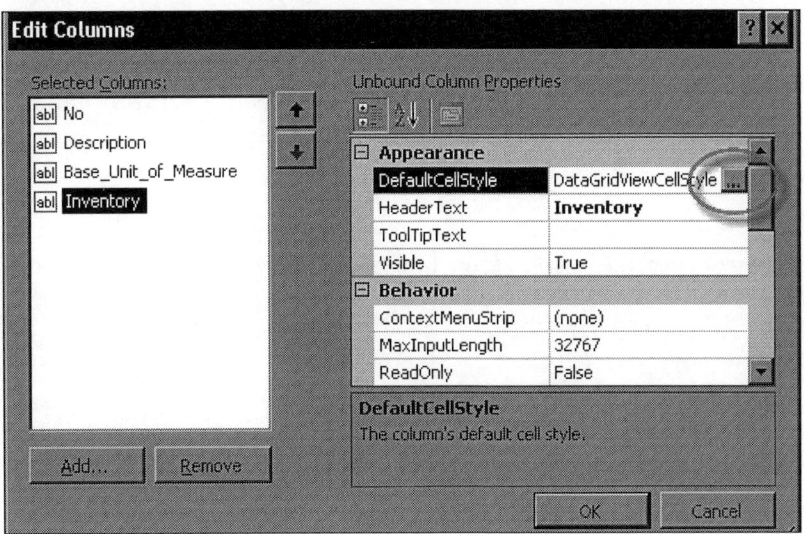

You can use the **Edit Columns** form to change the appearance of the columns. For instance, we want to change the **DefaultCellStyle** property of the **Inventory** field so that it is formatted as a number and is right-aligned. Click the ellipsis (three dots) to the right of the field.

Set the **Format** property to **N0** (that's N for numeric and 0 for zero decimal places), and set the **Alignment** property to **MiddleRight**.

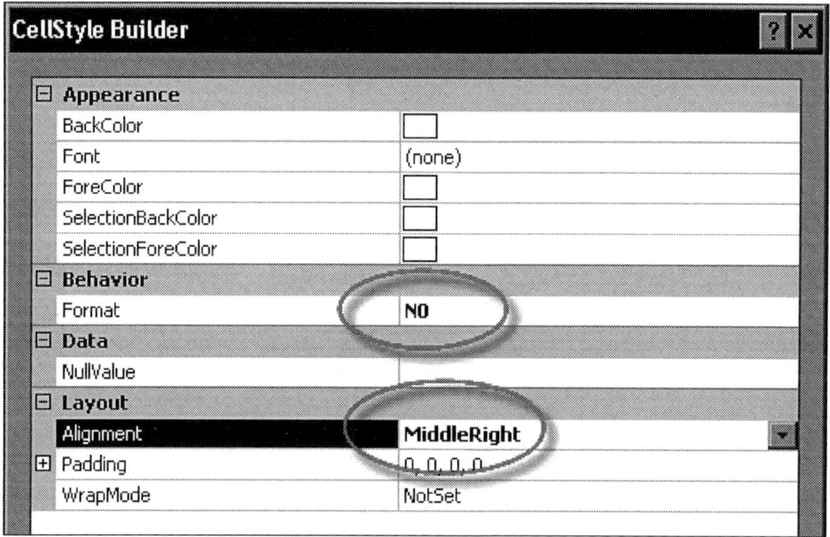

I suggest you also set the **HeaderText** property for the **Base_Unit_Of_Measure** field to something a little shorter (like UOM), and set the **AutoSizeMode** property for the **Description** field to **Fill**.

Now's a good time to run the form with *F5* to check that everything looks as it should. You can try resizing the form and see that the DataGridView expands and contracts and the Description field expands to fill the new space.

Getting some data

OK so we have a control to display our data, all we need now is something to put in it. As always we're going to take things one step at a time, so rather than trying to build all the functionality for matching strings in multiple fields with wildcards, we'll just get something to display to make sure everything is hooked up properly. Now it's time to add some code to our form; so double-click on the form and the `Form1.cs` code editor window will open with a new **Form1_Load** method created. We're going to put some code in there to find the first 100 records, but in order to do that we'll need to create a new method. The following is how your code should look:

```
using System;
using System.Collections.Generic;
using System.ComponentModel;
using System.Data;
using System.Drawing;
using System.Linq;
using System.Text;
using System.Windows.Forms;

namespace Item_Lookup
{
    using Item_Card_Ref; // Item_Card_Ref is our Web service
                         // reference

    public partial class Form1 : Form
    {
        // declare our Web service variable
        private Item_Card_Service ItemCardService;

        public Form1()
        {
            InitializeComponent();

            // Instantiate our Web service
            ItemCardService = new Item_Card_Service();

            // Use the default credentials
            // (i.e. the NAV Windows User)
            ItemCardService.UseDefaultCredentials = true;
        }

        private void Form1_Load(object sender, EventArgs e)
        {
            // OnLoad we'll display the first 100 records with
            // no filter
            FindRecords("");
        }

        // New method to find item records based on a filter
        // string and display them
        private void FindRecords(string filterString)
        {
            // Create a new item card instance
            Item_Card itemCard = new Item_Card();
```

```
                // Create a new List of Filters to be used to
                // filter the records
                List<Item_Card_Filter> filters =
                                      new List<Item_Card_Filter>();

                // Create a new filter on the No. field and add it
                // to the filter list
                Item_Card_Filter noFilter = new Item_Card_Filter();
                noFilter.Field = Item_Card_Fields.No;
                noFilter.Criteria = filterString;
                filters.Add(noFilter);

                // Find the records and set the resulting records as
                // the datasource for the grid
                dataGridView1.DataSource =
                     ItemCardService.ReadMultiple(filters.ToArray(),
                                                  null, 100);
            }
        }
    }
```

If all has gone well, you should now be able to press *F5* to compile and run the application and see something like this:

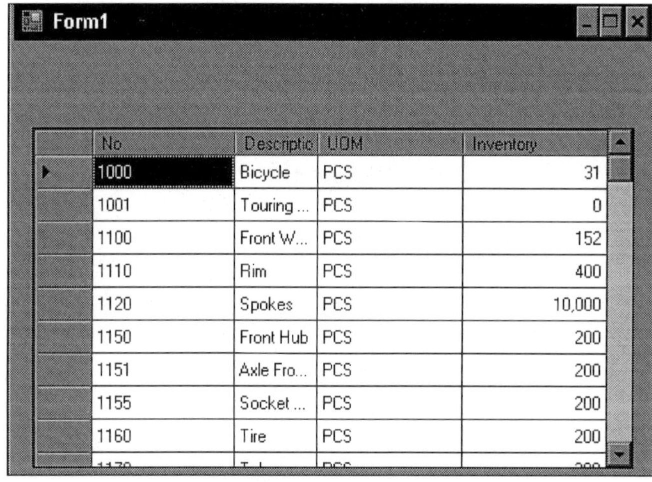

There're a few things to tidy up (like the starting columns sizes, the name of the form in the title bar, and the icon for the form), but these can all wait. The good news is we are displaying data from NAV 2009 in a Windows Application. Now let's add our filter text box and button to do the search.

Filter Box and Find Button

Drag a textbox and a button control on to our form and change the **Text** property for the button from **button1** to **Find**.

Double-click on the **Find** button so we can add some code to run when the user clicks the button. Not too much code to add this time; since we already have our method to do the work, we just need to call it with the contents of the text box.

```
private void button1_Click(object sender, EventArgs e)
{
    FindRecords(textBox1.Text);
}
```

Testing time

Press *F5* to run the application one more time so we can test our new search functionality. Since I'm watching the New Zealand men's soccer team get beaten by Brazil in the Olympics, let's search for some items with an Olympic feel. Type **????-?** into the text box (meaning any four characters followed by a minus sign followed by any character) and click the **Find** button.

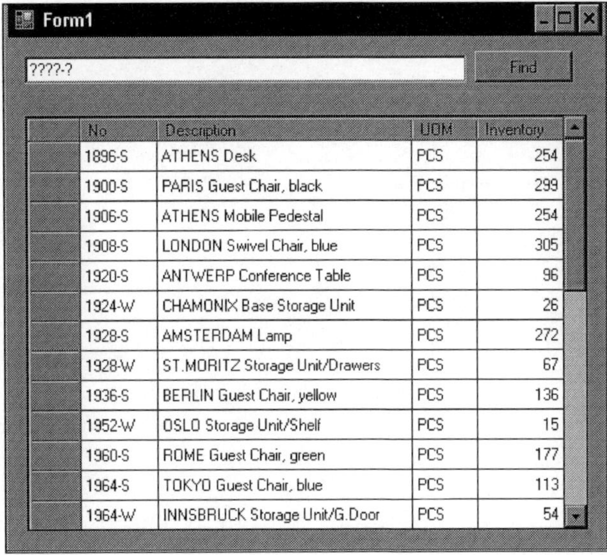

No	Description	UOM	Inventory
1896-S	ATHENS Desk	PCS	254
1900-S	PARIS Guest Chair, black	PCS	299
1906-S	ATHENS Mobile Pedestal	PCS	254
1908-S	LONDON Swivel Chair, blue	PCS	305
1920-S	ANTWERP Conference Table	PCS	96
1924-W	CHAMONIX Base Storage Unit	PCS	26
1928-S	AMSTERDAM Lamp	PCS	272
1928-W	ST.MORITZ Storage Unit/Drawers	PCS	67
1936-S	BERLIN Guest Chair, yellow	PCS	136
1952-W	OSLO Storage Unit/Shelf	PCS	15
1960-S	ROME Guest Chair, green	PCS	177
1964-S	TOKYO Guest Chair, blue	PCS	113
1964-W	INNSBRUCK Storage Unit/G.Door	PCS	54

Hmmmm, the **2008-S BEIJING Bar Stool, grey** doesn't seem to be there. Come to think of it where's the 1912 Summer Olympics in Stockholm or the 1916 games in Berlin? Phew, I checked the data in the Classic client and the problem is in the test data and not our form. Everything is working perfectly.

WinForms application summary

The product team has definitely made it easy for us with the thought they have put into the NAV Page Web services. There are some things that are just so easy when doing development in C/SIDE compared to .NET. For example, when you're editing data on a page, you don't need to worry about whether another user is trying to edit the same data. If you were to extend our example to include the ability to edit the data, you need to consider whether the data has been edited by someone else, possibly even deleted, and what you will do to handle the exception.

See if you can keep extending our little application to include all of the features described in the requirements section. You can download a complete version for study from our book's web site.

Sidebar gadget

A sidebar gadget is a simple single-tasked tool that sits in the sidebar on Windows Vista. If you don't have Windows Vista, I'm afraid you're out of luck and won't be able to run this sample. You can explore the free gadgets available for download at `http://gallery.live.com/`. Typical gadgets include:

- RSS Feed Readers
- News Readers
- Weather Reports
- Clocks
- Performance Monitoring Tools
- Mini Notepads
- Photo Slideshows

Hopefully you get the idea.

We're going to create a sidebar gadget that will use the Web service capabilities of Dynamics NAV 2009 to display a cue (a stack of documents similar to those shown in the RoleTailored client), based upon the document approvals features that have been available since NAV **5.0**. We want to display a document stack that represents the number of documents requiring approval from the current user and will allow the user to select the type of document as a configuration setting. In our example, clicking the document stack will show a list of documents and clicking an individual document will launch the RoleTailored client. There's no reason why you can't take this example and extend it to include the ability to display the actual documents and carry out the approval, all from the comfort of your Windows Vista desktop.

Design time

When we start to design NAV solutions, we use our knowledge of the standard application to create a solution that fits nicely within the NAV paradigm. We try to emulate the way the standard application solves common business problems and use the components that are used by the product team in a consistent manner.

Designing applications for .NET, or in this case for a sidebar gadget, follows the same conventions. First of all we need to understand a little bit about what makes a sidebar gadget so that we can know the constraints of our design.

What are little gadgets made of?

There is an excellent tutorial on MSDN Magazine's web site by Donavon West that tells you how to build a sidebar gadget for displaying MSDN Magazine articles in a news-ticker format with the ability to click an article to see more details and click another link to read the full article on the Web. We're going to use that article and the gadget provided for download as the basis for exploring what a gadget is, which will in turn help us to design our own gadget.

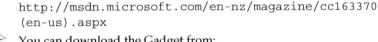

> You can read Donavon West's MSDN Magazine article at:
>
> 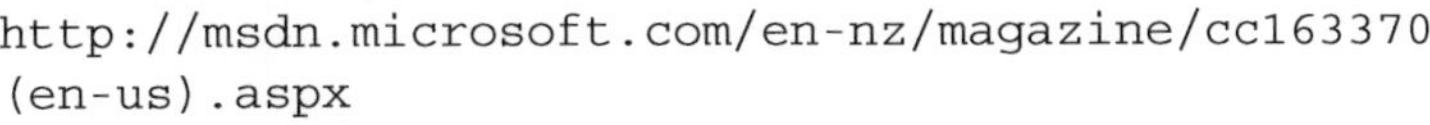
>
> `http://msdn.microsoft.com/en-nz/magazine/cc163370(en-us).aspx`
>
> You can download the Gadget from:
>
> `http://gallery.live.com/liveItemDetail.aspx?li=b21af41e-b846-46d9-a873-ac12a3c65ab3`

Essentially a gadget is little more than a mini web page (HTML file with some supporting resources such as images and JavaScript) and an XML definition file called `gadget.xml`. When we're writing a sidebar gadget for Windows Vista, the HTML page is rendered in Microsoft Internet Explorer 7, so there is no need to worry about cross-browser support. Which is nice.

If you download the gadget and save it somewhere instead of installing it, you will see an icon for the gadget like this:

Before we can use this gadget there is a little problem that needs to be fixed—unfortunately it is pointing to an RSS Feed URL that is not valid and therefore the gadget doesn't work correctly.

Donavon explains that a sidebar gadget is simply a collection of files that are stored in a ZIP or CAB file with a `.gadget` extension, so we can rename the file with a `.zip` extension and we should be able to open it as a folder. If you open the compressed folder, or extract it, you will see the following files:

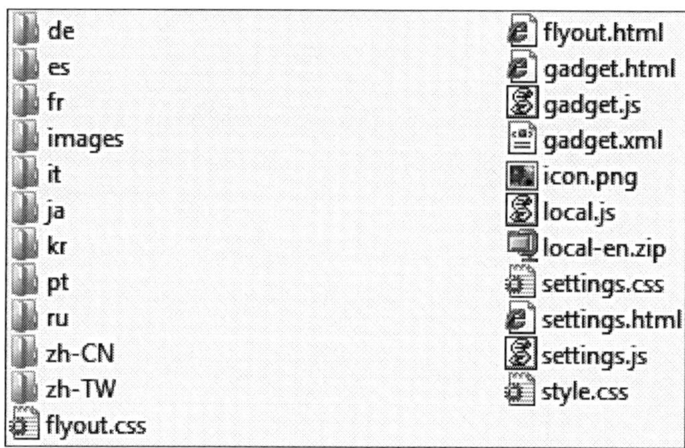

There is a file called `local.js` that we will need to edit in order to fix the problem. Gadgets support multi-language capabilities and if your language matches the folder names shown, you are going to need to open that folder and edit the `local.js` that it contains.

The languages supported by this gadget are as follows:

Folder Name	Language
de	German (Standard)
es	Spanish (Spain)
fr	French (Standard)
it	Italian (Standard)
ja	Japanese
kr	I don't think this is a valid language code, so we'll just ignore this.
pt	Portuguese (Portugal)
ru	Russian
zh-CN	Chinese (PRC)
zh-TW	Chinese (Taiwan)

You can get a full list of language codes at `http://msdn.microsoft.com/en-us/library/ms533052(VS.85).aspx`

According to the tutorial, whenever the sidebar tries to load a file, it searches for the file in folders in the following order:

- Full locale (en-us, es-us, ja-jp)
- Language portion of the locale (en, es, ja)
- Gadget root folder

So what does this mean? If your locale has a language component that is one of the folders listed in the table, you are going to need to edit the `local.js` within that folder in order for the gadget to work correctly.

When you edit the `local.js` file (any text editor will do), you will see the following:

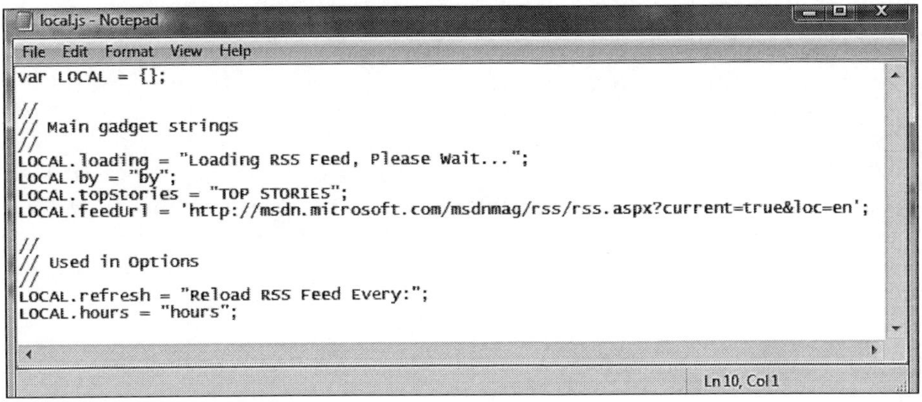

local.js - Notepad

File Edit Format View Help

```
var LOCAL = {};

//
// Main gadget strings
//
LOCAL.loading = "Loading RSS Feed, Please Wait...";
LOCAL.by = "by";
LOCAL.topStories = "TOP STORIES";
LOCAL.feedUrl = 'http://msdn.microsoft.com/msdnmag/rss/rss.aspx?current=true&loc=en';

//
// Used in Options
//
LOCAL.refresh = "Reload RSS Feed Every:";
LOCAL.hours = "hours";
```

Ln 10, Col 1

If you copy the `feedUrl` string and paste it into a web browser address bar, you will see a runtime error telling you this is not a valid address. A little bit of digging soon reveals an address that we can use for the gadget:

```
http://msdn.microsoft.com/en-nz/magazine/rss/default(en-us).
aspx?issue=1
```

You need to replace the old URL with the new one so that your line in the file looks like the following:

```
LOCAL.feedUrl = 'http://msdn.microsoft.com/en-nz/magazine/rss/
default(en-us).aspx?issue=1';
```

Now we can rename the file back to a `.gadget` extension and install it. This is to help us examine the main components of a sidebar gadget so we can consider how we will design our own gadget.

The gadget

The most obvious part of a gadget is the gadget itself. This is the gadget's main HTML page that is provided in the `base src` property of our `gadget.xml` file. For us, we want this to show a single document cue that represents the number of approval entries that are awaiting action for the current user. We want the main docked gadget to look something like this:

The image is meant to look like a cue from an **Activities Part** in a **Role Center**. The pencil sketch is there to give you an idea of what I am thinking. Since the 22 approval actions could be for multiple different document types, I think I will have some text underneath the stack of documents that tells me how many of each of the different document types there are. It could either fade in and out, or scroll horizontal like a marquee.

That takes care of the docked state of the gadget. When I undock it, I can get a larger area to play with, so I think it would be nice if the undocked state showed one stack of documents for each of the approval document types with the name of the document type shown underneath. This may be a little time-consuming, so maybe I'll add that to version 2. For now the undocked image will be the same as the docked image.

There are a couple of other pages that need to be considered: Flyouts and Options dialog.

Flyouts

When you click on a part of gadget, you can activate a flyout, which is basically a web page that gets displayed at the side of the gadget. The flyout file is specified by setting `System.Gadget.Flyout.file` to the name of the flyout HTML file. In the case of our MSDN Ticker gadget, the flyout looks like the following:

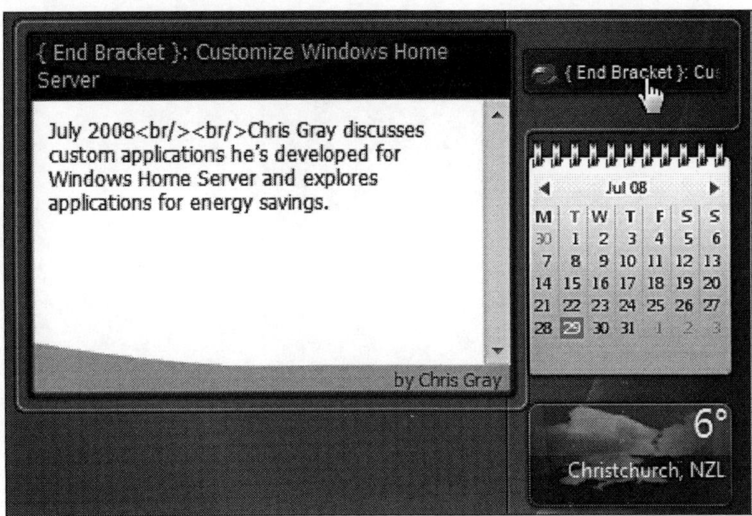

For our flyout, we are going to show a list of approval entries with the ability to click a hyperlink to open the approval entries screen. An obvious next extension to this gadget is to provide the ability to approve, reject, or delegate the approval entry directly from the gadget without needing to open the RoleTailored client. For now, we'll concentrate on making this work with our NAV Web service. After taking a quick look at the fields available on the approval entry screen, I think our flyout will look something like the following:

It's a simple table showing the documents with a document type and number, the ID of the sender and the amount that the document is for.

Options

There is one more part of the gadget to consider for our design and that is the options dialog page. Let's take a look at that for the **MSDN Magazine Ticker** sample gadget.

When I hover my mouse over the gadget, a mini tool bar appears allowing me to close the gadget, show the options, and drag the gadget to a different position. Click the spanner to show the options page.

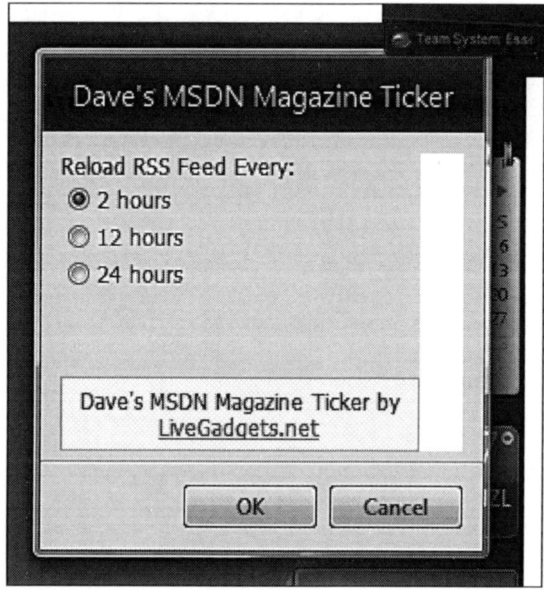

As you can see it's just another little web page with some options on it. You need to instruct the gadget to enable the options icon by setting `System.Gadget.settingsUI` to the name of the options HTML file, generally in the gadget initialization area of our script. Donavon's article explains how this is done, and provides sample code for how to set up a callback function for when the options dialog closes (so your gadget can read the new user preferences).

For our gadget we are going to need a place where we can enter the URL for our Web service. For more advanced options, we could possibly provide the ability to specify how often the gadget will call the Web service.

Our options page will look something like this:

These pencil sketches are just there to convey the intended layout of the pages; it's a lot quicker to scribble something on a piece of paper (for me) than to start playing around with graphics programs and although they're a little rough, if you squint at them, you can sort of work out what's intended in the final solution. Remember it's important to get an understanding of the design at this stage but it doesn't need to look great; form follows function.

The tricky bits

Now that we've done the high-level design for our sidebar gadget, and we know that a sidebar gadget is just a series of HTML pages, we can start to look at the technical design. There are a couple of tricky bits to take care of: how are we going to call our Web service from within what is essentially a web page, and how are we going to take our list of documents requiring approval and convert them into the table and graphics we want to display.

The great thing about sidebar gadgets and the way they are constructed is that you can simply rename the file and take a look at how they are doing what they do (and, of course, you can borrow ideas and code). If you search on the Web, you'll find quite a few examples of sidebar gadgets that call Web services, so there're plenty of examples to look at. I happened to pick an example from Microsoft that uses the Exchange 2007 Web service to display email, calendar, and task information. You can download it from:

`http://www.microsoft.com/downloads/details.aspx?FamilyID=F9A0D33C-C894-4EA1-AD20-4E418C715175&displaylang=en`

A quick search for **Exchange Web services Gadget** will help you locate it. Actually finding this gadget was a stroke of luck because it does pretty much everything we are after:

- It has a setup page with a time interval on it.
- It calls a Web service to find how many items there are in a folder and shows a summary.
- It displays a flyout with a more detailed view of the folder contents.

Finding good examples on the Internet and learning from them is a key skill for doing this kind of development.

Just a little bit of SOAP

Calling a NAV Web service from within a Visual Studio.NET project is dead easy as we've already seen. We just add our Web service as a web reference and Visual Studio does all the hard work for us. It creates a proxy class that allows us to call the member functions and access the properties of the service as though it was a piece of code that we had written ourselves and not just some black box at the end of a URL. But how do we do this when we don't have Visual Studio?

Essentially a Web service is just some text sent over the Internet that generates a response (which is also text). It just so happens that the text being sent and received is formatted as XML which is handy because there is lots of support for reading XML text. Web services typically use a protocol called **Simple Object Access Protocol** (or **SOAP**) to allow any system that can post a request to a URL (and read a response message) to call to a function exposed by the Web service. In order to do this for our sidebar gadget, we need two things: we need to know how to send and receive our request, and we need to know what the SOAP request should look like.

Figuring out the HTTP call and response handling isn't too hard and you can do this by looking at the Exchange Web service gadget source code or, once again, searching the Internet.

Looking at how Microsoft did it in their Exchange Web service gadget shows us we can use the native `Microsoft.XMLHTTP` object provided by Internet Explorer (remember that a sidebar gadget runs in Internet Explorer only, so we don't need to worry about cross-browser support) to make an HTTP post to our Web service and read the response.

Finding the XML for the SOAP request that is needed to invoke a NAV Web service is going to be a little trickier. If I do a Web search for 'how to view a soap request in Visual Studio?', it doesn't take much to find a link to a freeware product called Fiddler that will allow me to inspect messages to and from my web server. Here is the URL:

`http://www.fiddler2.com/fiddler2/`

If I use this tool on the simple example we started the chapter with, I can see the SOAP request is:

```
<soap:Envelope xmlns:soap="http://schemas.xmlsoap.org/soap/envelope/"
               xmlns:xsi="http://www.w3.org/2001/XMLSchema-instance"
               xmlns:xsd="http://www.w3.org/2001/XMLSchema">
    <soap:Body>
        <ConvertStrToUpperCase
                xmlns="urn:microsoft-dynamics-schemas/codeunit/NAV_Codeunit">
            <p_Str>hello nav2009!</p_Str>
        </ConvertStrToUpperCase>
    </soap:Body>
</soap:Envelope>
```

And the response is:

```
<Soap:Envelope xmlns:Soap="http://schemas.xmlsoap.org/soap/envelope/">
    <Soap:Body>
        <ConvertStrToUpperCase_Result
                xmlns="urn:microsoft-dynamics-schemas/codeunit/NAV_Codeunit">
            <return_value>HELLO NAV2009!</return_value>
        </ConvertStrToUpperCase_Result>
    </Soap:Body>
</Soap:Envelope>
```

I'm guessing I could have worked out this request and response format by reading the WSDL (pronounced 'wiz-dal'), that I get when I type the URL to the Codeunit in my web browser; however, I think that using Visual Studio to test calling my Web service is by far the easiest way, and using the Fiddler tool to be able to inspect and copy the SOAP Envelope XML has got to be better than thinking.

Now before I get too carried away trying to create a series of Web service calls to allow me to pull data from a page type Web service, I'm going to create a simple proof-of-concept web page that will make a JavaScript call to this NAV Web service with our `ConvertStrToUpperCase` function.

An HTML page that calls a NAV Codeunit

This next script is 72 lines of text, and it took me nearly 5 hours to write. That's pretty slow progress, but bear in mind I don't know JavaScript or HTML or SOAP (well I know a bit more now as I have finished the example), but the point of the exercise is to show how easy it is to do things in the .NET world even when you don't know what you're doing. I must apologize to any HTML uber-gurus out there for my hacked together code. I really just pulled bits from here and there and hacked it about until I got something that worked. I'm not proud of it, but it does the job. Here is the code in full; we'll go through it in detail later:

```
<HTML>
<HEAD>
  <TITLE>Hello NAV 2009 With JavaScript</TITLE>
</HEAD>
<BODY>
<b>Input: </b>hello nav2009!<br/>
<div id="resultContainer"><b>Output: </b></div>

<FORM Name="Form1" ACTION="">
   <INPUT TYPE=BUTTON VALUE="Call NAV" NAME="BtnHello" OnClick="Hello
NAV2009()">
</FORM>

<SCRIPT LANGUAGE="JavaScript">
<!--
  function HelloNAV2009 ()
  {

    var data = "";

    data += '<?xml version="1.0" encoding="utf-8"?>';
    data += '<soap:Envelope xmlns:soap="http://schemas.xmlsoap.org/
soap/envelope/" ';
    data += '                xmlns:xsi="http://www.w3.org/2001/
XMLSchema-instance" ';
    data += '                xmlns:xsd="http://www.w3.org/2001/
XMLSchema">';
    data += '  <soap:Body>';
    data += '    <ConvertStrToUpperCase ';
    data += '      xmlns="urn:microsoft-dynamics-schemas/codeunit/NAV_
Codeunit">';
    data += '     <p_Str>hello nav2009!</p_Str>';
    data += '    </ConvertStrToUpperCase>';
    data += '  </soap:Body>';
    data += '</soap:Envelope>';
```

```
    var xmlHttpRequest = new ActiveXObject("Microsoft.XMLHTTP");

    var url = 'http://ds-srv-01:7047/DynamicsNAV/ws/CRONUS_
International_Ltd/Codeunit/NAV_Codeunit';

    xmlHttpRequest.open("POST", url, false);

    xmlHttpRequest.SetRequestHeader("Content-Type", "text/xml");
    xmlHttpRequest.SetRequestHeader("SOAPAction", "urn:microsoft-
dynamics-schemas/codeunit/NAV_Codeunit:ConvertStrToUpperCase");


    xmlHttpRequest.onreadystatechange = readResponse;
    xmlHttpRequest.send(data);

    function readResponse()
    {
      if (xmlHttpRequest.readyState == 4)
    {
      var xmlDoc = new ActiveXObject("Microsoft.XMLDOM");

            xmlDoc.loadXML(xmlHttpRequest.responseText);

      resultText = xmlDoc.getElementsByTagName("return_value")[0].
childNodes[0].nodeValue;

           xmlDoc = null;

      resultContainerElement = document.getElementById("resultContaine
r");

            if (resultContainerElement != null)
            {
            resultContainerElement.innerHTML = "<b>Output: </b>" +
resultText;
      }

      xmlHttpRequest = null;
    }
      }
     }
//-->
</SCRIPT>
</BODY>
</HTML>
```

You can download the `HelloNAV2009.html` file from `www.teachmenav.com` (or `http://www.packtpub.com/support`). You may need to edit the file on the line where the `url` variable is assigned to point to the Web service URL available on your computer. When you open the file in your browser, you will need to allow the blocked content in order for the example to run (apparently my programming is potentially dangerous—how does the web browser know me so well?)

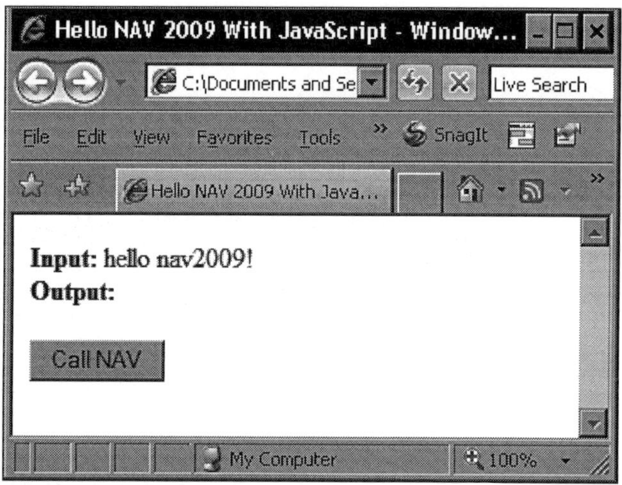

When you click the **Call NAV** button, the screen updates to show the following:

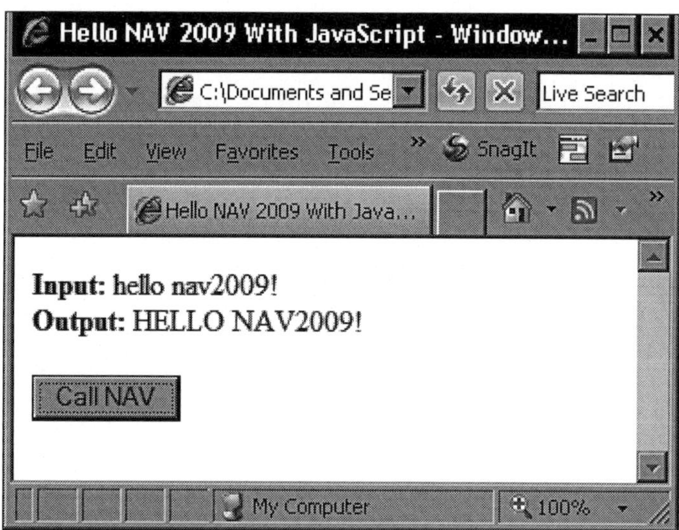

Wooohooo! It works!

OK, let's take a look at what's going on in the code. First of all I assign my variable called `data` to the XML for the SOAP request body (I found this by using the Fiddler application earlier). I haven't included that block of code for analysis, so let's move on.

This next block of code creates an instance of the Microsoft.XMLHTTP object that we are going to use to make the HTTP post and read the response.

```
var xmlHttpRequest = new ActiveXObject("Microsoft.XMLHTTP");

var url = 'http://ds-srv-01:7047/DynamicsNAV/ws/CRONUS_International_
Ltd/Codeunit/NAV_Codeunit';

xmlHttpRequest.open("POST", url, false);

xmlHttpRequest.SetRequestHeader("Content-Type", "text/xml");

xmlHttpRequest.SetRequestHeader("SOAPAction", "urn:microsoft-dynamics-
schemas/Codeunit/NAV_Codeunit:ConvertStrToUpperCase");
```

The highlighted text in the code caused me a good deal of grief. Without the **SOAPAction** request header, the response always contained the WSDL definition of the Web service (the XML document that is shown when you type the Web service URL into the address bar on your browser). Once again I found that this was the missing bit by looking at the results of the Fiddler application trace of my .NET application I wrote at the start of this chapter.

The following code will hookup the `readResponse` function to the `xmlHttpRequest` so that the response can be read when the call is finished. I borrowed this code from the Exchange Web service gadget (although I had to wade up to my armpits in functions in order to find the code that actually did the business).

```
xmlHttpRequest.onreadystatechange = readResponse;
xmlHttpRequest.send(data);

function readResponse()
{
  if (xmlHttpRequest.readyState == 4)
  {
    var xmlDoc = new ActiveXObject("Microsoft.XMLDOM");

    xmlDoc.loadXML(xmlHttpRequest.responseText);
```

This next bit of code assigns the `resultText` variable to the contents of the SOAP response and it took a while to figure out. I'm sure if I knew more about XML this would have been easier, but in the end I got this example from the W3 schools site by searching for Microsoft.XMLDOM (`http://www.w3schools.com/Xml/xml_dom.asp`).

```
resultText = xmlDoc.getElementsByTagName("return_value")
                              [0].childNodes[0].nodeValue;
```

The code is reading the text result from the SOAP envelope. A real example will have to do a lot more with this XML document but for now, this does the job.

Finally, we dispose of some objects and then inject the result text in to the body of our HTML page using the `innerHTML` property for our `resultContainer` div class.

```
xmlDoc = null;
resultContainerElement = document.getElementById("resultContainer");
if (resultContainerElement != null)
{
  resultContainerElement.innerHTML = "<b>Output: </b>" + resultText;
}
xmlHttpRequest = null;
```

I now know that we've broken the back of the problem. We have successfully called a NAV Web service from a web page (which is essentially all a sidebar gadget is). The next tricky bit is to see how to use a page Web service to get the records back that match our documents requiring approval. We'll use the same approach of first writing the code in .NET as a console application and then after we have this working the easy way, we'll convert the code into JavaScript. After that, it's just a case of tidying everything up and making it look pretty.

Hey, Good Lookin'

If there's one thing you need for a sidebar gadget, it's nice graphics. Vista is a beautiful operating system and, to be honest, if a gadget doesn't look good, I don't want it on my desktop. Now I'm really lucky to work for a company that is creative as well as technical, and I asked one of our creative design team members if he thought he could make a document stack for me. I explained that I thought I could use a single image and position the images on top of each other and explained how the image could be created by taking a document and flipping it and applying perspective. It's at this point that I have to take my hat off to the skills of creative people and web page designers. It would have taken me days (if indeed I could have done this at all) to have come up with these images. Here are the document stacks that Olmec produced after half an hour's effort one lunch time.

The images were created using Photoshop (and a lot of professional skill), and the original image that the stack is built from actually has the Microsoft Dynamics NAV logo at the top (how's that for attention to detail?) Here's the image of the document:

Olmec also produced the HTML to render these documents as a stack with the number floating over the top (in the same half-hour), and the HTML to produce the previous image can be found on the `www.teachmenav.com` site under the Simple Document Stack sample for this chapter.

I figured I would generate the HTML dynamically based upon the number of documents requiring approval. I took Olmec's HTML and manipulated it to give myself 12 document stacks that will be used by the application. The largest stack is 10 images high but I figured that this would be used to represent 31 or more documents. The question mark on the final empty stack shown in the following image will be used when the gadget gets no response from the Web service or has not been properly configured.

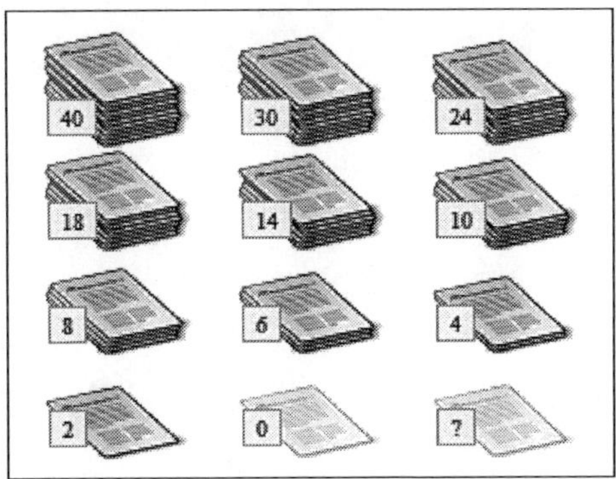

Now we have nearly everything we need to be able to put together the sidebar gadget. There's just one piece of the puzzle missing; we need to be able to call a Web service to tell us how many documents we have for approval and also return the details of those documents, the rest is just applying more of what we know and writing a lot of code.

We've covered calling a page Web service in an earlier example, so I won't go into details here but we do need to know what we are calling. As you know Web services from NAV can be based on either Codeunits or Pages, so which should we use?

The temptation may be to use a Page Web service as this will allow us to bring back the Approval Entry records for the current user, but we need to do far more than read the records. Our first interaction will be to get a count of the records for approval so we can display the gadget; we don't want the gadget to have a lot of work to do in order to draw its initial state, so ideally we want a quick call that will return just the number of documents and maybe the document name.

If you remember from the beginning, our gadgets are meant to be simple, single-tasked applications, so we want a single document approval gadget to work for any one document type. This way our users can have multiple gadgets on their desktop if they want to be notified on multiple document types. We can achieve this by using a Codeunit type Web service and have one of the parameters an identifier of the type of document we are interested in. The following is an overview of the functions we will need.

Operation	Description
`GetDocumentTypes`	On our configuration (options) page we want the user to be able to select a single document type from a list of document types supported by the gadget. I expect we will return this as an XML document.
`GetApprovalStatus`	This will be the main operation that is called when the gadget is refreshed. We actually want to return three pieces of information, so our return value is going to be an XML document. It will return the Document Name Singular and Document Name Plural (that is, Purchase Order when the number is 1 and Purchase Orders when it is 0 or greater than one). It will also return the Count, which is the number of documents that require approval from this user. Finally, it will return the Overdue Count, which is the number of documents that require approval from this user that are overdue.
`GetApprovalEntries`	This will return an XML document that has the record set of approval entries for a given document type.
`Approve`	This will set the approval status on the selected entry. It will require some kind of record key as a parameter to identify which record is to be updated. This could be as simple as the Entry No.

Operation	Description
`Reject`	This will set the approval status to rejected. It will take a record key and a reject reason.
`Delegate`	This will delegate the approval entry. Again a record key will be needed.
`ShowDocument`	This will not be implemented in the initial version as we will implement this by using the RoleTailored client to display the entry. The intention is that this operation can return an XML document that can be formatted by the browser. For the initial version, the ShowDocument feature in the user interface will simply activate a hyperlink that will show the document. The hyperlink could be implemented as a link to open the RoleTailored client, a link to a reporting services report, a link to an Employee Portal page, or a link to a bespoke ASP.NET web page.

The best thing you can do now, is download the final sidebar gadget from our book's web site (`www.teachmenav.com`), play with it (if you have Vista and Dynamics NAV 2009 installed), and then open up the source code contained within the gadget and take a look at how it's done. You'll also find some screenshots of the final gadget in all its glory.

Calling a Web service from NAV

Up to this point, we have looked at extending NAV by linking external applications to it through the newly introduced Web services enablement. Now we're going to look at the flip-side; we're going to see if NAV can *call* a Web service.

As the number of Web services available increase, it is more and more likely that we will want to consume them from within our ERP application. Some obvious examples are being able to pull-down the latest currency exchange rates, sending a business document to a trading partner, updating item prices by directly reading them from a vendor, or validate a postal address. There are numerous examples and believe it or not, it's not all that hard to do.

I really wanted a real practical example, and surprisingly I found it quite difficult to find a free Web service that I could use that would provide some real business value. In the end I discovered a site called `http://seekda.com/` that provides a searchable directory of Web services. I looked at the most frequently used services and came across a GlobalWeather Web service. Perfect!

Always take the weather with you

The service URL is `http://www.webservicex.com/globalweather.asmx?WSDL`, and I'm going to stick with my tried and trusted technique of getting it to work in Visual Studio (because it's easy), and then making it work from NAV. I'm going to use Dynamics NAV **5.0 SP1** for this example—just to illustrate that you don't need the Web services capabilities of NAV 2009 to be able to call a Web service.

Here's the WSDL for the service:

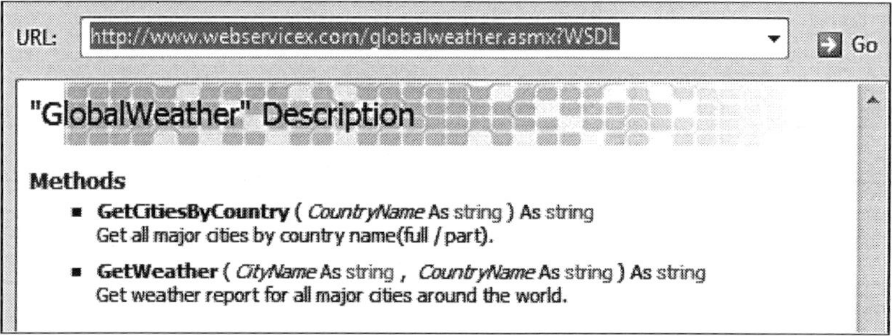

My plan is to use the GlobalWeather service to give some kind of weather report for a customer based upon the city and country on their address. This would work quite nice as a task part against the customer list place in NAV 2009—maybe you could extend the application to work in that way.

So my first part (and I'm not going to guide you through this step-by-step as you should be able to figure this out from the previous examples) is to make a simple console application that will take a **City Name** and **Country Name** as input and output something about the weather (not really sure what it returns at this point). Here's the output from my program:

Enter City Name: Christchurch

Enter Country Name: New Zealand

Calling Web service for Christchurch, New Zealand

<?xml version="1.0" encoding="utf-16"?>

<CurrentWeather>

<Location>Christchurch, New Zealand (NZCH) 43-29S 172-33E 30M</Location>

<Time>Aug 11, 2008 - 04:00 AM EDT / 2008.08.11 0800 UTC</Time>

<Wind> from the SSW (200 degrees) at 3 MPH (3 KT):0</Wind>

<SkyConditions> mostly cloudy</SkyConditions>

<Temperature> 39 F (4 C)</Temperature>
<DewPoint> 37 F (3 C)</DewPoint>
<RelativeHumidity> 93%</RelativeHumidity>
<Pressure> 29.83 in. Hg (1010 hPa)</Pressure>
<Status>Success</Status>
</CurrentWeather>

And this was generated by the following code:

```
using System;
using System.Collections.Generic;
using System.Text;

namespace ConsoleApplication1
{
    using com.webservicex.www;

    class Program
    {
        static void Main(string[] args)
        {
            GlobalWeather gw = new GlobalWeather();

            string city;
            string country;

            Console.Write("Enter City Name : ");
            city = Console.ReadLine();

            Console.Write("Enter Country Name : ");
            country = Console.ReadLine();

            Console.WriteLine("");
            Console.WriteLine("Calling Web service for {0}, {1}",
                                                     city, country);

            Console.WriteLine("{0}",  gw.GetWeather(city, country));
            Console.ReadLine();
        }
    }
}
```

And using Fiddler, here is the SOAP envelope for our successful call:

```
<?xml version="1.0" encoding="utf-8"?>
<soap:Envelope xmlns:soap="http://schemas.xmlsoap.org/soap/envelope/"
             xmlns:xsi="http://www.w3.org/2001/XMLSchema-instance"
             xmlns:xsd="http://www.w3.org/2001/XMLSchema">
   <soap:Body>
       <GetWeather xmlns="http://www.webserviceX.NET">
          <CityName>Christchurch</CityName>
          <CountryName>New Zealand</CountryName>
       </GetWeather>
   </soap:Body>
</soap:Envelope>
```

And here is the response:

```
<?xml version="1.0" encoding="utf-8"?>
<soap:Envelope xmlns:soap="http://schemas.xmlsoap.org/soap/envelope/"
          xmlns:xsi="http://www.w3.org/2001/XMLSchema-instance"
             xmlns:xsd="http://www.w3.org/2001/XMLSchema">
   <soap:Body>
       <GetWeatherResponse xmlns="http://www.webserviceX.NET">
          <GetWeatherResult>
             &lt;?xml version="1.0" encoding="utf-16"?&gt;
             &lt;CurrentWeather&gt;
             &lt;Location&gt;Christchurch, New Zealand (NZCH) 43-29S
                                     172-33E 30M&lt;/Location&gt;
             &lt;Time&gt;Aug 11, 2008 - 04:00 AM EDT / 2008.08.11
                                         0800 UTC&lt;/Time&gt;
             &lt;Wind&gt; from the SSW (200 degrees) at 3 MPH (3
                                           KT):0&lt;/Wind&gt;
             &lt;SkyConditions&gt; mostly cloudy
                          &lt;/SkyConditions&gt;
             &lt;Temperature&gt; 39 F (4 C)&lt;/Temperature&gt;
             &lt;DewPoint&gt; 37 F (3 C)&lt;/DewPoint&gt;
             &lt;RelativeHumidity&gt; 93%&lt;/RelativeHumidity&gt;
             &lt;Pressure&gt; 29.83 in. Hg (1010
                          hPa)&lt;/Pressure&gt;
             &lt;Status&gt;Success&lt;/Status&gt;
             &lt;/CurrentWeather&gt;
          </GetWeatherResult>
       </GetWeatherResponse>
   </soap:Body>
</soap:Envelope>
```

Now that we have proven the technique, let's look at how to call this from within NAV.

Calling out around the world

The principle is quite simple; we are going to use an existing Automation control that is available without additional programming or installation to make an HTML post (similar to our sidebar gadget example where we called the Web service from within JavaScript). In practice, we should probably be using XMLPorts to format the SOAP envelope for the call and parse the response. As usual, we're going to keep things as simple as possible and just create the SOAP envelope as a string. For the response, I'm going to copy the stream to a file so I can take a look at what I get back.

SOAP or COM?

There are two ways of calling the Web service from within NAV. One is to make an HTTP Post with a SOAP envelope that we have built up, and the other is to write an Interop enabled COM component and use it as an Automation variable in NAV. The SOAP method we have outlined here is certainly quick to get going, and doesn't require any extra components to be installed on the client (which is one reason I used it). The NAV 2009 architecture means that the COM component only needs to be installed on the server since it will be accessed there. This could make the COM component a better option going forward.

There are also limitations to what you can do using this HTTP Post technique, and as soon as we need to handle binary objects or UTF characters in our Web service call or response, this approach is unworkable. For details on how to get around these problems and how you can make a simple COM component to handle the Web services, take a look at Freddy Kristiansen's blog: `http://blogs.msdn.com/freddyk/default.aspx`

First of all let's create a simple test Codeunit to try to recreate the results of the previous console application.

We'll need to add an Automation control with type:

'Microsoft WinHTTP Services, version 5.1'.WinHttpRequest

Don't use the subtype with an 'I' infront, called IWinHttpRequest, otherwise you'll run into problems when you try to use the Automation control.

WinHTTP **5.1** is now an operating-system component of the following systems:

- Windows Server 2003
- Windows XP Service Pack 1 (SP1)
- Windows 2000 Service Pack 3 (SP3) (except Datacenter Server)

And I'm guessing it's also available in Vista Business as that's what I have. You can find out more at `http://msdn.microsoft.com/en-us/library/aa384273.aspx`.

I called my local variable for this Automation control **l_WinHTTPServices** if that helps you to understand the following Codeunit code.

```
// Instantiate my 'Microsoft WinHTTP Services, version 5.1'.
WinHttpRequest control
CREATE(l_WinHTTPServices);

// Change this file name if you don't have the file path D:\Dynamics
NAV\Web Service Demo\
l_FileName := 'D:\Dynamics NAV\Web Service Demo\WeatherResult.XML';

// Create my HTTP Post request.
l_WinHTTPServices.Open('POST',
  'http://www.webservicex.com/globalweather.asmx');

// Set the SOAPAction so the Web service will be called.
l_WinHTTPServices.SetRequestHeader('SOAPAction',
  '"http://www.webserviceX.NET/GetWeather"');

// Without this it will not work
l_WinHTTPServices.SetRequestHeader('Content-Type', 'text/xml');

// Build the SOAP envelope XML String
l_Data += '<?xml version="1.0" encoding="utf-8"?>';
l_Data += '<soap:Envelope xmlns:soap="http://schemas.xmlsoap.org/soap/
envelope/"';
l_Data += '             xmlns:xsi="http://www.w3.org/2001/XMLSchema-
instance"';
l_Data += '             xmlns:xsd="http://www.w3.org/2001/XMLSchema
                                                              ">';
l_Data += '  <soap:Body>';
l_Data += '      <GetWeather xmlns="http://www.webserviceX.NET">';
l_Data += '         <CityName>Christchurch</CityName>';
l_Data += '         <CountryName>New Zealand</CountryName>';
l_Data += '      </GetWeather>';
l_Data += '  </soap:Body>';
l_Data += '</soap:Envelope>';

// Make the call
l_WinHTTPServices.Send(l_Data);

// Wait for a response and throw an error if none received
IF NOT l_WinHTTPServices.WaitForResponse(60) THEN
  ERROR('Request timed out.');
```

```
// Create a file to dump my result to. In a real-world scenario
thiswould be a
// temp file or maybe a BLOB field. Or better still I would load the
stream into
// an XMLDOM object
l_File.CREATE(l_FileName);

l_File.CREATEOUTSTREAM(l_OutStream);
l_InStream := l_WinHTTPServices.ResponseStream;

REPEAT
  l_InStream.READTEXT(l_Data);
  l_OutStream.WRITETEXT(l_Data);
UNTIL l_InStream.EOS;

l_File.CLOSE;


HYPERLINK(l_FileName);
```

The following is the result of running the Codeunit:

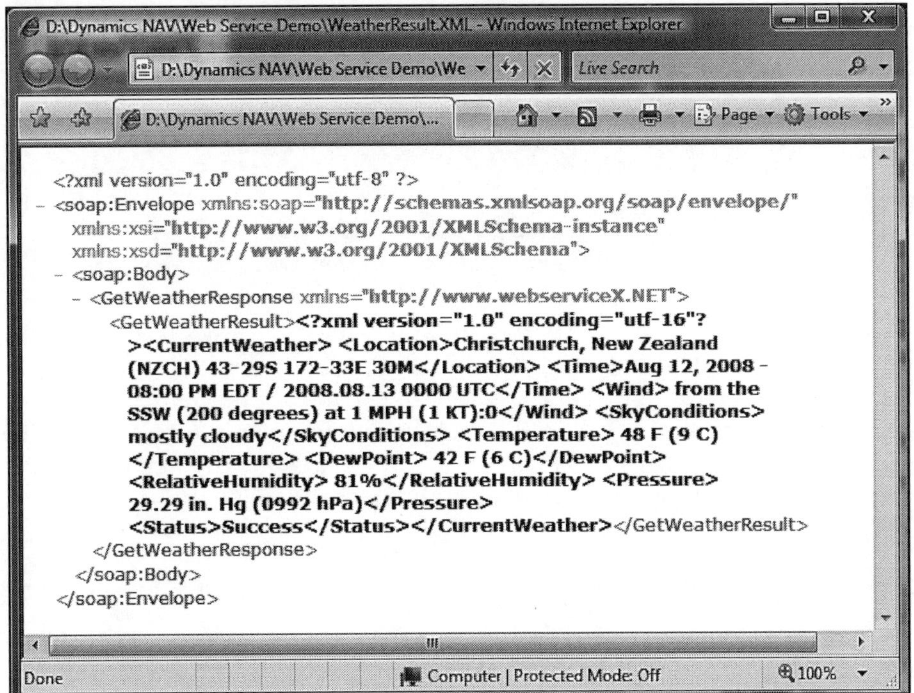

As you can see, it's still cold. I'm not going to take you through decoding this result string and building the final example, but you should be able to take this and extend it to meet the requirements set out at the beginning. If you get stuck, you can look on `www.teachmenav.com` for a working solution download. When you do start to use NAV calls to Web services, make sure you encapsulate the methods in their own Codeunits so you can simply call the function from a Codeunit rather than needing to put all that SOAP in your main code. It may be a good idea to create a single Codeunit for each Web service you want to call, or possibly keep all of your Web service calls in one Codeunit.

Service oriented or service enabled?

Most of us will have heard of **Service Oriented Architecture** or **SOA**, but does the new functionality in NAV 2009 make it an SOA? Well, in a word, no. The thing is that a service oriented architecture requires more than just Web services. In fact according to Krafzig, Banke, and Slama in their book *Enterprise SOA*, 'an SOA is based on four key abstractions: *application frontend*, *service*, *service repository*, and *service bus*.' We certainly have an application frontend (at least one), but what about the others?

When is a service not a service?

Is a NAV Web service a *service* in an SOA sense? Not really. An SOA service typically encapsulates a business concept such as 'open customer account' or 'raise purchase order'. While it is true to say that with NAV Web services we can insert purchase order headers and lines and also create customer records, this is not the same as the business processes an SOA would expose. For example, opening a customer account may start with a request which may require the collection of certain information such as name and address. The account will need some grouping for reporting and details of how related financial transaction should post to the General Ledger. The account will need a credit limit, and should be approved after a credit check has been performed. It is important to understand that the definition of a service such as this is far more than the formal service interface definition that is provided by WSDL, and can involve long running transactions and humans to make decisions.

Service repository

A service repository allows us to discover the services available in our SOA. You could argue that the list of services we get when we use `http://localhost:7047/DynamicsNAV/ws/CRONUS_International_Ltd/Services` URL is a service repository, but just as the formal interface definition from WSDL does not provide a service definition, this list of services does not really serve as a service repository. As well as the service definition for each of the available services, the service repository could include details of the service owner, access rights, a history of versions, performance, and scalability details. Krafzig et al, go on to say that although you can achieve many benefits of an SOA without a service repository, a repository is indispensable in the long term.

Service bus

In an SOA, the service bus glues the other components together. It allows the frontend (any frontend) to discover the services from the repository and call them. In addition, it can provide auditing, logging, and other technical functions such as message transformation and transaction handling.

Don't worry, be happy

There does not seem to be a universally accepted definition of SOA, and there are many interpretations of precisely what SOA means—so you may need to do some additional reading if you really need to understand it.

It seems that SOA has become one of those buzzwords that makes it on to everyone's wish list; even though they don't necessarily understand what it is, they still want it.

There are a good number of people that are saying that NAV 2009 has an SOA and this is not true. Often the people that are saying that NAV 2009 is SOA do not understand what SOA is but know that it will help them sell more product to people who want an SOA.

Just because NAV 2009 is not SOA, don't feel let down. The Web services enablement is fantastic, and if you are really involved in an SOA project it is going to make your life much easier—but you are still going to have to do a lot of work. Exposing a business process as a service requires a lot more thought than exposing a function as a Web service.

Any questions?

We've covered a lot on extending the application through Web services but there still remain a few unanswered questions:

- What happens if I use a document type page as a Web service, how does the system expose the header and the lines?
- Can I expose a Role Center page as a Web service?

- Can my Codeunit Web services take complex data types (such as table records) as parameters?
- What happens if I try to return a complex data type from a Codeunit?
- I've heard that I can use an XMLPort as a parameter to a Codeunit to allow me to pass complex data types. How does this work?
- Can I extend my page Web service to add other functions?
- What happens to applications that consume my Web service if I add or remove fields from a page?

Let's answer each of these questions in turn.

Document Pages as Web services

I don't want to sound cynical, but I was surprised to find that this just works. Those guys at Microsoft have thought of everything! I added Page 50 (Purchase Order) to my Web services and the purchase order page was available for my .NET application as a web reference.

There were a number of classes that I could instantiate:

- `Purchase_Order`
- `Purchase_Order_Filter`
- `Purchase_Order_Line`
- `And of course Purchase_Order_Service`

The great thing is that we get the purchase order line as a strongly typed object, which means the page lets us work with the header and the lines on the page; but how do we access the lines of the purchase order?

One of the 'fields' on the purchase order is called `PurchLines` and this is actually an array of objects of type `Purchase_Order_Line`. This allows you to write code such as the following (don't try compiling this; it's not the full program, just enough to illustrate the use of `PurchLines`):

```
Purchase_Order myPO = new Purchase_Order();

myPO = PO_s.Find(PO_fList.ToArray(),null,1)[0];

Console.WriteLine("\n\nPurchase Order No. {0} : {1}", myPO.No, myPO.
Buy_from_Vendor_Name);
Console.WriteLine("\n\nHas {0} Purchase Lines...\n", myPO.PurchLines.
GetLength(0));
```

```
foreach (Purchase_Order_Line POL in myPO.PurchLines) {
   Console.WriteLine("{0}, {1}, {2}", POL.Type, POL.No, POL.
Description);
}
```

This will produce the following output:

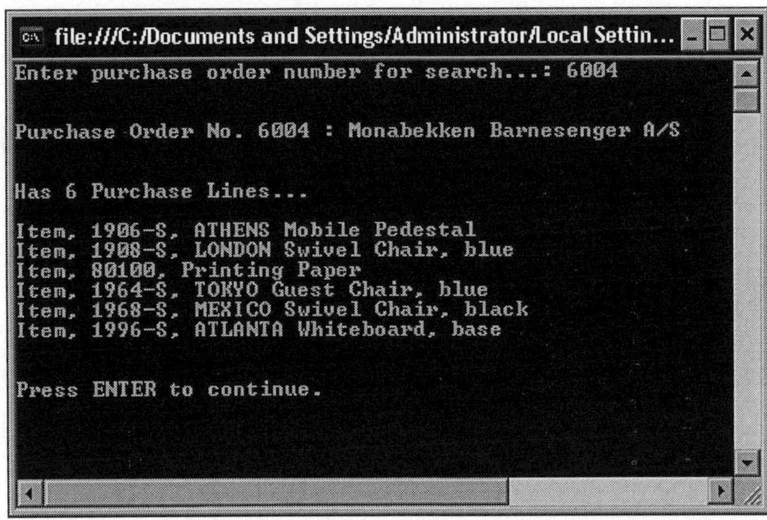

You can download the full source code for this simple Console application from our web site.

Role Center as a Web service

Now I really, really, didn't think this one would work, and I was quite shocked when I was allowed to add **Page 9001** (**Account Manager Role Center**) as a Web service and publish it. The new page even appeared in my list of available services, but alas I wasn't able to do anything with the suggested service URL for the page. It doesn't work, which isn't surprising because a Role Center page is whole bunch of containers that contain other pages and custom parts, some of which are quite complex. Since I can't think of a reason to do this (other than to write your own RoleTailored client) it's no big deal, but what about some of the pages that are on the Role Center, such as the Activities Part page, can they be used? Well sort of. You can create the Web service and even call some of the standard methods, but there are no fields on the Activities Part for you to read, so there's very little point. If you really want to write your own RoleTailored client (seriously why would you do that?), you should be looking at creating a Codeunit to give you the information you need to build your cues.

Records as parameters to Codeunits

Nope you can't do this. You can get as far as exposing the Codeunit but when you try to add it as a web reference, you get an unhandled exception for the type of record. The best thing to do is to write a function that takes a unique reference to the record that you want to work with. If you want to update records, you should use a Page type Web service. If you merely want to include a reference to the object, you should use the fields that you know to be in the primary key as parameters to the function. If you are going to use Codeunits to change records, you need to make sure you check that no one else has modified or even deleted the record since you read it from the Web service. When using Page type Web services, the system handles the concurrency for you, but with Codeunits you have full control (and therefore full responsibility).

Codeunit functions that return complex data types

This would mean creating a function that returned a complex data type, such as a customer record.

Err, you can't do this in C/AL, so there's no chance of doing this in a Web service. Let's just pretend I never asked this question and move on to the next one...

XMLports as parameters to Codeunits

By using an XMLport as a parameter to a Codeunit function, we can create services that can receive complex data types, such as records or documents as parameters. A good example would be if we wanted to create a purchase order in a single transaction. I don't remember where I got this idea from, possibly it was suggested in one of the early Microsoft Whitepapers but initial tests on the released product indicate that this is possible.

If you don't want to create an XMLport, one way to get around this may be to use a Codeunit function parameter of type BigText that can be used to pass an XML document (up to 2GB in size) to the function by reference. The BigText can then be decoded using the XMLDOM automation control in NAV.

More functions on a Page

Page Web services are great and for creating, reading, updating, and deleting records (known as CRUD), and they're really simple to use. There are times when you need more from your page, such as releasing a document for approval, or posting a journal. If you take a look at the *Microsoft Dynamics NAV 2009 Developer Help* in the topic *Walkthrough: Creating a Web Service using Extension Codeunits*, you can see an example of how this is done.

Can I break it?

Of course you can, and really this isn't hard to do, so be careful when tinkering with Codeunits and pages that have been exposed as Web services. To test this I renamed the 'subform' control on my **Purchase Order** Page to be **PurchLines2** from **PurchLines** and guess what? My sample application that read the purchase order and printed the details of the lines stopped working with an unhandled exception. Our recommendation is that whenever you expose a Codeunit or page from NAV as a Web service, you add a comment to the documentation trigger with the name of the service you have created. This will tell developers to be careful with their changes; renaming controls and removing fields can break things that are using the Web service and should be avoided.

You need to take care when executing code that initiates some kind of user interaction (such as `FORM.RUNMODAL`) during a Web service call. The call will fail with a strange error message: *Callback functions are not allowed*. You can avoid this error, by making sure that the user interaction code is within an `IF` statement that uses `GUIALLOWED` (see the section *Handling UI Interaction When Working with Web Services* in the online help for more details). Some areas of the application (such as the Sales Order Page) are relatively well shielded from this error through the use of `GUIALLOWED`, but you should still be aware of this issue when using NAV Web services, test the Web service calls thoroughly, and use the Code Coverage tool to search for the C/AL commands that are likely to cause problems.

It's also a good idea to keep a central repository of information about your services and for developers to document how they are using the services. This is similar to the idea of the Service Repository in the SOA model—it could be a series of SharePoint sites for the various services that allow the consumers of the Web service to detail what they are using the services for. This is going to help you when you are looking at upgrading and need to consider which systems need to be tested.

Presentation layers

As well as the RoleTailored client (and the Classic client), we can expect a SharePoint client. Sadly, the SharePoint client is not available for me to write about but when it is, I'll add something to the `www.teachmenav.com` web site. As for the Dynamics Mobile interface, we'll look at that in Chapter 10 when we'll design a mini-add-on using Dynamics Mobile.

Summary

We've only scratched the surface of the possibilities that Web service enablement presents. I expect there will be a plethora of samples on web sites and blog posts when NAV 2009 starts to take off and the NAV gurus decide to show off their skills. If you are non-technical, hopefully you found enough in this chapter to keep you interested, and you now have a better understanding of what NAV 2009 means in terms of extensibility. If you are a technical consultant and programmer, this chapter will provide a foundation for exploring the world of NAV 2009 and Web services, but there is plenty more for you to experiment with on your own.

Here're some more ideas you can try for homework:

- Build a Codeunit that takes an XMLport as a parameter to allow a 'Create Purchase Order' service to be exposed as a Web service—try the same exercise using a BigText parameter.
- Create an InfoPath form for creating new customers in NAV—for bonus points, you can deploy this to the Forms Server component of MOSS.
- Download the Dynamics AX samples for Dynamics Snap from `http://www.microsoft.com/dynamics/product/snap.mspx` and make them work with NAV.
- Create an ASP.NET or Silverlight application that will allow you to create, edit, and update customers in NAV

Enjoy!

8
The Development Lifecycle

"The sooner you start coding, the later you finish." *Unknown author.*

There is much more to development than programming. It starts with understanding what the customer really needs, and usually extends way beyond the system being deployed into the production environment. Development can be a phase of an implementation project, a topic we have already covered in detail in Chapter 4, or it can happen standalone, completely outside of an implementation. This chapter will focus on the development itself, and what it takes to get from a concept to a live and working application functionality.

You will learn:

- What is the difference between development and programming
- What a development lifecycle looks like
- What it takes to bring an idea to a fully working application feature
- What the standard application contains under the hood

Why is development different than programming?

If you ask an average person how software comes to be, odds are you'll get this answer: software is programmed. And essentially, it is true, at least as much as it is true that buildings come to be by laying bricks.

Programming is translating the requirements—something understood by people, into application code—something understood by computers. It's instructing computers how to do whatever we want them to do. There is no software product in the world, built from scratch or customized, that wasn't programmed.

Development is a process with a lifecycle of its own. It starts with understanding the requirements, an enormously intricate and often underestimated task, and ends with a software product release or a solution deployment, popping champagne being an integral and obligatory part of it.

If you look up the verb *develop* in Merriam-Webster's online dictionary, it says it means to *create or produce especially by deliberate effort over time*, or *to come into being gradually*. Wiktionary says it means *to progress through a sequence of stages*.

Programming is just one of the stages. It's the core task, it is where most effort is usually exerted, and it produces the most visible results. But no matter how complex the problem, in the perspective of all development stages, programming is the easiest of them all.

Development in Microsoft Dynamics NAV

Microsoft Dynamics NAV implementation projects are often confused for software development projects. Whether or not software development is done during implementation, these two are not in the same ballpark. In Microsoft Dynamics NAV, software development comes with many faces.

Most often it is an integral part of the implementation project. Typically, out-of- the-box software won't satisfy our customer, so we must do some development to get it there for them.

Sometimes we simply develop a software solution based on Microsoft Dynamics NAV, totally unrelated to a customer or an implementation project. Vertical add-ons such as retail management that we might sell as products, or horizontal solutions such as a payroll that we can include with all our implementations, are typical examples.

Every once in a while, long after the customer has implemented Microsoft Dynamics NAV, they may come back with extra needs and requirements—these are then addressed by a typical solution development approach, not as an implementation.

When we discuss software development in this chapter, we are not necessarily regarding it as part of implementation. Everything we say here applies equally to any kind of development work with Microsoft Dynamics NAV.

The lifecycle

Development is a curious beast. While we could draw as many parallels between building software and building houses as our hearts desire, there is an important perpendicular that crosses them all: we can't develop software as a series of consecutive steps.

While it's true that the software development goes through several distinctive phases, starting with the analysis of requirements, and ending with the deployment, or even maintenance, it is rarely true that this process can really happen with these phases being strictly consecutive.

It may easily happen that the requirements will not be completely understood before the first design blueprints have been drawn, or that whole design will not be completed before any programming has started, or that all programming will not be finished before any testing has started. This is especially true if there aren't too many dependencies between different features being developed.

Microsoft solutions framework

There are many different approaches to software development, such as the waterfall approach, the iterative and incremental approach or the spiral approach, and many different formal methodologies, such as **Microsoft Solution Framework** (**MSF**), **Rational Unified Process** (**RUP**), or **Extreme Programming** (**XP**). Whichever approach or methodology you choose, you are better off than with the cowboy coding approach.

For better or worse, we chose MSF as the foundation for the development lifecycle guidelines we lay here, primarily for the follwoing reasons:

- It's Microsoft's official solution development methodology, designed with Microsoft's technology in mind, and field-tested with it over past decade and half. It's true that Microsoft Dynamics NAV didn't grow on the same branch as Microsoft's other products, on the contrary—it was engrafted into the portfolio at its mature stage, as much as it's true that MSF can't be applied as an overall Microsoft Dynamics NAV implementation methodology. However, certain aspects of it align perfectly with the software development aspect of any Microsoft Dynamics NAV implementation project, and especially well with non-project related development.
- Most of the development work with Microsoft Dynamics NAV is highly iterative in nature, which is precisely the way MSF approaches solution development.
- Sure Step, Microsoft's official methodology for implementation of all Microsoft Dynamics products, draws many of its principles directly from Microsoft Solution Framework.

Why is it that software development projects are best approached iteratively? Among many reasons, let's pick this one: the requirements. There are two things about them: they change, and they are rarely completely understood at the beginning.

MSF doesn't use the term *phase*, it uses the term *track* instead. Since most of the Microsoft Dynamics NAV development lifecycle phases don't correspond directly to MSF tracks, we decided to stick with the term *phase* throughout this chapter.

Understanding the requirements

Development starts with the requirements. The customer explains their situation, which we usually refer to as a *business problem* or a *business need*—our job is to provide a solution for it. This is where the requirements are born. The requirements are a translation of business needs into sets of conditions that must be met by the system. As with any translation, much can be lost in this process.

The most important question about requirements is: what is it that the customer really wants to achieve? In this, there are two levels of understanding at work.

First, we must understand the customer's need. We need to understand it fully, from their point of view.

The second level of understanding is much easier, but equally as important. We need to understand how Microsoft Dynamics NAV addresses the customer's problem. We should always start from a simple premise: Microsoft Dynamics NAV is a business management system, it is made for businesses, and it solves a lot of business problems out of the box. Does a solution exist in the system that addresses the customer's problem? If so, does it cover the customer's needs completely?

Get familiar with Microsoft Dynamics NAV functionality. You don't need to know all the features in detail, or be a world-class expert in them, but at the very least you need to know which features are there, and what they are used for.

Apart from the lost-in-translation syndrome, and from the incorrect mapping of the customer's need to the standard solution (both of which happen pretty often), there is a bigger problem with requirements: they change.

They change during design, then during build, then during stabilization. They sometimes change even after deployment, when the solution is live and functioning in the production environment. They don't change only because the customer's need evolves; they also change because the customer's understanding of their own needs gradually develops over time.

Try to understand the customer's perspective. They most likely have an old computer system, which they have used for probably a long while; now they want to implement a new one. They know very well how their old system works; they don't know too much about Microsoft Dynamics NAV. When they express their requirements for the first time, they do it heavily biased by the habits their old system influenced over time. Especially if their existing system has come of age, their expressed needs may not be what they really need, but what they believe they need.

If you design and program a solution simply based on such requirements, the first time your customer sees it, they will say something like this: *nice, but that's not exactly what we need.*

Imagine trying to custom-design a car for someone who's only seen a horse. They have no clue what a car truly is or what they can do with it—whatever they say they need from their new vehicle better fits on a horse than into a car. You need to sit them in a car and take them for a test drive. Then you can start talking business.

Requirements are abstract, so are design specifications. The sooner your customer sees the real thing, the better chances of success the project has. With conventional software development, it is somewhat difficult to show anything to your customer before the first prototypes have been completed.

With Microsoft Dynamics NAV the situation is different, and you have a chance to show the application to your customer up front, before the requirements are completely articulated. That's why you should start the key-user training early during requirement analysis phase—it will give your customer a chance to get the feel for the application. To you, it will give a chance to see them work with the system and learn from the steps they make. You will receive more meaningful and valuable feedback from them, as well as a much clearer articulation of their true needs.

After this, when you design the prototype of their customized solution and show it to the customer for the first time, you stand far better chances of having your customer understand the concept.

Finally, if your customer has a chance to work with the application for a while, they may rethink their needs. We learn best from the things we do and try, not from the things we hear or see. With key users trying out the solution, there will be quite a few *Aha!* effects and conclusions that certain things can better be done the standard system way.

Designing the solution

Once we understand the requirements, both from the customer's and Microsoft Dynamics NAV perspectives, we can start working on the design.

The first design choice we need to make is about the approach. With development, there are basically two approaches that can be adopted:

- We extend the existing Microsoft Dynamics NAV functionality. This means that we build upon a foundation that is already there. If there is a high degree of fit between the requirement and standard functionality, extending the system will be the most reasonable approach.
- We develop a completely new functionality. Either there are no touching points between the requirement and what Microsoft Dynamics NAV has to offer, or modifying the system brings too many risks of breaking some important standard functionality. In situations like these, we need to design a whole new application area, which will provide something completely new, and at the same time work in perfect harmony with the existing functionality.

Let's take a look at these two approaches in more detail.

Extending existing functionality

There is one prerequisite for this approach: there has to be at least some functionality in Microsoft Dynamics NAV that satisfies the customer's requirement. If this is true, the easiest and definitely the cleanest approach is to lean on standard functionality and build upon it.

Building upon existing functionality comes at a cost. Whenever you touch any standard functionality, you need to thoroughly test your modifications to make sure not only that new functionality works well, but that everything that was affected by the change still works well. But there is a hidden, delayed, and much higher cost of extensions. Any extension of standard functionality makes the solution less upgradeable to a future version, because any changes that we introduce at this moment may conflict with the future standard functionality.

When we work with standard functionality, our first task is to list all the objects that we are going to affect with our change. We need to be particularly careful about any posting routines or ledger entry tables, because any problems we introduce with such extensions easily propagate far beyond what we thought was the boundary of our additions. Adding new fields is usually innocent. Branching original logic based on values of new fields is often not very much so. This is not to say that you shouldn't do it, or that you should avoid it—you should only make sure that you are perfectly aware of exactly what kind of change you are introducing, and what kind of regression effect it might have on the system as a whole.

There are three major mistakes with extending existing functionality that designers and developers commonly make:

- We might fail to notice that there is an opportunity to extend the existing system. Even if at first it seems that a requirement is not covered, or that there are no touching points between what the customer wants and what Microsoft Dynamics NAV offers, odds are that the opposite is true. Microsoft Dynamics NAV covers the majority of typical business processes, and often application functionality exists that is close to what the customer needs, and extending it wouldn't really break the original purpose. Try to find it, and you might save yourself from reinventing the wheel.
- We might overdo it. If the foundation for the customer's requirement exists in the system, but the customer's need is radically different from how Microsoft Dynamics NAV handles it, it is better to opt for designing a new solution, rather than deciding to extend the standard one, and then introduce so many changes that the original part ends up as a tiny portion of the complete solution, usually completely unusable, at least in the way that it was originally intended.
- We might decide we don't need the existing standard functionality, so we repurpose it instead and redesign it to do something completely different from what it was originally intended. This decision may cost us dearly if we later find out that we need the standard functionality back. If this happens, we might need to rollback all our modifications, which can be incredibly difficult, depending on the amount of work we have done.

In any case, we should try to drive our design choices carefully, not to fall into any of these traps. When we extend the existing functionality, we should strive to retain as much standard functionality as possible so that we maintain its original purpose, and keep it consistent with the rest of the application.

Designing a completely new functionality

Often we will find out that the system simply doesn't fit the customer's need. It doesn't have anything to do with a process being industry standard, or market standard. It may just be that it is not covered in the system at all.

There are many examples of this, the most notable being the payroll. Microsoft Dynamics NAV doesn't come with payroll functionality, although there is a limited Human Resource Management functionality already there. Payroll is something most customers do, but still it didn't make its way into the standard system. The reason is simple: Microsoft Dynamics NAV is a global solution, available in more than 150 countries, and while accounting standards in effect are basically the same in most of those countries, and supply chain management knows no borders anyway, payroll is something that is handled in many different ways; it is highly dependent on local regulations, and there are no international standards governing the payroll rules. This means that whoever needs payroll functionality, will have to develop it from scratch.

Developing from scratch doesn't necessarily mean there will be no touching points between what is being developed, and what's already in the system. In fact, there are always at least some touching points, because if you need to develop a completely isolated application area with nothing at all in common with the rest of the Microsoft Dynamics NAV application, then you shouldn't even do it in Microsoft Dynamics NAV.

Usually, you will extend a few master tables, such as Customer or Vendor, and you will also extend some standard posting codeunits such as Sales-Post or Item Jnl.-Post Line, but the bulk of the work will be developing something completely new. To be able to understand how to develop something new, we must first understand how the standard application functions from the inside.

Let's take a closer look at the standard application. A typical standard application area comes with some master data, and some setup and supplementary information. Then there are working documents, posted documents, and a register of all posted transactions. In the very center there is a ledger table structure comprising one or more entry tables. Typically, there is also a journal, which is used both as intermediary during posting of documents and for registering transactions into the ledger directly without any documents involved. There is also an infrastructure of codeunits used to transform working documents and journal lines into posted documents and ledger entries. When creating new application areas, we should try to mimic this model as much as possible.

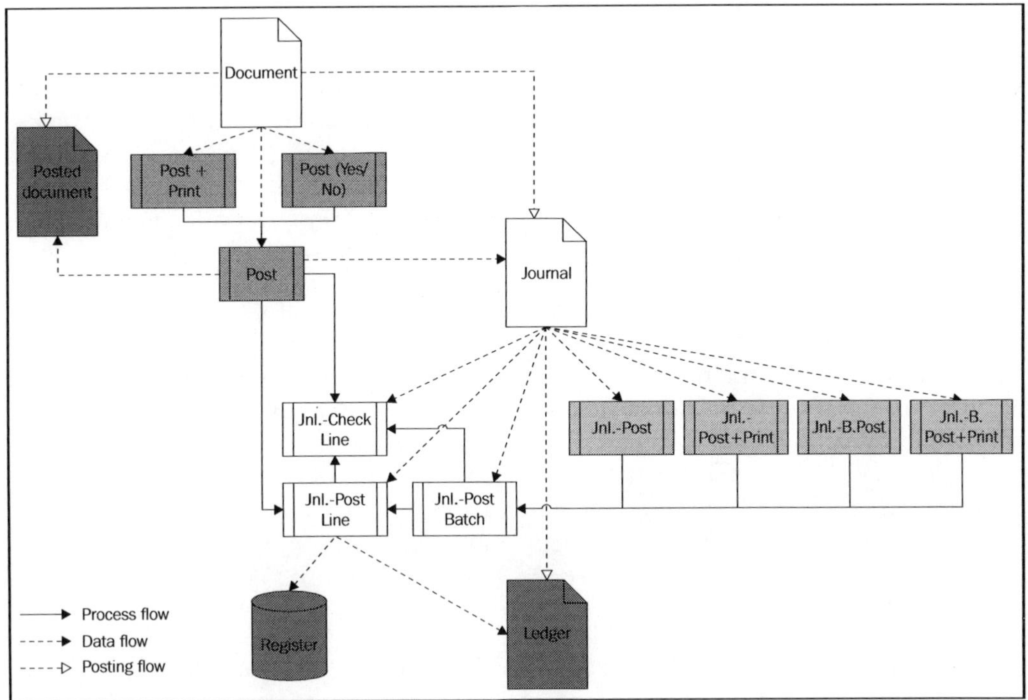

Designing tasks

After we have decided which approach works best for our scenario, we are ready to start the actual design work. There are three application layers we need to address here:

- Data model
- User interface
- Application logic

Data model

As abstract as any database can seem and get, data stored in it actually represents real life. Vendors we are buying from and customers we are selling to, as well as interactions we have with them—all these have their data representation in our databases.

Whatever the customer's need may be, our first task is to translate it to an abstract data model. A data model consists of tables and their relationships.

A table is used to store structured information. This means that all the information in the table is organized in the same structure and conforms to the same set of rules. Information in tables is stored in rows, also called records, which describe individual pieces of information. Tables are divided into fields, which describe certain attributes of stored information. Fields are the smallest building block of all data, and they are atomic. Information stored in a field cannot be divided further. Fields have data types, such as text, integer, or date, which make sure that every single piece of information stored in a field always conforms to the same rules.

Every single table should represent a single real-life object, or a single entity. Sometimes it is easy to recognize what an entity really is, and there will be a single table describing an object. Tables such as Customer, Vendor, and Item all belong to this category. At other times there can be many tables describing a single real-life object. For example, a purchase order is represented using two tables: Purchase Header and Purchase Line. There are complex examples, such as a production order, which is represented using eight tables: Production Order, Prod. Order Line, Prod. Order Component, Prod. Order Routing Line, Prod. Order Capacity Need, Prod. Order Routing Tool, Prod. Order Routing Personnel, and Prod. Order Rtng Qlty Meas.

Tables also contain keys, which are used to identify records and facilitate finding records. There are two types of keys: primary keys and secondary keys. The primary key is used for identification, and no two records in a table can have the same value in the primary key. Secondary keys are used to make it easier for the system to find and sort records. Although in typical relational databases keys are primarily used by the system, and not by the end users, in Microsoft Dynamics NAV keys are also used by end users for sorting, and it is only possible to sort information by a field if there is a key that starts with that field. This limitation obviously drives table design, because we need to include as many keys as there are fields by which the end users will want to sort information, but keys are not for free. While keys are intended to speed up certain operations, such as reading, poorly designed keys can slow down database performance considerably.

SQL Server is smart enough to sort data without an index. When defining keys for sorting purposes only, and running on SQL Server database (which you should be with Microsoft Dynamics NAV 2009), don't forget to switch their **MaintainSQLIndex** property to **No**. This will enable sorting, but won't create any SQL Server indexes.

The last building blocks of a data model are relationships. Relationships define how entities of various types relate to each other. Purchase order lines belong to a purchase order, a purchase order belongs to a vendor, a general ledger account contains entries, a customer is assigned to a discount group. Relationships are realized through fields of one table having the same values as fields (usually primary key fields) of another table. For example, the Purchase Header table has the field Buy-from Vendor No., which is related to the field No. of the Vendor table. By establishing this relationship we have effectively declared a rule by which every purchase document needs to belong to a vendor.

Relationships don't need to be defined at the data model level, and the world won't come to an end if a relationship is forgotten, but having them defined ensures data integrity. In Microsoft Dynamics NAV if there is a relationship defined, the system will make sure not only that a valid value is entered into a field belonging to a relationship, but also that any change to a field to which other tables are related is propagated to those tables.

Database design is often visualized using Entity Relationship diagrams, or simply ER diagrams. These diagrams represent entities (tables) and their relationships in an easy to follow and understand way, and depending on the level of detail or the phase your database design is in, they may look like the following example.

Other than simply depicting entities and their relationships, ER diagrams can show a lot more information, such as primary keys, foreign keys, cardinality, relationship types, or cascading actions. Some diagramming tools, such as Microsoft Office Visio, can even connect to the underlying database, and model the database as you model the diagram.

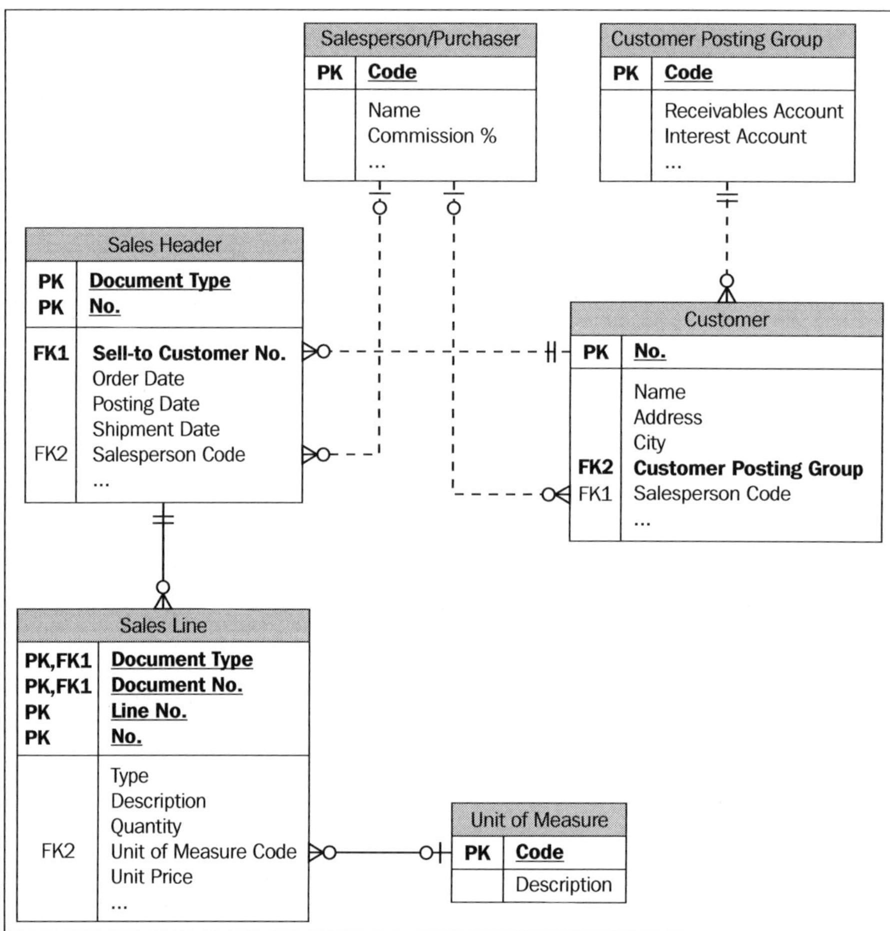

To be able to effectively design a data model representation of a real-life object, you should understand a little bit of relational database design theory. It helps if you understand the normalization process, but if you don't, you can still design a decent data model for your Microsoft Dynamics NAV solution. To do so, you need to ask yourself several questions:

- What does this object consist of? Go, and decompose it. If you store information about people, determine what attributes you need to effectively describe them—first name, last name, title, height, weight, age, gender, eye color, education, home address. Most of these attributes will translate into fields. Some may translate into tables in their own right.
- Is every identified attribute atomic? In plain English, if we can't describe the attribute itself with another set of attributes, the attribute is said to be atomic. Every attribute it is not atomic that is not atomic will be represented by another table. In our example above, we have home address, which consists of many other attributes, such as street, number, ZIP code, city, country, and possibly a few more.
- Is any of these attributes repeatable for a single entity? This means, can this object have more of these? If so, again we need a separate table to keep track of such an attribute. In the example above, education would be such an attribute. A person may have graduated from two universities, hold three PhD's and four MBA's, and we may need to keep track of all of these. The only correct way to achieve this is to list this information in a separate table.
- Is any of these attributes repeatable across entities? Or more simple, can several entities have the same value for this attribute? Obviously, several people can have the same height, weight, age, gender, and eye-color. These are typical candidates to break into separate tables, but we don't simply do so before we ask the final question.
- Does this attribute need consistency? Most of them do. This means that if several entities have the same attributes defined, we really want it to be recorded in exactly the same way every time. Consistency can be achieved by field types: height, weight, and age are numbers, and we simply define these fields as any of the numeric data types applicable. On the other hand, title, gender, and eye-color are textual. We might want to have consistent representation of genders for all persons, such as only being able to record M or F (instead of letting users enter free-text information). In this case, we will make this an option field. For titles, we might want to keep consistency, but allow users to enter new titles as they come across them, so we create a new table with a lookup field. For eye color we might simply not care at all, therefore we leave it as free-entry text field.

With these questions answered, we get all the information we need to create a decent data model, which will provide an adequate entity relationship and storage structure and all the data consistency we need.

User interface

Designing the user interface is much easier than designing the data model. User interface consists of pages, forms, and reports.

Pages are used for data presentation and data entry by the RoleTailored client, while forms are used for the same purpose by the Classic client. With Microsoft Dynamics NAV 2009 you need to develop both pages and forms, unless you are absolutely positive that only the RoleTailored user interface will be used.

Always design and develop both forms and pages. You can never tell what the future will bring, and sometimes it might happen that for one reason or another some users will need to use the Classic client instead of the RoleTailored one. Customers may want to implement an add-on solution that doesn't yet work with RoleTailored client, or they may take the web server offline for maintenance. The only way you can be sure that everything will still work as expected is if during development you addressed both RoleTailored and Classic clients.

Aim for consistency

When developing something new from the ground up, there is a great opportunity to introduce inconsistency. Any inconsistency is bad, because no matter the grounds of our conviction why we might believe that our approach is better than that of the standard application, it will make it very difficult for users to really master the application.

Why does consistency matter?

Once users get comfortable with how an application works in one area, they are much faster in mastering other areas as well. When there is a certain logic to how the application works, users involuntarily start to recognize patterns, which results in a steeper learning curve, higher proficiency levels, and increased productivity. If every application area works in a different way, or even when functions in the same application area work differently, it takes much longer before users start working productively, and users have less confidence in their acquired skills.

Inconsistency comes in many flavors. The most visible one comes with the user interface. With previous versions of Microsoft Dynamics NAV it was possible to create user interfaces that resembled Microsoft Dynamics NAV only in as much as they ran in the same client application. If you didn't want to include a **Functions** menu button at the bottom right of the screen of your custom card form, and decided to replace it with several buttons arranged all around the form, there was no mechanism that could prevent it.

In Microsoft Dynamics NAV 2009, at least for the RoleTailored part, this possibility is gone. The system itself takes control over layout and placement of user interface elements, with the developer having only limited ability to specify where a field control or an action button will be placed. Therefore it is much harder to create an inconsistent user interface. When we are designing pages, we have much less freedom than with designing forms, so there will be no more colorful buttons and edit boxes. In the end, the user interface will have the same familiar look and feel across the application, and users won't be able to tell a custom developed page from a standard one, or custom added fields from standard ones.

Because there are now forms and pages, which are functionally equivalent, to avoid any inconsistency you should never design them explicitly as forms and pages. Instead, you should design *screens*, and simply explain which fields are shown on the screen, how they are grouped, and which functions are available in which menus. It will be the programmer's job to make two physical objects from a single specification.

Reports

Reports are used primarily to print out information from the system. Design specification should include printout definitions of any necessary reports.

Microsoft Dynamics NAV 2009 RoleTailored user interface utilizes the ReportViewer .NET control, which means that reports are defined using RDLC (Report Definition Language Client-side). As with pages and forms, programmers will need to separately develop two layouts, but thankfully both of them are stored using a single C/SIDE report object.

While it is still possible to have two completely separate layouts for C/SIDE and RDLC representation of the same report, there is a built-in **Create Layout Suggestion** tool which can be used to transform any C/SIDE form layout definition into an equivalent RDLC. This means that while designing reports you only need to define a single design, and programmers will actually only need to prepare a single object out of this specification. The system will take care of everything else.

Application logic

The last layer of design is the application logic. The success and efficiency of programming work later on depends a great deal on how you approach your application logic design. Yet, many developers usually skip this part and jump directly into coding. Don't fall into this trap.

Technical documentation needs to be completed anyway, and it is much better to prepare it before the programming commences. Opponents of this approach will say that this is futile, because the final solution rarely looks exactly the way it was initially designed, and this is true. During build, stabilization, and testing phases of the development, you will frequently change the design, but you will have far less revisions if you think about it and write it up front.

Application logic in Microsoft Dynamics NAV 2009 is contained in the C/AL code, which can be found in all types of objects, except for **MenuSuite** objects. Typically, during application logic design, we address two types of code:

- **Data rules**: These are part of the data model, and consist of table and field triggers. They are used to enforce data integrity and consistency that cannot be obtained by simple mechanisms such as field types or table relations. Typical examples of data rules are assignment of the next available number from a number series, preventing deletion of a vendor for which there are outstanding invoices, or calculating a shipment date for a sales order line after selecting the item. Data rules are coded within `OnValidate` field triggers, and `OnInsert`, `OnModify`, `OnDelete`, and `OnRename` table triggers.
- **Application code**: this is any code that is not related to either user interface (including printable reports) or data model, which is used to perform certain operations typically invoked by user. Typical examples of application code are posting routines, production order refreshing, requisition plan calculation, or cost adjustment of item entries.

In Microsoft Dynamics NAV there is very little user interface code because most of user interface functions, such as lookups, drilldowns, or running forms, pages, and reports, are intrinsic functions of C/SIDE and can be achieved simply through properties. During design phase you don't need to address the user interface code, unless it is really complicated and the programmer wouldn't otherwise know how to implement it correctly. Instead, you simply need to describe any functionality related to user interface without deep technical specifications, and then the programmer will decide what can be achieved by coding and what by setting page, report, or form properties.

During application logic design there are many different approaches you can take. Whether you design your code with detailed UML diagrams, or you just create a declaratory specification of necessary codeunits and their functions, doesn't really matter as long as you are consistent with it, and as long as you communicate valuable information to the programmer. If your design specification is ignored by the programmer, then it's probably not about their attitude, but about the way you did the specification.

When designing a new solution, have in mind that Microsoft Dynamics NAV is a highly configurable system. You can achieve a lot by parameterization (or configuration), and try to design your solution to exhibit the same quality. Detect repeatable patterns, determine common denominators, and solve classes of problems instead of just what's within sight. Development is a dynamic process; what's beyond horizon today, will come into sight tomorrow—try to anticipate it and design the solution so that new requirements don't take you off guard.

Planning for performance and scalability

Microsoft Dynamics NAV offers fairly good out-of-the-box performance and scalability that will satisfy the majority of small and medium businesses. What usually hurts performance and scalability is custom development work, and the changes we the developers introduce. It is much easier to plan for performance and scalability than to add these later when you find out we need them badly, but they are nowhere to be seen.

There are several steps that you can already take during the design that can affect the performance and scalability of the solution.

Keys

For each of the tables, define the keys you need, and don't let new keys be created at will. Only the keys that have been specified in the design specification should be created. Each key should be carefully considered, defined, and documented, and that's why some application logic design should occur before coding, to help identify all the keys necessary for various search operations.

If you only need a key for sorting purposes in forms and reports, you can create it with **MaintainSQLIndex** property set to **No**. This will enable sorting by the specified field, but won't affect write performance because the index is not created on the SQL Server. Be advised that this can severely affect read performance on very large tables.

Keep the keys short, and don't put too many fields in there. For any key that is not going to be used as a covering index, there will be little performance benefit for any key more than five or six fields long, but the cost is usually huge. Also, keep the overall length of keys as short as possible, and never include text fields in keys (except possibly in master tables), especially not on SQL Server databases with a case-sensitive collation.

Generally, keep the number of keys for each table as low as possible, especially with ledger entry tables. Keys introduce significant overhead during write operations, and the ledger entry tables are the busiest of all. Most scalability issues arise during long write transactions due to heavy locking, and too many keys will just make these transactions longer.

When defining keys, always check existing keys first. You don't need to create a new key that starts with exactly the same fields in the same order as an existing key. For example, creating a new key `Document Type,Sell-to Customer No.,No.,Order Date` for table Sales Header makes no sense, because the key `Document Type, Sell-to Customer No.,No.` already exists. Adding the field `Order Date` to the end of the existing key, as opposed to creating a completely new key, will relieve you from some overhead that comes with every new key.

User interface

Try keeping the user interface logic to its minimum. With Microsoft Dynamics NAV 2009 all of the C/AL logic is executed on the server, regardless of whether it is a codeunit function or an `OnAfterGetRecord` trigger of a page. With a lot of users working at the same time, and a lot of server time dedicated to serving the user interface needs, you can degrade the performance of both the user interface and the application logic for all users.

This is especially true for the pages displaying data-bound parts, such as Sales Lines on Sales Order. If there are too many data-bound parts on the same page, linked using `SubFormLink` properties, and if there is heavy user interface logic in all of them, the scalability can decline dramatically.

Build

The build phase of a development lifecycle addresses what is commonly called programming or coding. However, calling it that wouldn't be fair, because coding is just a part of the build cycle. Build comprises all tasks necessary to bring the vision and the design to a fully functional solution or feature. These include creating tables, creating user interface elements (forms and pages), defining reports, and coding.

As soon as a design for a feature has been completed, we can start building it. In fact, we don't really need to wait for everything to be finished, and we may start creating tables as soon as entity relationship design has been finished, and creating forms and pages as soon as user interface design is completed.

Quality of work during the build phase is largely affected by the quality of the design, and the better the design, the less wandering around the build phase will contain. If design phase has been omitted, the programmer must make design decisions on the spot, often without knowing all the implications such decisions will have on the system. Hopefully, most of the decisions that are necessary to create a quality solution have already been made during the design phase, so the developer only has to follow the design specification.

Bugs happen during the build phase. It is possible that things have been designed the wrong way—these can be considered bugs as well—but the majority of bugs come out of insufficiently attentive programming work.

Team approach

Building a Microsoft Dynamics NAV solution is kind of austere. C/SIDE knows of no fancy features such as built-in version control or check-in/check-out of source files, which makes it exceptionally difficult to do any team development. Nevertheless, only the simplest of projects will see a lonely developer building the whole shebang.

With a second developer added to the team, the risk of losing work is increased by an order of magnitude. Development teamwork on Microsoft Dynamics NAV projects calls for utmost discipline. Here are few pre-emptive steps you can take to prevent the *who-trampled-my-work* frustration:

- Assign one developer as a code-responsible developer. Their task is to compare and merge developed features, publish them to the development server, and manage code base versions.
- When assigning development work, make sure that two different persons never work on features affecting the same objects simultaneously. If there are two features affecting codeunit **80 Sales-Post**, either have them assigned to the same developer, or make sure that the second developer starts their work only after the first one has finished theirs, meanwhile working on something else.
- Make sure nobody ever develops directly on the development server. All the development work must be done on personal development databases, with one database per developer. Completed features are submitted to the code-responsible developer for merging.
- Developers start every feature development by first importing the latest code base version from the development server to their personal development database.

Building the data model

Design specifications contain the descriptions of the data model: the tables, fields, keys, and relationships. At this phase your task is to create Microsoft Dynamics NAV tables based on these specifications.

> Make sure you define all the important table properties such as **Caption**, **CaptionML**, **LookupFormID**, and **DrillDownFormID**, and field properties such as **Caption**, **CaptionML**, and **TableRelation**. These can easily go overlooked, especially if there is a lot of work on the data model.

Part of building the data model is also implementation of any data integrity and consistency code, such as field validations or assignment of number series.

Building the user interface

As soon as the data model has been built, the user interface is the logical next step. Pages and forms for cards and lists for all master data and lookup lists, as well as any setup pages, are the simplest to create because they usually contain very little user interface code, so you should proceed with these first.

Other types of forms and pages may need some coding as well: journal pages and forms, open documents pages and forms, various worksheets and similar.

Finally, you need to create pages and forms for any statistics, entries lists, and posted documents. These typically contain little code, but depending on data model and the complexity of requirements this may not be so true.

In any case, user interface code looks best in codeunits—if at all possible, try not to keep anything but the codeunit function calls within user interface objects themselves. We'll explain this shortly.

Beware the page

With the introduction of pages, Microsoft Dynamics NAV 2009 has brought along a completely new kind of fun for programmers. With the RoleTailored interface running in parallel with the Classic one, it is now possible to produce a kind of inconsistency that calls for extreme caution during development.

Pages and forms are physically distinct objects, but C/AL makes them implicitly equivalent. When you write `FORM` in C/AL or declare a variable of type **Form**, and then run that code within the RoleTailored client, the C/AL will implicitly translate `FORM` into `PAGE`, or substitute the variable of type **Form** by one of the type **Page**, with the same object ID. This is a great feature, because it reduces code complexity, by making it unnecessary to write things like this:

```
IF ISSERVICETIER THEN
  PAGE.RUN(21,Rec)
ELSE
  FORM.RUN(21,Rec);
```

Instead, you can just write:

```
FORM.RUN(21,Rec);
```

These two will execute just the same, regardless of the client which executes this: both of these pieces of code will display form 21 in the Classic client and page 21 in the RoleTailored client

However, if you add a function `Foo` to the **Customer Card** form, but forget to add it to the **Customer Card** page, the following code will execute correctly only in Classic client, but won't execute as expected in RoleTailored one:

```
CustCard.Foo();
CustCard.RUN();
```

In fact, the C/SIDE compiler will only check whether function `Foo` is declared in the form object, but won't check its existence in the page object. This means that if you forget to declare this function in the **Customer Card** page, the compiler will not throw a compiler error. Even during run time, if the function `Foo` is not declared in the Customer Card page, the execution silently skips over it, not even showing the error message that would happen in C/SIDE if the function called wasn't declared:

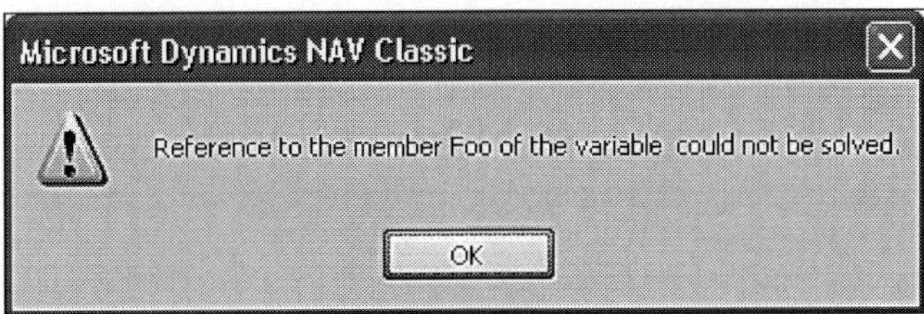

Effectively, a careless developer could inadvertently introduce an inconsistency, which may cause the system to behave in completely different ways when accessed through Classic and RoleTailored clients. It is the developer's job to prevent this and to make sure this never happens.

Never put any code directly into page or form objects, because sooner or later you will lose consistency. Instead, create a codeunit in which you will create a new function for every page or form trigger where you would normally put your custom code. Then put your custom code into the codeunit function, and call the function from within the form and page trigger, while passing any necessary context to the codeunit.

Let's look at an example. Carry out the following steps using C/SIDE **Object Designer**:

1. Design form **39 General Journal**.
2. Click **File | Save As...** and save the form as **51001 Special Journal**.

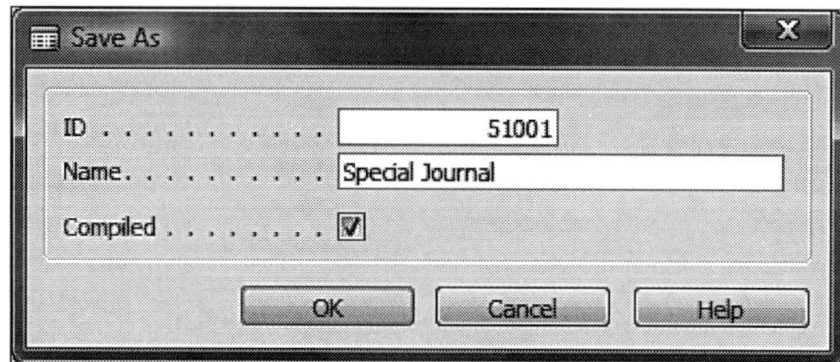

3. Close the form designer.
4. Design page **39 General Journal**.
5. Click **File | Save As...** and save the page as **51001 Special Journal**.
6. Take a look how these two handle the `OnOpenForm` and `OnOpenPage` triggers respectively. Both of these triggers contain the following code:

```
BalAccName := '';
OpenedFromBatch := ("Journal Batch Name" <> '') AND ("Journal
  Template Name" = '');
IF OpenedFromBatch THEN BEGIN
  CurrentJnlBatchName := "Journal Batch Name";
  GenJnlManagement.OpenJnl(CurrentJnlBatchName,Rec);
  EXIT;
END;
GenJnlManagement.TemplateSelection(FORM::"General Journal",
```

```
  0,FALSE,Rec,JnlSelected);
IF NOT JnlSelected THEN
  ERROR('');
GenJnlManagement.OpenJnl(CurrentJnlBatchName,Rec);
```

7. Create a new codeunit and save it as **51001 Form and Page Triggers**.

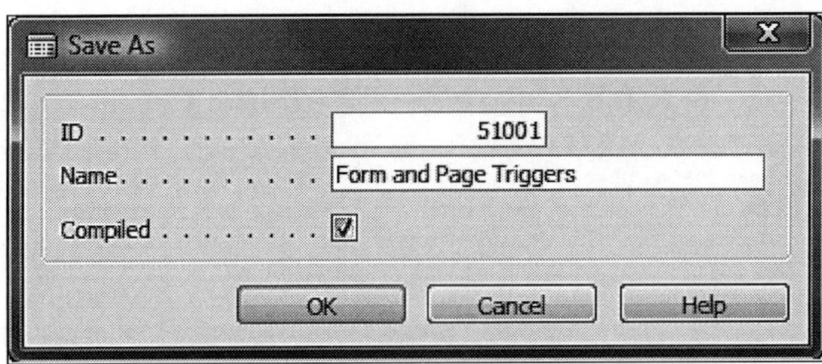

8. Add a new function named `SpecialJournal_OnOpen`.

   This new function will take the place of whatever code there was in the `OnOpenForm` and `OnOpenPage` triggers. It will contain the same code, and you will need to pass all the necessary context if you want it to work as expected.

9. Copy all the code from `OnOpenForm` trigger in form **51001**, and paste it into `SpecialJournal_OnOpen` function in codeunit **51001**.

10. Pass all the necessary context in the function as variables passed by reference.

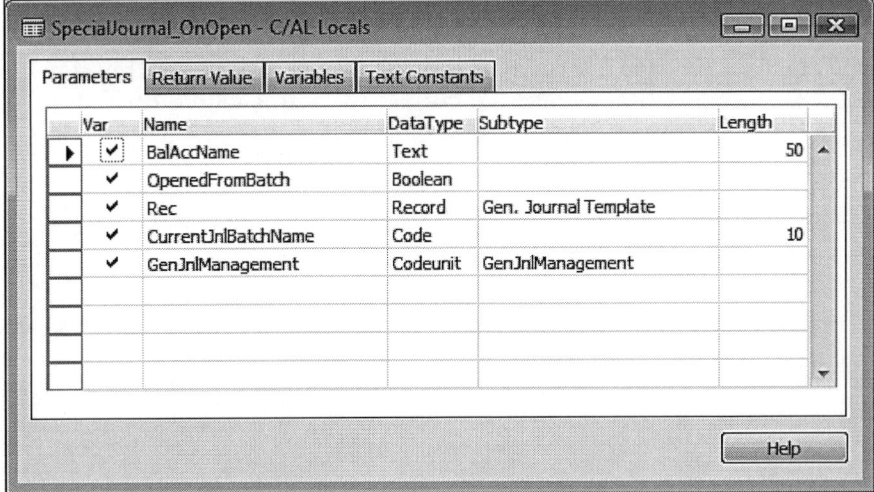

Only pass context for global variables—`Rec`, `xRec`, and similar built-in variables. Don't pass context for local variables—simply declare them as local variables in the codeunit function.

When you have finished, the `SpecialJournal_OnOpen` function should look like this:

```
SpecialJournal OnOpen(VAR BalAccName : Text[50];VAR OpenedFromBatch : Boolean;VAR Rec :
BalAccName := '';
OpenedFromBatch := ("Journal Batch Name" <> '') AND ("Journal Template Name" = '');
IF OpenedFromBatch THEN BEGIN
  CurrentJnlBatchName := "Journal Batch Name";
  GenJnlManagement.OpenJnl(CurrentJnlBatchName,Rec);
  EXIT;
END;
GenJnlManagement.TemplateSelection(FORM::"General Journal",0,FALSE,Rec,JnlSelected);
IF NOT JnlSelected THEN
  ERROR('');
GenJnlManagement.OpenJnl(CurrentJnlBatchName,Rec);
```

11. In form **51001**, declare a global variable `FormPageTriggers` of **Type Codeunit, Subtype 51001**.
12. Replace the code in OnOpenForm trigger with the following line of code:

```
FormPageTriggers.SpecialJournal_OnOpen(BalAccName,OpenedFromBatch,
  Rec,CurrentJnlBatchName,GenJnlManagement);
```

13. Repeat steps 11 and 12 for page **51001** and the OnOpenPage trigger.

With these changes, the application logic hasn't changed a single bit, but the consistency has been improved considerably. If you do this with all your form and page triggers, it will surely take a few extra minutes per trigger, but in the long run, it will pay off generously.

There is another intrinsic benefit of this approach: it will enforce functional consistency, and will make it especially difficult for you to introduce any inconsistency. If you ever wanted to add any code to the `OnOpenForm` or `OnOpenPage` triggers, you would sort of be forced to put it into the `SpecialJournal_OnOpen` function instead, because all the logic is contained there anyway.

Pages

Now that we got to know about them, we can take a look into what kind of pages we might need for our solution. We have already seen the types of pages that simply match the forms of the Classic client, but with the RoleTailored interface, we need a little bit more:

- **Role Centers**: These are your users' home pages, the first thing they see when they log onto the system, and the only place where they hang out. They look a lot like dashboards, and contain a lot of useful info and everything needed to navigate the application the RoleTailored way.
- **Activities**: These belong to role centers, and provide access to various tasks and to-dos. Users no longer need to click around the numerous items in the navigation pane in order to find out whether there is something waiting on their attention—everything they need to do is displayed in activities pages.
- **FactBoxes**: These belong to master data lists and cards and documents mostly, but can easily make their way into role centers. They provide some important factual information, typically about currently viewed records, and are RoleTailored counterparts of information panels in the Classic interface.
- **Chart Parts**: These can go wherever your heart desires, but are most useful as parts of role centers. They are similar to FactBoxes in that they provide factual information about something, only graphically.
- **Other Parts**: The good thing about the RoleTailored interface is that you can create a lot of pages that you can use as parts on other pages. Typically, you will use these parts in FactBox panes of various pages, as well as in role centers. Typical examples of parts are **My Customers**, **My Vendors**, and **My Items**, which are seen frequently in default role centers included in the standard application.

Reports

There are two kinds of reports: old C/SIDE reports that render within the C/SIDE application and leave much to be desired, and new RoleTailored reports based on SQL Server Reporting Services technology and allowing advanced features such as saving to Excel or PDF. Unlike pages and forms, reports in Microsoft Dynamics NAV 2009 have remained a single object type.

When designing reports, you need to design its Request Page and Layout. The request page is simple—it's the request form, only RoleTailored. Layout is tricky, because it takes you out of the comfort of the C/SIDE designer, into the world of RDLC (Report Definition Language Client-side). Not that there is something particularly scary about this, it's only that Microsoft Dynamics NAV developers never had to do any object design work outside the C/SIDE—now they do. In the new world of the services tier, things like this will be increasingly common.

However, there is a helpful tool, **Create Layout Suggestion**, safely nested within the **Tools** menu of the C/SIDE report designer:

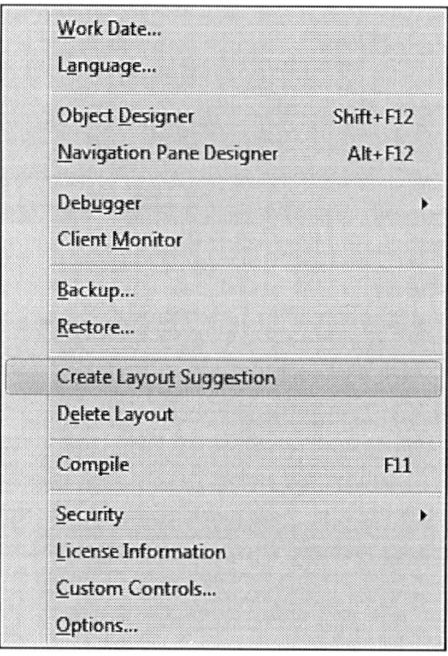

This tool lets you translate the C/SIDE report sections into RDLC, which is all you will need in the majority of situations.

User interface integration

When all the user interface elements have been built, it is time to integrate them into the user interface. The first task of user interface integration is to link various pages or forms together. You need to link things like list and card pages for master data and documents, and to make available related pages or forms and reports through actions on pages or menu buttons on forms.

Then you need to integrate the user interface elements into RoleTailored user interface and the navigation pane of the Classic user interface.

> Always integrate forms and reports into the navigation pane through a MenuSuite object. Whatever is available in the Classic client in the navigation pane will be available in the RoleTailored user interface's Departments menu.

The most important part of user interface integration in Microsoft Dynamics NAV 2009 is making all the necessary pages available through related role centers.

[You can read more about role centers functionality in Chapter 2.]

Extending existing role centers

Microsoft Dynamics NAV 2009 comes with 21 predefined role centers. Most of the pages you have designed must find their way into one or more role centers.

The following list includes actions you may want to take to make your custom objects (pages and reports) available in the RoleTailored client:

- Make any master data, document, and journal pages you have added available in the navigation pane role center **Home** menu, using the appropriate role center's page designer (Action Designer).
- Add any cues you might have built for your users. Cues are an excellent way to visually alert the users about the tasks they need to do.
- Promote any actions to the **Activities** part of the **Role Center**.
- Add any custom parts that you want to display in the **Role Center**, together with standard parts.

A customized Production Planner Role Center looks like the following:

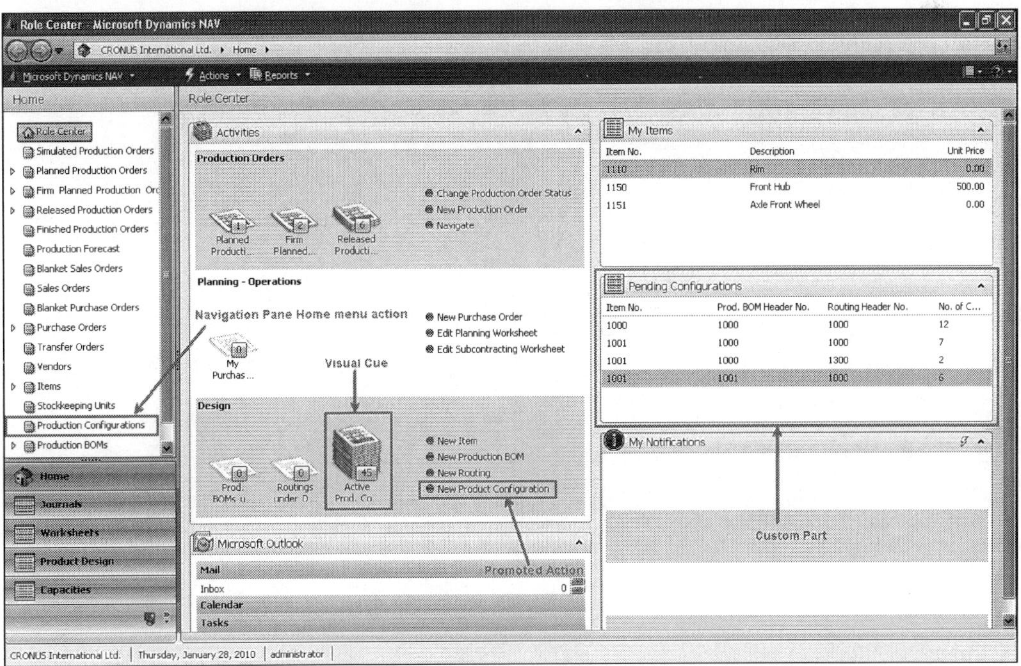

Creating new role centers

If you have developed a major new functionality, or a vertical add-on solution, or your customers simply don't fit into any of the 21 default roles, you will want to create new role centers. Adding new role centers is a lot like customizing an existing one; it just takes much more time.

> With role centers, you are not limited to two columns of parts, which is how many all standard role centers have. You can add as many columns as you need, and this applies both to standard and custom role centers.

When creating role centers, you need to create a root container of subtype RoleCenterArea. This container includes as many groups as you need—these will render as columns. Finally, each group contains parts, which can be any of the page types explained earlier.

The following is how it looks like in the designer:

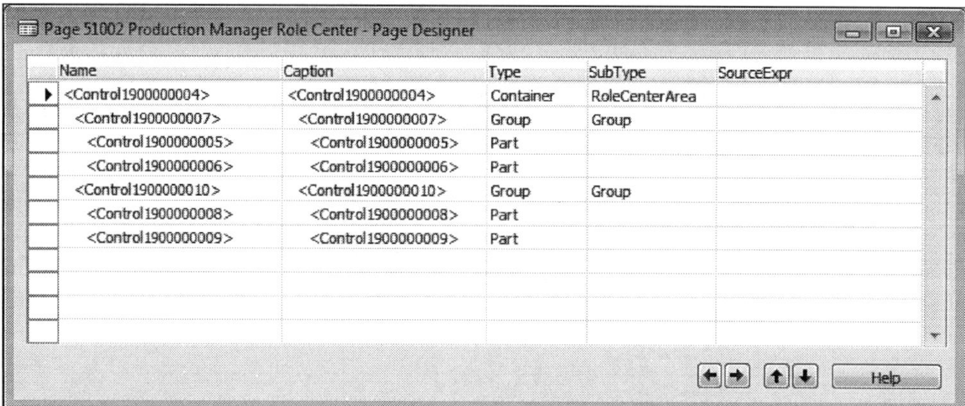

Building the application logic

The final step of the build cycle is usually the most complex one. It's also the riskiest part, because this is where the bugs hatch.

It's also the topic about which we have least to say. There is an excellent book by David Studebaker titled *Programming Microsoft Dynamics NAV*; it will teach you everything you need to know to be able to successfully build working C/AL code.

Security

Unless you are comfortable with your users working as members of the `SUPER` role, you need to set up security roles for any custom objects you added to your Microsoft Dynamics NAV solution.

Always plan to use the `ALL` role for all user accounts. This enables you to rely only on setting **TableData** security permissions. Otherwise, your life gets enormously complicated as you need—for every role—to list every possible table, form, report, dataport, XMLport, codeunit, MenuSuite, and page that users belonging to that role will ever need. Debugging such security roles may extend well into the operation phase of your projects.

Be careful when extending standard security roles with permissions for your custom objects—this can easily introduce security risks. If any of objects you added are required by all users, add them to the `ALL` role. For all other objects create new roles and define security permissions for these objects there, instead of in standard roles.

Testing

If it compiles, it's not good enough.

Programmers must test their code. It is comic how much this obvious fact needs to be emphasized over and over again. Sometimes programmers are *just sure* that their code works, sometimes they simply forget to test a feature due to the sheer number of other features they develop. Not so long ago, I had a chance to work with a programmer who literally said: *I am a programmer, not a tester—I don't need to test anything*. Whichever the reason is, failing to properly test the programming work is a bad habit—eliminate it without mercy.

You don't need to adopt an automated unit testing approach. If you can, it can't hurt, but it depends primarily on your budget. If it is too tight, you may do manual unit tests, or simply compile and run. Compile frequently, run frequently.

The goal of this kind of testing is to eliminate the most obvious bugs, those that get detected within the first seconds or minutes of testing. There is almost no fear that those would go undetected through stabilization phase, but if you release into stabilization something that wasn't unit tested, you introduce an unnecessary code merging and failed test documentation overhead if it only compiles, but doesn't work.

Feature Complete

After a feature has been programmed according to the design specification, and has been unit-tested by its developers, it is ready for the next phase in the development lifecycle: Stabilization. When all features have been completed according to the specification, *Feature Complete*, an important milestone of the development lifecycle has been reached.

> The official MSF milestone term is *Scope Complete*. We are using a more widespread term: *Feature Complete*.

It is not necessary to reach the Feature Complete milestone before stabilization can start. In fact, you start stabilizing a feature as soon as it is complete, and as soon as all features upon which it depends have been completed.

Object versioning

An important development concept with Microsoft Dynamics NAV is object versioning. Objects have a **Version List** property, which is often both misunderstood and mistreated by developers.

Version List contains what its name suggests: the list of versions that have modified that object. A few typical version lists are:

```
NAVW15.00.01.14
NAVW13.70.01,NAVHR5.00.01
NAVW15.00,NAVHR5.00.01
```

Let's take a look at these, and understand what they really mean. In the version tag `NAVW15.00.01`, the `NAV` stands for standard Microsoft Dynamics NAV object. `W1` stands for a non-localized worldwide version of the application. The numbers that follow represent the product version, with `5` meaning version 5, `.00` standing for major release, `.01` meaning Service Pack 1, and `.14` standing for a published hotfix not yet included in any release version or service pack. Accordingly, version tag `NAVW13.70.01` stands for standard worldwide object from Microsoft Dynamics NAV **3.70** (version 3, major release 7), Service Pack 1.

With version tag `NAVHR5.00.01` we have a different story. `NAV` and `5.00.01` mean exactly the same thing; the only difference is that `W1` is replaced with `HR`, which means this is an object belonging to Croatian localization.

Let's take a look at **Object Designer** over a standard Microsoft Dynamics NAV 2009 database:

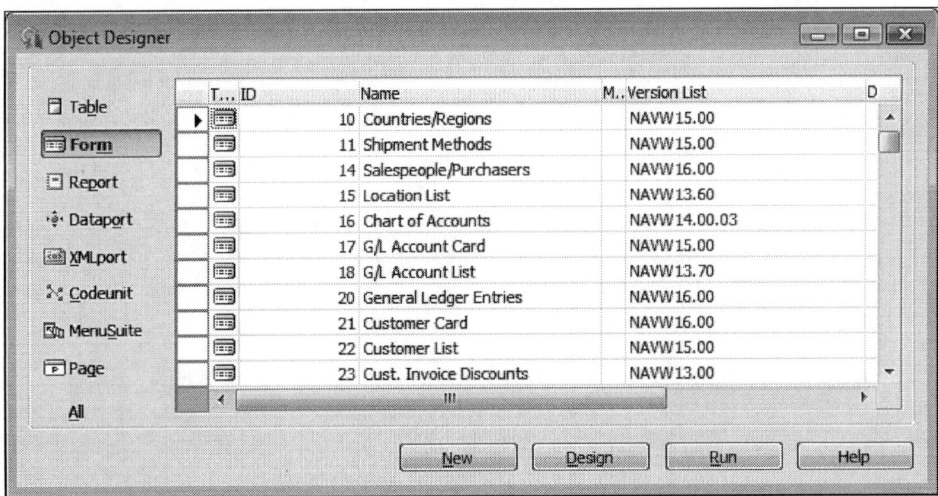

Obviously we can find objects belonging to various versions: 3.00, 3.60, 3.70, 4.0 SP3, 5.0, and 2009.

The same screen in version **4.0 SP2** looked a bit different:

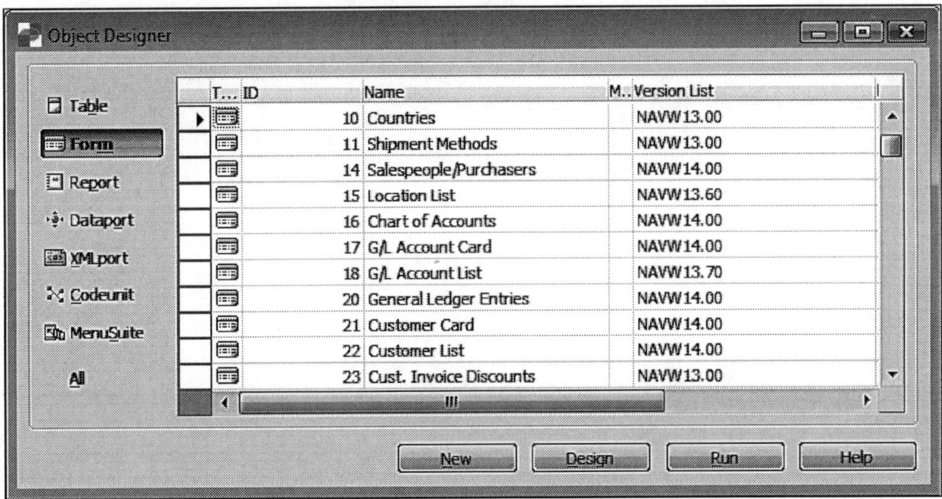

From what we can see, as far as standard Microsoft Dynamics NAV is concerned, for W1 there is only one version tag. Even though an object existed in version **3.00**, and was later modified in version **5.00**, it retains only the latest version tag. Thus, you will never find a version tag looking like this: `NAVW13.00,NAVW15.00`; this will simply become `NAVW15.00`. Please note that in the examples discussed, we have `NAVW13.70.01,NAVHR5.00.01`, and not only `NAVHR5.00.01`. This means that the Croatian version doesn't simply replace the worldwide version—these two are considered distinct versions, so both are preserved.

There is lot to learn from standards, and object versioning teaches us an important lesson: the version list should be considered as a list of distinct standard versions, localizations, add-ons, or modifications, not the list of all versions ever having anything to do with an object.

For all modifications you do during an implementation project for a customer, design a single version tag code, containing three or four letters, and only increase version numbers. If your customer is called Cronus International Ltd., a good choice for version tag is `CRON`. During the implementation project, you can start with version `CRON0.10.01`, which would indicate version 0, major release 10, minor release 01. For each development iteration during implementation, you can increase the version to `CRON0.10.02`, `CRON0.10.03`, and so forth.

Do the same for any add-ons you might have that are not related to a specific customer. If you developed a payroll add-on, a decent version tag code is `IGPAYR`, indicating both your company and the add-on. A typical version tag looks like `IGPAYR2.20.03`, indicating payroll add-on, version 2, major release 20, and Service Pack 3.

After the development is finished, and the project is deployed to the customer, set the version tag to `CRON1.00`, indicating the first version. After the project goes live, for any later work you can set versions as in the following table:

Change type	Explanation	Action	Example
Large-scale modification	Modifications primarily introducing new major functionality or comprehensive feature sets	Increase major release number	`CRON1.`**01**
Minor change requests	Modifications primarily modifying existing features	Increase minor release number	`CRON1.00.`**01**

Change type	Explanation	Action	Example
Hotfix	Modifications addressing bugs discovered in the production environment, or very minor change requests, such as adding fields to forms	Increase Hotfix number	`CRON1.00.00.`**01**
Upgrade	Upgrade to a new Microsoft Dynamics NAV version, or implementation of a new add-on product	Increase version number	`CRON`**2**`.00`

When adding version tags never touch standard Microsoft Dynamics NAV, localization, or third-party add-on version tags. Simply add your version tags to the list, and always to the end of the list. Never insert your tags at the beginning or in the middle of existing tags. For example, if you modify form **18 G/L Account List**, which has version list `NAVW13.70,NAVHR5.00.01`, this is good:

```
NAVW13.70,NAVHR5.00.01,CRON1.00
```

And this is bad:

```
NAVW13.70,NAVHR5.00.01,CRON1.00
```

The **Version List** property can handle a maximum of 80 characters—use this limited space responsibly. Never accumulate version tags in the end of the list. If the same object has been modified by two minor releases, `CRON1.00.02` and `CRON1.00.03`, this is good:

```
NAVW13.70,NAVHR5.00.01,CRON1.00.03
```

And this is bad:

```
NAVW13.70,NAVHR5.00.01,CRON1.00.02,CRON1.00.03
```

Never assign completely new version tags based only on change requests or bug fixes, or include developer initials or similar designations. If Jane Doe added three new fields to page **18 G/L Account List** upon customer request, don't let her stick `JD01` to the end of the version list, simply increase the Hotfix number, for example, `CRON1.00.00.05`. Accordingly, if Charlie Brown implemented a change request PCR017 for your payroll add-on, don't let him attach `PCR017` to the version list; instead have him increase the add-on minor version, for example, `IGPR2.20.04`.

Certainly, there are some benefits with having version lists such as this:

```
NAVW13.70.01,NAVHR5.00.01,CRON1.00.03,FIN017,JD01,FIN031,CRON1.00.04,
GEN018,CB01
```

This version tag tells you a lot, and you can immediately see which versions and change requests ever changed this object as a part of a controlled release, as well as which developers laid their hands on this object ad-hoc. However, the problem with this approach is obvious—you can't add anything else to this version tag. As soon as you need to update this object with Hotfix `CRON1.00.04.47`, you are toast. You'll need to drop some parts of the version tag, in the process dropping all the reasons to use this approach in the first place as well. Hence, don't use this approach at all.

Instead, document all your changes in the Documentation trigger and in a release notes document for every new release or Hotfix you make. The Documentation trigger is a great place to keep a log of all changes, because it doesn't come with any limit, let alone an 80-characters one.

If your Documentation trigger contains the following:

```
CRON1.00.03 - 2008-01-04
  - Added action "Posting - Allowed to..." to action group "Account"
  - Added factbox 50119 "Posting Allowed FactBox"
CRON1.00.03.01 - 2008-03-12 - Jane Doe
  - Change Request FIN017
    - Rearranged field order in repeater group
    - Added factbox 50132 "Balancing Information FactBox"
CRON1.00.03.01.16 - 2008-04-15 - Jane Doe
  - Ad-hoc changes based on customer call
    - Added fields to repeater group:
      - 6 "Global Dimension 1 Code"
      - 7 "Global Dimension 2 Code"
CRON1.00.03.03 - 2008-05-20 - Charlie Brown
  - Change Request FIN031
    - Added factbox 50134 "Budget Factbox"
    - Added calculated field to repeater group:
      - "Remaining Budget"
CRON1.00.04 - 2008-06-03
  - Consolidated hotfix changes from all previous hotfixes.
CRON1.00.04.01 - 2008-06-20 - Jane Doe
  - Change Request GEN018
    - Added field to repeater group:
      - 51030 "Source Type"
```

```
CRON1.00.04.12 - 2008-07-02 - Charlie Brown
  - Ad-hoc changes based on customer call
    - Rearranged field order in repeater group
CRON1.00.04.47 - 2008-07-19 - John Smith
  - Fixed bug with incorrect calculation of "Remaining Budget" with
    entries inserted from manufacturing costing.
```

...your version tag doesn't lack a single bit of useful info if it stays as simple as `NAVW13.70.01,NAVHR5.00.01,CRON1.00.04.47`, and there is plenty of room left for it to accommodate new version tags if necessary.

Developers don't need to assign version tags immediately during development. Instead, have a dedicated person, the one who performs merging of changes into the code base, keep track of version tags for all of your modifications and add-ons, and assign correct version tags to all objects modified in scope of a modification.

Should I change the Modified flag?

Whenever an object is saved through C/SIDE **Object Designer**, the **Modified** flag is turned on automatically. There are several ways to reset this flag to its default unchecked state:

- By manually switching it off using C/SIDE **Object Designer**
- By importing a new version of the object from a `.fob`, `.txt`, or an `.xml` file, if the imported object has this flag switched off
- By modifying it programmatically using the `Object` virtual table

The **Modified** flag is used to tell whether an object has been designed through **Object Designer**, which means it was created or opened, and then saved. This simple mechanism comes in extremely handy during development, because it can help distinguish modified objects from untouched ones. As long as the development is in progress, nobody should ever change the Modified flag for any objects.

The only situation in which this flag has to be switched off is when a modified object has been inspected, merged with the code base, and included in a release or Hotfix. Actually, any time you create an official release or a Hotfix, you should switch the Modified flag off for any objects included in the release or the Hotfix—this will help you distinguish between officially released and deployed objects, and those still in development.

The best approach is never to turn off the Modified flag manually, but to use a programmatic method. You can create a simple worksheet form which can help you do so, or you can download the Version Tracking tool from our book web site `www.teachmenav.com`.

Never deploy objects to the production environment if their Modified flag is switched on. If all objects in the production environment have Modified flag always switched off, an object with this flag switched on can only mean that it was modified directly in the production environment.

When customers play developers

It is completely legal that a customer purchases the Table, Form, or Report Designer, or even the Solution Developer granule, and then does the development work on their own. If they are technically savvy, they can do simple modifications, or even large-scale development, completely without a consultant's involvement. This is very handy for the customer, but extremely risky for the consultant.

If your customers intend to play the developer role, educate them that they shouldn't switch off the Modified flag for objects they have changed. Instead, try to establish an equal code management process for their modifications to that which you have with your own. Then you can review all the modifications, group them into version releases, and include them into your code base.

Documentation

As much as programmers really hate this part, this is an important aspect of the build phase. If you are a programmer, then you might get an excuse, but if you want to be a real developer, this chore is all over you.

A lot of documentation must be completed during build phase, and here we list the most important pieces of it:

- **Deployment guide** (or **plan**): It's not enough to pop up at your customer's with an installation DVD and a lot of goodwill. To properly deploy a solution you need a plan. There are a lot of deployment decisions that must be made long before you get to start the installation procedure, and all of these must be documented: which software goes on which server, which versions of SQL Server are going to be installed, where data files go, and where transaction logs go, and so forth. Before final deployment, you get a chance to debug this guide too: all the steps contained here you need to follow first in the test environment; this will be your chance to find out whether you missed something important.

- **Functional specification**: This one got written earlier, during analysis phase, but any approved change requests must make their way into it as well. Sometime during build phase you need to freeze this document and not allow any more changes to it. You can't proceed to stabilization phase if you haven't frozen your functional specification, or at least parts of it.
- **Test scripts**: Testing is not just pressing buttons and clicking around at will—you need to do it systematically. Test scripts closely follow the functional and design specifications, and they document the kinds of tests you need to submit your solution to, and the kinds of results you expect to get from it. These will be mostly used during user acceptance testing, but your application consultants may use them during stabilization phase as well.

Stabilization

The Feature Complete milestone doesn't mean the programming work is over. In fact, the real frenzy is just about to start.

The goal of the stabilization phase is to bring the solution from a Feature Complete milestone to a fully tested and stable solution ready to be released in the production environment. Stabilization phase consists of intense solution testing, documenting the results, reporting of any issues or bugs found, and reworking them until everything works as expected.

The tests conducted are not unit tests, or code tests; here we are focused on functionality testing instead. Application consultants and customer key users are going to work with the solution in an environment closely resembling the production one.

When a solution enters the stabilization phase, bugs start being discovered, usually at a frightening rate. This can get so overwhelming that the rate of discovery of new bugs massively outpaces the rate at which they are resolved. Don't get scared by this—it's perfectly normal.

It is important to keep track of all the discovered bugs, to log them, and track their resolution progress, and then close them once the problem has been fixed. If you don't do this, you can never be completely sure that your solution is ready for deployment. Bugs are tricky. You can never tell how many of them will pop up, or how long it will take before they are resolved. But if you have a decent bug tracking system in place, you can tell at all times how many new bugs have been discovered, and how many bugs have been fixed.

From this point on, it is only about statistics, and there are two important statistical milestones you need to hit before you can start wrapping the solution up for deployment: *Issue Convergence*, and *Issue Log Cleared*.

> We are using the official MSF terminology for these milestones. Since MSF version **3.0**, the term *bug* was renamed to *issue*; therefore the *Bug Convergence* and *Zero Bug Bounce* milestones were renamed to *Issue Convergence* and *Issue Log Cleared* respectively. We stick with the term *bug*, however—it fits better with the development terminology than the more generic term *issue*.

Issue Convergence

When you compare the pace at which new bugs are found, you get an interesting picture. At the start of stabilization phase there are far more bugs discovered per day than there are resolved ones. As the testing and debugging progresses, the paces will shift, and at a certain point, the rate at which new bugs are found will fall below the rate at which they are fixed. This point is known as *Issue Convergence*.

Issue Convergence isn't reached the moment you resolved more bugs than there were new ones reported. Sometimes the rates of discovery and resolution may dance for a while, outpacing each other again and again, so to know when the Issue Convergence is reached you need to keep track of trends.

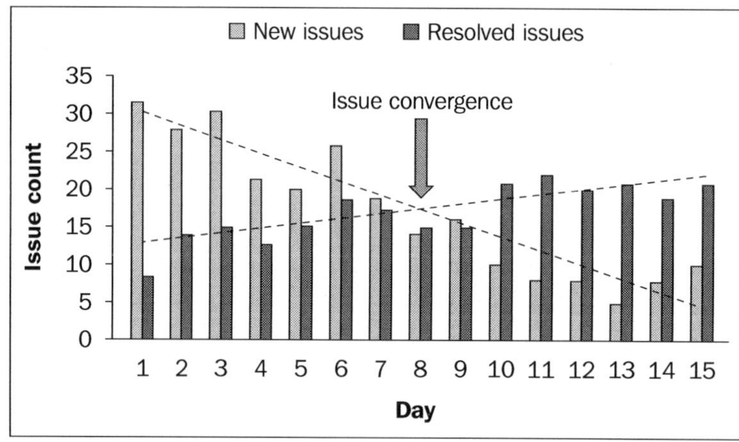

The discovery rate of new bugs is affected by two factors: the efficiency of the testing team, and the quality of the solution. If the testing team is equally efficient throughout the stabilization phase, the dropping rate of discovery of new bugs can only be because the solution is far more stable and there are increasingly fewer bugs left to be discovered: the more bugs there are, the easier it will be to spot them. Thence higher discovery rates early during stabilization.

On the other hand, resolution rate is affected by the efficiency of programmers and the complexity of the discovered bugs. Complexity isn't linear, and there is no firm correlation between the complexity of discovered bugs and the stabilization phase timeline. On the other hand, the efficiency of programmers is somewhat affected by the number of bugs discovered, because analysis and prioritization of bugs takes more time with a higher bug count. As the number of discovered bugs drops, programmers get a little bit more efficient. Thence the somewhat higher resolution rates later during stabilization.

Issue Convergence is the first indicator that the stabilization phase is nearing its end. When the resolution rate has outpaced the discovery rate, it takes elementary arithmetic to realize that, very soon, all of the known bugs will be resolved. At this point, the solution is starting to leave a *Beta* stage, and is heading steadily towards a *Release Candidate* stage.

Issue Log Cleared

Soon after Issue Convergence you can expect that all of the known bugs have been resolved. When this happens, you have reached the *Issue Log Cleared* point. This is only temporary—you can reasonably expect that the testing team will soon reveal new bugs. However, after the Issue Log Cleared milestone the peak number of open issues decreases steadily, and the issue log will be empty more often than not.

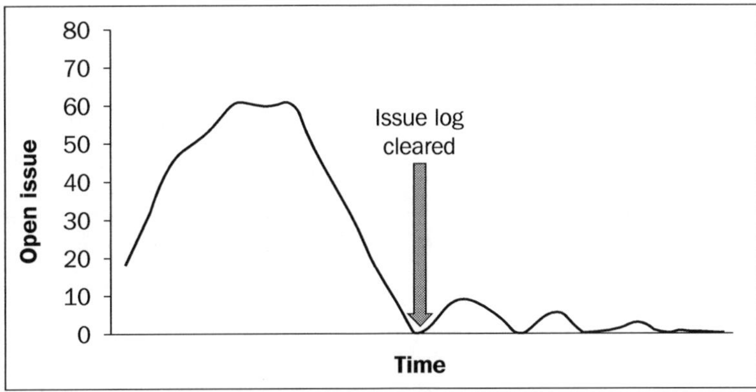

This milestone indicates that the solution will soon be ready for the first *Release Candidate*—a stable and fully working solution that you would immediately put into production if you didn't know better.

Final tests

Once you officially enter the *Release Candidate* stage of your solution, you should deploy the solution to the test environment and conduct the user acceptance tests. The deployment into the test environment gives you a chance to test your deployment procedures, and to note and resolve any issues you might find.

User acceptance tests are the final set of tests performed by the key users and selected end users with the goal of testing the whole solution. The focus this time is on the processes and integration, not on individual functions. We have discussed user acceptance testing earlier in Chapter 4.

Release Readiness milestone

After successful deployment into the test environment and testing and as soon as there are no open issues left, you can declare that the *Release Readiness* milestone has been reached. At this point, the solution is officially ready to be deployed into the production environment.

> Be determined with this milestone. The presence of bugs doesn't necessarily mean that the solution isn't ready for deployment—only critical bugs should be allowed to prevent proceeding into the deployment phase. Minor bugs can be detected at any time after user acceptance and after deployment—don't allow them to take you back to stabilization phase.

Finalizing development work

After all the development and testing has been completed, and the customer has given a sign-off on the results of the user acceptance tests, you should temporarily freeze all remaining debugging activities.

Before the solution goes into production, you need to assign the appropriate version tag to all modified objects, and switch off their **Modified** flag, as explained earlier in this chapter.

> Make sure that all modified objects get the same values for **Date** and **Time** properties. This is just one more safety mechanism that you can later use to tell whether something has been changed unbeknownst to you.

Deployment

Almost there. The solution has been thoroughly tested and has been deemed ready for deployment, and the deployment procedure has been validated and field-proven in the test environment. Now it's time to go live.

During deployment you need to follow the deployment guide you have prepared during build phase and tested during stabilization phase. There should be no surprises with this. You need to make sure that all the necessary software and hardware has been configured in the production environment, and validate once again that the deployed solution works.

From the development perspective, you still can't call off the development work. A little bit of stabilization is required for almost all deployments: there may be a few setup issues you need to address, or a minor bug may be detected that you need to fix.

Documentation

This is your last chance to prepare operational procedures, if they are necessary. These may include the service-tier troubleshooting guides, SQL Server maintenance guides, disaster recovery procedures, security configuration procedures, and similar.

Check the state of the technical documentation and specifications, and make sure they are all up to date. If they are not, make them so—it's the developer's job after all.

Deployment Stable and Deployment Complete

After you have completed all these chores, and the deployed solution is in daily operation, and no new critical bugs are discovered, you can declare the *Deployment Stable* milestone, the first step towards the official closure of the development lifecycle.

After the deployment has been declared stable, usually a short period ensues during which the team isn't active, but will respond to any bugs or issues identified. This period, also known as the *quiet period*, is useful for determining how the system works in day-to-day operation, and to estimate the amount of ongoing support. After this period has elapsed, which is typically no longer than a month, you have reached the *Deployment Complete* milestone, the final landmark, which officially closes the development lifecycle.

Of course, stabilization work can sometimes extend long into the production phase; every so often a new bug will be discovered that you will have to address, but these minor interventions don't belong to the development lifecycle. This is the part of the support and maintenance, and is of someone else's concern.

Summary

This chapter has explained what it takes to turn a programmer into a developer, and why these two are completely separate beasts. We have seen that development has several important phases, requirements analysis, design, build, stabilization, and deployment, and have given a broad overview of them all. At certain places we have made a deep dive into important concepts with several phases, and have put emphasis on Microsoft Dynamics NAV 2009 specifics, such as page objects. We have also got to know all the important milestones that help us keep track of the work.

9
Troubleshooting

> *"The measure of success is not whether you have a tough problem to deal with, but whether it is the same problem you had last year."* John Foster Dulles

After the system is alive and in production, but also when it grows, there are periods when new unpredicted problems arise, and when their source is far from obvious. This chapter will focus on tools and techniques available to detect the problem, pinpoint the source, and help eliminate it painlessly and quickly. A decent share of problems can be avoided with proper planning undertaken before the system is even designed, so this chapter also explains the measures you can take into account when planning.

You'll learn how to:

- Identify problems
- Detect and exterminate bugs
- Troubleshoot performance issues
- Plan ahead to avoid typical pitfalls
- Get help if none of the above helps

Identifying problems

Nothing is perfect. This adage is universal and common sense, and so is the truth behind it. Sometime, somewhere, something will most certainly go wrong, the thing will stop working as expected, and the better prepared you are for it, the more chance you have of quickly determining the cause and eliminating it efficiently.

As a multi-tiered application with several distributed components, Microsoft Dynamics NAV 2009 can get troubled by many kinds of problems. The most common issues, however, are these:

- Bugs, when the system doesn't produce expected results
- Performance issues, when the system doesn't perform as expected

- Scalability issues, when the system can't accept any more users
- Concurrency issues, when users have trouble accessing the database at the same time

These problems may originate in the application itself, or outside of it. To remove the problem, you must first identify the real cause of it, and sometimes this is not as simple as it seems. A slow report can happen to be tracked to a clogged network interface after days of tweaking and tuning the indexes, or a suspected C/AL code bug can turn out to be a poorly defined table relation.

There are many tools at your disposal that you can use for troubleshooting the issues you may encounter during any phase of an implementation project, or even far into the live production stage of the solution. Sometimes it will take a minute in a debugger to correctly diagnose the problem, but often you will need to combine several tools before you get to the root of the problem.

But there is good news for you: all the tools you need are already available to you, because they are already included in the operating system, SQL Server, or Microsoft Dynamics NAV.

Debugging

When code doesn't execute the way it was initially intended by the programmer, we say we have a *bug*. *Debugging* is a process of detecting such code and effectively removing it.

> An urban legend goes that the term *bug* has its origin in the early days of computing, when an insect trapped within the computer circuitry could easily cause the sensitive electronics to malfunction. An actual incident in 1947, when two engineers at Harvard University lab found a real bug trapped in a relay, contributes to this legend.
>
> The truth is different. *Bug*, as an engineering term for designating engineering faults, has been in use for many decades, and as early as 1878 it was most likely already widespread, when Thomas Edison mentioned it in a letter to his associate Tivadar Puskás.
>
> *Debugging* is also not of computational origin. A 1945 article in the *Journal of the Royal Aeronautical Society* mentions the term in the context of airplane engine testing. It wasn't until mid 1950's that these two terms took on widespread usage among computer scientists.

Bugs come in many forms. A missing piece of code, which the programmer didn't write for any conceivable reason, an extra line of code, an incorrect condition branching, a variable that wasn't reset—these are examples of bugs that frequently happen, and are fairly easy to detect and correct.

Other types of bugs can get uglier: perfectly working code suddenly stops working after another part of code has been changed. Adding parameters to existing functions, adding new options to the middle of existing option fields, changing the length of text or code fields, adding another option field to the table—all of these are examples of operations that can cause perfectly working code to stop behaving as expected. We call these the *regression issues*.

All of these are the situations where you need some debugging tools—those that can help you detect and remove any bugs. However, a debugger can come in handy not only for removing bugs. Sometimes perfectly legal situations, such as error messages indicating that some invalid conditions have occurred, can be analyzed and troubleshot using a debugger.

There are two ways you can go about debugging in Microsoft Dynamics NAV:

- **Debugging the Classic client**: By using a debugger built into the C/SIDE development environment of the Classic client, it is possible to debug business logic contained in all kinds of objects except pages.
- **Debugging the Service Tier**: To address the limitation of the Classic clients in respect to debugging page objects, you can use Microsoft Visual Studio to debug the Service Tier. Microsoft Dynamics NAV 2009 translates the C/AL code into C#, which is then compiled into .NET assemblies. By attaching Visual Studio to Microsoft Dynamics NAV Server service, it is possible to debug the business logic in the Service Tier.

Debugging the Service Tier

Microsoft Dynamics NAV 2009 made a step forward towards integrating the development with mainstream Microsoft development tools: .NET, C#, and Visual Studio. While it is still not possible to develop Microsoft Dynamics NAV solutions using Visual Studio, you can make a good use of the fact that all C/AL code is internally translated into C#, and debug that C# using Visual Studio.

Debugging of the Service Tier is not enabled by default. To enable it, you must switch some configuration settings in the Service Tier configuration XML file.

Start Visual Studio and from the **File** menu, choose **Open**, then **File**. Browse to the Service Tier application folder (if you installed Microsoft Dynamics NAV using default options, it should be `C:\Program Files (x86)\Microsoft Dynamics NAV\60\Service`), locate the file `CustomSettings.config`, and click **Open**.

If you have no previous experience configuring .NET applications, you should know that the majority of them come with a `.config` file, which allows configuring some application-wide settings by editing this file directly. For Microsoft Dynamics NAV Server, it's the `CustomSettings.config` file you've just opened.

Different configuration settings are stored in `<add>` tags. Each `<add>` tag contains two attributes: `key` and `value`. Search for the `EnableDebugging` key, set its value to `true`, and save the file.

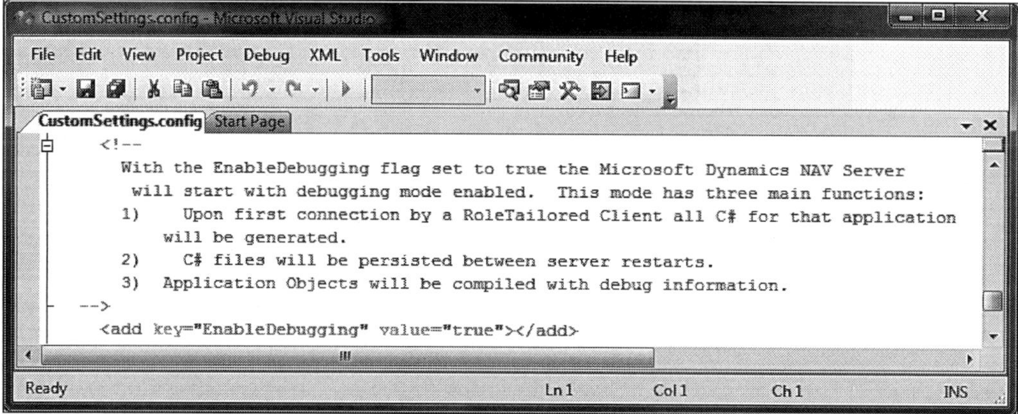

The configuration change you have made won't take effect until Microsoft Dynamics NAV Server service is restarted. You can do so by restarting it using Services console in your administrative tools, or by typing this into your command prompt:

```
net stop MicrosoftDynamicsNavServer
```

After it has completed, type this:

```
net start MicrosoftDynamicsNavServer
```

> Create a batch file that contains these two commands one after another, and save it as `Restart Service Tier.bat`. Every time you need to restart the Service Tier for whatever reason, simply double-click this file.

Now go back to Visual Studio, and from the **Debug** menu choose the **Attach to Process...** option. It will display the **Attach to Process** dialog. This is used to attach the Visual Studio to an external process you want to debug.

If you are doing this for the first time, make sure to switch on both **Show processes from all users** and **Show processes in all sessions**. Because the Service Tier runs in a session other than your logon session, also in the context of a user account other than your own, without these two options switched on, the list of processes won't include it.

In the **Available Processes** list, locate `Microsoft.Dynamics.Nav.Server.exe` and click the `Attach` button:

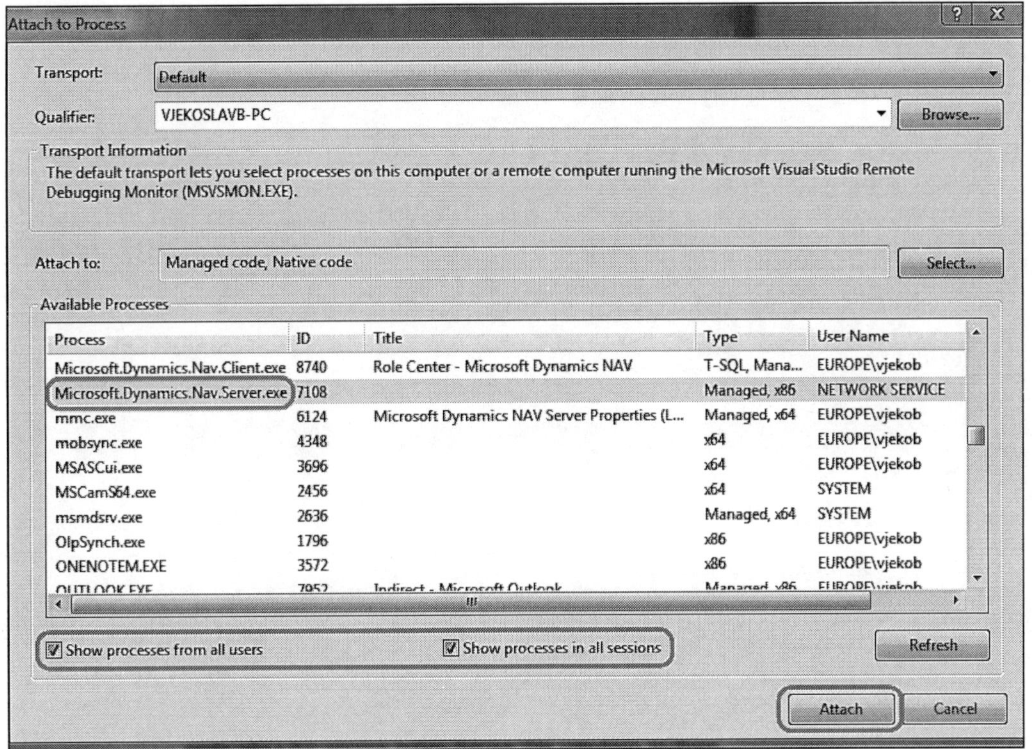

This has enabled the debugging in the Service Tier and made your Visual Studio ready to debug some Microsoft Dynamics NAV C#.

The next step is to create C# files for all application objects. Thankfully, this is something that is done automatically when the first RoleTailored client connection is made to the server for which debugging is enabled. Start the RoleTailored client, and lean into your chair: it might take a few minutes before the Service Tier completes its chore.

The RoleTailored client being completely started means that all of the C# translations of underlying application C/AL code have been saved as individual C# files ready to be debugged. To confirm this has happened, browse to folder `C:\ProgramData\Microsoft\Microsoft Dynamics NAV\60\Server\MicrosoftDynamicsNavServer\source`, and make sure it is not empty. It should contain the following folders: `Codeunit`, `Page`, `Record`, `Report`, and `XMLport`.

One folder represents each application object type you can debug, with the `Record` folder representing tables. The Service Tier cannot execute dataports and forms, therefore these objects are never saved as C# files, and you can't use Visual Studio to debug them.

In each of these folders there is one file per C/SIDE object, and files are named in a consistent and logical way: object type, followed by object ID, ending in a `.cs` file extension. For example, codeunit 80 Sales-Post is saved as file `Codeunit80.cs`.

Let's debug page 21 Customer Card. Open file `Page21.cs` in Visual Studio and observe its structure. Every C/AL trigger and function has been translated into a C# function. For example, search for the `OnOpenPage` trigger, and see how it looks like in C#:

```
protected override void OnOpenPage()
{
  using (NavMethodScope __local = new NavMethodScope(this, @"OnOpenPage"))
  {
    NavCodeunitHandle mapMgt = new NavCodeunitHandle(__local, 802);

    // ActivateFields;
    ActivateFields();
    // IF NOT MapMgt.TestSetup THEN
    if(!(( (Boolean)(ALCompiler.ObjectToBoolean(mapMgt.Target.Invoke(1, new Object[]
    {
      //   MapPointVisible := FALSE;
      mapPointVisible = false;
    }
```

It's much more of a mouthful than the same thing in good old C/AL:

Page 21 Customer Card - C/AL Editor

```
OnOpenPage()
ActivateFields;
IF NOT MapMgt.TestSetup THEN
  MapPointVisible := FALSE;
```

Obviously, with C# there is a lot of overhead with type conversion and .NET infrastructure, but fortunately every original C/AL line has been preserved as a comment line above the matching C# line. This makes reading and understanding much easier.

Now, set a breakpoint on the `ActivateFields();` line by positioning the cursor on that line, and from the **Debug** menu choose **Toggle Breakpoint** (or press *F9*):

```
// ActivateFields;
ActivateFields();
// IF NOT MapMgt.TestSetup THEN
if(!(( (Boolean)(ALCompiler.ObjectToBoolean(mapMgt.Target.Invoke(1, new Object[]{
{
```

Now, any time the Customer Card page is opened in the RoleTailored client, the execution will be suspended, and the control will be passed on to Visual Studio and its debugger process.

You can easily confirm this by opening a customer card for any of the customers. If you use the default Sales Order Processor role, you can do it by choosing **Customers** from the **Home** pane in the navigation pane, then opening any customer from the list. As soon as the execution hits a breakpoint, Visual Studio is brought into focus, with the execution point line highlighted in yellow, and indicated by a yellow arrow to the left:

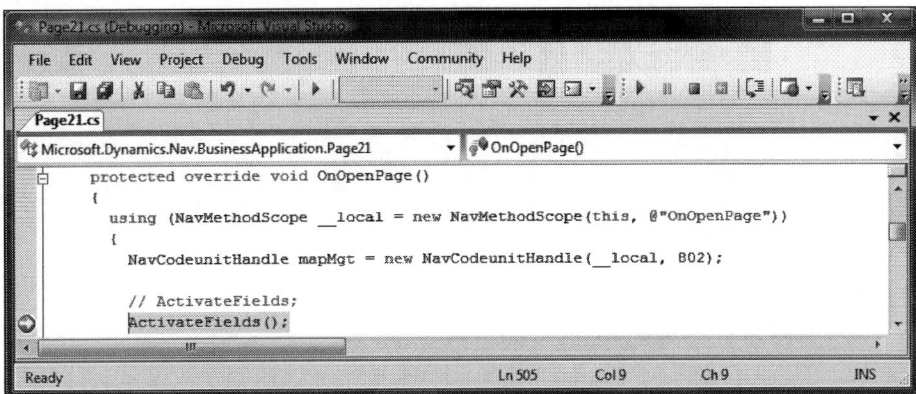

A wealth of Visual Studio debugging options is at your disposal, and you can now debug your Microsoft Dynamics NAV application in much the same way as you would debug any .NET application.

As long as Visual Studio is attached to the Microsoft Dynamics NAV Server process, any runtime error caused by C/AL code will also suspend execution and pass control to Visual Studio, which will ask the user whether to debug, or to continue:

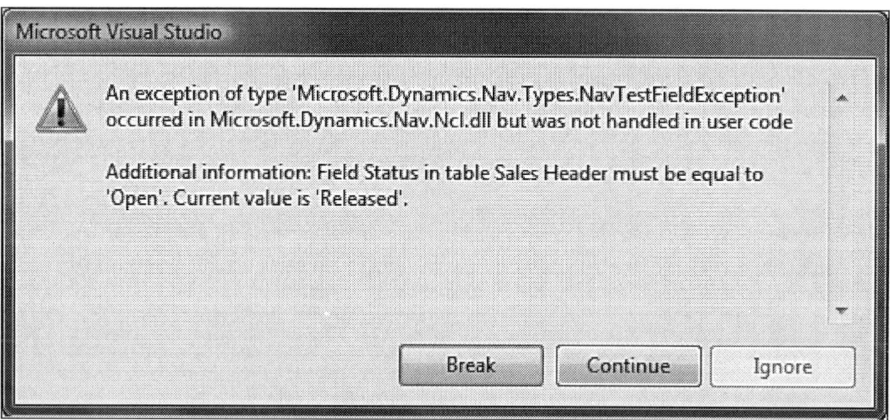

Clicking **Break** will open the source file for the object that caused the error and will start debugging, while hitting **Continue** will relinquish control back to Microsoft Dynamics NAV Server.

Although debugging using Visual Studio provides a deep insight into Microsoft Dynamics NAV Service Tier processing and .NET concepts at work, this kind of debugging is only a workaround that makes it possible to debug page objects—something that is otherwise impossible using the Classic client and built-in Microsoft Dynamics NAV debugger. Translated C# code is much more difficult to follow than native C/AL code, so for debugging all other object types, you'll probably want to stick with the Classic client.

Never debug the Service Tier directly in production or any multi-user environment. As it's not possible to specify which user process you are debugging, your breakpoints will be hit for all users, and any runtime errors will halt the execution for users, and pass the exclusive control of the Service Tier process to your debugging session. Always debug on a dedicated single-user machine.

Debugging the Classic client

You might decide not to deploy the Microsoft Dynamics NAV 2009 Classic client into production, but you will still spend a lot of time with it during debugging. As much as Visual Studio provides a fancy user interface with numerous options, for the majority of debugging tasks of business logic debugging, you'll probably want to stick with the Microsoft Dynamics NAV Debugger. This kind of debugger is built-in and integrated with the Classic client, and you can use it to debug all kinds of objects, except pages.

To activate debugger, from the main menu choose **Tools**, then open the **Debugger** submenu. It contains the following options:

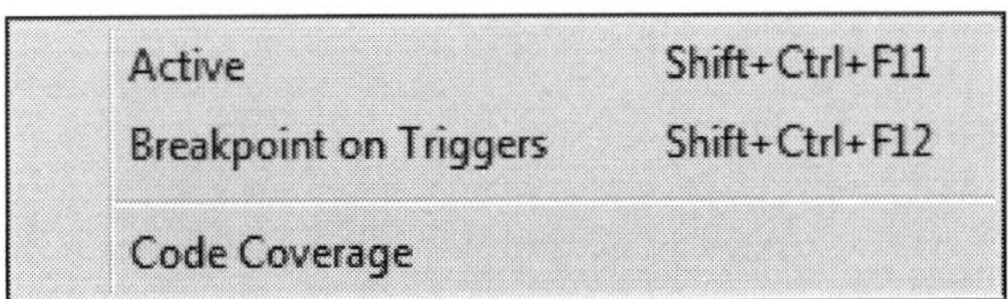

Activating the debugger is a no brainer: clicking **Active** or pressing the *Shift+Ctrl+F11* keystroke combination will set it waiting for a debugger triggering condition to occur.

When it is active, there are three conditions that can trigger the debugger:

- **An error**: Whenever a C/AL function results in an error, before the error message is shown, the Microsoft Dynamics NAV Debugger is invoked and control is passed to it.
- **Starting of any trigger or function**: If you switched on the **Breakpoint on Triggers** option in the **Debugger** menu, Microsoft Dynamics NAV Debugger will be invoked as soon as any trigger or function executes.
- **A breakpoint in code**: you can set a breakpoint on a line of code where you would like the C/AL code execution to halt and pass control to the Microsoft Dynamics NAV Debugger.

The first two situations are obvious and require absolutely no user input before the debugger is invoked. Breakpoints are places in code where you want the execution to stop and debugging to start, and these places be can only manually set by you.

To set a breakpoint, open the object you want to debug, place the cursor on the line of code where you want the execution to halt, and press the *F9* key or choose **Tools | Debugger | Toggle Breakpoint** from the main menu. The breakpoint is indicated by a small dark red disk to the left of the code:

```
Table 36 Sales Header - C/AL Editor
Sell-to Customer No. - OnValidate()
● TESTFIELD(Status,Status::Open);
IF ("Sell-to Customer No." <> xRec."Sell-to Customer No.") AND
   (xRec."Sell-to Customer No." <> '')
THEN BEGIN
  IF ("Opportunity No." <> '') AND ("Document Type" IN ["Document Type"::Quote,
    ERROR(
      Text062,
      FIELDCAPTION("Sell-to Customer No."),
      FIELDCAPTION("Opportunity No."),
      "Opportunity No.",
```

After you set a breakpoint, it doesn't come into effect automatically. You must first completely close any open windows belonging to the designer of that object (C/AL Editor, Table Designer, Form Designer, Request Options Form Designer, Section Designer, and similar).

For the sake of an example, design **Table 36 Sales Header**, locate the field `Sell-to Customer No.`, and invoke the C/AL Editor by pressing *F9* or choosing **C/AL Code** from the **View** menu. Position the cursor on the first line of code and set the breakpoint. Close the **C/AL Editor** and **Table Designer**.

To test the breakpoint, open a `Sales Order`, select the field `Sell-to Customer No.`, and press *F2* to invoke the field validation. This will bring up the **Microsoft Dynamics NAV Debugger application**:

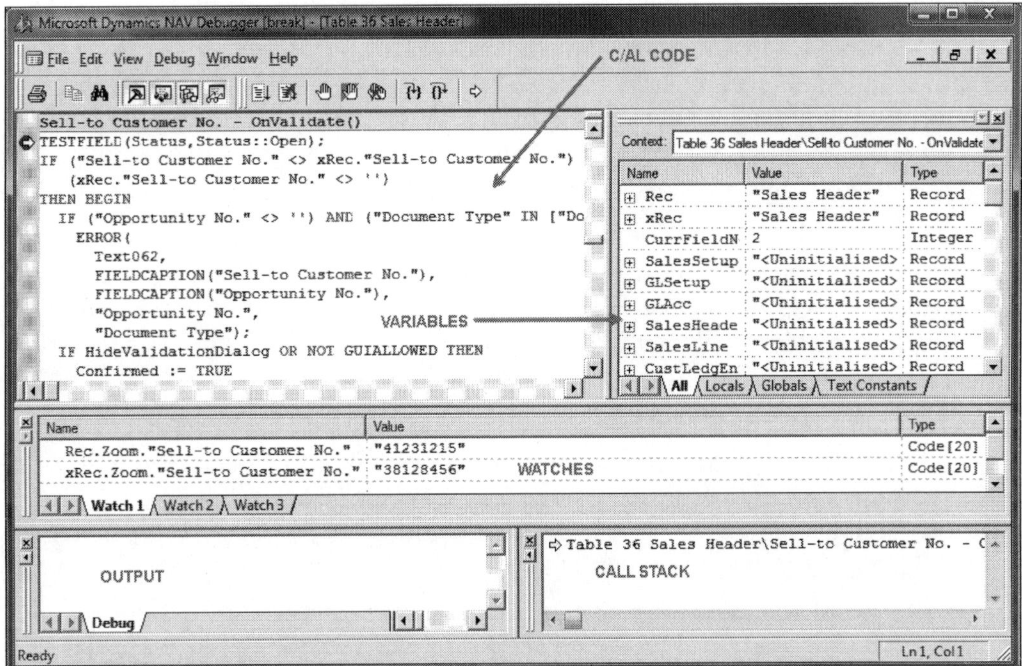

The default screen layout you get might not look exactly like the one above, and you can rearrange the screen elements to suit your needs. The elements displayed are the following:

- **C/AL Code**: shows the C/AL code of the currently executed object. The current execution point is indicated by a yellow arrow pointing to the line of code which will be executed next.
- **Variables**: show the values and types of variables the in scope of the current C/AL function. There is a tab for viewing variables of different scopes—**Locals** and **Globals** show local and global variables respectively; **Text Constants** shows both local and global text constants; and **All** shows local and global variables but no text constants.
- **Watches**: show the values and types of user-selected variables. This is useful when there are too many global or local variables, and you only need to watch values of a few variables at a time.
- **Output**: displays `Break On Error` if the debugger was invoked as a result of an error condition.
- **Call stack**: displays the list of all active partly executed functions, which were called as part of current execution thread before the current execution point was reached.

When the debugger is called, you can execute it line by line and monitor the changes of variables, which helps you determine the cause of any code-related problems and detect the sources of bugs. You can advance code in two ways: by stepping over a function, or by stepping into it. Stepping over will execute a function by calling it in the background and returning control to the debugger at the next line of code. Stepping into a function will call the function and set the debugger execution point at the first line of code within that function.

The debugger leaves much to be desired, and is by no means a perfect application. We don't intend to grumble about missing features such as conditional breakpoints and dynamic variable assignments, something that comes for free with Visual Studio debugger, but some features that are inside sometimes behave unpredictably. Here are a few especially annoying behaviors:

- If the debugger is invoked because of an error, any record variables will display the value of `<Uninitialised>`. This makes debugging of error conditions difficult, but can be effectively mitigated by placing a breakpoint in front of the line that generated the error.
- The execution point indicator may not point to the correct line. It is quite common for it to point to a comment line instead of the code line immediately after it, or to stop at `BEGIN`, but skip the very next line. Otherwise, debugging error conditions works much better in Visual Studio debugger.
- Watches don't follow the usual C/AL syntax, but must be specified using syntax valid only inside the debugger. This can be addressed by dragging-and-dropping variables from the **Variables** list into a **Watch** list. Still, this is better compared to the Visual Studio debugging experience, where there is a lot of .NET overhead around the whole context, including variables.
- Stepping over the next line of code might execute the remainder of the debugged function (or code altogether) without ever stopping again. This can be addressed by setting extra breakpoints or by stepping into such lines of code, which may enter a lengthy function, which we don't want to debug step by step. If this behavior annoys you, use Visual Studio to debug in situations when this happens.

After a few tries, debugging will probably start feeling like a stepparent: you may never grow fond of it, but you had better learn to get along with it. Otherwise, you'll experience even more pain by programming debugging code and making sure you remove it completely before shipping the code out to the customer.

Sometimes the debugger will become so stubborn that the only way to debug code is to insert some `MESSAGE` or `ERROR` lines to display the values of variables or indicate that execution has reached a certain point.

If you are not a programmer, don't bother too much with the debugging, it's the programmer's chore after all to clean up any problematic code. But even if you don't know how to debug, you can make good use of the debugger to help the programmer understand problem conditions quicker.

For example, you can test the application with the debugger switched on. On any unexpected error you can take a screenshot of the debugger and send it to the programmer. This will make fixing errors much easier, because the programmer might not need to repeat a lengthy operation to understand the error.

Code Coverage

Another feature you can use for troubleshooting code execution is Code Coverage. It's a utility built into the Classic client that monitors the code executed, and gives you an overview of executed and non-executed lines of code afterwards.

Similar to the Debugger, it must first be activated. You can do this by choosing **Tools | Debugger | Code Coverage** from the main menu. This opens the **Code Coverage** form. Click **Start** to begin monitoring the coverage of C/AL code.

After you have started the Code Coverage monitoring, execute whatever operations you want analyzed. For example, create and post a **Sales Order**, selling a single line of type **Item**. Then return to the **Code Coverage** form and click **Stop**.

The **Code Coverage** you collected will look similar to the following:

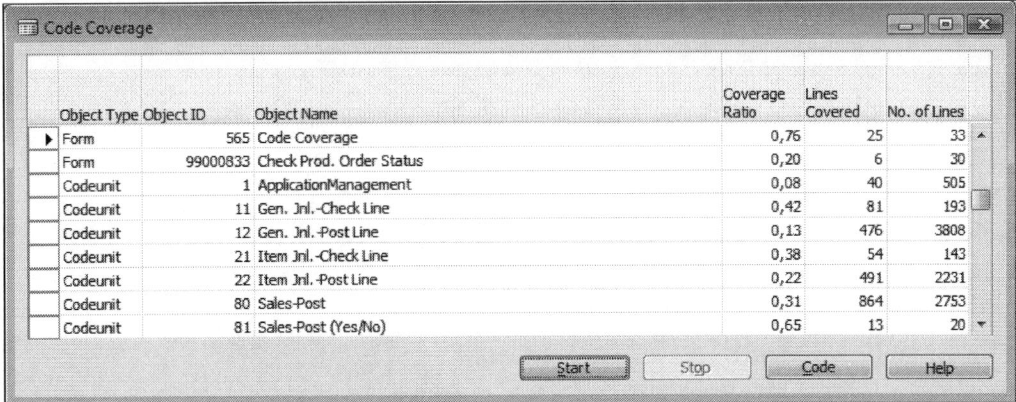

Object Type	Object ID	Object Name	Coverage Ratio	Lines Covered	No. of Lines
Form	565	Code Coverage	0,76	25	33
Form	99000833	Check Prod. Order Status	0,20	6	30
Codeunit	1	ApplicationManagement	0,08	40	505
Codeunit	11	Gen. Jnl.-Check Line	0,42	81	193
Codeunit	12	Gen. Jnl.-Post Line	0,13	476	3808
Codeunit	21	Item Jnl.-Check Line	0,38	54	143
Codeunit	22	Item Jnl.-Post Line	0,22	491	2231
Codeunit	80	Sales-Post	0,31	864	2753
Codeunit	81	Sales-Post (Yes/No)	0,65	13	20

Every object whose C/AL code has been executed in the course of the operation you performed is listed here together with the most basic information:

Field	Description
Object Type, Object ID, and Object Name	Type, ID, and name of the object
No. of Lines	Total number of lines of C/AL code inside the object
Lines Covered	Total number of executed lines
Coverage Ratio	Ratio of the number of executed lines to the number of total lines

To see exactly which lines of code have been executed, select an object you'd like to inspect, such as **Codeunit 80 Sales-Post**, and click the **Code** button. This will invoke the **Code Overview** form:

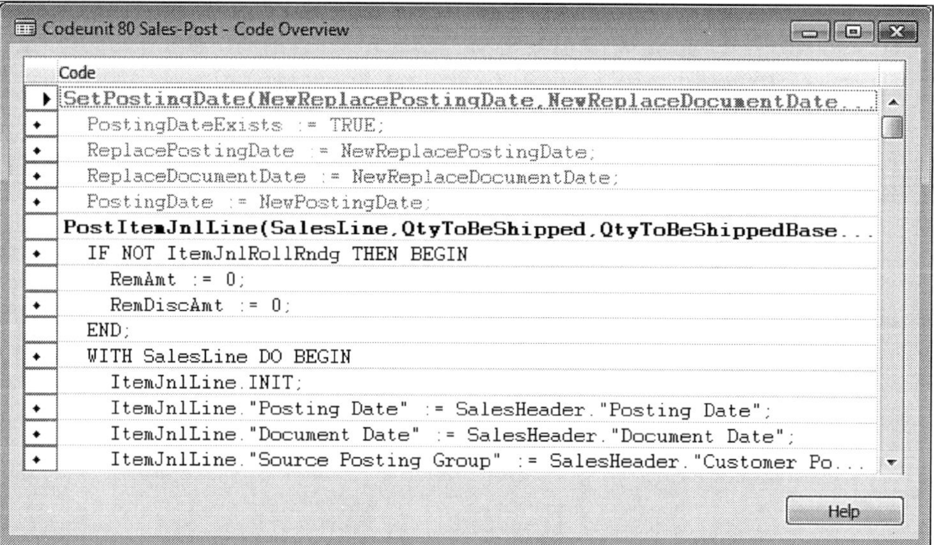

Black lines represent the executed lines, while red lines represent those lines that were skipped. This is royally confusing for every first-time user, but after a while you get used to it.

Code Overview is not a feature built into the Classic client, but is a normal C/SIDE form: **566 Code Overview**. You can customize it and replace the default red color for non-executed lines with a light-gray one; it can better convey the fact that a certain line wasn't executed.

To do this, design the form 566, select the **Code** column, and press *F9* to invoke the C/AL Editor for `Line - OnFormat` trigger. There, replace the following line of code:

```
CurrForm.Line.UPDATEFORECOLOR := 255;
```

...with this:

```
CurrForm.Line.UPDATEFORECOLOR := 13684944;
```

Code Coverage is especially good at detecting silent bugs though. When you notice that the results of a transaction are inconsistent with your expectations, and no error occurred, you can start debugging by putting the Code Coverage feature to work. It will tell you which lines of code haven't been executed, which is exactly what you will be looking for with most silent bugs. After detecting the branching conditions that caused important parts of code to be skipped, you can set a few breakpoints and engage in a regular debugging activity.

While analyzing Code Coverage, you can also set filters and search for certain operations, such as insertions, deletions, or modifications. If you decided to modify the form **566 Code Overview**, you may add other fields from the underlying virtual table **2000000049 Code Coverage** to this form: `Object Type`, `Object ID`, `Line No.`, `Line Type`, and `No. of Hits.`; this will turn code coverage into a really powerful tool for code analysis.

Performance tuning

You could deliver a feature-complete perfectly functioning solution, but if it lacks two important ingredients, your users won't be able to tell your space shuttle from a wheelbarrow. They are *performance* and *scalability*. These two distinct terms are often used synonymously and interchangeably, which is wrong. Imagine a horse: its performance is how fast it can run, and its scalability is how many people it can carry on its back.

Performance and scalability are not equally important. While the majority of customers will be happy with default scalability levels, performance is a substance that we can never have enough. Even slight performance problems can adversely affect productivity and user experience, while major performance issues can have a detrimental effect on scalability even when scalability itself is not so important. This makes performance one of the top priorities of most implementations.

The system is only as fast as its slowest component, and if Microsoft Dynamics NAV performs poorly, there can be number of reasons. Sometimes, the problem is caused internally, by the application itself; sometimes it is caused by an external component, something that doesn't belong to the Microsoft Dynamics NAV application itself.

Let's take a look at typical external and internal sources of poor performance.

The following are typical external sources:

- **Client hardware**: Slow hardware on the client side can be a problem, especially with the Classic client. Low memory and slow disks are typical culprits, and the combination of the two is a sure performance killer.
- **Server hardware**: With the RoleTailored client, the Service Tier carries most of the workload of the system; slow or inadequate hardware running the Service Tier will almost certainly result in unacceptable system performance.
- **Database server hardware**: With either the RoleTailored or the Classic client, the database server is responsible for how swiftly the data is handled. Data is accessed synchronously, which means that the client has to wait until any **read** or **write** requests have been processed by the database server before it can go on about its business. A slow database server means more waiting time and degraded application performance.
- **Database server disk subsystem**: The single most important ingredient of a healthy database server is its disk subsystem. Like any ERP system, Microsoft Dynamics NAV reads and writes data intensively, and most transactions consist of long series of consecutive reads and writes. Therefore, the disks need to handle both read and write operations equally well.
- **Network**: Microsoft Dynamics NAV is not easy on the network; to be totally honest it's a network hog. Client-side cursors, which are how data is handled by the Service Tier and the Classic client, require incessant database server calls and the data packets that travel back and forth are usually very heavy. With the Classic client deployed in a non-terminal services environment, network can easily become a bottleneck.

- **Client software**: The Microsoft Dynamics NAV client is competing for system resources with system services and other applications running at the same time, and this can become a serious problem, especially in a terminal services environment. If your users need to run other applications at the same time, make sure that the hardware is sized accordingly.
- **Server software**: Microsoft Dynamics NAV Service Tier and SQL Server have the same issue on server machines as the client application has on a client machine. If a server is not a dedicated machine, other services can simply consume too much system resources and leave the Service Tier puffing and panting under pressure from unrelenting client requests.

Often you don't have to search for the reasons for poor performance outside of Microsoft Dynamics NAV. Like it or not, sometimes it was we who made bad design or coding decisions, and no matter how good our hardware is, or how much bandwidth our network has, the system will run slowly.

The two most common internal sources of poor performance are these:

- **Database design**: How your data is laid out in a relational database can have great influence on data reading and writing speed. Normalization can reduce the database footprint, but Microsoft Dynamics NAV isn't especially good at handling normalized data; indexes can help retrieving the information more quickly, but they can significantly slow down the write operations. There are a number of tough design choices you need to make when designing the database, which ultimately influence the overall performance of the system.
- **Application logic**: Bugs are not the only application logic problem—poor performance can be, too. It may be a sub-optimal algorithm, or an incorrect key chosen for a data operation, or too many or unnecessary data reads or writes, or many other things.

With so many components that can cause poor performance, how do you know which one is to blame? Fortunately, there are many tools available that can aid you in the process.

Client Monitor

By far the best tool for analyzing performance issues in Microsoft Dynamics NAV is Client Monitor. This powerful tool monitors the communication between client and database server by logging database function calls, together with an abundance of useful information about each call, which can help detect and expose any performance issues originating in the business logic part of the application.

As good as this tool is, there are some limitations as well. It can only analyze the performance of C/AL code that results in database calls, and it can only be used with the Classic client.

Client Monitor consists of two components: the built-in utility inside the Classic client application, and the Client Monitor helper objects, a set of C/SIDE objects (tables, forms, dataports, and codeunits) that can be called from Object Designer. The built-in part comes embedded into the Classic client application, while the C/SIDE objects are not included and come as a part of both the Database Resource Kit and the SQL Server Technical Kit.

Built-in Client Monitor functionality

Client Monitor is a built-in utility that attaches itself to the execution of any database-related function within the Classic client application, which includes execution of any C/AL code, but also other operations, such as creation of objects, getting database statistics, and many more. It has to be started manually from within the Classic client, and while it is running, it will collect information about database functions and log it into the virtual table **2000000024 Monitor**.

To start the Client Monitor, open the Classic client, click **Tools**, then **Client Monitor**. The **Client Monitor** window is displayed.

The **General** tab lists the database function call information, and by default it is empty. To start logging the functions, you must first click **Start**. Before you do, make sure to check the *carte du jour* of the **Options** tab; there is plenty to choose from:

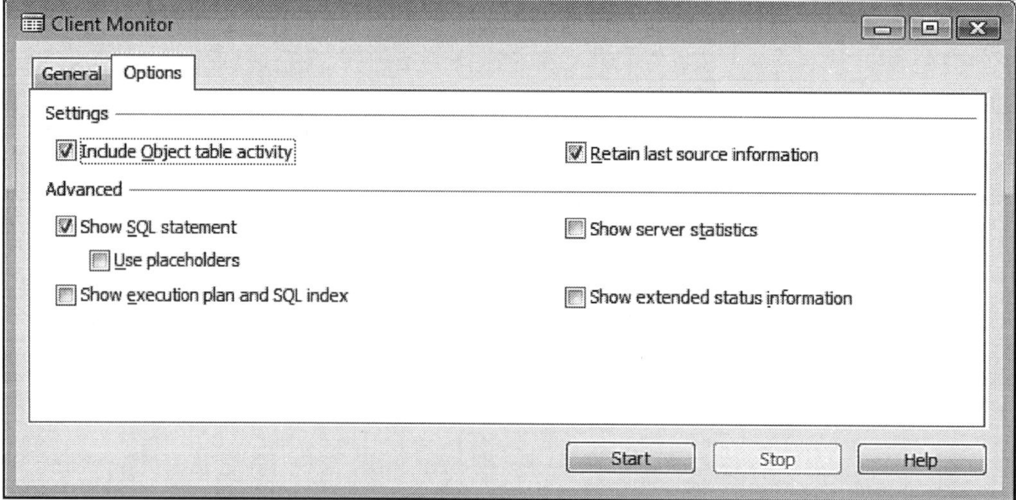

The options have the following meaning:

Option	Explanation
Include Object table activity	Specifies whether you want to log any operations on the Object table. Typically you can't optimize the access to the Object table beyond increasing the **Object Cache** option, so there is little value in monitoring these operations.
Retain last source information	Most database operations happen as a result of a C/AL function call. However, there are certain operations that are inherent to the client application. Properties pertaining to the C/AL code execution (**Source Object**, **Source Trigger/Function**, **Source Line No.**, and **Source Line**) won't be included in the log unless you switch this option on, in which case any non-C/AL operation will retain the C/AL-related properties of the last C/AL source object.
Show SQL statement	Specifies whether you want to include in the log the SQL statements that were sent to the server.
Use placeholders	Specifies whether you want to see actual filter values or placeholders for any filtered calls.
Show execution plan and SQL index	Specifies whether the SQL Server execution plan will be included in the log. Getting the execution plan through Client Monitor can be a very time-consuming operation, and you are better off obtaining this kind of information using SQL Server Profiler.
Show server statistics	Specifies whether you want SQL Server statistics information included in your collected log. The properties that will be included are **Server Time**, **Logical Reads**, and **Records Read**.
Show extended status information	Specifies whether additional SQL Server information, such as cursor types, optimizer hints, transaction types, and similar, is logged. Again, SQL Server Profiler is a better tool for collecting this kind of information.

The options you will switch on depend on what kind of troubleshooting you are doing, but for simple performance troubleshooting leaving the default options switched on will do just fine.

There are two kinds of performance troubleshooting you can do with Client Monitor:

- **General troubleshooting**, when you aren't sure if any operation is taking too much time, and you only want to collect statistics to find out if there are operations that could benefit from optimization. For this type of troubleshooting, you simply start the Client Monitor and start performing normal operations. After an extended period of time (such as a few hours), you stop the monitor, collect the results, and do the analysis. This will help you determine which operations take the longest in the normal course of working with the system.
- **Targeted troubleshooting**, when you know that a certain operation takes a long time to execute, and you want to analyze why. In this case, you start the Client Monitor, execute the lengthy operation, stop the monitor, collect the results, and analyze them.

To make a simple test, start the Client Monitor with the default options switched on, and create and post a sales order with a single sales line of type **Item**. When you are finished, stop the Client Monitor by pressing the **Stop** button.

Never start Client Monitor too early into the session. Too many overhead operations, such as reading compiled objects from the database or preparing the SQL execution plan, occur in the first several minutes of the user's work, which can distort the results. If possible, before you start monitoring the client, *warm up* the database by performing the operations you need to monitor at least several times.

After you start Client Monitor, it is not necessary that the Client Monitor window is displayed all the time. You can start the monitoring and close the window. When you have completed executing the tasks you monitored, you simply open the Client Monitor again, and all operations that have been executed meanwhile have been logged.

Client Monitor's **General** tab lists all the logged operations, and for a simple posting of a sales order, about twenty thousand lines were logged, exposing a great deal of detail about the database operations that have occurred. The following is what you can see there:

Column	Description
Date	Starting date of the operation.
Time	Starting time of the operation.
Entry No.	Ordinal number of the database operation. You will immediately notice that there are several lines for each Entry No., and each line explains only a single property of a database call, not the whole call.
Function Name	Database function that was called. The value in this field corresponds to the C/AL function that was called, but can contain many other values, corresponding to behind-the-scenes database calls.
Parameter No.	Numeric code representing the type of parameter passed to the database call, or returned from it. The exact meaning of each numeric code is contained in the Parameter column.
Parameter	Textual explanation of the parameter passed to the database call, or returned from it.
Number	Numeric value of the parameter passed to the database function, or returned from it.
Data	Textual value of the parameter passed to the database function, or returned from it.

Client Monitor helper objects

With each database call being explained using about a dozen lines, finding anything useful just by looking at the list collected by the built-in Client Monitor utility is utterly difficult. The true value of Client Monitor becomes obvious the moment you import the Client Monitor helper objects using the Object Designer.

Client Monitor is part of the Database Resource Kit, which isn't shipped on the product DVD, and is not included in the application by default. You need to download it and import it manually. You can download the Database Toolkit, including Client Monitor helper objects, from PartnerSource at the following URL:

`https://mbs.microsoft.com/partnersource/downloads/supplements/databaseresourcekit.htm`

When you download and unpack the Database Resource Kit, in its root folder you'll find a folder called `Objects`, which contains a file called `Client Monitor.fob`. Import this file into Microsoft Dynamics NAV using Object Designer.

Start form 150020 Client Monitor. Every time you start a Client Monitor object it will first check if anything new has been logged by the Client Monitor utility, and any new information will be processed. Processing basically transforms the multiple-line per function call format of built-in Client Monitor into the more usable one-line per function call format of the Client Monitor helper objects. After the processing is finished, the form contains processed information:

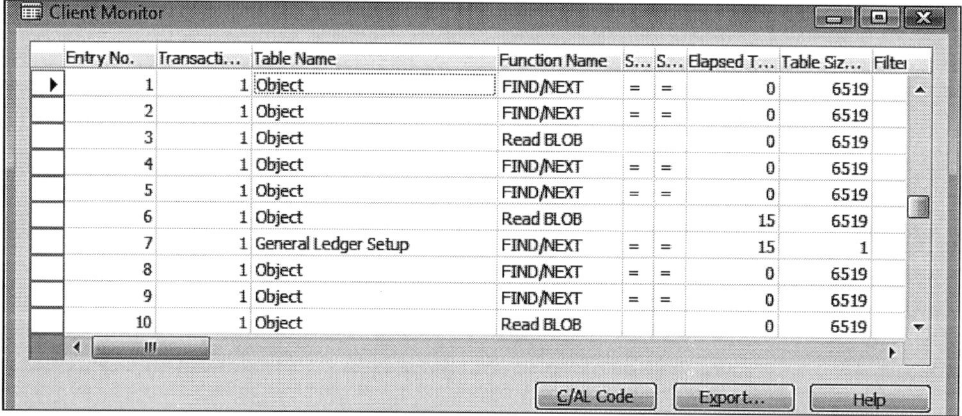

Entry No.	Transacti...	Table Name	Function Name	S...	S...	Elapsed T...	Table Siz...	Filter
1	1	Object	FIND/NEXT	=	=	0	6519	
2	1	Object	FIND/NEXT	=	=	0	6519	
3	1	Object	Read BLOB			0	6519	
4	1	Object	FIND/NEXT	=	=	0	6519	
5	1	Object	FIND/NEXT	=	=	0	6519	
6	1	Object	Read BLOB			15	6519	
7	1	General Ledger Setup	FIND/NEXT	=	=	15	1	
8	1	Object	FIND/NEXT	=	=	0	6519	
9	1	Object	FIND/NEXT	=	=	0	6519	
10	1	Object	Read BLOB			0	6519	

As you can see, there is now a single line for each entry. The original table contained multiple lines per entry, with each property on a separate line. Processing has consolidated this information into one line per entry, with each property mapping to a specific column. Now the information is much more readable, and we can start some serious analysis.

You can do some smart filtering on the **Table Name** and **Elapsed Time** columns, and analyze what each call consisted of and how long it took to execute it, but it will be hard to come to any real conclusions just by looking at this form alone. If at this point you thought of how handy Excel's PivotTable feature would be, you are on the right track.

Analyzing performance with Excel

There are at least three ways you can get this data into Excel for detailed analysis. The first one is the old-fashioned manual way. Click the **Export** button in the **Client Monitor** form, specify the export file destination of your choice, and click **OK**. Then open Excel, go to the **Data** tab, then click on **From Text** in the **Get External Data** group:

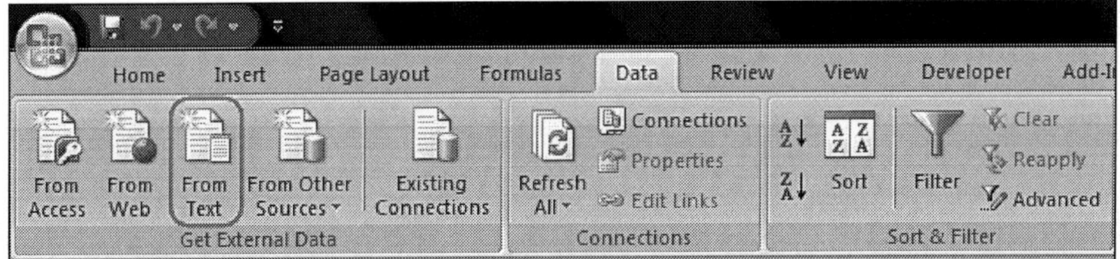

Excel will ask you for the location and file name of the text file; simply browse to the location where you saved the export file from Classic client, and click **Import**. This will launch the **Text Import Wizard**. This wizard is normally used to specify the format of the imported text file, but Client Monitor was nice enough to prepare it so it can be imported with all the default options, so you just press **Finish**.

Last, the Excel will display a dialog box requiring you to specify where to place the imported data. Either select **Existing Worksheet** and type `=$A$1` into the textbox, or choose **New Worksheet**, then click **OK**. That's it, quite a task to get a bunch of lines from Classic client to Excel.

Another way—courtesy of Classic client—is by clicking the **Send to Microsoft Office Excel** toolbar button, or by simply pressing *Ctrl+E*. This will automatically open Excel for you, and export the data into a worksheet using the default stylesheet for sending to Excel. If you use this handy feature, please note the value in the **A1** cell: **Client Monitor**. It may cause you headaches later while defining the pivot data source, so clear the value of this cell, or delete the whole first row before you continue the analysis.

Finally, you can do the good old copy-and-paste trick, and get the data into Excel by copying it to the clipboard in Classic client, and pasting it to Excel. Depending on the volume of information, this can be very slow, and can cause the Classic client to hang for an extended period of time.

There are many advantages of manual export and import, and although it takes far more steps, it is well worth every step it takes.

Only the manual export and import procedure will get all of the fields into Excel. The other two options will import only what's displayed on the screen, where the following fields aren't shown: **Wait**, **Commit**, **Good Filtered Start of Key**, **Key Remainder**, **Key Candidate Fields**, and **Order**.

Also, with manually imported data in Excel, you can call Refresh in Excel to read new information from the external file. This will allow you to create a big fat Excel worksheet with as many analyses as you like, and then simply pull data inside with a single click, instead of starting from scratch every single time.

Now that the data is in Excel, select the columns **A** through **AK** or **AR** (depending on how you imported the data into Excel) by clicking on the **A** column header and dragging your mouse all the way to **AK** (or **AR**) while maintaining the left-click. When you're done, click on the **Insert** tab in the ribbon, then the **PivotTable**:

This will open the **Create PivotTable** dialog, which allows you to set some additional options, such as data source and target placement of PivotTable.

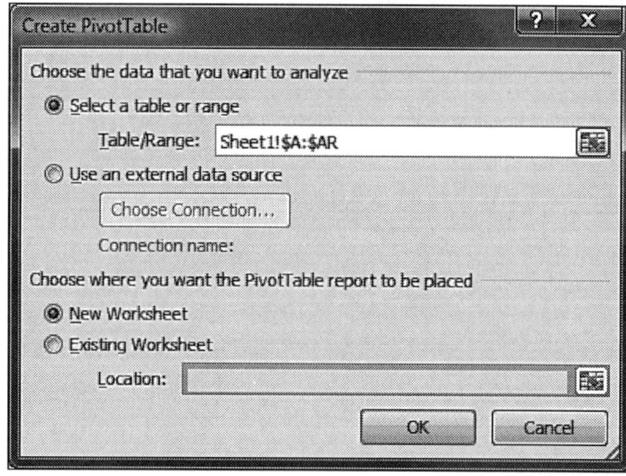

The selection you made earlier will be automatically placed into the **Table/Range** text box. Choose **New Worksheet** to place your new PivotTable analysis into a blank new worksheet, rather than an existing one (no special reason for this, other than saving you a few unnecessary mouse-clicks), and click **OK**.

For greatest versatility with future analyses, make sure that the range specified is `$A:$AR`. This will allow for easy data refresh in the future while keeping all the pivot analyses you made meanwhile completely untouched.

Analyzing data

If you followed all the steps correctly, at this point your Excel will look like this:

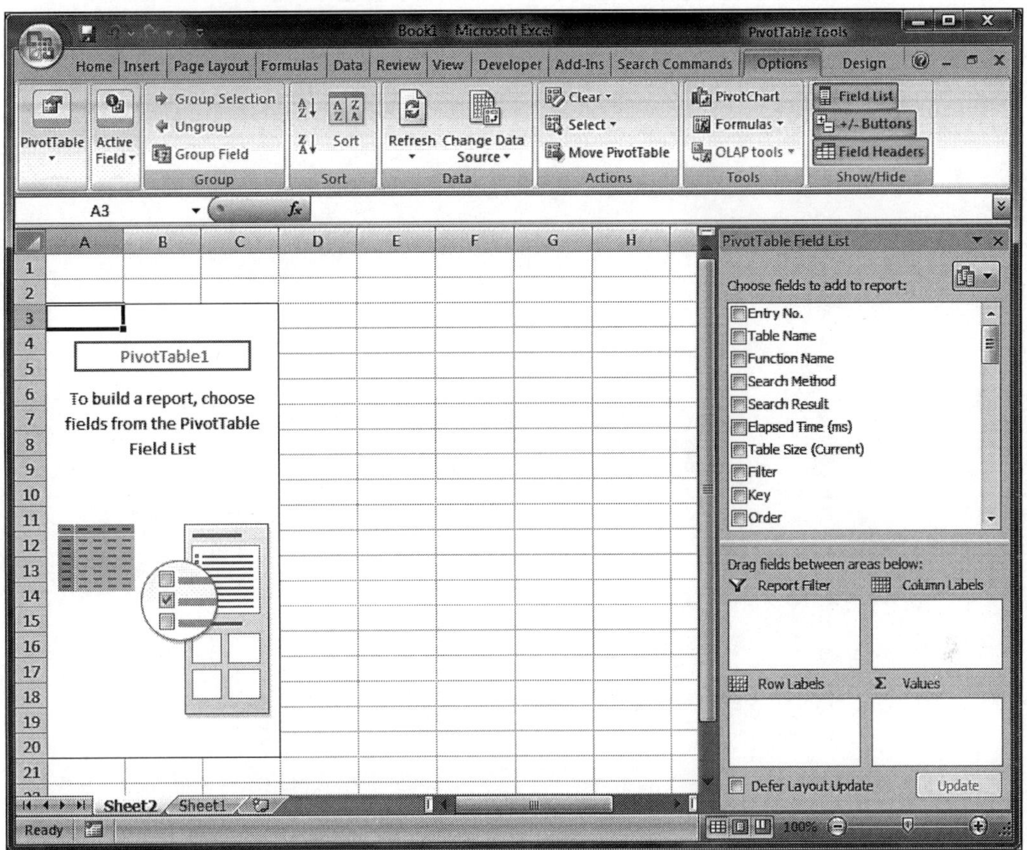

Let's do several analyses to establish what was going on with the database while we posted a sales order.

Analyzing tables

When performance slows down, you'll typically want to know which tables are to blame. To determine slow tables using PivotTable analysis in Excel, put a check mark into the box next to **Table Name** in the **PivotTable Field List**. Next, drag the field **Elapsed Time (ms)** from the field list into the **Values** box. If you have done everything correctly, the following is how the bottom part of the **PivotTable Field List** looks:

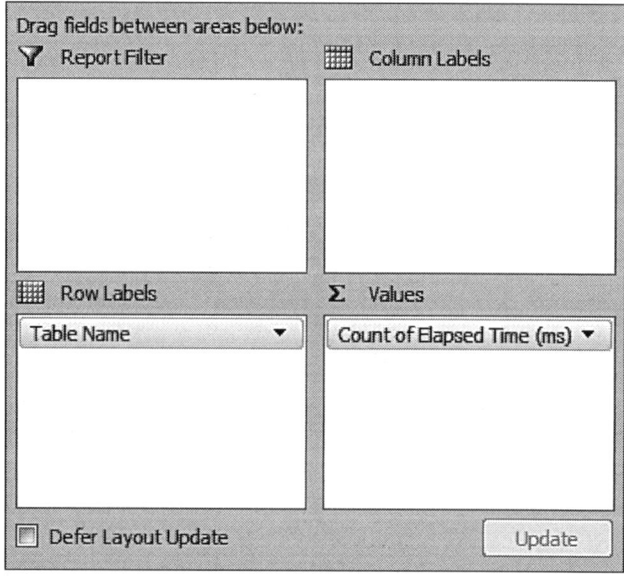

This default view gives you a breakdown of the number of occurrences of Elapsed Time (ms) per table. While this in itself might not seem as a useful metric, because Elapsed Time (ms) has exactly one occurrence per operation, what this actually tells you is number of operations per table. Knowing how many operations per table you have can help you focus your performance optimization efforts: small performance improvements on tables with a large number of operations can result in higher performance gain than large improvements on tables that barely exhibit any activity.

To see how much time was spent on each of the tables, you need to switch from Count to Sum calculation. The easiest way to do it is to right-click the **Count of Elapsed Time (ms)** cell in the PivotTable, click **Summarize Data By**, and choose **Sum** from the drop-down menu:

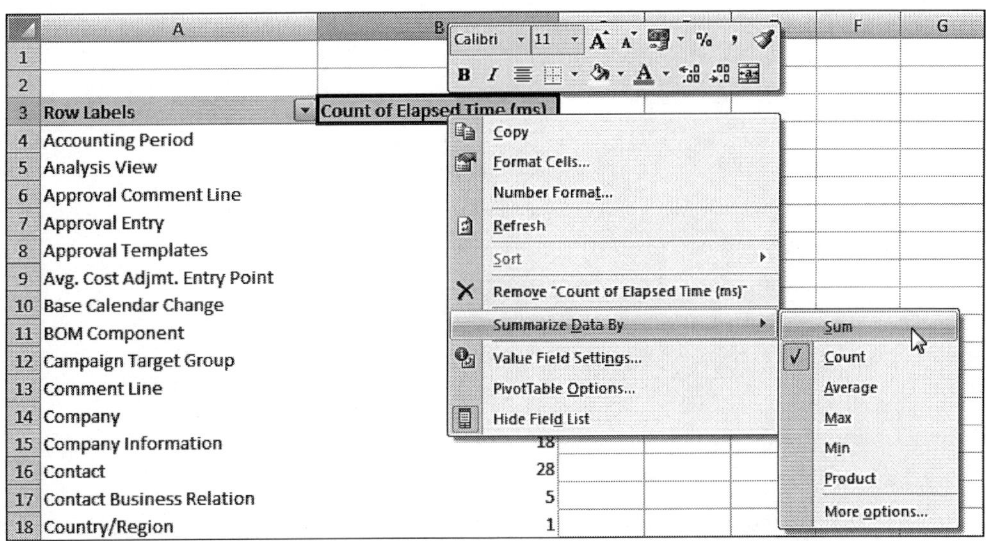

This will turn the heading of the column into **Sum of Elapsed Time (ms)**, and show sums instead of counts. You are almost there. Sorting the data by elapsed time will give you a clearer picture of what happened. To do so, select the first value in the **Sum of Elapsed Time (ms)** column (not the header, but the first value below), then click the **Options** tab under PivotTable tools and choose descending sort order in the **Sort** group:

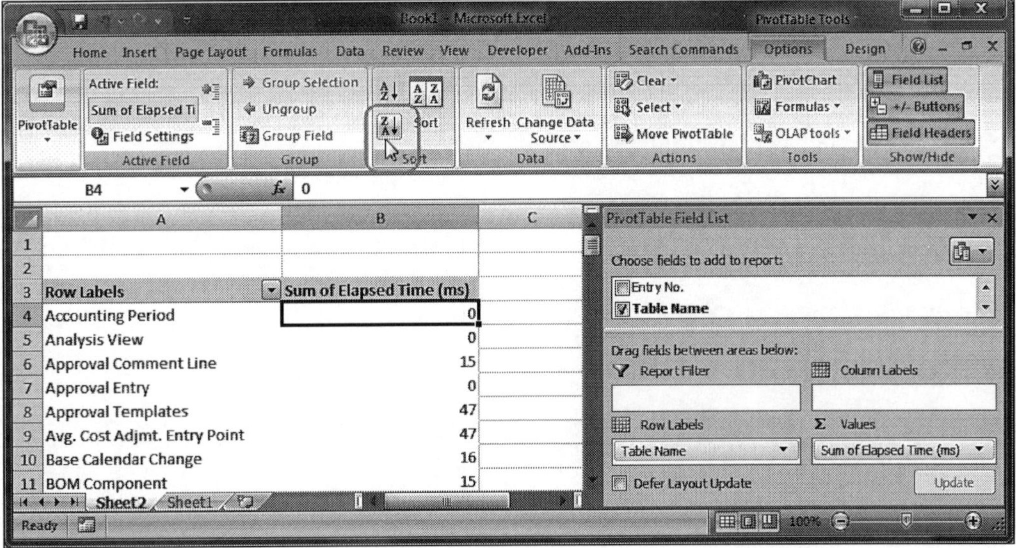

Now that the data is sorted, you immediately see the tables that took the most time during the sales order creation and posting operation. Depending on the overall speed of your computer, the results might look somewhat like this:

Row Labels	Sum of Elapsed Time (ms)
Object	1606
Sales Line	1386
(blank)	827
Sales Header	299
Item Analysis View Entry	172
Item	157
Reservation Entry	143
...	...
Grand total	6692

The first line doesn't tell you much—while you were executing your task, 1606 milliseconds were spent on reading the **Object** table, not anything you need to optimize.

You can ignore any **Object** table results in the PivotTable, or you can filter them out by clicking the drop-down button next to the **Row Labels** column heading, removing the check mark next to the **Object** table name in the drop-down list, and confirming the choice by clicking the **OK** button.

A better way to exclude the **Object** table from Client Monitor results is to switch off the **Include Object table activity** check mark in the **Options** tab of **Client Monitor** built-in utility.

When analyzing tables, another row you'll normally want off the screen is **(blank)**. This one represents database operations that relate to no single table. Normally, this is only the `COMMIT` function. You can hardly do anything to optimize the performance of database commits (except maybe on the hardware level at the database server), and having these operations in your PivotTable can only confuse you. Filter them out using the technique described above.

In our example above, most of the time during our test went on various operations on the **Sales Line** table. This is somehow expected: with this table being the central table of all the sales operations, you can reasonably expect this table to carry the bulk of the job.

PivotTables wouldn't be too useful if they simply summed information in rows. The true power of PivotTable analysis in Excel becomes obvious when you first try to see some breakdowns. In our case, a breakdown of elapsed time per operation per table would be more useful than simply looking at table totals.

To create this breakdown, drag the **Function** field from the field list into the **Column Labels** box. The PivotTable will now contain as many columns as there are different functions that were called on each table.

Breakdowns are extremely useful, because they show quickly how two various measures relate to each other. We now see how functions relate to tables, and which functions on which table took most time to complete. However, with as many rows and columns as we now see, finding the information we need can become increasingly more difficult. We need some filtering.

Let's first remove all those operations that took no time to complete. These are various operations that mostly had their results already cached on SQL Server, such as retrieval of setup tables. Numbers we got from these operations don't tell us anything useful, but clog our analysis view, so they look best when off the screen. To exclude zero-time operations from analysis, drag the **Elapsed Time (ms)** field from the field list into the **Report Filter** box.

This has added the **Elapsed Time (ms)** field above your PivotTable. Right next to it you will find the text **(All)** with a drop-down arrow. Click that drop-down arrow to see the list of all different values in the **Elapsed Time (ms)** field. Make sure **Select Multiple Items** is selected, and uncheck the box on the left of the value **0**. Finally, click **OK**.

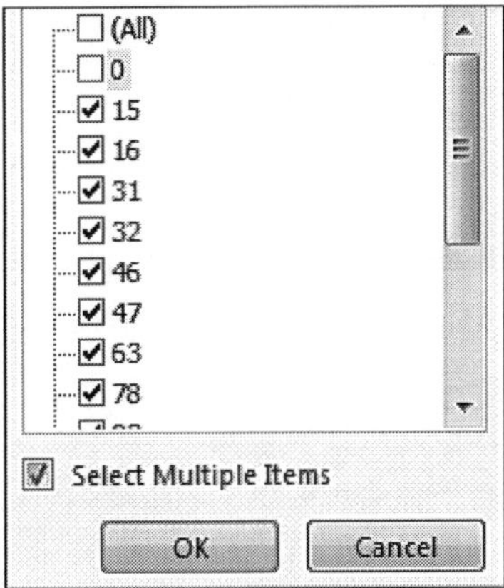

The PivotTable has shrunk significantly as the result of your operation, leaving only those operations included in the analysis that actually took some time for the database to chew on.

Still, the view might look a little bit clogged, and Excel provides fantastic features to help us find useful info in the jungle of information we see. One of such features is called Conditional Formatting, and it helps by adding some visual hints to the displayed numbers.

Select any cell within the PivotTable that actually contains a number, go to the **Home** tab in the ribbon, and click on **Conditional Formatting** in the **Styles** group. For example, choose **Color Scales**, and select a scale starting with the red color on top, so as to indicate the *less-is-better* type of formatting.

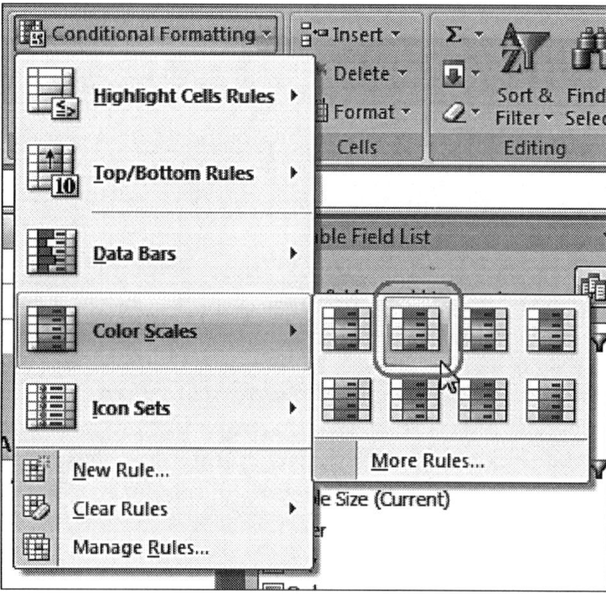

This will have the selected cell formatted according to the formatting rule you selected, but we want the same rule to apply to all numeric cells. Click the **Formatting Options** smart tag right next to the field you just formatted, and click **All cells showing "Sum of Elapsed Time (ms)" values for "Table Name" and "Function Name"**.

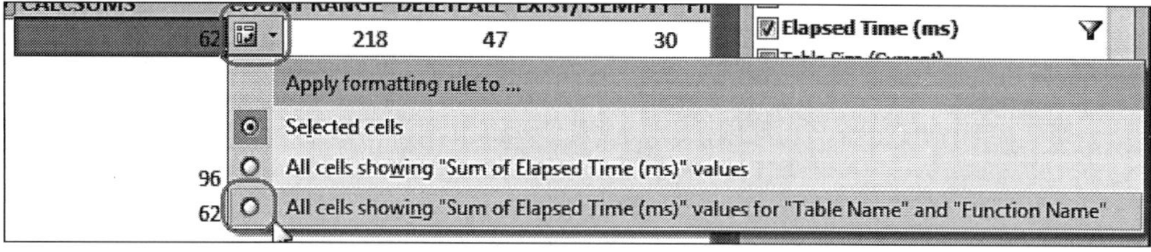

If you followed these steps exactly as described, Excel now displays a very useful analysis with a lot of visual hints that point you in the right direction at the very first sight:

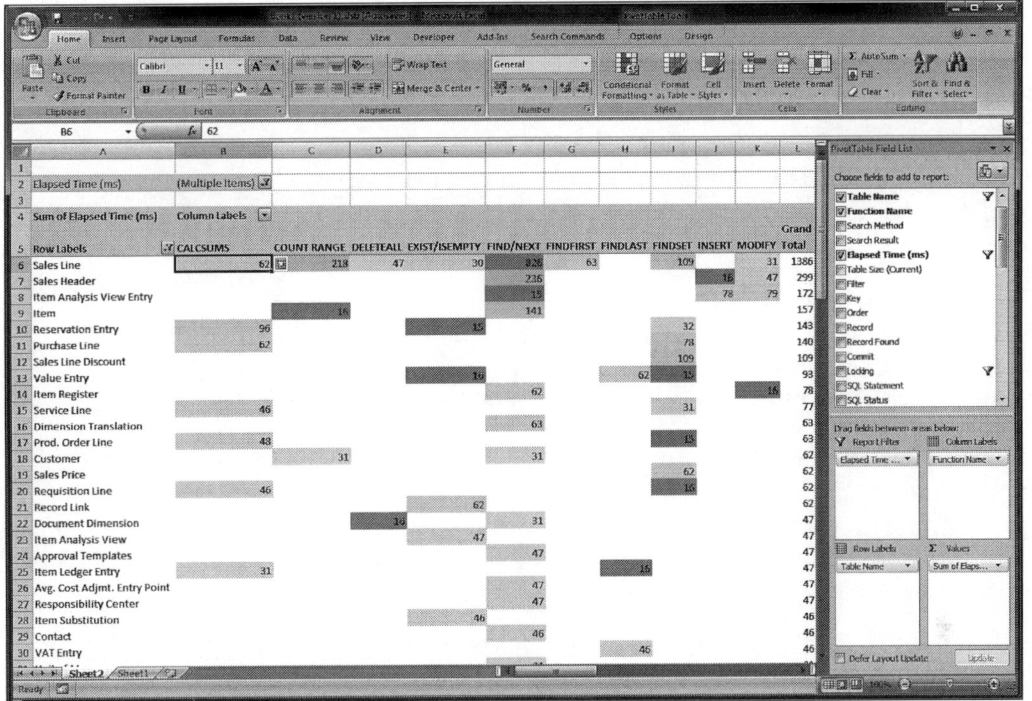

Another useful Excel feature, which helps getting to the very source of any information contained in the PivotTable, is the **Show Details** functionality, which allows drilling into any summary information by displaying the exact lines of the import file that make up the selected number. For example, if we wanted to know where the 826 milliseconds of the **FIND/NEXT** operation over the **Sales Line** table come from, we can double-click the number in cell **F6**, or right-click it and choose **Show Details** from the drop-down menu.

This will open a new Excel sheet, which will include only those lines of the imported text file that make up the sum we decided to drill into. This is typically the last step you do after you have already pinpointed the most problematic operation.

Analyzing objects

Tables tell you only a part of the story. By knowing the slowest performing tables in your database you can focus your optimization efforts there, and squeeze a few milliseconds out of the troublesome operations.

However, fine-tuning the database can be beating a dead horse if the true source doesn't hide in table indexes. For example, you may find out that there are a thousand calls on a table, which take ten seconds to complete, with average of ten milliseconds per operation, and optimizing the table indexes you find out that there is absolutely nothing to do. The database is as optimized as it gets. This still doesn't mean that there is nothing to do—maybe you can optimize the code, and reduce the thousand operations down to two hundred, effectively reducing execution time by a factor of five.

You do these kinds of optimizations in Microsoft Dynamics NAV C/AL code, and to detect possible candidates for code optimization, invest some time to analyze the objects instead of tables.

To prepare for new analysis, you can create a new PivotTable from the same selection you used when you created the first one, or you can remove all the fields from it by selecting every individual field in the **Report Filter**, **Column Labels**, **Row Labels**, and **Values** boxes and choosing **Remove Fields** from the drop-down menu.

When your PivotTable is empty, start the analysis by clicking the checkbox next to the **Source Object** entry in the field list. This will list the names of all objects participating in the monitored operation as rows of your PivotTable. To analyze how much time the execution of code in any of these objects took, add **Elapsed Time (ms)** to the **Values** box.

With **Object** and **(blank)** filtered out, you'll get something like the following:

Row Labels	**Count of Elapsed Time (ms)**
Codeunit 5790 Available to Promise	234
Codeunit 408 DimensionManagement	225
Codeunit 1 ApplicationManagement	205
Codeunit 7171 Sales Info-Pane Management	185
Codeunit 7000 Sales Price Calc. Mgt.	181
Table 37 Sales Line	128
Codeunit 80 Sales-Post	79
Table 348 Dimension	74
Codeunit 7600 Calendar Management	57
Form 42 Sales Order	41
...	...
Grand Total	1800

This gives you an overview of how many database operations were initiated by any of these objects. There are two kinds of analyses you will typically do on objects: table coverage analysis to see which tables were most called from an object and function coverage analysis to detect which functions take most time to complete.

To do table coverage analysis, in the field list, click the checkbox next to the field **Table Name**. This will break down the objects by table names, by listing both of them as rows. In our example above there were 205 database operations in **Codeunit 1 ApplicationManagement**. Filter the **Row Labels** to show only **Codeunit 1 ApplicationManagement**, and the filtered list should look like this:

Row Labels	Count of Elapsed Time (ms)
Codeunit 1 ApplicationManagement	205
Dimension	98
General Ledger Setup	101
Item Charge Assignment (Sales)	1
Reservation Entry	1
Sales Header	1
Sales Line	1
Warehouse Request	2
Grand Total	205

There are a total of 101 calls of the **General Ledger Setup** table, and even without looking at **Show Details** we can be fairly sure they are all of the `GLSetup.GET` kind. This means that there were 101 database calls reading exactly the same record from the database. If this was a time-consuming operation, this would be a perfect candidate for C/AL code optimization: by implementing a simple caching mechanism, we could replace the 101 database calls with a single database call and 100 reads from cache.

Another way to detect possible C/AL code optimization candidates is to do function coverage analysis. This means that instead of breaking down objects by tables, you'll break them by their functions. Uncheck the checkbox next to the **Table** field in the field list, and check the checkbox next to the **Source Function/Trigger** field. If you kept the filter on **Row Labels**, the results will look similar to these:

Row Labels	Count of Elapsed Time (ms)
Codeunit 1 ApplicationManagement	260
AutoFormatTranslate(AutoFormatType,AutoFormatExpr)	39

Row Labels	Count of Elapsed Time (ms)
CaptionClassTranslate(Language,CaptionExpr)	19
DimCaptionClassTranslate(Language,CaptionExpr)	199
GetGlobalTableTriggerMask(TableID)	2
Rounding := ReadRounding()	1
Grand Total	260

What you see here is that function **DimCaptionClassTranslate** made **199** database calls. Further analysis by **Show Details** will reveal that this function made 98 database calls to the **Dimension** table, and that these 98 calls were in fact 7 identical calls sent 14 times each. Situations like these signal possible code optimization spots.

This specific situation won't cause any performance issues, because none of these operations took more than a millisecond to complete. However, if you notice any patterns such as this in your analyses, and you notice that the operations take considerable time to complete, you may achieve significant performance gains by optimizing your C/AL code.

A few ideas to find sources of major performance issues

Now that you have got the gist about how to shuffle the Client Monitor numbers around the PivotTable, you are ready to walk on your own. There are thousands of questions you can ask here and get answers that can pinpoint the source of your performance issues.

The following are a few ideas:

- Make a *what-if* analysis by comparing sum, count, and average of elapsed time per table. To the right to the PivotTable you can add another column where you can enter the percentage of estimated improvement and another column where you calculate total time if you achieve that improvement. This tells you the kind of overall improvement you will get if you focus on optimizing certain tables.
- Detect the slowest tables during `INSERT`, `MODIFY`, or `DELETE` operations by putting **Table Name** into PivotTable rows, **Function Name** into columns, and **Average of Elapsed Time (ms)** into values. This tells you where there may be too many keys, or keys might benefit from some fine-tuning.

- Pinpoint the most detrimental scalability hogs by crossing **Table Name** in rows and **Locking** in columns. Put **Sum of Elapsed Time (ms)** in values, and show only values where **Locking** is **Yes**. This gives you the picture of how long certain tables were locked out for other users. Add **Source Text** to rows to find out the exact source line where the locking occurred.
- Determine the poorest performing keys by crossing the **Table Name** and **Good Filtered Start of Key** in rows with **Function Name** in columns, while displaying **Average of Elapsed Time (ms)** in values. This tells you which keys can be good candidates for performance tuning in SQL.

These are just a few suggestions. As you get more familiar with what kinds of useful information you can pull out of PivotTables by crossing, slicing, and dicing certain fields, you'll be able to come up with a number of other useful analyses.

Recycle your analyses

When you have created a useful analysis, don't close Excel without saving. Save the file and you can reuse the analysis in the future. When you complete another round of collecting Client Monitor statistics, export the results to a file, then open the saved Excel analysis, go to the **Data** tab of the ribbon, and click the **Refresh All** button. This will replace the original data with the contents of the imported file, and let you analyze away.

This effectively allows you to create a set of useful analyses, pivot tables, and charts, save the file and use it for every Client Monitor analysis you ever do, without ever having to design your pivots or import data manually again.

Multi-user issues

Performance issues are ugly, and they can cause headaches, but true problems never happen in a single-user environment. So far, we have been troubleshooting from a single user's perspective only.

As soon as other users start connecting to the database, another kind of problem starts happening: locking. When a user needs exclusive access to a table (typically when they want to write information), the SQL Server locks the table for them, so nobody else can access it until the operation is completed. If another user requests access to a locked table, they must wait until the first user releases the lock.

Waiting for lock releases can cause major performance issues, as well as scalability issues, especially if there are many transactions accessing the same table. To make things worse, transactions rarely access a single table; in our example, the posting procedure alone has accessed 26 tables. If transactions can lock that many tables, it is critical that the tables are always locked in the same order, otherwise a condition known as a deadlock can occur. A deadlock is when two users need exclusive access to two different tables, but don't lock them in exactly the same order.

Imagine there was only one tap and one glass, and two people were thirsty. To relieve their urge, both of them need exclusive access to both the glass and the tap. If the first person took the glass, and the second took the tap, you have a deadlock: both of them remain thirsty.

In the database it may look like this:

Transaction 1	**Result**	**Transaction 2**	**Result**
Try locking table Customer	Success		
		Try locking table Cust. Ledger Entry	Success
Writes to table Customer	Success		
		Writes to table Cust. Ledger Entry	Success
Try locking table Cust. Ledger Entry	Wait (table locked)		
		Try locking table Customer	Wait (table locked)

DEADLOCK

(each transaction is waiting on the other to release the lock)

If this case occurs in reality, the system will detect the deadlock condition, and will terminate a transaction at random, while throwing the following error message at the user:

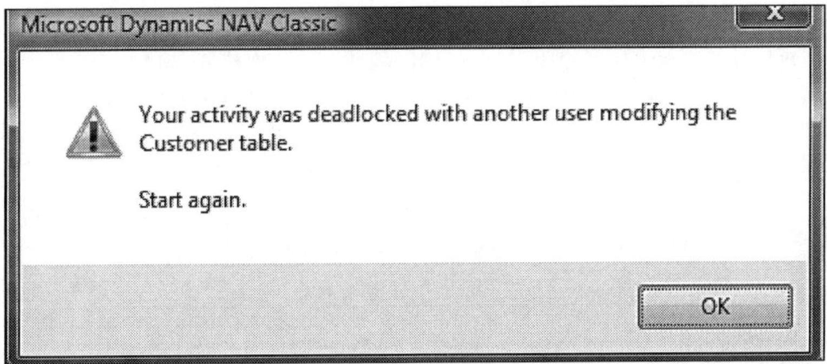

Client Monitor can be effectively used to detect both locking issues and transactions that could potentially cause deadlocks.

Analyzing locking situations

To detect any locking issues that can arise with multiple clients accessing the database simultaneously, you can apply the knowledge acquired so far: you simply start the Client Monitor on all of the clients you want to monitor.

Clocks must be synchronized on all machines for multi-user monitoring to work as expected. If all client machines belong to the same Active Directory domain, this will most likely already be the case. If not, you can use the same terminal server, or you can manually synchronize the time on the machines by running the following line of code in the Command Prompt:

```
net time \\computername /set
```

...where `computername` is any computer in the network to which you can connect.

After the Client Monitors are up and running, go and perform normal transactions. It is unlikely that any realistic locking situations will occur in a small timeframe with only two clients involved. For more realistic locking analysis, start Client Monitor on several clients, and leave it running for an extended period of time, such as several hours.

Multi-user monitoring can prove vital for system testing, user-acceptance testing, or performance testing during the deployment phase of your project. Start the Client Monitors on every machine and have users perform their normal daily routine, and you'll collect a wealth of useful information.

After all the operations you decided to monitor have been completed, on each of the machine perform the following two-step procedure: stop the Client Monitor, and start form **150020 Client Monitor**. Finally, start form **150024 Client Monitor (Multi-User)** from any of the computers connected to the same database. This is a typical output:

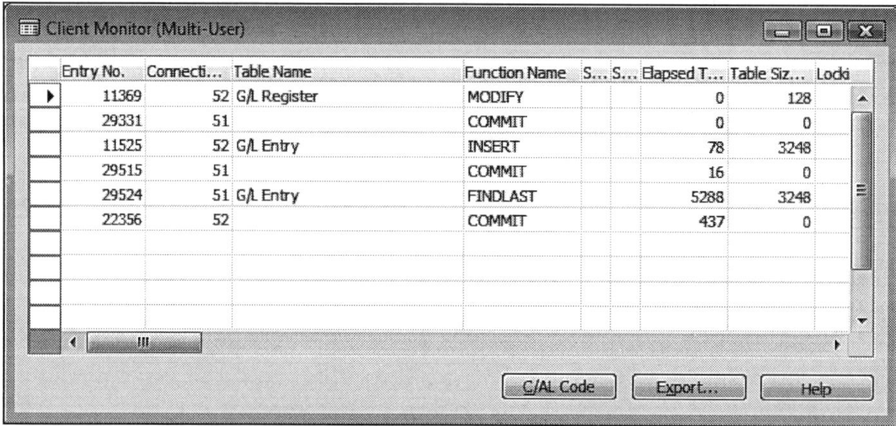

This form will first analyze the information in the Client Monitor table to detect any locking situations. If operations belonging to different transactions were accessing the same objects at the same time, potential locking has occurred, and the transaction is marked as potentially blocked. After this process is over, the form displays the potentially blocking operations in all transactions.

Depending on the thoroughness of your tests, this table might contain too little information to call for detailed analysis using Excel, and in many situations all the information you need is already listed here. You'll mostly be interested in checking the **Elapsed Time (ms)** column to see how long transactions had to wait on other transactions to unlock the resources. If there is a huge number of potentially locking transactions, you can export the data to Excel and perform analysis in much the same way as you do it for single-client monitoring.

Avoid using Client Monitor in a live environment, especially if you switched on the advanced flags for SQL Server monitoring. Client Monitor can significantly slow down the code execution, increasing lock times for other clients, thus causing even more performance and concurrency problems. For any performance troubleshooting you should use a copy of the production database, preferably on separate hardware, so that none of your tests interferes with normal operations.

Detecting deadlocks

To prevent transactions from getting deadlocked, you can use the **Locking Order Rules** feature of Client Monitor helper objects. This requires some manual setup.

Start form **150029 Locking Order Rules**:

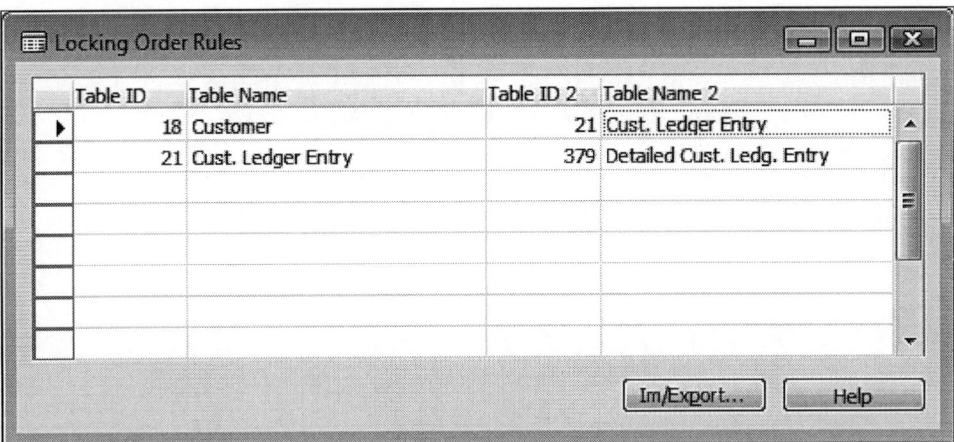

This form contains list of locking order conditions represented as table pairs. **Table ID** has higher locking order than **Table ID 2**, which means that any table specified in **Table ID** cannot be legally locked if the table specified in **Table ID 2** has already been locked in the same transaction.

In this example, it means that we can't lock table **Cust. Ledger Entry** if table **Detailed Cust. Ledger Entry** has already been locked in the same transaction, or that we can't lock table **Customer** if table **Cust. Ledger Entry** has already been locked in the same transaction.

> The system checks for locking rules violations by inspecting every locking operation and every consecutive locking operation after the inspected one within the same transaction. Then it checks if there are any locking rules where **Table ID 2** equals any of the consecutive operation's **Table ID** and **Table ID** equals the inspected operation's **Table ID**. If such a rule is found, the inspected transaction is marked as violating the locking rules.
>
> To support this decision algorithm, after you set up the locking rules, the system inserts any necessary entries (such as `Table ID=18; Table ID 2=379` in our last example). These system-created entries exist as physical entries in table **150025 Locking Rule**, but are not visible to the user in form **150029 Locking Order Rules**.

When you have specified all the locking rules you want to check your code against, start Client Monitor and execute the operations you suspect of violating these rules. This can be done in single-user mode, because the system merely checks the locking order within single transactions, and doesn't need to compare anything with the transactions executed at other machines.

After execution of these operations, stop Client Monitor and start form **150027 Transactions (Locking Rules)**. This form will list all transactions that occurred while the Client Monitor was running, and will clearly mark those transactions that violated the locking rules by placing a check mark into the **Locking Rule Violations** column.

This is what it looks like:

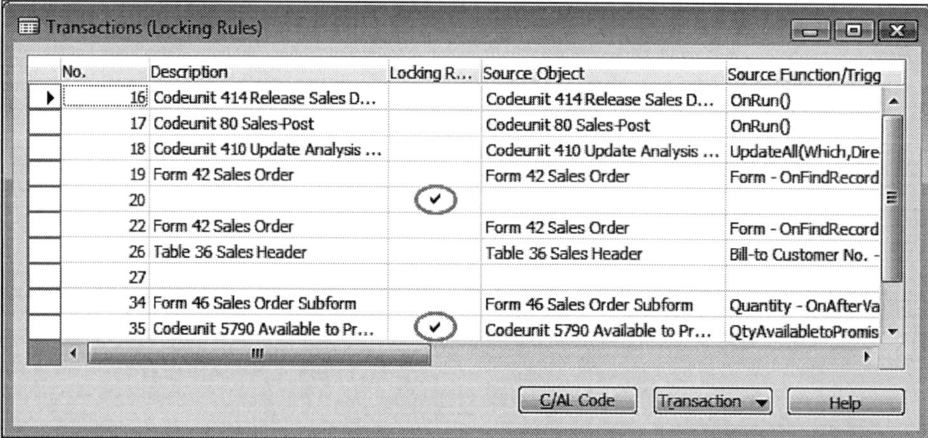

To see which rules were violated for these transactions, you can click the **Transaction** button, and choose **Locking Rules Violations** from the pop-up menu. You'll see all of the locks that were placed in violation to rules you specified earlier. In our example, we got the following violations:

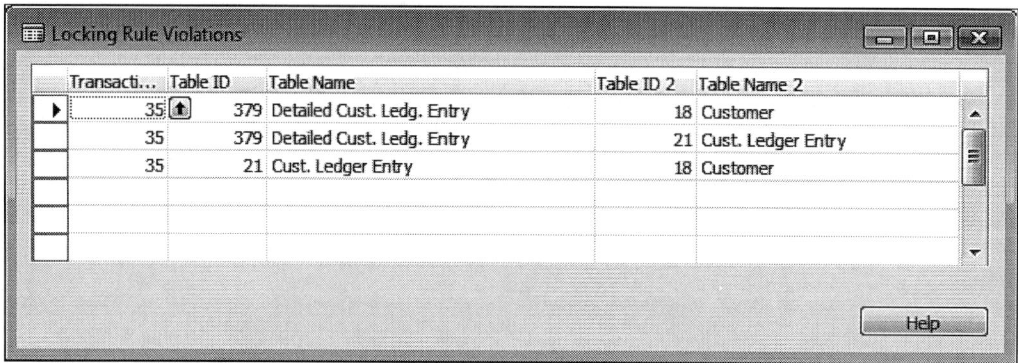

Obviously, each of the three rules we specified earlier was cold-bloodedly violated by **Transaction No. 35**.

To get to the heart of the problem, you need to check which objects have caused incorrect locking order. To do so, go back to form **150027 Transactions (Locking Rules)**, select the transaction that violated the locking rules, click on the **Transaction** menu button, and choose **Locking Order**. This will open the **Transaction Locking Order** form:

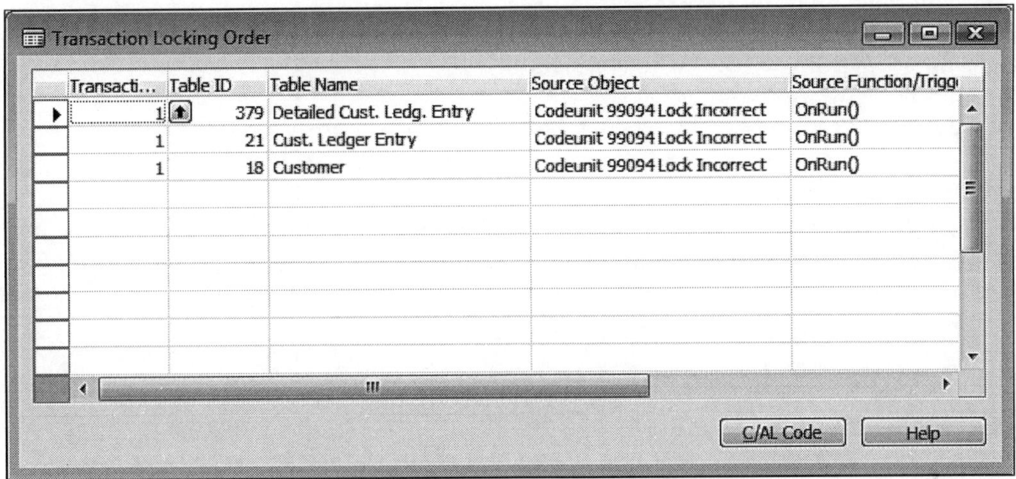

In the example above, we can easily confirm that all of the violations occurred within a single object (**Codeunit 99094**), and a single function (**OnRun**). This is all the info we need to go and restructure the C/AL code in this object to make it adhere to the rules we defined.

While it might happen that no deadlocks occur even if there is an occasional locking rules violation, deadlocks are as unpredictable as they are annoying, and it is better to address them before you release any code into the production environment. The last thing you need is users frustrated over a cancelled transaction due to a reason no less cryptic to them than cuneiform tablets.

Combining Code Coverage and Client Monitor

The Client Monitor and Code Coverage tools can work hand in hand to provide even more useful info than either of them is capable of providing if used alone. If you start Code Coverage simultaneously with Client Monitor, all the C/AL code that ever got executed as part of monitored operations will be accessible through C/AL buttons in the majority of Client Monitor helper objects.

When used together, these two tools slow down the execution considerably, which can distort the reported **Elapsed Time (ms)** of analyzed operations. Any performance analysis using PivotTables in Excel over statistics collected with both Client Monitor and Code Coverage tools running might be unreliable, so use these tools together only when absolutely necessary.

After you have detected which operations cause performance or locking issues, and you suspect that the problem lies in C/AL code, you can double up these two tools to locate the exact place in the C/AL code that causes your headaches.

Start the Client Monitor and Code Coverage tools in any order, execute the operations that are causing trouble, and finally stop both of the tools. Start form **150020 Client Monitor** and locate the operation that caused the trouble. Click the **C/AL Code** button to invoke the **Code Overview** form. The form will display only the code for the object involved in the selected operation, and will position the cursor on the exact source line where the selected database operation was initiated.

How about the RoleTailored client?

It's a pity that the RoleTailored client didn't come with a built-in tool for troubleshooting performance. The Code Coverage and Client Monitor tools can be used exclusively with the Classic client. Troubleshooting the RoleTailored interface, at least with the first release of Microsoft Dynamics NAV 2009, is next to impossible, with the only troubleshooting tools being the built-in system utilities—and these can be used to detect primarily hardware or operating system issues. So, with the RoleTailored client, you are primarily on your own.

This is not such a big problem, because properly transformed pages will run almost the same client code anyway, and transactions that cause most locking issues can be successfully debugged using the Classic client.

Other tools

When the tools we described are not enough, or a problem clearly lies outside the realm of C/AL code or business logic, we must reach for other tools. We are not going to describe how to use each of them—we are merely providing you a list of the tools that are already available to you as parts of the operating system or SQL Server. If you want to learn more about them, consult the documentation or help files.

Let's make the inventory of the arsenal, just to give you an idea what to use in which situations.

Event Viewer

Previous versions of Microsoft Dynamics NAV didn't use much of the event logging technology of Microsoft Windows. The only component able to log its events in the Windows Event Log was Application Server. Things have changed for the better.

With Microsoft Dynamics NAV 2009, the application log in the Event Viewer abounds in Microsoft Dynamics NAV events, explaining all sorts of Service Tier and RoleTailored client events, including information, warnings, and errors. Sometimes when you have a critical application condition that doesn't bubble up all the way to the user interface, don't forget to take a peek at the Event Viewer; it might be able to tell you quite a lot about why things aren't the way you'd like them to be.

SQL Server Profiler

This versatile troubleshooting tool can give you more answers than you will likely ever have questions to ask. It attaches to a running SQL Server process, and allows you to subscribe to any number of available events, while enabling you to filter the results on the fly.

SQL Server Profiler is extremely useful, and not only can you use it by itself to find out what's going on deep in the database engine, you can combine it with Database Engine Tuning Advisor, another utility from the SQL Server stack, which can analyze the trace results produced by the Profiler to suggest changes in index structures to achieve optimal database performance.

Performance Monitor

This standard Windows administrative tool is a weapon of choice of many system administrators, and can be used to detect hardware and operating system-related issues. It works by attaching to system counters—the system components' metrics, such as operation speeds, availability and consumption of various resources, or frequencies of certain occurrences.

Typically, you will use Performance Monitor to detect hardware-related bottlenecks, such as slow disks, clogged network interfaces, slow processors, low memory issues, and similar problems.

The most useful information is obtained from Performance Monitor when various counters are used together, so combining counters such as Memory, Physical Disk, and Network Interface can give you the more comprehensive information.

Finally, you can log the history of counter values into a log file or directly into a database, which allows you even more thorough analysis using external tools, such as Excel PivotTables.

Dynamics management views and functions

A lot of useful information about the health and status of SQL Server can be returned using dynamics management views and functions. They give information about virtually every aspect of SQL Server, but for troubleshooting and analyzing issues with Microsoft Dynamics NAV, the most useful categories are those pertaining to query execution, database status, indexes, I/O operations, and transactions.

You can best harness the power of dynamic management views in two ways:

- Prepare a set of administrative T-SQL scripts for analyzing specific aspects, such as the state of indexes or query execution, and then use these scripts when you want to perform the analysis.
- Create a set of views over which you create linked tables in Microsoft Dynamics NAV. You can then use these views from the Microsoft Dynamics NAV application itself. You can take this to a completely new level by developing an administrator Role Center for the RoleTailored client, and include all these views as pages or charts there.

> Dynamics management views and functions are internal, version-specific system views and functions, which means that they can change with no previous announcement in any of the future releases or service packs.

Task manager

Before frowning upon the usability of this ubiquitous Windows applet, be assured that it can help you in quickly determining the most common issues with memory, processor, or network interfaces. It doesn't provide as detailed insight into the heartbeat of the system as Performance Monitor, but what it gives can be classified as *just enough* in most cases. Not to mention that it is both more user-friendly, and more readily understood by average users.

Planning ahead

As an old saying goes, prevention is better than cure. The majority of the issues we have learned how to mitigate here can be prevented with as much effort, or even less. If you plan for performance and scalability from the very beginning of the project, you will most likely make any design decisions with performance and scalability goals clearly present in your mind. If you thought you could add these two later, the troubleshooting hassle you went through when you first had to deal with performance or scalability issues in a live system when all the code has been written, probably demonstrated vividly how false this belief is.

Luckily, planning for performance and scalability is much easier than it might seem at the first glance. It primarily consists of proper hardware sizing, simple coding choices, and common sense with database design decisions.

Hardware Guide

Nowadays hardware is a commodity, but companies are reluctant to give up on their previous hardware investments, so many of them will seek to retain as much of their existing hardware infrastructure as possible after the deployment of Microsoft Dynamics NAV. This decision might not be bad at all, but don't let the spur of the moment make it for you—before deciding whether to keep a vintage server or to replace an old switch, it might be worthwhile to consult the Hardware Guide.

The Hardware Guide is an official document published by Microsoft, and updated regularly for the latest versions of Microsoft Dynamics NAV, which specifies the guidelines for selecting adequate hardware architecture for your solution. It addresses questions such as number of processor cores, system memory, operating system and SQL Server version, disk layout, and many more.

After you confirm that existing hardware infrastructure can be retained, or has to be upgraded, a good idea is to make your hardware choices a part of your design specification, and have your customer sign it off.

The Hardware Guide is just a rule-of-thumb document, and it provides a good starting point. In certain situations, such as high concurrency deployments or multi-purpose SQL Servers, you might conduct a Sure Step Architecture Assessment engagement with your customer, or even engage a third-party expert to validate your sizing.

Indexes

If there was a double-edged sword in any relational database, it would be indexes. They provide performance benefits on one front, while cutting down on performance on another. The formula for a perfect balance is a sort of a database design philosopher's stone.

Luckily, there are many tools that can make up for bad design decisions, but rather than having your users notify you of bad performance, try focusing on delivering premium performance up front. There are many rules you can follow when designing your indexes. Keep in mind that many indexes easily gobble up memory and processor and disk time at write operations, while giving little performance benefits in return at read operations, so think twice before adding an SQL-maintained index to a table.

During an implementation project, include index optimization as a post-go-live task in the Operation phase activity plan. Several months after go-live, when there is enough information in the database to reflect the real use of the system, conduct this optimization using SQL Server Profiler or similar tools.

Database Resource Kit

By now you should be more than familiar with this valuable resource, abundant in useful tools and documentation that can help you squeeze the last atom of performance out of your Microsoft Dynamics NAV installation. Make sure to apply any of the knowledge and best practice gems explained in the documentation, especially in the Design section.

Although the latest version of Database Resource Kit at the time of publishing of this book was aimed at Microsoft Dynamics NAV **5.0**, the majority of advice applies equally well on Microsoft Dynamics NAV 2009, so don't hesitate to apply it in absence of an updated version.

Technical Presales Advisory Group (TPAG)

Microsoft Dynamics partners have access to many valuable online resources, one of them being the Microsoft Dynamics Technical Presales Advisory Group portal and TPAG Evaluation tool. The goal of TPAG as a group is to provide technical assistance with properly sizing and scaling implementation projects, while the online

Evaluation tool can help you estimate the risk of proceeding with certain deployment scales before you start the project. This can save you from probably futile attempts at achieving 5,000 concurrent users of the manufacturing module.

If the online form doesn't give you all the information you need to decide whether to proceed with a risky implementation, you can get in direct touch with TPAG, and obtain further services, such as architecture assessments.

Access the TPAG portal at the following URL:
`https://mbs.microsoft.com/partnersource/support/tpag`

Getting help

Troubleshooting is a very wide topic, and we didn't try to cover all of it here. Tools that you mastered while reading these pages will help you get through the majority of problems you'll encounter during your implementation projects. Planning activities you do should be aimed at avoiding as many of these as possible. Still, sometimes you'll find yourself in a new situation, where existing knowledge might not help too much.

There are many resources available to help you troubleshooting and optimizing your implementations. Some of them are available in the documentation provided on the product DVD, but the majority of them are available online.

In case nothing we have covered so far helps, you can reach for the online resources we list next.

Microsoft Dynamics NAV tools overview

This page lists various external tools you can use to help your Microsoft Dynamics NAV implementation efforts. It doesn't contain only performance troubleshooting tools, but many other tools you might need as well. Access the page at the following URL:

`https://mbs.microsoft.com/partnersource/newsevents/news/newsgeneral/dynnavtoolsoverview.htm`

SQL Server Technical Kit for Microsoft Dynamics NAV

This kit is a comprehensive set of documentation and tools for optimizing Microsoft Dynamics NAV on SQL Server. As with Microsoft Dynamics NAV 2009 you don't have another option, you'll want to add this invaluable resource to your arsenal. The Database Resource Kit is included in this kit as well.

Access the SQL Server Technical Kit here:

`https://mbs.microsoft.com/partnersource/downloads/supplements/mdnavsqltechkit.htm`

Summary

Troubleshooting various issues is a usual part of the process of bringing Microsoft Dynamics NAV to life. If your project included programming, odds are you will need to debug your custom code; if you extended the data model with new tables, relations, and indexes, you might need to tweak the performance; if your solution plays at the limits of attainable scalability of Microsoft Dynamics NAV, you might try to locate the pieces of code that could be improved to cut down the transaction wait time.

Microsoft Dynamics NAV comes with a selection of tools, either built-in or downloadable, which help you detecting, tracking, and eliminating most issues, and learning how to effectively use the tools and leveraging their potential should be as important as learning the technical and functional capabilities of Microsoft Dynamics NAV itself.

Remember, on every project you'll have to spend at least some time troubleshooting the problems; this is perfectly normal, but don't approach the experience as a mere nuisance. Never miss a chance to learn from your troubleshooting experiences—any lessons you learn from them you can successfully apply in the future, during designing, developing, deploying, and operating your next Microsoft Dynamics NAV solution.

10
Sample Application

There are two ways of constructing a software design. One is to make it so simple that there are obviously no deficiencies, and the other way is to make it so complicated that there are no obvious deficiencies. The first method is far more difficult. – C.A.R. Hoare.

You've learnt about the standard application and what you can do to configure it, how you can extend it, and how you can distort it beyond all recognition (although hopefully you've also learned to keep your modifications consistent with the standard product). You have also picked up enough good advice, tips, and tricks to have the confidence to tackle almost any project. Now it's time to put this all into practice and build something. We're going to try and cover as much as we can from NAV and the surrounding stack in one simple solution, starting with the requirements gathering and ending with a delivered prototype and solution design. This is not a full implementation of NAV, just a little bit of everything we've covered and some new things thrown in. The purpose of this chapter is not to teach you how to program but how to get to a point where we could begin programming.

In this chapter we'll cover:

- How to gather requirements using interviews
- How to propose a solution design using use-case modeling
- How to design and build a prototype for a multi-tiered application for Dynamics NAV 2009

Sample code download

The source code for all components can be downloaded from the usual places on the PACKT web site as well as `www.teachmenav.com`. It may be that you find this application useful and can extend and adapt it in some of your implementations. To make a fully working solution, there is definitely more to do than what we are covering in this chapter, but remember, it's not about the destination but the journey. Fasten your seatbelts and ensure that your tray-tables and seat-backs are in an upright position, we're about to take off.

Gathering requirements

There are a number of techniques for gathering requirements: interviews, shadowing users, and workshops. For me a combination of shadowing key-users in their daily tasks and follow-up interviews works best. In this sample application, we're going to look at how this process can work from the beginning by looking at how some the interviews for a new implementation may have gone. If you're an old-hand with implementing ERP and requirements gathering, you may want to skip ahead to our section on *Functional requirements* or *Use-case modeling*.

> *Seek First to Understand, Then to be Understood. – Steven Covey (The Seven Habits of Highly Effective People).*

In his excellent book *The Seven Habits of Highly Effective People*, Steven Covey warns that giving advice before having empathetically understood a person and their situation is likely to result in rejection of that advice. This principle should be applied to implementing software solutions, and it is for that reason that I like interviewing as a requirements gathering technique. Not only are you able to get a first-hand understanding of the people and the problems they face, you are also letting them know that you have listened to them before proposing your solution. This will definitely help in the long run by increasing end user buy-in and ultimately the success of the project.

If you've never had to gather requirements from users before, read on to learn how one of our interviews may have gone.

The scenario

Peter Parker is a Dynamics NAV implementation consultant working on the NAV implementation project at Arch N.M.E. Inc. He is an old-hand NAV consultant and developer with over ten years' experience. Peter loves the new architecture of Dynamics NAV 2009 and he can't wait to design and build something that really breaks the mold.

Peter works for 'Intelligent Business and ERP Ltd.' (IBERP): a Microsoft Gold Partner specializing in Dynamics NAV, .NET, SharePoint, and Mobile Solutions. He understands the components of the Dynamics NAV 2009 technology stack but also knows that he cannot be an expert in all of the products; instead, he has learnt the capabilities of the products, how they fit together, and who to call upon when things get tricky.

The training sessions have been completed and the Arch NME super users are very happy with the product. We join Peter in his interview with John Jameson, the CFO, discussing some of the requirements raised in the training sessions.

"The accounts handling capabilities of NAV look good," comments John, the CFO. "I'm sure we're not going to have any issues but there is something I've been thinking about that I want to raise. My biggest headaches happen at month end when I need to get all of the expenses approved and posted so they can be included in the payroll and the customer invoice runs. It takes such a lot of effort and we make no money; we just pass the expenses on to our customers, where we can. I really like your suggestion of posting the expenses in NAV as purchase invoices against an employee-related vendor account but I want something to make the whole process faster, more agile."

"Tell me more about the business processes," says Peter as he starts to take notes. "Walk me though some typical scenarios from start to finish."

"I think the problem comes when the guys leave things to the last minute," grumbles John. "It makes me howl sometimes, they go out to visit our customers and often we don't see them for days on end. They bring their receipts in at the last minute and spend most of the day keying the details into our expense claim spreadsheet. They're pretty smart guys, they have to be in this business, but we must get a dozen calls every month asking which code to enter the expenses against, I guess the spreadsheet could be made a bit easier to follow. Next, the spreadsheets are printed and sent to the office administrator who checks that all of the receipts are attached and all of the details are complete. At the same time the spreadsheet is e-mailed to the office manager for approval."

"What happens then?"

"The office manager checks the spreadsheet for personal expenses that should not be claimed," adds John as he holds up a sample printed expense sheet. "He is also checking that all recoverable expenses are marked with a customer and project code. If there are any problems, the office manager sorts it out with the staff member directly, and a revised spreadsheet is fed back to the office manager, who reattaches the receipts and resends the electronic copy to the office manager."

Peter realizes this is getting a bit complicated and decides to start drawing on the whiteboard. Sometimes it helps people visualize a process when they can see a diagram. As Peter draws each step in the process he repeats what he has learned back to John. Peter knows that trying to explain a process to the domain experts is a good way of ensuring that his understanding is correct.

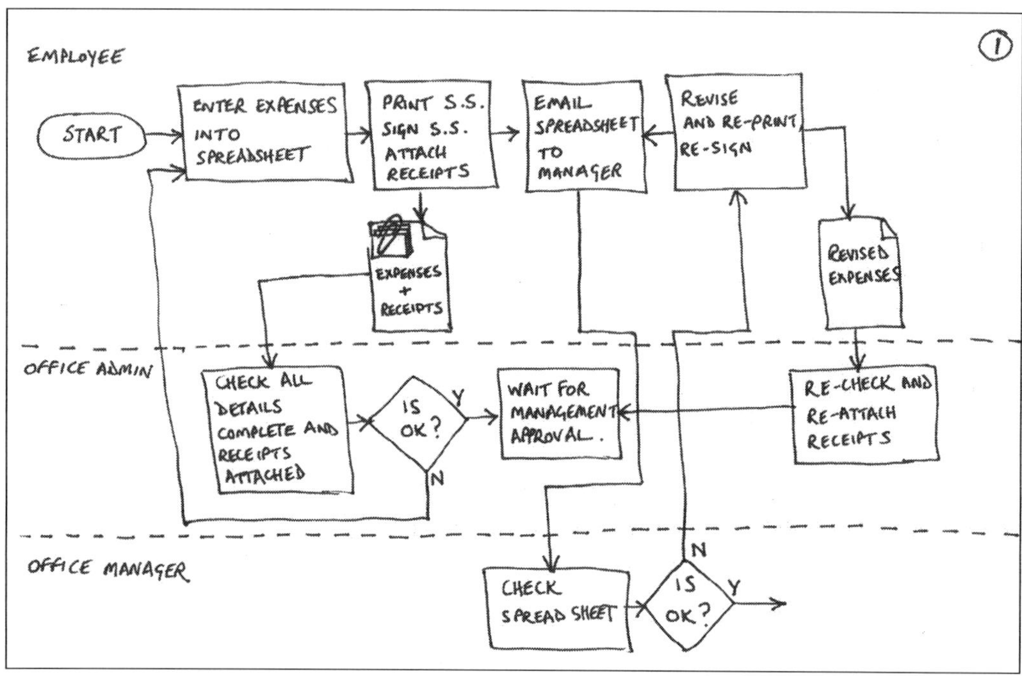

Peter uses a swim-lane flow diagram as he finds this most useful when trying to capture a process that spans multiple departments.

"OK," says Peter as he makes the finishing touches to the diagram, "let's say that the expenses are correct. What next?"

"Well, the office manager emails the spreadsheet to the accounts department and copies the office administrator, who'll find the paper copy with the receipts and send it to the accounts department via snail mail. Sharon's the one who handles them from then on."

"What's Sharon's role?"

"She's the accounts payable/accounts receivable clerk."

"So," prompts Peter, "Sharon receives the envelope of expenses and then what does she do?"

"Well we don't wait for the envelope to arrive, that just gets filed," continues John. "Instead Sharon works from the electronic approved spreadsheets she receives." John draws the new boxes and arrows on the whiteboard as he carries on talking.

"She creates a sales invoice for each customer and enters each expense as an invoice line with the date, project, employee, and description. Obviously she also enters the amount and the account code. Once all expenses are entered, she updates the sales invoices and puts the printouts to one side so they can go out with the project-related billing."

"OK, so how does the employee get paid?"

"Well at the moment', says John, "the expense amount gets entered directly into the payroll system, but I like your idea of using a purchase invoice. That way we'll have some way of tracking the details back and doing some reporting. If we use purchase invoices, can we get the expenses into the payroll without having to key them in again?"

"We'll certainly try and reduce the amount of re-keying of data wherever possible," says Peter diplomatically.

"I just want to make the whole process faster," grumbles John. "It costs us a fortune in admin time and is of no real value-add to the business. Plus we end up having to pay the employees for the expense at the end of the month but it takes us another month to get the money out of our customers, sometimes longer."

"I've been thinking," says Peter, "what if we could get the employees to key their expenses directly into NAV?"

"That would help, I guess," says John suspiciously, "but won't that mean we need more licenses?"

"Not necessarily," says Peter, "NAV 2009 has a pretty smart architecture that means it's much easier to glue systems together. People can use the applications that suit them, such as Excel, Outlook, or Windows Mobile, and let the computers do the work. Named users still need a license but it's much cheaper than a full license."

"I like the sound of that," says John with a grin. "Hey, our sales guys all have Windows Mobile phones; it would be great if they could enter the expenses at the time they get them. It would have to be simple though, you know what salesmen are like. If it works for them, we could give all the staff a smart phone. I've been looking for an excuse to upgrade the phones and this could really work."

"Well let me have a think about the solution," says Peter not wanting to commit to something he'll regret later. "I'll get back to you with some ideas. I just want to confirm I have your requirements at a high level: you want to reduce the effort in processing expenses and invoice your customers faster to improve your cash flow; you want to reduce the number of times data gets keyed to reduce mistakes; and you want to reduce the uncertainty about which account to select, whether VAT is applicable, and so on."

"That's right," says John with a nod.

"You also want to have some sort of reporting over your expense transactions," continues Peter. "You want to make the approvals process easier, and you want the expenses to go directly through to the payroll system."

"Correct," says John. "If we can reduce the time spent by the office managers, that would be a bonus. I'm not sure I want those guys going into the accounts system though."

"Don't worry," says Peter, "we can use SharePoint for the approvals process. NAV 2009 makes it easy for users that don't need to use the full application to get access to some of the features through a web browser."

"Sounds good," grins John. "When can I see more?"

"Well, we're still going through the analysis phase, gathering requirements. Once we've finished that we'll talk about how much customizations are likely to cost and whether you want us to design a solution. If you decide to go ahead with these requirements after we've given you a ball-park, we'll work with you to prototype a solution so you can get a feel for it as we go along."

"Can I get a copy of the spreadsheet that is filled in for expenses?" Asks Peter as he takes a photo of the whiteboard drawing.

"Sure," says John, "why do you want that?"

"If I have the spreadsheet, I can ensure that any solution I design has exactly the same information that you are currently capturing. If you could send it via email, that would be best. That way I will have an electronic copy for our records."

Peter returns to the office and decides the first thing to do is to write down the functional requirements he has captured while they are still fresh in his mind. He knows he wants to use several components to the solution, so he is probably going to need to talk to one of the architecture guys or produce some kind of architecture diagram as well.

Functional requirements

Now that we have our interview notes, hand-drawn flow diagram, and sample spreadsheet, we can think about creating our functional requirements document. Did you notice in the interview that most of Peter's comments were questions that were getting John to keep talking? Even if you think you know how to provide a solution to a problem, or that you understand the problem fully, you need to resist the temptation to explain how you would solve the customer's problems until you have heard all they have to say. The functional requirements document is our chance to show the customer that we have been listening, and get them to confirm that we have understood their issues correctly.

Process flow diagram

Peter gets his colleague Liz to redraw his whiteboard diagrams using Visio so that it can be included in his functional specification.

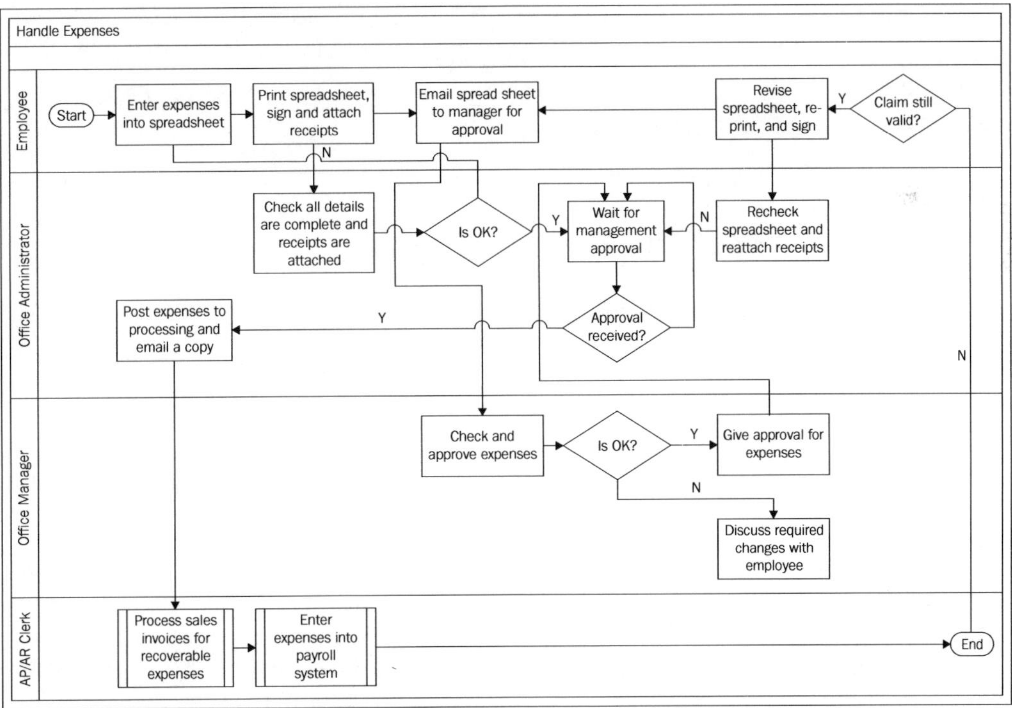

The process flow diagram is useful for getting an overview of what is happening currently, but this is not really going to help Peter to confirm a design for the new system. For this he will need to use something else, and this is where use-case modeling can help clearly define the requirements.

Use-case modeling

Peter wants to use use-case modeling for his functional requirements. He likes use-case modeling because it is basically telling a story about how people use the system. A use-case description provides a narrative of how a system and its actors collaborate to achieve a specific goal. The purpose of the use-case is to describe functionality and therefore does not contain details of the user interface; this is to allow the reader to focus on the functionality and not the presentation.

Learn about use-case modeling

For an excellent introduction to use-case modeling, you should read *Use-case Modeling* by Kurt Bittner and Ian Spence.

A set of use-cases are not complete without some supporting information. Peter knows that he will also need to produce a glossary of terms and a conceptual model. The glossary of terms allows the flow of the use-case to remain clutter-free by referring to the terms that are defined in greater detail elsewhere. This allows the reader to focus on the interaction with the system and not get bogged down in the specifics of the data being entered. The conceptual model shows the relationships between the different terms within the system. The model can be used to capture the business rules that are being enforced.

Peter's first step is to identify the actors within the system. This is not the same as the roles you will find in the Dynamics Customer Model (which tend to be based around the role a person plays within the organization) but is instead based upon the role played when interacting with the system. In use-case modeling terminology, these are called **actors**.

Defining the actors

An actor defines a role that a user can play when interacting with the system. The reason we use the term *actor* and not *user* is that an actor can either be an individual or another system.

From the notes Peter has collected and the swim-lane diagram, it is pretty clear there are initially four actors: the employee, the office administrator, the office manager, and the AP/AR clerk. But hold on—these are job descriptions not actors. An actor is defined by the interaction they have with the system. It may be that the parts of several actors are actually played by a single person so don't get actors confused with people. For each actor, Peter will provide a description of the role they play within the system so that it can be included in the glossary of terms for the system.

Expense Claimant

The expense claimant is the employee that has incurred the expense and wants to recoup the money from the company.

Expense Checker

The expense checker ensures that the expense claimant has provided all the necessary information, and that the receipts are also provided. The expense checker will ensure that only valid expenses get forwarded for posting.

Expense Approver

The expense approver will ensure that all expenses are recoverable (they can be billed on to customers) or in the case of non-recoverable expenses that there is a valid reason for incurring the expense.

Expense Processor

The expense processor will ensure that the sales invoices are raised for the expenses that can be recovered and post the necessary transactions through to the payroll and General Ledger to ensure that the employee gets paid and the expense is correctly accounted for.

Defining the use-cases

Peter needs to identify the use-cases in the system. He needs to do some design work now because he is no longer simply documenting what he has found out, he is documenting how the proposed system will work.

Peter knows that in his new system design he would like to capture as much information as possible at the time of incurring the expense. He wants to make it easy for people to use but needs to cater for those with smart phones and those without. One of the requirements was to reduce re-keying of data and, in order to do that, Peter wants the data entered by the expense claimant to be directly entered in to Dynamics NAV.

In order to come up with this initial high-level design, Peter will simply use his imagination. He will imagine being a person playing the role of the actor and think about the goals of the actor and how the actor will interact with the system to achieve those goals. Initially he comes up with seven use-cases. He writes down the headings and a short description of the use-case.

Mobile Capture of Expense

This use-case is specifically for the smart phone users. It will cover how an expense claimant with a smart phone will capture details of their expense while out of the office.

Prompt Expense Claimant to Submit Expenses

Peter thinks it would be useful if the system could somehow tell the expense claimant that they need to submit their expenses on the right date, and possibly even give them the form they need to print if they have previously captured their expenses using a mobile device.

Edit and Submit Expenses

The users without smart phones (or maybe those that have them but didn't bother to use them) will need to get their expenses into the system somehow. Even if the expenses have been captured already, the expense claimant will need to print out their expense claim form, attach their receipts, and submit their expenses for checking.

Check Expenses

Someone needs to ensure that for every expense claimed, there is a valid receipt. They also need to check that the amount on the expense claim matches the amount on the receipt, and that if the VAT number is on the receipt, then the VAT component is split out on the expense and it correctly matches the receipt.

Approve Expenses

This use-case is all about whether the office manager thinks the employee should be paid for the expense. It could also be that the expense should be charged on to the customer but the employee has not marked the customer and project on the expense. It is often an opportunity for the office manager to discuss correct procedures with the employee (such as claiming their expenses in a timely manner and allocating the expense to the correct Expense Code).

Post Expenses

When everything has been checked and agreed, the expenses need to be posted in the system (meaning that they turn into posted financial transactions). This will create a liability for the company showing an amount of money due to the employee. The expense may be on-charged to a customer and as such posting the expense will also create a sales invoice.

Pay Expense Claimant

As far as the employee is concerned, this is more than likely the most important part of the system. They probably don't care how it is done, just as long as they get their money back.

Use-case diagram

Peter creates a use-case diagram for his system. The diagram shows the actors and use-cases which we have already listed so this is not new information. However, the diagram also shows the association between the actors and the use-cases. This is useful information that is not represented elsewhere. The arrow indicates the direction of the interaction which tells us how the interaction was started, did the actor initiate the interaction or did the system?

I'm not a huge fan of use-case diagrams but they do serve a purpose by providing a very fast overview of what the system does. It doesn't take long to draw, so it can be useful to include it with your functional requirements. Remember the purpose is to confirm your understanding of the requirements with the domain experts (and not to give the diagram to a developer and say 'here, build this!')

The diagram shows the actors (stick men), the use-cases (ovals), and how they interact (lines with an arrow indicating who initiated the interaction, the actor or the system).

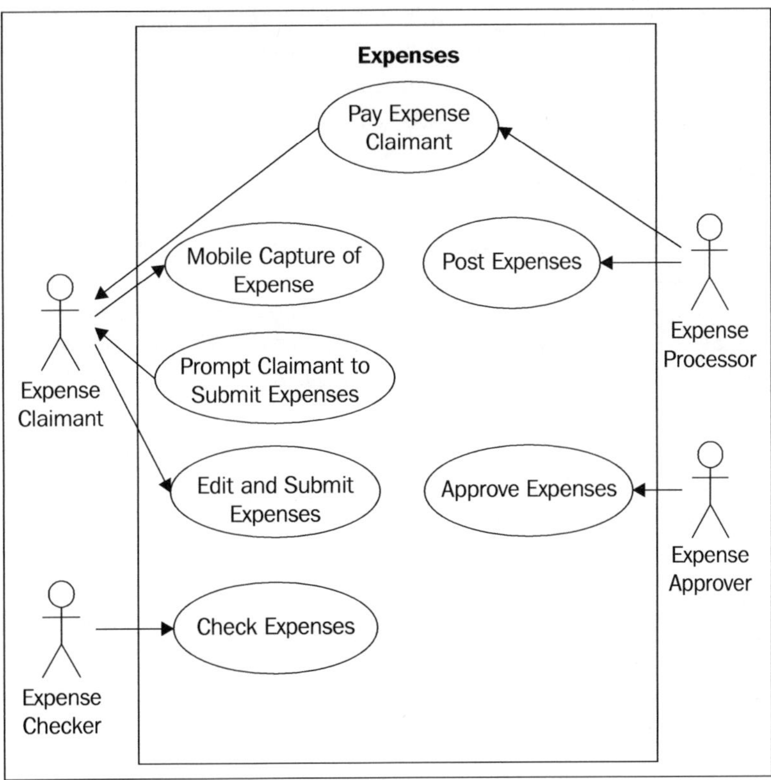

Now it's probably a good idea to get confirmation that the solution design is on the right tracks. Peter will need to flesh out these use-cases with the users, so he arranges another meeting with John and asks him to invite some other members of the team that are involved in the expense handling processes. Peter suggests that a user of a smart phone, an office administrator, an office manager, and Sharon (the AP/AR Clerk) would be a good starting point.

Before going to the meeting, Peter wants to take a look at the existing spreadsheet used for capturing expenses and make sure he has understood all of the data required. He will start to compile his glossary of terms and domain model that will be used to support the use-case descriptions.

Glossary of terms

The glossary of terms is where the real action happens. This is where you list all of the entities and attributes that will eventually form your data model. Terms are the foundations upon which any system is built. You may think that it is not necessary to define terms, particularly if they seem obvious, but I have found that it is the seemingly obvious terms that can cause the most trouble. For more details on terms and how to identify and define them, you can consider reading *Principles of the Business Rule Approach* (Addison-Wesley Information Technology Series) by Ronald G. Ross. Let's carry on with our scenario and see what Peter does next.

Peter starts by examining the expenses spreadsheet he received from John and listing each of the pieces of information it contains as a term. Peter uses his experience to group each of the individual fields on the spreadsheet into entities. He also knows that each line on the spreadsheet is going to be a repeating entity and each field that does not appear on each line is going to be on a related entity. He decides to call each line an expense and the entire sheet an expense claim.

Expense

An expense is a single claim for reimbursement of money spent by an employee. Each expense relates to either a single receipt for goods or services purchased, a travel claim for a distance traveled in the employee's own vehicle, or a per diem allowance. An expense can be either recoverable (in which case a customer must be specified) or non-recoverable. An expense has the following attributes:

Attribute	Description	Type
Employee ID	This is the employee ID of the employee that incurred the expense.	Must be a valid existing employee.
Date of Receipt	Date on the physical receipt. For a per diem or car journey, this is the date of travel or per diem date.	Date.

Attribute	Description	Type
Is Recoverable	If true then a customer must also be specified.	True or False.
Customer	Customer account that a recoverable expense will be invoiced to.	Must be a valid existing customer.
Description	Notes explaining the reason for the expense. This is intended to help match the expense to the receipt.	Text.
Distance	Number of Miles or KM.	Decimal.
Rate	For distance traveled type expense claims, this is the cents per unit that the claim is made at.	Decimal.
Is VAT Receipt	For overseas expenses, this will be false.	True or False.
Expense Code	Indicates what the money was spent on.	Select from a list of: • Assets • Cleaning Products • Computer Operations • Computer Software • Consumables/ Stationery • Couriers • Entertainment • Training • Travel & Taxis.
Department	For non-recoverable expenses, this is the department that will incur the expense.	Must be a valid existing department.
Date of Claim	This date links the expense to the expense claim.	A link to an expense claim that the expense was submitted on.
Checked By	Employee that checked the expense and verified that the receipted amount matched the claimed amount.	Must be a valid existing employee that is allowed to check expenses for the office the employee belongs to.
Amount	For goods or service expense, this is the total amount including VAT.	Decimal.

Expense claim

Expenses are not claimed one at a time but are collected together and submitted in a batch of expenses. An expense claim is a collection of expenses with some additional attributes:

Attribute	Description	Type
Employee ID	Identifies the employee that this expense claim is for. The employee is the claimant.	Text.
Date of Claim	Date that the expense claim was submitted.	Date.
Approved By	Employee that approved the expense claim.	Must be a valid existing employee that is allowed to approve expenses for the employee.

Employee

Employees can submit expense claims. Other employees can check expense claims to verify that the receipt matches the claimed amount and can approve the expense.

Attribute	Description	Type
Employee ID	A unique identifier for the employee.	Text.
Office	The office that the employee belongs to. This is used to determine which employees can check expenses from this employee.	Must be a valid existing office.
Is Checker For	A link to the office that the employee is a checker for.	Must be a valid existing office.
Approver	A link to the employee that has been granted the permission to approve expense claims submitted by the employee.	Must be a valid existing employee.

Office

An office is a grouping of employees. Each employee belongs to an office and only certain employees are designated as being checkers for any given employee.

Department

The department is the financial dimension that will receive the charge for the expense being claimed when the claim is not recoverable.

Customer

The customer is the trading partner that procures goods or services from the company. The customer will be invoiced for the expenses if they are marked as being recoverable.

The domain model

When dealing with a complex system (such as Dynamics NAV) it is difficult to produce a comprehensive domain model. Dynamics NAV has hundreds of entities and relationships and you don't want to really have to start modeling something that already exists. Instead, you should focus on what you are trying to achieve: you are trying to get the domain experts (the users) to understand what it is that you are proposing, and you are trying to get confirmation that your understanding of their domain is correct. Don't get too carried away with this diagram, it is simply a means of agreeing a common understanding of the problem domain. Once that understanding is reached, you can throw the diagram away.

For the domain model, Peter decides to use **Object-Role Modeling (ORM)** to describe the objects and the roles they play. He could have used **Entity-Relationship Modeling**, but he likes the way ORM allows more than one object to be joined in a single relationship (something he finds hard to express using ER diagrams). He also likes the fact that by not using ER diagrams, he is not going to get the users asking for an ER diagram of the entire system; he wants to simply focus on the problem at hand.

What is ORM?

It is not the intention of this book to teach you about Object-Role Modeling; however, it would be a bit unfair to introduce the diagrams without giving some explanation of the syntax used. Here's a description of the common symbols.

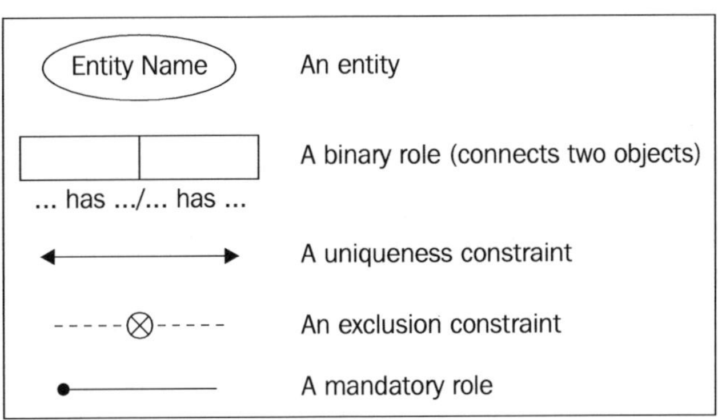

If you want to learn more about ORM, take a look at Dr. Terry Halpin's web site at `http://www.orm.net`. It's all fairly intuitive apart from the way uniqueness constraints are applied. The arrow-line is drawn above the box that represents the column that must be unique in any set of sample data—we'll explain this with an example later on.

Employee
office
... works in .../... has ...
Customer
Department
... is claimed by .../... makes ...
... is to be changed to ... /... Gets changed from ...
... Is to be changed to ... /... Gets changed from ...
Expense Claim
Expense
... has ... / ... is on ...
Is for goods or services
Is a claim for travel
Is a daily allowance

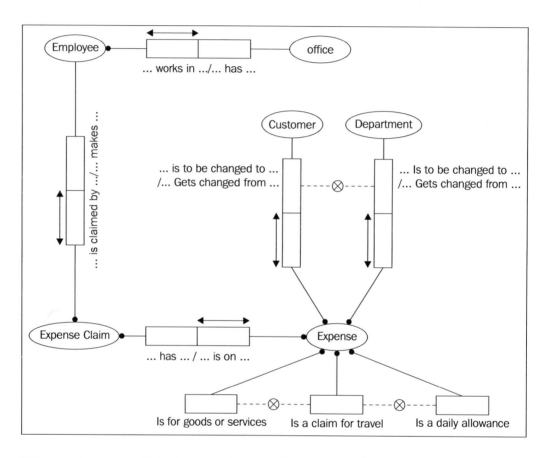

Peter sends a copy of his glossary of terms, domain model, use-case diagram, and list of actors to John so that he can distribute the team ready for the use-case design workshop. He tells John not to worry too much about what they mean as he will be explaining the meaning at the start of the workshop.

Use-case workshop

The purpose of this section is to help you understand how you could typically go about running a use-case workshop. Unless you get the opportunity to shadow someone delivering one of these workshops, it's difficult to understand how it should be conducted, so let's see what Peter, our consultant, does.

Explaining the ORM diagram

Peter starts by introducing himself to the team and explaining the purpose of the workshop: to come up with a design for a system that will improve the expense claim and approval process and help to realize the goals stated by John (to reduce the effort in processing expenses, to invoice customers faster to improve cash flow, and to reduce mistakes by providing an intuitive solution that minimizes the number of times data gets keyed). He then goes on to explain the design documents he has sent through starting with the ORM diagram.

"OK," starts Peter, "let's take a look at the ORM diagram. The purpose of this diagram is to help you to quickly see if my understanding of the problem is correct. This diagram simply offers a quick way of notating the relationships between the entities we have identified."

"The diagram doesn't cover every entity in the system but just those that help us to understand the significant parts of the problem. If we look at each of the entities in the diagram, we can write a sentence that explains the relationship the entity has to another entity. Let's start with the **Employee** and work our way out."

Peter points to the first role in the diagram between the **Employee** and the **Office** objects and explains, "An employee works in an office."

"Nice one Peter," says John, the CFO, with a grin. "Now I know why we pay you the big bucks."

The group chuckles and Peter smiles and carries on, knowing that it's soon going to get a lot more complicated.

"The dot next to the **Employee** is a mandatory constraint," explains Peter, "meaning that an employee must work in an office. The double-arrowed line above the **works in** part of the relationship between **Employee** and **Office** means that for any set of sample data that expresses the 'Employee works in Office' relationship, the 'Employee' part of the relationship must be unique."

Peter draws a table on the whiteboard with the names of the employees in the room (including himself) and the offices that they work in.

Employee ID	Office ID
John	New York City
Sharon	New York City
Phineas	Buffalo
Peter	Forest Hills
Otto	Rochester

"As you can see from this list, the Office ID is not unique," he says. "We have two entries in the list with the same Office ID of New York City. The Employee ID in the list, however, is unique. It is not possible for an employee to work in more than one office."

"Hey that's not true!" says Phineas, the engineer from Buffalo. "I spend half my week working in Buffalo and the other half in Lackawanna."

"Hmmm," says Peter. "Maybe 'works in' isn't the correct relationship here. What I'm trying to say is that an employee can only have a single office for checking their expenses and approving them."

"Ahh, OK," says Phineas, "so maybe 'is linked to for administration purposes' is a better description of the relationship."

"Hold on Phineas," says John. "Let's keep it as 'works in' because it's easier to write, but it's good to know the distinction. Carry on Peter."

"OK. The only other thing you need to know about in the diagram is the circle with the cross inside it," says Peter. "This is an exclusion constraint."

"My ex-wife has one of those against me," says Otto, an overweight salesman with huge grin on his face.

"Err, right," says Peter. "In this case, the exclusion is used to indicate that two or more roles are mutually exclusive meaning that a single entity can only fulfill one role or the other."

"For example, we can see that a single expense can be charged to a customer or charged to a department but not both," continues Peter. "We can also see that an expense can be for goods or services, a claim for travel, or a daily allowance. The little dot against the expense side of these roles means that each expense must be fulfilling one of these roles. The exclusion constraint means that expense can only fulfill one of these roles."

"If we were to write all of these relationships out long-hand, it would result in ten different rules for us to read. There is no way to look at this list and get a quick understanding of the number of entities involved or the complexity of their relationships."

Peter puts the following list of rules on the projector to illustrate his point:

An employee must work in one (and only one) office.
An office may have zero, one or many employees.
An employee makes zero, one or many expense claims.
An expense claim must be made by one (and only one) employee.
An expense claim must have one (at least one) or many expenses on it.
An expense must be on one (and only one) expense claim.
An expense must be either charged to a customer or must be charged to a department.
A customer may be charged for an expense only once.
A department may be charged for an expense only once.
An expense must be for either goods or services or a claim for travel or a daily allowance.

Mobile expense claim

With the ORM diagram explained, everyone is on the same page, it's time for Peter to move on to fleshing out the use-cases.

"Now it's time to take a look at each of our use-cases, and describe them in more detail," he says. "The description of the use-case will mainly take the form of a story of interaction between the user, or actor, and the system."

"The description is independent of user interface design, which allows us to focus on the interaction itself and not get bogged down with how screens should look. Let's start with the Mobile Capture of Expense use-case and see if we can define the goals for the use-case."

"That's easy," says Otto with a grin. "My goal is to get my money back from 'the Wolfman' over there before I need to pay my credit card bill."

Otto gestures to John, who makes a growling noise. Peter can see this Otto character is going to be trouble.

"That's a good starting point," says Peter. "We're going to include details of the actors and the goals in a brief description at the start of the use-case description."

Peter writes the following description for everyone to see on the projector.

Use-case: Mobile Capture of Expense

This use-case describes how the Expense Claimant actor can use the system to capture the information relating to a single expense so that it may be later submitted as part of an expense claim.

"If we take a look at our glossary of terms for the Expense entity, we can see the details we need to capture. We can also see from the ORM diagram that the expense will require different information to be captured depending on the type of expense and whether it is recoverable or not. It might make sense to capture this information first so that we only need to get the relevant information later on. We're going to write a series of steps with numbers against them to describe the interaction."

Peter writes the following steps on the whiteboard:

1. The use-case begins when the Expense Claimant selects an option to create a new Expense.
2. The system displays a screen with the Date of Receipt set to today's date and with the ability to specify the Expense Type (Goods or Services, Travel Distance, or Daily Allowance) and whether the expense can be recovered from a customer or not.

"Now it's getting interesting," says Peter. "Depending on what we select, different things will happen. In use-case modeling, these different paths are called 'flows'. We are currently describing the 'basic flow', which is the most common path through the interaction. For the sake of argument, we'll say that our basic flow is for Goods or Services that are going to be recovered from a customer account. Let's carry on with the next steps in our use-case."

Peter writes the next step on the board.

3. The Expense Claimant selects the option for Goods or Services and indicates that the expense can be recovered from a customer.

"O-oh! Big problem-o," says Otto excitedly. "Sometimes I simply don't know if an expense is going to be recoverable or not. How can I say yes or no if I don't know, do I just pick one and hope it's right?"

"OK," says Peter, making a mental note to not invite Otto to the next session, "so maybe we need the facility to say we don't know when we're capturing the expense. This is a good chance for us to start capturing our alternate flows. One of our alternate flows at this point may be called 'Recoverability Unknown'. Who is likely to know if the expense is recoverable or not?"

"Well," says John, "that's going to depend on the terms of the service contract. The customer service manager will be able to answer that but they'll need to know the customer that the expense relates to and some details of why the expense was incurred."

"Great," says Peter. "We can maybe build some workflow into our solution so the customer service manager gets to specify if the expense is recoverable or not." Peter notices that Otto is still not happy.

"What if the customer service manager doesn't provide the missing details before pay day?" asks Otto. "Will that mean I don't get my money?"

"Not necessarily," says Peter. "We can get the workflow to split at that point so that getting paid is not dependent on knowing whether the expense is recoverable or not. It seems from this discussion that we are missing a use-case and an actor. We need to add **Customer Service Manager** to the use-case diagram and also a **Prompt for Expense Recovery Details** use-case."

Peter adds the new use-case and actor to the diagram.

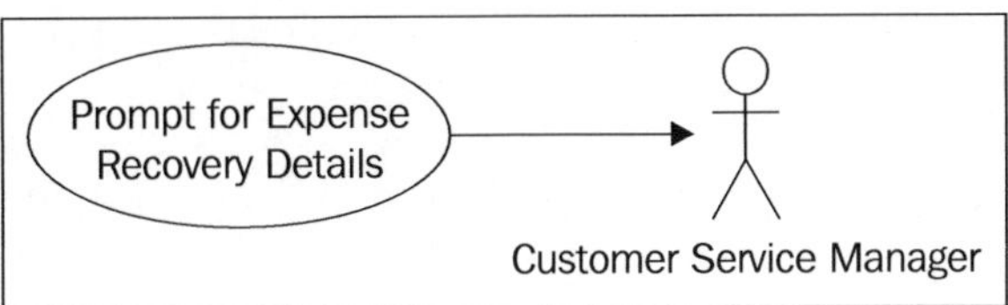

"OK, let's carry on with the next step," says Peter as he writes the next step on the board.

4. The system displays a screen prompting the Expense Claimant to specify a Description of the expense, whether this is a VAT receipt, the Expense Code, The Total Amount including VAT, and the VAT amount stated on the receipt and the Customer that this expense will be charged to.

"There's quite a lot of details in that step, and it's starting to detract from understanding the flow," says Peter. "We can move details like that out to the glossary of terms by defining a new term for our glossary."

"Let's create a new term called 'Recoverable Goods or Service Expense Details' and add that to the glossary."

Peter puts up the new definition and revises the step in the use-case.

Recoverable Goods or Service Expense Details

Information to be collecting in relation to an expense that is for goods or services and can be recovered from a customer: description of the expense, whether the receipt is a VAT receipt, the expense code, the total amount including VAT, and the VAT amount stated on the receipt and the Customer that this expense will be charged to.

5. The system displays a screen prompting the Recoverable Goods or Service Expense Details to be entered.
6. The Expense Claimant enters the Recoverable Goods or Service Expense Details.

"When we use a term that is further defined in the glossary in the use-case description," explains Peter, "we tend to use a dotted-underline to indicate that there are more details elsewhere."

"This keeps all of the information but means it's easier to read the use-case without having too much information. Now we can enter the last couple of steps for the basic flow."

7. The system stores the expense details so that it can be included on the next expense claim.
8. The use-case ends.

"Now we've completed our basic flow," says Peter, "let's try and list out our alternate flows. This is as simple as walking through our use-case step-by-step and trying to identify when something different could happen. Let's look at our complete use-case description as we have it so far and write the different scenarios under each step."

Peter writes the alternate flows beneath the steps where they exist.

1. The use-case begins when the Expense Claimant selects an option to create a new Expense.
2. The system displays a screen with the Date of Receipt set to today's date and with the ability to specify the Expense Type (Goods or Services, Travel Distance, or Daily Allowance) and whether the expense can be recovered from a customer or not.

3. The Expense Claimant selects the option for Goods or Services and indicates that the expense can be recovered from a customer:
    - Possibly the expense is for a different date.
    - The expense could be for travel.
    - The expense could be for a daily allowance.
    - The expense could be non-recoverable.
    - We may not know if the expense is recoverable or not.
4. The system displays a screen prompting the **Recoverable Goods or Service Expense Details** to be entered.
5. The Expense Claimant enters the Recoverable Goods or Service Expense Details.
6. The system stores the expense details so that it can be included on the next expense claim.
7. The use-case ends.
    - Maybe we want to carry on capturing other expenses.

"You can see that most of the alternate flows happen at step 3 when the expense could be for different expense types and could be non-recoverable or unknown," says Peter. "We need some way of hooking our alternate flows into our main flows. We could just make reference to the step number, but that causes problems when we need to add a step into our basic flow as it means we need to update all of our alternate flows to use the new step numbers."

"We're going to use labels in the use-case description. A label is just some text in curly brackets. We can use the labels as though they are headings to help us find our way through the use-case. It should be possible to read the use-case at a high level by just reading the headings. Our first task is to put the headings into the use-case and then list the alternate flows at the end of the basic flow with details of where they cut in and under which circumstances they occur."

Peter extends the use-case description to include the labels.

Basic flow

{Begin Mobile Capture of Expense}

1. The use-case begins when the Expense Claimant selects an option to create a new Expense.

{Capture Expense Form Displayed}

2. The system displays a screen with the Date of Receipt set to today's date and with the ability to specify the Expense Type (Goods or Services, Travel Distance, or Daily Allowance) and whether the expense can be recovered from a customer or not.
   {Today's Date Used for Expense}

{Select Recoverable Goods or Service Expense}

3. The Expense Claimant selects the option for Goods or Services and indicates that the expense can be recovered from a customer.
4. The system displays a screen prompting the Recoverable Goods or Service Expense Details to be entered.

{Enter Recoverable Goods or Service Expense Details}

5. The Expense Claimant enters the Recoverable Goods or Service Expense Details.

{Save Expense Details}

6. The system stores the expense details so that it can be included on the next expense claim.

{Use-case Ends}

7. The use-case ends.

Peter then goes on to list the alternate flows by making reference to the labels at which they occur.

Alternate flows

Different expense date

At **{Today's Date Used for Expense}** if the expense claim is for a different date.

Non-recoverable goods or service expense claim

At **{Select Recoverable Goods or Service Expense}** if the expense claim is for goods or services but is non recoverable.

Possibly recoverable goods or service expense claim

At **{Select Recoverable Goods or Service Expense}** if the expense claim is for goods or services but it is not clear as to whether the expense is recoverable or not.

Recoverable travel expense claim

At **{Select Recoverable Goods or Service Expense}** if the expense claim is for travel and is recoverable.

Non-recoverable travel expense claim

At **{Select Recoverable Goods or Service Expense}** if the expense claim is for travel and is non-recoverable.

Possibly recoverable expense claim

At **{Select Recoverable Goods or Service Expense}** if the expense claim is for travel but it is not clear as to whether the expense is recoverable or not.

Recoverable daily allowance expense claim

At **{Select Recoverable Goods or Service Expense}** if the expense claim is for a daily allowance and is recoverable.

Non-recoverable daily allowance expense claim

At **{Select Recoverable Goods or Service Expense}** if the expense claim is for a daily allowance but is non recoverable.

Possibly recoverable daily allowance expense claim

At **{Select Recoverable Goods or Service Expense}** if the expense claim is for a daily allowance but it is not clear as to whether the expense is recoverable or not.

Multiple expense claims

At **{Save Expense Details}** if the Expense Claimant wishes to enter another expense.

Peter notices that everyone seems happy with the technique he is explaining and decides to go on a little further.

"Normally we don't bother going any deeper into defining the alternate flows at this stage in the workshop," explains Peter. "While I have you all here together, it's more beneficial to go through the other use-cases in the system and define the goals, the basic flow, and the alternates."

"If there's time at the end of the session, we can always go back and start to flesh out the alternate flows, but for now, since this is your first introduction to use-cases, I'm going to define the first couple of alternate flows in full."

Peter writes the alternate flow descriptions on the board.

Alternate flows

Different expense date

At **{Today's Date Used for Expense}** if the expense claim is for a different date:

1. The Expense Claimant enters the date for the expense.
2. Resume the basic flow at **{Select Recoverable Goods or Service Expense}**.

Non-recoverable goods or service expense claim

At **{Select Recoverable Goods or Service Expense}** if the expense claim is for goods or services but is non recoverable:

1. The Expense Claimant selects the option for Goods or Services and indicates that the expense cannot be recovered from a Customer.
2. The system displays a screen prompting the **Non-recoverable Goods or Service Expense Details** to be entered.
3. The Expense Claimant enters the Non-recoverable Goods or Service Expense Details.
4. Resume the basic flow at **{Save Expense Details}**.

Everyone seems pretty happy with the use-case modeling technique and Peter continues with the group to define all of the use-cases and alternate flows.

Finishing the functional requirements

You should now have a pretty good idea of how use-case modeling can help you to capture and describe functional requirements. Our scenario continues with more of the same; each of the use-cases is defined in the workshop and the alternate flows are provided and where possible expanded.

Peter, our consultant, returns to the office with his newly found information and completes the functional specification which includes:

- An overview of the problem and the high-level requirements.
- A use-case diagram and a set of use-cases.
- Supplementary requirements. These are business rules that do not form part of the process flow but are important parts of the functional specification.
- A glossary of terms.
- A domain model.

We've seen enough sample dialogue to learn how the process works, and we're going to leave it there and focus on the design and build. In our story, Peter would walk through the completed use-cases and functional specification with the end user design team in order to get final approval that his understanding of the problem is correct and to iron out any kinks. For more details of the functional specification, take a look at our *Sample Application Functional Specification* download on `www.teachmenav.com`. Since we are no longer looking at requirements gathering, workshop facilitation and interview techniques, it's time to say goodbye to Peter Parker and move on to the solution design. So long Peter, until next time.

Architectural design

Now we have a completed functional specification that tells us how the users want the actors to interact with the system to achieve their goals. We have walked through the complete functional specification with the users to ensure we are on the right track and have validated the use-cases. There are no user interfaces defined, and this is a good thing since it means that we are focusing on the functionality and not how the screens look.

Once we have acceptance for the functional specification, it's time to start thinking about how we will be realizing the actual implementation of the functionality to meet these requirements. We can build our system pretty much any way we please, so what are the things that are going to constrain our design?

Supplementary requirements

Our users have stated that they want to be able to capture expenses using a mobile device, more specifically the Windows Mobile devices that are currently in use by the sales reps. This requirement is definitely going to be a constraint for our design. If we don't design something that meets this requirement, we won't have succeeded (or at least we will have failed to meet some of the requirements).

Existing architecture and framework

Let's face it, when we're designing solutions for NAV, we're not working from a clean palette. We're designing a system that will work with Dynamics NAV, and we need to be able to use the tools at hand. This means that it is highly likely that some of our components will use pages in the RoleTailored client as the primary interface. We know we also want to use the SharePoint client to allow office managers to approve expenses, but is this really the best tool for the job? Let's go back to our requirements for that part of the solution:

- We want our users to be able to perform the approval without needing to use the RoleTailored client.
- We need a thin client so that there is no need to install software and the process can run over our wide area network.
- The system must be easy to use since it will be used infrequently.
- We need to easily deploy and maintain the application by using a self-updating or web-based front-end.

There are a number of possibilities that will allow a system that meets these requirements, so how do we decide what to build?

Budget

When you have a number of possibilities that will meet the requirements for an architectural design, the final decision often comes down to how much the various options are going to cost. If we take our expenses approval process as an example, here are just some of the possibilities that will meet our requirements:

- SharePoint client deployed NAV page
- Custom built SharePoint web part
- Custom built ASP.NET web application
- A Silverlight application
- XAML Browser Application (XBAP)
- Clickonce deployed client application (Smart client)
- Office Business Application (OBA)
- InfoPath forms
- MOSS and InfoPath Forms Services

What a lot of options? The cost of building each of these options is going to depend on the skills your organization has, the resources you have available, and whether you have done it before. It may be that you have just written a Silverlight-based Invoice Approval application that uses NAV Business Web Services to communicate with the back-end. If this is the case, this option may seem quite attractive. In reality, most partners are not going to be able to create half of these applications, and there is one standout option that requires no extra development: the SharePoint client deployed NAV page solution.

What's cool?

There may be strategic reasons for picking a particular approach. It could be that you want to show off your technology muscles or promote a new technology. Maybe your client has specifically asked for a particular technology, such as XBAP, because they think it's cool and want to be associated with cool technology. Personally I think that a solution that meets the requirements that will not have any additional development costs is pretty cool, and I think the majority of customers are going to agree.

The key to a successful implementation is to involve the stakeholders at every step. Don't pick a technology because you want to build it, talk to the customer and find out what they want. By all means, offer your expert advice and guidance but ensure that the customer is fully behind the solution architecture.

And the winner is...

Our architecture for this solution is clear as the client has pretty much stipulated in the supplementary requirements that we will be using three main components:

- Dynamics Mobile for mobile capture of expenses
- Dynamics NAV RoleTailored client for all functions
- SharePoint client for expense approval and possibly expense submission

Build—technical design

It's nearly time to build something. We have defined our architecture and functional requirements and this has all been approved with the customer. Very often no one is going to be 100% sure that they are happy with a design until they see something real. It's a good idea to start some prototyping work as soon as the fundamentals have been agreed. This way, we can get something in front of the customer quickly and verify that we are on the right tracks.

Our starting point will be to build the tables, forms, and pages in the NAV client and get this in front of the customer. We may even be able to create the SharePoint environment so that we can demonstrate the web-based functionality, but since this is going to be a mirror of our RoleTailored experience, this will come later.

If we go through our functional specification document (focusing on the glossary of terms and the conceptual model), we can see that our design will require many new tables. Depending on the size of your team, you may need to produce a technical design document that will include details of what needs to be created so you can give it to a junior developer. Even if you are going to do the development yourself, it's always a good idea to write down what you are going to do before you actually do it. Remember, the sooner you start programming the later you'll finish.

When your system is all up and running and someone asks you for a list of the objects in the solution, it would be nice to have the technical design document you prepared at hand, rather than needing to go through your development and document what you have done. Another advantage of preparing the field names in a Word document is that you can ensure that you don't build spelling mistakes into your code. The developer can cut and paste a spell-checked field name into the field name property.

Tables

Looking at the conceptual model, there are a number of entities that we can use from the standard NAV application: Employee, Customer, and Department. We also have some new entities to create: Office, Expense Claim, and Expense. It is likely that there may be some supporting tables, such as setup tables, required, and these will come to light as we go through a more technical design process.

Mapping the entities to the standard system can be difficult sometimes. The Customer entity maps nicely to the standard Customer table, but for the Employee entity we need to decide how to handle this. We could use the User Setup table (used by document approvals), Salesperson/Purchaser (since the initial roll out will be sales reps, this is a good candidate), Employee (this would seem a perfect match as the table is used to represent the entity we want to work with. However, the Employee table is part of the Human Resources functionality and our client is not going to be using that part of the system).

For me, creating the data model specification is where the design really comes to life. There is no option but to think about how tables are going to relate and how information is going to flow. It only really becomes clear at this point that an Expense can exist without an Expense Claim and the user will manage a list of unclaimed expenses for their own user name. When they submit their expenses (and they can put expenses on hold so they do not get submitted), they can specify the Date of the Claim which will create the Expense Claim with a status of Submitted.

Expense (new table)

Create a new table called Expense. Primary Key = Expense ID. Other Key = Claimed By, Expense Claim Date, On Hold with SumIndexField: Amount (LCY).

Field Name	Data Type (Length)	Description
Expense ID	Integer	Unique identifier of an Expense. Set AutoIncrement property to Yes.
Date of Receipt	Date	
Is Recoverable	Option	No, Yes, Not Known.
Customer No.	Code (20)	`TableRelation=Customer."No."`.
Description	Text (250)	
Distance UOM	Code (10)	`TableRelation="Unit of Measure".Code`.
Distance	Decimal	
Distance Claim Rate	Decimal	
Is VAT Receipt	Boolean	
VAT Amount (LCY)	Decimal	
Expense Code	Code (20)	Relation to the Dimension Value will depend on the setup and will be done in code.
Department Code	Code (20)	See Expense Code.
Expense Claim Date	Date	
Claimed By	Code (20)	`TableRelation="User Setup"."User ID"`
Checked By	Code (20)	`TableRelation="User Setup"."User ID"` Note that some additional validation will be required because the employee must be a checker for this claimant's office.
Amount (LCY)	Decimal	
Amount	Decimal	
Currency Code	Code (10)	`TableRelation=Currency.Code`.
Currency Factor	Decimal	
Posting Date	Date	
Document No.	Code (20)	
On Hold	Boolean	
Type	Option	<blank>, Goods or Services, Travel Distance, Daily Allowance.
Daily Allowance Start Date	Date	
Daily Allowance End Date	Date	
Daily Allowance Quantity	Integer	

Expense Claim (new table)

Create a new table called Expense Claim. Primary Key = Claimed By, Date. Other Key=Office, Claimed By, Status.

Field Name	Data Type (Length)	Description
Claimed By	Code (20)	`TableRelation="User Setup". "User ID"`
Date	Date	
Status	Option	Submitted, Approved, Posted
Approved By	Code (20)	`"User Setup"."User ID" WHERE (Is Expense Approver=CONST(Yes))`
Office	Code (10)	`Location.Code WHERE (Is Expense Claim Office=CONST(Yes))`
Total Claimed Amount (LCY)	Decimal	`Flowfield, CalcFormula= Sum(Expense."Amount (LCY)" WHERE (Expense Claim Date=FIELD(Date),Claimed By=FIELD(Claimed By),On Hold=CONST(No)))`

Location (Modify Table ID=14)

We are going to use the Location table to represent our office because it already has a lot of the attributes we need. When we are working with the Expenses system, it would be good to filter out the locations that are used for inventory, so we will have a new field on the Location table called Expense Claim Office.

Add the following fields to the Location table.

Field Name	Data Type (Length)	Description
Is Expense Claim Office	Boolean	
Expense Approver	Code (20)	`TableRelation="User Setup"."User ID" Where "Is Approver"=Yes`

Department (no changes to existing table)

For our list of departments, we are going to use the standard Dimension Value table. We will need a setup table to allow us to specify which Dimension Code we are using as our department.

Customer (no changes to existing table)

For our customers that we can charge expenses on to, we are going to use the standard Customer table. Whenever we use part of the standard system in our solution design, we need to check that the end-customer has bought the granules that this table belongs to. This will come up in testing (as long as you are using the customer's license when doing the testing) but it will be better to catch this early so you can decide whether the end-customer needs to buy the missing granule or whether the design should be changed to use another table or create a new table.

Expense Claim Setup (new table)

Create a new table called Expense Claim Setup. Primary Key = Primary Key.

Field Name	Data Type (Length)	Description
Primary Key	Code (10)	
Distance UOM	Code (10)	TableRelation="Unit of Measure".Code
Currency Rate Discrepancy %	Decimal	
Daily Allowance Rate	Decimal	

User Setup (modify Table ID=91)

We are going to use the User Setup table to represent our employee. We need to add some attributes to specify the office an employee belongs to and which office the employee is a checker for. We also want to specify the approver (another record on the User Setup table) that can approve the expenses for this employee.

Add the following fields to the User Setup table.

Field Name	Data Type (Length)	Description
Expense Claim Office	Code (10)	`TableRelation=Location.Code WHERE (Is Expense Claim Office=CONST(Yes))`
Checker for Office	Code (10)	`TableRelation=Location.Code WHERE (Is Expense Claim Office=CONST(Yes))`
Is Expense Approver	Boolean	
Expense Vendor No.	Code (20)	`TableRelation=Vendor."No."`

Points raised by table design

Creating the table definitions has raised some additional design points that did not come up in the functional specification. For example on the Expense table, adding some of the attributes to the table tells us that we should really have the default Distance UOM specified on an Expense Claim Setup table so that new expense records automatically specify the unit of measure that the distance is in.

Also, our Expense Code is going to be a look-up to a dimension value code. Again our Expense Claim Setup table should allow us to specify which Dimension Code is going to be used to represent this attribute. This highlights a possible enhancement for our solution design. It would be nice for the user to be able to specify any number of dimensions against our expense, and it would also be good for the system configuration to allow us to say which dimensions must be specified on an expense before it can be claimed. Things like this will come up frequently throughout the technical design and you must consider a number of options before going ahead and doing it.

- Extra features cost money. Who is going to pay?
- Does the customer want the extra features?
- Is this development going to be used as a standard add-on?

The first point is the one that most developers forget. It may be that this is a small change at the programming side but this will add cost all through the lifecycle. Extra features means more for people to learn, more things to test, more things that can go wrong. Just adding something in because it will make the system better is known as 'Developer Gold-Plating'—be aware of this and stop yourself from doing it (by all means raise it with the team/customer, but don't ever just go ahead and add the feature).

It may be that what seems like an improvement to you is not wanted by the customer. They may be quite adamant that, in this case, they prefer to have a single field called Expense Code on their Expense entity rather than having a field called Shortcut Dimension Code 1.

On some occasions, you may take the additional cost of the improvement because you can see the potential for this development being a standard add-on. If the customer is really insistent they do not want the new feature, you need to find a way of incorporating what the customer wants and the extra functionality into your add-on. In this particular example, the resolution would be to have the ability to link any number of dimensions to the expense (probably using the document dimensions table) and to also have an Expense Code field on the expense that will automatically populate the correct dimension.

New items to consider

Here is a list of all the design points that came up when defining the tables. Some of these items have been incorporated to our design and others have been put on hold (possibly for a later release).

- Expense Claim Setup requires Default Distance UOM field.
- Unlimited Dimensions on Expense.
- Expenses can be in a foreign currency— the claimant can specify the exchange rate.
- There should be a tolerance of allowed difference between the standard system exchange rate and the one being claimed for foreign currency expenses.
- Should a checker be able to check expenses for more than one office? If so we will need a new table for the relationship because this would become a many-to-many relationship.
- It would be nice to show posted expenses when navigating and to be able to navigate from the expense to other ledger entries.
- When submitting expenses on an expense claim it would be nice to hold certain expenses so that they are not included on the claim (possibly they are being disputed or the receipt cannot be found).
- Should there be some way of delegating approval responsibilities to another user? This would mean that instead of there being an approver for an office, we can specify multiple approvers with a date range.

Additional development tasks

Going through the table designs has made things a lot clearer and it is now possible to define a number of additional programming tasks, such as creating the forms needed to maintain the data in the tables we have just created. I find it easier to create the tables at the same time as writing the specification for them; then, as I go through the tables, I make a note of the additional programming activities that will need to be done in order to make everything hang together. You may find it easier to complete the table designs and then go through the definitions and consider what actions or additional programming will be required for each of the fields on the table. Then consider how the records will get into the system, how they will be maintained, and what functions the user will be table to run against the records.

At the very least, you should be trying to estimate the time needed to carry out these tasks. For some of the tasks, you may decide to actually do the work (creating a form or page using the Wizard is pretty easy and it will probably take longer to write down exactly how you want the form to look than to do it yourself).

Give each of your tasks a unique ID since you are going to need to allocate this work or at the very least, keep a record of what work is outstanding. Here are the tasks that came up as a result of building the table definitions and making the table modifications. The obvious place to keep track of these items is in a spreadsheet. Try to give item a title so you can easily refer to it later on.

Task ID	Description	Est. Time (h)
1	**Expense Form (List and Card)** Create Form and Page to allow users to Create, Read, Update, and Delete their own Expenses. To follow the conventions of the standard system we will have a List page that will show all of the expenses for an Employee, and when they double-click on an expense, a Card is created allowing the details to be entered.	8
2	**Expense Form Submit Function** Allow a user to submit their expenses for checking and approval. This option can be called from the Expense Form or Page. Any expenses that are not marked as On Hold will be submitted if they meet the criteria. Criteria for submission is that all mandatory fields are specified for the type (that is, amount for goods or services, distance and distance UOM for travel, quantity and from date/to date for daily allowance). Once submitted, this will prompt for the claim date and create an Expense Claim record for the Employee and Date. The items will be linked to the claim and will be non-editable. If there is an existing Expense Claim of status Submitted, the user can choose to add these expenses to that claim. See the supplementary requirements in the Functional Specification for a complete list of rules.	8
3	**Expense Claims for Approval List** This list will show all the submitted expense claims for the office that the current user is an approver for if the user is an approver. If the user is not an approver, it will show only the users own expense claims. For each claim, the list should show the Office, Claimed By, Date, and Total Claimed Value (LCY). Double clicking a claim will open the Expense Claim Approval page.	8

Task ID	Description	Est. Time (h)
4	**Expense Claim Approval Page** This page allows individual expenses to be removed from the claim (that is, rejected) and for the entire batch to be approved. A rejection comment can be attached to the expense (this will use the Note feature of NAV 2009 which is a Record Link record of type Note). Ideally, the note will be automatically allocated to the claimant.	8
5	**Post Expenses** This routine will take all approved expenses and, for each employee, create a purchase invoice and post it. We will need to have a Vendor account number linked to our Employee record.	16

Working through the use-cases

In addition to looking at the table designs in order to determine the work to do to complete the system, we can go through each of the use-cases and decide whether the specifications we have written so far will allow us to perform the activities required by the use-case. This exercise highlights the following additional programming tasks:

Task ID	Description	Est. Time (h)
6	**Build Dynamics Mobile Tasklets** Create the Dynamics Mobile tasklets to allow the expenses to be captured in the Mobile Capture of Expense. This includes setting up the architecture and getting the synchronization working.	40
7	**Expense Claim Sheet** Create the report with the expense claim details.	8
8	**Check Expenses Page** The Expense Claim approval page (Task 4) will also be used to set the Checked flag. Only the expense checker can set the checked flag.	4
9	**Prompt Claimant to Submit Expenses Workflow** This will just be a report or Codeunit that will generate an expense claim report as a PDF with all of the currently un-submitted and not held expenses on it (see task 7). The report will then be sent to the claimant using the SMTP mail features.	8

Task ID	Description	Est. Time (h)
10	**Prompt Customer Service Manager for Expense Recovery Details** Need a routine will send an email to the designated account manager for the customer in question indicating that the claimant does not know if the expense should be recovered or not. If the Customer Card does not have an Account Manager, the notification will be sent to the Expense Approver.	8
11	**Specify Account Manager Employee on Customer Card** Just a small change to allow an employee to be specified as the account manager for a customer. This will require adding a new field to the customer record and page.	2
12	**Set Recovery Details Page** A list is required for the account manager to see the expenses that have been claimed with an unknown recoverability status that has the current user as the account manager. The account manager needs to be able to specify if the expense is recoverable.	8
13	**Expense Claim Schedule** The prompting of submission for expenses and the date for the expense claim are going to be driven centrally, meaning there will be an Expense Claim Schedule table that indicates the periods that expenses can be claimed for and the dates that other activities will be triggered. There should be a Functions menu button that will contain a single option to Create Schedule.	8
14	**Expense Claim Setup** A setup card to allow the parameters to be configured for the expense claim system. Take a look at some of the other setup cards in the system for how they handle creating the record when it is first run and not allowing deletes and inserts. For a hint, take a look at the Insert Allowed, Delete Allowed properties and also at the OnOpenForm trigger.	2
15	**Create Expense Claim Schedule** This will be a non-printing report that creates the Expense Claim Schedule records based upon a date formula. This will operate in a similar manner to the report ID=93 Create Fiscal Year.	4
16	**Employee Details on User Setup** Add the new fields to the User Setup form.	1

Do you want the good news or the bad news?

Well the good news is that now we have worked through the conceptual model and the use-cases, we have a really good idea of the data model and the programming activities needed to complete our solution. The bad news is we have just estimated over 130 hours of development and that's not including any testing, documentation, training, or project management.

It's not uncommon to get to this position in a project. Some projects will be able to swallow additional costs like this and some simply won't. There's only one thing to do and that's make the best estimate you can of the remaining work (trying to include all of those other activities like testing, fixing defects, documentation, project management, training, deployment) and schedule a meeting with the customers to discuss.

It's better to go back to the customer with your news as soon as you have it, than to take an overly optimistic view. One common mistake is to look at estimates like this and, based upon nothing more than knowing the customer will not like it, trim the estimates to make a more acceptable cost. Now is a good time to remember our time, cost, scope triangle from Chapter 4—if you want to reduce the cost, you need to reduce the scope.

Build—prototype

Fortunately for this chapter, our customer has reviewed our estimates for this functionality and decided that it is acceptable. They have agreed for us to build our prototype which we have estimated to take 40 hours. The prototype is going to include:

- All tables
- NAV Classic Forms for all data entry processes with empty menus for functions on the forms,
- MenuSuite for Classic client
- Some RoleTailored pages depending on available time
- Some RoleTailored MenuSuite options depending on available time
- Some Windows Mobile tasklets depending on available time

The deliverables for the prototype will include a demonstration of the prototype to the users. For screens that have not been developed, mock-ups will be provided. Probably the most important deliverable is a more accurate estimate for the remaining work. Based upon the prototype and the costs at the end of this phase, the customer may decide that this is not for them after all. For our prototype we are going to quickly build the forms for the classic client and then use the Form Transformation tool to create our RoleTailored Client pages.

Additional tables

For the prototype, we are going to make the additional programming changes to our table definitions that came out of the review of our initial design. The table changes are listed in the following sections:

User Setup (modify Table ID=91)

We are going to use the User Setup to represent the Employee. Since we want the posting of expenses to create a Vendor Invoice, we will need a Claimant Vendor No. field on the User Setup table.

Add the following fields to the User Setup table:

Field Name	Data Type (Length)	Description
Claimant Vendor No.	Code (20)	`TableRelation= Vendor."No."`

Expense Claim Schedule (new table)

Create a new table called Expense Claim Schedule. Primary Key=Claim Date.

Field Name	Data Type (Length)	Description
Claim Date	Date	
Latest Submission Date	Date	
Approval Reminder Date	Date	

Customer (modify Table ID=18)

Modify the Customer table to add our account manager field.

Field Name	Data Type (Length)	Description
Account Manager	Code (20)	`"User Setup"."User ID"`

Time to build

By now, we have covered enough technique on form building for you to be able to build these application forms yourself. Here is a nice simple list for you to tick off when you have completed the development. If you want to see what you should have at the end of this stage, you can download the Expense Claim Tables and Forms Prototype from our book web site. Build the tables first and use the Form Designer Wizard to create the forms in this order.

Task	Name	Form ID
14	Expense Claim Setup	50000
13	Expense Claim Schedule	50001
11	Customer Card	21
16	User Setup	119
1	Expense List	50002
1	Expense Card	50003
3	Expense Claim List	50004

Once you have built the forms, it should become clear that some of the fields need to be made non-editable.

I love the Classic client

This book is about a new product, NAV 2009, with a new user interface. Personally I think the RoleTailored client looks fantastic and has customization functionality that has never been seen before in NAV. Having said that, the Classic client is an amazing rapid development environment. I managed to complete the modifications and build of the forms for the prototype in a little under an hour. I could probably have done this a lot quicker if I wasn't trying to write a book at the same time. My point is that when it comes to quickly building a prototype, you cannot beat the power of the NAV environment. If you have defined your tables correctly, creating the forms is a breeze. Let's take a look at the new forms with some dummy data keyed in.

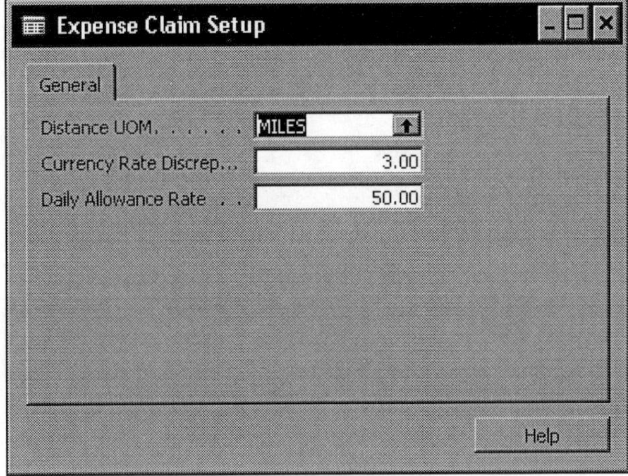

Our simple setup form contains only three fields on a single tab.

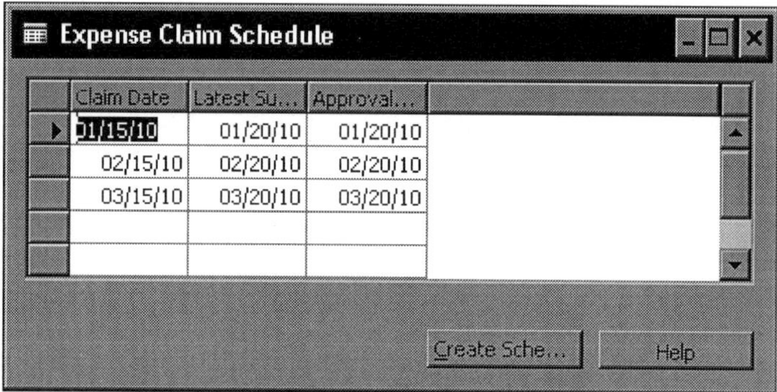

Notice that I added a **Create Schedule** button to this form. The button runs report ID=50000 which I created as a place holder for my Create Expense Schedule routine. The report has a single line of code in the `OnPreReport()` trigger as follows:

```
ERROR('TODO: Not implemented yet.');
```

This non-implemented report allows us to demonstrate the intended functionality in our prototype without needing to do too much work.

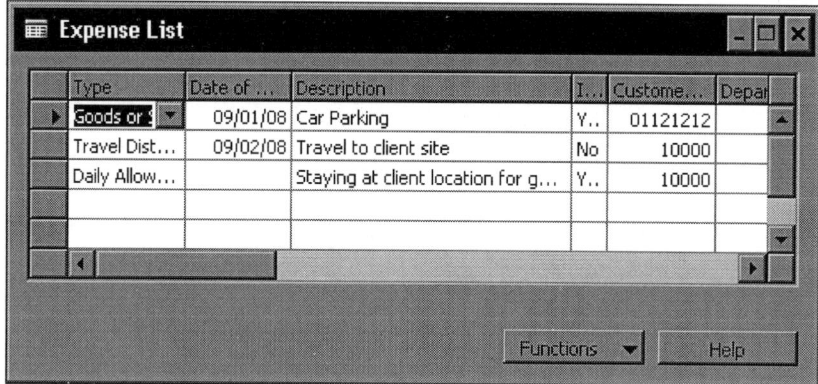

This basic list form can be used for people to key in their expenses in the Classic client or serve as the main point of enquiry and place to launch the Expense Card in the RoleTailored client. The expense list is also used by the expense checker to mark an individual expense claim as being checked. For this we could either have created a new Expense menu button with two options: **Mark as Checked**, and **Mark All as Checked**. Alternatively, we can have a **Functions** menu button with the same options. The **Expense** button will be automatically transformed into the **Related Information** group and will appear as follows in the RoleTailored client.

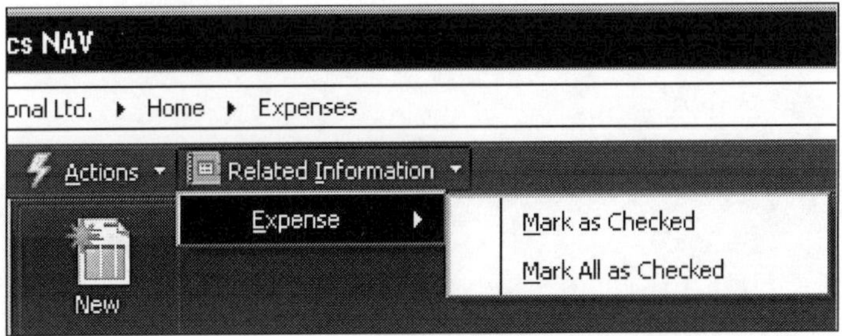

If we use a **Functions** button instead, the action is placed in a **Functions** submenu in the **Actions** menu. If we want it to appear on the action pane, we are going to need to specify some additional input to the transformation tool—but more on that later. If you don't specify some code or a RunObject property against the menu button items, they will not get created in the Page by the transformation process.

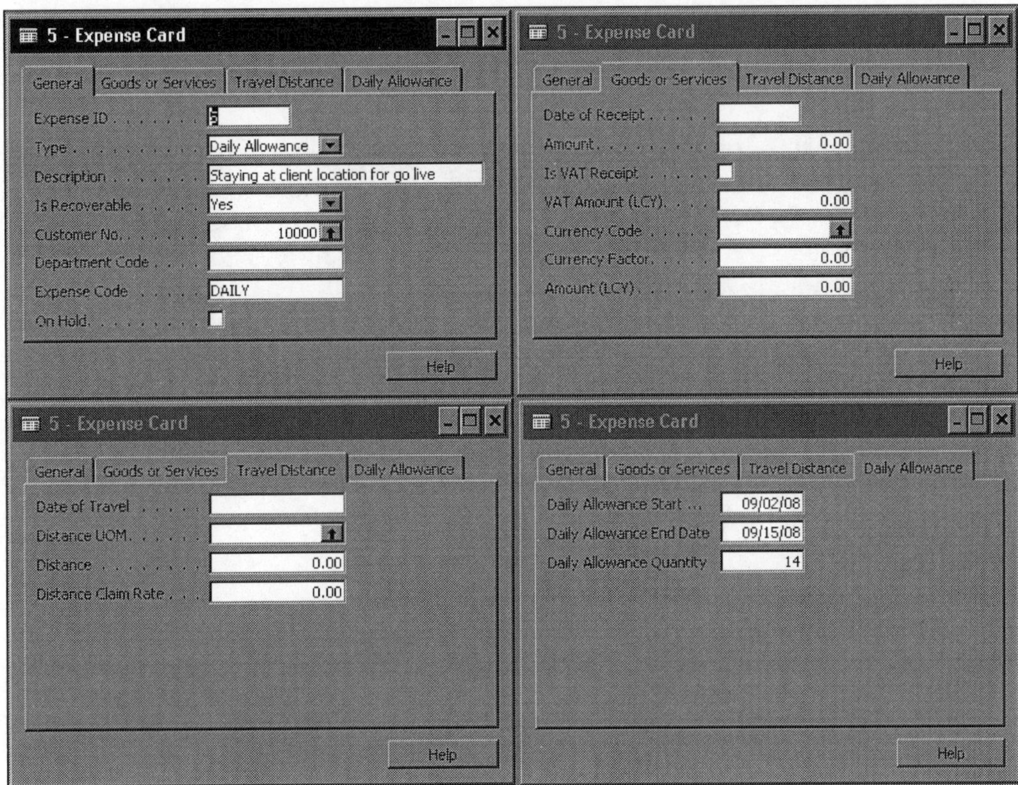

The **Expense Card** has four tabs of information, a general one, and one for each type of expense. It may be nice to implement this card as a Wizard type form later on, to improve the user experience.

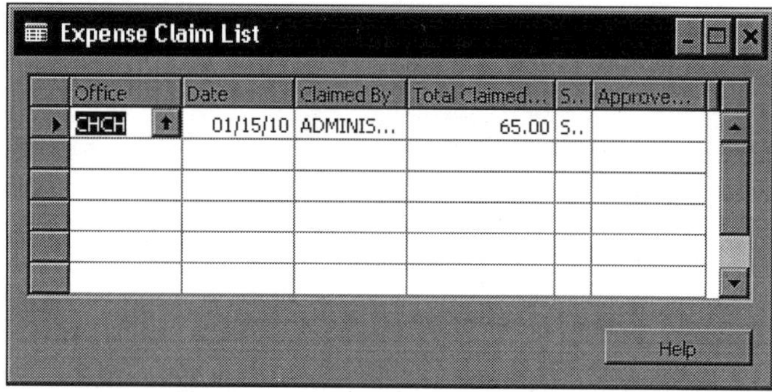

Now we have our forms, let's see if we can transform them into pages using the Form Transformation tool.

Transformers, robots in disguise

Having two different user interfaces for one system, each with their own screen definitions, causes somewhat of a problem. You need the forms in the classic client because that is where you're going to get everything working and how you're going to easily debug problems should something go wrong (you can debug in the RoleTailored client but it is not as easy as running the application with a menu option selected). But the RoleTailored client is where the users want to be; it's cool and if you can't deliver your solution for the RoleTailored client, you're not realizing the potential of NAV 2009.

Let's assume that you decide to take our advice and have the same functionality in the Classic and RoleTailored clients; what options are there for creating the duplicitous interface? The options are simple:

- Do the work twice.
- Use the Form Transformation tool

I can't say I'm particularly thrilled about either of these options. I don't like doing work once, let alone doing it twice so that option seems unlikely for me, but I've also heard bad things about the transformation tool, but how bad can it be?

Microsoft provides documentation on how to use the transformation tool to partners and also provide the tool on the product DVD or download. The online help also has a walkthrough that tells you how to use the tool to make transformations.

I'm assuming that you've installed the tool and imported the FOB files into the Classic client; you won't be able to do the following until you have done this.

From the **Object designer**, run form **177000 Transformation Forms**.

From the **Setup** menu button, select the **Get Forms** option.

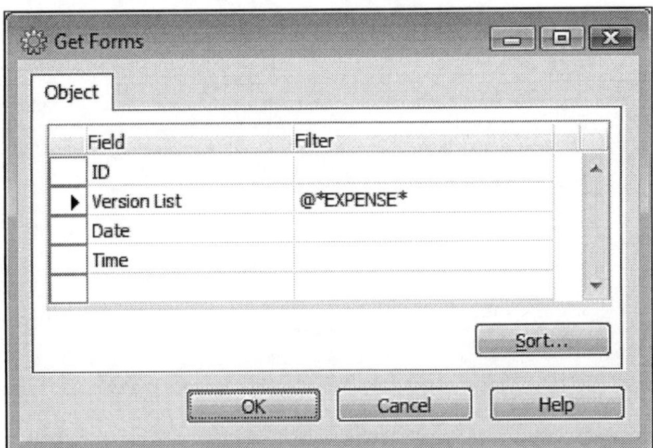

I used the word **EXPENSE** in my version list for all of the forms I worked on, so I can use this to filter the objects I am bringing in. This gives me eight forms to transform.

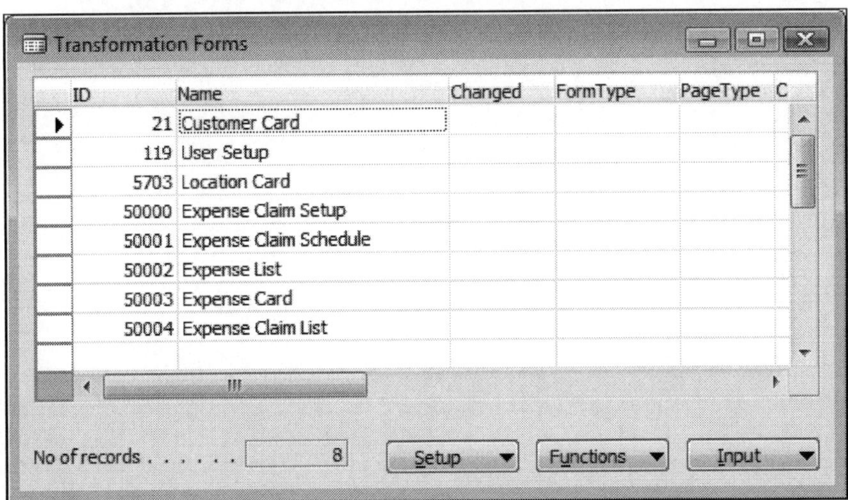

Use the **Import FT-PT Mapping** option on the **Setup** button to import the `FormToPageTypeMapping.txt` file that comes with the transformation tool. This text file contains the descriptions of the various form types, you'll see this when you click the look up button on the **FormType** field.

Importing the text file is only necessary when you are using the transformation tool for the first time.

For each form, specify the mandatory properties as follows:

Form ID	Name	FormType	PageType
21	Customer Card	Card	Card
119	User Setup	List	List
5703	Location Card	Card	Card
50000	Expense Claim Setup	Card	Card
50001	Expense Claim Schedule	List	List
50002	Expense List	List	List
50003	Expense Card	Card	Card
50004	Expense Claim List	List	List

Set the **CardFormID** property for the **Expense List** to be **50003**.

The Location Card and the Customer Card have some elements that we don't want to be transformed. Fortunately in our case, it is mostly the standard forms that are going to be causing special problems, so we can use the standard XML files that come with the transformation tool. The only XML files we will need to generate are the TranformPages.xml and MoveElements.xml files. I think it's a good idea to take a backup of the transformation XML files before accidentally overwriting them. You can always get them back by re-installing the tool, but it's easier to just take a copy of these files before you write over them.

- `DeleteElements.xml`
- `IgnorePages.xml`
- `MoveElements.xml`
- `MovePages.xml`
- `TransformPages.xml`

Thankfully, the objects we have modified in this example do not contain any elements that require the use of `DeleteElements`, `IgnorePages`, or `MovePages` but we do want to promote the actions on our Expense List form and for this we will use the `MoveElements` input file.

Since we are using standard forms and want to apply the general rules for moving elements to these forms, we need to first import the standard `MoveElements.xml` file. Click on the **Import** menu button on the **Transformation Forms** form and select the **Move Elements** option. We can now add our own movement instructions to the ones that already exist for our Customer and Location cards.

To promote our new actions on the **Expense List**, click the **Input** menu button and select **Promote Action by Caption**.

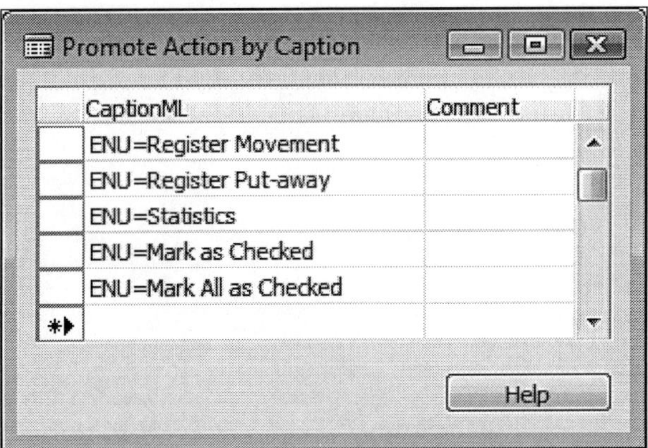

Add the two lines shown at the bottom of the previous screenshot for **Mark as Checked** and **Mark All as Checked**. You should also add the lines in the **Move Action by Caption** form (select **Input | Move | Action by Caption** and insert the two new lines shown at the bottom of the following image) so that the actions will appear in the action pane.

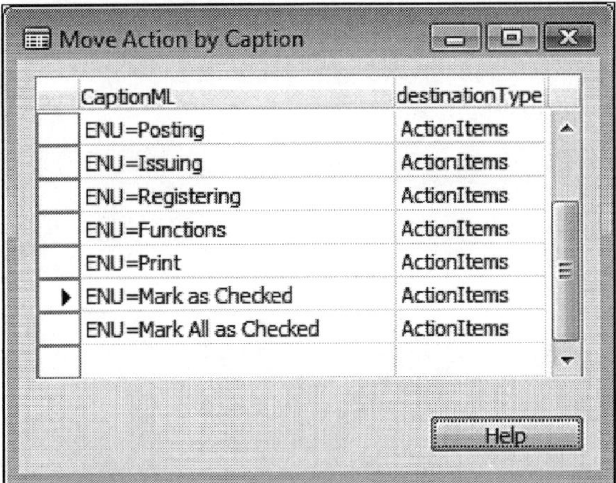

Finally, we want to make sure the **Mark as Checked** action has a nice big button on the action pane. To do this, select **Input | Add by Caption | Big Image to Action**.

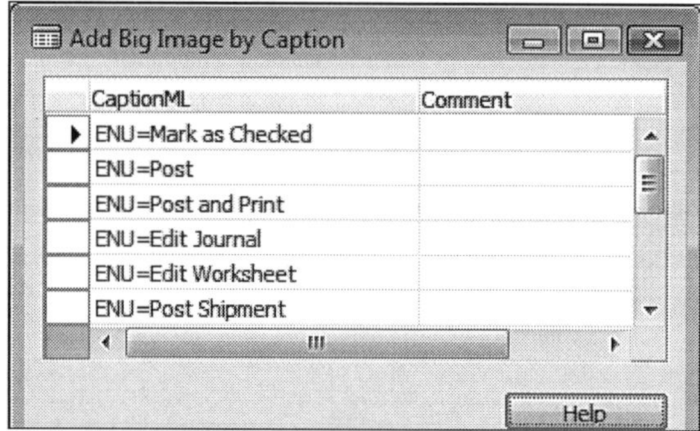

Insert a line with our **Mark as Checked** caption. You should note that these elements will apply to all forms that you are transforming so if, for some reason, you do not want a **Post** action to have a big button, you will need to transform that form separately. If you want to select one of the standard images for the action buttons, you can select from the list of available images on the **Input | Add by Caption | Image to Action**.

Before you generate your `TransformPages.xml` and `MoveElements.xml` files, you must select all records. If you don't, you may get a shock when all but one of your forms in the **Transformation Forms** list disappear (although the system will prompt you telling you only one object is selected). If this happens, you can get the missing forms back by selecting **Show All**.

Make sure all of your lines are selected as shown below:

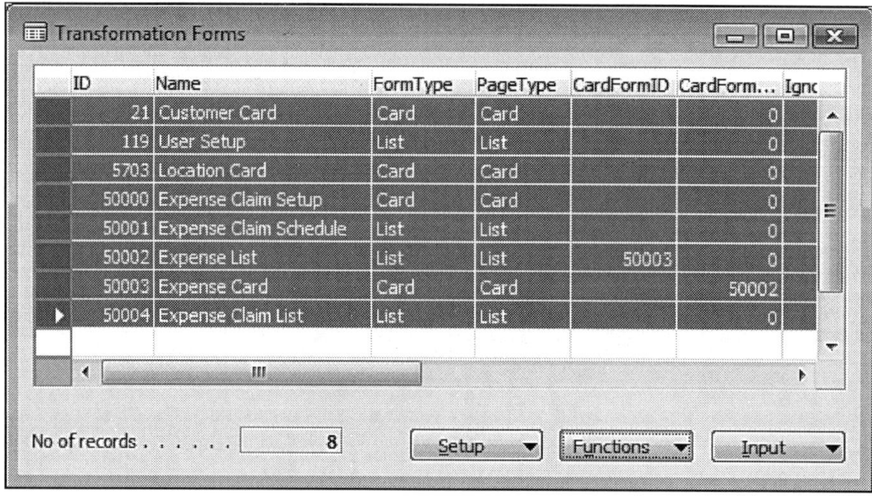

ID	Name	FormType	PageType	CardFormID	CardForm...	Ignc
21	Customer Card	Card	Card		0	
119	User Setup	List	List		0	
5703	Location Card	Card	Card		0	
50000	Expense Claim Setup	Card	Card		0	
50001	Expense Claim Schedule	List	List		0	
50002	Expense List	List	List	50003	0	
50003	Expense Card	Card	Card		50002	
50004	Expense Claim List	List	List		0	

Then select the **Functions | Create All Transformation Input**. This will save all five transformation input files to the directory you specified in the **TIF path Export** field on the **Transformation Setup** card but if you do this, you may get caught out. The files that we are not using, `DeleteElements.xml`, `IgnorePage.xml`, `MovePages.xml`, get created by the routine but they are empty XML files which are not valid for the transformation. You can't just delete the files because the transformation tool insists that the files are there. The best thing to do is to copy the files that ship with the tool back in to our transformation directory (you did take that backup of the files didn't you?)

Now we have our input files ready to rock, we need to export the forms themselves in XML format. Select the forms from the **Object Designer** and use the **File | Export** menu option. Don't forget to select the file type as XML. Save the file as `Forms.xml` and put it, yes you guessed it, in the directory that contains the transformation tool.

Now it's time to run the tool and see what happens.

What did that message say?

Rather than running the transformation tool by double-clicking the `FormTransformation.exe` we recommend that you open a command window and change the directory to the location of your transformation tool. This way you can read the progress messages instead of watch them flash past in a command window making you think something you needed to know about was happening.

The tool has produced a `TransformationLog.xml`, `Transformation.log` (containing any exceptions if there were any, which in this case there should not be), and a `Pages.xml` file that contains our new pages.

Use the **Object Designer | File | Import** option to import the `Pages.xml` file. Don't forget to set the file type to XML.

If all went well, you should now have the following pages with the **EXPENSE** text in the **Version List**.

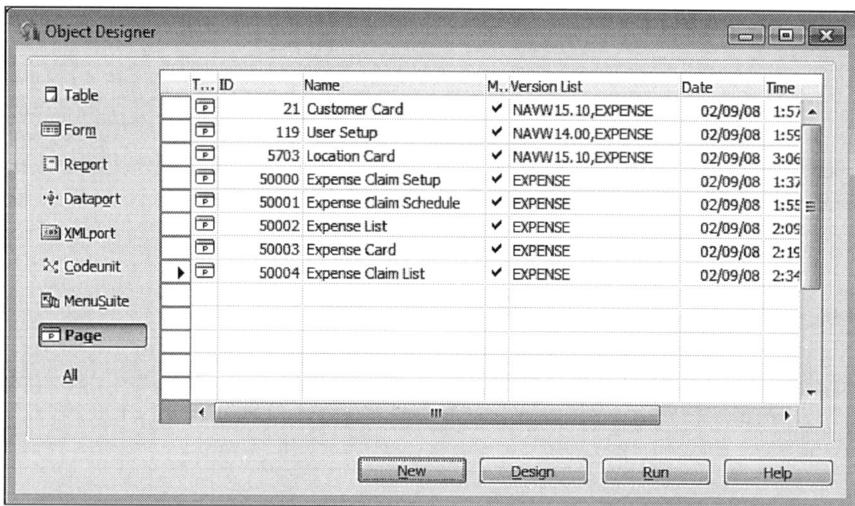

Importing objects from an XML file leaves them in an un-compiled state, similar to the way older versions handled text files. Select your list of pages and press *F11* to compile them.

When developing for the RoleTailored client, you are going to go through this cycle a number of times, and I would definitely recommend building the form, setting up the transformation rules, and using the tool to transform the form to a page rather than doing the development twice. The benefits of having a repeatable process far outweigh the pain in setting up the transformation tool. Until you have come to terms with the various transformation rules, you will find yourself repeating the steps over and over:

1. Build and test the form in the Classic client.
2. Export the XML transformation files (the ones you have changed).
3. Export the form as XML.
4. Run the transformation tool.
5. Check the log file for problems.
6. Import the `Page.xml` file.
7. Compile the pages.
8. Start the RoleTailored client to check the changes you have made meet your requirements.
9. Go to step 1 and repeat until you are happy with RoleTailored pages.

Until the development tools for the RoleTailored interface improve, you will need to add a lot of extra time for development.

A quick way to run pages

If you just want to see how your page looks in the RoleTailored client after the transformation but don't want to add the page to a MenuSuite in order to be able to run it, there is a fast way to run a RoleTailored page (or report for that matter).

Try typing the URL given in parenthesis into your Internet Explorer address bar or in a Run command prompt (`dynamicsnav:////runpage?page=21`) and (assuming you have NAV 2009 installed and running) the correct page will be run in the RoleTailored client.

Take a look the Microsoft Dynamics NAV 2009 Developer Help topic called Creating and Running Hyperlinks for more details.

MenuSuite and navigation pane

If we want to run our new pages from the navigation pane in the RoleTailored client, we'll need to create some menu items first.

The menu options are created using the Navigation Pane Designer that has been available since version **4.0**. For the Classic client, we need to edit the MenuSuite with ID 90, for the RoleTailored client, it will be 1090. When you select the **New** button in the Object Designer, a new form makes it perfectly clear what you need to do.

We don't need to worry about the standard items because they are already in the Departments Place but for our custom pages in the 50000+ range, we need to find a new home to launch them from.

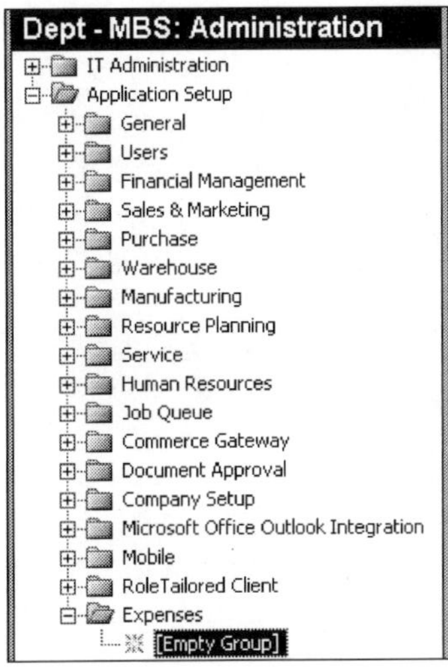

Create a new menu group called **Expenses** in the **Administration | Application Setup** menu. This is going to be the home for two of our new pages.

Create another group called **Expenses** in the **Financial Management | Payables** menu. This is where we will put our **Expense List** and **Expense Claim List**, but we will need to change the caption for these options as shown in the next screenshot:

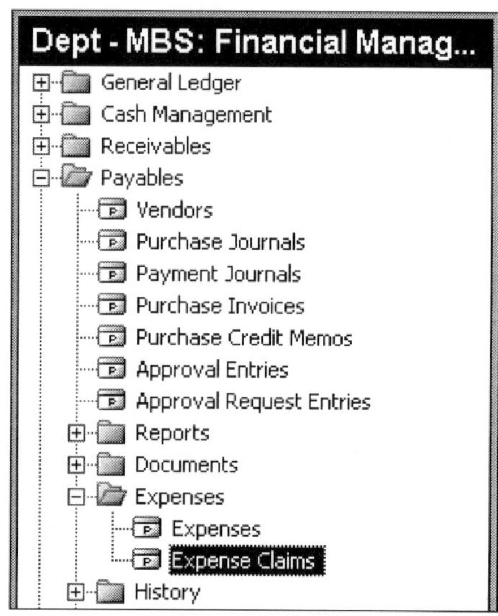

Form ID	Name	Menu Path	Department Category
50000	Expense Claim Setup	Administration, Application Setup, Expenses, Expense Claim Setup	Tasks
50001	Expense Claim Schedule	Administration, Application Setup, Expenses, Expense Claim Schedule	Lists
50002	Expense List	Financial Management, Payables, Expenses, Expenses	Lists
50003	Expense Card	None - this gets called from the Expense List and does not get run directly	
50004	Expense Claim List	Financial Management, Payables, Expenses, Expense Claims	Lists

We'll think about the role centers later but for now, let's fire up the RoleTailored client (note that the refresh button isn't going to pick up changes to the MenuSuite so if you have it running already, you will need to restart the RoleTailored client).

If everything has gone according to plan, you will be able to go to **CRONUS International Ltd.** | **Departments** | **Financial Management** | **Payables** | **Expenses** | **Expenses** and see the following list place displayed:

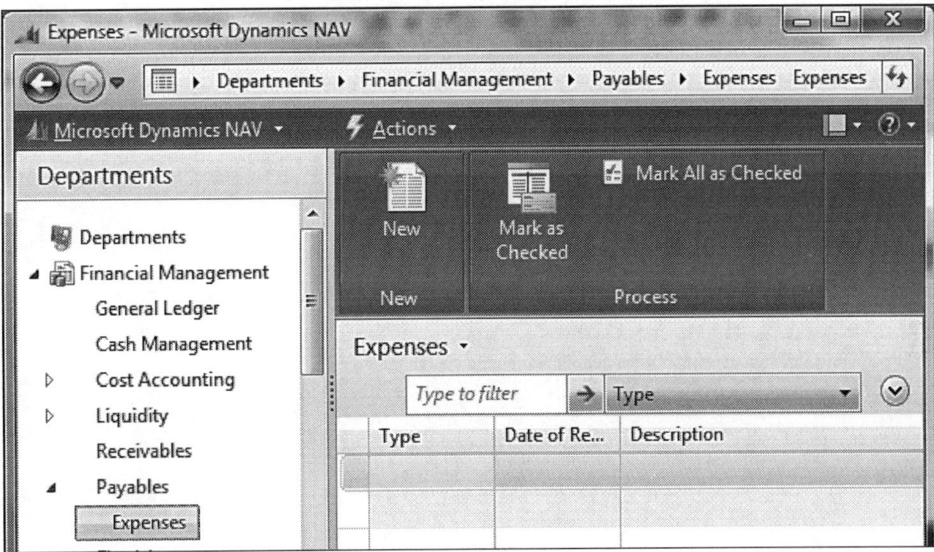

For the sake of the prototype walk-though, we can add the **Expenses** and **Expense Claims** list places to the navigation pane in the RoleTailored client by right-clicking the options in the **Departments** place and selecting the **Add to Navigation Pane** option.

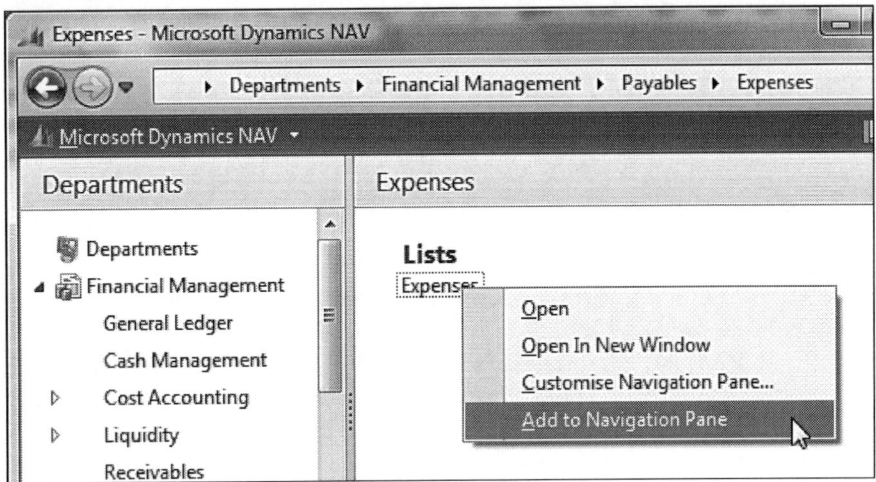

This is a nice and easy way to make the new options readily accessible for the user, but in reality, we will need to look at our profiles and decide which ones will need expense handling functionality. It would also be a good idea to provide cues (stacks of documents) to represent the following things:

- Expense Claimant Cue Group
  - Un-submitted Expenses
  - Pending Expense Claims
  - Approved Expense Claims
- Expense Checker Cue Group
  - Expense Claims for Checking
  - Checked Expense Claims
  - Approved Expense Claims
- Expense Approver Cue Group
  - Expense Claims for Approval
  - Approved Expense Claims
- Expense Processor Cue Group
  - Approved Expense Claims
  - Processed Expense Claims

Dynamics Mobile

The Dynamics Mobile Framework has been around for a little while now and in our scenario, the client is interested in including a mobile application as a means of capturing expenses for staff members that are on the road. There's a lot to this framework and, sadly, we won't be able to cover much of it in this short chapter, however; we should be able to cover enough to help you understand how to design mobile applications for Microsoft Dynamics NAV.

Applications built on the Dynamics Mobile Framework comprise a series of mini-applications or tasklets that are strung together into an application by using an orchestration. This neat design means that the tasklets in the application can be reused for different applications and that the behavior of the tasklet can change according to the requirements of the task and the rights of the user.

The business logic of a mobile application is described using the `UserRole.xml` file that controls the interaction between tasklets.

An application is made up from one or many orchestrations that each define a single business activity.

Dynamics Mobile home page

If you have access to PartnerSource, you can access many Dynamics Mobile resources at the following URL: `https://mbs.microsoft.com/partnersource/solutions/mobile/`

The documentation that comes with the Dynamics Mobile Framework is excellent and there isn't much we can add to it. If you want to learn how to use orchestrations to build a mobile application, we suggest you read the *Guidelines for Using Orchestration to Build a Mobile Application* topic in the `MobileOrchestration` help file that comes with the download. If you haven't downloaded the toolkit yet, here are the highlights:

1. Design the flow through the tasklets of the mobile application.
2. Define the business activities.
3. Define the orchestrations.
4. Define the tasklets.
5. Define the flow through the application.
6. Determine the data transfer between tasklets.
7. Identify and define data transfer to the business solution.

Overview tasklet

In our application, we will have a single overview tasklet that will contain icons to launch the main orchestrations within the application. The icons will represent:

- Capturing an expense
- Editing captured expenses
- Synchronize

To help the users to visual the design, we have created some hand-drawn screen mock-ups to illustrate the layout. Paper-prototyping is fast and forces the users to focus on the functionality of the system rather than the color of the graphics or position of the buttons.

Capturing Expense

This option will launch a wizard orchestration that will display the tasklets needed to capture an expense. The orchestration will basically follow the flows outlined in the Mobile Capture of Expense use-case. The following are some sample screen mock-ups of the basic flow:

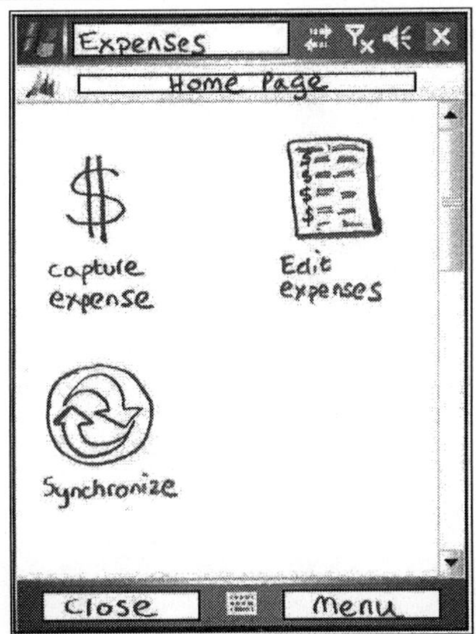

The system displays the Overview screen.

The Expense Claimant selects the option to capture an expense.

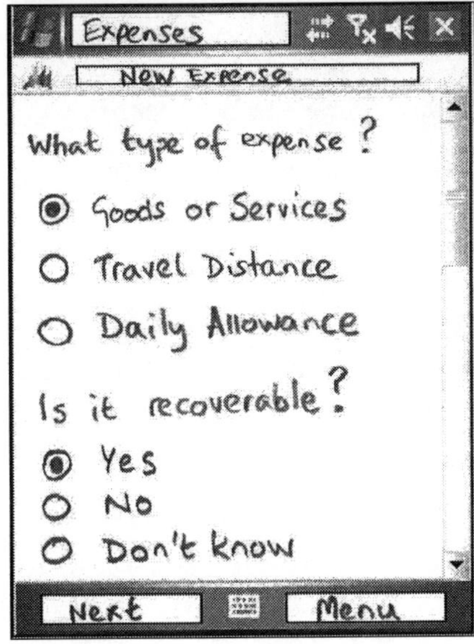

The system displays a screen with the ability to specify the Expense Type (**Goods or Services**, **Travel Distance**, or **Daily Allowance**) and whether the expense can be recovered from a customer or not.

The Expense Claimant selects the option for **Goods or Services** and indicates that the expense can be recovered from a customer and clicks **Next** to continue with the Wizard.

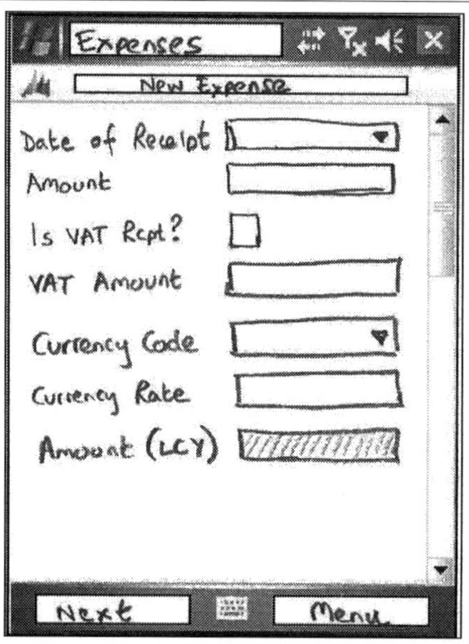

The system displays a screen prompting the Goods or Service Expense Details to be entered.

The Expense Claimant enters the Goods or Service Expense Details and clicks **Next** to continue with the Wizard.

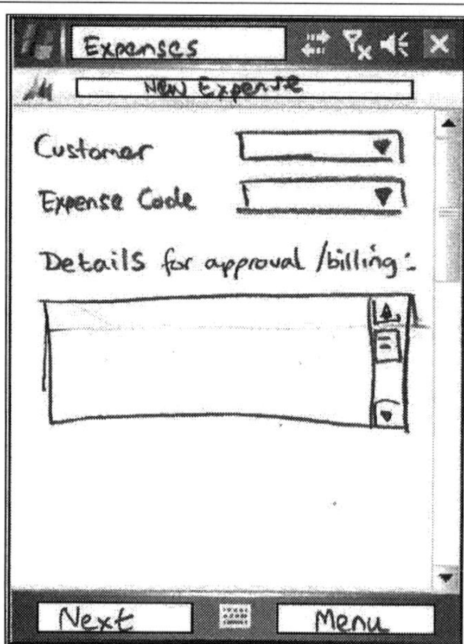

The system displays a screen prompting for the Recoverable Expense Approval and Billing Details to be entered.

The Expense Claimant enters the Recoverable Expense Approval and Billing Details and clicks **Next** to continue with the Wizard.

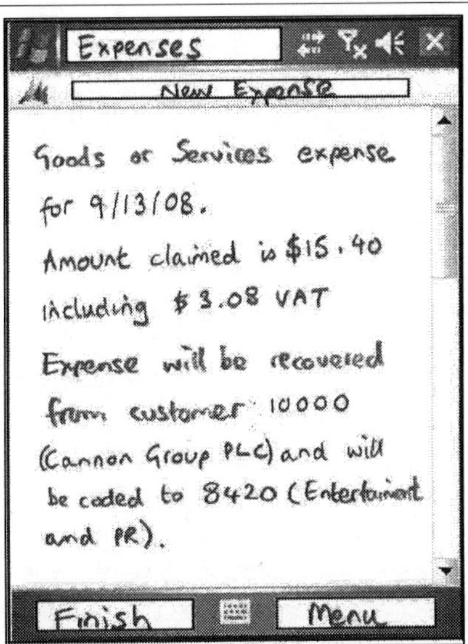

The system displays the Summary of Recoverable Good or Services Expense Details.

The Expense Claimant clicks **Finish** to continue.

The system displays the Overview screen.

Editing Captured Expenses

This option will run a list tasklet of all captured (but not submitted) expenses for the current user. The user can scroll through the expenses in the list, view the expense details, delete the expense, or modify the expense (that will launch the Capture Expense Wizard orchestration using the details already captured).

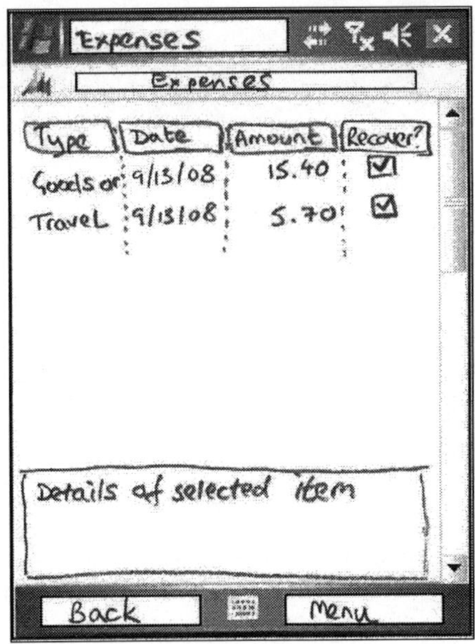

Synchronize

Selecting this option will run the synchronization process which will persist captured expenses back to NAV so they can later be submitted, and will also update the reference data such as departments, customers, expense codes, and other configuration options.

Prototype, demonstrate and iterate

Way back in chapter 4, we talked about using prototyping to design our solution. Iterative prototyping allows the design to evolve based upon the input from the domain experts and the technical designers. In our sample prototype demonstration of the Mobile Capture Expense use-case, you may have noticed that the information to be captured is actually different to the details set out in our use-case description. When designing the screen layouts, it became clear that since the date of the expense has a different label for different expense types, it made sense to capture this detail after the expense type is known. As a result the capture use-case changed so that the first screen simply asks for the expense type and whether it is recoverable or not.

It's OK to change the design in this way, in fact, that's why we're doing prototyping. The functional specification is history; it helped us to produce the designs and prototypes and move forward with the solution, but there is no need to go back and update the use-cases when our approach changes. It is, however, important to ensure that our test cases (developed in conjunction with the prototypes) and the user documentation (to be written just prior to and during the stabilization phase) include the correct options.

Summary

In our sample application chapter, we have focused on requirements gathering, functional requirements specification, design and prototype build. We've explored use-case modeling and object-role modeling techniques, and have seen how these can be applied to NAV applications. We've also touched upon building an application for NAV 2009 and how to overcome some of the challenges the new user interface presents for developers.

So long, farewell, Auf Wiedersen, Adieu

Microsoft Dynamics NAV 2009 is an amazing product. It is by no means perfect, but it has definitely reinvigorated the NAV platform. In this book we wanted to share what we have learnt about the new 2009 version of NAV and also help you understand how to put some of the theory into practice. There are a number of experts on NAV in the world and you can get help from the many forums and user communities, not to mention Microsoft through CustomerSource and ParnerSource. We'll provide links to additional sites and resources on our book's web site `www.teachmenav.com`.

We tried to make this book fun, and not to take ourselves too seriously, yet still impart some of the experience we have gained from our many years of consulting and programming. I have learnt many things in writing this book, through researching, experimenting, and doing a lot of thinking (not to mention the things I have learnt from Vjeko). I hope that you have found it useful and have learnt some things too.

Finally, I would like to acknowledge David Studebaker, author of Programming Microsoft Dynamics NAV. It was reading David's book that inspired me to co-author this book. When I read David's book, I found it odd that he chose to end it with a quote from a song. Now, as I write these final few lines, I understand how he must have felt, after such a huge effort, there doesn't seem to be an easy way to stop.

The time is gone, the song is over,
Thought I'd something more to say.
– Mason, Waters, Wright, Gilmour

Index

A

accounting
about 184
bookkeeping 184, 185
chart of accounts 184, 190
dimensions 185
financial data, analyzing 200-204
hippo's bottom 184
hippopotami analogies 193
transactions 193, 194
accounting manager profile, role
actions, adding 114-116
configured pages, clearing 113, 114
customer card layout, changing 119, 120
customizing 111
reports, adding 114, 118
actors, use case modeling
expense appover 463
expense checker 463
expense claimant 463
expense processor 463
analysis phase
about 152
approval process, planning 154
considerations, data migration analysis 157
data integration, detailed analysis 159
data migration 156
detailed analysis 158
detailed analysis XE 158
functional requirements document, detailed analysis 160
interfaces, detailed analysis 160
key users, training 154, 155
kick-off meeting 154
master data migration 156
past transactions migration 156
path, preparing 152
resources, planning 153
user roles, detailed analysis 159
architectural design, sample application
about 481
budget 482, 483
components 483
cool technology 483
existing architecture 482
supplementary requirements 481

B

breakpoints 415
build, development lifecycle
about 382
application logic, building 392
C/SIDE reports, user interface 389
code testing 393
data model, building 384
deployment plan, documentation 400
documentation 400
existing role center, extending 391
feature complete 394
functional specification, documentation 401
new role centers, creating 392
object versioning 394-398
pages, user interface 389
reports, user interface 389
RoleTailored reports, user interface 389
security 393
teamwork 383
test scripts, documentation 401
user interface, building 384
user interface integration 390

C

cards
about 51
assist edit button, FastTab 55
browser button, FastTab 55
drop-down button, FastTab 54
email button, FastTab 55
FactBox pane 56
FastTab 52, 53
phone button, FastTab 55
categories, tasks pages
cards 51
documents 56
journals 57
list plus 58
lists 56
matrices 59, 60
wizards 60
chart of accounts, accounting
about 190
assets, balance sheet 192
balance sheet 192
designing 190
dividend, balance sheet 193
expenses, income statement 192
gains, income statement 192
income/revenue, income statement 192
income statement 191
liabilities, balance sheet 193
losses, income statement 192
shareholder's equity, balance sheet 193
client monitor
about 423
built-in client monitor functionality 424
client monitor helper projects 427, 428
code coverage, combining with 447
data, analyzing 431
deadlocks, detecting 445-447
general troubleshooting, performance troubleshooting 426
locking situations, analyzing 443, 444
multi-user issues 441
objects, analyzing 437-440
performance, analyzing with Excel 428-430
performance troubleshooting 426
sources of performance issues, finding 440, 441
tables, analyzing 432-437
targeted troubleshooting, performance troubleshooting 426
Client Tier
about 18
components 18
code coverage 419
components, Client Tier
data binder 18
form builder 18
RoleTailored client 18
components, of reports in Classic client
data items 289, 290
data items properties 290
request form 294
section designer 291
sections 291, 292
components, Service Tier
application component 19
business web services 19
metadata provider 19
Microsoft Dynamics NAV Class Library 19
Microsoft Dynamics NAV Service 19
Cues 27
customize menu, RoleTailored client
about 86
arrange by option, customize this page option 88
chart part, customize role center page 97
choose column option, customize this page option 89
customize actions option 86
customize activities page, customize role center page 94
customize reports option 87
customize role center page 93
customize task page, with FastTabs 92
customize this page option 88
display option, customize this page option 88
FactBoxes option, customize this page option 90
list part, customize role center page 96

Microsoft Outlook, customize role center page 95
notification part, customize role center page 97

D

data migration, RIM toolkit
about 232
data migration tool 233
dataports issues 232
limitations, data migration tool 240
data migration tool, RIM toolkit
about 233
example 233-240
limitations 240
data model, extending
field groups 257
fields, adding 254
properties, or objects 253
table keys 256
table relationships 254, 255
tables, creating 252
debugging
about 408
behavior, Visual Studo debugger features 418
breakpoint, setting 415
breakpoint, testing 416
C/AL code, elements 417
call stack, elements 417
Classic client, debugging 409-419
code coverage 419-421
debugger, activating 415
debugger, triggering 415
elements 417
output, elements 417
Service Tier, debugging 409-414
variables, elements 417
watches, elements 417
ways 409
departments page, RoleTailored client
about 48
departments 49
financial management page 49
deployment, development lifecycle
about 405
deployment complete milestone 405
deployment stable milestone 405
documentation 405
deployment phase
about 172
activities, planning 172
end user training 175
environment, configuring 172, 173
go-live activity 175, 176
load test 174, 175
UAT (user acceptance test) 173, 174
design, development lifecycle
designing tasks 373
keys, performance and scalability 381
NAV functionality, extending 370
new functionality, designing 371, 372
new functionality, developing 370
performance, planning for 381
scalability, planning for 381
user interface, performance and scalability 382
designing tasks, development lifecycle
application code, application logic 380
application logic 379
consistency, user interface 378
data model 373
data rules, application logic 380
entity relationship diagram, data model 375, 376
pages, user interface 378
relationships, data model 375
reports 379
table, data model 374
user interface 378
design phase
about 162
demonstrate 164
imagination, using 163
iterate 164
paper prototyping 163
problem, understanding 163
products of design 165
prototype 163
standard application, understanding 162
development
about 366
in Microsoft Dynamics NAV 366

lifecycle 366
requirements, understanding 368, 369
solution, designing 370
development lifecycle
about 366
Microsoft solutions framework 367
rational unified process 367
development phase
about 166
application functionality 168
customer testing 171
data migration development 169, 170
documentation 170
end user documentation 170
environment, setting up 167
planning 166
security issues 170
technical documentation 171
diagnostic phase
about 143
business issues 143
comprehensive analysis 147
detailed analysis 149
fit/gap analysis 145-147
Microsoft Dynamics Business Modeler 148
out of scope 150
project scope, drafting 144, 145
technical requirements 150
wrapping up 151
dimensions, accounting
about 185
basic flow diagram 221
default dimensions 220
default dimensions, setting 221
document dimensions 220
how 188
journal line dimensions 198
posted document dimensions 220
types 221, 222
what 187
when 187
where 188
who 186
why 188
Dynamics Customer Model
about 99
departments and work view 101
issues, in previous Dynamics NAV 100
new beginning 100
people and departments view 101
role, in Dynamics NAV 2009 101
Dynamics Mobile
about 508
captured expenses, editing 513
expense, capturing 510-513
overview tasklet 509
synchronization process 514
Dynamics Mobile Framework 508

E

ERP 7
existing role, extending
sales order processor profile 120
external sources, of poor performance
client hardware 422
client software 423
database server disk subsystem 422
database server hardware 422
network 422
server hardware 422
server software 423

F

fit 145
forms, customizing
button 263
controls, adding 260-262
form properties 259
forms, creating 258
menubutton 263
properties, for defining actions 263
subform control 262
subform control, properties 262
functional areas, Microsoft Dynamics NAV 2009
financial management 13
human resources 14
jobs 14
manufacturing 14
purchase management 13
resource planning 14
sales and marketing 13
service management 14

warehouse management 13
functional requirements
about 461
process flow diagram 461
use case modeling 462
use case workshop 471
future product versions, Microsoft Dynamics NAV 2009
business vision + software 22
company + ecosystem 23
people + processes 22

G

G/L entry
about 209, 211
VAT bus. posting group 212, 214
VAT prod. posting group 212, 214
vendor posting group 211
gap 145
general ledger 185

H

human resources, functional areas 14

I

implementation
about 135-137
implementation tasks 137
implementation, Microsoft Dynamics NAV 2009
phases 142
implementation tasks
standardized software, implementing 137
internal sources, of poor performance
application logic 423
database design 423

J

journal line dimensions, accounting 198

K

kick-off meeting 154

L

limitations, data migration tool
data templates 244
dimensions 241
dimensions, programmer's path 243
dimensions, programmers path 244
dimensions, way of consultant 241, 242
known issues 244
slow performance 244

M

MenuSuites
about 301
creating 304
customizing 301
designing 305-307
editing 303
levels 250
methodology
about 141
importance 141
Microsoft Dynamics Business Modeler 148
Microsoft Dynamics NAV
development 366
development lifecycle 366, 367
future 21
methodology 141
Microsoft Dynamics NAV 2009
about 7, 8, 11, 12
application areas 13
architecture 9, 10
Classic client, debugging 409
common issues 407, 408
data model, extending 251
debugger, activating 415
debugging 408, 409
debugging ways 409
Dynamics Customer Model 101
existing role, discovering 105-107
existing role, extending 120
forms, customizing 257
functional areas 13
future 21
implementation 142
implementing 10, 11

MenuSuites, customizing 301
modifying, for non-programmers 248
new role, creating 132
object designer, role center page 108, 110
object designer basics 249
objects, customizing 308
pages, customizing 264
problems, identifying 407, 408
project issues 180
regression issues 409
reporting in Classic client 288
reporting in RoleTailored client 295
reports, customizing 287
resources 133
role, customizing 111
roles 101, 102
role center thinking 105
RoleTailored, need for 8, 9
RoleTailored, used 8
Service Tier, debugging 409
sure step methodology 141
understanding 247, 248
Web Service Enablement 311
Microsoft Dynamics NAV 2009 architecture
about 9, 10, 15
Client/server architecture 15
Client Tier 18
fat client architecture 16
Service Tier 18
thin client architecture 15
three tier architecture 15-17
two tier architecture 15, 16
Microsoft Dynamics NAV Service Tier. *See* also Service Tier
mobile expense claim, use case workshop
about 473, 474
alternate flows 478, 480
basic flow 477, 478
modifications for programmers, Microsoft Dynamics NAV 2009
data exporting 249
data importing 249
data model, extending 248
reporting 249
user interface, modifying 249

N

navigation window, RoleTailored client
about 29
action command, local commands 33
address bar 29, 30
command bar 31, 32
customize command 33
departments activity button 35
departments activity button, navigation pane: 35
help command 34
home activity button, navigation pane: 35
local commands 33
navigation pane 34
posted documents activity button, navigation pane: 35
related information command, local commands 33
reports command, local commands 33
role center navigation page 37
status bar 36
NAV web service
calling 314, 315
exposing 314
web service, calling 317-322
web service, creating 316

O

Object-Role Modeling. *See* ORM
object designer basics 249-251
objects
codeunits 308
customizing 308
dataports 308, 309
XMLports 309
object versioning, development lifecycle
development work, by customers 400
modified flag, reseting 399
operation phase
change request, accepting 178
documentation 177
final acceptance 179
planning, not needed 176

project review 179
transition 177, 178
ORM 469

P

page designer
about 275
Action, actions types 284
ActionContanier, actions types 281
action designer 281
ActionGroup, actions types 283
ActionItems container, ActionContanier 281
actions 280
actions, defining for a page 280
actions, promoting 286
actions types 281
ActivityButtons container, ActionContanier 282
chart parts 279
containers 276
ContentArea, containers subtype 276
CueGroup, groups subtypes 276
determining factors, fields 278
FactBoxArea, containers subtype 276
fields 277
FixedLayout, groups subtypes 276
Group, groups subtypes 276
groups 276
HomeItems container, ActionContanier 282
NewDocumentItems container, ActionContanier 281
page controls 250, 253
page parts 278
parts 278
positioning control 279, 280
promoted actions 285
RelatedInformation container, ActionContanier 282
Repeater, groups subtypes 276
Reports container, ActionContanier 282
RoleCenterArea, containers subtype 276
RunFormView property, Action 287
RunObject property, Action 286
SystemPartID property, parts 279
system parts 279
pages, customizing
card, page types 265, 266
CardPart, page types 268, 269
ConfirmationDialog, page types 273
document, page types 270
form transformation tool 287
list, page types 266
ListPart, page types 269
ListPlus, page types 271, 272
NavigatePage, page types 274
page, creating 264
page designer 275
page properties 265
page types 265
role center, page types 267, 268
worksheet, page types 271
performance, tuning
client monitor 423
external sources, of poor performance 422
internal sources, of poor performance 423
phases, Dynamics NAV 2009 implementation
analysis phase 152
deployment phase 172
design phase 162
development phase 166
diagnostic phases 143
operation phase 176
planning, for performance
about 451
database resource kit 452
hardware guide 451
indexes 452
technical presales advisory group 452
posting groups
about 205
another invoice, creating 215
copy document feature 215
copy purchase document 216
G/L account card 219
G/L account entries 220
G/L accounts 209, 210
G/L entries revisited 211
G/L entry 209
gen.business posting group 218
general ledger entries 217

general posting setup 219
purchase invoice, creating 205-208
Registers feature of Dynamics NAV, using 217
VAT entry 210
vendor ledger entry 210, 211
programming 365
prototype, building
additional tables 494
customer, additional tables 494
expense claim schedule, additional tables 494
forms, building in Classic client 495-498
FormTo PageTypeMapping.txt file, importing 500
log files, checking for options 503
menu group, creating 506
MenuSuite 505
MoveElements.xml file, importing 500
navigation pane,RoleTailored client 505, 507
new actions, promoting 501, 502
page.xml file, importing 504
pages, compiling 504
RoleTailored client, starting 504
tables, building 494
transformation forms, running 499
transformation forms list 502
transformation tool, running 503
user setup, additional tables 494
XML file, exporting 503
XML file, using 500

Q

queries, web service
codeunit web service, returns complex data types 360
document pages, as web services 359
fields, adding or removing from page 360
page web service 360
role center, as web service 360
XMLports, used as parameters to codeunits 360

R

Rapid Implementation Methodology. *See* **RIM**
REP document 147
reporting in Classic client
C/SIDE objects, used 288
components, of reports 288
layouts, of report wizards 288
report logic 295
reports, creating 288
reporting in RoleTailored client
about 295, 297
components 298
data items, components 298
RDLC layout definition, components 298
request page, components 298
Report Viewer
about 61-63
print report task page 61
report, printing 63
RIM 223
RIM toolkit
about 223
components 223
data migration 232
setup questionnaire 224
role
about 101, 102
accounting manager profile, customizing 111
customizing 111
role center navigation page
about 37, 38
action pane 42, 43
activities part 38, 39
chart pane 45, 46
chart part 40
FactBox pane 47
filter pane 43, 44
list 44, 45
list part 39
list place navigation page 41, 42
notifications part 41
Outlook part 39

role center page, customizing
activities 94
chart part 97
list part 96
Microsoft Outlook 95
notification part 97
roles, Dynamics NAV 2009
finance, accounting manager-Phyllis 103
finance, accounts payable coordinator-April 103
finance, accounts receivable administrator-Arnie 103
finance, bookkeeper-Annie 103
IT and partners, IT manager-Tim 105
operations, customer service, dispatcher-Daniel 104
operations, customer service, outbound technician-Terrence 104
operations, logistics, purchasing agent-Alicia 104
operations, logistics, shipping and receiving-Sammy 103
operations, logistics, warehouse worker-John 103
operations, production, machine operator-Shannon 104
operations, production, shop supervisor-Lars 104
operations, professional services, project manager-Prakash 104
operations, professional services, resource manager-Reina 104
perations, production, production planner-Eduardo 104
President-Charlie 103
sales and marketing, sales manager-Kevin 105
sales and marketing, sales order processor-Susan 105
small business owner-Stan 103
RoleTailored
about 8
features 11
need for 8
RoleTailored client
about 26
departments page 48
navigation window 28, 29
personalizing 83
Report Viewer 61, 62
role center 26, 27
tasks pages 28, 50
terminologies 28
ways, of using 64
RoleTailored client, personalizing
actions, customizing 86
list places, adding to menus 85, 86
navigation pane, customizing 83-85
pages, personalizing 86
reports, customizing 87
role center page, customizing 93
task page, customizing 92
RoleTailored client, using
cash receipt, entering 67, 79-82
conclusion 82
customer, creating 65-68
invoice, posting for a sales order 72-79
sales order, creating 68-72
RoleTailored report
creating 298
creating ways 298
layout, transforming 299, 300
request option form, transforming 300

S

sales order processor profile, existing role
activities part, changing 120, 121
page ID of activities part, searching 122-124
priority customer field, adding 124-126
sales cue table, extending 128-132
source table of activities part, searching 124
sample application
architectural design 481
Dynamics Mobile 508
functional requirements 461
iterative prototyping 514
prototype, building 493
prototype demonstration 514
prototyping 514
requirements, gathering 456
sample code download 456
scenario 456-460
technical design 483

Service Oriented Architecture. S*ee* **SOA**
Service Tier
about 18
components 19
setup questionnaire, RIM toolkit
general ledger setup, before RIM 224, 225
general ledger setup, using RIM 226-232
sidebar gadget
about 334
designing 335
technical design 341
sidebar gadget, designing
flyout file 339
gadget 338
gadgets, making 335, 336
languages, supported by 337
options dialog page 340, 341
SOA
about 358
service bus 359
service repository 358
SOA service 358
stabilization, development lifecycle
about 401
development work, finalizing 404
final test 404
issue convergence 402, 403
issue log cleared 403
release readiness milestone 404
standard functionality 136
standardized software, implementing
business process reengineering 137, 139
configuration 139
customization 140
third party solution 140
sure step methodology, Microsoft Dynamics NAV
best practices 141
templates 142
tools 141
system configuration
about 183
accounting 184
categories 183
posting groups 205
RIM 223

T

tables, technical design
customer 487
department 486
expense 485
expense claiim 486
expense claim setup 487
location 486
user setup 487
tasks pages, RoleTailored client
about 50
categories 50
FactBox pane, cards 56
technical design, sample application
about 483
design points 489
development tasks 489-492
table design points 488
tables 484
use cases, working through 491
technical design, sidebar gadget
HTML page, calling NAV codeunit 344, 347, 348
SOAP 342, 343
terms, use case modeling
about 466
customer 469
department 468
employee 468
expense 466, 467
expense claim 468
office 468
tools, for troubleshooting issues
dynamics management views 450
event viewer 449
performance monitor 449
SQL server profiler 449
task manager 450
transactions
about 193
account types 195
credit accounts 194, 195
credit entry, posting 196-199
debit accounts 194, 195
debit entry, posting 196

G/L registers, launching 199
general ledger entries 200
real-world example of journal 194
tricks 195
ways, of getting transactions 194
troubleshooting
Microsoft Dynamics NAV tools overview 453
online resources 453
performance issues 421
SQL Server Technical kit for Microsoft Dynamics NAV 454

U

use case modeling
about 462
actors, defining 462
domain model 469, 470
terms 466
use case diagram 465
use cases, defining 463
use cases, use case modeling
expense claimant, paying 464
expenses, approving 464
expenses, checking 464
expenses, submitting 464
mobile capture of expense 463
post expenses 464
prompt expense claimant to submit expenses 464
use case workshop
about 471
mobile expense claim 473-477
ORM diagram, explaining 471, 472

W

waterfall model 142
web service
about 312, 313
calling, from NAV 351
intranet 313
solutions to queries 360-363
web service, calling from NAV
GlobalWeather web service 352, 354
Web Service Enablement 311
Windows application project, WinForms application
data, collecting 330, 332
filter box 333
find button 333
testing 333, 334
WinForms application
about 323
item look-up requirements 323
web service, exposing 323, 324
Windows application project 326-330

X

XML file, prototype
exporting 503
using 500

Z

ZUP files 112

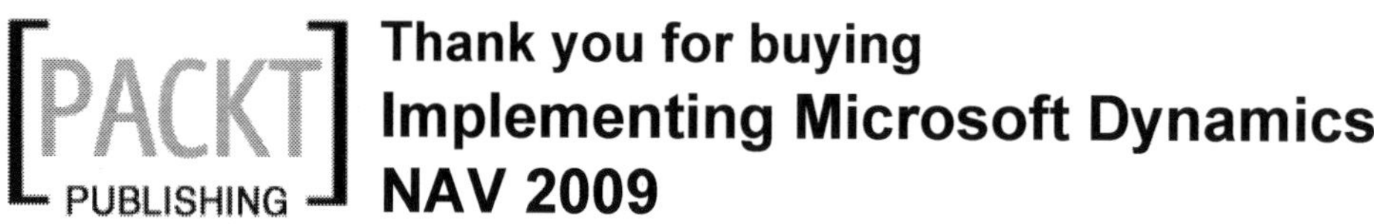

About Packt Publishing

Packt, pronounced 'packed', published its first book "*Mastering phpMyAdmin for Effective MySQL Management*" in April 2004 and subsequently continued to specialize in publishing highly focused books on specific technologies and solutions.

Our books and publications share the experiences of your fellow IT professionals in adapting and customizing today's systems, applications, and frameworks. Our solution based books give you the knowledge and power to customize the software and technologies you're using to get the job done. Packt books are more specific and less general than the IT books you have seen in the past. Our unique business model allows us to bring you more focused information, giving you more of what you need to know, and less of what you don't.

Packt is a modern, yet unique publishing company, which focuses on producing quality, cutting-edge books for communities of developers, administrators, and newbies alike. For more information, please visit our website: `www.packtpub.com`.

Writing for Packt

We welcome all inquiries from people who are interested in authoring. Book proposals should be sent to `author@packtpub.com`. If your book idea is still at an early stage and you would like to discuss it first before writing a formal book proposal, contact us; one of our commissioning editors will get in touch with you.

We're not just looking for published authors; if you have strong technical skills but no writing experience, our experienced editors can help you develop a writing career, or simply get some additional reward for your expertise.

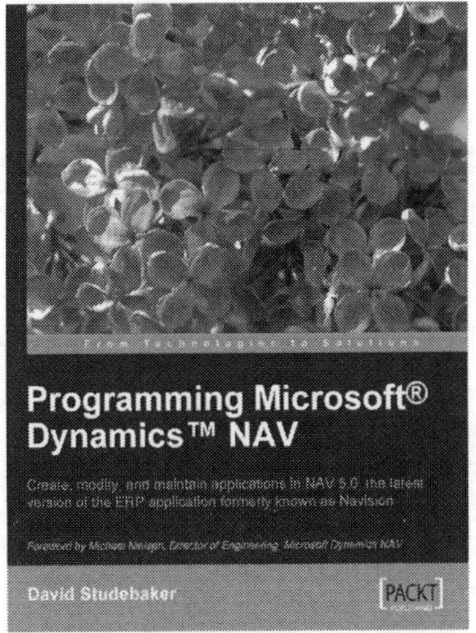

Programming Microsoft® Dynamics™ NAV

ISBN: 978-1-904811-74-9 Paperback: 480 pages

Create, modify, and maintain applications in NAV 5.0, the latest version of the ERP application formerly known as Navision

1. For experienced programmers with little or no previous knowledge of NAV development
2. Learn as quickly as possible to create, modify, and maintain NAV applications
3. Written for version 5.0 of NAV; applicable for all versions

---

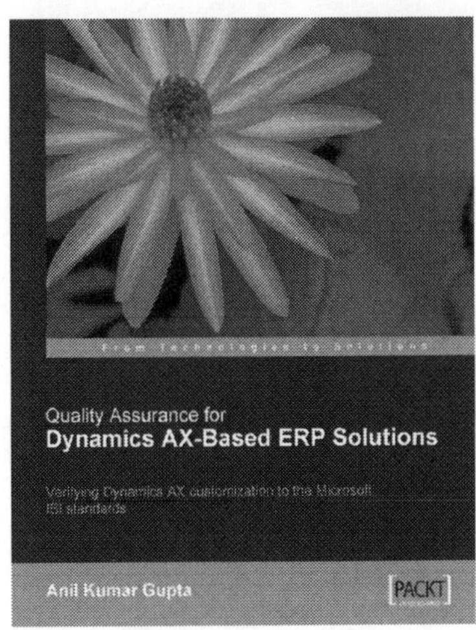

Quality Assurance for Dynamics AX-Based ERP Solutions

ISBN: 978-1-847192-91-2 Paperback: 168 pages

Verifying Dynamics AX customization to the Microsoft IBI Standards

1. Learn rapidly how to test Dynamics AX applications
2. Verify Industry Builder Initiative (IBI) compliance of your ERP software
3. Readymade testing templates
4. Code, design, and test a quality Dynamics AX-based ERP solution
5. Customization best practices backed by theory

Please check **www.PacktPub.com** for information on our titles